THE CAMBRIDGE HISTORY OF ARABIC LITERATURE

ʿABBASID BELLES-LETTRES

ʿABBASID BELLES-LETTRES

EDITED BY

JULIA ASHTIANY, T. M. JOHNSTONE †,
J. D. LATHAM, R. B. SERJEANT and G. REX SMITH

The right of the University of Cambridge to print and sell all manner of books was granted by Henry VIII in 1534. The University has printed and published continuously since 1584.

CAMBRIDGE UNIVERSITY PRESS
CAMBRIDGE
NEW YORK PORT CHESTER MELBOURNE SYDNEY

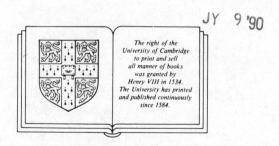

Published by the Press Syndicate of the University of Cambridge
The Pitt Building, Trumpington Street, Cambridge CB2 1RP
40 West 20th Street, New York, NY 10011, USA
10 Stamford Road, Oakleigh, Melbourne 3166, Australia

First published 1990

Printed in Great Britain at the University Press, Cambridge

British Library cataloguing in publication data

ᶜAbbasid belles-lettres. – (The Cambridge
history of Arabic literature).
1. Arabic literature, 750–1258. Critical
studies
I. Ashtiany, Julia
892′.7′090034

Library of Congress cataloguing in publication data

ᶜAbbasid belles-lettres.
(The Cambridge history of Arabic literature)
Bibliography.
Includes index.
1. Arabic literature–750–1258–History
and criticism. I. Ashtiany, Julia.
II. Series.
PJ7530.A18 1990 892′ 7′090034 82-23528

ISBN 0 521 24016 6

SE

CONTENTS

EDITORIAL PREFACE

This volume of the *Cambridge History of Arabic Literature* covers the literary production of a period of five centuries, from the accession of the ᶜAbbasids in 132/750 to the dynasty's end and the capture of its capital, Baghdad, by the Mongols in 656/1258. Geographically, the regions covered are those actually or nominally held by the ᶜAbbasids during part or most of this period: Iraq, Syria and Iran; Egypt and the Arabian peninsula. The scope of the volume appears self-explanatory, but a few words of clarification are nevertheless called for. The term ᶜAbbasid is neither a political nor a strictly chronological designation, but a cultural one: though the first century of ᶜAbbasid rule set its stamp on a literature, that literature was thereafter to develop independently of the regime in many regional centres. Moreover, many features or tributaries of ᶜAbbasid literature had their origins in an earlier period, and are treated here within the framework of that period where appropriate. But above all the use of the term *belles-lettres* requires explanation. The companion to this volume, *Religion, Learning and Science in the ᶜAbbasid Period*, deals with ᶜAbbasid writings on such subjects as grammar, philosophy, history and law. This division between *belles-lettres* and "technical" literature is not found in ᶜAbbasid authors themselves, and could not be strictly observed in the present volume without presenting a distorted picture of the output of a given writer or region; but for a fuller treatment of the development of technical or scholarly disciplines, the reader is referred to the companion volume.

The proliferation of both scholarly and *belles-lettristic* genres marks a striking difference between ᶜAbbasid literature and the Arabic literature which preceded it. No less striking is the high proportion of non-Arabs who contributed to the Arabic literature of the ᶜAbbasid period, and the learned and allusive stamp of the literature as a whole. Cosmopolitan, urban ᶜAbbasid writers were conscious of the distance which separated them from the classical models by which they defined Arab and Muslim culture: archaic bedouin poetry and the enduring human and aesthetic values they believed it to embody; early Islamic history, which could be seen, no less than the Qurʾān itself, as enshrining the fundamental choices set before believers. These models were pressed into service to vindicate a civilization which faced rival cultural influences and claims, and which was itself in the process of absorbing many new elements. The pervasiveness of literary, Quranic and historical allusion in ʿAbbasid writing, and the impressive growth of scholarly and critical writing side by side with *belles-lettres*, reflect a culture sustained by active and creative reference to tradition. It follows that modern readers must acquire some familiarity with that tradition in order to gain access to ʿAbbasid literature even at the simplest level; and this volume has tried to provide the general reader with such an introduction by quoting original material wherever possible.

In format, the volume consists of juxtaposed studies of individual authors and thematic surveys of genres, arranged as far as possible chronologically in two main sections, prose and poetry, with each section prefaced by a general introductory chapter. These sections illustrate the literatures of Iraq and Syria, the earliest and major centres of ʿAbbasid culture. Two chapters on the regional literatures of Egypt and the Yemen, which until recently have received less widespread attention, conclude the volume. As the type and arrangement of material reflect some characteristics of, or problems raised by, ʿAbbasid literature, a final word should be said on this subject. The printing of texts in scholarly editions began only in the last century, and the literature is not yet well enough mapped, in terms of the sum of its productions, the finer categorizations applied to them or the relative importance of all but the most outstanding figures, to supply us with a canonical framework for interpretation. Definitive editions of many authors are not yet available, attributions are sometimes uncertain, and many texts were by their nature fluid and might be altered several times by the author himself without producing a definitive version. In addition, while there are anecdotal and biographical sources for the lives of most ʿAbbasid men of letters, the aim of medieval biographers was not to lay bare the souls of their subjects nor even to give an exhaustive account of their careers. Thus only in exceptional cases can the lives and literary personalities of ʿAbbasid writers be convincingly portrayed in modern biographical terms; hence one reason for the alternation in this volume between individual and general studies. But no less important is the fact that the ʿAbbasid conception of character, whether personal or literary, is probably not to be approached in modern terms. Many writers will be found, in the following chapters, as competent practitioners of genres which have little in common and might appear to have less common ground in the writer's own personality than in the requirements of his patrons. An explanation must be sought both in the conditions of literary production and in ᶜAbbasid conceptions of literature itself, whose variety is perhaps most broadly illustrated in the surveys of the literatures of Egypt and the Yemen, in which the links between genres, whether "technical" or *belles-lettristic*, are brought to the fore.

In the hope that the volume may be of interest and use to readers with no knowledge of Arabic as well as to Arabists, references have been given wherever possible to material which has been translated into a European language. Similarly the bibliographies, which are not intended as exhaustive, generally list European in preference to Arabic secondary sources.

I should like to thank all the staff at the Cambridge University Press who have helped in the production of this volume, Mr. Colin Wakefield of the Bodleian Library, Oxford, for advising on the index, and Mrs. Barbara Hird for compiling it. I gratefully acknowledge the advice and encouragement of the editorial board; and my particular thanks go to Professor A. F. L. Beeston for the translations which appear above his initials in chapters 9, 16, 18 and 19.

J. A.

ABBREVIATIONS

CHALUP	*The Cambridge History of Arabic Literature: Arabic Literature to the End of the Umayyad Period*
CHIran	*The Cambridge History of Iran*
CHIslam	*The Cambridge History of Islam*
EI	*The Encyclopaedia of Islam*
GAL, GAL,S	C. Brockelmann, *Geschichte der arabischen Litteratur*, and *Supplements* I-III
GAS	F. Sezgin, *Geschichte des arabischen Schrifttums*
Shorter EI	*Shorter Encyclopaedia of Islam*

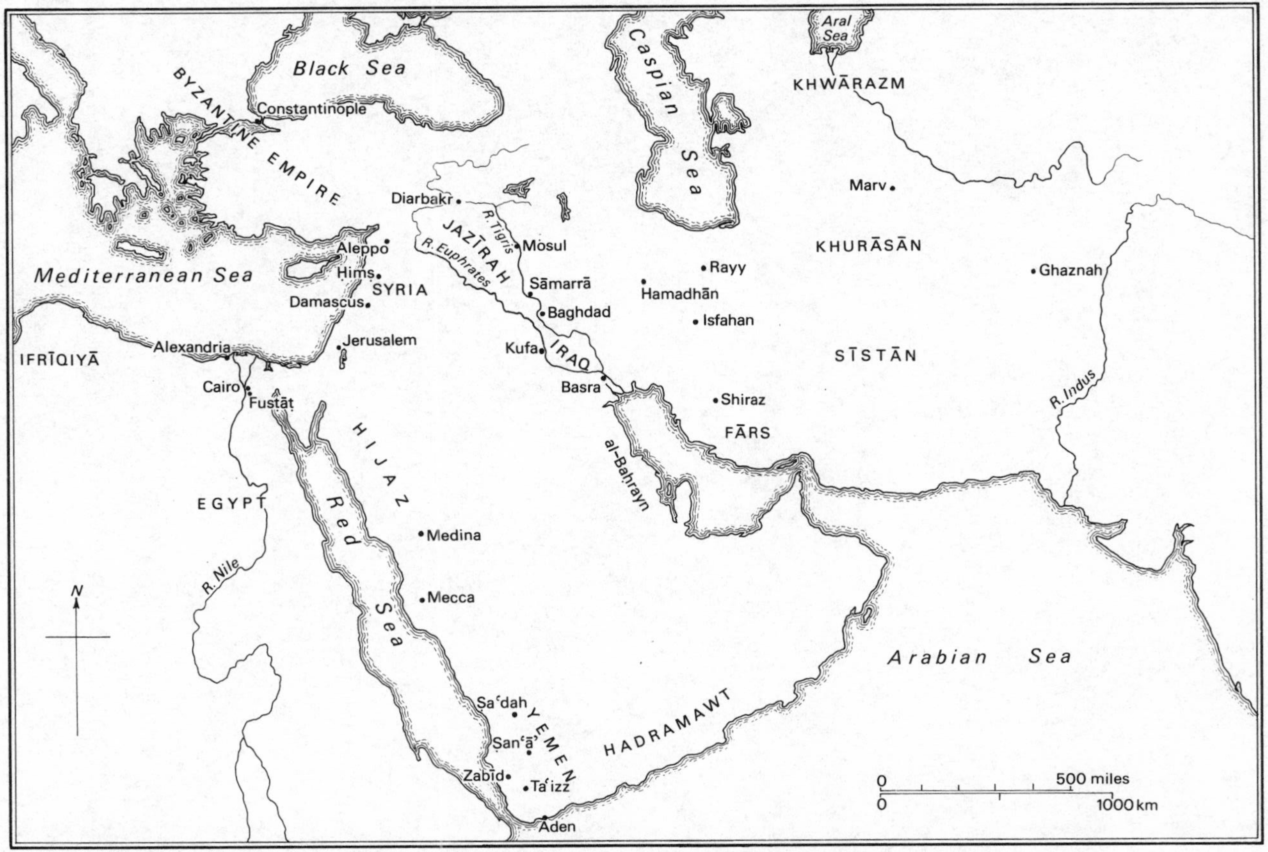

The Middle East during the ʿAbbasid period

THE ᶜABBASID CALIPHATE: A HISTORICAL INTRODUCTION

The ᶜAbbasid period opened with a major political revolution in the Islamic world. The ᶜAbbasid movement had developed in Khurāsān, the vast province which lay on the north-east frontiers of Islamic Iran, during the first part of the second/eighth century. The reasons for the revolt against the rule of the Umayyads in distant Damascus have been intensively debated by historians, and much remains unclear; but we can be certain that it was a movement among all the Muslims of the area, Arab and non-Arab alike, and it was intended to replace the Umayyad government, thought to be authoritarian and indifferent to both religion and the local concerns of the Khurāsānīs, by the rule of a member of the "Family of the Prophet" who would usher in an era of peace and justice. Perhaps because they came from a frontier province and had ample military experience, the Khurāsānīs were able to succeed where so many before them had failed;[1] marching westwards across the great plains of central Iran and through the passes of the Zagros mountains, they took Iraq in 132/749 and, while the leaders stayed in Iraq and Iran to consolidate their position, an expedition was sent to the west to defeat the demoralized Umayyad army and eventually to kill the last Umayyad caliph, Marwān b. Muḥammad, in Egypt, where he had taken refuge.

The military victory left many political problems to be solved. Like so many groups which come to power on the crest of a wave of revolutionary enthusiasm, the leaders of the ᶜAbbasid movement soon had to come to grips with the problems of reconciling revolutionary ideals with the practical problems of government. The first question was of course, who should be caliph. Revolutionary propaganda had simply called for "a chosen one" from the family of the Prophet, a cry which could unite many different interests; but it seems that the leaders of the movement had for some time been in touch with the descendants of the Prophet's uncle, al-ᶜAbbās, and when the victorious armies approached Iraq from the east, the ᶜAbbasid family had moved from southern Palestine to settle in Kufa. So it

[1] See *CHIslam*, I, 75–103.

was that in 132/750 a group of leading Khurāsānīs sought them out and proclaimed one Abū ʾl-ʿAbbās, known to history by his regnal title of al-Saffāḥ, as the first ʿAbbasid caliph. Not everyone was satisfied by this and it seems that there was a considerable number of people who held that only the direct descendants of the Prophet through his daughter Fāṭimah and ʿAlī b. Abī Ṭālib should be accepted as leaders of the Muslim community. At this stage they were too weak to mount a major political challenge, but they continued to pose an ideological threat which the ʿAbbasids were never completely able to master; those who felt that the revolution had been betrayed, or that the ʿAbbasid government had failed to establish a truly just and Islamic society, could always look to the ʿAlid family for leadership.

The first ʿAbbasid caliph, and his brother and successor, al-Manṣūr (136–58/754–75), were also faced with a second problem – the extent of the powers of the caliph. On the one hand, there were those who felt that the Umayyad regime had become too authoritarian and that the Muslims of the various provinces of the empire should be effectively in control of their own affairs, in particular that the taxes collected in the provinces should be spent on the stipends of the Muslims settled there, an idea which went back to the *dīwān* (list of those entitled to state salaries) of the second "Orthodox" caliph ʿUmar b. al-Khaṭṭāb. On the other hand, there were those who felt that the caliph should play the role of religious leader as well as secular administrator, deciding on the true interpretation of Qurʾān and *sunnah* (the precedents set by the Prophet, which were used as a basis of law) and, as God's representative on earth, enjoying an almost absolute power.

The differing ideas about who should be ruler, and the powers he was to enjoy, were the main bones of political contention under the ʿAbbasid caliphs. For their part, al-Saffāḥ and al-Manṣūr were determined to steer a middle course. They did not claim semi-divine powers, a fact which drove some of their supporters to violent discontent, but on the other hand they established a strong state, in which the caliph would be the effective ruler and would appoint governors to and collect taxes from all the provinces of the Islamic world (except Spain, which was tacitly abandoned at this time). Thus, when the leader of the ʿAbbasid movement in Khurāsān, Abū Muslim, attempted to secure his own independent rule over the province, al-Manṣūr had no hesitation in having him murdered, despite his previous services to the dynasty.

Although many of its leading figures originally came from Khurāsān, the early ʿAbbasid state was firmly based in Iraq and the rulers derived a large proportion of their incomes from the rich and flourishing agricultural economy of the Sawād, the "black land" or irrigated lands of lower Iraq. It was at the northern end of the Sawād, on a site conveniently close to the two great rivers, Tigris and Euphrates, and the roads to Khurāsān through the passes of the Zagros mountains, that al-Manṣūr, in 145/762, founded his capital at Baghdad which was to be the most important cultural centre in the Muslim world for the next three centuries. This concern for Iraq and its revenues led to the development of that most characteristic feature of ᶜAbbasid administration, the consolidation of a highly educated élite of administrative secretaries (*kuttāb*), the mandarins of the early Islamic world, whose power and wealth were based on the fact that they alone could administer the revenue-collecting machinery on which the regime depended. In many cases these were men of Persian or Nabaṭī (Aramaean) origin whose families had been established as small landowners in the Sawād since Iranian times but who now lent their expertise to the state. Under the leadership of the Barmakid family (the Barmecides of the *Arabian Nights*), themselves of eastern-Iranian origin, the *kuttāb* became an important political force during the reign of the third ᶜAbbasid caliph, al-Mahdī (158-69/775–85), and even after the dramatic fall of the Barmakids in 187/803, during the reign of Hārūn al-Rashīd (170–93/786–809), the *kuttāb* maintained and increased their influence.[2] These people were immensely important for the development of the literary culture of the age. Not only were they themselves literate, as their profession demanded – and sometimes, like Ibn Muqlah (d. 328/940), famous calligraphers – but they were also important as patrons of poets and prose-writers alike. The language of administration was Arabic, and it was Arabic literature that the *kuttāb* composed and patronized; but many of the *kuttāb*, like the Barmakids, were of Persian origin and looked back with some nostalgia to the great Persian imperial past, seeing in its achievements a form of reply to the Arab pride in the Qurᵓān and early Arabic culture. The Persian heritage, and to a lesser extent the Aramaean, was thus incorporated into the Arabic–Islamic cultural tradition, where it proved extremely influential and provided the intellectual background to the *Shuᶜūbiyyah* movement in literature, a reaction among non-Arab Muslims to Arab claims of superiority. The scene of this cultural activity was of course at the political capital in Baghdad, which had, by the beginning of the third/ninth century, come to replace all other cultural centres; the independent traditions of Kufa, Basra and the Hijaz were taken over and adapted by the new metropolitan centre. Besides the patronage of court and *kuttāb*, Baghdad also offered a separate and equally important cultural milieu, the world of the *ḥadīth* scholars or traditionists. This was largely a middle-class movement. The rapid economic growth of Baghdad led to the develop-

[2] For a comprehensive discussion of the *kuttāb*, see D. Sourdel, *Le Vizirat abbaside* (Damascus, 1959–60).

ment of a genuine bourgeoisie whose fairly modest wealth was derived from trade and manufacture rather than from government office or extensive landed estates. From the third/ninth century these people became increasingly concerned with the science of *ḥadīth* (the sayings and doings attributed to the Prophet), and this led in turn to much early history writing, culminating in the great *Taʾrīkh* ("History") of al-Ṭabarī (d. 310/923), who, although a landowner of private means from northern Iran, owed his training and intellectual development to the Baghdad milieu. The full development of Arabic literature in the third/ninth centuries is inconceivable without Baghdad as the great melting-pot and crucible of this culture. And Baghdad owed its existence and continued prosperity to the ʿAbbasid dynasty.

The period of stability and prosperity under the early ʿAbbasids reached its apogee during the reign of Hārūn al-Rashīd, which left its mark on literature with the poetry of Abū Nuwās and Abū ʾl-ʿAtāhiyah and is recalled in popular legend, including *Alf laylah wa-laylah* (the *Arabian Nights*), as the "golden age" of the ʿAbbasids; but this peace was shattered in the years after the caliph's death in 193/809 by a prolonged civil war which profoundly affected the course of ʿAbbasid history. Hārūn had decided that he should be succeeded by two sons in turn (some sources mention a third son but he did not play an active part in the war), Muḥammad al-Amīn and ʿAbdullāh al-Maʾmūn, and that meanwhile al-Maʾmūn should be essentially al-Amīn's viceroy in the East, i.e. Khurāsān, including all of eastern Iran. This complicated arrangement, detailed in solemn agreements displayed in the Kaʿbah at Mecca, was designed to solve a number of problems; those of coping with the vast size of the empire, of assuring an orderly pattern of succession, but above all the problem of taxation. In the years that followed the ʿAbbasid revolution, many Khurāsānīs had settled in Baghdad and their descendants formed an influential part of the population, known as the *abnāʾ al-dawlah* (literally "sons of the [ʿAbbasid] state"); but despite their long residence in Iraq, they were still paid from taxes collected in Khurāsān whence their families had originally come. It seems to have been resentment at this from those presently living in Khurāsān that led Hārūn to divide his heritage, and one of the most important features of the agreements between the two brothers was that taxes collected in Khurāsān were to be spent there. After the caliph's death, the elaborate agreement soon broke down; the leaders of the *abnāʾ* in Baghdad felt unable to tolerate the fiscal autonomy of Khurāsān and launched a major invasion to deprive al-Maʾmūn of his inheritance and to reconquer their native province. The attempt backfired disastrously; under the leadership of Ṭāhir b. al-Ḥusayn, al-Maʾmūn's supporters swept westwards into Iraq and took Baghdad after a long and hard-fought siege in 198/813. The civil war dragged on for almost a decade after that. It was only gradually that al-Maʾmūn and his supporters, notably Ṭāhir and his family and the caliph's younger brother Abū Isḥāq (soon to be caliph himself with the title of al-Muᶜtaṣim), were able to re-establish ᶜAbbasid authority over the central Islamic lands.

Al-Maʾmūn was succeeded in 218/833 by his brother al-Muᶜtaṣim, and it was under him that the new, middle ᶜAbbasid regime took shape. It was distinguished by a highly centralized financial administration and the development of a new army, a new capital and a new ideology. The new army consisted almost entirely of horsemen of Turkish origin, many of whom were barely Muslim or Arabic-speaking. Both the Arab tribes who had supported the Umayyad regime and the *abnāʾ*, who had supported the early ᶜAbbasids, were effectively excluded from participation, and it is the development of this new army, much more than the ᶜAbbasid revolution, which marks the moment when the Arabs lost control of the empire they had created. To avoid friction between this new army and the *abnāʾ* of Baghdad whom they had supplanted, al-Muᶜtaṣim founded a new capital, at Sāmarrā on the Tigris about eighty miles north of Baghdad, which distanced the military and government centre from the economic and cultural metropolis of Baghdad. The new ideology was adherence to the Muᶜtazilī doctrine of the createdness of the Qurʾān. This doctrine held that the Qurʾān, while of course the Word of God, was created in time, rather than being, as Sunnī theologians later held, coeternal with God. The importance of this was that if the Qurʾān was created in time, then it was for that time and could be interpreted or even possibly modified by a divinely guided caliph/imam to suit changing circumstances. There were a number of reasons why the middle ᶜAbbasid government was attached to this position; in part it was an attempt to reconcile the supporters of the ᶜAlids to ᶜAbbasid government, and the caliphs began to use the title imam at this time, emphasizing their religious status. The Muᶜtazilī position also allowed the caliph greater freedom for manoeuvre on dogmatic and legal questions since he was not bound by the developing tradition (*sunnah*) of the Prophet (clearly, if the Qurʾān itself could be reinterpreted, much of the early tradition which sought to explain it could be viewed as obsolete and disregarded). The middle ᶜAbbasid government made acceptance of the Muᶜtazilī position on the createdness of the Qurʾān the touchstone of loyalty to the Sāmarrā regime, and government officials were obliged by the *miḥnah* (inquisition) to pledge their loyalty to it. In opposition to these policies there developed in Baghdad a passionate concern for, and interest in, the traditions of the Prophet as a defence against the pretensions of

Sāmarrā, and the foundations were laid, by Aḥmad b. Ḥanbal and others, of the movement which was to develop into the fully fledged Sunnism of the fourth/tenth century. This development reached its intellectual maturity in the work of Abū ʾl-Ḥasan al-Ashʿarī (d. 324/935), who used the debating techniques of the Muʿtazilīs to produce a reasoned defence of tradition, and the general acceptance of Ashʿarism by the Sunnī community effectively closed the argument.

The Sāmarrā regime was comparatively short-lived. The marginal and alien soldiers whom al-Muʿtaṣim and his successors had imported to be their military backers felt threatened by any change of caliphal policy, and an attempt by the caliph al-Mutawakkil to broaden his power base by recruiting soldiers from elsewhere led to his murder at the hands of his Turkish guards in 247/861. There then followed ten years of anarchy in Sāmarrā, with rival groups of Turks and their supporters among the *kuttāb* fighting to ensure that their candidate became caliph and that, when he did, he looked after their interests. It was a grim period for the ʿAbbasids, and one which saw the beginnings of the disintegration of the empire into numerous different states. The accession of al-Muʿtamid in 256/870 effectively marked the end of the anarchy in Sāmarrā, not because of the caliph himself, who was something of a figurehead, but because his brother Abū Aḥmad, called al-Muwaffaq, slowly rebuilt the ʿAbbasid army and secured its loyalty to the dynasty. The anarchy had seen many of the provinces pass into the hands of the local rulers; in Egypt Aḥmad b. Ṭūlūn, himself of Turkish origin from Sāmarrā, took over and, while acknowledging the formal authority of the caliph, was effectively independent. In eastern and southern Iran power was seized by a war-lord from Sīstān, Yaʿqūb b. Layth al-Ṣaffār ("the Coppersmith"),[3] who was soon in a position to threaten Iraq. Closer to the centre, northern Syria and Iraq were claimed by local adventurers while, most dangerous and humiliating of all, the Zanj, black slaves who worked the latifundia of southern Iraq, overran the area which had been the heartland of ʿAbbasid power and sacked the great trading city of Basra at the head of the Gulf. Al-Muwaffaq and his son, the caliph al-Muʿtaḍid (279–289/892–902), both of them great soldiers, made a determined effort to restore the position, al-Muwaffaq by subduing the Zanj in a series of campaigns in the marshes of southern Iraq and by keeping back the threat from the Saffarids, and al-Muʿtaḍid by bringing northern Jazīrah (northern Mesopotamia) and much of western Iran under control. The high point of the ʿAbbasid revival was during the reign of al-Muktafī (289–95/902–8), when Egypt was briefly recovered for the caliphate.

All this good work was, however, brought to nothing during the

[3] See *CHIran*, IV, 106–17.

disastrous reigns of al-Muqtadir (295–320/908–32) and his successors, al-Qāhir (320–2/932–4) and al-Rāḍī (322–9/934–40). The reasons for this collapse were partly connected with the circumstances of al-Muqtadir's reign. He came to the throne young and inexperienced and was shamelessly manipulated by viziers, court factions and the military, all out to get what they could. But there was more to the collapse of the caliphate than the inadequacies of one individual. The most fundamental cause was the economic decline of Iraq. The early ᶜAbbasid caliphate, as has already been seen, had flourished on the agricultural prosperity of Iraq. From the time of the long civil wars which followed the death of Hārūn al-Rashīd in 193/809, this prosperity began to decline. The wars of the anarchy in Sāmarrā and the protracted struggle against the Zanj simply intensified the damage to the rich but fragile irrigation agriculture of the area. The problems which defeated al-Muqtadir and his experienced viziers like Ibn al-Furāt and ᶜAlī b. ᶜIsā, "the good vizier", were in the end economic; the government simply could not support the burden of providing for the vast court and military establishment. As the ᶜAbbasids gave away more and more lands and rights, frequently in the form of *iqṭāᶜ* or quasi-fief,[4] to solve temporary financial embarrassments, their enemies became more powerful and their own prospects for recovery diminished still further. In 324/936, the caliph al-Rāḍī was obliged to call on a local war-lord, Ibn Rāᵓiq, to enter Baghdad and assume the title of *amīr al-umarāᵓ* (amir of amirs, generalissimo) with complete control over military, political and financial affairs.[5] The ᶜAbbasid caliphs became simply ornamental figures, isolated in their palaces and devoid of any real power. The idea of a powerful and vigorous caliph exercising effective control of the Muslim world, an idea born with Abū Bakr and ᶜUmar, and fostered by Umayyads and early ᶜAbbasids alike, was now at an end.

THE SUCCESSOR STATES

The breakup of the caliphate saw the emergence of a large number of successor states of different background and character. It is easy to see the breakup of the caliphate as a disaster, and in some ways it was; never again was the Islamic world to have a central political focus of the sort which the ᶜAbbasids provided, and the effect on Baghdad and much of southern Iraq was to introduce a new era of economic decline in the area which had been the political centre of a major empire. But in other ways the breakup of the caliphate allowed the development of other political and cultural centres which had hitherto been overshadowed by Baghdad and the ᶜAbbasid court; in Egypt, Syria and Iran, new Muslim states emerged to provide

[4] See *EI*², "Iḳṭāᶜ". [5] See ibid., "Amīr al-umarāᵓ" and "Amīr".

different centres of cultural patronage; these competing centres allowed a wonderful variety of writing to flourish, and in many ways the century which witnessed the collapse of the caliphate was also a period of unrivalled literary activity.

This activity was stimulated by another important change, the growing pace of conversion to Islam. It is difficult to speak with confidence on this subject, but it would appear that the fourth/tenth century was the time when Muslims came to form the majority of the population in the central Islamic lands, although the speed obviously varied from area to area: faster in Iraq but probably slower in Egypt, where it would seem that mass conversion did not really get under way until after the Fatimid take-over in 358/969. It would be difficult to overestimate the importance of this change for the development of Arabic literature; educated Muslims in Egypt, Syria and Iran all expressed themselves in Arabic and if they made a contribution to literature, they made it to Arabic literature. Only when there was a considerable body of Muslims could centres like Egypt or Isfahan make a major contribution to Arabic writing as they did in the fourth/tenth century. Arabic high culture was no longer confined to a few centres but had become much more widespread. At the same time sectarian divisions became much more firmly established in the Muslim community. The emergence of militant Isma^cilism, which led to the rebellion of the Qarāmiṭah (Carmathians) in the Syrian desert and al-Baḥrayn, and to the emergence of the Fatimid caliphate, first in North Africa from 297/909 and in Egypt from 358/969, led to this sharpening of divisions.[6] In Baghdad itself there developed a deep split between those who supported the party of the Imāmī (Twelver) Shīʿīs and those groups who opposed them. (Twelver Shīʿīs believed that the line of visible *imām*s had ended with the eleventh imam, and that the twelfth would return to rule the world only at the end of time, as *Mahdī*; meanwhile, however, mankind was guided by the invisible line of his successors.) This split widened throughout the fourth/tenth century and was exacerbated if not originated by Buyid (or Buwayhid) amirs, who supported the Shīʿah in the hope of winning some popular support for their rule. One effect of these disputes was to encourage the development of polemical literature, all written in Arabic, which attempted to define and defend religious positions. The hub of this activity was Baghdad which, despite its appalling political and economic problems, never ceased to be the centre of religious learning.

The *kuttāb* continued to be important as patrons or creators of literature, and a good education in classical Arabic was still a passport to bureaucratic success. The role and origins of the viziers of this period were different

[6] See p. 12.

however. The *kuttāb* of the early ᶜAbbasid period owed their position to their ability to run a complex taxation system, especially in the Sawād of Iraq. The viziers of the successor states served more as intermediaries between the rulers and their subjects. The early Buyid rulers in both Iraq and central Iran were ill-educated; Muᶜizz al-Dawlah (amir of Iraq 334–56/945–67) hardly knew Arabic although he ruled Baghdad for over twenty years, and was heavily dependent on his viziers, notably the famous al-Muhallabī. It was from this Buyid milieu too that the most celebrated of the literary viziers, the Ṣāḥib Ibn ᶜAbbād, renowned both as poet and patron, emerged, as well as the most distinguished historian of the age, Abū ᶜAlī Miskawayh. Viziers who fell out of favour in one area could seek employment elsewhere, and even the great Ibn Sīnā (Avicenna) took service with the local rulers of Isfahan. Religious and political diversity had, in many cases, a stimulating effect on culture; even in the Buyid domains, where a dynasty of Iranian origin ruled over a predominantly Iranian population, the language of government and court culture was Arabic. Only in the extreme east of Iran, in the realms of the Samanid rulers, was the position of Arabic threatened by the emergent New Persian language.[7]

The Buyids or Buwayhids

Of the states which succeeded the dormant ᶜAbbasid caliphate, the most extensive was the confederation of amirates ruled by the Buyid family. The Buyids came originally from the area of Daylam at the south-west corner of the Caspian Sea and they were supported in their rise to power by the martial energies of the mountain people of the area, the Daylamīs. The Buyid dominions were not one state but at least three and sometimes more, combining and dividing according to the interests of the members of the family and their supporters. The first and most important of these amirates was the one founded in 322/934 by ᶜImād al-Dawlah (d. 338/949). Buyid rule, which lasted in Fārs until around 440/1048, was something of a golden age of peace and prosperity for the area. By contrast the history of the Buyid amirate of Baghdad was a catalogue of disasters. The financial problems which had plagued the later ᶜAbbasids were aggravated by the strife between Buyid princes and the war within the city between Sunnīs and Shīᶜīs and Turks and Daylamīs. Outside Baghdad, the countryside was increasingly under the control of bedouin chiefs like the ᶜUqaylids of the Jazīrah, or the Mazyadid chiefs of the Banū Asad in the Ḥillah area. Only when a strong ruler like ᶜAḍud al-Dawlah (amir in Baghdad 367–72/978–83) could use the resources of Fārs to sustain his rule in Baghdad was

[7] *CHIran*, IV, 145.

anything like peace and security established. Otherwise the first half of the fifth/eleventh century saw most of Iraq under the control of the bedouin tribes, while the unfortunate Buyid ruler of Baghdad, Jalāl al-Dawlah (416–35/1025–44), was obliged by poverty to dismiss his servants and set loose his horses since he could no longer feed them.

The third Buyid amirate, based on Rayy, Isfahan and Hamadhān in central Iran, was always separate from the other two, ruled at first by Rukn al-Dawlah (333–66/947–77) and later divided between a western Hamadhān and Isfahan state and an eastern one based on Rayy. Real power in this state lay as much with the viziers, the elder and younger Ibn al-ᶜAmīd and above all the famous Ṣāḥib Ibn ᶜAbbād, as it did with the Buyid princes themselves. The Buyid amirate in central Iran disappeared a full generation before those in Fārs and Baghdad; in 420/1029 Rayy fell to the Ghaznavid ruler Maḥmūd advancing from the East, while at about the same time Hamadhān passed into the family of the Kakuyids, related to the Buyids, who ruled it until the coming of the Saljuqs.

Despite its chaotic political history, the period of Buyid rule saw many achievements in the field of Arabic literary culture; apart from ᶜAḍud al-Dawlah, none of the rulers seems to have been greatly interested in learning or literature and the patronage came rather from the viziers, who, with their great wealth and power, were able to make up for the deficiencies of the semi-educated rulers; al-Muhallabī and Fakhr al-Mulk in Baghdad, Bahrām b. Māfannā in Shiraz in the early fifth/eleventh century, and Ibn ᶜAbbād, greatly encouraged literature and learning. Stress is frequently laid on the fact that the Buyids were Shīᶜīs, but too much weight should not be attached to this. In Baghdad some Buyid amirs certainly tried to manipulate Shīᶜī opinion in their own interests, a process which led, in the early fifth/eleventh century, to the re-emergence of the ᶜAbbasids, not as a political force but as spiritual leaders of the Sunnīs. In Fārs and central Iran, by contrast, the religious affiliations of the rulers seem to have caused few problems and there is no evidence that the Buyids encouraged Shiᶜī propaganda; indeed they sought the support of the ᶜAbbasid caliphs against the much more radical claims of the Shīᶜī Fatimids. The Buyids also tried to make use of the old Iranian heritage, adopting the title Shāhanshāh for the leader of the Buyid confederation and using Iranian personal names (ᶜAḍud al-Dawlah for example was called Fanā-Khusraw), but this was no thoroughgoing Iranian revival; the language of administration and literature remained Arabic throughout the Buyid period.

The Hamdanids

Of the various small amirates which succeeded the ᶜAbbasid caliphate in northern Iraq and Syria, the best known was the state of the Hamdanids. The Hamdanid ruling family came from the bedouin tribe of Taghlib, established in the Jazīrah since pre-Islamic times, and it was their power as tribal leaders which initially attracted the attention of the ᶜAbbasid authorities at the beginning of the fourth/tenth century when they were looking for allies against the Qarāmiṭah in the Syrian desert. The leaders of the family made their way as generals in the ᶜAbbasid army and, despite setbacks, they were able to take advantage of the final disintegration of the ᶜAbbasid state to carve out principalities for themselves, Nāṣir al-Dawlah (317–58/929–69) in Mosul and his more famous younger brother Sayf al-Dawlah (333–56/945–67) in Aleppo. Despite the bedouin origin of their families, the Hamdanid rulers tended to model their government on the later ᶜAbbasids, keeping armies of Turkish soldiers rather than relying on bedouin tribesmen, and living in cities rather than in nomad encampments. While Nāṣir al-Dawlah's long reign and that of his son Abū Taghlib (358–69/969–79) were comparatively undistinguished, being largely occupied with the struggle to keep Mosul independent from the Buyid amirate of Baghdad, Sayf al-Dawlah achieved immortality as a leader of the Muslims against resurgent Byzantine power. The early days, up to the mid-third/ninth century, when the Muslims usually held the initiative, were long since past; by Sayf al-Dawlah's time a strong and aggressive Byzantine empire was pursuing a policy of expansion against a deeply divided Muslim world, an expansion which culminated in the fall of Antioch to the Byzantines in 358/969. Despite a good deal of popular enthusiasm for the *jihād* (holy war) in Baghdad and elsewhere, Sayf al-Dawlah was effectively left to bear the brunt of the Byzantine attack on his own. In the end, he was not militarily very successful: much territory was lost by the Muslims, and Aleppo itself was sacked by the enemy; but his bold and spirited campaigns against greatly superior forces captured the imagination, and his prowess and patronage, celebrated by such poets as al-Mutanabbī, raised him to the status of a great Arab hero. After Sayf al-Dawlah's death in 356/967, the state he had founded declined rapidly. His son Saᶜd al-Dawlah (356–81/967–91) had great difficulty in establishing himself in Aleppo and was unable to defend his principality against outside aggression. The Hamdanid state was now squeezed between the Byzantines in the North and West and the Fatimids in Egypt and could no longer thrive in these changed circumstances. From 414/1023 Aleppo was a semi-independent buffer state between the two great powers, ruled, with interruptions, by the Mirdasid family, chiefs of the Banū Kilāb bedouin, who lived in the deserts to the east and south of the city.

The Fatimids

The most formidable of the states which replaced the ᶜAbbasid caliphate in the Middle East was the Fatimid caliphate of Egypt. Early Islamic Egypt was a wealthy country, but Arab settlement in the area had been restricted to a few areas, notably the capital city of Fusṭāṭ (Old Cairo), Alexandria and some of the desert areas. This had meant that conversion to Islam was fairly slow and that Egypt did not play as important a political role as its size and wealth would suggest. In 254/868, during the anarchy of the ᶜAbbasid caliphate at Sāmarrā, power in Egypt was assumed by the governor Aḥmad b. Ṭūlūn who made himself independent ruler not only of Egypt but also of most of Syria and Palestine as well; he built up an army of Turks and Nubian slaves and demonstrated that Egypt could be ruled as an independent state. The dynasty he founded ended with the ᶜAbbasid reconquest of 292/905, but others took up the idea of an independent Egypt. From 323/935 until 358/969 the country was ruled by the Ikhshidid family, another military dynasty of eastern Iranian origin, although for much of the time from 349/961 onwards effective power was in the hands of the Nubian slave Kāfūr, one of the patrons of the poet al-Mutanabbī.

The Ikhshidids were in their turn overthrown by the Fatimids. The Fatimids were adherents of the militant Ismāᶜīlī branch of the Shīᶜah. The first ruler of the dynasty, called, in disparagement by his enemies, ᶜUbayd Allāh, a diminutive of ᶜAbdullāh, began to proclaim that he was not only a direct descendant of ᶜAlī and Fāṭimah through the seventh imam – by Ismāᶜīlī reckoning – Ismāᶜīl, but also that he was the long-awaited *Mahdī* (divinely guided leader). He began his mission in Syria but was forced to leave by the Qarāmiṭah, a rival sect of Ismāᶜīlīs who refused to accept the Fatimid claims to the imamate. ᶜUbayd Allāh moved to Ifrīqiyā (Tunisia) where a supporter of his had already been conducting missionary activities. Here in 297/909 he seized power and proclaimed himself caliph and imam. The Fatimids claimed to be the rightful rulers of the whole Islamic world, but for the first sixty years they were confined to North Africa; they made two unsuccessful attempts to invade Egypt and conducted a protracted struggle with the Umayyad caliphate of Cordoba for the control of North Africa. In 358/969, however, the Fatimid general Jawhar finally took Egypt, and shortly afterwards the Fatimid caliph al-Muᶜizz abandoned his Tunisian capital of al-Mahdiyyah and moved to Egypt, where he established his court at the newly founded city of Cairo (al-Qāhirah, "the Victorious"), which lay just to the north of ancient Fusṭāṭ.

The coming of the Fatimids to Egypt marked a major revolution in the Islamic world. There were now two rival caliphates, the active and expanding Shīᶜī caliphate of the Fatimids and the shadowy ᶜAbbasids of Baghdad, effectively controlled by their Buyid protectors, and these two powers struggled for influence. The scenes of the conflict were essentially Syria and Palestine, which the Fatimids sought to control as the Tulunids had before them. They faced the opposition of the Byzantines and the Buyids and, most seriously of all, of the bedouin of the Syrian desert who continually threatened Fatimid control of the inland cities. The conflict with the ᶜAbbasid caliphate was greatly exacerbated after the strongly Sunnī Saljuqs, a Turkish dynasty, took Baghdad in 447/1055, and established themselves as protectors of the ᶜAbbasids; when the Crusaders arrived in the East in 491/1097, the Fatimids' first thought was not to defeat these new enemies of Islam, but to see if they would be useful allies against their Sunnī Saljuq enemies.

Within Egypt, Fatimid rule was, on the whole, a period of great prosperity. This was partly because of the agricultural wealth of the country, but also because of the textile industry and the growing importance of Egypt in international trade. From the beginning of the fifth/eleventh century, the Fatimid dominions saw the arrival of a growing number of merchants from the Latin West, notably from Italy, not only in Egypt itself but also in the Fatimid-ruled ports of the Levant. The Mediterranean was becoming once again, as it had been in classical times, a major route for international commerce, and the Fatimids were the main beneficiaries.

Writers at the time comment on the contrast between the wealth and prosperity of Fatimid Egypt and the poverty and misery of much of the Islamic East. The Fatimid period seems to have seen a great increase in the proportion of Muslims in the Egyptian population, although non-Muslims, especially Christians, remained important in the Fatimid bureaucracy. It was at this time that an indigenous Arabic culture was developed in Egypt, and Arab Egypt, so to speak, came of age to the extent that it was able to rival older centres like Baghdad as a seat of learning and intellectual activity.

It might be imagined that the coming to power of the Shīᶜī Fatimids in largely Sunnī Egypt would create serious religious tensions, but this does not seem to have been the case. The Ismāᶜīlī faith remained the belief of the ruling class and the city of Cairo with its newly founded mosque of al-Azhar a centre of Ismāᶜīlī education, but most of the country was allowed to adhere to its traditional beliefs, and the old city of al-Fusṭāṭ was a stronghold of Sunnism; only in the time of the unbalanced caliph al-Ḥākim (386–411/996–1021) was there any serious religious persecution, and by and large Egypt saw less tension between Sunnī and Shīʿī than contemporary Baghdad. (Al-Ḥākim, who seems to have believed himself divine, persecuted Sunnīs, Shīʿīs and Christians alike and seems, in the end, to have abandoned Islam entirely. After his death, a section of the Shīʿah who accepted al-Ḥākim's claims established themselves in Syria and Lebanon, where, known as Druzes, they survive to the present day.)

Rulers of the Yemen

In the Yemen, as elsewhere in the Islamic world, ʿAbbasid authority had largely disappeared by the end of the third/ninth century. From then on the country was the scene of confused struggles between local dynasts and representatives of powers from elsewhere in the Islamic world. Perhaps because of its remoteness, the Yemen became a centre of Shīʿī activity. From about 280/893 Ṣaʿdah and the north of the country were ruled by Imams of the Zaydī division of the Shīʿah (which was also influential in the areas to the south of the Caspian Sea in Iran). Their efforts to assert their control over the whole area were thwarted, partly by a local family, the Yuʿfirids of Shibām, and partly because missionaries from the rival Fatimid Ismāʿīlī Shīʿīs were active there as well. Between 439/1048 and the end of the fifth/eleventh century, power in the south of the country was in the hands of the Sulayhids, who gave their allegiance to the Fatimids, and conducted correspondence with the Fatimid caliph al-Mustanṣir (427–87/1036–94), although the country never came under effective Fatimid control. With the fall of the Sulayhids, Ismāʿīlī power waned, although the Zaydī Imams continued to retain their position in the north of the country. Thereafter power was shared in the area between the Zaydīs in the north and, after the Ayyubid conquest in 569/1173, two staunchly Sunnī dynasties: the Ayyubids (569–628/1173–1229) and the Rasulids (628–858/1229–1454). The Fatimids may have been interested in the commerce passing through the ports of the Yemen; the Ayyubids certainly were, and took an active part in it, the Egyptians and Yemenis both being concerned to foster Red Sea trade. The complexity of political affairs did not inhibit the development of a significant local literary culture, and the period was an important one for Yemeni civilization.[8]

[8] See R. B. Serjeant, "Yemeni merchants and trade in Yemen 13th–16th centuries", D. Lombard and J. Aubin, *Marchands et hommes d'affaires asiatiques* (Paris, 1987).

The Saljuqs

Other areas of the Middle East saw the emergence of dynasties of local, often tribal, origin at this time; some, like the ᶜUqaylids of Mosul and the Mazyadids of Ḥillah, were Arab; others, like the Hasanuyids of the central Zagros mountains or the Marwanids of Mayyāfāriqīn, were Kurdish. The history of these small states is complex, but they shared certain characteristics; they were all Muslim and acknowledged the authority of one of the caliphates, and they all used Arabic as their official and administrative language. Political divisions did not impede cultural unity and the interchange of scholars and ideas. The careers of such figures as Avicenna and the poet al-Mutanabbī show how the existence of these different centres could actually stimulate and encourage cultural developments.

The whole face of Middle Eastern history was changed by the arrival of the Ghuzz Turks under their Saljuq leaders during the course of the fifth/eleventh century.[8] Unlike the previous Turkish immigrants into the Muslim world, who had been either military slaves or professional soldiers, the Ghuzz came in a series of tribal migrations, and the changes they caused were ethnic as well as political, people like the Kurds of the Zagros and the Greeks of Anatolia being displaced from their homelands by these new arrivals. The Saljuqs swept away the last of the Buyids in Shiraz and, in 447/1055, in Baghdad, and forced the bedouin chiefs of Iraq and Syria to accept their authority. Only the power of the Fatimids could resist them. Saljuq rule had many achievements in terms of administration and architecture to its credit, but in terms of Arabic literature the coming of these Turkish-speaking rulers and their Persian-speaking bureaucrats marked the end of a great period. That is not to say that there were no longer religious scholars and historians producing Arabic writing, but the insistence on Sunnī orthodoxy seems to have muzzled something of the vigorous discussion that was possible in the more open, pre-Saljuq society when the free-thinking speculation of Abū ʾl-ᶜAlā al-Maᶜarrī or the humanist political philosophy of Miskawayh could be developed. If the Saljuqs did patronize literature, it tended to be Persian rather than Arabic, and the numerous little courts which had contributed to the cultural activity of the previous century were swept into oblivion.

[9] See C. Cahen, *Pre-Ottoman Turkey* (London, 1968); *CHIran*, v.

CHAPTER 1

ADAB AND THE CONCEPT OF *BELLES-LETTRES*

Adab, the general term used in modern Arabic for literature or *belles-lettres*[1], is often also applied by Arab and western scholars to a body of medieval writings (such as those described in chapters 2 to 6 of this volume) which has come to be regarded as constituting a specific literary genre. At the same time, the term *adab* is frequently encountered among medieval Arab writers in a variety of applications, and, though some of these have literary connotations, none corresponds exactly to either of the modern meanings of the word *adab*. C.A. Nallino first noted these divergencies and attempted to outline the development of the term.[2] *Adab* was widely used in the Middle Ages in the sense – among others – of "philology", "literary scholarship", "literary culture", and perhaps it was this use of the word that led nineteenth-century translators to adopt the plural *ādāb* to designate European works of literature. In so doing, they lent the word an added dimension, since the new application coincided with the introduction of new notions of what constituted literature and literary studies. Nevertheless, Nallino argues convincingly that there are medieval precedents for the use of *adab* to designate something like the modern concept of literature (taken, in the limited sense, as comprising verse, prose and historiography); thus we find the word applied to "witticisms, aphorisms, anecdotes, elegant verse" "pieces of poetry, curious tales"; philologists, meanwhile, used *adab* in the more precise sense of poetry and artistic prose. More recently, Charles Pellat has questioned the appropriateness of Nallino's acceptance of *adab* as a term for "literature" on historical grounds. Taking "literature" in a much wider sense than Nallino, he objects that the medieval concept of *adab* was too restricted to designate all existing literary production, since it included neither religious nor technical writings – which make up the bulk of medieval Arabic prose – nor poetry as such (this last statement, as we shall see, requires some qualification).[3] The following pages attempt to

[1] A longer and more technical version of this chapter was originally submitted in 1975. Part of the footnotes have been cut and the text has in some places been simplified. Ed.

[2] *La Littérature arabe*, 7–28.

[3] "Variations", 21–2.

retrace the medieval history of the term *adab*, and to discuss to what extent the use of categories such as "*adab* works" and "*adab* literature" can be justified.

PRE-LITERARY USAGES

The medieval dictionaries list a considerable variety of meanings for the term *adab*, for example "disciplines of the mind", "good qualities and attributes of the mind and soul", "good breeding", etc. Lane, in his *Lexicon*, says that *adab* in the sense of the "philological sciences" is post-classical, and could find no instances of *adab* meaning "polite literature" in a medieval dictionary – no doubt because the lexicographers are generally only concerned with classical usage. Pellat observes that in post-classical texts *adab*, in its widest sense, appears in three different spheres which are nevertheless closely related: the moral, the social and the intellectual.[4] Though these are not always easily distinguishable, the question of how the same term came to find a place in all three remains to be answered. Nallino suggests that *adab* originally meant "ancestral custom" and was therefore a near-synonym of *sunnah* (customary practice); hence, he suggests, *adab* came at an early date to be used for "knowledge", not only of social and ethical precepts but also of practical matters, moving eventually into the intellectual sphere. Early sources do not yield unambiguous evidence in support of this theory. Not only is it rarely possible to date or authenticate the earliest source-material, poetry, with absolute certainty (even in authentic, datable pieces individual words may have been changed at a later period to suit contemporary taste), but, in these early texts, *adab* and its derivates seldom appear in contexts where their meaning can be accurately determined. A case in point is a line by the *mukhaḍram* (pre- to early Islamic) poet Sahm b. Ḥanzalah al-Ghanawī, quoted by Nallino:

> People do not withhold from me what I want, but I do not give them what they want; what a good *adab* this is!

Here *adab* could well mean "custom" or even "ancestral custom", but the poet is probably commenting ironically on his own bad manners. The same ambiguity is found in a line by the, possibly early Islamic, poet Abūʾl-ʿIyāl al-Hudhalī:

> Sometimes the nobility of his grandfather and *adab* show a man the way to deeds of good repute.[5]

Here *adab* could mean "ancestral custom", but "upbringing" or "education" might fit the context equally well. Nevertheless, there are early

[4] See p. 83. [5] Sukkarī, *Sharḥ ashʿār al-Hudhaliyyīn*, I, 427.

examples which lend some support to the translation of *adab* by "custom" or "ancestral custom", and, though such material is probably not as old as that just quoted, it may still reflect what was common usage at an earlier date. A well-known *ḥadīth* states that a father can confer nothing better on his son than a good *adab*;[6] the women of Quraysh (the Prophet's tribe) catch the habit – *adab* – of the women of the Anṣār (the Helpers, Muḥammad's supporters in Medina) of speaking against their husbands;[7] the poet Ḥamzah b. Bīḍ (d. 116/734), addressing the son of the Umayyad governor Yazīd b. al-Muhallab, calls him a man brought up in the *adab* of a family to whom East and West had to submit and praises the way they raised (*addabū*) him.[8] As this last example shows, the borderline between custom and the knowledge and teaching of custom is tenuous; elsewhere, the association of *adab* with education is often explicit. In a number of examples dating most probably from pre-Islam or from the first century of Islam, we find the verbs *adaba* and *addaba* in the sense of "to educate", "to bring up", "to chastise" in the moral sense, and of "to train" an animal, and the adjective *adīb* in the sense of "well-trained". Examples from the first century of Islam confirm the association of *adab* with training; according to one *ḥadīth*, the master of a slave-girl will earn a threefold heavenly reward if he trains her well (*addabahā fa-aḥsana taʾdībahā*), instructs her well (in the tenets of Islam?), then frees her and marries her.[9] The subject of the verb *addaba* may be the experiences that make a man wise: the poet Aʿwar al-Shannī (a contemporary of ʿAlī b. Abī Ṭālib) claims that he has no need to ask anyone for advice, for he has schooled himself (*addabtu nafsī*) to act cunningly towards people who deserve to be treated with caution.[10] Of the term *adab* itself we find one example that, if authentic, can be dated to the first century: a line by ʿUmar b. Abī Rabīʿah (d. 93/711–12 or 103/721) who speaks of placating his angry beloved "with gentleness and *adab*".[11] *Adab* here should probably be translated by "diplomacy, courtesy" as social virtues, or "tact, grace" in the ethical sphere. The association of *adab* with social and ethical virtues is clearly supported by what the ʿAbbasid poet and anthologist Abū Tammām (d. 231 or 232/845–6) sees as ancient Arab *adab*; his interpretation is implicit in the choice of examples which make up the chapter "*Adab*" in his anthology of bedouin poetry, *al-Ḥamāsah*, which was intended to illustrate the old Arab virtues (it takes its title from the first chapter, "*Bāb al-Ḥamāsah*", which exemplifies hardihood). As Nallino observes, the material quoted deals with moral precepts and good qualities of the soul (fear of

[6] Wensinck, *Concordance*, I, 36b.
[7] Bukhārī, *Ṣaḥīḥ*, III, 174–5; VIII, 36; this tradition may date from the second/eighth century.
[8] Abū ʾl-Faraj al-Iṣfahānī, *Aghānī*, XIV, 15.
[9] Wensinck, *Concordance*, I, 36b.
[10] Buḥturī, *Ḥamāsah*, 103.
[11] Abū ʾl-Faraj al-Iṣfahānī, *Aghānī*, I, 59; on this poet, cf. pp. 152 and 204, below.

incurring blame, abhorrence of immoral deeds, politeness, indulgence towards friends, etc.), in short, everything that guides people in their conduct. The quotations actually contain only one example of the use of the term *adab*, and that of uncertain date, but what is important is how Abū Tammām, an expert on ancient poetry, sees pre-Islamic and Umayyad *adab*: in the verses he quotes, there is never any question of practical knowledge, still less of specialized knowledge. The quotations extol character and wisdom and related virtues and behaviour. Thus an anonymous, possibly ᶜAbbasid poet of the tribe Fazārah boasts that he always, politely, addresses people by their *kunyah*s (agnomens):[12]

> I have been brought up (*uddibtu*) to do so, and it has become part of my character:
> For I have found that nurture (*adab*) holds the reins of nature.[13]

However, if terms derived from the root ʾ*db* are often connected, in early examples, with upbringing and training, it is hard to believe that this education would always have been associated exclusively with social and ethical virtues, even though the examples in *al-Ḥamāsah* do not support a wider interpretation. There is no clear evidence, however, that *adab* moved into the intellectual sphere before the end of the first/seventh century. From this latter period Nallino quotes an example by the poet Abū ᶜAṭāʾ al-Sindī (end of Umayyad/beginning of ᶜAbbasid period), in which the term *adīb* appears in the sense of "instructed about a particular matter":

> If you send someone as a messenger to deal with an affair, make him understand it thoroughly and send him well-briefed (*adīb*).[14]

Ismāᶜīl b. ᶜAmmār, a poet of the same period, addresses some verses to a singing slave-girl who is being trained up to be offered as a gift to an Umayyad caliph, but whether, in referring to her education (*taʾdīb*), he means her training in singing, or education in a wider sense, is not clear.[15]

ADAB, LITERATURE AND CULTURE

Beginning with the second/eighth century, and possibly even earlier, *adab* appears in relation to literature, mainly poetry, but also some famous proverbs and speeches. To the question of how this new application derives from the earlier usages several answers may be suggested. From this period, *adab* in a literary context may refer either to literary creativity, or else to literature as an object of philological study or to knowledge of literature as a

[12] "Father of . . .", "Mother of . . ."; on Arabic nomenclature, see *CHALUP*, 18–22.
[13] Marzūqī, *Sharḥ Dīwān al-ḥamāsah*, 1146. [14] *La Littérature arabe*, 12.
[15] Abū ʾl-Faraj al-Iṣfahānī, *Aghānī*, x, 138.

mark of erudition. However, these two senses, with their respectively active and passive connotations, are not always clearly distinguished. For example, the second/eighth-century poet Bashshār b. Burd boasts of his own achievements in terms that leave no doubt he is referring to his literary talents:

A visitor of kings, endowed with splendour, known for his poetry (*shiʿr*) and speeches (*khuṭab*),
How excellent are the pearls hidden in his breast that are relentlessly sought after!
Wherever people are gathered, pearls come forth from his mouth as the light of the candle comes forth from its flame . . .
He is a jester to whom kings turn their attention, learning both from his earnestness and from his frolicking.
At daybreak people crowd at his door in haste to acquire his *adab*.[16]

Although, as a Persian and a Shuʿūbī (a protagonist of the virtues of the non-Arabs against Arab claims to superiority), Bashshār may be asserting his own cultural superiority, it is tempting, in this context, to translate *adab* simply by "literary production(s)", and there are texts from later periods which seem to justify this rendering. Speaking of his own poetry, al-Mutanabbī (d. 354/965) observes sarcastically:

It is as though the blind are studying my *adab*, and my words are received by those who are deaf;[17]

while in his *Risālat al-Ghufrān*, Abū ʾl-ʿAlāʾ al-Maʿarrī (d. 449/1058) at one stage makes his "hero", Ibn al-Qāriḥ, on an imaginary journey through Heaven and Hell, contemplate collecting some of the *ādāb* of the jinn, which consist of poetry, in which, he is told, the jinn are infinitely more prolific than humans. But simply to translate *adab* by "poetry", even in such contexts, is to overlook the fact that the word has connotations which set it apart from technical terms such as *shiʿr* and *qarīḍ* for poetry and *qawāfī* for lines of poetry, poems. A second passage from Bashshār tells how the poet tries to win over his beloved by sending her a message through a slave-girl who not only "recites poetry from memory" but is also "conversant with *adab*",[18] an amplification which suggests that she would be able to recite poetry suitable to the occasion, as a result of having a thorough grounding in literature. Similarly, it should be remembered that al-Mutanabbī gave lectures on his own poetry, while in the passage referred to from *Risālat al-Ghufrān*, *adab* is presented as an object of study. In the examples where Bashshār and al-Mutanabbī speak of their own *adab*, it may be imagined that the poets see their works as models for contemporaries or posterity; and, in

[16] *Dīwān*, II, 157–61. [17] Ibn al-Qifṭī, *Inbāh*, 54–5. [18] *Dīwān*, I, 177.

any case, if *adab*, in these contexts, is rendered as "poetry", it should be borne in mind that the poet may well be suggesting that his compositions are the fruit of his literary scholarship. For although much has been made of the early ᶜAbbasid "quarrel of the Ancients and the Moderns",[19] there is no evidence that the critics of the second–third/eight–ninth centuries felt that there had been, or that poets desired that there should be, a clean break with pre-Islamic tradition. Al-Mubarrad (d. *c.* 285/898), an influential and supposedly conservative critic, observes that the poetry of Ibn Munādhir (d. *c.* 198/814) shows the forcefulness of the idiom (*kalām*) of the bedouin and the sweetness of the "new" (*muḥdath*, i.e. early ᶜAbbasid) poets' style, the one resulting from his knowledge of ancient poetry and his *adab*, the other reflecting contemporary taste.[20] In a famous passage, the poet Abū ʾl-ᶜAtāhiyah (d. *c.* 210/825) deprecates his own poetry and comments on that of his contemporaries. Though he apparently makes a distinction between the old school and that of Bashshār and Ibn Harmah (Ibrāhim b. ᶜAlī b. Harmah, d. *c.* 176/792), he seems to imply that they, unlike himself, might well be able to live up to the standards of the early masters. There is no clear evidence that *adab* was used *before* Bashshār's time of the erudition of the poet who, in matters of form at least, adhered to the old conventions, but, once established, the association of *adab* with learning continues throughout the second/eighth to fourth/tenth centuries. Its specific association with knowledge of classical literature (and also grammar and lexicography) hardly seems open to question. Abū Tammām derides the Egyptian poet Yūsuf al-Sarrāj ("Yūsuf the Saddlemaker") for his use of lexical rarities (*gharīb*): he has never, he says, heard of a saddlemaker who is also an *adīb*.[21] The poet al-Buḥturī (d. 284/897) no doubt refers to his own qualifications as a scholar when he stresses that want and obscurity do not befit a man of *adab*:

If the *adīb* accepts a life of obscurity, what benefit will he derive from the *adab* that he has studied (*al-adab al-mustafād*)?[22]

– a good example (whether or not the line is authentic) of *adab*/*adīb* with both an active and a passive connotation. But the possession of *adab* was not confined to the scholar–poet, and *adab* itself need not be exclusively classical. The Spanish poet ᶜAbbās b. Nāṣiḥ (d. 238/852) is in the habit of questioning travellers about the emergence of new talent in the East; upon hearing of the rise of Abū Nuwās he travels to Baghdad and introduces himself to the poet as a man who is eagerly seeking *adab*.[23] The patron as well as the poet or man of letters might be an *adīb*: the philologist Ibn al-

[19] See pp. 155–6 [20] *Kāmil*, 1225. [21] See p. 415. [22] *Dīwān*, IV, 2551.
[23] Zubaydī, *Ṭabaqāt al-naḥwiyyīn*, 285.

Aʿrābī (d. *c.* 231/845-6), on his way to visit the singer and poet Isḥāq al-Mawṣilī, praises him, in the words of the poet Abū Tammām, as "a king from whose wealth and *adab*" he will benefit;[24] the context makes it likely that Ibn al-Aʿrābī associated *adab* with connoisseurship and taste as well as creative talent.

How then is the association of *adab* with literary scholarship and literary production connected with the earlier use of *adab* for training and the social and ethical virtues? If early uses of *adab* to designate a specific form of training, or specialist knowledge, could be found, the derivation of "literary scholarship" from *adab* would need no further explanation, and *adab* as "literary production" would in turn derive from *adab* as "learning" by the process described above. However, the twofold, and often simultaneous, active and passive connotations of literary *adab* perhaps suggest another line of descent. Though the examples of literary *adab* given so far relate to poetry, we have noted that *adab* and *shiʿr* are not simple equivalents. *Adab*, we saw, has wider connotations; and indeed, in the later third/ninth century, we find al-Mubarrad using the plural *ādāb* not only of poetry but of several other forms of literature as well. In the introductory paragraph to *al-Kāmil* he says:

> This is a book which we have composed in order to bring together various *ādāb*: prose, good verse, famous proverbs, eloquent homilies, and a selection of celebrated speeches and stylish letters. Our intention is to explain every unusual expression appearing in this book as well as every concept that is not readily understandable, and to offer detailed comments on every syntactical problem that might occur, so that the book can stand by itself and will not oblige the reader to have recourse to anyone else for explanations.

This list covers the whole spectrum of outstanding early ʿAbbasid literature; it seems that, to al-Mubarrad, speaking of his own discipline, *adab* had a very definite meaning: all prose and poetry that was aesthetically gratifying and therefore worth quoting and explaining.

The fact that *al-Kāmil*, like many other works that have also been classified as *adab*, is a miscellany, suggested to H.A.R. Gibb one explanation of how a term originally linked to the teaching of social and ethical concepts came to be applied to literature. Gibb seems to suggest that, since the word *adab* appeared in the titles of books produced by the secretarial school of letters representing Iranian literary and socio-ethical traditions, the opponents of this school (al-Jāḥiẓ, and perhaps some of his second/eighth-century precursors) used the same term in their own collections to make clear what they thought was the *adab* their readers should adopt.[25] More

[24] Abū ʾl-Faraj al-Iṣfahānī, *Aghānī*, v, 55.

[25] *Studies*, 71–2; cf. *CHALUP*, chs. 4, 23, and ch. 2, below.

detailed research has been done, since Gibb wrote, on the early *kātib*s (administrative secretaries, civil servants), which makes it less easy to advance broad hypotheses as to the significance and impact of their writings, and Gibb's view of early Arab *adab* as essentially anti-Shuᶜūbī, i.e. essentially polemical and political, cannot be accepted uncritically. Even before Gibb, Nallino had put forward a more discriminating explanation. He dates back to the beginning of the third/ninth century the use of the term *adab* for certain social graces which include the ability to entertain others with "aphorisms, anecdotes, elegant verse and stories; the use of allusive digressions and analogies"; Nallino appears to see the use of *adab* for literary erudition as resulting from the demands of a highly civilized society, from the requirements of social integration rather than those of social polarization. He may not be correct in suggesting that *adīb* is a synonym of *ẓarīf*, an adjective referring to the polished manners of a man of the world,[26] though the social connotations of the literary erudition of the *adīb* appear clearly in, for example, the introduction to the *Dīwān al-maᶜānī* (an anthology of literary theory) of Abū Hilāl al-ᶜAskarī (d. *c.* 400/1009). However, Nallino probes the social significance of *adab* more deeply when he observes that, to those who preferred knowledge of the humanities to other ways of earning social prominence, *adab* meant "all literary compositions of style and distinction, and not simply elegant extracts". This type of *adab* he sees as comprising "existing types of knowledge, exclusive of matters pertaining to religion" (the latter statement may require modification, as we shall see), and he adds that this usage, common in the first and second centuries of Islam, was, until the second/eighth century, restricted to knowledge that was typical of the Arabs (though it might be more exact to say that Arab lore formed the core of such knowledge). This line of reasoning would explain how *adab* came to have the active sense of "literary skills"(eloquence being deemed the Arab characteristic *par excellence*) as well as the passive sense of "literary scholarship" and "the classical literary heritage" that was the object of such scholarship. But the points inherent in Nallino's explanation – the emphasis on the complexities of a civilized society, the concept of the humanities,[27] and the consciousness of a certain tension between secular and religious learning – can be taken further, and used to refine Gibb's explanation of the significance of *adab*. Social, religious or political considerations may indeed have contributed to the use of the term *adab* for literature. To speak of poetry as *adab* qualified it as "education" rather than an idle pastime. The knowledge of Arab lore kept alive associations with those ancient virtues which gave the Arabs their title to glory and which later generations still

[26] Cf. pp. 208–9 [27] See below, chs. 4, 6.

strove to emulate despite the influence of foreign civilizations. On the one hand, it opened the way to countering the pretensions of the *Shuᶜūbiyyah*, who challenged the superiority of the Arabs in cultural and ethical matters; on the other, it gave a positive stimulus to the concept of practical virtue. *Adab* is sometimes associated with *muruwwah* (originally the pagan ideal of manly virtue), by which we should understand, in the Islamic context, the sum of those virtues that are typical of ancient Arab culture in so far as they are in agreement with the ethics of Islam. However, *adab* also appears in connection with specifically Islamic concepts of virtue. A famous scholar of *ḥadīth*, Ibn Kunāsah (123–207 or 209/741–823 or 824), is said to have had a pupil who studied *ḥadīth* and Islamic law with him, "making a show of *adab* and devotion". Upon discovering his lack of sincerity, Ibn Kunāsah wrote a poem which begins:

> He who studies *adab* but does not act on it and fails to control his passions is no *adīb*.

Two more lines follow which repeat that the student must practise the good conduct he has learned, and that it is not enough to simply to know the correct answers.[28]

ADAB AND THE PROFESSIONS

Perhaps in order to clarify the bearing of *adab*, which by the third/ninth century had already acquired many applications and shades of meaning, Ibn Qutaybah (d. 276/889) cites a much-quoted saying which contrasts the *ᶜālim*, who specializes in a single branch of knowledge, with the *adīb*, who practises various branches of knowledge.[29] Another, unpublished text of the same period, the *Muṣannaf* of Abū Bakr b. Abī Shaybah (159–235/775–6–849), subsumes various miscellaneous branches of *ᶜilm* under the heading of *adab*.[30] In this sense, the *adīb* may perhaps indeed correspond to the *ẓarīf*, Nallino's polished man of the world (see above). But the relation of *adab* to *ᶜilm* is not necessarily a simple relation of the general to the particular, for the one development in the applications of the term *adab*, which Nallino observes as early as the third/ninth century, is its use in the sense of "knowledge indispensible to a particular profession" or "rules of conduct pertaining to a particular social group". Nallino links this development with two different connotations of the earlier meanings of *adab*. These are, firstly, *adab* as a synonym of what he believes to be a pre-Islamic concept of *sunnah*; as examples, he cites such instances as the chapters on *adab al-*

[28] Ibn Qutaybah, *K. al-Shiᶜr*, 560. [29] *ᶜUyūn al-akhbār*, II, 129.
[30] Rosenthal, *Knowledge Triumphant*, 74–5.

ḥukamāʾ wa ʾl-ʿulamāʾ ("The usage of sages and men of learning"), and on *al-adab fī ʾl-mujālasah* ("How to behave in polite society"), in Ibn ʿAbd Rabbih's (d. 328/940) *al-ʿIqd al-farīd*, and chapters such as *adab al-akl* ("Table-manners") and *adab al-nikāḥ* ("The proprieties of matrimony"), in al-Ghazālī's (d. 505/1111) *Iḥyāʾ ʿulūm al-dīn* ("The Revival of the Religious Sciences"); these Nallino characterizes as rules of conduct to be observed while engaged in some specific art, science or other activity. Secondly, in support of *adab* as a social or intellectual quality, he cites Ibn Qutaybah's *Adab al-kātib*, which provides knowledge requisite for secretaries, Kushājim's (d. *c.* 350/961) *Adab al-nadīm* – rather, as the title says, a treatise on rules of behaviour for boon-companions of the great than a collection of apt quotations to be produced in social gatherings – and books with such titles as *Adab al-wuzarāʾ* ("The Proper Conduct of the Vizier"), or *Adab al-qāḍī* ("The Proper Conduct of the Judge"). As a working model, Nallino's distinction between custom and quintessence may still be valid, though there seems little point in pursuing problematic etymologies too closely: it is doubtful whether *adab* can be identified with *sunnah*, as Nallino suggests (by a double derivation of *adab* from the noun *daʾb*, "custom", and the root *ʾdb*), and it is questionable, in any case, whether the material cited by Nallino fully supports his argument. Rather, in contexts such as the above, *adab* should be interpreted according to its immediate social or intellectual terms of reference, and for this finer categories are needed than those established by Nallino – if, indeed, such categories can be established at all. In the introduction to his *Adab al-kātib*, to cite only one example of the difficulties of attempting a firm classification, Ibn Qutaybah intimates that secretaries should have more than a purely linguistic training. The introduction has moralizing overtones and stresses that the book was written with a didactic purpose in mind, although the text itself offers only lexicographical information; yet clearly for Ibn Qutaybah *adab* was more than lexicography: at one point he observes that abstruse or unintelligible vocabulary was unacceptable "in the good old days when *adab* had not yet lost its freshness".[31] More is implied by *adab*, here, than a mechanical set of rules and guidelines.

A last development of the specialized applications of *adab* to which Nallino draws attention is an understanding of the term which, he believes, originated among Muslim theologians and jurists. To this group it was *ʿilm al-adab* (the knowledge or study of ancient literature) which enabled them to understand the texts which could be used to explain the Qurʾān and *ḥadīth* and so to evolve law and doctrine. This manner of understanding *adab* differs from *adab* in the sense of literary scholarship only in so far as the goals

[31] *Adab al-kātib*, 15.

that it envisages give literary erudition a different, intermediate place in the hierarchy of learning. This is nowhere expressed more clearly than in a commentary on Ibn Qutaybah's *Adab al-kātib*, the *Iqtiḍāb* of Ibn al-Sīd al-Baṭalyawsī (d. 521/1127): "the lower [or: more obvious] goal of *adab* is to acquire the skills which enable one to compose poetry or prose; the higher goal is the interpretation of the Qurʾān and *ḥadīth*, and this is what the theorists of Islamic law have in mind when they engage in the study of *adab*."[32] As a logical consequence of this approach, which sees *adab* essentially as a subsidiary of a higher goal, Nallino suggests that philological disciplines such as syntax, rhetoric and prosody should be classified as branches of *adab*. This, of course, would mark both a systematic extension and a conceptual limitation of the term since, according to this model, *adab* is no longer recognized as an end in itself, and can no longer have any bearing on the activity of the creative artist; on the other hand, it now covers a number of specializations. But to use the term *adab* in this way is to impose a sometimes inappropriate interpretation on the works to which it is applied; much of the voluminous literature on, for example, poetic theory and criticism was intended as much for the creative artist as for the student of literature, and its primary aim was to produce sound practice in poets (as well as aesthetic appreciation in amateurs): if the role of such works is subsidiary, it is subsidiary to wider literary, not extraliterary aims.

To try to update Nallino's outline in every detail would carry us too far, and, though his argument is not always based on the strongest evidence, attempts to supplement his material serve only to underline the difficulty of drawing hard and fast distinctions or establishing firm affiliations between the various meanings of *adab* (and also, incidentally, that of pinpointing the chronology of their emergence), rather than to disprove Nallino's general thesis. However, the distinction, often blurred, between *adab* and *ʿilm*, referred to above, does suggest further observations. The conclusions drawn by Franz Rosenthal from his study of the concept of *ʿilm* in Islam supplement Nallino's conclusions regarding *adab* in several respects. Speaking in general terms of the role of *ʿilm* in *adab* works, Rosenthal notes that, though medieval authors seldom manage to make a clear distinction between the two terms, *adab* and *taʾdīb* are frequently used as synonyms of the Greek *paideia* and *paideusis* from the time when philosophical views of education began to be articulated after Greek works began to circulate in Arabic. With reference to the chapter on *ʿilm* and *adab* in Ibn ʿAbd Rabbih's *al-ʿIqd al-farīd*, Rosenthal adds that the two are considered an inseparable

[32] *Iqtiḍāb*, 14–15. The author was an Andalusian philosopher and polymath; his writings included grammatical treatises and both legal and literary scholarship.

pair, "twin poles" round which the world revolves and which separate man from the brute creation, but that *adab* would seem on the whole to designate knowledge of which active use is made.[33] Of *adab* used in specialized contexts, such as those reviewed above, we should therefore perhaps conclude that, however miscellaneous the material to which it may be applied, it can most often be found to refer to some general concept of human activity, either as an object of observation or as a model for behaviour.

ADAB AS A GENRE

The above examples show how the literary and socio-ethical concepts of *adab*, especially *adab* taken in the "passive" sense, tended to merge. Far from the ᶜAbbasid concept of *adab* excluding, as Pellat maintains, all non-*belles-lettristic* writing, it appears in a number of technical contexts whose association with "literature" is sometimes only marginal. Yet almost all western handbooks on Arabic literature make use of the terms "*adab* literature", "*adab* works" – even "*adab* topics" – to describe what is felt to be primarily a literary category. The last question we must ask is whether there is good reason to continue using such terms. The definitions of *adab* as a genre put forward by historians of Arabic literature are far from uniform. However, it is generally felt that *adab* works are usually miscellanies of one sort or another and are encyclopaedic and didactic in their aims, though non-technical in their approach; al-Jāḥiẓ is almost invariably seen as the originator of the genre. Yet we find the term applied to works of very diverse character and form, to monographs and to wide-ranging anthologies, which may be purely entertaining in intention or which may, on the other hand, demand considerable intellectual effort and expertise of their readers. *Adab* may, in addition, be used both of secondary works of the type cited in the preceding section of this chapter, and of creative writing such as the *maqāmāt*, which are fictitious narratives in rhymed prose (*saj*ᶜ). Almost no attempt has been made to define the genre "*adab* literature" in terms of what it does *not* include, though Rosenthal has tried to clarify its applications by presenting them in a historical formulation. He argues that the monograph essay may have been the earliest form of *adab* literature and that, very soon after, larger collections appeared, made up of what could be viewed as an assemblage of monographs, designed to cover the entire existing range of *adab*; both monographs and anthologies continued to be produced, with anthologies in particular enjoying uninterrupted popularity, and these could be viewed as the basic forms of *adab* literature.[34] From the point of view of content too, the early, ᶜAbbasid, formula remained

[33] *Knowledge Triumphant*, 200, 276, 284, 286–7. [34] Ibid., 252–3.

largely unchanged: verse and prose, anecdote and aphorism were drawn from the fields of political, ethical and religious thought, and from many other areas of learning as these multiplied, the anthologists' aim always being to stress the curious, the entertaining and, above all, the linguistic and *literary* merits of the material presented. Formulations such as this, though they have the merit of combining formal criteria (monograph, anthology) and conceptual ones (the author's aim must be to amuse and instruct through the medium of literature), are perhaps less definitions than generalizations and, loose as they are, a number of medieval "*adab* works" appear to conform to them, though not necessarily to support the classification of *adab* as primarily a "literary" genre. Thus *Kitāb al-Maḥāsin wa ʾl-masāwī* ("The Good and Bad Sides of Things"), by Ibrāhīm b. Muḥammad al-Bayhaqī (*fl.* Iraq, end third/ninth – beginning fourth/tenth centuries), opens with several quotations in praise of *adab*, some of which connect *adab* with the written word, followed by a eulogy of books and writing; however, though the book contains a chapter on *adab* which includes discussions of literary topics, the bulk of the book is more than literary – or entertaining – in scope: it deals with good and evil, the harmful and useful, the pleasant and unpleasant. These are essential to the human condition; man is expected to be aware of such opposite forces to make life meaningful. In the fourth/tenth-century Andalusian Ibn ʿAbd Rabbih's *al-ʿIqd al-farīd* we find, possibly for the first time in the history of the term, a statement clearly connecting *adab* with the contents of the book. Like al-Bayhaqī, Ibn ʿAbd Rabbih speaks of *adab* as the cream of past speech and wisdom which has been stored up and selected from by succeeding generations. His own book is meant to contain the choicest examples of such *adab* (*jawāhir al-adab*) and superior instances of pithy eloquence. It is also, however, intended to include most of the topics (*maʿānī*) commonly discussed by people in all walks of life. Like *al-ʿIqd al-farīd* and the *Kāmil* of al-Mubarrad, *Zahr al-ādāb* by the North African scholar and poet Abū Isḥāq b. Ibrāhīm al-Ḥuṣrī (d. 413/1022) contains a statement of what *adab* means in terms of the author's intentions. Al-Ḥuṣrī wrote the book on the invitation of a patron who had gathered examples of contemporary eloquence on a journey to the East; he wished al-Ḥuṣrī to make a selection from this material and to enlarge it with additions of his own: "And so . . . I composed for him this book in order that he should be able to dispense with all [other] *adab* books (*kutub al-adab*)" – by which al-Ḥuṣrī meant, specifically, such works as the prose epistles of famous contemporaries like al-Hamadhānī and al-Ṣāḥib Ibn ʿAbbād. However, it may be inferred from the paragraph that follows that by *adab* itself al-Ḥuṣrī means examples of eloquence occurring in poems and stories or in shorter prose extracts (*al-*

fuṣūl wa ʾl-fiqar). The *Lubāb al-ādāb* of the Syrian nobleman Usāmah b. Murshid . . . b. Munqidh al-Shayzarī (usually known as Usāmah b. Munqidh, d. 584/1188) has a long chapter on *adab*, from which it appears clearly that these are moral, and to a lesser extent social, virtues; only in the first section of the chapter is any association of *adab* with literature implied. The next chapter, on eloquence (*balāghah*), also has a section on *adab*, but though it quotes poetry, it does so only to illustrate social and moral precepts. To Usāmah, clearly, *adab* was a concept too obvious to need defining: in relation to the format of the book, it probably meant quotations of a certain literary merit, but in terms of the work's content, it referred to the socio-ethical meanings of the term.

But if the works just described conform to some degree to current definitions of "*adab* literature", there are many other so-called "*adab* works", often cited as such by modern scholars, which do not. Conversely, there are many instances of works described by their authors or by ʿAbbasid bibliographers as *adab* which have little or nothing in common with the genre as defined by literary historians. Among works classified today as *adab*, Ibn Qutaybah's *Adab al-kātib*, and the *Amālī* ("Dictations") of al-Qālī (d. 356/967)[35] – the latter consisting of transcribed course-notes taken down by students of philology and literature – were intended for specialists, not for general readers. Other so-called *adab* works are too narrow in scope to suggest that their authors' aim was to provide a general education, for example Abū Ḥayyān al-Tawḥīdī's (d. 414/1023) *al-Ishārāt al-ilāhiyyah* ("Divine Intimations"), has been variously described (by Nallino) as a collection of prayers and homilies and (by Keilani) as a mystical work,[36] while *Ḥikāyat Abī ʾl-Qāsim* ("The Story of Abū ʾl-Qāsim") by Abū ʾl-Muṭahhar Muḥammad b. Aḥmad al-Azdī (fifth/eleventh century) is not a compilation, although it uses quotations, but a work of creative literature of a novel and highly structured artistic form.[37] By contrast, among works in whose titles the word *adab* appears, literature may have figured only in a subsidiary capacity, if at all; in his *Fihrist*, a biblio-biographical dictionary completed in 377/987–8, Ibn al-Nadīm (or al- Nadīm) refers to *kutub adabiyyah* (*adab* books), and *kutub muṣannafah fī ʾl-adab*) (books on *adab*), as though they formed a separate category; of the titles which can still be identified, a few indeed deal with literature, criticism, grammar, lexicography, etc., but others refer to such subjects as music, history, agriculture or ethics. When the biographer Ibn Khallikān (d. 681/1282) speaks of al-Khaṭīb al-Tibrīzī's (d. 502/1109) commentary on Abū Tammām's *Ḥamāsah* as a book on *adab*, he is reverting to the

[35] Abū ʿAlī Ismāʿīl b. al-Qāsim al-Qālī; taught in Baghdad and in Spain.
[36] Keilani, *Abū Ḥayyān*, 62–3. [37] See Mez, *Sittenbild*, xv–xvi; Kilito, *Séances*, 42–8.

specialized notion of literary and linguistic scholarship. Moreover, few authors of "*adab* works" actually refer to them as such or use the term *adab* in their titles; a case in point is al-Jāḥiẓ, supposedly the originator of the genre. Al-Jāḥiẓ's younger contemporary Ibn Qutaybah refers to *adab* several times in the introduction to his *ᶜUyūn al-akhbār*, but not, apparently, in such a way as to identify the whole contents of the book as *adab*, and though *ᶜUyūn* forms a sequel to *Adab al-kātib*, we have seen that the latter itself eludes firm classification. In general terms, *ᶜUyūn* is an anthology covering a wide range of topics, many of them non-literary, with which Ibn Qutaybah expects every educated Muslim to be conversant.

Such discrepancies suggest that the current definitions of *adab* as a literary genre are too broad to provide a workable analytic framework, and bear little relation to what the ᶜAbbasids themselves might have understood by the term. Rather than abandon altogether as empty or anachronistic a classification which evidently fulfils a real need – since Arabic literature can seldom be described as accurately in terms of western literary categories – we might put forward a more restricted definition, based initially, perhaps, on one particular aspect of the ᶜAbbasid meaning of *adab*, such as the "passive" meaning of "the literary scholarship of a cultivated man" presented in systematic form. Such a definition still raises difficulties, but it usefully restricts the field by providing both formal and conceptual criteria, and the dual emphasis on literature and general culture would enable Ibn Qutaybah's *ᶜUyūn al-akhbār* to be included in the genre, as well as all more or less systematically arranged anthologies and monographs that emphasize the principle of drawing on literary quotations of aesthetic merit to illustrate their thesis. On the other hand, pure miscellanies and undigested scholarship, such as transcribed course-notes, would probably have to be excluded – for example al-Mubarrad's *Kāmil* and al-Qālī's *Amālī* – and specialized works on, for example, literary theory, literary history or geography would require to be re-classified under those headings. Similarly, letters and speeches in ornate prose, such as those of Abū Bakr Muḥammad b. al-ᶜAbbās al-Khwarazmī (d. 383/933), Ibn Nubātah (d. 374/984–5) and al-Ṣāḥib Ibn ᶜAbbād could no longer be classed as *adab*, nor could *Ḥikāyat Abī ʾl-Qāsim* or the *maqāmāt* of al-Hamadhānī and al-Ḥarīrī, all of which are original literary productions, despite many learned allusions to older literature.

CHAPTER 2

SHU^cŪBIYYAH IN ARABIC LITERATURE

One of the most striking movements in Arabic cultural history and literature, especially during the third/ninth century, is that assertive movement, collectively known as *Shu^cūbiyyah*, which represented a powerful, sometimes extreme, backlash amongst the conquered peoples against the Arabs of Arabia in particular, and has been characterized as "a more or less successful attempt on the part of the different subjected races to hold their own and to distinguish, at least, between Arabism and Islam".[1] The whole movement, however diversified and uncoordinated it may have been, extended from Spain and the furthest Maghrib to the remoter parts of Central Asia, and was especially espoused by the Persians and by the Aramaeans (Nabaṭ) of Iraq.

Opinion now favours the view that the bitter attacks directed against the Arabs in the literature of the third/ninth century were probably not the expression of nationalism, Persian nationalism in particular, but rather a movement, widespread among the new middle class of mixed race and the influential government secretaries (*kātib*s), aimed at remoulding the political and social institutions and the whole spirit of Islamic culture on the model of Sasanian institutions and values, which were then in favour and which the new urban society and the administrative class held forth as the highest ideal. It is clear, though, that the movement was not confined to secretaries, but was wider, nor can its aims be so clearly defined. Amongst the conquered peoples the culture of Islam had not yet become sufficiently widespread and assimilated to resolve the dilemma between Arabic language and native thought; nor did it assure equity of status between Arab and non-Arab, Muslim and non-Muslim or between Arabs and Muslims of non-Arab origin; many groups and classes throughout the empire were therefore left with grievances and unsatisfied aspirations. But while the political impact of *Shu^cūbiyyah* is hard to assess, it was undoubtedly of notable impact in the history of Arabic literature and consequence for the evolution of Islamic doctrines.

[1] *EI*[1], "Shu^cūbīya".

ANTECEDENTS

It is sometimes overlooked, however, that the seeds of regional or ethnic discontent which had been planted following the first Arab conquest, and which burst into vigorous bloom in the age of the early ʿAbbasid caliphs, especially during the reigns of Hārūn al-Rashīd and al-Maʾmūn, had already germinated in the Umayyad age. It would be wrong to ignore the zealous tribal loyalty and partisanship (*ʿaṣabiyyah*) deeply rooted among the Arabs themselves during the first/seventh and second/eighth centuries and to regard these as something different in kind from much of the *Shuʿūbiyyah* which followed. The feud between the northern Qays and the supposedly Yemeni Kalb, for example – which dictated the battle of Marj Rāhiṭ (64/684) that sealed the victory of the Umayyad Marwān I over the anti-caliph ʿAbdullāh b. al-Zubayr – and the bitter hostilities between the putative descendants of ʿAdnān and Qaḥṭān, the Arabs of the north and south of the peninsula, deepened the antagonism of two distinct Arabian ethnic identities over the entire breadth of the Islamic world and, in literature, inspired partisan boasting or deprecation. Examples may be found in the fourth/tenth-century poetic anthology, *Kitāb al-Aghānī* ("The Book of Songs"):

> Negroes are better, when they name their sires,
> Than Qaḥṭān's sons, the uncircumcised cowards:
> A folk whom thou mayest see, at war's outflame,
> More abject than a shoe to tread in baseness;
> Their women free to every lecher's lust,
> Their clients, spoil for soldiers of all ranks.[2]

Such sentiments are harbingers of a wider *Shuʿūbiyyah* based on anti-Arab sentiment rather than internecine Arab rivalry, and advocates of anti-Arab *Shuʿūbiyyah* were to make telling use of hardened Arabian tribal sentiments, which Islam, as preached by the Prophet, was dedicated to suppressing; they transferred such themes as those illustrated by the poem just quoted from tribe to conquered nation, and intensified their vehemence, refining the subtlety of their literary barbs and employing them in the service of peoples of varied ethnic background, class and group, each as proud of their pre-Islamic past as were the Himyarite Yemenis. Moreover, internecine and anti-Arab *Shuʿūbiyyah* were often associated. That the Yemeni Arabs, for example, were promoters of Shuʿūbī sentiments among the Copts of Fusṭāṭ on the morrow of the Arab conquest is beyond doubt, as has been convincingly demonstrated in a recent study.[3] The resourceful

[2] Abū ʾl-Faraj al-Iṣfahānī, *Aghānī*, XIII, 51; trans. amended from Nicholson, *Literary History*, 200.
[3] Vadet, "L' 'Acculturation'".

Yemenis saw the Copts as allies in their combat against the arrogance of the northern Arabians who held the reins of power; this alliance in the cause of inter-Arab animosity had its literary manifestation, as can be seen in the Persian-influenced romances attributed to Wahb b. Munabbih, a Yemeni who extolled his country's legendary past.[4] According to the Yemeni transmitters of *ḥadīth*, too, the Egyptian population were worthy of respect: had not the Prophet himself especially recommended to his successors this people, amongst whom was born his slave-wife, Māriyah? A similar view received support from the Kufan traditionists: "Be full of attention in regard to Egypt, and do not mow or crop it as you would a field of sprouting grass". According to the Yemenis, their ancestors the Himyarites and the Egyptians in the age of the legendary Yemeni king ᶜAbd Shams b. Sabaᵓ had been brothers. Yemen had not only been the seat of the true-believing Tubbaᶜ kings,[5] but had also been the depository of the most ancient wisdom of Hermes Trismegistus, whose seat was in Memphis in Egypt. As J.-C. Vadet remarks: "One of the great events of the literary history of the Arabs could have been the work of simple bedouins who turned, in the teeth of present vexations, towards the glories of their 'Sabaean' past – more or less happily transported on to the banks of the Nile. Egyptianised thanks to its Yemenites, Fusṭāṭ is accordingly supposed, from the dawn of its history, to have looked towards Memphis, which was always, to the Arab imagination, the ancient city of Hermes."[6]

Equally significant in the furtherance of early Shuᶜūbī sentiments were the Khārijīs.[7] According to H. A. R. Gibb: "The original *shuubiya* were the Kharijites, who on religious grounds maintained the doctrine that no race or tribe enjoyed inherent superiority, and in particular opposed the theory of the inherent right of the Quraish [the tribe of the Prophet] to the caliphate." However, "In rejecting any exclusive superiority attaching to the Arabs, the Kharijite *shuubis* equally rejected any superiority of the Persians; whereas the third-century *shuubis* proclaimed the superiority of the Persians (or of other non-Arab races) to the Arabs, and defended their claim by social and cultural, not religious, arguments."[8]

In addition to Yemeni patriotism and Khārijī ideas of equality, two other, literary, factors which first appeared in the Umayyad period may be cited as having contributed to the outburst of nationalist sentiment in the age of the ᶜAbbasids. The first of these was the influence of Persian books and stories extracted from the history of ancient Persia which were already in fashion during the reign of Hishām (105–25/724–43). As an example, the ᶜAbbasid literary historian Abū ᵓl-Faraj al-Iṣfahānī calls the poet Ismāᶜīl b.

[4] Cf. p. 138, and ch. 23, n.51. [5] Cf. ch. 23, n.22. [6] Vadet, "L' 'Acculturation'", 14.
[7] Cf. pp. 186–8. [8] *Studies*, 69.

Yasār a Shuᶜūbī, because he had extolled the Persians to the caliph Hishām, and was thrown into a tank of water for boasting in verse of his Persian descent, which, he maintained, stemmed from princes who rivalled Chosroes, Shāpūr, etc., in their renown and in their knightly courage against the Central Asian Turks and the Greeks. The second such factor was the growth in the critical study of lineages and genealogical archaeology. Daghfal b. Ḥanẓalah, who lived during the reign of Muᶜāwiyah and was associated with prominent Khārijīs, was a close contemporary of ᶜUbayd b. Sharyah al-Jurhumī[9] and the early Yemeni romancers. Daghfal concerned himself with the faults and weaknesses of tribes and with the shameful points (*mathālib*) in their history, though their good points were not wholly ignored but relegated to the background among these genealogical preoccupations. The "science" of vices and virtues (*mathālib* and *manāqib*) was to become increasingly central and came to occupy the foreground in the literary works of the *Shuᶜūbiyyah* of the ᶜAbbasid era.[10] It should be noted, however, that although the seeds of full-blown *Shuᶜūbiyyah* were sown in the Umayyad period, the examples cited above cannot fully account for the phenomenon; thus, to quote Gibb again: "There is no evidence that the founders and early leaders of the secretarial school [often, as we saw at the beginning of this chapter, associated with Shuᶜūbī ambitions], such as Abd al-Hamid[11] or even Ibn al-Muqaffa were *shuubis*", either in the egalitarian sense espoused by the Khārijīs or in the partisan, ethnic and cultural sense.

ᶜABBASID *SHUᶜŪBIYYAH*

The ᶜAbbasid age supposedly marked the end of the period in Islamic history where a clearly defined distinction was drawn between Arab and *mawālī* (non-Arab Muslim clients of an Arab tribe); or rather, in the third/ninth century, *mawālī* and the subject peoples were now in a position of power and influence which allowed them to give open vent to their resentment against the arrogance and monopoly of the Arab aristocratic élite who had been in the ascendant under the Umayyads. From the days of al-Manṣūr, and during the reigns of al-Mahdī, Hārūn al-Rashīd and al-Maʾmūn in particular, the ex-*mawālī* enjoyed the influence of the vizieral Barmecide family at court, and then, after their fall, the continuing dominance of Persian culture and literature, especially within the

[9] See *CHALUP*, 385, and ch. 23, n.51, below.

[10] Cf. also such ambiguous examples of the genre as Jāḥiẓ, *K. Manāqib al-Turk*, *K. Fakhr al-Sūdān*, pp. 85, 87, below.

[11] *CHALUP*, 164–79.

enormously powerful and influential network of the secretarial system. Ignaz Goldziher cites the following anecdote as typical:

The caliph al-Maʾmūn did not conceal the fact that he valued the Persian race higher than the Arab, and when an Arab reproached him for favouring the inhabitants of Khurāsān above the Arabs from Syria, the caliph characterized the Arabs thus: "I have never bidden a man of Qays descend from his horse but he ate up all my treasure to the last dirham; the southern Arabs (Yemen) I do not love and they love me not; the Quḍāᶜa Arabs await the arrival of the Sufyānī [the *Mahdī* of the followers of the Umayyad dynasty][12] in order to join him; the Rabīᶜa Arabs are angry with God that he chose his Prophet from the Muḍar tribe, and there are no two amongst them but one is a rebel."[13]

While in the Umayyad period it had been dangerous for a poet like Ismāᶜīl b. Yasār, who ridiculed the pre-Islamic Arabs, to boast of Persian descent, it was a different matter under the ᶜAbbasids. One poet deliberately derided the *Muᶜallaqah* of Imruʾ al-Qays when he remarked in a poem, "I am not one who leaves the *īwān* of Chosroes [the arch of Ctesiphon] for Tūḍiḥah or Ḥawmal or Dukhūl", the last being toponyms in the *Muᶜallaqah*; the poet Isḥāq b. Ḥassān al-Khurramī (d. 200/815) gloried in his Iranian descent, boasting of his Soghdian ancestry; and Maᶜbad, a boon-companion of the caliph al-Mutawakkil, exclaimed: "I am the son of nobles from the seed of Jam [legendary Persian king and hero], the possessor of the estates of the kings of al-ᶜAjam [Persia]."[14] Bashshār b. Burd, despite being accused of sympathies with the *zindīq*s (dualists or dangerous free-thinkers, see below), openly avowed his national sentiments, his descent from "the Quraysh of the Persians" and his sympathies with the Persian *mawālī*; Abū Nuwās likewise declares, "the Arabs in God's sight are nobody". Clearly, *Shuᶜūbiyyah* as a literary pose had become fashionable. Nevertheless, although *Shuᶜūbiyyah* was a fashion in thought rather than a creed, and although the literary evidence suggests that "the central issues for the *shuᶜūbīs* were not overtly political; that is, they were not primarily concerned with the creation of new governments",[15] many of its opponents perceived *Shuᶜūbiyyah* as a source of distinct evils and dangers. Al-Jāḥiẓ (d. 255/868–9), who, as we shall see, was one of its most vociferous opponents, has left us in little doubt that *Shuᶜūbiyyah* had grave religious implications:

The bulk of those who are sceptics in regard to Islam, at the outset, were inspired by the ideas of the *Shuᶜūbiyyah*. Protracted argument leads to fighting. If a man hates a thing then he hates him who possesses it, or is associated with it. If he hates [the Arabic] language then he hates the [Arabian] peninsula, and if he hates that peninsula then he loves those who hate it. Thus matters go from bad to worse with

[12] See Madelung, "The Sufyānī". [13] *Muslim Studies*, I, 138–9.
[14] Ibid., 151–2. [15] Mottahedeh, "The Shuᶜūbiyyah controversy", 162.

him until he forsakes Islam itself, because it is the Arabs who brought it; it is they who provided the venerable forebears and the example worthy of imitation.[16]

The attitude of Jāḥiẓ, and of others like him who were at heart anti-Shuᶜūbī in their sentiments and convictions and who associated *Shuᶜūbiyyah* with destructive and irreligious tendencies, led Gibb to conclude that the phenomenon, viewed in its historic entirety: "was not merely a conflict between two schools of literature, not yet a conflict of political nationalisms, but a struggle to determine the destinies of the Islamic culture as a whole . . . The dangers of the *shuubi* movement, lay not so much in its crude anti-Arab propaganda (in spite of its appeal to the still lively hostility to the Arabs amongst the lower classes in Iraq and Persia) as in the more refined scepticism which it fostered among the literate classes. The old Perso-Aramaean culture of Iraq, the centre of Manichaeism, still carried the germs of that kind of free thinking which was called *zandaqah*, and which showed itself not only by the survival of dualist ideas in religion, but still more by that frivolity and cynicism in regard to all moral systems which is designated by the term *mujun*."[17] These, however, are general perceptions of the significance of *Shuᶜūbiyyah*, and it is possible to discern at least three clear-cut points of view amongst the men of letters of the early ᶜAbbasid period:

That the Arabs were supreme among the nations

This was the view of many of the lettered, including a number who were non-Arab in origin. The unique position of the Arabs was to be seen in all its glory in Islam itself. The Apostle of God was born of Arab stock, as was undeniable. Other nations had qualities worthy of praise: the Persians had been mighty conquerors in ancient times; the Byzantines were technicians and fine artisans; the Chinese were refined artists, and the Indians had sired noteworthy, if "pagan", philosophers. But apart from the faith, the Arabs, and more especially the bedouin, had a unique and instinctive ability to express themselves in eloquent speech. Ibn al-Muqaffaᶜ, the early *kātib*, himself of Persian origin, is said to have defended, in the course of a discussion, the bedouin Arabs, tent-dwellers and men of great hospitality, whom God had chosen to proclaim the faith and to found the caliphate. The historian al-Balādhurī (d. *c.* 279/892), likewise a Persian, also refuted the Shuᶜūbī claim, and shared the opinion of Jāḥiẓ that to hear bedouins declaim in pure Arabic was to hear speech at its most telling and perfect.

[16] *Ḥayawān*, VII, 220. [17] *Studies*, 69. On the term *mujūn*, cf. pp. 162, 281, 430ff, below.

That the Arabs were neither better nor worse than other nations

This position rests on the view that all men are equal, as proved by passages in the Qurʾān, for example *sūrah* xlix.13: 'And We made you *shuᶜūb* and *qabāʾil* in order that you may know." Each of these rather vague terms distinguished a people or grouping; the former, *shuᶜūb* – and some saw a significance in the word-order – could be held to indicate the ᶜAjam (non-Arabs), and the latter, *qabāʾil*, the tribes of the Arabs. "Each knew the other," the Quranic commentator al-Bayḍāwī (d. *c.* 685/1286) explains, "but this was not for vying with one another in superiority of ancestors or of tribes." There were also *ḥadīth* supporting the principle of equality between Arab and non-Arab believer: what mattered far more than boasting of lineage (*nasab*) or personal status and achievement (*ḥasab*) was obedience to God and piety, both of which enabled the believer, whatever his ethnic origins, to be envied for his virtues among his fellows. Many noteworthy defenders of the Arabs against their opponents held this view. Ibn Qutaybah (d. 276/889), a non-Arab, having defended the Arabs and acknowledged their superiority in a number of respects, proclaimed without equivocation the absolute equality of all men. Nevertheless, he attempted to woo the Persian upper class by arguing that they too had lineages as genuine as the Arab lineages. He believed that the new Arab ruling class and the older Iranian ruling class could indeed have a shared genealogical prejudice against their subordinates, who had no ties of kinship.[18] Paradoxically, this group – people or peoples without lineage or position, who resented their lack of privilege – was later confused with the *Shuᶜūbiyyah*, although it never merited this name. It was the most worthy representative of that other name applied indiscriminately by pro-Arabs to any who were less than unequivocal in their support of Arab superiority, "the levellers" (*ahl al-taswīyah*). The first use of this latter name to categorize *Shuᶜūbiyyah* as a whole appears in the writings of Jāḥiẓ, more specifically in his *Kitāb al-Bayān wa ʾl-tabyīn* ("The Book of Eloquence and Exposition").

That the Arabs were surpassed by other nations in virtues and abilities

It was this view which most truly reflected the beliefs of the classical exponents of *Shuᶜūbiyyah*, whose self-appointed task it was to expose the spurious claim which had been made on behalf of the Arabs, and of the pre-Islamic Arabs in particular. Islam, they argued, is the religion of all mankind. The claim of the Arabs to a monopoly in its revelation was untenable. All the prophets had been non-Arabs except for Hūd, Ṣāliḥ,

[18] Mottahedeh, "The Shuᶜūbiyyah controversy", 180.

Ismāʿīl and Muḥammad himself.[19] The pre-Islamic Arabs had no distinguishing mark worthy of the name to place them on a par with the Greeks, the Persians and the Indians. These adverse criticisms, and others like them unknown to us (for it must be recalled that few works by Shuʿūbīs and little pro-Shuʿūbī literature have survived), were the common language of a disparate company of literary men from among the subject people, the Persians, the Aramaeans (Nabaṭ), the Copts and the Andalusians. Their arguments frequently converged or followed parallel lines, although their goals differed quite markedly. Among the Persians, particular emphasis was laid on independence and military expertise, and forms of *zandaqah* were mainly to be found among the Persians. The so-called Nabaṭ of the Sawād (irrigated agricultural lands) of Iraq were fanatically proud of their historic land and their methods of agriculture, and they believed in their superiority over the bedouin. The Copts plotted to gain their liberty and staged an unsuccessful revolt in the days of al-Maʾmūn; thwarted, their sentiments were expressed in word and by pen. In al-Andalus, as will be seen, Shuʿūbī literature took an individual Maghribi form. It may also be found among the Berbers, first in the heresy of the Barghawāṭah confederacy in Morocco, which lasted for some three centuries from the third/ninth century and had its own Berber Qurʾān, and at a later period in the books which praised the Berbers for their deeds (*mafākhir al-Barbar*). All these writings contributed to the manifold and diffuse arguments of the *Shuʿūbiyyah*. In time, however, any tendency to question Arab superiority was held to be Shuʿūbī whether its holder was a Khārijī, secretary or *zindīq*, and was felt to be aimed at the basis of Islam itself.

THEMES OF PRO-SHUʿŪBĪ POLEMIC

Rhetoric and oratory

The Arab claim to excellence in rhetoric and oratory was baseless, so it was argued, nor was there evidence to support their claim to an intuitive flair and native genius for the Arabic language, or indeed any language, since the Arabs were notorious for pointless mannerisms and dependence on elocutionary aids when they spoke in public. The Shuʿūbīs mocked them for their gesticulations, their use of a stick or staff to drive home a point, or their habit of leaning on a bow to deliver an address. This, together with the foppish manner in which the Arabs adjusted their turbans before speaking, had no connection whatsoever with true oratory. Quite the reverse: it distracted the thoughts of the listener and diverted his attention, and

[19] For the non-biblical Hūd and Ṣāliḥ, see *Shorter EI*.

revealed a failure on the part of the Arabs to grasp the essentials of the rhetorical art. In the same way, the better and more accomplished singer was the one who dispensed with the rhythmic beat sustained by an instrument when he sang his air. The Shuᶜūbīs scorned the Arabs for their rhythmic deficiency, although Arabs, they suggested, tried hard to hide this defect in metre and rhyme when they contended with their opponents. Shuᶜūbīs derided the Arabs' lack of skill in rhymed prose (*sajᶜ*) and the bedouins' use of the simple, improvisatory *rajaz* metre when they went to draw water, or in battle, or when they settled a dispute by wrestling with a rival. Equally laughable in their behaviour was the use of rhyming prose in speech-making when receiving blood-money, making peace or sealing convenants; while to cement alliances over a fire or covenants over salt was particularly gauche, stupid and ridiculous. (These criticisms and others are countered by Jāḥiẓ in his *Kitāb al-ᶜAṣā* ("Book of the Rod", a subsection of "The Book of Eloquence and Exposition").[20] Like an anthropologist, he points out the social purport of these customs attested in pre-Islamic verse and Prophetic *ḥadīth*. Since oratory was common to all men, the Persians, the Greeks and even the barbarous Zanj – the black slaves imported to work the agricultural estates of lower Iraq – no nation had a monopoly of its skills. Within Persia itself some towns and regions were especially renowned for proficiency and artistry; for example the people of Ahwāz were particularly fluent and eloquent in the Pahlavi language.)

Weapons and military skill

This polemic theme, like the preceding one, is based on antiquarian evidence furnished by bedouin poetry and lore. The Shuᶜūbīs, more especially those familiar with Sasanian chivalry, mocked the Arabs for their deficiency in the military art and their vain boast about their weaponry. The Arab spear was made from the hard wood of the dogwood tree (Lat. *murrān*, Ar. *cornus mascula*). It was heavy, while the Persian spear was hollow and much lighter. The Persians knew that it was far more effective a weapon for foot-soldiers than it was for the cavalry unless they merely wished to prevent a fleeing enemy from escaping. The Arabs, they maintained, were unfamiliar with the very short spears (*maṭārid*) which were of particular value in hunting. The merit of length or shortness lay not in the object itself but in the way it was used in military tactics. The bedouin Arabs were in the habit of riding bareback in battle; even if they had a saddle, it was made from skin; they were ignorant of the stirrup which allowed the rider to

[20] *Bayān*, III, *K. al-ᶜAṣā*, 5ff. For another example of anti-Shuᶜūbī polemic by Jāḥiẓ, see p. 88, below.

stand or sit as he chose and to use his weapon with the maximum freedom and to maximum effect. The Arabs did not fight at night nor had they any idea at all of the ambush, the use of ditches, or the power of siege catapults or ballista (*manjanīq*, pl. *majānīq*). They had no pavilions, domed tents, drums or waving banners, and their military tactics were crude and inflexible since they had no practice in the employment of flank movements either to the right or left. In almost every respect, so they alleged, the Arab performance in battle lacked the skill, science and efficiency of their opponents. (Jāḥiẓ, again in *Kitāb al-ʿAṣā*, produces evidence in verse to show that the Arabs had indeed fought on occasion by night and by day, that they had in fact known of the use of stirrups and that their spears were of sundry lengths and varieties. Many were their sorties; they used both ends of the spear in their fighting, and some of their swords were long as well as short.)

The arguments of minority peoples: the Nabaṭ

The Nabaṭ were the remnants of the Aramaic-speaking population of Syria and Mesopotamia. Among their number were some who desired to show that they were worthy to participate in ruling the empire, alleging kinship with Quraysh by a fictitious tradition of descent from ʿAlī b. Abī Ṭālib. Their historical claim rested on their past connections with the Babylonian empire. The most characteristic expression of their reaction against the Arabs is in a book entitled *al-Filāḥah al-nabaṭiyyah* ("Nabataean Agriculture"), compiled by Ibn Waḥshiyyah; it is a work of pseudo-science, written in the third/ninth century, and allegedly a translation of Chaldaean or Babylonian works. Despite the debate over the overall authenticity of the book, it remains nonetheless a unique example of non-Persian *Shuʿūbiyyah*, and also exemplifies the varied ways in which Shuʿūbī sentiments could be expressed. According to Goldziher: "Ibn Waḥshiyyah, moved by a grim hatred of the Arabs and full of bitterness about their contempt for his compatriots, decided to translate and make accessible the remnants of ancient Babylonian literature preserved by them in order to show that the ancestors of his people, so despised by the Arabs [*nabaṭī*, "peasant/oaf", was a standard term of abuse], had had a great civilisation and had excelled in knowledge many peoples of antiquity. The author intended to contrast the insignificance of the ancient Arabs in science and culture with the great achievements of his own race in order to answer the limitless arrogance of the ruling race."[21] In fact, the Nabataean challenge went far deeper than archaeology. It was espoused by noted men of letters, for example the Muʿtazilī Ḍirār b. ʿAmr al-Ghaṭafānī, whose views were also widely shared

21 *Muslim Studies*, I, 146.

by Jāḥiẓ, and Thumāmah b. Ashras, a leading Muᶜtazilī and adviser to the caliph al-Maᵓmūn. Despite his Arab descent, Ḍirār was deemed a Shuᶜūbī on account of his teaching about the superiority of the Nabataeans and the way in which he introduced this premise into basic teachings about the Islamic doctrine of the state and the caliphate. There are several references to the views of these "Nabataean" Shuᶜūbīs in the historian al-Masᶜūdī's (d. 346/957) *Murūj al-dhahab*; one passage in particular contains a reply to the bizarre assertions of certain Nabataean Shuᶜūbīs regarding their superiority over the Arabs and how they had attained a status denied to the Arabs. The Shuᶜūbī argument runs on the following lines: God had singled out two categories of men. The first were those to whom God had given bliss without equal, by decreeing that his Prophet should be born among them. The second was the category of the dispossessed, among whom God had decreed that his Prophet should *not* be born, whom he had thus stripped of every honour of which they could boast, and who had suffered the most grievous of all afflictions. No bliss can be higher for the former and no test and trial more grievous than the loss of prophethood for the latter (the Nabataeans). Nevertheless, to such belongs the superior merit of pursuing virtue in adversity. Al-Masᶜūdī confutes this challenge by apparently arguing (in a difficult and debatable passage) that the merits of adversity in fact belong to the Arabs, who possessed the Prophet, but lost him by death, whereas the Nabataeans had never possessed him.[22]

The *zindīqs*

Among the Shuᶜūbīs there were undoubtedly some whose private religious convictions placed them completely outside orthodox Islam. Most of them were believers or dabblers in Manichaeism or in a Zoroastrian dualism, and were dubbed *zanādiqah* (sing. *zindīq*, supposedly, according to one medieval source, from the Zend, a book produced by the Manichaean schismatic Mazdak),[23] a word which in Muslim law denotes any heretic who is a danger to the state. To the *zindīqs*, the claims of the Arabs, as Muslims and as Arabs, were totally unacceptable. Ibn al-Nadīm, in his fourth/tenth-century index of authors and books, *al-Fihrist*, mentions a certain Muḥammad b. al-Ḥusayn, nicknamed Daydān, who was a secretary to the governor of Isfahan in the second/eighth century and was sympathetic to those who sought a restoration of Sasanian power. He was a philosopher and astrologer, "Belonging to the *Shuᶜūbiyyah*, he was bitter against the Islamic government. He believed with certainty in [such neo-Platonic and un-Islamic – or Ismāᶜīlī – abstractions as] the Universal Soul (*al-Nafs*), the

[22] *Murūj*, II, 170–1. [23] Cf. ch. 3, n.18.

Intelligence (*al-ᶜAql*), Time (*al-Zamān*), Space (*al-Makān*) and Matter (*al-Hayūlā*). He also supposed that the stars exercised control and spiritual action over the world",[24] and that they predicted a return to Persian rule and to the religion of the Magi. Such beliefs, which were allied to academic snobbery and to deprecation of Arabism, were widespread in certain circles in Baghdad and Basra. Among their best-known manifestations is a poem attributed to Abū Nuwās addressed to Abān al-Lāḥiqī[25] and quoted by Jāḥiẓ in his *Kitāb al-Ḥayawān*; the poem takes the form of an argument between Abū Nuwās and Abān al-Lāḥiqī:

> I said, "Glory to God" and he said, "Glory to Mānī";
> I said, "Jesus is an Apostle" and he said, "of the Devil";
> I said, "Moses is the Interlocutor of the Benevolent Watcher";[26]
> He said, "Your Lord, then, has an eyeball and a tongue?[27]
> His very essence brought Him into being; if not, who did?"
> I rose up there and then offended by an infidel to be shunned,
> Who argues by denying any belief in Him, the Lord Most Merciful.

Clearly, as Jāḥiẓ, however hotly he might disagree with the trivialization of profound truths and beliefs in this way, admitted, the *zindīq*s were far from ignorant of Arabic and Islam and their literature; their scepticism as to the validity of the Islamic faith arose from what the *zindīq*s saw as its naivety; and Charles Pellat has argued that *zandaqah* is an extreme manifestation of Shuᶜūbī sentiment arising in the first instance from a sense of wordly superiority, and only thereafter spilling over into spiritual matters.[28]

Ishmael and Isaac

Shuᶜūbiyyah sharpened the discussion within the body of Islam between those who were without question believers, but who made the issue of lineal descent from Sarah, the free-woman (Sārah *al-ḥurrah*), and Hagar (Hājar), the slave, the mothers of Isaac and Ishmael respectively, a major topic of dispute and a formidable argument in their attempt to denigrate the Arabs – though the Prophet himself was tactfully ignored in this debate or else piously excluded from it by the Shuᶜūbīs. Père René Dagorn has examined this phenomenon and has concluded that the gradual promotion of Ishmael, son of the slave, above Isaac, son of a free mother (despite the Prophet's own statements that no distinction should be made between them), and the spread of the varied stories forming part of the so-called *Geste d'Ismaël*, were furthered, exacerbated and even shaped to no small degree by the Shuᶜūbī debates of the third/ninth and later centuries.[29] (The

[24] *Fibrist*, Tajaddud, 239–40/Dodge, 1, 469. [25] Cf. ch. 11, n.28. [26] See ch. 14, n.90.
[27] A denial of the divine attributes. [28] *Le Milieu basrien*, 220–1. [29] *La Geste*, 220–34.

subject was also popular among the Spanish Shuᶜūbīs, who based their case on the premise of descent from Sarah). Hence the names of the Patriarchs became a sort of code in which the bitterest of nationalist contests was fought within Islam by men of letters. (There was, of course, a positive and constructive side to all this since it heightened interest in the exploration of biblical sources and in seriously weighing up the biblical contribution to Islam.) Ibn Qutaybah, notwithstanding his Iranian origin, was one of the stoutest defenders of the Abrahamic claim of the Arabs. In his *Kitāb al-ᶜArab*, he hotly rebutted the assertions of their opponents, showing that there was no tie between the Persians, or the Nabataeans, and Abraham. Esau was the father of the Byzantines (al-Rūm), the yellow-hued (*al-aṣfar*); and the mother for al-Rūm was Ishmael's daughter, so he allowed the Byzantines an ascendance to Abraham on the maternal side. He defended the honour and chastity of Hagar and her son against the Persians, who claimed that both of them were of servile status and that Hagar was impure (*laknāʾ*, foul-smelling or uncircumcized?). Furthermore, Ibn Qutaybah pointedly added that slave-women of great beauty and intelligence had given birth to famous caliphs. Jāḥiẓ, slightly his elder, was among those who were aware of the inherent blasphemy and inconsequence of the Shuᶜūbī position, which smeared the reputation of Ishmael yet avoided any insult to the Prophet himself. He made it clear in his writings that the Shuᶜūbīs were guilty of "impugning the Prophet's rod and stick, and also the rod of Moses".[30]

Language and lineage

Among the varied fields in which the Shuᶜūbī and his pro-Arab opponent competed, none was more prominent than the weighing up of Arab virtues against their vices. This literary hobby, as we have seen, derived from the study of Arabian lineages (and not only those of men, but also those of famous horses) by Daghfal b. Ḥanẓalah and others; transferred to the interests of the philologists of Basra and Kufa, it was extended across the whole field of comparative poetic genius and mastery of language. Those philologists with Shuᶜūbī sympathies tried to prove that the non-Arabs, especially the Greeks and the Persians, had far surpassed the Arabs in linguistic skill and literary flair; furthermore, a study of the Arab poets, their tribes and histories, revealed many of the lineages claimed by the Arabs to be fabricated. Abū ᶜUbaydah (d. 209/824–5), a grammarian of non-Arab, possibly Jewish, origin, who, incidentally, was much admired by Jāḥiẓ, was held up as the foremost exposer of the vices of the ancient Arabs

30 *Bayān*, III, *K. al-ᶜAṣā*, 89.

and of spurious genealogies. Yet opinion differs with regard to his true position in the controversy; was he in fact at heart a Khārijī who primarily sought equity and racial equality along with factual accuracy in his philological pursuits; or was he, as Goldziher would have us believe, a true Shuᶜūbī, hating the Arabs whom he accused of aping the Persians?[31] Many of his contemporaries or near-contemporaries shared his views. Such works as *Manāqib al-ᶜAjam* ("The Virtues of the Persians") by Saᶜīd b. Ḥumayd al-Bakhtakān (d. 240/854–5), *Mathālib al-ᶜArab* ("The Vices of the Arabs") by al-Haytham b. ᶜAdī (d. 207/822–3), "The Names of the Whores of Quraysh in pre-Islam" by Sahl b. Hārūn (d. 245/859–60), and the book on Arab robbers by Abū ᶜUbaydah himself – some of these works having been written in the courtly circle of the caliphate or as polemics reflecting the bitter personal rivalry among philologists – set the tone which characterized the sharpest exchanges in this literary debate.

The rejoinder to the Shuᶜūbīs was to come in master-works on the etymology of Arabic tribal names. The earliest known is the *Kitāb al-Ishtiqāq* ("Book of the Derivation [of Proper Names]") by Ibn Durayd (d. 321/933). He was followed by Ibn Fāris (d. 395/1004), the teacher of Badīᶜ al-Zamān al-Hamadhānī, in his work *al-Ṣāḥibī fī fiqh al-lughah* – written for the Ṣāḥib Ibn ᶜAbbād, the Persian vizier of a Persian ruler – in which he defended Arabic against the vicious attacks made on it by Shuᶜūbī philologists and historians such as Ḥamzah al-Iṣfahānī (d. 356/967), whose aims included the recounting of the Himyaritic past of the Yemen, and the etymological explanation of the original Persian forms of geographical names which Arab philology had tried to explain by far-fetched Arabic etymologies. To Ibn Fāris, Arabic was the best and richest of all languages, which could not be translated into any other language, nor could non-Arabs compete with Arabs in the use of metaphor. *Iᶜrāb* (grammatical inflexion) enabled Arabic to articulate its utterances with the utmost clarity, and in its richness of synonyms the language was without equal: "In Persian the lion must rest content with but one name, but we give it a hundred and fifty." By the time al-Zamakhsharī (d. 538/1143), himself a Persian by descent, wrote his *Mufaṣṣal*, the debate was nearing its close; an unconscious identification of Islam with (linguistic) Arabism had taken root in the conscience of believers, and Zamakhsharī was able to thank his Maker for ordaining his preoccupation with philology in order to fight the Lord's battles against the party of slander and mockery. Centuries before him, Jāḥiẓ, in *Kitāb al-Bayān*, had expressed similar sentiments:

When you take a Shuᶜūbī by the hand and cause him to enter the land of the pure bedouin Arabs, the source of perfect eloquence, and acquaint him with an

[31] *Muslim Studies*, I, 181–3.

accomplished poet or an eloquent orator, he will know that what you say is the truth, an evidence clearly visible to the percipient eye. Understand what I say in this, and know that you have never seen a people more wretched than these Shuᶜūbīs, nor more hostile to its religion, nor more vehement in ravaging its honour, nor greater bores.[32]

SHUᶜŪBIYYAH IN AL-ANDALUS

A later, characteristic, and yet unusually interesting Shuᶜūbī literature was to be written in al-Andalus in the fifth/eleventh century. Despite many borrowings from the East and from earlier masters in Iraq and Iran, it is stamped with a markedly Maghribi character. Furthermore, it is among the most comprehensive of all Shuᶜūbī literatures, and, as it has now been edited and translated into English,[33] it offers the best introduction to *Shuᶜūbiyyah* from any aspect, whether geographical, chronological or in point of style, choice of subject and use of quotations. Derivative it may be; nonetheless, the wine poured into old bottles is of a quality sufficient to impress the modern reader.

James T. Monroe suggests that Shuᶜūbi sentiment in al-Andalus was provoked by conditions similar to those which gave rise to it in the East: "It is known for example that in the ninth century AD the Arabs were installed in the best and most fertile lands of Andalusia and the eastern portion of the Peninsula. This permitted them during the tenth century to live in Cordoba and to enjoy the privileges of absentee landlordism so that towards the end of the caliphal period the Arabs constituted the upper echelon of society." Thereafter the "Slav" and Berber elements [mainly praetorians like their Turkish counterparts earlier in the East), who rose to power after the ruin of the Cordovan caliphate, were a fertile field for Shuᶜūbī ideas. One "Slav", Ḥabīb, a man of letters in the time of Hishām II (366–400/976–1009), composed a work setting forth Shuᶜūbī pretensions called "Clear and Convincing Proofs Against Those Who Deny the Excellencies of the 'Slavs' ". However, the *Risālah* ("Epistle") of Abū ᶜĀmir b. García, a noted poet and secretary, remains the masterpiece of Andalusian and possibly of all Shuᶜūbī literature, in Monroe's words: "a veritable mosaic of allusions to Arabic literature and history, containing quotations from the Koran, from poetry and proverbial wisdom, all this . . . expressed by means of a highly elaborate rhymed prose of the kind that was so much in vogue among the prose writers of the fifth century of Islam, and . . . decorated with all the ornaments of Arabic rhetoric." As a spokesman of all the non-Arabs, more especially the "Slavs", Ibn García boasts of his descent from Sarah and

[32] *Bayān*, III, *K. al-ᶜAṣā*, 29.

[33] Monroe, *The Shuᶜūbiyyah in al-Andalus*.

derides the Arabs because of their descent from Hagar, the slave. Throughout the *Risālah* the Arabs are depicted as uncouth bedouin, without breeding or manners, borrowers of other men's ideas and attainments (though the Prophet himself is exempted from the charge). The non-Arabs are contrasted with them in every way; they were "clear, grave, not camel herders or diggers tilling the soil; great kings, not burners of camel dung for fuel. Intelligent, they [wore] brocade and fine silk cloth [not] a coarse garment suitable for both summer and winter weather made up of the collected wool of six ewes". They were "warriors, not guardians of palm branches or planters of palm shoots; kings who recognized no overlords, not one of whom in quenching his thirst drank of the milk of milch camels; nay, their drink was wine, and their food roasted meat, not the mouthful of colocynth seeds in the deserts or the eggs of lizards taken from their nests".[34]

Over a period of roughly a century, no less than five still extant refutations of Ibn García appeared. These rejoinders contain anti-Christian invective, abuse of the "Slavs", praise of both Sarah and Hagar and disparagement of both Persians and Byzantines. Several lack the freshness and spontaneity of Ibn García, while the constant harking back to bogus pre-Islamic and early Islamic mythical history is somewhat forced and often tedious. This passage from Abū ᵓl-Ṭayyib b. Mann Allāh al-Qarawī (d. 492/1099) is fairly typical:

Do not fear, the Arabs straitened nations before you, they bent down the crowns of heads because they were the most noble men of the age, the masters of the ideas which then prevailed. Among them were the ᶜArab al-ᶜĀribah,[35] and from them came ᶜĀd,[36] the conquering, the discerning, men huge in build, likewise Iram of the Columns created without an equal in the land . . . Among the Arabs were the *Tubbaᶜs* . . . Dhū ᵓl-Qarnayn, the builder of the barrier and the dam[37] . . . Allāh, Almighty, has said: "Are they better then the people of the *Tubbaᶜ*?" [Qurᵓān, xliv.37]. Thus they became a byword for greatness.[38]

Shuᶜūbiyyah as a literary movement or vogue was to last long and was wide in its appeal. It might at times be a facile literary pastime, or manifest itself in ways that are confusing and difficult to translate into socio-political terms. (As an example, Mālik b. Wuhayb, who lived in Morocco at the court of the sixth/twelfth-century Almoravids, wrote "The Clipped Gold Piece (*Qurāḍat al-dhahab*), wherein mention is made of the ignoble among the Arabs of the Jāhiliyyah and of Islam"; it was hailed as an unsurpassed masterpiece;

[34] Trans. Monroe, *The Shuᶜūbiyyah in al-Andalus*, 25–6; cf. ch. 16, n.11, below. [35] Cf. ch. 23, n.26.

[36] An ancient nation which perished, leaving behind mighty ruins often identified with "Iram of the Columns", see ch. 8, n.15; frequently cited in the Qurᵓān, however, as an example of human vainglory. [37] A legendary Tubbaᶜ king; see ch. 8, n.13.

[38] Trans. Monroe, *The Shuᶜūbiyyah in al-Andalus*, 39.

yet, paradoxically, Ibn Wuhayb's master was a Berber who claimed Himyarite descent, for the Almoravids spared no effort to prove that they were Arabs by lineage and that there was no glory to compare with that of the Arabs.) But so pervasive and inescapable was the legacy of early *Shuᶜūbiyyah* that one is often mistakenly tempted directly or indirectly to attribute every manifestation of "patriotism" or intellectual ferment to its influence. Thus some have urged that Muᶜtazilī rationalism was the orthodox response to *Shuᶜūbiyyah*, while others have suggested that the whole *geste* of Ismāᶜīl was powerfully enhanced by Shuᶜūbī claims. All are agreed, however, that *Shuᶜūbiyyah* reflected a profound stirring and questioning in the Islamic world of the early Middle Ages. Yet even the most fanatical Shuᶜūbī expressed his sentiments in the tongue first spoken by the Arabian lizard-eaters he so despised.

CHAPTER 3

IBN AL-MUQAFFAᶜ AND EARLY ᶜABBASID PROSE

LIFE

In the annals of Arabic literature Ibn al-Muqaffaᶜ occupies a central position. For it is with his work that the history of ᶜAbbasid prose literature begins; it is he who opens the door to the golden age of Arabic prose writing; it is by him that a wide humanistic concept of letters is introduced to the Arabs. Though rightly classified as an ᶜAbbasid writer and littérateur, Ibn al-Muqaffaᶜ lived most of his life in Umayyad times, and it was under the Umayyads that he served his literary apprenticeship and began his career as a chancery secretary (*kātib*). Like his Umayyad precursor and older contemporary, ᶜAbd al-Ḥamīd al-Kātib,[1] he was to become the luminary of the secretarial school of his day. As such, he won for himself unprecedented renown as a master of Arabic prose and contributed signally – though no more so perhaps than ᶜAbd al-Ḥamīd – to the development of a written artistic prose tradition.

Born in Fīrūzābād in Fārs some time in the very early years of the second/eighth century, Ibn al-Muqaffaᶜ was the son of an Umayyad tax-officer of noble Persian origin and, indeed, bore the Persian name Rōzbih until at a mature age he converted to Islam from Manichaeism and took the name ᶜAbdullāh. The date of his execution at the age of thirty-six is imprecisely known, but it was not earlier than 139/757 and in all likelihood fell in that very year.[2] His command of literary Arabic he acquired in Basra, where in early life he lived in high literary circles and learned scrupulously to observe the proprieties of the language from magisterial exponents of the classical ideal. The first glimpse we have of Ibn al-Muqaffaᶜ as an Umayyad *kātib* is in Fārs not long after the appointment of ᶜAbdullāh b. ᶜUmar b. ᶜAbd al-ᶜAzīz as governor of Iraq (126/743–4). The latter's replacement of Ibn al-Muqaffaᶜ's master, al-Masīḥ b. al-Ḥawārī, brought both *kātib* and master into open physical conflict with the new appointee, Sufyān b. Muᶜāwiyah al-Muhallabī. Partly, though not wholly, for his part in the affair, Ibn al-

[1] See *CHALUP*, ch. 4. [2] Sourdel, "Biographie", 318.

Muqaffaʿ was some years later to suffer a painful death at Sufyān's hands. But in the short term he survived Sufyān's eventual victory over al-Masīḥ in 129/746–7, and we find him next in Kirmān, apparently amassing a fortune in the secretarial service of lieutenants of Ibn Hubayrah, the new governor of Iraq. Umayyad *kātib* though he may have been, Ibn al-Muqaffaʿ had no difficulty in adapting his life to changing circumstances; for, after leaving Kirmān, he took up with ʿĪsā b. ʿAlī b. ʿAbdullāh b. al-ʿAbbās b. ʿAbd al-Muṭṭalib and his brother Sulaymān, paternal uncles of the future ʿAbbasid caliph al-Manṣūr. With ʿĪsā he forged a particularly close bond as his *kātib*. This part of his life he spent mainly in Basra, which from 133/751 to 139/756 was governed by Sulaymān. Plainly a man of fertile counsel and consistent purpose, he comes across as an adventurous climber, scaling the heights close to the summits of power.

The accounts we have of our *kātib*'s behaviour in the ʿAbbasid phase of his life are tales that can have lost nothing in the telling. Yet, when stripped of embellishment and read with discrimination, they do permit us to form an impression of his personality which, if correct, may contribute to a broad understanding of his work and the fate that befell him. His reported conduct suggests a fastidious man of refined manners, steeped in the old culture, traditions and etiquette of the Persian nobility, yet ever observant of the values of Arab society and passionately devoted to the cause of purism in the use of Arabic. In his extravagant generosity and the lavishness of his hospitality, it seems almost as if he sought to outclass the most munificent of Arabs. In the purity of his Arabic he outshone the members of the Arab ruling class. In company he was witty and entertaining. But, for all his qualities and attainments, there was an unendearing side to his character in which we detect an insensitivity to the feelings of those for whom he cared little. His wit could be caustic, his tongue sarcastic, his manner arrogant, and his air superior. Prone to belittle with ridicule, he could be offensive with his strictures if an Arab's command of Arabic did not measure up to his demands. And so, among the duller members of the proud and elusive Arab élite, he must have made many an enemy from whose vengeance only the potent shield of his patrons can have saved him. But nemesis in the end overtook him and put a sudden end to his hubris by delivering him up to a victim of his acts of aggression and ridicule, namely Sufyān b. Muʿāwiyah.

Reports that it was Ibn al-Muqaffaʿ's un-Islamic beliefs and behaviour, or *zandaqah*, that were his undoing need not be taken at face value. Whether he was indeed a back-slider or heretic seems hardly relevant; for, as has recently been suggested, Manichaeism "was not yet as heretical as it became from the reign of al-Mahdī . . . The need for administrative cadres was at that time still greater than the need for orthodoxy".[3] What is relevant is that Ibn al-Muqaffaʿ, whether willingly or under orders, committed an act of egregious indiscretion by making what seemed to the caliph a highly importunate approach to him on a sensitive political issue. The train of events preceding the deed grew out of Sulaymān b. ʿAlī's fear for the safety of his brother, ʿAbdullāh. As a defeated rebel against their nephew, al-Manṣūr,[4] ʿAbdullāh had been allowed to live unmolested in Sulaymān's household, but, once the caliph had felt strong enough to end the arrangement, he had made his wishes known. Before complying, however, Sulaymān had requested safe conduct and free pardon (*amān*) for his brother, but, for his pains, had been instantly replaced (Ramaḍān 139/February 757) as governor of Basra by Sufyān b. Muʿāwiyah. The involvement of ʿIsā b. ʿAlī in this family affair soon followed and, inevitably, that of Ibn al-Muqaffaʿ. On behalf of the branch of the ʿAbbasid family which he served, the *kātib* indited the text of the *amān* for what amounted to the caliph's unconditional acceptance. He thus became the target of the caliph's fury. For this, various reasons can be advanced. One possibility is that al-Manṣūr saw in him the brains behind the political ambitions of the Banū ʿAlī. Whatever the truth, it was left to Basra's new governor Sufyān, for long the implacable foe of Ibn al-Muqaffaʿ, to inflict exemplary punishment on him in the form of death by torture, while the caliph turned a deaf ear to all the protests and entreaties of his patrons.

TRANSLATIONS AND ADAPTATIONS OF NON-ARABIC WORKS

Kalīlah wa-Dimnah

Today Ibn al-Muqaffaʿ is chiefly remembered for his transmission, through the medium of Arabic, of a collection of old Indian fables. Such was the popularity acquired by the collection that by the end of the eleventh century AD it had entered the Byzantine world in a Greek version and by the middle of the thirteenth was awaiting, in a Castilian version, the attentions of the cultural world of Alfonso the Wise in Spain. The collection to which Ibn al-Muqaffaʿ had access was in its essence a Pahlavi, or Middle Persian, adaptation of a work in Sanskrit made in the time of Anūshīrvān Khusraw I (531–79) and traditionally attributed to one Burzōē, who, if the identification is correct, was his court physician.[5] Known in Sanskrit as the *Pañcatantra* (roughly, "Five Occasions of Good Sense"), the work in its Pahlavi adaptation – no longer extant – took its title, *Kalīlag u Dimnag*, from

[3] Van Ess, "Fragments", 161; on *zandaqah*, see also pp. 41–2, above and p. 195, below.
[4] See pp. 49, 64. [5] *CHIran*, III, 161; *EI*², "Kalīla wa-Dimna".

corrupt forms of Karataka and Damnaka, the Sanskrit names of two jackals who dominate the opening narrative. From the Pahlavi, of course, comes the Arabic title by which Ibn al-Muqaffaᶜ's work is best known: *Kalīlah wa-Dimnah*.

Kalīlah wa-Dimnah is basically made up of a series of animal apologues developed through and around the two jackals so named. In the interconnected episodes within an encompassing narrative framework, animals and birds, behaving as humans as in Aesop's fables, point morals and utter maxims for the benefit of those living in the world of practical politics, and illustrate shrewd and worldly-wise reactions to human predicaments. The Pahlavi version, said to have been produced on the spot in India, carried, in addition to its core of fables, Burzōē's autobiography, and, done into Arabic by Ibn al-Muqaffaᶜ, it forms the introduction to the body of his work. The whole is prefaced by Ibn al-Muqaffaᶜ's own prologue.

To define precisely the nature and quality of our *kātib*'s *Kalīlah wa-Dimnah* poses a problem that has so far defied solution. A detailed discussion of the matter in all its complexity has no place here. Suffice it therefore to notice only its essential elements. As regards content, it is appropriate first to call attention to an extant Syriac translation of Burzōē's Pahlavi text made more than half a century or so before the advent of Islam. The direction in which the evidence of this translation points is that Ibn al-Muqaffaᶜ expanded the Pahlavi text by making certain additions possessed of the same general features as those characterizing the Indian substructure so faithfully preserved in his work. Much as suspected additions of this nature – which we may characterize as episodic – may have aroused legitimate scholarly curiosity, there is one addition of a very different order that has been found even more intriguing. This is the translator's putative insertion into Burzōē's autobiography of an excursus in which we encounter a sceptical view of the revealed religions in the light of their mutually contradictory positions on the one hand, and, on the other, a recognition of the place of human reason alone in the development of religion. The whole content of the excursus seems quite out of character with the Burzōē we discern in the rest of the autobiography. For in the former we see a man who, though not averse to the idea of the enjoyment of worldly goods, yet evinces a spirit of marked asceticism, reinforced by a pessimistic outlook on the woes that attend man from the cradle to the grave. Nöldeke was inclined to accept the excursus as the product of Ibn al-Muqaffaᶜ's own pen and to attribute the ascetic element to Indian influences. Others, however, notably Kraus and Christensen, have cast serious doubt on this line of thinking on the grounds that the same kind of freedom of thought and criticism of revealed religions as well as the ascetic spirit can be shown to have been current in the Iran of Anūshīrvān.[6] On the specific point of asceticism and the desire to withdraw from the world Christensen's position has been well summed up by Mary Boyce: "Christensen found its source in influences within 6th century Iran itself, from Christianity, Gnosticism, Manichaeism and Mazdakism." Thus he held that that aspect of the autobiography was typical of the reign of Khusraw I. In short, Ibn al-Muqaffaᶜ may or may not have been responsible for the insertion of the excursus; but, even if it could be supposed with a high degree of certainty that he was, it does not follow that he was in fact the author.

If the form and substance of our Arabic *Kalīlah wa-Dimnah* are problematical, its originator's translation is no less so. His original is lost, and the earliest known manuscript post-dates his death by more than four and a half centuries, and the second oldest by almost six. Through how many intermediate copies these codices derive from the original we cannot say. What we can say is that the wording of the one differs markedly from that of the other and that all available evidence has shown them to be but part of a varied and uncertain tradition. Hence the way in which Ibn al-Muqaffaᶜ adapted the resources of the Arabic language to his purpose is not a matter of precise knowledge, but of informed conjecture. That said, it is generally agreed that his approach to the translation was not slavishly literal, but that of an able master of Pahlavi and Arabic concerned to produce an idiomatic rendering of *Kalīlag u Dimnag* suited to the taste and grasp of his Arab readers. All indications are that, in so doing, he forged an Arabic prose style that was plain and free and distinguished as much by the ease and straightforwardness of its syntactical structures as by its clarity of expression and simplicity of diction. To apply to his style, as has been done, such epithets as "polished", "graceful", and the like, seems in the absence of the original text less fitting than to say with Gibb that "he posed the problem of finding a smooth and palatable prose style".[7] That he solved the problem by achieving a pleasing and effective style is not in doubt, and certainly no medieval Arab critic is known to have questioned its quality.

Despite the widespread popularity that *Kalīlah wa-Dimnah* enjoyed in aftertimes, it was originally produced for an exclusive readership within court circles. Seen as didactic, its function was to illustrate what should or should not be done by those who would succeed in life. Sporting a golden thread of diversion in a ground of edification, it was intended to serve in Arabo–Muslim court circles the same purpose as it had served at the Sasanian court, whose values and political wisdom so dominated the

[6] See Boyce, *Tansar*, 13; cf. *EI*[2] (III, 883), "Ibn al-Muḳaffaᶜ". [7] *Arabic Literature*, 52.

secular thinking of Ibn al-Muqaffaᶜ and others of the same secretarial class of the same era.[8] But to regard *Kalīlah wa-Dimnah* as less than a masterpiece of Arabic literature in its own right simply because of its unoriginal content would be seriously to misjudge it. Ibn al-Muqaffaᶜ's achievement is comparable to that of Jacques Amyot, who in the Renaissance conspicuously contributed to the shaping of a French prose style by his translation of Plutarch. Like Amyot, Ibn al-Muqaffaᶜ merits recognition as a magisterial pioneer. His *Kalīlah wa-Dimnah* illumined the path along which others would move and served as a stimulus to the development of a style suited to the needs of a creative prose literature. At the same time, through the subject-matter it so well interpreted, it opened for the Muslim world a window on a source of inspiration for imitators, artists and poets.

Because *Kalīlah wa-Dimnah*, largely through the popularity of its content, has survived in essence, and because the work as we know it today has posed problems that have attracted much scholarly attention, there is always a danger of detaching it from the context in which it ought properly to be viewed. To put the matter in perspective, it should be seen as nothing more than just one of several works of old Sasanian court literature which Ibn al-Muqaffaᶜ set out to introduce to the new masters of Islam's destiny. To interpret his intention as a conscious endeavour to set an entirely new literary trend would be to misinterpret his primary objective. Motivated by an evident sense of didactic mission, he was, rather, concerned to promote a cultural reorientation that would extend the political and social norms of the old order. In short, his main aim was to graft congruent Sasanian shoots upon the old Arab stock of secular culture in order to produce and regulate an Arabo–Islamic culture embodying what he saw as a proven, potent strain of political wisdom.

The Khudaynāmah

Among Pahlavi texts of which Arabic versions are said and believed with a measure of certainty to have been made by Ibn al-Muqaffaᶜ the *Khwadāy-nāmag* ("Book of Kings") is perhaps the most important. Neither the original nor the Arabic version is extant, but the nature of the work is retrievable from a number of sources. Compiled towards the end of the Sasanian period, this part-legendary, part-mythical and part-factual chronicle of the rulers of pre-Islamic Iran was a quasi-official national history inspired by a vision of kingship as a well-ordered autocracy with a sacred duty not merely to rule its subjects, but also to regulate their ethics and social conduct within a clearly defined and rigid class system.[9] Into the

[8] Cf. Gibb, *Studies*, 62–6. [9] *CHIran*, III, 342, 359ff.

fabric of an engaging saga of kings, princes and warriors, there was interwoven a pattern of maxims, morals and musings characteristic of *andarz*, or "wisdom" literature, combined with explicit admonitory pronouncements and practical advice on a range of matters both civil and military. Clearly a socio-politically oriented chronicle, the *Khwadāy-nāmag* was in the Sasanian historical tradition, which was "concerned less with determining historical facts than with providing an insight into the past and a vision of the future".[10] That Ibn al-Muqaffaᶜ did not put into Arabic all that was contained in the Pahlavi work is clear from the unequivocal testimony of Ḥamzah al-Iṣfahānī, who completed his famous "Annals", or "Chronology", in 350/961, and one suggestion is that Ibn al-Muqaffaᶜ may have chosen to omit or modify subject-matter that his readers would not readily understand.[11] At the same time, our translator is also believed to have introduced into his Arabic version at least one item not included in the original, namely an account of Mazdak son of Bāmdād, from which, it has been argued, later Perso-Arab historians derived much of their information on Mazdak and the movement named after him.[12] But the extent of Ibn al-Muqaffaᶜ's omissions, interpolations and modifications cannot be quantified: if anything of his Arabic version survives at all, it amounts to nothing more than fragments of varying length preserved by Ibn Qutaybah (d. 276/889) as extracts from what this writer styles without ascription *Siyar mulūk al-ᶜAjam* ("Lives of the Persian Kings") – an evident Arabic rendering of the neo-Persian *Khudaynāmah*.[13] That these extracts do in fact derive from Ibn al-Muqaffaᶜ's Arabic text is a presumption that can rightly be said to be strongly based, if for no other reason than that Ibn Qutaybah, both in his *ᶜUyūn al-akhbār* and his *Kitāb-Maᶜārif*, displays unquestionable familiarity with the *kātib*'s writings. Be that as it may, such fragments are, for obvious reasons, of limited heuristic value.

The Āyīn-nāmah

In addition to the "Book of Kings", Ibn al-Muqaffaᶜ is credited with the production of Arabic versions of other Middle Persian works. Listed in the celebrated fourth/tenth-century *Fihrist* of Ibn al-Nadīm are an *Āyīn-nāmah* (or *Āʾīn-nāmah*), a *Kitāb al-Tāj* and a *Kitāb Mazdak*. As in the case of the "Book of Kings", Ibn Qutaybah is thought to have preserved for us parts of the *Āyīn-nāmah*; for in his *ᶜUyūn al-akhbār* are a number of passages, quoted without ascription, but opening with the words "I have read in the *Āʾīn* [or, *Kitāb al-Āʾīn*]". The passages bear on various subjects, ranging from court manners and customs to military tactics, from divination and

[10] Ibid., 393. [11] Ibid., 419f. [12] Cf. n. 18. [13] Gabrieli, "L'opera", 208ff.

physiognomy to archery and polo. Two main questions are posed by these fragments. First, do they derive from a single work of almost encylopaedic scope? Secondly, are they in fact from Ibn al-Muqaffaᶜ's Arabic version of that work? For his part, Gabrieli, though strongly inclined to answer both questions in the affirmative, is acutely aware of the circumstantial nature of the evidence and rightly remains cautious.[14]

Of what the *Āyīn-nāmah* consisted it is not precisely known. The actual title is from the Pahlavi *Āyīn-nāmag* ("Book of Rules [of Propriety])", but this was seemingly a title applicable to any one of a number of preceptive works treating of Sasanian institutions, court protocol, the powers and prerogatives of the social classes, general *savoir faire*, the arts of entertainment, and so forth. To judge from what is reflected of them in Arabic sources, they were written in a rhetorical, sententious and hortatory vein and were designed "to extol and establish the virtues associated with Iranian tradition".[15]

Kitāb al-Tāj

The *Kitāb al-Tāj* ("The Book of the Crown") is the object of as much, if not more, speculation than the *Āyīn-nāmah*. It is to the *Tāj* that Ibn Qutaybah is thought to refer in his *ᶜUyūn al-akhbār* when introducing quotations prefaced by "I have read in the *Tāj*".[16] There is, however, a puzzling aspect to the matter: whereas the *Tāj* is said in Ibn al-Nadīm's *Fihrist* to have been a biography of Anūshīrvān Khusraw I, three-quarters of Ibn Qutaybah's extracts pertain to Parvēz Khusraw II. Nöldeke's considered opinion was that the *Fihrist* incorrectly describes the *Tāj*'s contents, and with good reason Gabrieli shares this view. For him, Ibn Qutaybah's quotations are indeed extracts from Ibn al-Muqaffaᶜ's *Tāj*, in which he sees, however, not so much a chronicle as a "mirror for princes".[17]

Kitāb Mazdak

The nature of the *Kitāb Mazdak* ("The Book of Mazdak": *Mazdak-nāmag*) is held to be deducible from the contents of certain later Perso–Arab writings in which material borrowed from the work has either been detected or deemed to be such with a degree of probability verging on certainty. It is named, of course, after the leader of the Mazdakite revolutionary movement whose disruptive socio-religious tenets led to his execution at the end of Kavād's reign (531 AD) and against whose followers it then fell to Khusraw I to act with relentless severity. The book offered neither a factual

[14] Ibid., 214. [15] *CHIran*, III, 363, 393. [16] Gabrieli, "L'opera", 215. [17] Ibid., 216.

biography of Mazdak nor an account of his tenets; it was, rather, a work of entertaining historical fiction slanted towards disparagement of Mazdak.[18]

The "Letter of Tansar"

Another significant product of Ibn al-Muqaffaᶜ's translational activities was the so-called "Letter of Tansar/Tōsar",[19] a Sasanian political treatise of no mean literary merit. With this work we move on to very much firmer ground than that hitherto traversed. For, although the Arabic version is lost – presumed no longer extant – it was known to the Persian historian Ibn Isfandiyār, who translated it into neo-Persian around the beginning of the seventh/thirteenth century, and incorporated it in his *Tārīkh-i Ṭabaristān* ("History of Ṭabaristān").[20] From available evidence, it is demonstrable that Ibn al-Muqaffaᶜ expanded the original Pahlavi text by adding Quranic and biblical quotations as well as various illustrative verses. It is equally demonstrable that the neo-Persian rendering – which also carries some additions – in no way reflects or remotely evokes the style and spirit of Ibn al-Muqaffaᶜ's Arabic version. Prolix and vapid, it lacks body and vigour. Yet for all that, it has preserved for us the essential subject-matter transmitted through the Arabic.

Tansar, the putative author of the "Letter", was a powerful and influential Zoroastrian priest and chief counsellor of the first Sasanian king, Ardashīr, who reigned *c.* 224–40 AD. On the ascription scholarly opinion is divided, raising the question, is it a late forgery uttered for Khusraw I's political ends, or is it a product genuine in the sense or to the extent that it had been developed from an essentially authentic nucleus?[21] The problem need not concern us. All that interests us here is the epistle's content. Its writer first offers a sketch of Iranian history up to the time of Ardashīr. He then goes on to recount how Gushnasp (Ar. Jashnasf), one of the local kings of a divided Iran reluctant to submit to Ardashīr, had been able to profit from a respite contrived by Ardashīr to write to Tansar, the king's most trusted counsellor, listing the reasons for his withholding allegiance. To each point raised by Gushnasp, Tansar diligently responds, and his replies form the body of the letter. Taken as a whole, what we have is an apologia for political, religious, social and legal institutions which, if not, as asserted, established by Ardashīr, were at any rate familiar in later Sasanian times. The superiority of race and country and the king as its *fons et origo* are the linchpin of the system defended and justified by the author. This position he explains thus:

18 On Mazdak and the Mazdakite movement, see *CHIran*, III, 994ff.

19 In neo-Persian *Nāma-yi Tansar*. *Tosar* is probably correct, but "the form *Tansar* has by now gained too wide a currency for it to be usefully displaced", Boyce, *Tansar*, 8.

20 See *EI*², "Ibn-i Isfandiyār".

21 Boyce, *Tansar*, 15ff, 22.

we are called "the Iranian people", and there is no quality or trait of excellence or nobility which we hold dearer than this, that we have ever showed humility and lowliness . . . in the service of kings, and have chosen obedience and loyalty, devotion and fidelity. Through this quality our works were established and we came to be the head and neck of all the climes.[22]

Tending towards the didactic, the tract owes some of its essential flavour to such characteristic ingredients as the aphorism and the apologue. All in all then, the "Letter" is very much in the tradition so dear to Ibn al-Muqaffaᶜ.

There is so much that is conjectural about Ibn al-Muqaffaᶜ's Arabic translations and adaptations that an evaluation of his achievement may seem an impertinence. In particular, the pursuit of his style through material that may have been reworked, even if originally the fruit of his labour, is hazardous in the extreme. To try to pursue it through an inferior Persian translation would be utterly reckless. Nevertheless, available evidence suggests a simple, direct, functional prose such as may be expected of one not only able to exploit the resources of Arabic to meet new needs, but also sufficiently sensitive to literary form to suit his style to didactic and preceptive subjects.

ORIGINAL WORKS

Kitāb Ādāb al-kabīr ("al-Adab al-kabīr")

The *Kitāb Ādāb al-kabīr* (hereafter *Ādāb*: "The Comprehensive Book of Rules of Conduct") is commonly, but incorrectly, styled *al-Adab al-kabīr* – a title which conveniently distinguishes it from *al-Adab al-ṣaghīr* ("The Lesser Book of Conduct"). Though long thought to be the companion to the *Ādāb* and thus the work of Ibn al-Muqaffaᶜ, *al-Adab al-ṣaghīr* can no longer safely be regarded as such.[23] The description of it as "merely a pseudepigraphic cento of *ḥikam* [aphorisms] drawn partly from *Kalīlah wa-Dimnah*"[24] is almost certainly correct. It need not therefore concern us here.

The *Ādāb* comprises four parts. The first is clearly a preface, accounting for only some 250 words of the Arabic text.[25] Its brevity is apt to belie the importance of its function, for, as a rhetorical retrospect on the ancients, it is in fact the justification of all that it prefaces: without ancestral excellence there would be no heritage of spiritual or temporal knowledge, no tradition of literary or moral learning – in short no fund of human experience on which to draw.

The concept of a golden age long past is implicit in the opening declaration that in early times men were physically and mentally superior to

22 Ibid., 52. 23 ᶜAbbās, "Naẓrah, 578". 24 *EI*², "Ibn al-Muḳaffaᶜ".
25 Kurd ᶜAlī, *Rasāʾil*, 40–1; for the texts of the other three parts, see ibid., 42–54, 54–70, 71–106.

the author's contemporaries, and by virtue of great longevity acquired superior experience of life. Unselfishly they had passed on their sum of knowledge to posterity; they had committed it to books in writing. So rich was their legacy that latter-day lesser intelligences had but one task before them – that of elucidating minutiae from the corpus of weighty maxims bequeathed to them. The legacy referred to is not hard to identify as Sasanian, and, as he wrote, Ibn al-Muqaffaᶜ doubtless had to the forefront of his mind the wisdom literature through which the Sasanian establishment expressed so many of its political and social views.[26]

The second part of the treatise, amounting to less than one-fifth of the whole, is a "mirror for princes" in miniature. If we can accept as genuine a similar composition contained in ᶜAbd al-Ḥamīd's "Epistle to the Crown Prince",[27] Ibn al-Muqaffaᶜ's mirror is the lesser literary achievement both in scope and style. It is none the less a landmark in the history of the genre. The addressee, taken to be the caliph's son, is apostrophized as one seeking to acquire *adab* – Cowper's "polish'd manners and fine sense". He is counselled first to learn the basic rules (*uṣūl*) of conduct and not permit them to be displaced by secondary rules (*fuṣūl*). To illustrate, the author takes religion, health, courage, generosity, the spoken word, and the management of resources, enunciating for each topic the basic principle and indicating the general direction in which it may be developed. The framework for all is the same: "The basic principle in . . . is that . . . Then, if you can . . . all the better." Thus, he writes of health in the following terms: "The basic principle in maintaining physical health is that you make only light demands on the body in the way of food, drink and coitus. Then, if you can get to know all those things that will benefit or harm it and learn how to profit from your knowledge, all the better."[28]

He then turns to pitfalls awaiting a prince. He warns against the love of flattery and in particular against the dangers of allowing others to detect it. On the more positive side he urges the prince to make the acquaintance of men of religion and moral perfection (*muruwwah*; literally, "manliness") with a view to their becoming his aides, close friends and confidants. He should not fear to seek and take advice from those qualified to give it. In his general dealings he will be unable to please all men, nor should he try, but seek, rather, to please only the best and most intelligent. As for those in authority under him, he should do his utmost to keep himself informed of their conduct and see that they know what and what not to expect from him. Unpalatable opposition to his views from judicious, mature and honourable men is something he must learn to tolerate. He must also see that he does not concern himself with trifles to the detriment of matters of

[26] *CHIran*, III, 398, 400. [27] *CHALUP*, 167–72. [28] Kurd ᶜAlī, *Rasāʾil*, 42.

moment; that he is not indiscriminately lavish with money and honours; that he does not overwork; and so on.[29] In due course three bases of kingship are identified: religion, which is the best; the resolve to rule, which creates stability but may arouse opposition; and personal fancy, which produces transitory results. Here the author strikes a clear Sasanian note. There next follow various pronouncements on the need for caution and prudence in particular circumstances, exhortations to seemly conduct, accompanied by the reasons for such, and sundry observations on statecraft. The section concludes with a statement of the pivotal role in government of two interdependent factors: power and an attractive public image.

The third part of the *Ādāb* is longer than the second. Again the addressee is apostrophized in the second person singular, but it is now the turn of the courtier, counsellor or minister, as the case may be, to be advised of the rules of conduct appropriate to his status in the ruler's service. Familiarity with the ruler should never be allowed to breed contempt, so to speak. The limit of familiarity is indirectly set by the maxim: "If you see the sovereign making a brother of you, make of him a father."[30] Implicit in the injunction is that, under the circumstances stated, the ruler should be accorded all the respect and obedience that a son owes his father. A detailed analysis or extended summary of all that follows this precept is not called for here. The tenor, style and presentation of material are fundamentally the same as in the second part of our treatise. Moreover, the difference in content is not so much a radical change in substance as an adjustment of orientation appropriate to an exposition of the basic techniques of handling a ruler on the one hand, and the senior members of his household and "government" on the other. As a pragmatic guide to survival for a ruler's intimate, minister, or other high official in a potentially precarious position at the top, it is based on the requirements of common sense expressed through dicta that may well be moral but are primarily rewarding, and through instructions and prohibitions largely savouring of the self-regarding rather than of the altruistic or purely ethical. A counsellor's advice, for instance, must always be disinterestedly sincere, but it must be such for practical, not ethical, reasons as the following directive makes clear: "If you want your advice to be taken, give a disinterested opinion. Under no circumstances blend with it any element of private interest, for your opinion will be taken from you by an enemy, and your private interest thrown back at you by your lord and master." The potentially dangerous consequences of shaping counsels to accord with one's own predilections prompt Ibn al-Muqaffaᶜ to take the matter one step further: he warns his

[29] This section is translated in Beeston, *Samples*, no. 3.

[30] Kurd ᶜAlī, *Rasāʾil*, 54.

reader never to be suspected by a ruler of allowing personal considerations to influence his judgements since rulers regard such conduct as deception, treachery and ingratitude. The consequences of ignoring his advice are left to the imagination.

It is noteworthy that on a purely moral issue Ibn al-Muqaffaᶜ abandons his prescriptive approach in favour of presenting a choice between alternatives. Taking the case of a ruler reckless of his subjects' welfare, he merely points out that one either sides with the ruler against his subjects and thereby forfeits the next world, or sides with the subjects and thereby forfeits this world since "you have no choice but to die or decamp". There is no question here of his indicating, much less advocating, the virtue of dying in the cause of justice and righteousness. But why, after all, should there be? His moral thought has no basis either in philosophical principle or in religious ethics or spirituality. Thus it is inappropriate, however tempting, to contemplate any comparison between his thinking and that of the moral philosopher or spiritual teacher. His didacticism is essentially that of a man conversant with the age-old vagaries of despots and their entourages. As we are taken step by step through a variety of circumstances and predictable situations calling for tact, diplomacy and discretion, our author makes it increasingly clear that his concept of the most advantageous code of conduct for the highly placed courtier is based first and foremost on the latter's ability to discipline himself to regard his own wishes and reasoning as irrelevant to the many situations he will be called upon to meet. Accordingly, in the especially desirable blend of qualities and modes of behaviour commended to the reader, patience, self-restraint, humility and self-subordination are readily identifiable as, in Ibn al-Muqaffaᶜ's view, cardinal assets. Courtesy and magnanimity toward spiteful, carping rivals, personal kindness and affability towards colleagues, and general *bonhomie* are, of course, sensible desiderata, but all are secondary to the thinking behind the note struck in the closing words of the section, exhorting the reader to be "submissive if they wrong you, agreeable if they anger you; otherwise put yourself as far from them as possible, and treat them with the utmost caution".

As in the third, so also in the fourth and longest part of the *Ādāb*, it is *savoir faire* in the domain of human relationships that Ibn al-Muqaffaᶜ seeks to impart. But now his preoccupation is with relations between a man and his colleagues and associates in what – since he is not specific – we are left to surmise is the secretarial and administrative fraternity. With his opening exhortation, "Give generously both your blood and your goods to your friend",[31] he strikes the key-note of the discourse on which he is about to

[31] Ibid., 71.

embark – friendship, a theme to which almost all that follows is directly or indirectly related. His style and treatment are, as always, didactic and heavily dependent on the aphoristic, and the framework within which his discourse develops conveys the impression of a structure ill-suited to unity of purpose and systematic thinking. In his approach he is still the pragmatist: the theme of friendship subsumes that of enmity, and he is as concerned to communicate the art of avoiding occasions of enmity that may lose a man his friends and gain him enemies as to press home a man's need not only to cultivate true friendship, but also to be popular in the circles in which he moves.

Our *kātib*'s concept of true friendship is that of a sincere relationship rooted in the intention that it shall be permanent and therefore not be undertaken unadvisedly, lightly or wantonly; for to break a friendship, however justifiable the cause, is considered discreditable, opprobrious, and even tantamount to treachery. The choice of a friend, then, must be a judicious choice resulting from patience, circumspection, and discrimination, and culminating in a relationship that will be sustained by such virtues as fidelity, loyalty and devotion, and be secure against such vices as deceit, depravity and wickedness. The bond of friendship thus envisioned cannot but evoke the traditional Christian concept of the marriage bond in its non-carnal aspects. But any similarity there may be between the two evaporates before the recommendation that it is with one's better, not with an inferior, that a bond of friendship should be formed. Albeit justified on the ground that to make friends of inferiors is a mark of the reprehensible trait that is envy, the advice but thinly disguises its essential pragmatism as the reader is told:

> you will reap a handsome reward from having as your friend and companion one who is superior to you in learning, so that you may acquire learning from his learning; superior to you in power, so that he may protect you with his power; superior to you in wealth, so that you may profit from his wealth; superior to you in status (*jāh*), so that you may attain to the fulfilment of your wishes through his status; superior to you in religious observance, so that you may be the more pious through his piety.[32]

In striking contrast to the true friend, women rank low in Ibn al-Muqaffaᶜ's estimation. To shed a friend is to put honour at risk; but to divorce a woman is a discretionary matter of no great consequence. His hostility to women and their allure is almost philosophical and is redolent of that of some moralists of classical antiquity:

> You must realise that one of the things that does most to dishonour religion, most to exhaust the body, most to entail financial ruin, most to impair the mind, most to

[32] Ibid., 84.

detract from manliness and is most swift to sweep away dignity and bearing is a passion for women. One affliction suffered by a man with such a passion is that his appetite for such women as he has is forever cloyed and his eyes on the look-out for such women as he does not have.[33]

Contending that there is nothing to choose between one woman and another, he goes so far as to insist that food has more variety and, by the comparison thus implied, comes perilously close to a depersonalization of women.

But, interesting as they may be, these succinct references to women are only incidental to the content of this last part of the discourse, in which the writer's main interest is the promotion of good fellowship, companionship, amity and concord in the circles that concern him. Here is not the place to itemize the techniques that he advocates for the attainment of that purpose; but the loftier of them cannot be better adumbrated than they are, unwittingly, by Cardinal Newman in his well-known *Scope and Nature of a University Education*. Essaying the definition of a true gentleman, he observes that: "he is mainly occupied in removing the obstacles which hinder the free and unembarrassed action of those about him: and he concurs with their movements rather than takes the initiative himself . . . [He] carefully avoids whatever may cause a jar or a jolt in the minds of those with whom he is cast; all clashing of opinion, or collision of feeling, all restraint or suspicion . . . or resentment: his great concern being to make everyone at their ease . . . He has his eyes on all his company: he is . . . merciful towards the absurd. He can recollect to whom he is speaking: he guards against unseasonable allusions, or topics which may irritate. He is seldom prominent in conversation, and never wearisome . . . He never speaks of himself except when compelled, never defends himself by a mere retort, he has no ears for slander or gossip . . ." Whatever differences might have separated Ibn al-Muqaffaᶜ and Newman, could they ever have met in discussion, there would, it is clear, have been some common ground on which they could have stood together.

Of the content of the *Ādāb* there is little else that calls for comment here. It remains only to say of the Greek elements that are detectable in the work that they need cause no surprise: Persian moral thought had not developed in total isolation from the influences exerted by the translations from the Greek under the auspices of Shāpūr I and Khusraw I and at the Christian schools of Nisibis and Gondēshāpūr.[34]

Without a detailed analytical study of the vocabulary, diction and rhythms of the *Ādāb*, a precise stylistic appraisal is clearly out of the question; we must make do with general observations and impressions.

[33] Ibid., 89. [34] ᶜAbbās, "Naẓrah", 554ff; *CHIran*, III, 161, 573.

The parallelistic style of the early *khuṭbah* (oration, or address) had already, in Umayyad hortatory compositions, been expanded and elaborated without any marked invasion of the sort of rhyming that came to characterize later ʿAbbasid prose.[35] Not surprisingly then, this same style is the most distinctive feature of the *Ādāb*. Like ʿAbd al-Ḥamīd, Ibn al-Muqaffaʿ is alive to the stylistic potential of semantic, structural and acoustic parallelism and to the value of sophisticated patterning wherever it serves the purpose of driving home a point by the verbal expansion of an idea or ideas. At the same time, he shows no predilection for the lengthy circumstantial clauses so dear to ʿAbd al-Ḥamīd, and his manner is not so diffuse or prolix. Sensitive to the effect of epigrammatic point and of antithesis in admonitory discourse, he has on the whole accommodated his stylistic method well to his subject. To point his contrasts and enforce his parallels, he makes full use of a range of devices that could have been drawn straight out of the teachings of the ancient schools of classical rhetoric: alliteration, assonance, antithetical isocola, interlocking antithetical phrases, anaphoras, epistrophes, rhetorical repetitions of phrases and structures, rhythmic balance, measured terminations, and so on.

As examples of the author's use of just one or two of the devices just mentioned, the following must suffice: *iḥtaras min sawrati ʾl-ghaḍabi wa-sawrati ʾl-ḥamiyyati wa-sawrati ʾl-ḥidqi wa-sawrati ʾl-jahl* (alliterative quasi-anaphoristic repetition of *sawrah*): "Be on your guard against excessive wrath, excessive hubris, excessive rancour, and excessive folly"; *dhallil nafsaka bi ʾl-ṣabri ʿalā jāri ʾl-sūʾi wa-ʿashīri ʾl-sūʾi wa-jalīsi ʾl-sūʾi* (epistrophic repetition of *sūʾ*): "School yourself to suffering patiently a bad neighbour, a bad companion or a bad associate"; *wa -ʿlam anna faḍla ʾl-fiʿli ʿalā qawli zīnah: wa-faḍla ʾl-qawli ʿalā fiʿli hujnah* (alliteration and repetition of *faḍl*, *fiʿl* and *qawl* in the antithetical isocola *faḍla . . . zīnah* and *faḍla . . . hujnah* together with rhythmic balance and measured terminations ∪∪ – / – ∪ – – familiar from the poetical metre *madīd*): "Mark well that the primacy of deeds over words is an ornament and the primacy of words over deeds a vice"; *(i)lbas li ʾl-nāsi libāsayni laysa ʾl-ʿāqili buddan minhumā* (alliteration with a metrical pattern from *nāsi* to *minhumā* close to that of the poetical metre *basīṭ*): "For [the eyes of] men have two garments to put on which every man of good sense must have"; *ikhwāna ʾl-ṣidqi hum khayru makāsibi ʾl-dunyā hum zīnatun fī ʾl-rikhāʾ: wa-ʿuddatun fīʾl-shiddah: wa-maʿūnatun fī ʾl-maʿāshi wa-ʾl-maʿād* (*inter alia* metrical rhythms familiar to the Arab ear from the poetical metre *basīṭ*); *makāsibi ʾl-dunyā, hum . . . shiddah* and *maʿūnatun . . . maʿād*: "true friends are the best of earthly acquisitions [that a man can make]: they are an ornament in good times and a resource in bad: a support both in this world and in the next [perhaps an allusion to a *ḥadīth* which could be translated "in

35 *CHALUP*, 174ff.

the hereafter we will be judged according to the virtues of our associates in this world"].[36]

Risālah fī ʾl-ṣaḥābah (Kitāb al-Ṣaḥābah)

The place of political thought in Ibn al-Muqaffaʿ's literary output is nowhere more conspicuous than in a piece of writing that is significantly different in purpose, content, length and style from any other of his writings so far discussed. Of the two Arabic titles assigned to it, the more appropriate would seem to be *Risālah fī ʾl-ṣaḥābah* (hereafter *Risālah*: "Epistle on the Companionage"). A freer, but perhaps more apposite, English rendering would be "Memorandum on the Caliph's Entourage"; for what we have is essentially an administrative document, proposing measures designed to ensure the stability of the realm.[37] In rather less than 5,000 words (Arabic text), the writer treats of specific governmental problems in a clearly identifiable historical context and of the means of tackling them. That the addressee is the caliph al-Manṣūr is fairly plain from internal evidence. The *Risālah* must therefore date from somewhere between 136/754, the year of the latter's accession, and 139/757, the most likely date for Ibn al-Muqaffaʿ's death. Whether in producing it Ibn al-Muqaffaʿ acted on his own initiative or was prompted by the caliph's paternal uncle, ʿĪsā, whom he served, is a moot point, as is also the question whether it ever reached al-Manṣūr. This last matter need not concern us here: all we need say is that if it did reach him and he read it, he ignored its contents and acted as if he had never had sight of it.

The considerable historical interest attaching to the *Risālah* is reason enough to examine its content in detail. But first something must be said of the background against which it was written. The climate in which al-Manṣūr – as Abū Jaʿfar – had succeeded Abū ʾl-ʿAbbās al-Saffāḥ, the first ʿAbbasid caliph, was not one in which all his subjects were likely thereafter to be "godly and quietly governed". Disaffected elements abounded not only in Syria, the home of the dethroned Umayyads and heartland of their empire, but also inside Iraq, the new metropolitan province and home of the ʿAbbasid administration. The first threat to the dynasty came from within its own ranks in the shape of a revolt by the caliph's uncle, ʿAbdullāh, early in 137/summer 754. As governor of Syria since the fall of the

[36] Kurd ʿAlī, *Rasāʾil*, 81, 82, 92, 78, 80.

[37] The text (Kurd ʿAlī, *Rasāʾil*, 117–34) has been edited, translated and studied by Pellat (*Ibn al-Muqaffaʿ*); references are to the latter edition. The nine parts into which it is broken down below are to be found in Pellat (Arabic text with facing French translation), 16–22, 22–36, 36–40, 40–6, 46–50, 50–7, 58–60, 60, 60–6.

Umayyads, he had painstakingly cultivated the military leaders of the Syrians, whom he had defeated only four years before. And so, on hearing of Abū ᵓl-ᶜAbbās's death, he readily enlisted Syrian support for his claim to the caliphate and made for Iraq with a largely Syrian army. A Syrian victory was ultimately averted only by the solicited intervention of a Khurasanian army led by Abū Muslim, the very man who had so ably managed the Khurasanian revolutionary movement that had brought the ᶜAbbasids to power. The reward for his pains was assassination by al-Manṣūr's Khurasanian guard: he had outlived his usefulness and, though a spent force in Iraq and the west, he could still command some support in Khurāsān, where he was plainly determined to resume authority. His death sent not a ripple of disturbance through the ranks of the imperial army in Iraq, and, even in the east, it provoked only limited reaction. Clearly al-Manṣūr had gained the legitimacy necessary to command the respect and loyalty of his Khurasanian army –an army comprising not only Iranians but also Arabs, however much Persianized, of old Iraqi stock.

Not the least of al-Manṣūr's problems was that created by the expectations of many who had supported the revolution in the belief that it would result in a religious leadership with a programme of radical reform. A strong tinge of Shiᶜism had run through the propaganda that had won the movement so many of its adherents. But the caliph was no Shīᶜī. He claimed no divine right, nor did he aspire to charismatic leadership of the Muslim community. Though of the House of Muḥammad, he was purely and simply *amīr al-muᵓminīn* (Commander of the Faithful), and, as such, seen by the Shīᶜīs as little better than a continuator of the old regime. And so throughout the empire there ran a wide spectrum of Shīᶜī feeling, ranging from bitter disappointment to a violent sense of outrage. In Iraq itself, where the situation called for unremitting vigilance, the greatest cause for concern came from two leading members of the ᶜAlid family, namely Muḥammad b. ᶜAbdullāh – known as al-Nafs al-Zakiyyah ("the Pure Soul") – and his brother Ibrāhīm, by reason not so much of their presence as of their disappearance and the protracted failure of caliphal agents to track them down. Al-Manṣūr's anxiety over the whereabouts of these known potential rebels can only have been heightened by his awareness of a strong ᶜAlid presence in Kufa, which until he could take up residence in his newly founded capital, Baghdad, in 145/762 – several years after Ibn al-Muqaffaᶜ's death – retained its importance in the ᶜAbbasid administration. None of the revolts generated either by Shīᶜī discontent or by the extremism of men swayed less by Islam than by the influence of the old Iranian religions, has any relevance here. What *is* relevant is the widespread heterodoxy of which they were manifestations. Likewise in law, both in the domain of jurisprudence and in the day-to-day administration of justice, there was no more unity than in the realm of religious belief. Indeed by the second half of the second/eighth century, legal development was almost synonymous, as it were, with diversity. Most conspicuous, perhaps, was the legal rift dividing Medina and Kufa, whose differences were ultimately to be reflected in the Mālikī and Ḥanafī schools of law respectively. Apart from the Medinese and Kufan schools, there were a number of others, as well as schools within schools, with all the resultant conflicts of laws. As we shall see, nobody was more conscious of the problems created thereby than Ibn al-Muqaffaᶜ.

Let us now turn from the background of the *Risālah* to the work itself. If we break down the content according to subject-matter, nine constituent parts of widely varying length result. In the order in which they occur these are: (i) eulogy of the caliph; (ii) the army; (iii) Iraq; (iv) the law; (v) Syria; (vi) the caliph's entourage; (vii) taxation; (viii) Arabia; (ix) education of the people.

If the eulogy of the caliph with which the *Risālah* opens is "long and rather strained", it is not mere rhetoric or encomium for its own sake, but a purposeful *captatio benevolentiae*.[38] Put plainly, it is the sugar on the unsolicited pill to be prescribed for the caliph's swallowing. With the utmost tact and diplomacy, Ibn al-Muqaffaᶜ begins by contrasting the caliph's knowledge and readiness to question and hearken on the one hand, with his predecessors' ignorance, self-conceit and complacency on the other. And not for the last time does he use the tactic of contrasting the caliph's virtues with other men's vices. Thus not for nothing does he laud the caliph's disciplined view of riches: he knows the ways of tax-collectors, and he will have occasion later to denounce them. The odd "white lie" or statement in conflict with his subsequent testimony does not unduly disconcert him: his first objective is seemingly to humour his addressee lest his submissions go unread. Consistent with such a view of his motive is his evident concern to allay any suspicion of his playing tutor to the caliph. No man of judgement familiar with the latter's ways, he observes, would consider it his business to do more than keep the *amīr al-muʾminīn* informed of items of news that may not have reached him or refresh his memory on what he already knows. Although conscious of the need for the kinds of compliment that his delicate task demands, Ibn al-Muqaffaᶜ avoids unduly extravagant panegyric and does in fact remark that he would hate to be thought at pains to be singing his ruler's praises. Indeed his concluding comments on the caliph's devotion to his subjects' welfare seem more an appropriate justification for the *Risālah* than mere perorational flattery.

[38] Goitein, *Studies in Islamic History*, 154; Pellat, *Ibn al-Muqaffaᶜ*, 4.

The writer now moves on to the subject of the army (*jund*) – the caliphal Khurasanian troops in Iraq. His praise for them is lavish: unique in the history of Islam, they are highly disciplined and remarkably well-behaved towards the civilian population. Yet, being an ethnically mixed body with officers of extreme persuasions commanding men uncertain of their beliefs, they are in need of edification. The caliph should therefore issue a concise, but clear and comprehensive, religious code (*amān*)[39] for committal to memory by officers and for the obedience of all ranks. For among the officers there are too many religious instructors (*mutakallimūn*)[40] predicating of the caliph such superhuman or unacceptable powers that 'were he to order mountains to move, they would move, and, were he to order the prayer to be performed with men's backs to the *qiblah*, it would be done".[41] Such a view of unquestioning obedience prompts a digression in which an attempt is made to define the measure of obedience that a head, or imam, of the community can command. Too literal an interpretation of the maxim, "No obedience to any creature disobeying the Creator", points the way to anarchy, while blind obedience to the imam, regardless of his conduct, debases authority and brings it into disrepute, since it "results in abominable and outrageous legitimization of publicly paraded disobedience to God".[42] The maxim is to be interpreted as applicable only where the imam countermands Quranic duties and sanctions. Unqualified obedience on the other hand means obedience to the imam and *him alone*, wherever he is not bound by the Qurʾān and the *sunnah* (the precedents set by the Prophet or sanctioned by him). And so, in the absence of religious impediments, policy and administration are the imam's prerogative and subject to his discretion; for where religion is silent, rulers must have recourse to judgement (*raʾy*) inspired by reason (*ᶜaql*), that second principle on which man's earthly welfare turns.

Reverting to the army, Ibn al-Muqaffaᶜ strongly advises against allowing the combination of fiscal with military duties; for the collection of land-tax (*kharāj*) – the mainstay of the economy – is a corrupting occupation, encouraging extortion, and unbecoming the dignity of a soldier. He then suggests measures clearly aimed at raising the army's morale and guaranteeing its continued support. These include: recruitment of officers from deserving members of the ranks; religious education; inculcation of integrity and a sense of loyalty, and of the same virtues of thrift and unpretentiousness as the caliph himself displays; and regular payment, at predetermined intervals, of stipends based on calculations allowing for

[39] This rendering of *amān*, which Ibn al-Muqaffaᶜ invests with an usual but unequivocal sense, seems preferable to "catechism" (Goitein, *Studies in Islamic History*, 157) or "règlement" (Pellat, *Ibn al-Muqaffaᶜ*, 6).

[40] On the sense of *mutakallim* in this context, see Crone, *Slaves*, 64, 246, n. 1. Pellat does not translate the word (*Ibn al-Muqaffaᶜ*, 24).

[41] Pellat, *Ibn al-Muqaffaᶜ*, 25.

[42] Ibid., 27.

inflation. Finally, great stress is laid on the importance of maintaining, regardless of cost, an efficient intelligence service throughout Khurāsān and the peripheral provinces.

Next comes a shortish account of the general situation in Iraq, leaving us in no doubt of an undercurrent of discontent. Since the Basrans and Kufans, we are told, are on the best of terms with the local Khurasanians, they are potentially the caliph's most natural supporters. To keep himself informed of their activities, he would do well to enlist the aid of the Khurasanians, even if local relationships are something of an obstacle. In other words, there are in the two main cities (*miṣrān*) of Iraq disaffected elements who need to be watched. One cause of discontent among the Iraqi professional classes is made quite plain: lack of opportunity for employment in government service. In a spirited defence of the Iraqis, whom he portrays as much maligned and the long-suffering victims of Syrian oppression and abuse, Ibn al-Muqaffaᶜ stresses the qualities that fit them for service, at the same time warning against the danger of recruiting incompetent but plausible sycophants.

Quite unpredictably, the next topic for discussion is that of law reform – a subject that has assured the writer a distinctive niche in the history of Islamic law, not because of any contribution to its development, but because of his percipient diagnosis of the malady afflicting the legal system and the bold remedy he prescribed.[43] That there is widespread disarray among the jurists and judges is a fact that he underlines by noting that in vital areas of the civil and criminal law Kufan practice is the reverse of that of al-Ḥīrah and that, even within Kufa itself, the law may differ from quarter to quarter. Nor are matters helped by the Medinese-Kufan legal rift. The situation is such that a *qāḍī* (judge), dispensing death, will invoke the *sunnah* in support of his judgment, but close questioning will finally elicit a response suggesting Umayyad practice as his sole authority. He has in fact been guided by personal opinion (*raʾy*), and he cares nothing that he is alone in an opinion that he will admit is based on neither the Qurʾān nor the *sunnah*. The remedy lies with the caliph: he would serve the interests of uniformity, were he to order the compilation of a corpus of all conflicting judgments and procedures together with their reasons and, after scrutiny, deliver on each his own judgment as God inspires, firmly abide by it and permit no other. The writer then goes on to identify the main causes for divergences as the perpetuation of different local precedents and analogical juristic reasoning (*qiyās*) that is either faulty or carried to absurd conclusions. *Qiyās*, he stresses, is not an end in itself, but the servant of justice, and, if it leads to manifest injustice, it must be abandoned. He

[43] See Schacht, *Origins*, 58f, 95, 102f, 129, 137, and *Introduction*, 55f; cf. Coulson, *Islamic Law*, 52.

concludes the section by showing how strict adherence to a good principle can produce a bad result.

Somewhat abruptly, there comes the problem posed by the conquered Syrians. Recognizing them as a potential thorn in the caliph's flesh, he advocates a policy of cautious clemency, based on a division of sheep from goats, as it were, with the recruitment of a hand-picked Syrian élite into caliphal service, the removal of ruinous economic sanctions, and an equitable distribution of foodstuffs in the Syrian military districts. For all their past misdemeanours, the Syrians will create no trouble if justly treated.

And now at length we come to the entourage, or Companions, of the caliph – "the splendour of his court, the ornament of his council, the spokesmen of his subjects, his helpers in the making of decisions, the recipients of his bounty, and the elite of his commonalty,"[44] From behind the ideal thus portrayed there soon emerges the reality of an entourage whose ranks have been penetrated by men unworthy of access to the caliph's presence. The secretaries and ministers (*wazīr*s) of his predecessors – the opening ascription is tactful – brought membership of the entourage (*ṣuḥbat al-khalīfah*) into such disrepute that men of standing eschewed what should be an honour. For membership had gone to men of no education, no breeding, and no known personal worth, but, rather, of reprehensible judgement and notorious immorality – men who, moreover, had spent most of their lives as artisans working with their hands and had not even won any claim to military fame. Influence had been the secret of their success and given them precedence over not only descendants of the Muhājirūn and Anṣār (the Emigrants, who fled with the Prophet to Medina, and the Helpers, his supporters there), but also members of the caliph's own family. Their allowances were twice those of many of the notables of Hāshim and Quraysh, but apart from service in the office of *kātib* or *ḥājib* (chamberlain), they had no qualifications for their status, whether religious, literary, military or familial. Immense injustice and suffering had resulted for the Quraysh in particular and many worthy men in general.

An unmistakably forceful statement of the caliph's duty follows. Unlike a private overlord, free to dispense favours as and where he will, the caliph must dispense an important public kind of justice that takes account of claims to preferential treatment. To eliminate existing injustices that dishonour authority will cost nothing and provoke no disturbance of any kind. The types of individual that our author would single out for preferment are: men possessed of some special talent; kinsmen; men with a record of distinguished service; men combining nobility with judgement

[44] Pellat, *Ibn al-Muqaffaᶜ*, 51.

and conduct becoming the caliphal council (*majlis*); serving soldiers combining proven valour with personal merit and integrity who can be suitably elevated by transfer to caliphal service; men of virtue versed in religion who can be sent to serve among the people and profit the latter by their example and teaching; and incorruptible and uncorrupting men of noble lineage. For their part the social climbers – and those who would advance them – will have to be content with acts of charity and kindness. Climbers must be kept in their places: no secretary should have the power to raise or lower a salary, nor should any chamberlain have the power to expedite or delay an audience. Finally, the caliph is urged to consider the princes of his house, his consanguine brothers, the descendants of ᶜAlī b. Abī Ṭālib and of al-ᶜAbbās b. ᶜAbd al-Muṭṭalib; for among them are men who could be trusted with high office and be of assistance to others.

In his section on land-tax, Ibn al-Muqaffaᶜ is mainly concerned with a system – or the lack of one – which greatly facilitates the ruthless exploitation of cultivators by predatory collectors (*ᶜummāl*, sing. *ᶜāmil*), who either arbitrarily take all they can wherever they can, or, after a simple survey (*misāḥah*), tax those who have sown and exempt those who have not. Particularly hard hit are those who have been enterprising enough to work the poorest land. Fiscal justice would be best assured and the public interest best served by the introduction of a system governed by known rules and regulations and official registers. The idea will not win ready acceptance, and the benefit will be felt only in the long term. The only alternative lies in the seemingly unprecedented steps already taken by the caliph to ensure that collectors are handpicked and then supervised, and, where necessary, chastised or replaced.

The *Risālah*'s shortest section, bearing on Arabia, runs to no more than a few lines and suggests merely that the caliph, if willing to allow such regions as the Hijaz, the Yemen and al-Yamāmah to retain sums from legal alms (*ṣadaqāt*) and the like, may be minded to choose for them the best available governors whether from his own house or from elsewhere.

The closing section of the *Risālah* calls for the commons to be schooled in correct behaviour and conduct under loyal instructors versed in the religious sciences. Stripped of the rhetoric with which they are adorned, Ibn al-Muqaffaᶜ's proposals can be simply described as measures aimed at achieving uniformity of "orthodox" belief through what we may term a programme of mass education. There would be no question of the exercise of personal opinion (*raʾy*) by the tutored. A properly paid body of professional instructors, working peacefully and sympathetically among the rank and file, would ensure stability and create a situation in which troublemakers would be unable to operate unobserved. Prosperity and public welfare depend on an ordered society, which in turn depends both at its upper and lower levels on its imam. The *Risālah* at this point moves to its conclusion with an expression of pious hopes and prayers for the caliph and his people.

The *Risālah* has been variously described as "a remarkable memorandum on government", "a complete political program", "an illuminating report on the art of governing", and more melodramatically, a "blueprint" for a "showdown with the *ᶜulamāᵓ*" and "a truly imperial vision of Islam presented without a single reference to Kisrā, Buzurjmihr or anything Persian".[45] Whether or not such descriptions are accurate or apt is a question that need not detain us; they are cited merely to demonstrate the lively interest aroused by the *Risālah*. In particular, students of Islamic history and political theory have been concerned to identify the respects in which its author's ideas either presaged later developments (e.g. Islamic military feudalism, military religious education) or failed to gain acceptance in orthodox Islam (e.g. central control of religion and law).

Of the structure of the *Risālah*, nothing need be said apart from the fact that, as the reader will already have gleaned, there is no well-ordered plan to which the writer works in the presentation of his subject-matter. There is more to be said of style. In this respect the *Risālah* is noticeably different from the *Ādāb*. The difference in manner is perhaps largely attributable to the difference in matter: to proffer general advice along sententious and aphoristic lines is one thing; to propose particular solutions to particular problems at the risk of causing offence to the caliph is another. Whatever the truth of the matter, it is clear that the prose in which the *Risālah* as we know it is written has little of the stylistic ease and lucidity that we are often led to believe are characteristic of Ibn al-Muqaffaᶜ. The style is in fact difficult, and, as Pellat rightly points out, not only is the sequence of ideas, in periods of surprising length for the time, often far from clear, but also the manner of expression is in a number of places irritatingly obscure. Indeed, Beeston draws attention to some twists of thought "almost Jahizian in complexity" as well as to a stylistic "foretaste of the writing that was to become normal a century later", and wonders whether an unpublished document from the caliphal archive has been "worked over and polished up for publication at some later date".[46] Whether such a thought ever occurred to Pellat in the course of his study of the text he does not say; he tells us only that he was prepared to take the work as authentic.

For the translator the difficulty of the *Risālah* lies less in the domain of

[45] Goitein, *Studies in Islamic History*, 150, 155; Shaban, *Islamic History*, 22; Crone, *Slaves*, 69, 70. *ᶜUlamāᵓ* (sing. *ᶜālim*) is a blanket term for those regarded, or who regarded themselves, as the guardians of the law, tradition and the creed.

[46] Pellat, *Ibn al-Muqaffaᶜ*, 1; Beeston, *Samples*, 9.

syntax or complexity of thought than in the realm of vocabulary. For, however cumbersome and awkward some structures may be,[47] they present few, if any, insoluble problems. By contrast, in the absence of a well-developed technical vocabulary, the assignment of a multiplicity of meanings to one and the same word or to cognates not infrequently throws up a barrier of obscurity and uncertainty that is hard to surmount. That this should be so is scarcely surprising in the light of the fact that to all intents and purposes the range of vocabulary on which the *Risālah* is based does not extend much beyond 1,000 words.[48]

Rhetorical devices similar to those characteristic of the *Ādāb* are also observable in the *Risālah* and call for no special comment. Use is also made of rhythmical patterns and measured openings and terminations deriving their measures from the metres of Arabic poetry or savouring of the prosodic. To illustrate, we may take the following: *li-anna ʾl-mubtaghī laysa ʿayna ʾl-qiyāsi yabghī* (∪ – – / – ∪ – / – ∪ – / – ∪ – / ∪ – – with the patterning ABBBA): "For it is not for its own sake that one should seek *qiyās*"; *fa-inna man arāda an yalzama ʾl-qiyās* (the opening words from *fa-inna* to *yalzama* constitute a hemistich in the metre *sarīʿ*, namely, ∪ – ∪ – / ∪ – ∪ – / – ∪ –): "For whosoever would cling to *qiyās*"; *fa-yaghramu man ʿammar: wa-yaslamu man akhrab* (∪ – ∪ / ∪ – – – / ∪ – ∪ / ∪ – – – is the metre of the second hemistich of *ṭawīl* acatalectic): "Those who cultivate the land are taxed, and those who leave it waste get off scot-free"; *zālati ʾl-umūru ʿan marākizihā: wa-nazalati ʾl-rijālu ʿan manāzilihā* (the first member, carrying three feet from the *basīṭ* tetrameter, namely, – ∪ – / ∪ – ∪ – / ∪∪ – , is followed by a complete hemistich of the same in the second member, namely, ∪∪∪ – / – ∪ – / ∪ – ∪ – / ∪∪ –), loosely: "There will be dislocation and disruption of the established order"; *wa-qallamā yaridu fī samʿi ʾl-sāmiʿ : illā aḥdatha fī qalbihi rībatan wa-shakkā* (the first member carries three feet deriving from the *rajaz* trimeter catalectic, ∪ – ∪ – / ∪∪∪ – / – – – , while the second from *fī* to *shakkā* is a complete hemistich of the *basīṭ* trimeter catalectic, – – ∪ – / – ∪ – / ∪ – –): "Such talk rarely reaches one's ears without its raising a suspicion and a doubt in one's heart."[49]

The Manichaean "apologia"

Of the various works attributed, rightly or wrongly, to Ibn al-Muqaffaʿ, there are two of which we have nothing other than longer or shorter fragments in the form of quotations and therefore only a very imperfect knowledge. One of the two, opening with an obviously Manichaeistic

47 For examples, see Pellat, *Ibn al-Muqaffaʿ*, 14f.

48 Ibid., 13f (a detailed analysis).

49 Ibid., 45, 59, 41, 25.

version of the *basmalah* ("in the name of God, the Compassionate, the Merciful") – "In the name of Light (*nūr*), the Compassionate, the Merciful" – lends itself to interpretation as an anti-Islamic tract delivered in an aggressive spirit of mocking scepticism in the name of a strongly rationalist Manichaeism. All that we know of the actual text derives from a series of extracts preserved by a writer of Muᶜtazilī persuasion whose sole purpose is to refute the arguments they encapsulate or generate. The nature of the subject-matter, however, is not hard to discern if to these extracts we add a body of pertinent material drawn from the refutations. The work in which the extracts – varying from a few words to a few lines – survive bears the clear-cut title *Kitāb al-Radd ᶜalā ʾl-zindīq al-laᶜīn Ibn al-Muqaffaᶜ* ("The Refutation of the accursed Heretic, Ibn al-Muqaffaᶜ") and has as its author the Zaydī Imam al-Qāsim b. Ibrāhīm (d. 246/860).[50]

In a history of Arabic literature neither the substance nor the literary style of what little of Ibn al-Muqaffaᶜ's original composition remains in the *Radd* justifies protracted discussion or analysis. There is little to be gained from expatiation on his views of anthropomorphic expression in the Qurʾān or speculation on his exposition of Manichaean cosmogony or his approach to the mythology of Mānī's religion, or anything of that kind. It is more pertinent and rewarding merely to cast an eye over a fragment – one of the longer extracts cited by the Imam al-Qāsim – in which the efficient principle of his philosophy is plain for all to see. It runs as follows:

Dismiss the authority of the ignoramus who insinuates ignorance into you and commands you neither to inquire nor to quest, but commands you to believe in what you do not know and to accept as true what you do not comprehend. Were you to take your money to the market to make some purchases, and were a vendor of the goods you had in mind to approach you with an invitation to buy from him, swearing an oath to you that there was nothing better to be had in the market than what he had offered you, you would be loath to believe him for fear of being the victim of fraud and deception and think [any faith you would have in his word to be a sign of] your being too weak to base your choice on the evidence of your own eyes and to turn for help to someone from whom you could hope to gain assistance and support.[51]

Such are the words in which the writer declares his belief in the unacceptability of any mode of thought requiring an act of faith as the basis of knowledge. This is the creed of the rationalist.

In style and diction the hallmark of the fragments is simplicity, as may be seen from parts of the text from which the foregoing translation is made: *akhrij sulṭāna ʾl-jāhili ʾlladhī yusirru ᶜalayka ʾl-jahālah wa-yaʾmuruka allā tabḥatha wa-lā taṭlub . . . law atayta ʾl-sūq bi-darāhimika tashtarī baᶜḍa ʾl-silaᶜ fa-atāka ʾl-rajulu . . . fa-*

[50] See Guidi, *La lotta*, iiif; for the Zaydī Imams and their polemics, see ch. 23.
[51] Guidi, *La lotta* (Arabic text), 26f.

daʿāka ilā mā ʿindahu wa-ḥalafa laka annahu laysa fī ʾl-sūqi shayʾun afḍalu mimmā daʿāka ilayhi la-karihta an tuṣaddiqahu . . .

Wansbrough seems disinclined to accept Ibn al-Muqaffaʿ's authorship of this work: he contrasts its "trivial argumentation" with "the pious" and "substantially sophisticated" *Risālah*; sees its *bismi ʾl-nūr* as "childishly inept humour", to be taken seriously "only as a caricature"; and notes al-Qāsim's criticism of the author's Arabic.[52] But even if we accept the arguable point – which cannot be debated here – that the argumentation is trivial, may we not suppose the work to date well before the *kātib*'s conversion to Islam? In any case the validity of any comparison between a theological tract and a policy document addressed to a caliph is highly questionable. As for the *bismi ʾl-nūr*, van Ess has pointed out that it is neither childish nor humorous, but "stands in a larger context which seems to have the form of a hymn".[53] As regards the Arabic of the fragments quoted by the Imam al-Qāsim, it is in fact superior to al-Qāsim's own – a point which van Ess also notes – and the criticisms made of it seem to be mainly nit-picking quibbles from a pedant who, for all we know, may have been misled by a copyist's orthography or errors, or both. Finally, Gabrieli has drawn attention to the fact that "the rationalistic criticism of fideism in general" as it emerges, say, in the passage translated above "presents a striking analogy with certain passages from the autobiography of Burzōē in *Kalīla wa-Dimna*".[54] Be that as it may, the problem of authenticity remains a thorny one, and it may never be resolved unless new evidence comes to light.

Muʿāraḍat al-Qurʾān

The second work attributed to Ibn al-Muqaffaʿ and known to us only through fragmentary extracts is *Muʿāraḍat al-Qurʾān* ("Imitation of the Qurʾān"). Curiously enough, these fragments, like those of the Manichaean tract, are of Muʿtazilī-Zaydī provenance, in that they have come down to us in a Muʿtazilī-oriented commentary on parts of a work by the Zaydī Imam Aḥmad b. al-Ḥusayn al-Muʾayyad bi-ʾllāh (d. 411/1020). Entitled *al-Risālah al-ʿasjadiyyah fī ʾl-maʿānī ʾl-Muʾayyadiyyah* ("The Golden Treatise on al-Muʾayyad's Rhetorical Usages"), this commentary was written some three centuries later by a certain ʿAbbās b. ʿAlī al-Ṣanʿānī.[55] Seven fragments from the *Muʿāraḍah* embedded in al-Ṣanʿānī's commentary have recently been studied by van Ess, who finds their attribution to Ibn al-Muqaffaʿ not at all improbable.[56] Despite some uncertain readings, the text of the passages is sufficiently sound and illuminating to permit a tentative assessment of the

52 *Quranic Studies*, 160. 53 "Fragments", 162. 54 *EI*², "Ibn al-Muḳaffaʿ".
55 Van Ess, "Fragments", 151. 56 Ibid., 161.

nature of the work. Four of the fragments, which for present purposes are of greater interest than the other three, may be characterized as follows: a rearrangement of Quranic formulae under a different *saj^c* (balanced and rhyming prose) intended to produce a similar effect; an invocation, in early Meccan style, of God as "The Lord of Mecca" (*ṣāḥib al-balad*), characterized by a series of staccato phrases turning on *al-balad* as the key word; a variation on Qur'ān lxxxix, 6–14, with the Syrians cast in an ^cĀd-Thamūd role as doomed to exemplary destruction, like the haughty peoples of old, and the Khurasanians ("those bringing their tents from the east") as their conquerors; and a parody, introducing the Iraqis in terms familiar to us from al-Ḥajjāj's famous Kufan *khuṭbah*: *Yā ayyuhā 'l-nās qad nusiba ahlu 'l-^cIrāq ilā 'l-shiqāq wa'l-nifāq* ("O men, the people of Iraq have been charged with hypocrisy and dissension").[57]

Van Ess sees nothing in any of the seven fragments to suggest that the *Mu^cāraḍah* was either a vehicle of anti-Quranic or anti-Islamic polemic or an instrument for the infiltration of pagan beliefs. It seems, rather, to have been an experiment in rhetoric calculated to demonstrate that in the author's time something *stylistically* comparable to the Qur'ān could be composed without, however, attracting the same acclaim for elegance of style and expression. For such a theory the author's own testimony can be adduced from his argument that the Book's unequalled stylistic reputation rests on men's long familiarity with its text through repeated recitation. That the *Mu^cāraḍah* had anything to do with the *content* of the Scripture seems to van Ess unlikely. His verdict on the evidence before us is: "In the first half of the second century *saǧ^c* was quite unusual. It was . . . in this respect that Ibn al-Muqaffa^c's attempt was revolutionary and perhaps shocking. But there was, strictly speaking, no heresy about it . . . for [Ibn al-Muqaffa^c] did not doubt the message of the Qur'ān and its contents, nor did he necessarily doubt the *i^cǧāz* [the Qur'ān's "inimitability", which was proof of its divine origin]. We may assume that there was already something of a common belief in the language of the Qur'ān being better than anything else; he seems to react against this in his final remark. It is possible that such an opinion was primarily held by Arabs, and that Ibn al-Muqaffa^c disliked it because he was a Persian and aware of his literary talent."[58]

Other compositions

In addition to the preceding works the section devoted to Ibn al-Muqaffa^c in Kurd ^cAlī's *Rasā'il al-bulaghā'* contains the following: (a) a composition

57 See *CHALUP*, 119. 58 Van Ess, "Fragments", 160.

styled *Yatīmah thāniyah* ("A Second Peerless"); (b) a *risālah* entitled *Yatīmat al-sulṭān* ("Authority's Peerless [Pearl]"); (c) a doxology (*taḥmīd*), followed by a series of passages and sentences, for the most part extracted from letters and other epistolary compositions and useful as examples of expressions of congratulation, condolence and the like; (d) a collection of aphorisms (*ḥikam*).[59]

The *Yatīmah thāniyah* is so styled by the modern editor Kurd ᶜAlī because, in his *Rasāʾil al-bulaghāʾ*, he placed it immediately after the *Ādāb*, for which he considered *al-Durrah al-yatīmah* ("The Peerless Pearl") to be either its true or alternative title.[60] Since the text derives from an early source, Ibn Abī Ṭayfūr's *Kitāb al-Manthūr wa-ʾl-manẓūm*,[61] its ascription to Ibn al-Muqaffaᶜ may well be correct, but we cannot be certain. Supposedly a reply to a friend or colleague, the composition is a shortish epistle in sententious vein, treating of good and bad rulers, good and bad subjects, and combinations of both. A prominent feature is the writer's elaborate eulogy of the reigning caliph and the Prophet – in that order.

Since the *Yatīmat al-sulṭān* has been shown beyond reasonable doubt to be spurious,[62] it calls for no comment here. As regards the *taḥmīd*, this is almost certainly not the work of our author. Some of the passages and sentences that follow, on the other hand, may well be authentic and come from a work of which we know only the title from the *Fihrist*, namely *Yatīmah fī ʾl-rasāʾil* ("A Peerless [Composition] on Epistles"). The title suggests a manual of instruction on the art of epistolary composition in which we can reasonably expect the reader to have been offered examples of style and phraseology, and so on, appropriate to given circumstances and particular occasions. As for the *ḥikam*, these are thought to be unauthentic and the work of a copyist or some devotee of the aphorism.[63]

For all that Ibn al-Muqaffaᶜ has won almost universal acceptance as the most outstanding writer of the early ᶜAbbasid period and enjoys a pre-eminent position in the history of Arabic literature, the dimensions of his contribution to the development of Arabic prose cannot be measured in precise terms. The reasons are not far to seek: not all that is ascribed to him is his, and even where there is no misattribution, uncertainties are created by textual corruption or contamination, which in some cases are such that the original fabric can be but imperfectly discerned beneath patches or embroidery, or both. From what we can see or deduce, his prose style was far from uniform. But then stylistic uniformity should not be expected of one so obviously ready to experiment in the language to which he was

59 Kurd ᶜAlī, *Rasāʾil*, 107–11, 145–72, 135–44, 112–16.

60 On the title and the problems posed by it, see Gabrieli, "L'opera", 218, n. 1.

61 See *EI*², "Ibn Abī Ṭāhir Ṭayfūr".

62 ᶜAbbās, "Naẓrah", 555–8.

63 Gabrieli, "L'opera", 219; ibid., n. 2, 235.

devoted and, indeed, very likely conversant with the teachings of the ancient schools of rhetoric on gradations of subject-matter and the different levels of style (e.g. sublime, intermediate, lowly) appropriate to the same.

Be that as it may, the importance of Ibn al-Muqaffaᶜ in the history of Arabic prose writing is of the highest order and has never been questioned. Of that importance there can be no better assessment than that encapsulated in Gabrieli's verdict on the man: "His works, both as translator and original writer, soon became classic in the great ᶜAbbasid civilization and, by their form as well as their subject-matter, exerted an influence that cannot be exaggerated on the cultural interests and ideals of the succeeding generations. Today, it is even possible to speak of an Ibn al-Muqaffaᶜ myth which has dominated the renaissance of neo-Arabic literature."[64]

[64] *EI*², "Ibn al-Muḳaffaᶜ".

CHAPTER 4

AL-JĀḤIẒ

Abū ᶜUthmān ᶜAmr b. Baḥr b. Maḥbūb al-Kinānī al-Baṣrī, known as al-Jāḥiẓ, is one of the best-known and most prolific of early ᶜAbbasid prose-writers and Muᶜtazilī theologians, and also one of the most controversial. Little is known of his origins, apart from the fact that he was born in Basra, probably around 160/776, to a humble family of freedmen (*mawālī*) who were clients of the Banū Kinānah (a tribe related to Quraysh). Jāḥiẓ's forebears were probably of African descent; his grandfather was black, and he himself retained some of the pigmentation of his ancestors; his ugliness, caused by his bulging eyeballs, became proverbial and earned him the nickname of *jāḥiẓ* (pop-eyed). Nothing is known of his father, who died soon after his birth, and little of his mother, to whom Jāḥiẓ must have been a source of considerable anxiety; she had managed to send him to the local Quranic school, but when he left he refused to be tied down to any regular work. It is said that he was once seen selling fish, and this, if true, confirms what other anecdotal sources say about his idle way of life. His idleness, however, was to give him an exceptionally broad experience of human nature. As he strolled around Basra he made an assortment of friends who doubtless fed and sheltered him, and who also gave him the opportunity to indulge his precocious fondness for observation, argument and reading, for despite his intelligence and insatiable thirst for intellectual and factual knowledge, he had no access to any kind of formal training higher than that given in his Quranic school. However, other kinds of education were freely available to him. He mixed with the groups of educated idlers which were springing up all over Basra, especially at the mosque, and which discussed all manner of topics, and he watched what was going on around him in the streets of Basra. He also went to the Mirbad, the great open space on the outskirts of the city where the bedouin halted and were questioned by the philologists, whom Jāḥiẓ would then follow to the Friday mosque to hear their public lectures on the information they had collected. Among these scholars were such well-known figures as the great "triumvirate" of al-Aṣmaᶜī, Abū ᶜUbaydah and Abū Zayd al-Anṣārī, who played a key role in the development of Arabic culture: the material that they amassed on *ḥadīth*, lexicography and ancient poetry was classified into monographs which became the nucleus of the Arabic humanities, handed down by their pupils to later generations. Merely to listen to their teaching was, for Jāḥiẓ, to master contemporary literary and historical learning and to gain a thorough grounding in the Arabic language. But besides being, together with Kufa, the main centre of philological research, Basra was also the home of Muᶜtazilism[1] and of a form of rationalism which was in sharp contrast to a nascent trend towards conformism (a trend which was later to find its embodiment in Jāḥiẓ's younger contemporary, the Sunnī apologist and *adīb*, Ibn Qutaybah, d. 276/889). For grammar and lexicography were not the only interests of Basran intellectuals; they also held lively discussions on less dry, more general subjects, such as the harmonization of faith and reason, the legitimacy of the ᶜAbbasid caliphate, the part played by the Khārijīs[2] and Shīᶜīs in shaping Muslim history, and the threat posed to Arab supremacy in the Muslim world by such opposition as that of the Shuᶜūbīs. It was probably through the friends he made among the early Muᶜtazilīs that Jāḥiẓ gained entry into "good" society and was able to attend, and later to take part in, a great many often heated debates on such general topics, which he later remembered vividly enough to be able to make extensive use of them in his own works. His contacts with affluent and educated circles also gave him the opportunity to read voraciously, in particular the translations from Greek and Pahlavi that were then beginning to appear. But all this while, unlike middle-class intellectuals, Jāḥiẓ remained in contact with people of his own background, the lower classes, artisans and seamen, still mixed with idlers, and even took an interest in the activities of the underworld to which a city as cosmopolitan as Basra was bound to give birth. These were the basic influences on Jāḥiẓ's development; it was perhaps inevitable that a city as intellectually advanced as Basra undoubtedly was should produce a genius marked with its stamp, and Jāḥiẓ was in every way a true representative of his birthplace; Basra was a microcosm whose every facet Jāḥiẓ knew and was able to translate into literature.

We do not know when Jāḥiẓ began to write, but his first works must certainly date from before the end of the second/eighth century, since by that time he must already have been a writer of some standing, to judge by a passage in one of his later works,[3] which reveals that, through the good offices of a Basran grammarian called al-Yazīdī, who was in favour at the court of Baghdad, Jāḥiẓ had been encouraged, if not actually commissioned, to write on the imamate, and that his efforts had been very well received by the caliph al-Maʾmūn; this was in about 200/815–16. At that

[1] See p. 5. [2] See pp. 186–8. [3] *Bayān*, III, 374–5.

time Baghdad was attracting many talented men from the provinces, eager to make their mark on the new capital and to win fame and fortune; grammarians dreamed of being made tutors to princes, poets hoped to obtain great rewards through their panegyrics, and ambitious men of letters were gratified to receive a post as a clerk (*kātib*) in the administration. Jāḥiẓ, who was neither a grammarian nor a poet, nor even ambitious, was nevertheless well enough educated to have become a *kātib*, but was of too independent a nature to endure the constraints of an official post. After receiving the caliph's congratulations for his tract on the imamate he duly settled in Baghdad, but it seems that in the whole of his career he only worked as a *kātib* for three days, at some indeterminate date (he may also briefly have acted as assistant to Ibrāhīm b. al-ᶜAbbās al-Ṣūlī[4] in the chancellery). According to some accounts, he earned a meagre living as a teacher and, in his old age, the caliph al-Mutawakkil once engaged him as tutor to his children – but cancelled the appointment when he saw how ugly Jāḥiẓ was. As against this last, probably fanciful story, the only precise information we have as to how Jāḥiẓ earned his living is that he received substantial gratuities from various ᶜAbbasid officials for books dedicated to them, some of which, however, seem to have been too slight to merit such generosity. There is reason to believe that he was paid a pension during the caliphate of al-Mutawakkil, and he may well have drawn a state salary or received secret payments for unofficial services to the government. For his career was largely determined by his early writings on the imamate, writings which led to a series of works designed to legitimate the ᶜAbbasid caliphate or to justify important government measures; these were assured of a ready market, and, in addition, Jāḥiẓ also wrote letters and reports to those in charge of government policy, which at this period assumed a frankly religious garb. In other words Jāḥiẓ acted as an adviser to and apologist for the government, and seems to have exercised this role quite openly, for though he was not the intimate of caliphs, he maintained close ties with the vizier Ibn al-Zayyāt (d. 233/847) and the caliph's adoptive brother, general and *kātib*, al-Fatḥ b. Khāqān (d. 247/861),[5] as well as with the chief *qāḍī* (*qāḍī ᵓl-quḍāh*), Aḥmad b. Abī Duᵓād (d. 240/854–5), and his son and deputy Muḥammad (d. 239/854), despite occasional differences of opinion. He is also known to have been closely involved with leading Muᶜtazilī figures such as al-Maᵓmūn's adviser Thumāmah b. Ashras,[6] as well as with some less prominent members of the movement. Meanwhile he

[4] Poet, *kātib*, and an influential figure in government circles (d. 243/857). His (originally Turkish) family produced several men of letters, notably Abū Bakr al-Ṣūlī (d. *c.* 335/946), who edited the *dīwān*s of several Modern poets, including that of Abū Nuwās.

[5] He was also an important figure in literary circles, see *EI*², "al-Fatḥ b. Khāḳān".

[6] See *EI*¹, "Thumāma b. Ashras"

kept in close touch with his native city through the large colony of Basrans who were more or less permanently settled in Baghdad, and he returned to Basra itself on several occasions. During his stay in Baghdad he also spent a short time in nearby Sāmarrā, which became the seat of government from the time of al-Maʾmūn's successor al-Muʿtaṣim,[7] but his travels never seem to have taken him any further afield than Syria, unlike so many of his contemporaries who travelled tirelessly "in search of knowledge", in accordance with the Prophetic injunction to "seek knowledge though it be in China". We do not even know if he ever performed the pilgrimage to Mecca, and a geographical work of his, *Kitāb al-Amṣār* (see below), was criticized by later geographers for its numerous blunders, resulting from his lack of first-hand knowledge. In fact, travel was superfluous to Jāḥiẓ; the experience that he had gained in Basra and built up in Baghdad was all he needed. He earned what was probably a comfortable living by his pen, all the while adding new knowledge to his store and broadening his outlook by reading the new translations from the Greek made during al-Maʾmūn's reign; at the same time he continued to elaborate the theological doctrine which he had begun to develop under his master Abū Isḥāq Ibrāhīm b. Sayyār al-Naẓẓām (d. between 220–30/835–45). Al-Mutawakkil's reaction against Muʿtazilism was very likely the reason why Jāḥiẓ, already old and paralyzed, decided to leave Baghdad and retire to Basra, where he died in Muḥarram 255/December 868–January 869. A late tradition claims that Jāḥiẓ, who had written so affectionately and eloquently of books, was smothered to death under an avalanche of books; *se non è vero . . .*

The quantity of Jāḥiẓ's output is by no means unique in Arabic literature, but it is remarkable that he managed to produce so much at a time when writing materials were very expensive and paper only just coming into use: the most recent published catalogue of his works lists 231 authentic works,[8] of which, however, only two dozen have survived intact. In range as well as quantity, Jāḥiẓ's output is unusual for the period, and displays a remarkable breadth of intellect. This may not always have appealed to later generations; on the other hand, the elegance of his style has long been held up as an example by the best judges. Thus works of doubtful authenticity and those known to be apocryphal are generally well preserved, which shows that they satisfied public demand and that Jāḥiẓ continued to enjoy great prestige for some time after his death; while the fact that later anthologists, who probably had access to complete texts, seem often to have reproduced only extracts of some forty of Jāḥiẓ's works suggests that they may have found their style more interesting, or perhaps more congenial, than their

[7] See p. 5. [8] Pellat, "Nouvel essai d'inventaire".

content: the decline of Muʿtazilism must certainly be one of the reasons why comparatively few of Jāḥiẓ's works have survived; many lost works are the very epistles and short treatises which would have contained the most information about Jāḥiẓ's doctrinal position. However, but for the efforts of the anthologists, a still greater proportion of Jāḥiẓ's short works would have been lost; Jāḥiẓ himself and, at the end of the following century, Ibn al-Nadīm,[9] refer to a large number of works which have disappeared completely. Most of those which are now considered lost are unlikely ever to be recovered, and texts which to date have simply been overlooked are most probably minor works, to judge by *Kitāb al-Burṣān* (see below), which was discovered in Morocco fairly recently. In fact the likeliest sources for surviving fragments of important texts are manuscripts of later works, in which they may occur as quotations; we may take heart from the results of a piece of detective work carried out by J. van Ess, who partially reconstructed the *Kitāb al-Nakth* of al-Naẓẓām through passages of the *Kitāb al-Futyā* of Jāḥiẓ which in turn are preserved only in the *Kitāb al-ʿUyūn* of al-Shaykh al-Mufīd (d. 413/1022), which is itself partially reproduced in the *Fuṣūl Mukhtārah* of al-Sharīf al-Murtaḍā (d. 436/1044)![10] As for Jāḥiẓ's major works, *Kitāb al-Ḥayawān*, *Kitāb al-Bayān wa ʾl-tabyīn*, *Kitāb al-Bukhalāʾ* and *Kitāb al-ʿUthmāniyyah* have been preserved virtually intact, as have a very few shorter works, notably *al-Tarbīʿ wa ʾl-tadwīr* and *Risālat al-Qiyān*; several of the surviving epistles are also probably very little mutilated.

Editions of Jāḥiẓ's apocryphal works appeared at an early date in the East, but it was G. van Vloten who first drew attention to the authentic works by his publication of several of the treatises, and of *Kitāb al-Bukhalāʾ* in 1900. *Kitāb al-Ḥayawān* was not published until the beginning of this century, in a poor edition; today, however, a number of Jāḥiẓ's works have become widely available thanks to the efforts of eastern and western scholars to reinstate him. Some of the existing editions are of variable quality, but standards of Jāḥiẓ scholarship are steadily improving.

In attempting to establish a descriptive bibliography of Jāḥiẓ's works, it must be borne in mind that references to lost works may be cryptic or misleading and cannot be dealt with adequately in a chapter of this length. The following account is therefore almost entirely restricted to those complete works and fragments which are extant.[11]

Brockelmann suggested classifying the works of Jāḥiẓ under the following headings: theological and politico-theological writings; history;

[9] *Fihrist*, Tajaddud, 210–12/Dodge, I, 402–9. [10] Van Ess, *K. al-Nakṯ.*

[11] Details of editions are given in the Bibliography to this chapter. In the case of works published as part of a collection, page references are given in the text of the chapter and translations are referred to in brackets. References to English versions of extracts from otherwise untranslated texts are given in the footnotes.

anthropology; general ethics; professions; animals; languages; geography; anthologies; polemics; with the lost works covering the further categories of: games; plants and other substances; literary history; works of entertainment.[12] However, a reading of the works published or discovered since Brockelmann's time suggests that his classification is, if anything, too clear-cut; in order to gain a balanced picture of Jāḥiẓ's output, account should be taken of his much-criticized tendency to ramble from subject to subject within a single work. What is needed is a full and detailed listing of all the topics discussed by Jāḥiẓ in whatever context they may occur. Until this task has been accomplished, a broader classification based on a given work's overall function might prove more satisfactory than Brockelmann's listing by topic.

Jāḥiẓ had two main fields of activity; firstly, theology and politics, and secondly, *adab*. As a writer on matters political and theological, Jāḥiẓ's aim was to act as an apologist for the ᶜAbbasids and the Arabs respectively, on the one hand, and, on the other, to uphold and spread Muᶜtazilism and to prove the existence of God by rational argument and the direct observation of nature. At the same time, Jāḥiẓ was an *adīb*, a man of letters who hoped to educate his readers, and to do so by a process more attractive than that of contemporary scholarship. We may assume *adab* to be of three basic types, according to whether it aims to instil ethical precepts, to provide its readers with a general education, or to lay down guiding principles for members of the various professions; Jāḥiẓ was a practitioner of all three types. By adding to these functional criteria a further, purely formal distinction between those works which are built around quotations upon which Jāḥiẓ provides a commentary, and original works which give an unhampered view of his own style and opinions, we may, provisionally, classify his writings as follows: political and religious works; works modelled on, or developing out of, conventional scholarship; *adab*.

POLITICAL AND RELIGIOUS WORKS

Jāḥiẓ's earliest works are probably his writings on the imamate, of which there remain only fragments of *Kitāb Istiḥqāq al-imāmah*/*Bayān madhāhib al-Shīᶜah* ("The Necessity of the Imamate"/"An Exposition of the Different Kinds of Shiᶜism", S, 241–8), and *Jawābāt fī ᵓl-imāmah* ("Replies Concerning the Imamate", S, 249–59). *Istiḥqāq*/*Bayān madhāhib* argues that, at the time of the Prophet's death, the community did not unanimously favour his son-in-law, ᶜAlī b. Abī Ṭālib, as its leader, and that the presence of a single imam, the best Muslim of his time, is necessary in every age.

[12] *GAL*, SI, 241–7.

Jawābāt deals with the qualities required of the imam (these subjects are also treated elsewhere in Jāḥiẓ's works).[13] ᶜAbbasid propaganda was necessarily directed in the first instance against the Shīᶜīs, with their rival claim to legitimacy, and especially against the most moderate and therefore potentially attractive Shīᶜī sect, the Zaydīs.[14] Jāḥiẓ's largest work on these subjects is *Kitāb al-ᶜUthmāniyyah*; this declares the legitimacy of the first three "Orthodox" caliphs, develops Jāḥiẓ's ideas on the imamate, attacks the ᶜAlids on the ground that ᶜAlī failed to dissociate himself from the murder of ᶜUthmān, by which he himself succeeded to the caliphate, and thereby justifies the accession of the ᶜAbbasids. The defence of the ᶜAbbasids was probably further developed in a *risālah* (epistle) entitled *Fī ᵓl-ᶜAbbāsiyyah* ("Of the ᶜAbbasids", S, 300–3), though the only remaining fragment of this work seems unconnected with the subject. As a logical sequence to invalidating Shīᶜī claims to the imamate, Jāḥiẓ went on to attack the Umayyads and their later supporters who instituted a posthumous cult of the first Umayyad caliph, Muᶜāwiyah, in *Kitāb Taṣwīb ᶜAlī fī taḥkīm al-ḥakamayn* ("Vindication of ᶜAlī's Resort to Arbitration"), which recognizes the validity of the arbitration of Ṣiffīn.[15] The superiority of the ᶜAbbasids to the Umayyads is further demonstrated in *Faḍl Hāshim ᶜalā ᶜAbd Shams* ("The Superiority of the House of Hāshim to that of ᶜAbd Shams"),[16] and the *Risālah fī ᵓl-Nābitah* (or *fī Banī Umayyah*, S, 67–116; trans. Pellat, *Annales de l'Institut des études orientales*, Algiers, 1952) includes a report to the son and deputy of the chief *qāḍī* Aḥmad b. Abī Duᵓād on the current political situation and the claims of the "young generation" (*nābitah*) of Ḥanbalīs – followers of the Sunnī theologian and jurist Aḥmad b. Ḥanbal (d. 241/855)[17] – who idealize the Umayyads and Muᶜāwiyah and use theological argumentation as a weapon. Clear evidence that Jāḥiẓ acted as adviser to ᶜAbbasid officials on political and religious matters is provided by this *risālah* and others, particularly another epistle written for the son of Aḥmad b. Abī Duᵓād, *al-Risālah fī Nafy al-tashbīh*, which condemns anthropomorphism, an anti-Muᶜtazilī tenet, *Kitāb al-Futyā* ("The Book of Legal Opinions") and a dedicatory epistle to the recipient of *Kitāb al-Futyā*, *Risālah ilā Aḥmad b. Abī Duᵓād yukhbiruh fīhā bi-Kitāb al-Futyā* (H, I, 313–19),[18] and *Kitāb al-Radd ᶜalā ᵓl-Naṣārā* ("Refutation of the Christians",

[13] Pellat, *Jāḥiẓ*, 62–4, 64–6; see Pellat, "L'imamat".

[14] The Zaydīs put forward a pragmatic theory of the imamate: it could be held by any male member of the Prophet's House (*ahl al-bayt*), and any imam could be ousted by a better-qualified candidate; the presence of single imam in every age was not necessary: there could be several, or none.

[15] Pellat, *Jāḥiẓ*, 72–82, 56–8, 66–72; on the arbitration of Ṣiffīn, cf. p. 186, below.

[16] See Pellat, *Jāḥiẓ*, 58–62.

[17] *CHALUP*, 216. Aḥmad b. Ḥanbal opposed the Muᶜtazilī doctrine of the createdness of the Qurᵓān and taught that the attributes of God, which the Muᶜtazilīs interpreted allegorically, were real; for the political significance of this stance, see pp. 5–6.

[18] Pellat, *Jāḥiẓ*, 51–2.

Finkel, *Three Essays*, 10–38, trans. Finkel, *Journal of American Oriental Society*, XLVII, 1927, 311–34), which is linked to the measures taken by al-Mutawakkil against the "People of the Book" (*ahl al-kitāb*), non-Muslims whose religions were founded on scriptures recognized by Islam and who were entitled to Muslim protection. In a similar "official" vein, *Kitāb Manāqib al-Turk wa-ᶜāmmat jund al-khilāfah* ("The Merits of the Turks and of the Caliphal Army in General", H, I, 1–85), addressed to the Turkish commander al-Fatḥ b. Khāqān, deals with the composition of the caliph's army, particularly the Turkish troops.[19]

Though theological points are dealt with in several of the above works which Jāḥiẓ produced for official consumption, most of the writings in which he gives a more or less systematic account of his own doctrinal position have been lost, and it is difficult to reconstruct his Muᶜtazilī beliefs without drawing upon the writings of the later Muᶜtazilīs, al-Khayyāṭ (d. *c.* 300/913) and ᶜAbd al-Jabbār (d. 415/1025),[20] and the heresiographers. For strangely enough, though he differed enough from his teacher al-Naẓẓām to give rise to a separate Muᶜtazilī school, the Jāḥiẓiyyah (which the heresiographers cite without naming its adherents), Jāḥiẓ's own writings tell us less about his own beliefs than about those of other Muᶜtazilīs, especially al-Naẓẓām. Apart from *Kitāb al-Futyā*, a striking example of this is *Kitāb al-Akhbār wa-kayfa taṣiḥḥ* on the authenticity of *ḥadīth*, the first part of which discusses the beliefs of the pre-Islamic Arabs, the Indians, Persians and Byzantines, while the second part is given the significant title "Ein unbekanntes Fragment des Naẓẓām" by its German editor and translator J. van Ess. Surviving fragments of other doctrinal works include a eulogy of dogmatic theology, *Risālah fī Faḍīlat ṣināʾat al-kalām* (unpublished), another work on the authencity of *ḥadīth*, *Kitāb Ḥujaj al-nubuwwah* ("Proofs of Prophethood", S, 117–47), which also discusses the inimitability (*iᶜjāz*) of the Qurʾān, and *Kitāb Khalq al-Qurʾān* (S, 147–54), which tackles the thorny issue of the createdness (*khalq*) of the Qurʾān and the persecution of Aḥmad b. Ḥanbal, who opposed the official Muᶜtazilī doctrine of createdness, by the Inquistion (*miḥnah*) of al-Maʾmūn.[21] Finally, *Kitāb al-Masāʾil wa ʾl-jawābāt fī ʾl-maᶜrifah* ("Questions and Answers on the Subject of Knowledge") must have been an account of the teachings of the different Muᶜtazilī schools on the knowledge of God, the only surviving fragment of which suggests that Jāḥiẓ believed that God can only be known by a process of ratiocination and not by intuition, which implies that ᶜAlī b. Abī Ṭālib could not have had an innate knowledge of God, and could not therefore be seen as having had an intrinsically better claim than other

[19] Ibid., 91–7. [20] See ch. 5. [21] See Pellat, *Jāḥiẓ*, 32–3, 38–48, 48–50.

Muslim converts to the imamate after the Prophet's death.[22] *Fī ᵓl-Shārib wa ᵓl-mashrūb* ("Drinkers and Drinks", S, 276–84), an epistle on the licitness of date-wine (*nabīdh*), must be included among Jāḥiẓ's writings on religious matters proper, though another epistle on the same subject, *Fī Madḥ al-nabīdh* ("In Praise of Date-Wine", S, 285–91), should probably be treated as a work of *adab*.[23]

SCHOLARLY WORKS

In terms of form, Jāḥiẓ's political and religious writings fall into the category of works which include but are not structured around quotations. Jāḥiẓ's scholarly works are more mixed in form, some making sparing use of quotation while others rely heavily on secondary material, but all can be viewed as marking a transition between conventional scholarship and Jāḥiẓ's own branch of *adab*. Both literary and scientific topics are discussed and analyzed; Jāḥiẓ sifts through the mass of lore and tradition collected by his predecessors, examines their authenticity and, in so doing, suggests the framework within which general culture should evolve and expand. His aim being to instruct without tedium, Jāḥiẓ's approach tends to be digressive and untidy; he switches from topic to topic by simple association of ideas and intersperses even the most serious material with comic anecdotes. Because of his playful style and often mordant wit, Jāḥiẓ has often been considered something of a joker, even a buffoon; but his works have a serious undertone. The "scientific" writings are theological too in so far as they are intended to prompt the reader to reflect and discriminate when making use of existing knowledge (and, in the case of the lengthiest work, *Kitāb al-Ḥayawān* ("The Book of Beasts"), to draw edifying lessons from the observation of nature); the "literary" writings are likewise designed to stimulate the reader's critical faculties. An example of this approach is *Kitāb al-Tarbīᶜ wa ᵓl-tadwīr* ("The Square and the Round"), a short treatise now mutilated and interspersed with fragments of other works, in which Jāḥiẓ, while remaining just within the bounds of religious prescriptions and the pronouncements of the Qurᵓān, probes the accuracy of conventional interpretations of natural phenomena and questions "established" facts and generally credited legends; the work is an invitation to leave the ranks of the conformists and join those of the Muᶜtazilīs, who exercise their powers of reason and accept nothing without critical examination. In *al-Tarbīᶜ* Jāḥiẓ avoids giving answers to the issues he raises, but he does propose some solutions in one of his two crowning works,

[22] Pellat, *Jāḥiẓ*, 33–7; see Vajda, "La connaissance naturelle de Dieu", and van Ess, *Aṣḥāb al-maᶜārif*".
[23] Pellat, *Jāḥiẓ*, 52–4, 54–5.

Kitāb al-Ḥayawān, an anthology supposedly centred on a number of animals, but which in fact covers so vast a range of subjects as to make it a veritable encyclopaedia.[24] The ostensible aim of *al-Ḥayawān* is to prove that the early Arabs knew as much about zoology as did the Greeks, and especially Aristotle, who is often quoted and criticized; but the main idea which emerges from the work is that everything in nature has a meaning and a use, and that everything proves the existence and wisdom of God. Quotations from archaic poetry and comic stories rub shoulders with passages of philosophy, metaphysics, sociology and anthropology, providing invaluable source-material for modern research, and there are observations on animal psychology, the evolution of species and the influence of climate on animals and man that often have quite a modern ring to them, though how many of these ideas are Jāḥiẓ's own it is difficult to establish; many are clearly borrowed from his contemporaries. As a good rationalist, Jāḥiẓ even carries out experiments to check the validity of conventional wisdom about animals, though he does not always interpret the results correctly or realize that the conditions of the experiment are faulty, as when he accepts the idea of spontaneous generation on the evidence of seeing flies hatch in a sealed bottle. The monumental *al-Ḥayawān*, which Jāḥiẓ never completed, was followed by a short work, *Kitāb al-Qawl fī ʾl-bighāl* (H, II, 211–378), which deals with the mule, a hybrid well-calculated to arouse Jāḥiẓ's curiosity.

Altogether different is *Kitāb al-Amṣār wa-ʿajāʾib al-buldān* ("Metropolises and Geographical Curiosities"), only a fragment of which has survived.[25] This cannot be called a geographical treatise in the true sense of the word, for, though it deals with cities and countries, Jāḥiẓ presents them in literary rather than scientific terms, describing the tales and legends surrounding them; nevertheless, the work could be seen as an early specimen of human geography. The notion of the influence of soil and surroundings on their human inhabitants which is common to this work and to *al-Ḥayawān* is also developed in a curious text, *Kitāb Fakhr al-Sūdān ʿalā ʾl-Bīḍān* (H, I, 173–226), in which Jāḥiẓ vaunts the superiority of the black races to the white.[26] Despite his origins, it seems unlikely that Jāḥiẓ genuinely wished to disparage the whites; rather it seems that his aim was obliquely to undermine Persian Shuʿūbī pretensions to racial and cultural superiority to the Arabs; by using the kinds of argument employed by the Persians themselves, Jāḥiẓ shows that mere racial characteristics are not a mark of divine favour or displeasure, but of climatic conditions. Also to be included under the heading of ethnology is the last chapter of *Kitāb al-Bukhalāʾ*, which is probably identical with *Kitāb Aṭʿimat al-ʿArab*; this deals with the

[24] Ibid., 130–85. [25] Ibid., 185–8, 188–95. [26] Ibid., 195–8.

foodstuffs of the ancient Arabs, whose curious and sometimes revolting nature is set against the bedouins' proverbial hospitality and is explained in terms of environment – a dig at those Shuᶜūbīs who mocked the supposedly barbaric habits of the Arabs. The work is similar to a conventional lexicographical monograph, with an added dash of irony, for the material includes verses on cannibalism and provides a good example of Jāḥiẓ's slyly humorous method:

It was customary among the early Arabs to attribute the wrongdoing of a single individual to his entire tribe; similarly, a whole tribe might win commendation for the acts of one man alone. Thus . . . tribes would vilify each other as dog-eaters or man-eaters on the strength of an isolated incident – which might itself, upon examination, prove to have been perfectly excusable . . . A poet accordingly mocks the tribe of Bāhilah thus:

Ghifāq got eaten by Bāhilah; fie!
They sucked his bones and skull quite dry;
Now Ghifāq's mother pipes her eye.

. . . And the whole tribe of Asad were stigmatized as cannibals because of what happened to Ramlah bint Fāᵓid . . . who was eaten by her husband and her brother Abū Arib (who for their part declared that they only ate her out of exasperation at her unsuitable behaviour). The poet Ibn Dārah upbraids them thus:

Ramlah was wife to one of your family, sister to another; now her name spells infamy.
Abū Arib! is this your clan's style of blood relationships, bloated as you all are on the flesh of the lady's hips?

and thus:

After what happened to Ramlah Fāᵓid, no Faqᶜash man can find a bride;
A newly-wed but yestere'en, her flesh now graces your tureen.[27]

A similar spirit of irony informs *Kitāb al-Burṣān wa ᵓl-ᶜurjān wa ᵓl-ᶜumyān wa ᵓl-ḥūlān*, a selection of anecdotes, verse quotations and items of vocabulary relating to lepers, cripples, the blind, cross-eyed and otherwise physically defective.

The remaining works in this section deal with literary topics. *Kitāb al-Bayān wa ᵓl-tabyīn* ("The Book of Eloquence and Exposition") is an anthology of poetry and oratorical prose which constitutes a kind of selective inventory of the Arabic humanities, by means of which Jāḥiẓ tries to demonstrate Arab superiority to all other nations in the literary field, and so to add to the arguments directed against members of other cultures who claimed that the Arabs were barbarians, unfit to lead the Muslim community.[28] Although Jāḥiẓ does little to explain his choice of literary material, he sketches an outline of poetic theory, leaving the reader to define the rules of literary criticism. *Kitāb al-Bayān* is such a rich source of material that it has tended to overshadow other shorter but equally

[27] *Bukhalāᵓ*, 234, 236; trans. J. Ashtiany (hereafter J.A.). [28] Pellat, *Jāḥiẓ*, 100–11.

interesting works, such as the epistle *Fī ʾl-Balāghah wa ʾl-ījāz* ("Of Eloquence and Concision", unpublished), the brief surviving fragment of which shows that Jāḥiẓ was anxious not to neglect prose as a subject of literary discussion, and to lay down one fundamental rule of composition for Arabic prose-writers, namely concision (*ījāz*). In a short essay with the enigmatic title, *Fī Ṣināʿāt al-quwwād* ("The Skills of the Guild-Masters", H, I, 375–93), Jāḥiẓ represents several people using the jargon of their professions to describe a battle and compose love poetry; the effect is comic and illustrates the dangers of professional conditioning, over-specialization and the lack of a broader culture. Jāḥiẓ himself favours all-round development, and expounds his views in *Kitāb al-Muʿallimīn* ("Schoolmasters"), the surviving portion of which is a serious treatise on teaching, though the lost portions may well have presented schoolmasters in a satirical light.[29]

In *al-Ḥayawān* and *al-Bayān* Jāḥiẓ acted as a compiler, arranging notes and using his own personal observations to link them, but in the shorter treatises he emerges as a constructive critic and – himself at best a mediocre poet – an advocate of prose as an equal and a rival to verse. He himself sets the example by writing an elegy (*rithāʾ*) in prose, *Fī Mawt Abī Ḥarb al-Ṣaffār*, and a prose satire (*hijāʾ*) of a well-known member of the Barmakid family, *Hijāʾ Muḥammad b. al-Jahm al-Barmakī*. Other, unpublished fragments of the same type have survived in manuscript. Finally, *Fī Dhamm al-zamān* (S, 310–11) is a veritable prose poem on the "evils of the age".[30]

ADAB

Moral decline and neglect of customary practices are recurrent themes both of paraenetic and of professional *adab*. To the latter category doubtless belonged a lost *Kitāb Akhlāq al-wuzarāʾ*, which must have been a manual for the use of viziers. The surviving *Kitāb al-Tāj* ("The Book of the Crown"), which deals with rules of conduct for the great, is clearly apocryphal, as may also be *Kitāb al-Ḥijāb* (H, II, 25–85), on the office of chamberlain (*ḥājib*). Good manners are the subject of *Risālat al-Maʿād wa ʾl-maʿāsh fī ʾl-adab wa-tadbīr al-nās wa-muʿāmalatihim* ("Epistle for the Next World and This on Manners, Managing Men and Social Relations", *Majmūʿ*, 1–36, French trans. Vial, *Quatre Essais*, I, 33–66). This treatise falls to some extent under the heading of *adab* as Ibn al-Muqaffaʿ for example conceived it, and Jāḥiẓ sets a still more individual stamp on paraenetic *adab* and the study of manners and morals, analyzing character and emotion and building up

[29] Ibid., 11–12, 114–16, 112–14. [30] Ibid., 116–21, 122, 122–4.

pictures of entire social groups characterized by some particular moral or psychological feature.

To judge by the titles to which references have survived, Jāḥiẓ must have devoted a number of epistles to such qualities as forgiveness and clemency, energy and resolve, etc., and he makes tantalizing allusions to these themes in other works. Some works of this kind survive; the keeping of promises is discussed in the fragmentary *Fī ᵓstinjāz al-waᶜd* (*11 Risālah*, 173–7), anger and its consequences in *Fī ᵓl-Jidd wa ᵓl-hazl* ("Earnestness and Jesting") – the title describes the tone of the epistle rather than its contents (*Majmūᶜ*, 61–98, French trans. Vial, *Quatre Essais*, I, 99–148), envy in *Fī Faṣl mā bayn al-ᶜadāwah wa ᵓl-ḥasad* ("On the Difference Between Enmity and Envy", trans. Beeston, *Journal of Arabic Literature*, XVIII, 1987) and in *Fī ᵓl-Ḥāsid wa ᵓl-maḥsūd* ("The Envier and the Envied", *11 Risālah*, 1–13),[31] indiscretion in *Kitāb Kitmān al-sirr wa-ḥifẓ al-lisān* ("On Keeping Secrets and Guarding One's Tongue", *Majmūᶜ*, 37–60, French trans. Vial, *Quatre Essais*, I, 67–97), whose overly dogmatic assertions Jāḥiẓ tones down in *Tafḍīl al-nuṭq ᶜalā ᵓl-ṣamt* ("Speech is Better than Silence", *11 Risālah*, 148–54),[32] where the value of speech is acknowledged. Snobbishness and pride are discussed in *al-Nubl wa ᵓl-tannabbul wa-dhamm al-kibr* ("Real and Assumed Superiority and a Condemnation of Arrogance") and narrow-mindedness in *Fī ᵓl-Wukalāᵓ wa-muwakkilīn* ("Of Stewards and Those Who Appoint them", *11 Risālah*, 170–2).[33] But by far the most famous and extensive work in this category is *Kitāb al-Bukhalāᵓ* ("The Book of Misers"). It consists of anecdotes and epistles which illustrate the vice of avarice, and begins with an introduction in which meanness is illustrated in great depth. By stressing the greed of the protagonists – many of them Persians – Jāḥiẓ seems to be trying to accentuate, by implication, the proverbial generosity of the Arabs, but what makes the book a masterpiece is Jāḥiẓ's gift for sheer story-telling:

A man from Marv [in Persia] used constantly to be travelling on business and pilgrimages; he used to stay with an Iraqi, who would entertain him liberally and see to all his needs. Often and often the man from Marv would say to the Iraqi: "How I wish you would come to Marv, so that I could repay all the kindnesses you've done me and the goodness you show me every time I come here. Of course here in your home town, by God's grace, you have no need of my hospitality." Now it so happened, a long while after, that the Iraqi had some business in that quarter [Marv], and he found the hardships of travel and the loneliness of being away from home considerably alleviated by the fact that he knew his friend was there. When he arrived in Marv he made straight for his house in his travelling dress, in his turban and tall hat and cloak, all ready to deposit his baggage and take up residence as a man does with a trusted friend and intimate. When he saw the man from Marv sitting among his cronies he threw himself into his arms and embraced

[31] Ibid., 221–2. [32] Ibid., 230–1. [33] Ibid., 235–6.

him; yet the man gave no sign of recognition and was as unforthcoming as if he had never set eyes on him before. The Iraqi said to himself, "Perhaps he can't recognise me through my dust-veil", so he took off his veil and began to ask his friend how he was; but the man was more offputting than ever. Then the Iraqi said to himself, "Most likely it's because of my turban", so he pulled it off, said who he was and renewed his enquiries; but his friend was as chilling as could be. "Perhaps it's because of my hat", said the Iraqi [and began to remove it]. The man from Marv saw that the game was up and that it was impossible to feign ignorance any longer. He said, "If you were to take off your skin I still wouldn't recognise you!"[34]

Kitāb al-Bukhalāʾ also contains an entire chapter on vagabonds, a subject also treated in the lost *Ḥiyal al-mukaddīn* ("Mendicants' Tricks"), of which two pages have been preserved by a slightly later writer, Ibrāhīm b. Muḥammad al-Bayhaqī, as has one page of *Ḥiyal al-luṣūṣ* ("Robbers' Tricks"),[35] to which Jāḥiẓ refers in *al-Bukhalāʾ*. These texts could be considered forerunners of the *maqāmah* and of *Ḥikāyat Abī ʾl-Qāsim* by Abū ʾl-Muṭahhar al-Azdī, and bear an affinity to the later genre of the *qaṣīdah sāsāniyyah*;[36] as transmitted via Spain through the quotations in al-Bayhaqī, they may even be related to the picaresque novel. *Kitāb al-Bukhalāʾ*, which has already proved a stimulus to literary and linguistic research,[37] would clearly repay further study.

Probably earlier in date than *al-Bukhalāʾ*, *Kitāb al-Qiyān* ("The Book of Singing Slave-Girls") contains a study of the manners and morals of the type as embodied in a seductive coquette and gold-digger, whose feigned or real feelings are analyzed with great subtlety:

The singing-girl is hardly ever sincere in her passion, or whole-hearted in her affection. For both by training and by innate instinct her nature is to set up snares and traps for the victims, in order that they may fall into her toils . . . But it sometimes happens that this pretence leads her on to turning it into a reality, and that she in fact shares her lover's torments . . . Sometimes she may renounce her craft, in order for her to be cheaper for him [to buy] . . . or she may allege that she is really a free woman, as a trick to get herself into the lover's possession, and out of anxiety for him lest her high price should ruin him . . . Yet for the most part singing-girls are insincere, and given to employing deceit and treachery in squeezing out the property of the deluded victim and then abandoning him. Sometimes a singing-girl may have three or four such victims with her, in spite of their own anxiety to avoid such an encounter, and their mutual jealousy when they do meet each other. Then she weeps with one eye to one of them, and laughs with the other eye to the second, and winks at the latter in mockery of the former . . . When they leave, she writes letters to all of them in identical terms, telling each one how much she dislikes the rest, and how she longs to be alone with him without the others.[38]

[34] *Bukhalāʾ*, 22, trans J. A. [35] *Maḥāsin*, 521–3, 622–4; see Pellat, *Jāḥiẓ*, 255–6, 253–4.
[36] See p. 101. [37] E.g. Mubārak, *Fann al-qaṣaṣ*; Blau, "Syntactic phenomena".
[38] Trans. Beeston, *Singing-Girls*, 31–4.

The epistle is ostensibly an apology for the rich businessmen who own, train and hire out the singing-girls, and, though bolstered by a typology of the affections and a history of the relations between the sexes in Arab society, is surely satirical in intent; but, though paradoxical and daring at times, it could hardly be considered shocking, unlike an anthology on natural and unnatural love, *Kitāb Mufākharat al-jawārī wa ʾl-ghilmān* ("Boasting-Match between Girls and Boys"; H, II, 91–137), in which Jāḥiẓ displays a marked hostility to homosexuality, as he also must have done in a lost work, *Dhamm al-liwāṭ* ("Condemnation of Sodomites"), and as he does in a witty essay, *Fī Tafḍīl al-baṭn ʿalā ʾl-ẓahr* ("On the Superiority of the Belly to the Back").[39] Passionate love is described at length in *al-Qiyān* and is also the subject of an epistle, *Fī ʾl-ʿIshq wa ʾl-nisāʾ* ("Of Love and Women"); this has survived only in mutilated form in combination with *Faṣl mā bayn al-rijāl wa ʾl-nisāʾ* ("The Difference between Men and Women", S, 266–75), an examination of the respective roles of men and women in which Jāḥiẓ shows himself to be resolutely feminist in a far from feminist environment.[40]

Several of the above works, *al-Bukhalāʾ* and *al-Qiyān* in particular, depict social classes, as do the epistles *Fī Madḥ al-tujjār wa-dhamm ʿamal al-sulṭān* (*II Risālah*, 155–60)[41] and *Dhamm al-kuttāb* (Finkel, *Three Essays*, 40–51, French trans. Pellat, *Hespéris*, XLIII, 1956, 29–50); as their titles indicate, the former compares merchants, very favourably, to civil servants, and the latter is an attack on the bureaucracy. The fact that a treatise in praise of civil servants is also attributed to Jāḥiẓ, and that several other sets of antithetical titles are listed in the sources, gave rise to the idea that Jāḥiẓ was particularly fickle and quite prepared to defend in turn "a case and its opposite", as Ibn Qutaybah says in a famous passage.[42] In fact this "fickleness" can be explained both in terms of literary convention[43] and of Jāḥiẓ's idiosyncratic ability to see the good and bad in everything. One last work, which should perhaps be included under the heading of portrayals of social groups, is a year-book of the singers of Baghdad for the year 215/830–1, *Fī Ṭabaqāt al-mughannīn* ("Classes of Singers", *II Risālah*, 186–9); Jāḥiẓ declares his intention of bringing it up to date each year, but only a short fragment has survived.[44]

As the above bibliography shows, in compilations such as *Kitāb al-Ḥayawān* or *Kitāb al-Bayān* Jāḥiẓ seems to follow the pattern of conventional scholarship, but he moves well beyond convention when he uses traditional

[39] Pellat, *Jāḥiẓ*, 270–1, 269. [40] Ibid., 257–9. [41] Ibid., 272–3.
[42] *Mukhtalif al-ḥadīth*, 71–2. [43] See Geries, *al-Maḥāsin wa ʾl-masāwī*, and p.28, above.
[44] Pellat, *Jāḥiẓ*, 124–5.

material as a vehicle for his own tastes and convictions. What is more, Jāḥiẓ always sets his own personal and utterly distinctive stamp on his source-material, however neutral. In the field of the Arabic humanities, it could well be said that while Jāḥiẓ's predecessors collected and sifted the raw materials, Jāḥiẓ himself was the artist who brought an original touch to the whole edifice. He raised the study of manners to the level of psychological enquiry and brought an analytical approach to scholarly and professional *adab*. Moreover, the structure of Arab–Islamic culture as presented by Jāḥiẓ is not merely founded on the traditions of the past corrected by the logic that Jāḥiẓ learned from the Greeks; it is an open culture, based on the recognition that the Arabs were not the first race to become civilized and that the progress of the human spirit did not cease with the Revelation. Unique in his own time, Jāḥiẓ, like Bacon or d'Alembert, embodies a process of development which can best be expressed in the formulae "memory, imagination, reason" or "scholarship, *belles-lettres*, philosophy". Since the chronology of his writings cannot be established precisely we cannot, perhaps, speak of his personal development in these terms; but his works take scholarship as their point of departure, enrich it with imagination, and are consistently rationalist in outlook. Though Jāḥiẓ is in no way comparable to the Muslim philosophers and thinkers of succeeding centuries, he nevertheless occupies a prominent place in the early history of Muslim thought. He was not, perhaps, a profound thinker, but he observed widely, and his shrewd comments are inspired by solid good sense and sound reason. Above all, though, Jāḥiẓ was a man of letters whose technical achievements mark a high point in the history of Arabic literature. Other writers before him had used a more sophisticated prose than that of the scholars and preachers, but Jāḥiẓ showed that the Arabs and Muslims, as the heirs of preceding civilizations, had attained an intellectual level which required its own medium of expression, at once more flexible than the prose of the early orators and simpler than that of the scribes – an unadorned prose which would be capable of conveying subtle shades of meaning and would derive its aesthetic quality from its own resources, without recourse to poetic ornamentation. Few writers were talented enough to follow his lead, and artistic prose soon drew upon rhyme and tropes and, once its original inspiration had dried up, lapsed into affectation and verbal acrobatics. The best critics have always rightly considered Jāḥiẓ as the greatest of Arabic prose-writers, though their judgement has been based less on precise analysis than on general impressions. But it must be conceded that Jāḥiẓ's style is hard to characterize. His sentences, which almost always dispense with internal rhyme, are often complex and extremely long, so long indeed as to mislead some editors who fail to grasp their flow into breaking them up at the wrong point. They are balanced by the juxtaposition of units of similar quantity and by the repetition of the same idea in two different forms, so that the reader may be sure to grasp its sense. His vocabulary is rich and as precise as the state of the language at that period allowed; foreign terms and neologisms are used with discrimination, and many passages seem quite modern. Nevertheless, Jāḥiẓ is a difficult writer to translate, so much so that, whenever the present writer has little trouble in turning into French a work attributed to Jāḥiẓ, he is inclined to consider it of doubtful authenticity. The difficulty stems from the often defective state of the texts, the richness of the vocabulary, and from Jāḥiẓ's untidy and confusingly digressive method of composition. But the untidiness is intentional and is, perhaps, less a result of Jāḥiẓ's pen trying to keep pace with his ideas than of his desire to vary his rhythm and subject-matter, to break down his reasoning into easy steps, and to make room for witticisms, anecdotes and pithy reflections. In an environment seemingly hostile to frivolity, Jāḥiẓ tackles the most serious questions, but at the same time gives the impression that he sees everything in relative terms and takes nothing wholly seriously. No reader can fail to be struck by the frequency with which Jāḥiẓ discusses laughter and feels the need to justify it, as though it were generally felt to be unnatural. To be sure, he repeats that the serious and the comic both have their place in the scheme of things, but to many Jāḥiẓ is still a mere entertainer whose only object is to raise a laugh. Some early writers were more clear-sighted and dubbed him *muᶜallim al-ᶜaql wa ᵓl-adab*, "the teacher of reason and polite learning", and for Jāḥiẓ *adab* was indeed a process of building up a new culture in which reflection, doubt, observation and even experiment were involved; but he also showed that man has the right to cast a satirical eye on the world about him and openly to enjoy such harmless pleasures as frank and healthy laughter.

Jāḥiẓ was bound to attract admirers, one of the most distinguished of whom was Abū Ḥayyān al-Tawḥīdī; he also inspired forgers and clumsy imitators but did not found a literary school as such, for his talents were too unique. However, the isolated position that Jāḥiẓ occupies in Arabic literature can largely be blamed on the ground lost by Muᶜtazilism to Sunnism and on one of Sunnism's chief apologists, Ibn Qutaybah, who served the Sunnī policy of the caliph al-Mutawakkil much as Jāḥiẓ himself had earlier served Muᶜtazilism, and who played a prominent role in shaping later Muslim thought. Ibn Qutaybah's understanding of the aims of *adab*, as well as his theology, was radically different from Jāḥiẓ's; he consequently misunderstood Jāḥiẓ, and succeeded in caricaturing him in the eyes of posterity.[45] In the long term, he can be said to have succeeded in ousting

Jāḥiẓ's conception of *adab* as progress and pluralism and in winning acceptance for his own tendency towards a safe and unadventurous singleness of outlook.

[45] Lecomte, *Ibn Qutayba*, 433–6; Ibn Qutaybah, *Mukhtalif al-ḥadīth*, 71–3; trans. Lecomte, *Le Traité des divergences*, 65–6.

CHAPTER 5

AL-ṢĀḤIB IBN ᶜABBĀD

One of the foremost prose-writers and poets of the fourth/tenth century, Ibn ᶜAbbād was also an able politician and administrator and a great patron, a *kātib* who for more than eighteen years successfully held office as vizier to a branch of the Buwayhid family. Biographical sources are agreed upon his name (*ism*) and genealogy (*nasab*): Ismāᶜīl b. ᶜAbbād b. al-ᶜAbbās b. ᶜAbbād b. Aḥmad b. Idrīs. They also agree on his agnomen (*kunyah*), Abū ʾl-Qāsim, which must have been given to him in childhood, since he had no son. Varying explanations are given of the honorific title (*laqab*) of al-Ṣāḥib usually prefixed to his name. Some sources say that the form of the title was originally *ṣāḥib* Ibn al-ᶜAmīd, "the companion of Ibn al-ᶜAmīd", because it was Abū ʾl-Faḍl Ibn al-ᶜAmīd, vizier to the Buwayhid amir Rukn al-Dawlah, who had trained him as a *kātib*. Others claim that the title in its full form was *ṣāḥib* Muʾayyid al-Dawlah, and that it was given in recognition of Ibn ᶜAbbād's loyalty to the Buwayhid amir of that name. Whatever the true explanation, it was soon forgotten, and the title al-Ṣāḥib thereafter entered the repertory of Muslim honorifics. The zeal and efficiency with which Ibn ᶜAbbād discharged his duties as vizier also earned him the more formal title of Kāfī ʾl-Kufāh, "the most competent of the competent".

It must not be supposed that Ibn ᶜAbbād's achievements were due solely to his own talents; for two generations, the Iranian family to which he belonged had already served the Buwayhids, his grandfather as vizier or at very least as secretary, his father ᶜAbbād as secretary to the amir Rukn al-Dawlah. The father, who had a reputation for great piety and religious learning, seems to have continued in office until his death, the date of which is disputed. Some sources claim that father and son both died in the same year, 385/995. A likelier date for the father's death is 334 or 335/946–7, and it is probable that Ibn ᶜAbbād became an orphan early in life. The date of his birth is unknown, although he came of a distinguished family which might have been expected to record the event, as indeed it probably did, since we know the exact day of the month on which he was born, 16 Dhū ʾl-Qaᶜdah.

The year is given variously as 320, 324 and 326/938;[1] the last figure being taken as the most probable gives us the date of 14 September 938. There is even more uncertainty about Ibn ᶜAbbād's birthplace; several towns and villages have been suggested, but as he bore the *nisbah* al-Ṭālaqānī and seems always to have been fond of Isfahan, where he built a Friday mosque and was finally buried, it would seem that he was born (and spent his early childhood) in the village of Ṭālaqān near Isfahan.

Assuming that Ibn ᶜAbbād was actually born in 326/938 and that his father died in 334–5/946–7, the latter may possibly have taught him the basics that every well-bred Muslim would acquire in childhood, though it is unlikely that he would have transmitted any *ḥadīth* to so young a child, as some sources claim. Since his family were well-to-do, his mother was probably able to send him to good teachers, but for this we have only indirect evidence; we are told that every day she would give him some coins to hand to the first needy person he met on his way to school. Thereafter his biographers cite a few scholars with whom he mixed at various stages of his career, all agreeing that it was to the vizier Abū ʾl-Faḍl Ibn al-ᶜAmīd, who took him under his wing after his father's death, that he owed his real training.[2] His education, as befitted his birth, was directed primarily towards a career as a *kātib*; this required a good command of Arabic and an all-round competence in letter-writing, official and private, and in versification, where considerable versatility was expected. Ibn ᶜAbbād also attended Ibn al-ᶜAmīd's *majlis* (social and literary circle), and later those of the Buwayhid amirs whom he served, Muʾayyid al-Dawlah and Fakhr al-Dawlah; when eventually he formed his own *majlis*, it attracted such celebrities as the grammarian Ibn Fāris, Abū Ḥayyān al-Tawḥīdī, the poet Abū Bakr al-Khwārazmī, the critic al-Qāḍī ʾl-Jurjānī,[3] and many others, including Badīᶜ al-Zamān al-Hamadhānī. He had access to extensive libraries, and soon built up a collection of his own which became a byword for its lavishness and came to include works dedicated to him, such as Ibn Bābawayh's (d. 381/991–2) *Kitāb ᶜUyūn akhbār al-Riḍā*, a Shīᶜī anthology,[4] and the foremost grammatical work of the period, *al-Ṣāḥibī*. It also contained a large section on theology (*kalām*) – subsequently burnt by the staunchly Sunnī Maḥmūd of Ghaznah (for Ibn ᶜAbbād, as we shall see, was a Muᶜtazilī). Indeed, so large and varied was Ibn ᶜAbbād's library and so great his fondness for books that one of the main excuses he is said to have given for declining a pressing invitation to become vizier to the Samanid ruler of Transoxiana and Khurāsān, Nūḥ II b. Manṣūr, was the problem of shifting

[1] Yāqūt, *Irshād*, VI (2), 171, 208; Tawḥīdī, *Akhlāq*.
[2] For a portrait of this influential statesman and polymath, see Kraemer, *Humanism*, 241–55.
[3] See pp. 375–9. [4] See *CHALUP*, 305.

all his books, which would have required "four hundred" camels, sixty for his lexicographical works alone; the library catalogue is said to have filled ten volumes. Even allowing for exaggeration, these, symbolic, figures give some idea of the range and depth of Ibn ʿAbbād's learning and interests.

At the time of Ibn ʿAbbād's birth, the amir Rukn al-Dawlah (d. 366/977) was ruling in Rayy; Ibn ʿAbbād's future guardian Ibn al-ʿAmīd became his vizier in 328/940, and brought Ibn ʿAbbād to continue his education in Rayy, later putting him to work as his private secretary. In 347/958, Ibn ʿAbbād was given the mission of accompanying Rukn al-Dawlah's son, the prince Abū Manṣūr (later to reign as Muʾayyid al-Dawlah), to Baghdad to ask for the hand in marriage of the head of the Buwayhid clan Muʿizz al-Dawlah's daughter.[5] In this year began Ibn ʿAbbād's association with the scholars of Baghdad, as well as with Muʾayyid al-Dawlah, whose secretary he became. Little is known of his movements for the next ten or so years, but in 358/968 we find him back in Rayy, still with Muʾayyid al-Dawlah, who became governor of Rayy and Isfahan on the death of his father in 366/977 and enjoyed a degree of autonomy, even though he was the vassal of his brother ʿAḍud al-Dawlah (324–72/936–83), who had succeeded Muʿizz al-Dawlah as head of the Buwayhid family.

Some years before, Ibn al-ʿAmīd, Ibn ʿAbbād's guardian, had died, and his son Abū ʾl-Fatḥ Ibn al-ʿAmīd (b. 337/947–8) had been appointed vizier in his father's place by Rukn al-Dawlah. When Rukn al-Dawlah was succeeded by Muʾayyid al-Dawlah, the latter dared not deprive the young and ambitious Abū ʾl-Fatḥ Ibn al-ʿAmīd of his office, though he knew that he was exceedingly jealous of his own personal secretary, Ibn ʿAbbād. In fact Abū ʾl-Fatḥ Ibn al-ʿAmīd incited the troops to rebel against Ibn ʿAbbād and kill him; yet Muʾayyid al-Dawlah took no action against his vizier, but sent Ibn ʿAbbād away, incognito, under cover of darkness, to Isfahan to escape the wrath of his enemy (with whom al-Tawḥīdī alleges Ibn ʿAbbād had earlier pleaded in vain).[6] Eventually Abū ʾl-Fatḥ Ibn al-ʿAmīd was put to death and Ibn ʿAbbād took his place.

In 369/979 he was sent to Hamadhān, to the court of ʿAḍud al-Dawlah, who received him with much honour. He stayed there so long that his master complained of his absence; this despite the fact that on his arrival he had recited a poem of his own composition in praise of his host parts of which were considered decidedly ill-judged.[7] It was also said that ʿAḍud al-Dawlah had considered having Ibn ʿAbbād murdered – he had apparently been in league for some time with the amir's brother and rival, Fakhr al-Dawlah. Sure enough, after the deaths of ʿAḍud al-Dawlah in 372/983 and

[5] Miskawayh, *Tajārib*, II, 168 (Ar.), V, 180–1 (trans.). [6] Tawḥīdī, *Akhlāq*, 535.
[7] Ibn ʿAbbād, *Dīwān*, 191.

Muᵓayyid al-Dawlah the following year, it was to Fakhr al-Dawlah, now head of the Buwayhid clan, that Ibn ᶜAbbād turned in order to preserve his vizierate. He paid the army, thus ensuring its support, and, taking a contingent of troops with him, went to see Fakhr al-Dawlah, then in exile, and made as if to tender his resignation; but the ploy was a pretence and the amir of course refused it, reminding Ibn ᶜAbbād that the vizierate was his due inheritance as was the amirate for himself. Ibn ᶜAbbād – now in effect a king-maker – then negotiated with Ṣamṣām al-Dawlah, the Buwayhid amir of Iraq, who might have tried to oppose Fakhr al-Dawlah's investiture by the caliph, and thereafter was free to govern as he wished in his master's name. His administration gave Fakhr al-Dawlah's subjects several years of relative peace and prosperity. Meanwhile Ibn ᶜAbbād himself led the army on several foreign campaigns, and is credited with having conquered fifty fortresses for his master; in 377/987 he put down a revolt in Ṭabaristān; in the following year he minted coinage in Jurjān in the name of Fakhr al-Dawlah and presented him with a gold coin weighing a thousand *mithqāl*s and inscribed on one side with seven of his own verses.[8] In 379/989 he even had the audacity to contemplate seizing Baghdad, but an intially successful campaign was ruined by a flood, and his troops sustained considerable losses at the hands of the enemy. Ibn ᶜAbbād was accused of engineering the defeat and plotting against his master's life, though the historian Ibn al-Athīr (d. 630/1234), who, in retrospect, saw Ibn ᶜAbbād as a model statesman, claims that Fakhr al-Dawlah brought the disaster on himself by disregarding his vizier's advice.[9] Despite the defeat, the grave charges levelled against him and his master's displeasure, Ibn ᶜAbbād remained in office until his death in Rayy on 24 Ṣafar 385/30 March 995. We are told that Fakhr al-Dawlah visited him during his last illness and seemed deeply afflicted by his death; the people were loud in their grief and prostrated themselves before the funeral procession as it left the house of the deceased. Only one person refused to share in the mourning, his protégé the *qāḍī* ᶜAbd al-Jabbār, for which Fakhr al-Dawlah is said to have had him arrested and dismissed from office, confiscating three million dirhams from him to boot. Fakhr al-Dawlah, and Ibn ᶜAbbād's deputy and successor Abū ᵓl-ᶜAbbās al-Dabbī, observed a long period of mourning, and a large number of elegies were composed by the poets of the day, notably the Shīᶜī man of letters al-Sharīf al-Raḍī (d. 406/1016).[10] Ibn ᶜAbbād's coffin is said to have been suspended from chains as a mark of honour before being taken to Isfahan for burial; however, according to another, perhaps less reliable account, Fakhr al-Dawlah ordered al-Ḍabbī to make good his predecessor's

[8] Yāqūt, *Irshād*, VI (2), 275, 318–19. [9] *Kāmil*, IX, 64–5.
[10] Quoted in Thaᶜālibī, *Yatīmah*, III, 253–61.

defalcations and confiscated Ibn ʿAbbād's property.[11] Nevertheless, there are many accounts which bear witness to the high esteem in which Fakhr al-Dawlah held his vizier, who was widely respected both at home and abroad, as is shown by the fact that Nūḥ II b. Manṣūr had tried to poach him from the Buwayhids at a time when he was still a relatively inexperienced statesman and had probably not yet become the magnificent figure described in the sources, which depict him clad in military dress, with a large retinue and lavishly maintained household, shielded from importunate petitioners by several chamberlains.

In his heyday, Ibn ʿAbbād commanded the deference of all the grandees in the kingdom, who were, or pretended to be, loyally devoted to him; needless to say, he was fawned upon by the flatterers who are always to be found at court, and himself claimed to have been eulogized by 500 poets in a thousand *qaṣīdah*s in Arabic or Persian.[12] Despite the obvious exaggeration, it is quite true that many poets and poetasters were attracted by his reputation for generosity, which is difficult to assess, although he is said to have given away 100,000 dinars every year. On the other hand, he inevitably aroused the hostility of potential rivals, and his haughty bearing and machinations often provoked sharp criticism. An example is his relationship with Abū Bakr al-Khwārazmī (323–83/934–93), the poet and epistolographer, who was employed by him as a spy besides singing his praises at court. The pair quarrelled; there was an exchange of epigrams, and, when his former friend died, Ibn ʿAbbād composed some extremely spiteful lines which revealed a most unpleasant side to his character:

I questioned a messenger from Khurāsān: "Is it true that your poet Khwārazmī is dead?"
He said, "Yes," "On his gravestone in letters of plaster write *God curse all such thankless wretches*," I said.[13]

Ibn ʿAbbād was famous for barbed witticisms of this kind. Then there was the dispute with the historian and philosopher, Miskawayh (d. 421/1030), whose *Tajārib al-umam* provides us with a political portrait of Ibn ʿAbbād; the quarrel, which arose in 358/968 at the *majlis* of Ibn al-ʿAmīd in Rayy, resulted in a coarse attack in verse by Miskawayh,[14] and may have been prompted by Ibn ʿAbbād's hostility towards philosophers generally, an attitude stigmatized by his other famous adversary, Abū Ḥayyān al-Tawḥīdī. Tawḥīdī may well have been biased against his subject, but his works are almost the only source to provide details on the conduct, character and capabilities of the Buwayhid vizier. Tawḥīdī had heard

[11] Abū Shujāʿ, *Dhayl Tajārib*, III, 170 (Ar.), VI, 278–9 (trans.).
[12] Yāqūt, *Irshād*, VI (2), 310, 317. [13] *Dīwān*, 285.
[14] Quoted in Thaʿālibī, *Tatimmat al-Yatīmah*, I, 100.

favourable reports of Ibn ʿAbbād (whom he had already met in Baghdad in 358/968) and of the warm welcome he extended to literary men; he went to Rayy hoping to find a better post which would enable him to give up working as a copyist. His first encounter with the vizier was something of a mixed success and, much to his disappointment, Tawḥīdī found himself once more engaged as a copyist. He was instructed by Ibn ʿAbbād's librarian to copy out his master's *Rasāʾil* ("Epistles"); the work in question already ran to thirty volumes, according to the newcomer, who suggested that he should somehow try to extract its quintessence, but to no avail. At Ibn ʿAbbād's *majālis*, Tawḥīdī seized every opportunity to confront and even publicly to belittle Ibn ʿAbbād, who no doubt looked upon him as a literary rival.[15] Tawḥīdī returned to Baghdad, and there wrote a biting study of Ibn ʿAbbād and his predecessor Abū ʾl-Fatḥ Ibn al-ʿAmīd, *Akhlāq al-wazīrayn* (also known as *Mathālib al-wazīrayn*, "The Characters [or Vices] of the Two Viziers"). His stay in Rayy also provided occasional material for another work, *al-Imtāʿ wa ʾl-muʾānasah* ("Delight and Entertainment").[16]

Though Tawḥīdī was not an impartial witness, it seems fair to conclude on his evidence that the outstanding features of Ibn ʿAbbād's character were his inordinate pride, which often took a malicious turn, and a feeling of superiority which rendered him so singularly proud of everything he achieved that he tended to despise anyone else's work. Tawḥīdī tells us that – no doubt at the start of his career – Ibn ʿAbbād used to write poems in his own praise and give them to another poet to recite as his own.[17] Tawḥīdī considered him harsh, irascible, jealous and somewhat naïve, and thought that he had been spoilt by being given the total confidence of the amirs whom he served. He had a tendency to pass off other people's stories as his own, and what is more was in the habit of repeating rather improper anecdotes, albeit in an amusing manner. It must be admitted that he did not always associate with the most desirable characters; one of his protégés was Abū Dulaf al-Khazrajī, author of the famous *Qaṣīdah sāsāniyyah* ("Poem of the Criminal Underworld"), which was probably inspired by al-ʿUkbarī, another of the vizier's more raffish companions.[18] Ibn ʿAbbād revelled in the cant of the underworld (Banū Sāsān) and had no qualms about using it occasionally in his own poetry. He admired and extended his patronage to Ibn al-Ḥajjāj (330–91/941–1001), the great exponent of *sukhf* (scurrilous verse), and, according to Tawḥīdī, admitted to his household a real ruffian, a convicted and consequently one-armed brigand called al-Aqṭaʿ al-Munshid al-Kūfī, whom he employed to recite his religious poetry. He openly proclaimed his devotion to dissipation and his homosexuality in

[15] See p. 121. [16] See ibid. [17] *Imtāʿ*, I, 56–8.
[18] Thaʿālibī, *Yatīmah*, III, 104, 321–2; see pp. 129–30, below.

verses addressed to another rogue.[19] It goes without saying that his ordinary habits were not those of a pious Muslim, and it is hard to tell how sincere he was when, at an indeterminate date, he decided to assume the garb of a religious scholar, withdrew for a week to a place of so-called "repentance", and had the *fuqahāʾ* (doctors of religious law) bear witness to his contrition, as a prelude to declaiming *ḥadīth* to a crowd which included the *qāḍī* ʿAbd al-Jabbār.[20]

Tawḥīdī admits that, for all his faults, Ibn ʿAbbād was an extremely cultivated man, and recognizes his achievements in the field of philology. In this connection it is worth mentioning his relations with the grammarians al-Sīrāfī, whom he greatly admired, and Ibn Fāris (d. 395/1004). Ibn Fāris had served Abū ʾl-Fatḥ Ibn al-ʿAmīd and bore a grudge against Ibn ʿAbbād, who in turn gave a cold reception and scant remuneration to Ibn Fāris's recently compiled lexicographical work *Kitāb al-Ḥajar* ("The Book of the Stone"). However, when Ibn Fāris was summoned to Rayy as tutor to Fakhr al-Dawlah's son, Ibn ʿAbbād's attitude changed, and he began to praise the grammarian and claim to be his disciple, while Ibn Fāris, for his part, dedicated a famous grammatical treatise to the vizier and named it *al-Ṣāḥibī* in his honour.

Besides literature, Ibn ʿAbbād, like his father before him, was interested in *ḥadīth*, although, according to Tawḥīdī, he cared little for traditional religious studies and seems to have reserved most of his energies for *kalām* (theology). This fits in with what we know of his religious and political beliefs. The Buwayhid milieu favoured Twelver Shiʿism, but was subject to Zaydī[21] and Muʿtazilī influences; consequently Ibn ʿAbbād was a Muʿtazilī, as his prose writings and some of his poetry prove, and a Shīʿī, as is shown by most of his surviving verse; the famous "dialogue-poem" is particularly revealing in this respect:

> She said: What religion have you chosen for your success?
> I replied, I am a Shīʿī and a Muʿtazilī.[22]

Elsewhere, Ibn ʿAbbād claims to be a Zaydī, which would be consistent with the moderate Shīʿī leanings of the Muʿtazilah in the fourth/tenth century. His position regarding the imamate is not clear; W. Madelung stresses the deep influence that Ibn ʿAbbād exerted on Shiʿism in Rayy but considers that he was fundamentally a Muʿtazilī and opposed to the idea that ʿAlī b. Abī Ṭālib had been designated by the Prophet as his successor; a passage from what is probably a youthful work, *al-Ibānah*, appears to confirm this view.[23] However, in the course of time Ibn ʿAbbād may have

19 Tawḥīdī, *Akhlāq*, 184, 187, 214–15. 20 Yāqūt, *Irshād*, VI (2), 312.
21 See ch. 4, n. 14. 22 *Dīwān*, 39. 23 Madelung, "Imāmism", 20–1; *Ibānah*, 28.

changed his opinions and come to agree that ᶜAlī was indeed the Prophet's designated successor; this at least is what he says here and there in his poetry (though the impression remains that he did not reject the imamate of the first three caliphs). Nevertheless, he upheld Muᶜtazilism vigorously, maintaining agents to spread the doctrine in different countries[24] and, according to Tawḥīdī, sending propagandists out into the market-place for the same purpose, which is more than anyone claims he did for Shiᶜism. His strong adherence to Muᶜtazilism is illustrated by anecdotal evidence, and was probably inherited from his father, who had written a book called *Aḥkām al-Qurʾān* in support of the doctrine. Ample additional proof is given by his relationship with ᶜAbd al-Jabbār, the leading Muᶜtazilī theologian of his day, whom he summoned to become chief *qāḍī* (*qāḍī ʾl-quḍāh*) of Rayy, Qazwīn, Suhraward, Qumm, Sāwah and their dependencies; Ibn ᶜAbbād is supposed to have drawn up the letter of appointment himself and copied out all 700 lines of it on to as many pages of high-quality paper, and later extended ᶜAbd al-Jabbār's jurisdiction to the newly conquered Ṭabaristān.[25] Writers have remarked on the long-suffering Ibn ᶜAbbād showed towards his protégé, who behaved towards him in a somewhat cavalier fashion and whose attitude at the time of his death has already been described. At any rate, a large proportion of Ibn ᶜAbbād's doctrinal works are concerned with Muᶜtazilism, as can be seen from the following bibliography, which attempts to classify the titles which have come down to us according to their subject-matter, known or conjectured.

THEOLOGY (*KALĀM*) AND WORKS OF A POLITICAL OR RELIGIOUS NATURE

1 *al-Tadhkirah fī ʾl-uṣūl al-khamsah*, a concise exposition of the five "principles" of Muᶜtazilism (*al-uṣūl al-khamsah*),[26] probably intended as a manual for the propagandists mentioned above. Published from a manuscript dated 813 (1410).

2 *al-Ibānah ᶜan madhhab ahl al-ᶜadl bi-ḥujaj al-Qurʾān wa ʾl-ᶜaql* ("An Exposition of the Beliefs of Those who Hold that God is Just [i.e. the Muᶜtazilah], Drawing its Proofs from the Qurʾān and from Reason"). Like *al-Tadhkirah*, probably written before Ibn ᶜAbbād became vizier, and probably likewise intended as a propaganda manual; it consists of a summary refutation of various doctrinal

[24] See Ibn ᶜAbbād, *Rasāʾil*, 218–20.

[25] Ibn ᶜAbbād, *Rasāʾil*, 42–6, 34–9. On ᶜAbd al-Jabbār, cf. Kraemer, *Humanism*, 73, n. 140.

[26] See *EI*¹, "Muᶜtazila".

points held by different sects and religions from the point of view of those Muᶜtazilīs who believed in "*tawḥīd*," i.e. that God and His attributes are one. Not mentioned in early sources; published from a late manuscript.

3 *Risālah fī ʾl-Hidāyah wa ʾl-ḍalālāh* ("Epistle on Guidance and Error"), a reply to a question on right and wrong and a defence of divine justice and free will. Not mentioned in early sources, but survives in a manuscript dated 364 (974–5) with a colophon in the author's hand dated 366. Published.

4 *al-Qaḍāʾ wa ʾl-qadar*,[27] a refutation of predestination. Lost.

5 *(Mukhtaṣar) Asmāʾ Allāh wa-ṣifātih* ("A Concise Exposition of God's Names and Attributes"). Lost.

6 *al-Imāmah* ("The Imamate") recognizes ᶜAlī's claim to the imamate but does not reject the imamate of the first three caliphs. Fragments survive in quotation.

7 *Nahj al-sabīl fī ʾl-uṣūl* deals with ᶜAlī's qualities and titles and with *ḥadīth* concerning him. Survives, in an extract which follows the text of *al-Tadhkirah* (no. 1 above), in a manuscript of 1055/1645. Published.

8 *al-Zaydiyyah* ("The Zaydīs"), on the Shīᶜī sect of that name, and perhaps

8a *Kitāb al-Zaydayn* (if not identical with 8, "The Two Zayds", i.e. Zayd b. ᶜAlī b. Abī Ṭālib, who gave his name to the Zaydī sect, and another ᶜAlid). Both works are lost. Perhaps also

8b *Nuṣrat madhāhib al-Zaydiyyah*, supposedly a transcription of a discourse by Ibn ᶜAbbād on the Zaydīs, as noted down by an anonymous admirer of the vizier. Published.

9 *al-Risālah fī Aḥwāl ᶜAbd al-ᶜAẓīm al-Ḥasanī* deals with an important ᶜAlid mentioned by almost all Shīᶜī biographers. Published from a late copy of a manuscript dated 516 (1122).

HISTORY

10 *ᶜUnwān al-maᶜārif wa-dhikr al-khalāʾif* ("An Epitome of Knowledge and an Account of the Caliphs"), a small treatise, possibly some kind of manual, which gives a short biography of the Prophet and then lists those who have held or usurped the title of caliph. Published from a manuscript of 420/1029.

Other, lost works which probably belonged to the same category are:

[27] For these terms see *EI*², "Ḳaḍāʾ", "Ḳadar".

11 *Taʾrīkh al-mulk wa ʾkhtilāf al-duwal* ("The History of Kingship and Dynasties") and

12 *Kitāb al-Wuzarāʾ* ("The Book of Viziers").

13 *Kitāb al-Anwār* appears to have dealt with the history of the imams of the Twelver Shīʿah; a few fragments survive in Ibn Ṭāwūs, *al-Yaqīn fī imrat amīr al-muʾminīn*.[28]

PHILOLOGY, LEXICOGRAPHY AND METRICS

14 *al-Farq bayn al-ḍād wa ʾl-ẓāʾ*, a short treatise for scribes, who often confuse the letters *ḍād* and *ẓāʾ*. Not mentioned in early sources; survives in one manuscript. Published.

15 *al-Muḥīṭ bi ʾl-lughah*, a dictionary arranged, like the earliest Arabic dictionary, *Kitāb al-ʿayn*, attributed to al-Khalīl b. Aḥmad,[29] according to the point of articulation of the first radical of the words from the back to the front of the mouth. Several incomplete manuscripts; one complete version in the Iraqi Museum, Baghdad. The first part (the letter *ʿayn*) has been published.

16 *al-Iqnāʿ fī ʾl-arūḍ wa-takhrīj al-qawāfī*: as the title indicates, a concise treatise on metrics, consisting of some general remarks followed by a technical discussion of the fifteen metres. Two manuscripts, of which Bibliothèque Nationale, no. 6042, is of forty folios. Unpublished.[30]

17 *Jawharat al-Jamharah* ("The Essence of the *Jamharah*"), an abridgement of Ibn Durayd's (d. 321/933) dictionary, *Jamharat al-lughah*; said to exist in a hitherto untraced manuscript.

18 *al-Ḥajar*, a lexicographical work on stones; quoted in *al-Ṣāḥibī* by Ibn Fāris, who had himself written a similar work.

19 *al-Waqf wa ʾl-ibtidāʾ* ("On Pausal and Initial Forms/Utterances"), a juvenilium. Lost.

(*al-Maqṣūr wa ʾl-mamdūd*, a grammatical work once attributed to Ibn ʿAbbād (ed. P. Brönnle, London, 1900) is probably by the fourth/tenth century grammarian Ibn Wallād.)[31]

LITERARY CRITICISM

20 *al-Kashf ʿan masāwiʾ shiʿr al-Mutanabbī* ("An Exposition of the Faults in al-Mutanabbī's Poetry"). Towards the end of 352/963, Ibn ʿAbbād invited al-Mutanabbī to Isfahan; the poet did not deign to

[28] Quoted in Āl Yāsīn, *al-Ṣāḥib b. ʿAbbād*, 242. [29] See *CHALUP*, 15.

[30] Summary and extracts, Āl Yāsīn, *al-Ṣāḥib b. ʿAbbād*, 202–6. [31] Ibid., 254.

reply, but accepted an invitation sent to him at the same time by Ibn al-ʿAmīd and was received by him with honour in Arrajān in 354/965. *Al-Kashf* cannot be dated precisely, but appears to have been written during the lifetime of Ibn al-ʿAmīd, probably before 360/970.[32] Ibn ʿAbbād claims to have composed the work in reply to a challenge to put his verbal criticisms into writing, and denies that it was written in a spirit of denigration. He acknowledges the influence of the great third/ninth-century scholars Mubarrad and Thaʿlab, but the work is representative of aspects of fourth/tenth-century criticism and probably to a great extent reflects the methods taught to Ibn ʿAbbād by his guardian Ibn al-ʿAmīd, specimens of whose criticisms are given at the beginning of the treatise. *Al-Kashf* prompted the then *qāḍī* of Rayy, al-Jurjānī, to write a reply, *al-Wasāṭah bayna ʾl-Mutanabbī wa-khuṣūmih*, in which he tried to steer a middle course between the poet's admirers and detractors.[33] Published.

21 *al-Amthāl al-sāʾirah min shiʿr al-Mutanabbī* ("Proverbial Passages in Mutanabbī's Poetry"), an anthology composed for Fakhr al-Dawlah; not mentioned in early sources. Published from a late copy of a contemporary manuscript.

CORRESPONDENCE AND *BELLES-LETTRES*

22 *al-Rūznāmajah*, a kind of journal – as its Persian title indicates – in which Ibn ʿAbbād noted down for Ibn al-ʿAmīd all that he saw and heard in Baghdad from 347/958. Extracts preserved in quotation by Yāqūt and al-Thaʿālibī. Published jointly with *al-Amthāl al-sāʾirah*.

23 *al-Rasāʾil* ("The Epistles"), Ibn ʿAbbād's longest and most important work, comprising his official and private correspondence. Tawḥīdī speaks of thirty volumes (see above); Yāqūt mentions only ten. Originally in fifteen volumes, according to the eleventh/seventeenth-century Ḥājjī Khalīfah's bibliography *Kashf al-ẓunūn*, it now survives only in the form of a selection in a Paris manuscript of 577/1182. This contains twenty sections, generally of ten letters each. These are archival documents of great historical interest,[34] but as yet under-researched. The chapters have received the following headings, which give a general idea of their contents:

> News of victories and conquests; letters of appointment; safe-conducts, orders of taxation, proclamations, directions for the observance of leap years; the Pilgrimage, public works, defence; on winning the hearts of

[32] Ibid., introd., 19. [33] See pp. 375ff. [34] See Mottahedeh, "Administration", 36–43.

the defenders of the [Muᶜtazilī] cause by acts of generosity; letters of conciliation, injunctions to civil obedience and censure of family strife; praise and eulogy; blame and censure; letters of congratulation and acceptance of congratulations; letters of condolence; letters to friends in affectionate and playful vein; letters of thanks; strictures of inefficiency and rebukes [for disobedience]; self-vindication and mollification; letters of intercession; injunctions to tax-gatherers to levy money, act honestly and conduct themselves properly; courtesies (*ādāb*) and homilies; select passages and postscripts; letters of particular beauty; letters on diverse subjects.

(The idea that Ibn ᶜAbbād was an expert on medicine arises from a letter included in last section, which was in fact written by al-Thaᶜālibī to Ibn ᶜAbbād's deputy al-Ḍabbī when the latter was ill.) Published.

23a *al-Kāfī fī ʾl-rasāʾil/al-tarassul*, probably a selection from *al-Rasāʾil*, listed in several sources. Lost.

MISCELLANEOUS

24 *Akhbār Abī ʾl-ᶜAynāʾ*, a monograph on the third/ninth century philologist, wit and poet. Lost.

25 *al-Aᶜyād wa-faḍāʾil al-Nayrūz* ("Festivals, and the Virtues of Nawrūz [the Persian New Year]"). Lost.

POETRY

26 *Dīwān*. Ibn ᶜAbbād's poetry was collected into a *dīwān* which is referred to by medieval and later sources, but the only surviving manuscript is a copy, dated 1172 (1758–9), of what is clearly only a selection, containing fifty-five pieces of varying length. To the material contained in this Hyderabad manuscript M. Ḥ. Āl Yāsīn, in his edition of 1384/1965, added a further 267 poems and fragments, mainly taken from al-Thaᶜālibī's *Yatīmat al-dahr*.[35] The second edition (1394/1974) adds a further twenty-seven short pieces. However, these editions may give a somewhat distorted idea of Ibn ᶜAbbād as a poet since they omit a number of pieces on grounds of obscenity. The two main topics treated in the published *Dīwān* are Muᶜtazilism, and the glorification of the Prophet and of ᶜAlī and some of his descendants; occasionally, as in *qaṣīdah* no. 1, the two

[35] Abū Manṣūr ᶜAbd al-Malik b. Muḥammad al-Thaᶜālibī (d. 429/1038); his *Yatīmah* and *Tatimmat al-Yatīmah* are major sources for the poets of the period, not least those of Ibn ᶜAbbād's circle, and contain a wealth of anecdotal material (cf. nn. 14, 18, above).

subjects are combined.[36] In addition, the *Dīwān* contains a number of impromptu verses, e.g. no. 151 (a description of apples), eulogies of Ibn ᶜAbbād's guardian Ibn al-ᶜAmīd (nos. 50, 146, 201, 202) and of his master Fakhr al-Dawlah (nos. 84, 229), and epigrams (nos. XXVII, 2, 3, 4). Noteworthy is no. 222, a highly abusive poem addressed to a Persian who had called the Arabs snake-eaters, a standard accusation of barbarity;[37] Ibn ᶜAbbād ripostes by accusing Persians of incest – an equally standard insult referring to the pre-Islamic Zoroastrian practice of consanguineous marriage. This suggests that, in spite of his Iranian origins, Ibn ᶜAbbād was no Shuᶜūbī; nor does he seem to have been influenced by Persian culture, though Persian was probably his mother tongue and, as we have seen, he may have patronized poets writing in Persian, and despite the fact that he himself wrote a monograph on the Persian New Year Festival (no. 25, above) – which, however, was widely observed in the Muslim world.

Some of the *qaṣīdah*s are neo-classical in form, but display a remarkable propensity for verbal acrobatics. Ibn ᶜAbbād is famous for a series of poems each of which was distinguished by the absence of one particular letter of the alphabet (though it is said he was unable to dispense with *wāw*); of these, two have survived; no. XXIX, in praise of the Prophet, which does not use a single *alif*, and no. XXXI, an eighty-five line piece in praise of ᶜAlī, without a single *sīn*. In a similar vein, no. XXXV consists of thirty-three lines in which the beginnings as well as the ends of all the lines rhyme in *ību*, while in no. XXXIII the twenty-eight first hemistichs begin with the twenty-eight letters of the Arabic alphabet, in order, followed by a word beginning with the same letter, as in "A is for apple", e.g. in the first line, *Alifun: amīru ʾl-muʾminīna ᶜAliyyū; Bāʾūn: bihī ruknu ʾl-yaqīni qawiyyū*, which might be loosely rendered "A, the Amir of the Faithful, ᶜAlī; B, Before whom the true faith doth rally"; proud of this *tour de force*, Ibn ᶜAbbād dedicated the poem to the Prophet in the hope that he would act as his intercessor. Another poem, no. II, sixty-five lines long, was considered so original that it was made the subject of a commentary and has survived in a separate manuscript; it has the form of a dialogue with an interlocutress who reproaches the poet with neglecting love-poetry (*ghazal*) and goes on to question him on points of doctrine; the first hemistich of each line

[36] Roman numerals refer to part I of the *Dīwān*, Arabic numerals to the supplement.
[37] See pp. 46, 88, and 279–80.

begins with *qālat*, "She said", and the second with *fa-qultu*, "I replied".

As well as writing poetry himself, Ibn ᶜAbbād apparently compiled an anthology of favourite pieces by other hands:

27 *al-Safīnah*; al-Thaᶜālibī quotes examples from it which he admits to having copied out by stealth, since Ibn ᶜAbbād seems to have kept the collection secret. Lost.

The remaining titles cannot be classified with any degree of certainty:

28 *al-Taᶜlīl*. Lost.

29 *al-Shawāhid*. Lost.

30 *al-Fuṣūl al-muhadhdhibah li ʾl-ᶜuqūl*, probably a collection of maxims. Lost.[38]

Judgement on Ibn ᶜAbbād by his contemporaries and by posterity has been based less on his achievements as a vizier than on assessments of his literary works or of his character; indeed, even when his personal conduct is under discussion, there is scarcely any mention of the fact that for most of his life Ibn ᶜAbbād enjoyed almost limitless power as head of the administration and the army, reaped victories, and managed to fill the coffers of the state without excessive hardship to the people, whose prosperity he was at pains to ensure; his government upheld the rule of law, and extended protection to men of religion and letters. Ibn ᶜAbbād's "Epistles" bear witness to the effectiveness of his administrative methods, but this was not how medieval writers saw them: they appreciated them for their style, which established Ibn ᶜAbbād as a writer against whom others were to be measured. Since his literary achievements inevitably aroused jealousy as well as admiration, the opinions of him expressed by contemporaries are often diametrically opposed: at one extreme are the unflattering and sometimes cruel portraits painted by several of Tawḥīdī's informants in *Akhlāq al-wazīrayn* (Tawḥīdī's own overall appraisal of Ibn ᶜAbbād is slightly more temperate); at the other are the adulatory expressions used by Thaᶜālibī, who speaks of the magic, indeed the inimitabilty (*iᶜjāz*), of Ibn ᶜAbbād's language, using a term which sets it on a par with the Qurʾān, and declares that words fail him to describe it,[39] while Ibn al-Nadīm calls him the nonpareil of the age, both for prose and for verse.[40] Modern histories of Arabic literature are scarcely less lavish in their praise.

[38] References to the sources which cite the works listed in the bibliography above are given in Āl Yāsīn, *al-Ṣāḥib b. ᶜAbbād*.

[39] *Yatīmah*, III, 169. For the critical concept of Quranic inimitabilty, see pp. 362–6, below.

[40] *Fibrist*, Tajaddud, 150/Dodge, I, 297.

Like most of his contemporaries, Ibn ᶜAbbād quotes frequently from the Qurʾān and from poetry and proverbs, and his prose is highly allusive and erudite; but it was the practice of using *sajᶜ* – rhymed and rhymically balanced prose – to enhance elegance, which was only just becoming fashionable when he wrote,[41] for which Ibn ᶜAbbād was most noted. But though he did not use *sajᶜ* indiscriminately, as did later writers, he attracted criticism as well as approbation. Tawḥīdī complains that he twists his ideas to fit the requirements of rhyme – a trick which his detractors sometimes caricatured. Ibn ᶜAbbād is also criticized for his excessive indulgence in alliteration, a concomitant of the quest for rhyme, and he uses copious and occasionally strained metaphors and comparisons, as might be expected in a medium which draws upon poetic devices. Nevertheless, his prose contains many graceful turns of phrase, even when dealing with as dry a subject as the duties of a *muḥtasib* (inspector of weights, measures and public morals),[42] and his conceits are often apt and his rhetoric functional, as in the following examples. To a bereaved friend:

When I heard of [the virtues of] the blessed deceased – God sanctify her passing and raise her to rank surpassing among righteous women – I mourned her as a man mourns an honoured mother, honourable kinswomen, and grieved even as my lord grieves, as one who shares alike in weal and woe. I will dwell no more on the image of my own sorrow, for I know that my lord will picture my feelings sooner than I can depict them.[43]

On a civil disturbance:

The unthinking among them [i.e. the inhabitants of Qazwīn] are the more infatuated, the fuddleheads the more befooled, that this folly is of no short date and has continued without abate; the pace has not been forced by us, matters have been let to run their course by us: therefore the people reckon that our tolerance and sufferance, our disregard and insouciance, will proceed as of ordinary in the manner that has become customary. Little do they heed that fate will not be deceived nor the sinner reprieved! [Cf. Qurʾān, iii.145][44]

Ibn ᶜAbbād himself is alleged to have said, "Prose is scattered hither and thither like flying sparks, but poetry will last as long as graven stone", and the fact that his younger contemporary, the North African anthologist al-Ḥuṣrī (d. 413/1022), who reported this saying,[45] collected more of Ibn ᶜAbbād's poetry than of his prose, may be taken as an indication of a general preference in the Middle Ages. To modern eyes, certainly, though Ibn ᶜAbbād's poetry shares the contemporary tendency towards verbal artifice,

[41] For the earlier history of *sajᶜ*, *CHALUP*, 175–6, 180–5, and pp. 62–4, above, 126, below.
[42] *Rasāʾil*, 39–41. [43] Ibid., 136; this and following trans. J. A. [44] Ibid., 92.
[45] *Zahr*, 640; the idea, often voiced by medieval Arab critics, is that the structure of poetry, its metre and rhyme, hold it together and enable it to be accurately preserved.

it is relatively simple and by and large less stiff than his formal prose. But, though the *Dīwān* consists mainly of eulogies of the Prophet and ᶜAlī and contains some very effective lines which bear the stamp of practised craftsmanship, it is difficult to detect in it any signs of genuine feeling, either religious or poetic; Ibn ᶜAbbād was a highly accomplished rhymer and nothing more. In sum, he was a *kātib*, a competent versifier and talented epistolographer, who came into his own at a time when rhymed prose was first becoming what it was long to remain, the favoured medium of administrative scribes. However, any attempts to assess Ibn ᶜAbbād's contribution to Arabic literary development must bear in mind that, of the surviving works that are attributed to him, part at least may be the work of other hands.

CHAPTER 6

ABŪ ḤAYYĀN AL-TAWḤĪDĪ

CONTEMPORARY PERSPECTIVES

Abū Ḥayyān ᶜAlī b. Muḥammad b. al-ᶜAbbās al-Tawḥīdī was born, in either Iraq or Fārs, between 310–20/922–32; he died in Shiraz in 414/1023. His life was spent under Shīᶜī Buwayhid rule, and on several occasions he served the Buwayhids, though himself a Sunnī; but, although his beliefs were not those of the Shīᶜī ruling classes, neither were they always congenial to his fellow Sunnīs. Consequently, though he now holds an acknowledged place in Arabic literature, he underwent a long period of neglect. Besides their literary merit, his writings are of considerable historical interest, and new editions of his works, together with manuscripts discovered over the past thirty years, provide valuable material for the detailed study of social and intellectual developments in the fourth/tenth century.

Medieval sources and modern studies alike (the latter beginning in 1883 with Aḥmad Fāris Shidyāq, one of the movers of the nineteenth-century Arab "renaissance" or *Nahḍah*)[1] reveal a wide range of interest in Tawḥīdī, a fact which indicates how varied, and sometimes controversial, were Tawḥīdī's own beliefs. Of the main sources, which date from the seventh/thirteenth to the ninth/fifteenth century, over half are hostile, and the complete lack of biographical sources during the two centuries following Tawḥīdī's death[2] is probably best explained by the fact of his intellectual non-conformism and unflinching promotion of humanist ideals, which made him a suspect figure in the eyes of many Muslims. Under the "Sunnī restoration" which followed the fall of the Buwayhids after Tawḥīdī's death, the political and religious climate may well have been such as to deter any writer from undertaking an apology or even a straightforward biography of Tawḥīdī. Yāqūt (d. 626/1229) first remarked on the lack of early sources, and himself composed an apt and eloquent biographical

[1] Bergé, "Continuité", 269.
[2] For citations of his works during this period, see Tawḥīdī, *Akhlāq*, introd., *ẓā*ᵓ.

sketch of the writer, whom he calls "the philosopher of cultured men, and a man of culture among philosophers" (*faylasūf al-udabā*ʾ *wa-adīb al-falāsifah*).[3] It is impossible, however, to apply a single label to Tawḥīdī, though the following points may be borne in mind as helpful to an understanding of his thought. Firstly, the juridical rite (*madhhab*) to which he belonged was probably Shafiᶜism;[4] secondly, he was deeply sympathetic to Sufism, and this sympathy pervaded his attitude to other issues. Thirdly, an opponent both of Shiᶜism and Muᶜtazilism, Tawḥīdī supported not only Sunnism, but also the use of reason (*ᶜaql*), but was nevertheless deeply mistrustful of dogmatic theology (*kalām*) and the sterile debates to which it gave rise. Consequently, though he was interested in contemporary intellectual developments and though Ashᶜarī[5] influences are discernible in his thought, he neither subscribed to nor, apparently, was ever claimed by any school of theology. However, if his support of reason did not make a *mutakallim* of him, still less can he be called a free-thinker (*zindīq*), an accusation often unfairly levelled at him over the centuries. The nineteenth- and twentieth-century writers who rediscovered Tawḥīdī after a break of several centuries make two, more general points about his beliefs. For them, Tawḥīdī is a Muslim humanist who, in seeking to understand both God and man, expresses and defines a human ideal, though well aware of the difficulties of achieving it. Modern scholars view Tawḥīdī's works as a rich source of spiritual and intellectual themes, which provided matter for contemporaries and successors alike and remains strikingly relevant today. Accordingly, many modern Muslims rightly believe that Tawḥīdī has a prominent role to play in cross-cultural dialogue and in providing a bridge between Islam and the wider contemporary world.

Not least important to an understanding of Tawḥīdī is his love of literature, of whose function he cherished a high ideal:

> [the ideal man of letters] will not think it the least of his duties to study fluency and command versatility, for he may be called upon to use his craft (*ṣināᶜah*) to soothe resentment and remove dissent and to fulfil missions of state, to render critical assistance to the great (*al-khāṣṣah*) and important service for the benefit of the commonalty (*al-ᶜāmmah*): hence his wit must always rove far afield and his pen must follow it.[6]

[3] *Irshād*, VI (5), 380.

[4] Its attraction for Tawḥīdī would have been that, at this period, Shafiᶜism "by restricting analogical reasoning within definite limits" aimed "to create for traditionalism a science which could be used as an antidote to *kalām* [the tool of the rationalist Muᶜtazilīs]", Makdisi, "Juridical theology", 12.

[5] See p. 6.

[6] *ᶜUlūm*, 289 [Ar.], 269 [French trans.].

BIBLIOGRAPHY AND CHRONOLOGY OF WORKS

Tawḥīdī's surviving works, which cover over 5,000 printed pages, may be classed under five headings:

1 *Adab* bearing on philosophical and religious themes:
al-Baṣāʾir wa ʾl-dhakhāʾir ("Insights and Treasures")
al-Imtāʿ wa ʾl-muʾānasah ("Delight and Entertainment")
al-Muqābasāt ("Conversations")
al-Hawāmil wa ʾl-shawāmil ("Searching [Questions] and Compendious [Answers]"), jointly with the historian–philosopher Miskawayh, d. 421/1030[7]
Risālat al-Ḥayāh ("Of Life")
al-Risālah fī ʾl-ʿUlūm ("Of the Branches of Knowledge")
al-Ṣadāqah wa ʾl-ṣadīq ("Of Friendship and Friends")

2 Prose polemics:
Akhlāq al-wazīrayn ("The Characters of the Two Viziers")
Riwāyat al-Saqīfah, a discussion of the imamate[8]
al-Risālah ilā ʾl-Qāḍī Abī Sahl ("Epistle to the *Qāḍī* Abū Sahl")

3 Literary history:
Taqrīẓ al-Jāḥiẓ ("In Praise of Jāḥiẓ")

4 Calligraphy:
Risālah fī ʿIlm al-kitābah ("On Penmanship")

5 Mysticism:
al-Ishārāt al-ilāhiyyah ("Divine Intimations")

Tawḥīdī's first work was *al-Baṣāʾir*, begun in 350/961 when he was in his thirties and still studying under the great scholars of Baghdad; it was completed around 365/975. His next works were written about 370/980 when he was in his late forties, had found his vocation as a writer and was anxious to find patronage in government circles: *al-Hawāmil*, *al-ʿUlūm* and *Akhlāq al-wazīrayn*, the latter written after he had broken with and left the service of al-Ṣāḥib Ibn ʿAbbād in Rayy. On his return to Baghdad, Tawḥīdī attended the gatherings (*majālis*) of the vizier Ibn Saʿdān, on which he based the forty "nights" of *al-Imtāʿ* (written between 373–5/983–5). During the same period he began work on *al-Ṣadāqah*. *Al-Muqābasāt* was composed about 382/992, probably in Shiraz when he was trying to attract the

[7] See Arkoun, "L'humanisme arabe".

[8] See Keilani, *Abū Ḥayyān*, 65–70. All Tawḥīdī's writings on law are lost; for the titles of these and of other lost or fragmentary works, see Bergé, *Humanisme*, 413–15; for fragments attributed to Tawḥīdī, see *EI*², "Abū Ḥayyān".

patronage of the vizier al-Dalajī. In 410/1019 he rewrote the first draft of *al-Ṣadāqah*, but later in the same year he burned all his works, an action which he explains in *al-Risālah ilā ʾl-Qāḍī Abī Sahl*. Nevertheless, he still enjoyed a following in Shiraz, and *al-Ishārāt* and *al-Ḥayāh* were written there at about this time, his last surviving works before his death in 414/1023.

Tawḥīdī's writings offer insights both into the thought and background of some of the leading figures of his day and into more general aspects of Islamic culture. In the fourth/tenth century, *adab* covered a wider range than ever before, reflecting the developments taking place in all aspects of contemporary thought, whether religion, mysticism, science or philosophy, art, aesthetics or the linguistic sciences. Echoes of all these concerns are found in Tawḥīdī's writings, and to this extent his works illustrate the age in which he lived. But if Tawḥīdī was shaped by Buwayhid society, he in turn, to some degree, helped to shape that society. Yet, however true it is that a writer's works cannot be understood without reference to the public for which they were designed, it is equally true that no writer is purely the product of his background, and it may be helpful to bear in mind the concept of "basic personality type", and to distinguish between Tawḥīdī as a "type" of the fourth/tenth century *adīb* in the first phase of his development, during which he assimilated background influences, and the later, mature Tawḥīdī, who had to some extent transcended direct influence.[9]

There is no record of Tawḥīdī's date of birth, but it may be deduced to within ten years from what he himself says in *al-Risālah ilā ʾl-Qāḍī Abī Sahl*, where he mentions that he is approaching ninety.[10] If he was over eighty in 400/1009–10, he must have been born before 320/932 and after 310/922. Differing accounts are given of his birthplace. Tawḥīdī himself throws little light on his origins. We do not know whether he was of Arab or Iranian stock, nor whether Arabic or Persian was his mother tongue. If he was indeed Iranian, it is hard to say how this may have affected his subsequent development, for though most sources claim he was born in Shiraz, we know him as an Arabic writer, and as a Sunnī hostile to the Shiʿism which flourished in the Iranian court circles in which he moved. If we are to go by an anecdote in *Akhlāq al-wazīrayn*, he was unable to understand some remarks which Ibn ʿAbbād made in Persian;[11] elsewhere, he extols the

[9] R. Linton, *The Cultural Background of Personality* (New York, 1945); for the application of the concept to Islamic studies, see M. Arkoun, "Révélation, vérité et histoire d'après l'oeuvre de Ġazâlî", *Studia Islamica*, XXXI, 1970.

[10] Yāqūt, *Irshād*, VI (5), 388. Shāljī argues that *tisʿīn* (ninety) may be a misreading of *sabʿīn* (seventy), and revises the chronology of Tawḥīdī's life and works accordingly, *al-Risālah al-Baghdādiyyah* (Abū ʾl-Muṭahhar al-Azdī, attrib. Tawḥīdī, ed. ʿA. Shāljī, Beirut, 1980), introd., 16–17.

[11] *Akhlāq*, 306.

pre-eminent virtues of the Arabic language and speaks of Persian – together with the languages of the Greeks, Hindus, blacks, etc. – as a tongue of which he knows little.[12] In any case, it seems that Tawḥīdī's parents took him to Baghdad when he was still a child, and that he grew up in an Arab, not a Persian, setting.

The Baghdad of Tawḥīdī's childhood came under the *de facto* rule of the Shīʿī, Iranian Buwayhids in 334/945. The Sunnī caliph was allowed to retain nominal sovereignty, but this did not prevent a growing antagonism and frequent clashes between the long-established Shīʿī and Sunnī populations of Baghdad. Contemporary historians describe many violent disturbances of this kind, often fomented by the popular preachers (*quṣṣāṣ*). Such scenes, to which Tawḥīdī must certainly have been a witness, were a visible reminder of irreversible sectarian and doctrinal differences. Little is known about Tawḥīdī's earliest years in Baghdad or about his family's social standing, though it has always been assumed that he came from a very humble background: some sources say that his father was a seller of dates (*tawḥīd*).[13] Perhaps the fact that Tawḥīdī himself never mentions his parentage may be taken as confirmation of his lowly origins. We know a great deal more, however, about the cultural setting in which Tawḥīdī passed his first thirty or so years. Throughout the Buwayhid empire, as earlier in the ʿAbbāsid empire, Arabic remained the language of polite literature, learning and the administration, and thus provided a bond between all intellectuals, whatever their background or beliefs. It is clear from Tawḥīdī's writings that he was familiar with Ismāʿīlī doctrines and had been personally acquainted with members of the Ismāʿīlī secret society, the Ikhwān al-Ṣafāʾ (Pure/Sincere Brethren).[14] He was, as we know, strongly attracted to Sufism, which he regarded as grounded on science and wisdom, and often quotes from Sufi masters. *Falsafah* too played an important part in Tawḥīdī's education. Greek philosophy was much in vogue in some Muslim and non-Muslim circles alike, but also aroused much unease, and there is no doubt that Tawḥīdī assimilated something of both attitudes. The most important influence on Tawḥīdī, though, was to be Ashʿarism. Ashʿarism was in some ways an offshoot of Muʿtazilism; and

[12] *Imtāʿ*, I, 77.

[13] Ibn Khallikān, *Wafāyāt*, V, 113, trans. de Slane, *Biographical Dictionary*, III, 264.

[14] Stern, "New information", 405–6. For Ismāʿīlī Shiʿism, cf. pp. 199, 420, 445, below. For the membership and aims of the group which anonymously produced the "Epistles of the Sincere Brethern" see *EI*², "Ikhwān al-Ṣafāʾ"; the "Epistles", encyclopaedic in range and eclectic in their intellectual sources, but heavily influenced by neo-Platonism, expound a doctrine which aims "secondarily at securing men's happiness in this world" but primarily at drawing the soul towards "a true and universal vision of the realities of creation" and so preparing it "to rise through the celestial spheres when at last released from the body, and later to merge itself in the universal Soul, and then, with the latter, in the Intellect" (ibid.).

though Muᶜtazilism itself had failed politically,[15] it survived as a doctrine whose reliance – some saw it as over-reliance – on reason (*ᶜaql*) could only be defeated by reason. As such it offered a worthy target to would-be champions of the Sunnī faith. Early on, Tawḥīdī also came under the influence of popular Sunnism of a brand akin to Sufism, as expounded by Ibn Samᶜūn, a fearless and independent preacher with a large following, who was admired by both Ashᶜarīs and Ḥanbalīs[16] but remained free of doctrinal ties and was bold enough to stand up to the Buwayhid amir ᶜAḍud al-Dawlah himself.[17]

The turning-point in Tawḥīdī's development came in 350/961, when he resolved to become a writer. He decided to write in prose – he was later to disclaim any talent for poetry[18] – and his aims, initially, were modest: *al-Baṣāʾir*, his first book, was to be no more than an anthology of anecdotes and aphorisms, covering his reading and encounters during the years 350–65/961–75.[19] Nevertheless, although, in this age of patronage, Tawḥīdī presents himself to his readers as an independent author who has received no commission and expects no remuneration, he lets it be understood that he is no amateur, takes his task seriously and is well aware of the rules of his craft: concision, appositeness and the avoidance of everything common-place. The aim of the book is to impart *adab*, a varied and demanding field of accomplishments to which Tawḥīdī devotes over thirty terms in his preface alone, and which he places on a high moral plane:

> I guarantee you that in perusing these pages you will not fail to find pearls of wisdom and treasures of edification, the foremost and sublimest of these being what is contained in the Holy Qurʾān, followed by the *sunnah* of the Prophet . . . the third source is . . . reason (*ᶜaql*), for reason is the king (*malik*) to whom we look for protection, the arbiter (*ḥakam*) to whose authority we turn on all occasions . . . Reason is the link between God and man, the stamp of God's word, the token of His Prophet . . . Its law (*sharīᶜah*) is truthfulness; it enjoins righteousness (*amruh al-maᶜrūf*); its aristocracy (*khāṣṣah*) is discernment (*ikhtiyār*), its vizier knowledge (*ᶜilm*), its edict discretion (*ḥilm*), its treasury kindness and its army good works . . . The fourth [source] is experience, and I shall also adduce something of the statecraft (*siyāsah*) of the Persians and the philosophy (*falsafah*) of the Greeks; for wisdom is the goal of all believers and must be taken wherever it is found . . . Wisdom is truth, and truth needs no lineage, rather all things derive their lineage (*nasab*) from truth.[20]

The writing and publication of *al-Baṣāʾir*, the first-fruits of Tawḥīdī's education, took fifteen years, and during this time he carefully noted how it was received by the public.[21] But if he was sensitive to contemporary opinion, he was no less conscious of the writer's – even the prose-writer's –

[15] See pp. 5–6. [16] Ibid. [17] Laoust, *Schismes*, 176. [18] *Imtāᶜ*, I, 134. [19] Ibid., 3.
[20] *Baṣāʾir*, I, 6; trans. J. A. [21] Ibid., III, 296.

debt to precedent, a debt acknowledged in the sources listed in *al-Baṣāʾir* (these include the works of al-Jāḥiẓ, Ibn al-Aʿrābī's[22] *Nawādir*, al-Mubarrad's *Kāmil*, Ibn Qutaybah's *ʿUyūn al-akhbār*[23] and Abū ʿAbdullāh Muḥammad b. ʿAbdūs al-Jahshiyārī's *Kitāb al-Wuzarāʾ* or "Book of Viziers"),[24] as well as in a separate work, *Taqrīẓ al-Jāḥiẓ* ("In Praise of Jāḥiẓ" preserved in Yāqūt's *Irshād*).

The first profession Tawḥīdī is known to have practised was that of copyist. This was no menial calling; it was often the prerogative of a highly educated élite of men of learning but no private means who could be relied upon to produce an accurate text. Many of Tawḥīdī's own teachers had been copyists, for example the Christian philosopher Yaḥyā b. ʿAdī.[25] The evidence suggests that Tawḥīdī earned a comfortable living. But in 362/972, after losing all his possessions as a result of political disturbances,[26] he realized the precariousness of his position, and later seems to have viewed his profession with scorn: "My sole reason for leaving Iraq to come knocking on this [i.e. Ibn ʿAbbād's] door, rubbing shoulders with those who seek patronage here, was to have done with that wretched profession, for there was no lack of work for copyists in Baghdad."[27]

He therefore decided to seek his fortune further afield. Of what kind of a wider world it was that Tawḥīdī now moved in his later writings give us some idea. The first of the forces governing society was the authority (*sulṭān*) of the rulers, which "is . . . nothing but force, coercion and caprice, pomp, pleasure and frivolity". As for the ruling classes generally, Tawḥīdī makes no distinction between rulers and their agents and hangers-on; all are tarred with the same brush, and they make common cause.[28] Even so, their power can never be absolute, for the common people are sometimes a force to be reckoned with, a topic which Tawḥīdī once discussed with the vizier Ibn Saʿdān after his return to Baghdad:

One night, the vizier said: "By God, I learn to my fury that the common people (*al-ʿāmmah*) discuss what we rulers say, talk of our affairs and try to pry into our secrets . . . I don't know what to do about them; I have a good mind, every now and again, to chop off a few tongues, hands and feet; perhaps that would make them have a proper respect . . . Why can't they mind their own business, ply their trades and stick to their duties?"[29]

22 Philologist and *rāwī* (transmitter of poetry), d. *c.* 231/846. 23 See p. 30.

24 See *EI*², "al-Djahshiyārī". A scholar, *adīb* and chronicler (d. 331/942) whose *K. al-Wuzarāʾ* was the product of his own close association with high administrative circles and "lays quite as much emphasis upon men's characters and intellectual qualities as upon their administrative or political activities" (ibid.).

25 D. 364/974; a pupil of al-Fārābī; see Ibn al-Nadīm, *Fihrist*, Tajaddud, 322/Dodge, II, 631.

26 Described in *Imtāʿ*, I, 160–1. 27 *Akhlāq*, 306. 28 *Ṣadāqah*, 5. 29 *Imtāʿ*, III, 85–6.

Tawḥīdī mentions the very lowest classes, the "dregs" of society, often referred to by contemporary historians as being at the bottom of disturbances:

The vulgar and mean . . . have no virtues worth mentioning, no vices worth proclaiming, which is why we call them the rabble, the riffraff . . . the vulgar herd, the offscourings, the canaille . . . So small-minded are they and so mean-spirited, so sordid by nature, that they could not possibly achieve any kind of fame or notoriety . . . yet there are reasons for this and I shall do my best to explain them . . . [Perhaps they have something better in them] which is conquered by forgetfulness, effaced by oblivion, pushed out of mind by the business of getting a living and wondering where the next meal is to come from, when they are without means or resources, and must scheme to get their hands on a rag or two, to cover their nakedness, not to adorn themselves. [The question always before them is] how to escape imminent evil, how to pursue elusive good fortune, how to seek help from those who will not assist them or complain to those who have no pity on them.[30]

This unorganized rabble is not the only burden on the sovereign; there are also the *ᶜayyārūn* (bands of brigands or brotherhoods of outlaws), who seize every opportunity of threatening established authority.[31]

Religion is the second major force in society – Tawḥīdī quotes the Buwayhid amir ᶜAḍud al-Dawlah's maxim that religion is the foundation of the state and the secular arm its guardian[32] – but men of true piety are, so Tawḥīdī observes, rare.[33] The representatives of learning, the *kātib*s (secretaries) and *ahl al-ᶜilm* (scholars), are another major social force, though bickering and jealousy are the chief characteristics of intellectual society. Wealth is represented by *al-tunnāʾ* or *aṣḥāb al-ḍiyāᶜ* (the great landholders), and by the *tujjār* (merchants), for whose crassly materialistic outlook Tawḥīdī has nothing but contempt.[34] Noticeably absent from Tawḥīdī's analysis is any mention of the great army leaders.

Tawḥīdī's intellectual gifts were bound to make him seek out the great and powerful, for this was a period in which viziers, as well as holding high office, were often highly cultivated. But it was no easy matter to gain admittance to court circles: "For everyone who tries to gain the ear of an amir or vizier there is usually someone else, great or small, bent on blocking his path."[35] On the other hand, as Tawḥīdī observes: "Fine as it is to withdraw from the world, this can only be achieved by those with sufficient means . . . it is quite impossible not to serve those in power unless a man has unwavering piety and his desires are all otherworldly."[36]

How well-equipped Tawḥīdī was to overcome such obstacles in his pursuit of recognition we may guess from the words of the courtier and

[30] *Ṣadāqah*, 6; trans. J. A. [31] *Imtāᶜ*, III, 160–1; for such brotherhoods, see *EI*², "Futuwwa".
[32] *Imtāᶜ*, II, 33. [33] *Ṣadāqah*, 6. [34] Ibid., 5. [35] *Imtāᶜ*, II, 1. [36] Ibid., I, 13.

mathematician Abū ʾl-Wafāʾ al-Muhandis, whose protégé Tawḥīdī later became:

> You are inexperienced, and you do not observe a proper demeanour in your dealings with the great and your intercourse with viziers. All this requires manners which are different from yours, skills of which you know nothing, and clothes which are not in the least like those which you wear.[37]

In a first move towards gaining access to government circles, Tawḥīdī turned to Abū ʾl-Fatḥ Ibn al-ʿAmīd (Ibn al-ʿAmīd the younger), who was then the Buwayhid vizier in Rayy in northern Iran. Ibn al-ʿAmīd visited Baghdad during the year 363–4/974–5, and cut a brilliant figure in political and intellectual society; Tawḥīdī attended his *majlis* in Baghdad, no doubt hoping to be admitted to his circle of intimate advisers, the qualification for such a post being the possession of enough "learning, wisdom, eloquence, experience . . . and *adab*" to make one's counsels (*naṣāʾiḥ*) palatable.[38] At first Tawḥīdī conceived a great admiration for Ibn al-ʿAmīd; he spoke of him later as a lively and accomplished young man of great promise.[39] But the association with Ibn al-ʿAmīd proved abortive; the young vizier was disgraced and executed.[40] However, the reputation that Tawḥīdī gained at his *majlis* ensured that he was immediately taken on by Ibn al-ʿAmīd's successor in Rayy, the Ṣāḥib Ibn ʿAbbād.

Tawḥīdī's chief motive in accepting Ibn ʿAbbād's protection was his belief that their relationship would be one of mutual respect and intellectual equality, since both men were *adībs*. In this he was mistaken. Ibn ʿAbbād's splendid library, in which Tawḥīdī had doubtless pictured himself browsing at leisure, required copyists of a high standard; Ibn ʿAbbād coveted Tawḥīdī's services not as a scholar but as a scribe. By Tawḥīdī's own account, he found life at the court of Ibn ʿAbbād barely tolerable. Neither he nor Ibn ʿAbbād would yield, and their strained relationship only lasted as long as it did because the two were in some respects indispensible to each other, if only as sparring partners. It was Tawḥīdī himself – or so he claims – who finally severed relations with Ibn ʿAbbād in 370/980–1. The relationship between Ibn ʿAbbād and Tawḥīdī gives a vivid picture of how a cultivated man in a position of power could be on quite familiar terms with a mere man of letters without ever contemplating any surrender of the prerogatives of his rank. Of the two men – both writers, brilliant conversationalists, well-versed in literature and grammar – Tawḥīdī had nothing to do but wait on the pleasure of his patron, and nothing tangible to offer in return but his skills as a copyist-cum-philologist and

[37] Ibid., 5. [38] Ibid. III, 212. [39] *Akhlāq*, 406.
[40] See p. 98, above. For details of his character and career, see Kraemer, *Humanism*, 255–9.

lexicographer; the great statesman, on the other hand, while able to offer his protégé the magnificent hospitality of his house, library and table, seldom missed an opportunity of making him feel his inferiority. Tawḥīdī got his revenge by meeting insolence with insolence:

Was I to blame [he asks] if, when he said to me: "Wherever did you get that gaudy, tawdry style you keep writing to me in?" I replied, "How could my style be otherwise than as His Excellency describes it, seeing that I pluck the fruits of his "Epistles",[41] drink at the fount of his learning, make his *adab* my guiding light, and do my humble best to draw a few drops from his ocean and strain a trickle of his outpourings?"[42]

The wounds to his pride that Tawḥīdī sustained in Rayy were to have lasting effects; his gifts and even his ambitions were unimpaired, but gradually took a more serious turn. At first conceived in terms of caricature, *Akhlāq al-wazīrayn* ("The Characters of the Two Viziers", i.e. Ibn al-ʿAmīd the younger and Ibn ʿAbbād) developed into a psychological investigation of the thoughts and motives of the two statesmen, and a social critique of Ibn ʿAbbād's misuse of authority. The following self-justification must belong to the same period:

Anger, though blameworthy in some cases, is praiseworthy in others. Just as a permanent state of vexation on all occasions is a form of vice, so a universal complacency is a form of hypocrisy. One should alternate between acceptance and anger, just as one does between ease and exertion.[43]

After the break with Ibn ʿAbbād, Tawḥīdī returned to Baghdad, where he was lucky enough to renew the acquaintance of Abū ʾl-Wafāʾ al-Muhandis. Besides being a celebrated mathematician,[44] Abū ʾl-Wafāʾ had twenty-two years' experience of political life in Baghdad and many useful connections. Tawḥīdī, though somewhat older and no less brilliant, was a failure in terms of worldly success. Abū ʾl-Wafāʾ listened kindly to Tawḥīdī's account of his sufferings[45] and took him under his wing. His first step was to secure him a post at the hospital (*bīmāristān*) in Baghdad; his second was to introduce him to Abū ʿAbd Allāh al-ʿĀriḍ, the future vizier Ibn Saʿdān.

With Ibn Saʿdān as his new patron, Tawḥīdī was at last able to achieve the kind of relationship that had so far eluded him. He asked, and was permitted, to use the familiar "thou" with the vizier so that they could converse more freely.[46] So it was that an "obscure" writer and a powerful statesman were able to discuss, as equals, a wide variety of issues, politics and religion not excluded. The result was *al-Imtāʿ wa ʾl-muʾānasah*, which Tawḥīdī composed as a record for his friend and benefactor Abū ʾl-Wafāʾ.

[41] See pp. 106–7, 110. [42] *Akhlāq*, 494–5; trans. J. A. [43] *ʿUlūm*, 298, para. 2; trans. J. A.
[44] See *EI*², "Abū ʾl-Wafāʾ al-Būzadjānī". [45] *Imtāʿ*, I, 4. [46] Ibid., III, 210–11.

After the death of Ibn Saᶜdān in 382–3/992–3, there is no further mention of Tawḥīdī in Baghdad, and we first hear of him again at Shiraz in Fārs, trying to establish himself with the vizier al-Dalajī. The years from 386–400/996–1009–10, towards the close of Tawḥīdī's life, seem to be the period in which his individuality found fullest expression, and were also his most fruitful period as a writer, for though he was to live another twenty-eight years, he seems to have felt a sense of urgency, putting intellectual fulfilment before ambition in accordance with the advice which he himself had earlier given Ibn Saᶜdān: "A man should strive to succeed from the start in all his undertakings, and not to wait for success to follow."[47] To these years belong *al-Muqābasāt*, a memorandum of intellectual life in Baghdad as Tawḥīdī had known it, in which the chief protagonists are the Christian Yaḥyā b. ᶜAdī and, above all, Abū Sulaymān al-Manṭiqī al-Sijistānī, both followers of the philosopher al-Fārābī. *Al-Muqābasāt* is not only our chief source for al-Sijistānī's thought,[48] but also a living record of debates and discussions between men of widely differing beliefs and origins from all over the Islamic world, covering religious, philosophical, literary and factual topics;[49] it contains, among others, the famous disputation between the Christian logician Abū Bishr Mattā b. Yūnus, an influential translator from Syriac, and the grammarian Abū Saᶜīd al-Sīrāfī, on the merits of logic as a universal tool.[50] Another work of this period, *al-Ishārāt al-ilāhiyyah*, was a new departure for Tawḥīdī, being devoted exclusively to mysticism.

Though his strength was now failing, Tawḥīdī continued to write, even reviving an unfinished and forgotten work, *al-Ṣadāqah*. But in, or shortly before, Rajab 400/February 1010, without any warning, Tawḥīdī experienced a spiritual crisis, and in Ramaḍān, the month of fasting, he burned all his books. In reply to a friend who reproached him for this act of vandalism, Tawḥīdī pleaded movingly that with the loss of his family and friends he had lost the compassionate audience that would have forgiven him his shortcomings, but also that his books were irrelevant to the chief concern of his life: citing famous precedents, he suggests that he burned his books for fear of "burning himself" on learning. His thoughts were now turned towards death:

Departure is imminent, short is our stay; hard is our resting-place, painful our station (*maqām*, used as a mystical term?); fearful the path, our helpers weak, and certain are we to stray.[51]

[47] Ibid., 221. [48] See Kraemer, *Humanism*, and *Philosophy*.
[49] See Keilani, *Abū Ḥayyān*, 56–8, and Jadaane, "Philosophie".
[50] See Mahdi, "Language and logic", and Endress, 'The limits to reason".
[51] Yāqūt, *Irshād*, VI (5), 389–90 = R. *ilā ʾl-Qāḍī Abī Sahl.*

An eye-witness describes Tawḥīdī's deathbed: "There were several people present; they said, 'Call upon God; now is a time of terror towards which we are all hastening.' They began to call upon God and to admonish Tawḥīdī, but he said, 'You behave as though I were about to go before a soldier or a constable; but I am going to meet a merciful master.' Then he died."[52]

Tawḥīdī's outstanding achievement is, perhaps, the honesty with which he depicts himself, the hopes and failures of his chequered career, in language of great versatility and unfailing expressiveness. He viewed the world through the eyes of a philosopher, a believer and a mystic; later he withdrew from the world and devoted himself to his craft, seeking that "spiritual peace" which is to be found "in striving for the goal in a manner which procures for the seeker . . . silence without constraint, abstraction (*ghaybah*) without inadvertence, boldness without rashness".[53] Tawḥīdī sought to give spontaneous expression to his perception of the truth; it was the clear-sightedness with which he did so that made him feel at once most apart from society and most actively involved in trying to show what society should really be. He imagined an ideal order, beyond the reach of mankind yet realizable in specific instances: the world is at odds, yet some men achieve harmony in friendship; the genius and fortunes of nations vary, yet all nations have virtues and in time come into their own.[54] Tawḥīdī seems to be striving for balance, coherence and objectivity, and it is this that gives him his humanity and makes him able to understand people as individuals, whether the outcasts of society or the rulers with their heavy burden of responsibility. As a defender of Sunnism, Tawḥīdī formulated ideas which were to contribute to the gradual elaboration of doctrine which led to the resurgence of "traditional" Islam, and his writings had a substantial influence on al-Ghazālī, as the great Ḥanbalī thinker Ibn Taymiyyah (661–728/1263–1328) was to show.[55] His own vision of the world is expressed in the doctrine of universal friendship (*ṣadāqah*) voiced by his master, the philosopher Abū Sulaymān al-Sijistānī:

> [Men associate only for conventional reasons, such as propinquity, profession or family, yet even then they are divided by uncharitable feelings] but if you were to befriend each other according to your higher nature . . . you would not yield to the promptings of your lower nature – for you are all human by species, animal by genus, able to become as angels when you choose well, and as liable to become devils when you choose ill. If you were to walk in the straight path (*al-ṣirāṭ al-mustaqīm*) [Qurʾān, i.6, etc.] and hold fast to the strong rope of reason (*ḥabl al-ʿaql al-*

[52] Ibn Ḥajar, *Lisān al-Mīzān*, VI, 370. [53] *Imtāʿ*, I, 206.
[54] *Ṣadāqah*, 2–5; *Imtāʿ*, I, 73–5. [55] Laoust, *Essai sur les doctrines sociales*, 82.

matīn)[56] and cling to the most firm bond (*al-ᶜurwah al-wuthqā*) [Qurʾān, ii.256; xxxi.22] of guidance and religion, you would be as one spirit in all things and . . . unity would flow from friend to friend, then to a second and a third, from lowly to great, from the people to their rulers . . . then indeed would you see God's sublime word [manifest] and sublime obedience to Him . . . [However little human nature lends itself to friendship, yet] this well-nigh impossible thing has been sought among all men, in all successive ages and places . . . in prayer after prayer . . . and if impediments make this goal remote in a general way, yet we must not despair of achieving it in some particular favourable circumstance. For if reason proves the fitness of this thing, it is impossible that it should not exist . . . and were it unattainable, then reason would not bespeak its fitness.[57]

[56] Cf. Qurʾān, iii. 103: "And hold you fast to God's rope together and be not scattered."
[57] *Ṣadāqah*, 56–7; trans. J.A.

CHAPTER 7

AL-HAMADHĀNĪ, AL-ḤARĪRĪ AND THE *MAQĀMĀT* GENRE

The telling and hearing of anecdotes has been a favourite pastime in all ages and places: round the bedouin camp-fire, in the literary salons of ᶜAbbasid Baghdad, in the English public house and over the after-dinner port. The nature of an anecdote varies enormously. In length it may range from the retailing of the briefest piece of repartee, to what is virtually a short story; in content it may deal with a humorous or pithy saying, a remarkable event, a piece of literary criticism, a riddle, or even (in the Arabic ambience) a grammatical observation or a well-expressed piece of religious homily. But the anecdote proper has three features. First, the point of the piece should be set against a background of circumstantial detail which adds to its vividness. Secondly, it is either true or presented as true: a repartee gains greatly in effect if presented, for instance, as "what Churchill once said to de Gaulle", even if it is manifest that the teller has no means of knowing what Churchill really said, and an anecdote is hence most often presented on the authority of a transmitter (Ar. *rāwī*) or narrator, whether historical or imaginary. Thirdly, each anecdote is a completely isolated and self-sufficient unit; though, of course, collections of anecdotes are often made, sometimes with the unifying principle of a common topic, and anecdotal collections set in a chronological framework can form the basis for a rather unsophisticated historical narrative, of the "Little Arthur's History of England" type (or, for that matter, al-Masᶜūdī's fourth/tenth century *Murūj al-dhahab*, which is essentially anecdotal history), or for the picaresque novel, in which the independent episodes are strung together by the presence of a single protagonist throughout.

Collections of anecdotes in Arabic literature can be said to begin with *ḥadīth*, inasmuch as these are organized into collections of historical anecdotes about the sayings and doings of the Prophet and his Companions.[1] Later, we get collections usually centred on a single topic, like the *Kitāb al-Bukhalāᵓ* ("Book of Misers") of al-Jāḥiẓ and *Akhbār al-ṭiwāl* ("Tales of Long-lived Men") of al-Dīnawārī (d. *c.* 281/894). But the most

[1] *CHALUP*, 271, 289.

voluminous of all come from Abū ʿAlī al-Muḥassin al-Tanūkhī (327–84/939–94), who after his retirement from active service as a judge (*qāḍī*) devoted his later years to the compilation of several anecdotal works, including the vast *Nishwār al-muḥāḍarah* ("Desultory Conversations") in ten volumes, of which over half are lost.

Something has already been said about the pre-ʿAbbasid oratorical (*khuṭbah*) style, marked by strong parallelism and "balance" but devoid of rhyme.[2] In the third/ninth century a new trend set in, whereby this style was married to ornamental features derived from verse, namely rhyming and tropes (the latter collectively referred to as *badīʿ*),[3] producing a new kind of *sajʿ* (to be distinguished from the so-called "*sajʿ* of the soothsayers"),[4] which rapidly achieved a tremendous dominance over prose writing. The critic al-Mubarrad (d. 285 or 6/898–9), already divides prose into the categories of *khuṭbah*, *kalām manthūr* (unadorned prose) and *sajʿ*, apparently regarding the last as primarily differentiated from *khuṭbah* by rhyme. An excellent example of the differentiation can be seen in two documents quoted by the historian Abū Jaʿfar Muḥammad b. Jarīr al-Ṭabarī (d. 310/923): one is an address of the caliph al-Muʿtazz delivered shortly after his accession in 252/866, in conventional *khuṭbah* style, markedly parallelistic but unrhymed; the other, a contemporary letter of Muḥammad b. ʿAbdullāh al-Khuzāʿī, criticizing those who supported the caliph's policy, which is rhymed and makes much use of poetical tropes.[5] The latter is significantly introduced by the historian with the verb *anshaʾa*, "he composed", and it is in fact an early specimen of what later came to be known as *inshāʾ*, "chancery style", regularly employed for diplomatic and chancery documents. The line drawn between *sajʿ* and *inshāʾ* is not easy to draw, but perhaps one could say that, while both use rhyme, the other adornments are more to the fore in *inshāʾ* than in *sajʿ*.

In the following century the prevalence of *sajʿ* made great strides. The most famous preacher (*khaṭīb*) of the age, Ibn Nubāṭah (335–74/946–84), used it for his sermons, and in the secular domain a variety of authors developed the *risālah* into the "ornate epistle", of which a noteworthy exponent was Abū Bakr Muḥammad b. al-ʿAbbās al-Khwārazmī (323–83/934–93).[6] At this stage *sajʿ* was still confined to the religious and political *khuṭbah* and *belles-lettristic* works of the ornate epistle type.

In the second half of the fourth/tenth century, a young man from Hamadhān in western Persia, Aḥmad b. al-Ḥusayn al-Hamadhānī (358–98/968–1008), set out to make an impression on the literary world, and in particular to challenge the position of al-Khwārazmī, at that time the

[2] Ibid., ch. 5. [3] See chs. 9, 16, 21. [4] *CHALUP*, 185.
[5] *Taʾrīkh*, IX, 366, 367–8; trans. Beeston, *Samples of Arabic Prose*, 15–16. [6] See p. 100.

acknowledged master of the ornate epistle. But Hamadhānī's "Epistles", though undoubtedly graceful, did not win him any recognized superiority over the older man. He then boldly invented a new genre – a feat which gained him the sobriquet of Badīᶜ al-Zamān, "Marvel of the Age", by which he has subsequently been known. His originality lay first and foremost in the use of *sajᶜ* as a vehicle for anecdotes of the kind collected by al-Tanūkhī (some of whose compilations must have appeared before al-Hamadhānī's *magnum opus*). In the second place, instead of doing as the anecdotists had hitherto done, and attributing the anecdotes either to a genuine historical personage, or to some verisimilous authority such as "my grandfather" or "one of my neighbours", he consistently throughout the work gives each episode on the authority of the same manifestly fictional narrator, whom he names ᶜĪsā b. Hishām. In this way he frankly acknowledges the fictional character of the narratives, and is the first Arabic author to compose a confessedly fictional prose work (the animal fables of the *Kalīlah wa-Dimnah* cycle, though in themselves fictional, are presented only within a frame story in which a purportedly historical character tells the fables).[7]

The novel use of *sajᶜ* for narrative purposes is perhaps the reason for the author's choice of title for his collection, which he called *Maqāmāt* ("Standings"): anecdotes in unadorned prose had normally been told at *majālis* (sing. *majlis*: sittings, sessions), where both narrator and audience were seated, whereas standing was the conventional posture for the orator (*khaṭīb*) using *sajᶜ*.The point has been obscured by many European translators with their use of either the ambiguous term "assemblies" for *maqāmāt*, or the outright mistranslation "sessions, seances".

Al-Hamadhānī's *Maqāmāt* comprise fifty-two pieces: the three main editions each have a total of fifty-one *maqāmah*s, but the Cairo and Istanbul editions have one that is not in the Beirut edition, while the latter has one that is not in either of the other two. There is a story that the author boasted of having triumphed over his rival al-Khwārazmī because he himself had composed "over 400" *maqāmāt* whereas the other could not produce even one. The tale cannot be taken at face value: forty and 400 have always been in the Near East idiomatic expressions for "an indefinite number", and there are no grounds for supposing that we only possess one-eighth of the original total.

There is a certain degree of structural irregularity in these *maqāmāt*. In a majority of them, the narrator is ᶜĪsā b. Hishām, but the protagonist is an individual named Abū ʾl-Fatḥ al-Iskandarī. Yet there are some in which the latter makes no appearance at all and the protagonist is the narrator himself;

[7] See pp. 50–3.

others in which Abū ʾl-Fatḥ is only dragged in peripherally, without having played any real part in the story. In the *maqāmah* "of the *Maḍīrah*" (a much relished item of cuisine), Abū ʾl-Fatḥ is indeed present, but plays effectively the role only of a second narrator, while the main gist of the story is the vulgar boasting of the *nouveau riche* host who invites him to a meal (English readers may care to look at chapter 56 of George Borrow's *Bible in Spain*, where Borrow's Moorish guide in Tangier delivers a harangue in somewhat the same style). Particularly striking is the very brief and unsatisfactory *maqāmah* "of the Ape", in which ʿĪsā b. Hishām sees a crowd of people and, having struggled through them with some difficulty, discovers that they are watching a showman with a performing ape – the showman being identified as Abū ʾl-Fatḥ; yet the whole piece is devoid of any point, beyond the description of the narrator's struggles to get to the front. It is difficult to avoid thinking that this is only a fragment, intended to be filled in later on by witty patter from the mouth of the showman, Abū ʾl-Fatḥ. One or two pieces (e.g. that "of the Lion") are made up of two separate episodes having only the slenderest link between them (and again, the narrator is protagonist, and Abū ʾl-Fatḥ appears only at the end, having played no part whatever in the narrative). It does not seem, moreover, that the author has given any thought to creating a recognizable personality for Abū ʾl-Fatḥ: he is sometimes young, sometimes an old man; sometimes thin and sometimes well-built; and although he is normally presented as master of a marvellous flow of language, this is not displayed in all cases (note the cases of "the *Maḍīrah*" and "the Ape" mentioned above).

Everyone will no doubt draw his own conclusions from all this. One possible view is that, having regard to the relatively early age at which the author died, his *Maqāmāt* are not in a fully finished state, and that, had he lived, he would probably have tidied up the work, e.g. by giving the ape's showman a speaking part, and dividing "the Lion" into two separate *maqāmah*s; it is more open to question whether he would have gone so far as to revise radically those pieces in which Abū ʾl-Fatḥ does not appear at all, so as to make him a real protagonist of a picaresque quasi-novel. On the other hand, J. N. Mattock has adopted a different standpoint, suggesting that the work as we have it is designed as a finished unity, and that the abnormalities are purposely inserted in order to create an effect of surprise that has its own entertainment value.[8] However, surprise can only be achieved if there is already an expectation of something different from what actually occurs; but, since the genre at this time was entirely new, it is not easy to see how there can have been an expectation on the part of the reader or hearer of any particular structure. As against this, referring to the

[8] "Early history of the *maqāma*".

structure of smaller entities than each separate narrative, A. Kilito has remarked that the individual *maqāmāt* draw upon a number of genres, themes and styles, and has suggested that "surprise", in this context, consists of identifying these prototypes and appreciating the novel manner in which they are applied and combined, while the still unfixed state of the genre teases the reader's expectation of how each narrative, taken as a whole, will develop.[9]

It is questionable how far the content of the *Maqāmāt* was Hamadhānī's original invention; many are elaborations or versions of what seem to have been common topoi in anecdotage – the theme of a ragged and destitute person who nevertheless proves to be a miracle of wit and eloquence appears in Tanūkhī's *al-Faraj baᶜd al-shiddah* ('Relief after Distress"),[10] and there are other echoes as well, though they are given a new look by being decked out in *sajᶜ*. Another of the *Faraj* stories turns on the point of a man saying to his neighbour, "How would you fancy a roast kid, a pot-au-feu and some cold dishes etc.?", but, when the neighbour turns up for the expected feast, he is told, "I only said, 'How would you fancy?', I never said I had the things, for my larder is empty": the same basic point is elaborated in a different way in Hamadhānī's *al-Maqāmah al-Nahīdiyyah* ("of Fresh Butter") and *al-Maqāmah al-Majāᶜiyyah* ("of Famine").

A feature of the social scene in Hamadhānī's time was a slightly prurient fascination with the seamy side of life – perhaps a reaction from the over-refined and over-sophisticated society of the great cities in ᶜAbbasid times. The literary manifestations of this trend have been exhaustively studied in C. E. Bosworth's *Medieval Islamic Underworld*. This underworld is summed up by the term Banū Sāsān, which in this context has nothing to do with genuine scions of the Sasanian dynasty, but alludes to a common type of boast made by beggars and rapscallions in all societies, of being persons of noble ancestry down on their luck. This term is an all-embracing one for vagabonds of every type, from highwaymen, cutpurses and housebreakers down to mendicants who extract charity by means of fraudulently simulated disabilities (sometimes, indeed, by actual self-mutilation), including also hypocritical hedge-preachers (*wuᶜᶜāẓ, quṣṣāṣ*) whose powerful sermons are in contradiction with their private life. This interest appears already in the third/ninth century in an anecdote in the *Kitāb al-Bukhalāᵓ* of Jāḥiẓ. Here an individual named Khālid b. Yazīd, on being approached by a beggar, fumbles in his pocket for a small copper coin (*fals*) but by mistake hands out a silver dirham; on discovering his error he demands the coin

[9] *Les Séances*, 13, 33.

[10] *Faraj*, II, 360–3, III, 306–13; this is a collection of anecdotes, mostly drawn from literary sources, which illustrate the workings of divine providence.

back, and, when the bystanders expostulate at this as unfair, he says, "I know this kind of fellow, he's only a farthing-beggar, not a sixpenny-beggar", and goes on to explain that his knowledge is due to the fact that he himself had formerly belonged to the Banū Sāsān and practised mendicancy in various guises. The anecdote continues, "and he was the person who gave a recommendation (*waṣiyyah*) to his son to follow the same path"; however, the phrasing of the recommendation which follows is a typical literary exercise, rather than a detailed exposition. For the latter we have to wait until somewhere in the early or mid fourth/tenth century, when a certain Abū Dulaf Misᶜar b. Muhalhil al-Khazrajī devoted a lengthy *qaṣīdah* to the trickeries of vagabonds, and an explanation of the canting terms they employ (only a few such had been mentioned in the anecdote of Khālid b. Yazīd).[11] To some extent, the *Maqāmāt* cater for similar tastes, but they are very far from going into the "curious" and somewhat scabrous detail of Abū Dulaf. (Though there is a *maqāmah* entitled *al-Sāsāniyyah*, it is a very slight thing, containing no more than a couple of pieces of versified beggar's patter.) Indeed, a recent study – which, as the examples below may suggest, perhaps somewhat overstates its case – has put forward the view that the *Maqāmāt* have an essentially moral purpose; J.T. Monroe observes, like Kilito, that they draw upon established antecedents, including *ḥadīth* and homily, and suggests that Hamadhānī parodies these elements or presents them in improper contexts or sequences, thus placing a burden of logical, and ultimately moral, discrimination upon the reader.[12]

It was practically *de rigueur* for any literary man of the time to have at least some capability for versifying; but Hamadhānī's excursions in this direction are extremely mediocre. Apart from some quotations from well-known poets, the bits of verse in his *Maqāmāt* are decidedly sparse, and to a large extent confined to fragments (hardly better than doggerel) put into the mouth of Abū ᵓl-Fatḥ as a sort of *envoi* at the end of an anecdote; it is noticeable that a similar piece is put into the mouth of the protagonist in the second of the *Faraj* anecdotes mentioned above.[13]

Writing in which the main point resides in a display of linguistic skill poses some intractable problems for a translator; yet most of Hamadhānī's *Maqāmāt* can be read with pleasure even in a version which perforce does not reproduce that feature. The following rendering of the *maqāmah* "of Armenia" may serve as an example of the narrative anecdote, albeit stripped of the allure of the language:

ᶜĪsā b. Hishām tells the following tale. We were once on our way home from a trading trip in Armenia, and while journeying through the desert we fell in with some of its sons on the fringes thereof; they forced our camels to halt in that land of

[11] Text and trans. Bosworth, *Underworld*, II.

[12] *Picaresque Narrative.* [13] Trans. Beeston, "Genesis".

the ostrich, until they had rifled our baggage and relieved our mounts of the burden. There we had to stay during the hours of daylight, held captive by that band, tied up in groups with leather thongs, while our horses were seized and picketed. But when night followed on the tail of departing day and the canopy of stars was spread, the band made off into the deep desert, while we made our way out of it. On we went until fair Aurora had laid aside her veil of modesty and the sword of sunrise was drawn from the scabbard of darkness; but its rising found us stripped to our pelts. Surrounded by perils, we could but face up to them as we cleaved the crust of the desert. At last we got to Marāghah, where each one of us selected a travelling companion and took to the road. To me there attached himself a youth of wretched appearance, dressed in rags, named Abū ᵓl-Fatḥ al-Iskandarī. Together we set off in quest of the staff of life, and found it where a brushwood fire was blazing in an oven. Iskandarī went up to a man and asked him for a handful of salt; then he said to the baker, "Lend me the top of the stove, for I'm frozen". Once mounted on it, he began to harangue the people about how badly off he was, and to describe his destitute condition. All the while, he was shaking out the salt from under his clothes, so as to give the impression that there was a nastiness in them [sc. that they were infested with lice]; whereat the baker cried, "Curse you! Tuck up your skirts! You've ruined our bread", and he rushed to throw the loaves away; but Iskandarī set about gathering them up and stowing them away under his arm. I expressed admiration of the clever way he had acted, but he replied, "Just you wait, and I'll find a way of getting something to go with the bread". He went to a man who had set out a number of clean jugs of milk, of various qualities, and asked how much they cost and whether he might have a taste. The man told him to go ahead, so he stirred his finger around in a jug, as if trying to find something he had lost; but then said, "I can't pay cash, but do you need the services of a barber-surgeon?" [*ḥajjām*, an unclean profession, because it included blood-letting]. "God damn you, is that what you are?" "Yes", was the reply, whereupon the man cursed his luck and made as if to pour the milk away, but Iskandarī said, "Better me than the devil". "Take it, and much good may it do to you," said the man. He took it, and the two of us went away out of sight and consumed the whole lot at one go. We resumed our travels, and came to a village where Iskandarī asked the villagers for some food. One of them ran off home and brought us a bowl of milk, full to the lip and brimming over. This we sipped to the very end, and asked them for some bread, but they would not give us this except at a price. "How is it," said Iskandarī, "that you are so free with milk but demand payment for bread?" "It was in a pan," said the lad, "and a mouse fell into it, so we charitably give it away to travellers." "Heavens above!" cried Iskandarī, and took the bowl and smashed it. "What a shame! What a terrible waste!" cried the lad. But our flesh crept, our stomachs turned over, and we brought up all we had eaten. "This serves us right for what we did yesterday," said I. But Iskandarī only declaimed:

> Of fastidiousness beware, clever men have no such care.
> He who sups with Fate must eat scanty meal or banquet rare.
> Don for one time garments new, for another ragged wear.

A riddling theme is found in the very brief *maqāmah* "of the Yellow One": ᶜĪsā b. Hishām tells the following story. When I was about to start for home after the Pilgrimage, a man came to me saying, "I have with me a lad of yellow paternity, who'd tempt you to join the ungodly fraternity; he dances on the fingertips, and much travel has polished him up. Charity impels me to come to you, to present his plea unto you; he seeks from you a yellow bride, admired beyond measure, to all eyes a pleasure. If you consent, there will be born of them a child that will reach all lands and all ears, and when you're bent on return and have wound up your concern, he'll be before you in your homeland, so will you please display what's in your hand?" This speech I relished, and the wit of his demand, so I did what he wished. In reply he declaimed:

The begging hand puts paid to pride,
but generosity has all on its side.

(Needless to say, the yellow pair are gold coins; their child is a reputation for generosity.)

During the following century, Blachère and Masnou list five authors who are credited with compositions styled *maqāmāt*,[14] but these are simply *khuṭbah*s clothed in *sajᶜ* and apart from borrowing the name *maqāmah* for this species of composition, they in no way resemble the individual character of Hamadhānī's *Maqāmāt*. That was reserved for an author of just a century after Hamadhānī, namely Abū ʾl-Ḥasan al-Qāsim b. ᶜAlī Ibn al-Ḥarīrī, usually known as al-Ḥarīrī (446–516/1054–1122), who in his preface explicitly acknowledges having been inspired by Hamadhānī. But despite this, his *Maqāmāt* show a distinct development beyond the model. So much is this the case that his work for many centuries after entirely eclipsed his predecessor's (until this was "rediscovered" in the second half of the nineteenth century), and it is the Haririan *maqāmāt* that have come to be considered as the typical examples of the genre; it is indeed not unknown for literary historians to describe Ḥarīrī's work as if such a description were applicable to all *maqāmāt* including those of Hamadhānī, notwithstanding the differences.

Ḥarīrī was a grammarian, and his other writings are of a grammatical nature, with special concern for normative grammar and the correction of errors. It seems probable that, just as Erasmus wrote his *Colloquies* in order to teach schoolboys correct Latin linguistic usage through the medium of entertaining matter, which they were expected to learn by heart, so one of the motives for the composition of Ḥarīrī's *Maqāmāt* may have been pedagogic. The work was certainly used in that way through many centuries, when it became a school textbook. The ornamental style of Hamadhānī is merely that which was becoming fashionable in his time, and the actual vocabulary of his *Maqāmāt* is relatively simple; it is far outdistanced by the style of Ḥarīrī, which almost inordinately coruscates with puns, and not a few rare expressions. It looks very much as if there was an intention on the author's part of providing instruction in language; the puns, for example, can serve

[14] *Maqāmāt (Séances) choisies*, app. I.

to inculcate the differentiation in sense between two words that differ only in voweling, and there are grammatical points which would serve as useful pegs on which a teacher could hang an exposition of some well-known grammatical crux. All this makes his *sajʿ* almost untranslatable.

Like his predecessor, Ḥarīrī presents his pieces as being transmitted by a narrator who appears throughout, and is here named al-Ḥārith b. Hammām; but the protagonist Abū Zayd al-Sarūjī also appears in every piece (unlike Abū ʾl-Fatḥ al-Iskandarī) and has a well-marked personality (again in contrast with Hamadhānī's protagonist). Despite his gifts of wit and eloquence, he is a hypocritical rascal – albeit a rather engaging one – and an unrestrained drunkard who, after a serious and moving religious homily, for example, which gains him alms from the auditory, dissipates the cash in low society at a tavern drinking wine; he himself is elderly, but occasionally has with him a youthful accomplice, whom he uses in playing crafty tricks for extracting money. Except for the absence of a chronological framework, the whole collection could be (and by some critics has been) regarded as a sort of picaresque novel.

But the most striking difference between the two authors lies in their use of verse. This is much more prominent in Ḥarīrī than in Hamadhānī, and is vastly more polished and elegant. One would hardly class Ḥarīrī among poets of the top rank, but he nevertheless displays talents of a high order in this field. One piece of special interest occurs in the *maqāmah* "of Damascus", the first line being:

lazimtu ʾl-sifĀRa wa-jubtu ʾl-qifĀRa wa-ʿuftu ʾl-nifĀRa li-ajnī ʾl-farAḤ

and it has the unusual feature that, in addition to the customary monorhyme repeated at the end of each line (here *AḤ*), there is in each line an internal rhyme (in the first line, quoted above, *ĀR*) occurring at quarter-line intervals, a device reminiscent of the stanzaic form of the *muwashshaḥ*[15] which was evolving at this period. Such a rhyme-scheme is rare in English, but can be exemplified in a couplet attributed to Burns: (cf. Scott's *Old Mortality*, ch. 9):

I am a son of Mars who have been in many wars and show my cuts and scars wherever I come;
This here was for a wench and that other in a trench, when welcoming the French at the sound of the drum.

The piece as a whole is a delightfully rollicking praise of bacchic antinomianism, something of the flavour of which may be gathered from the following rendering (though this lacks the allure of the rhymes and the puns):

[15] See pp. 231–2.

I'm constant in journeys, I wander the deserts, I've reticence spurned for the culling of joy,
and torrents I've waded and horses I've tamed for the sake of indulging in wanton delights.
I've laid aside gravity, sold all my property, so as to gulp down the goblets of wine;
and but for my longing to drink it I'd never have uttered my speeches so witty and fine,
and never have cleverly brought from Iraq my companions by telling of rosary beads.[16]
So do not be angry nor vex me with solemn reproaches, for which I've a ready reply,
and don't be surprised at an old man who battens on pasturage rich among winejars that brim:
it's wine that gives strength to the bones and is cure for all sickness and drives away trouble and grief.
The splendidest joy's when respectable conduct is shed and all shamefacedness cast aside,
and sweetest of moments in love is when lover declares all his passion without bashfulness.
So speak your love out and thus comfort your spirit wherein fiery anguish had planted its wound,
and cure all your sorrow and solace your care by that favourite remedy – daughter of vines;
and choose for your cupbearer one who will drive off with his tender glance the enamoured's distress,
who'll sing with a voice at which mountains of iron would melt when he raises his head for the song.
Don't heed the adviser who frowns on your clasping a pretty lad if the chance happens to come,
but play all your tricks to the utmost – and further; don't listen to gossip but take what seems good.
Abandon your father if he would restrain you; and spread out your nets for what game comes your way.
Be true to your friends and avoid the vile miser; do always what's handsome and generous too;
but make, ere your last hour, repentance your refuge, for he who knocks on grace's door is let in.

Ḥarīrī's *Maqāmāt* had tremendous influence in following centuries, and inspired a number of imitators, including a seventh/thirteenth century Spanish Jew, Judah ben Solomon Ḥarīzī, who wrote a collection of Haririan *maqāmah*s in Hebrew. The most recent example of the genre is the *Ḥadīth ʿĪsā b. Hishām* of Muḥammad al-Muwayliḥī (1858–1930), first

[16] This alludes to the theme of the anecdote, in which a party of travellers cross the Syrian desert in safety, thanks (so they believe) to the daily recital of a pious litany devised by Abū Zayd.

published as a series of articles and republished in book-form in 1906. This proclaims, by its use of the name ᶜĪsā b. Hishām for the narrator, its author's intention of writing in the tradition of Hamadhānī, yet its structure is different: it is a scathing satire on social mores in the Cairo of the end of the nineteenth century, expressed through the observations and misadventures of a resurrected pasha of the age of Muḥammad ᶜAlī, together with his constant companion, the narrator; and each of the separate and independent episodes is presented in two sections, an introductory one of varying length (but usually fairly substantial) in highly traditional *sajᶜ*, followed without any break or transition by one in everyday language.

Blachère and Masnou list some seventy authors, between Ḥarīrī and Muwayliḥī, of compositions either entitled "a *maqāmah*" or "*maqāmāt*", but some of these have practically nothing in common with the Hamadhanian-Haririan *maqāmāt* apart from the use of the word in the title, being non-anecdotal in character, and in content sometimes scientific, sometimes literary, but hardly distinguishable from the epistle (*risālah*) form.[17] The *maqāmah* considered as an identifiable literary genre, stemming from the Hamadhanian model, cannot however be satisfactorily described in terms of the very distinctive Haririan example, or even perhaps the Hamadhanian one. Its basic characteristics are that it is fictional, and presented through the mouth of a fictional narrator; it is episodic in structure, and anecdotal in substance (using the term "anecdote" in the widest sense, as at the beginning of this chapter); and it is stylistically drafted mainly in *sajᶜ*, though an admixture of verse or even (as in Muwayliḥī's work) of passages in unadorned prose is admissible.

[17] See *EI²*, "Maḳāma", for a fuller bibliography.

CHAPTER 8

FABLES AND LEGENDS

The ᶜAbbasid period was the golden age of Arabic story-telling: it was between the second/eighth and fourth/tenth centuries that the Arabic romantic tale was cast into an individual mould and took on its classical forms. Romances which were essentially ᶜAbbasid in imagery and vocabulary, adopted by popular writers and bards, were to continue in Arabic literature for centuries; a pseudo-ᶜAbbasid style remained the vogue long after the fall of Baghdad to the Mongols in 656/1258, and it is sometimes difficult to tell whether a version of a legend or romantic tale originated in ᶜAbbasid Iraq or Syria or was composed much later in Mamlūk Cairo.

Mia Gerhardt has suggested that Arabic popular literature of the early ᶜAbbasid period drew its inspiration from three main sources: Persia, the bedouin society of the Arabian peninsula and the Baghdad of Hārūn al-Rashīd (170–93/786–809) and al-Maᵓmūn (198–218/813–33).[1] From Persia came the idea of the attainment, marriage or capture of an unknown beloved: the hero, usually a prince, falls in love with a girl from a distant land, having heard her description or simply her name; after many adventures borne with great steadfastness, he woos and liberates her, and the couple found a dynasty which is blessed with good fortune. By contrast, bedouin Arabia contributed tales of the sad fate of sundered lovers. Often these evoke the pre- or early Islamic life of Arabia, but sometimes the bedouin setting is transformed into the life of an Iraqi village or city. There is a direct connection between such stories and the second/eighth century poems by, or attributed to, such ᶜUdhrī poets as Jamīl.[2] However, the bedouin inspiration of the tales seems to have been modified by the romantic nostalgia of the urban populations of Syria, Iraq and Persia. The story of the self-immolating Majnūn and his beloved Laylā is characteristic,

[1] *The Art of Story Telling*, 121–30.

[2] See *CHALUP*, 42, 424–5; and pp. 205–6, below; the poets of the tribe of ᶜUdhrah typified courtly, platonic and thwarted love.

and lent itself to wide diffusion.[3] The accomplishment of the Baghdad story-tellers lies in their realistic narrative technique and the sober and correct observation of attitudes and reactions. Most of these stories are set in the time of Hārūn al-Rashīd, and though composed later than his reign, they seem to typify the splendour, cosmopolitanism, affluence and intrigue of early ᶜAbbasid court life. The fourth/tenth-century *Fihrist* of Ibn al-Nadīm lists numerous titles of works about lovers, some passionate lovers of the pre-Islamic period, others famous ᶜUdhrī poets, and a few early ᶜAbbasids; also listed are tales of miscellaneous lovers, of constant and fickle maidens and stories of the loves between humans and jinn, in which many of the names seem to personify amatory states or concepts. Under the heading of "Fables", Ibn al-Nadīm also lists lewd and ribald versions of the love-story proper, telling of the exploits of harlots, adulterers and such characters as Laᶜūb the Boss-Lady and Ḥusayn the Homosexual.[4] (In the Baghdad stories of the *Thousand and One Nights* we find examples of both main types of amatory couples, the chaste and the sensual.)

Ibn al-Nadīm says that such tales were especially popular under the ᶜAbbasids, but in fact the period when popular courtly literature gained acceptance in its own right began in Umayyad times. The discovery of third/ninth century papyri in Egypt has enabled Nabia Abbott to postulate an early Syrian version of the *Thousand and One Nights*, *Kitāb fīhi ḥadīth alf laylah*, which shows a fusion of Arabian bedouin stories and Islamicized Persian tales from the Pahlavi *Hazār afsānah* ("Thousand Tales"), and this version seems to have been preceded by two second/eighth century Arabic translations, one a complete and literal rendition of *Hazār afsānah* entitled *Alf khurāfah* ("A Thousand Fables"), the second an Islamicized version of the same work under the title *Alf laylah* ("A Thousand Nights":[5] the selection of stories which Muhsin Mahdi, in the preface to his edition of the *Thousand and One Nights*, proposes as representing the earlier "core" of the work is very debatable). Still earlier the Umayyad caliph Muᶜāwiyah himself (41–60/661–80) was supposedly the recipient of the earliest collection of tales about legendary South Arabia, the *Akhbār* of ᶜUbayd b. Sharyah al-Jurhumī.[6]

Several other elements were common both to Umayyad and to early ᶜAbbasid story-telling. In both periods, a number of men of letters and

[3] Majnūn ("the Madman") fell in love with Laylā at first sight, was refused her hand in marriage and wandered half-naked in the wilderness until his death, communing with birds and beasts. The story became popular throughout the Muslim world and was also adopted into non-Muslim literatures; it was often depicted in miniatures and was used by Sufi writers as a type of the soul which yearns for union with God.

[4] *Fihrist*, Tajaddud, 365–7, 376/Dodge, II, 719–23, 736. On chaste, passionate and lubricious images of love in the poetry of the period, see p. 281.

[5] Abbott, "Fragment"; cf. *CHALUP*, 254.

[6] See *CHALUP*, 385, and ch. 23, n. 51 below.

traditionists were also *quṣṣāṣ*, story-tellers who used legendary or semi-legendary tales of prophets and heroes for edificatory purposes in their sermons and homilies, and the same material also found its way into scholarly writings. The Alexander Romance – the first full-length Arabic version of which is credited to ᶜUmārah b. Zayd (d. *c.* 200/815)[7] – was quoted by Muḥammad b. Sāᵓib al-Kalbī (d. 146/763) in his *Tafsīr* (Qurᵓān commentary), and numerous ideas from the Alexander legend are found in a variety of works. Fragments of the Alexander Romance occur in the writings of geographers of all periods and hide behind allegedly historical exploits reported by historians; Ibn ᶜAbd al-Ḥakam (d. 257/871), for example, in his history of the Muslim conquest of Egypt, *Futūḥ Miṣr*, draws upon the Alexander Romance in describing the adventures of the Companion of the Prophet ᶜUqbah b. Nāfiᶜ,[8] whose repeated question as he marches southwards through the Fezzan, "Does anyone live beyond you?" is an echo of Alexander's visit to the Fetid Sea; similarly, ᶜUqbah's halt at the Mare's Fount (*māᵓ al-faras*), where his dying comrades are refreshed by a hidden spring, has parallels in Alexander's search for the Water of Life. Alexander, the ruler wisely guided by Aristotle, had already figured in the works of the Umayyad *kātib* Abū ᵓl-ᶜAlāᵓ Sālim;[9] Alexander the philosopher-king was to figure later in the thought of Islamic philosophers. The later recensions of the *Thousand and One Nights* incorporate borrowings from the Alexander Romance, inserted into the plots of such tales as "Iram of the Columns" and "The City of Brass".[10]

Both Umayyad and ᶜAbbasid story-tellers could draw upon a fund of heroic themes. At an early date there were numerous legends of Muslim martyrs and warriors, but non-Muslim models were also provided by the flourishing Yemeni school of authors who gloried in the pre-Islamic past of the Himyarites; the material contained in such works as Wahb b. Munabbih's (d. 110/728 or 114/732) *Kitāb al-Tījān* (in the recension of Ibn Hishām, d. 218/833)[11] and al-Hamdānī's (d. 334/945)[12] *Iklīl* is no less genuinely South Arabian in stamp for all its borrowings from the Alexander Romance and from Persian tales and epics. The portrait of a Yemeni hero borrowed from Alexander stories can already be seen in a poem attributed to the pre-Islamic poet Imruᵓ al-Qays:

> Have I not told you that destiny slays by guile,
> A slayer most treacherous indeed, it consumes men's sons.
> It banished Dhū Riyāsh from lordly citadels,
> When he had ruled the lowlands and the mountains.

[7] *CHALUP*, 253; Nagel, *Qiṣaṣ al-anbiyāᵓ*, 154–8. [8] Trans. Gateau, *Conquête*, 63–5.
[9] *CHALUP*, 55–63. [10] See Abel, *Roman d'Alexandre*, 73. [11] Cf. ch. 23, n. 51.
[12] See p. 447.

He was a valiant king; by revelation he sundered the horizons.
He drove his vanguards to their eastern edges,
And, where the sun climbs, barred the hills to Gog and Magog.[13]

Legends of this kind also appear in the *maghāzī* literature, which told of the lives of the Prophet's Companions, especially their martial exploits. No doubt the bulk of this material, which was intended to portray an ideal Muslim knight, is late medieval, but it is also true that less elaborated versions already circulated in the early ᶜAbbasid period. The exploits of ᶜAlī b. Abī Ṭālib were among the most renowned and absorbed a constantly growing corpus of legends.

The themes of love, edification and adventure all figure in a noteworthy example of the Companion legends, the widely diffused story of the Lakhmid Tamīm al-Dārī Abū ᵓl-Fawāris ("the Father of Knights"), who was converted to Islam from Christianity.[14] Tamīm is said to have been the first to light lamps in mosques, and is supposed to have been the man who taught the Prophet the signs and wonders which would herald the appearance of the Antichrist. In the Tamīm legend, the Prophet, when about to die, prophesies that Tamīm will experience unheard-of adventures. Some are fantastic, others allegorical:

One day a hideous afreet kidnapped Tamīm from his home at the hour of prayer. He vanished for seven years. So long was his absence that his wife assumed that he had died; she asked permission from the caliph ᶜUmar b. al-Khaṭṭāb to remarry. The caliph hesitated, but in the end agreed, and she accepted the suit of a man of the tribe of ᶜUdhrah. On the day she was to be wed, Tamīm unexpectedly descended from the sky. No-one recognised him. A dispute arose between him and the ᶜUdhrī over possession of the wife, and the caliph was obliged to arbitrate. Tamīm then told his tale:

The afreet had transported him to an island; their flight had lasted half a night, although the distance they had traversed was equal to seventy years. The denizens of the island were horrible creatures, ape-men, dog-headed men and swine. Tamīm was tortured for his piety. Then, suddenly, at the end of two years, jinn who were true believers arrived on the island; Tamīm confessed to them that he was a Companion, and the king of the jinn assigned one of his party to return him to his homeland. The volunteer – an unbelieving afreet – promised to perform the journey in seven hours; the king warned Tamīm not to pray during the flight. The journey began, and Tamīm heard the symphony of the angels at prayer; enraptured, he forgot the king's warning and extolled God's unity; the afreet melted, and Tamīm found himself on a huge island. He walked around it for three months, and beheld towering mountains and a fortress of snow. The island was a "Land of

13 *Dīwān*, 158; for Imruᵓ al-Qays, see *CHALUP*. Gog and Magog (in Arabic, Yājūj and Mājūj) are giants typifying the nomad populations of central Asia, whom Alexander is said to have kept from overrunning the civilized lands by means of a wall of brass.

14 For the Lakhmids of al-Ḥīrah, see *CHALUP*, 462–4. For interpretations of Tamīm's *nisbah* of al-Dārī and of the significance of his Christianity, see *EI*¹, "Tamīm al-Dārī".

Camphor", and it contained abundant herbs and trees and a deserted city of one hundred thousand palaces in the air; the city had eight golden gates eighty leagues apart studded with silver, pearl and ruby, and seven thousand towers of white ruby and dwellings of gold; it was watered by four rivers, and had forests of palms and pomegranates. Tamīm slept in bliss, but on the morrow was warned to leave; he marched for five days and saw a man praying on a mountain. He came upon a palace of gold and silver, inside which he saw men dressed in green and armed with swords and spears; blood oozed from their wounds and their bodies smelt of musk; he also espied youths seated within enclosures of pearl. He saluted two knights dressed in silk and brocade and holding rods of light who told him that if he pressed onward he would meet a guide; then he was stopped by a shaykh who offered him dates and explained that the city was Iram of the Columns,[15] and that it had taken three hundred and sixty years to build; the man whom he had seen praying was an apostle of Christ; the youths were martyred believers, and the knights were the angels Gabriel and Michael. "I (said the shaykh) am Elias; continue on your way and you will find guidance, but do not leave the shore."

Tamīm walked on the beach, living on leaves and herbs, until he saw a ship and was taken aboard. The crewmen were not Arabs, but the oldest of them had a copy of the books of Moses which testified to the unity of God and the prophethood of Muḥammad. For six months they sailed towards the lands of Japhet, but suddenly huge black mountains appeared and the ship was dashed to pieces. Tamīm floated away on a plank, was cast up on an island and walked until he was exhausted. Then came a youth clad in green who fed him with dates; Tamīm recovered his strength and marched up to two mountains. At the first he met a beautifully-adorned maiden and at the second a black dog guarding a cave. Tamīm stepped inside and found himself face to face with a one-eyed greybeard who lay fettered and manacled upon a stone bed. When this creature heard Tamīm utter the Prophet's name he expanded until his body filled the cave. Then Tamīm came to a third mountain. He saw one thousand mosques and one thousand fortified retreats (*ribāṭāt*)at its base; within each *ribāṭ* were men clad in hair shirts who prayed to their Creator in adoration. Tamīm saw two beings in torment who had been suspended by their hair in a well with fires above and below them. He retraced his steps to the youth who had fed him with dates and was told that the maiden was the world, the one-eyed creature Antichrist, the two tormented ones Hārūt and Mārūt, two angels who had taught mankind the arts of sorcery.[16] Where the sun rose was the China Sea, behind it was Jabal Qāf which girdled the earth, and beyond it there were countless cities and worlds as far as the realms of the angels. Two cities, each with one hundred thousand gates, stood at the point where the sun rose and set.

Then two clouds formed above Tamīm; one was black and filled with angels of wrath, the other white and crewed by angels of mercy. The youth – who now declared himself to be al-Khiḍr or Idrīs[17] – asked those in the white cloud to return

[15] Cf. Qurʾān, lxxxix.6–8; a legendary ruined city in the deep desert, see *CHALUP*, 248–9.

[16] Qurʾān, ii.102. They suffer torment for first sneering at human sinfulness, then succumbing to human temptations.

[17] Qurʾān, xviii.60–2, tells of an unnamed servant of God, usually identified by commentators as al-Khiḍr (or al-Khaḍir), who accompanies Moses on a journey and performs a number of shocking actions which are later revealed to have been divinely inspired (cf. *CHALUP*, 252–3). He is an immortal figure associated with a number of legends, including those of Alexander, Idrīs (Enoch) and Elias; see Friedländer, *Chadirlegende*.

Tamīm to his people; the cloud descended and landed like a flat table on the ground, Tamīm climbed in and a year later was carried down to his former home.

The tale concluded, the caliph ᶜUmar now had to judge who was the lawful spouse. He consulted ᶜAlī b. Abī Ṭālib, the Prophet's son-in-law, who vouched for Tamīm's honesty, and the wife was given the final choice. She asked to be reunited with her husband, the ideal Companion.[18]

In the above story Islamic elements are emphasized, but such an emphasis is not uniformly characteristic of ᶜAbbasid story-telling. The legend of Tamīm may be compared with an early account of heroic exploits, the *Tārīkh* ("History") of Ibn Ḥabīb, a Hispano-Arab work dating from the third/ninth century which contains legends about Mūsā b. Nuṣayr, the conqueror of al-Andalus. Mūsā ordered Ṭāriq the Berber to embark near a rock and disembark at a brown hill close to which stood a foundry and the statue of a bull. The statue had to be shattered and command of the vanguard given to a tall man with a ruddy complexion who was squint-eyed and had withered hands. After the Muslim army had captured Algeciras, it fought an archer on horseback who guarded a bridge; after slaying two of Mūsā's men the archer fell to the ground and was found to be a figure of copper. Later Mūsā laid siege to a fortress of copper and discovered copper boxes filled with jinn which had been imprisoned by Solomon. Ibn Ḥabīb drew his fanciful inspiration from an Egyptian scholar, ᶜAbdullāh b. Wahb (d. 198/813).[19]

ᶜAbbasid story-telling not only absorbed and relaunched earlier themes and legends; it also contained the germs, not yet fully developed, of later story-telling. As examples, there is scant evidence to indicate that Abū Zayd al-Hilālī and ᶜAntarah b. Shaddād, later to be popular folk-heroes, were the subject of elaborated tales or were widely known in the ᶜAbbasid period.[20] The ᶜAbbasid writings which refer to the exploits of ᶜAntarah are *dīwān*s of verse which simply explain how the pre-Islamic warrior-poet, son of an Arab father and a black slave, gained his freedom and fought with mixed

18 Basset, "Les adventures merveilleuses de Temīm el-Dārī", 3–26. The journeys of Tamīm al-Dārī are referred to by Jāḥiẓ (d. 255/869), but the setting and some details of the above version recall the ideas and beliefs which accompanied the Almoravid and Almohad movements in the Maghrib during the fifth/eleventh and sixth/twelfth centuries. The person of Tamīm al-Dārī has been integrated into non-Arabic cycles of oral literature. Thus, amongst the Zarma of the Niger Republic, Tamimoun Dari has become the close companion of Zabarkâne (himself the Companion of the Prophet, al-Zibriqān b. Badr), who is held to be the progenitor of the Zarma heroes, Mali Béro and Issa Biro Krombi. It is not known when the Arab tales reached this part of Africa.

19 Egypt in the third/ninth century was a major source for Arabic legends, some of which were told in Spain, e.g. the legend of the opening of the tower of Toledo by King Roderick the Visigoth is Egyptian-inspired, see Basset, *Légendes arabes d'Espagne*. On Ṭāriq the Berber (Ṭāriq b. Ziyād), cf. *CHALUP*, 119.

20 The historical ᶜAntarah was a pre-Islamic poet (see *CHALUP*); in *Sīrat ᶜAntar*, he becomes the champion of Islam and of the Arabs and does battle both with pre-Islamic kings and with the Crusaders. The legendary Abū Zayd is portrayed as leading the fifth/twelfth century migration of the Banū Hilāl to the Maghrib; see *EI*², "Hilāl".

success for his tribe of ᶜAbs; the tale of his heroic death – based upon the death of Rabīᶜah b. Muqaddam of the Banū Firās – was to be added later. Evidence from ᶜAbbasid writers, for example al-Hamdānī's *Iklīl*, indicates that ᶜAntarah's love for ᶜAblah began as an example of the lyric tales of pairs of thwarted lovers referred to at the beginning of this chapter, and in ᶜAbbasid stories he is not yet the knight *par excellence* he later became in *Sīrat ᶜAntar*. In the early ᶜAbbasid age the knightly ideal was represented by the Yemeni warrior, ᶜAmr b. Maᶜdī Karib, who did battle with a fabulous sword, al-Ṣamṣāmah. Another Yemeni hero who, like ᶜAmr b. Maᶜdī Karib, appeared in ᶜAbbasid historical works, and by fusion with other heroes was to attain fame in later medieval literature, was Sayf b. Dhī Yazan, who freed his country from Abyssinian occupation prior to Islam. A version of the romance of Sayf existed in the fourth/tenth century. Ibn al-Nadīm in the *Fihrist* mentions the title of a work by Hishām b. Muḥammad b. al-Sāʾib al-Kalbī (d. *c.* 204/819), *Kitāb al-Yaman wa-amr Sayf*,[21] and the historian al-Ṭabarī (d. 310/923) devotes two chapters of his *History* to the story of Sayf or Maᶜdī Karib. In his account the brief biography of Sayf, included by Wahb b. Munabbih in his *Kitāb al-Tījān*, is considerably expanded by borrowings from Persian sources: Sayf is assisted in his struggle by an army of Persian archers and vagabonds from the court of Chosroes; Wahriz, their chief, who is half-blind, aims his mighty bow at the head of King Masrūq, the half-brother of Sayf; his arrow slays him and the Yemen is delivered. The blind archer who looses a fateful shot, probably a Greek inspiration, was to reappear quite often in Arab legend; Wahriz is perhaps the earliest mention of such a character. (It is worthy of mention that the lengthy *Sīrat Sayf b. Dhī Yazan* of the Mamlūk age has no organic connection with this earlier "pseudo-epic" material. The name of the chief hero is the same and the enemy is the land of Ethiopia and its king; otherwise, it draws its inspiration from diverse oriental and African material.)[22]

A noteworthy feature of the pseudo-historical or legendary literature of the ᶜAbbasid age was its attribution to leading men of letters, grammarians, lexicographers and philologists. One such was al-Aṣmaᶜī, the Basran grammarian (d. 213/828), to whom is attributed the composition of the Hijazi recension of *Sīrat ᶜAntar*. In fact there is no evidence to indicate that he, or a pseudo-Aṣmaᶜī, ever undertook this formidable task. On the other hand Ibn al-Muqaffaᶜ (d. *c.* 139/757) was the translator and part author of the most famous and distinguished work of animal tales in Arabic

[21] *Fihrist*, Tajaddud, 109/Dodge, I, 208.

[22] For a recent attempt to trace the early adventures of Sayf and to link them with those of his late-medieval successor, see Manqūsh, *Sayf b. Dhī Yazan*.

literature, his rendering into Arabic of the "Fables of Bidpai", *Kalīlah wa-Dimnah*. The moral of the book is addressed to the *kātib*s of the late Umayyad or early ᶜAbbasid court, and its function is partly didactic, its intention being to illustrate rules of conduct for princes and administrators. But the work plumbs other depths, philosophical and psychological; the animals who are introduced, their cruelty, cunning and will to survive, are a comment on, or parody of, human behaviour. Ibn al-Muqaffaᶜ had successors in this field, one of whom was the *kātib* Muḥammad b. ᶜAbdūs al-Jahshiyārī (d. 331/942), author of *Kitāb al-Wuzarāʾ*,[23] who began an encyclopaedic work which was planned to contain a thousand stories derived from Arabic, Persian, Greek and Indian sources. To quote Ibn al-Nadīm's *Fihrist*: "each section [i.e. story] was separate, not connected with any other. He summoned to his presence the storytellers, from whom he obtained the best things about which they knew and which they did well. He also selected whatever pleased him from the books composed of stories and fables." He collected 480 nights, each night (*laylah*) being a complete story of some fifty pages.[24]

Al-Jahshiyārī's stories, it seems, were juxtaposed. By contrast, in *Kalīlah wa-Dimnah* the animal fables are linked, by means of their narrators: at the end of each tale, an animal is selected from it to narrate the next. As this suggests, the collection and especially the translation of stories introduced not only themes and details but also methods of story-telling. Thus India was the source which inspired the invention of many of the fabulous creatures – dog-headed men, dragons and Amazon queens – which Arab geographers introduced to give colour and variety to their material. India too was the source not only of separate stories such as those collected by al-Jahshiyārī, but also of the Arabic Buddha legends, the most important of which is *Bilawhar wa-Būdāsaf*, a Middle Persian version of which was rendered into Arabic by an unknown translator, probably in the third/ninth century,[25] and which supplied Arabic writing with a group of themes, one of which will be discussed below. But India also passed on to Arabic story-telling a narrative technique, that of the frame-story. In the earliest parts of the *Thousand and One Nights*, where Shahrazād, faced by death in the morning, redeems her life and happiness by recounting story after story to her spouse, King Shahriyār, the stories are prolonged by making the characters within each story tell stories themselves; tales can be inserted at will within the framework of the main narration. Mia Gerhardt has analyzed three main categories of frame-story – i.e. stories contained within

[23] See ch. 6, n. 24. [24] *Fihrist*, Tajaddud, 363–4/Dodge, II, 714.

[25] This Arabic version was subsequently translated into Greek, and the Greek version became the source of the Christian legend of Barlaam and Josaphat. For earlier and subsequent Arabic versions of episodes from the Buddha romance, see *EI*², "Bilawhar wa-Yūdāsaf".

a "frame" or main narration – which she discusses in terms of the function they fulfil in relation to the "frame" itself.[26] Further categories could be added; and in many ways the framed story is an *idée fixe* in the entire literary repertoire of Arabic courtly romance. Any opportunity which enabled a sub-plot to develop within a narrative was used to the full. The nocturnal wanderings of Hārūn al-Rashīd, his vizier Jaᶜfar the Barmecide, and Masrūr the executioner from the palace into the streets, offer scope for unexpected plebeian episodes to be worked into the narrative. Hārūn follows his fancy and is delighted by his extraordinary encounters; as a result of them he redresses wrongs and injustices. He cares for the poor and needy. The scene is invariably Baghdad at night, and the river Tigris, its bridges, boats and fisher-folk are much in evidence. An Indian inspiration for this theme and several of its details may be found in the Arabic text of *Bilawhar wa-Būdāsaf* in "The Story of the Pagan King and his Wise and Devout Vizier":

That king, despite the error of his beliefs, was humble and affectionate, close to the people, easy and well-disposed and just towards his subjects, desirous of their well-being. The king and his vizier had remained good companions for a span of time. One night, after the people were peacefully settled, the king said to his vizier, "Would you like us to ride through the city and observe the state of the people in the depths of the night? We shall examine the effects of the rains which we have suffered of late." The vizier replied, "If this be your wish". So the king and the vizier rode forth at night and went round the quarters of the city. In one street they passed by a common dung-heap where people tipped their offal and dumped the rubbish from their dwellings and the sweepings from their houses. The king espied a light from a fire coming from the direction of the dung-heap, and said to his vizier, "This fire has a story to tell. Let us dismount. We shall go on foot until we come close to it and know all about it". When they reached the source of the light they found a hole which was like a mountain cavern. It had been dug out by one of the poor who beg for alms among the people. He had taken the dung-heap as a dwelling for his wife and himself. The king and the vizier heard sounds of singing and of stringed instruments before they peered into the hollow, and when they did so – in a manner which permitted them to remain invisible to the poor man and his wife – they saw a man who was deformed and clad in worn clothes, shabby rags from the dung-heap. He was resting on a support which he had fashioned from some object in the dung-heap; in front of him was a pottery vessel which held his drink, and his hands played a *ṭunbūr* [a long-necked stringed instrument]. His wife's state was similar to his own: she was deformed and clad in similar rags. She stood facing him, and poured him a drink whenever he asked for it; she danced for him whenever he played and saluted him as though he were a king whenever she came close to him. He called her the "mistress of women". They praised one another in words of honour and kindness and beauty; they were filled with joy, merriment and song; they manifested a deep love and a mutual devotion which defied description.

The king was amused and amazed. He shared his thoughts with the vizier, who saw his chance to speak to him of spiritual matters.[27]

[26] *The Art of Story Telling*, 377–416.

[27] Gimaret, *Kitāb Bilawhar*, 57–9.

In broad summary, ʿAbbasid story-telling introduced into Arabic written literature two main forms of composition, which were in turn profoundly to influence the art of the popular story-teller and the repertoire of the oral bard. The first, the frame-story, enabled the imagination of the raconteur to roam widely, though without losing sight of the central or principal plot of the tale. Suspense was maintained and considerable improvisation was allowed. The second narrative form, the edifying and epic *sīrah*, was to become fashionable in the age of the Ayyubids and the Mamlūks, though it certainly existed in the earlier ʿAbbasid period. In the *sīrah* – as in the lives of certain Christian saints which seem in part to have inspired the genre – the exploits of a hero or villain are unfolded in a series of linked episodes which often have little relation to one another. The main character is introduced and at the end bows and makes his exit; in between, a life-story is told or interest is sustained by a repetitive series of combats, amatory quests, fantastic escapades, poems and anecdotes. Something comparable is perhaps to be found in the *maqāmāt* of al-Hamadhānī and al-Ḥarīrī, a *belles-lettristic* genre, although its subject-matter is taken from low-life. For it should be emphasized that the ʿAbbasid age was an age both of *belles-lettres* and of "oral literature". I do not believe that there was ever a clear-cut distinction between the two; each influenced the other, and the literary genres to which this interaction gave birth were to be developed and eventually reached their peak in the age of the Mamlūks.

CHAPTER 9

ᶜABBASID POETRY AND ITS ANTECEDENTS

PRE-ISLAMIC POETRY

The difference between the formal ode (*qaṣīdah*) and the occasional poem (*qiṭᶜah*) seems to have been already fairly well established in pre-Islamic poetry. Despite the difficulties inherent in discussing the texts of pre-Islamic poems – which were transmitted and perhaps in some cases composed orally, so that there is some degree of fluidity in their structure and wording[1] – and despite the fact that in many instances we cannot be absolutely sure that what has come down to us as a *qiṭᶜah* was not originally part of a *qaṣīdah*, it can be said, with due caution, that stylistically there is a discernible difference between the two types of composition. Apart from its obvious freedom from the relative external structural rigour of the polythematic *qaṣīdah*, the *qiṭᶜah* is generally marked by the simplicity of its language. Examples are Imruʾ al-Qays's elegies on his father or ancestors, composed in a language considerably simpler than that of his *Muᶜallaqah* or his "Umm Jundab" *qaṣīdah*, with its elaborate descriptions of his mistress Umm Jundab and of his horse,[2] or Labīd's elegies on his half-brother Arbad, which may be contrasted with the much more formal and recondite diction of his *Muᶜallaqah*.[3] This simplicity of language is not just a feature of elegies, although these understandably tend to be closer to spontaneous and direct utterances of grief; it is also to be found in other types of poetic expression, as in Labīd's well-known lines on his old age or in the "religious" pieces attributed to Umayyah b. Abī ʾl-Ṣalt. Not all *qaṣīdah* poetry is devoid of such direct expression: examples that come readily to mind are al-Aᶜshā's description of wine, even though this is embedded in a longer work of panegyric, or parts of ᶜAmr b. Kulthūm's *Muᶜallaqah*, particularly the section dealing with the more urgent theme of his recent humiliation at the court of ᶜAmr b. Hind[4] (which, perhaps significantly, the fifth/eleventh-century scholar al-Tibrīzī omits from his edition of the

[1] See e.g. Zwettler, *The Oral Tradition.* [2] Cf. *CHALUP*, 90–1, 94–5, 61–2.
[3] Ibid., 54–5, 83. [4] Cf. ibid., 101, 76–7, 84.

poem). Nevertheless, it is probably valid in general terms to say that the occasional piece is of greater simplicity than the *qaṣīdah*.

Given the relative freedom and directness of the *qiṭᶜah*, it is perhaps not surprising that it is in the *qiṭᶜah* that the major developments in Arabic poetry during the Islamic period, which will be discussed briefly below, should be most easily noticeable. Yet it would be wrong to assume that later attempts to produce *qaṣīdah*s did not involve some changes in the nature and scope of the latter too. The pre-Islamic *qaṣīdah* was the product of a tribal desert society with its own ethos and values; it was created to celebrate these values, and by a ritualistic catharsis to enable its hearers to face issues of life and death in a usually harsh environment. The poet had an important social function to fulfil: to sing the praises of his tribe, to defend its honour and attack its enemies. Few societies, in fact, accorded their poets the acclaim and respect which, at least according to later tradition, were given to the pre-Islamic poet, and it was entirely appropriate for a recent scholar to write on pre-Islamic poetry under the rubric, "The poet as hero".[5] But the new religion of Islam, with its fundamentally different set of spiritual values, brought about a radical change in both the poet's social status and his role; so much so that to refer to the *qaṣīdah*s produced before and after Islam in the same terms can be seriously misleading. We may therefore usefully borrow the terms used by C. S. Lewis in his discussion of epic,[6] and refer to the pre-Islamic *qaṣīdah* as the Primary *Qaṣīdah*, to distinguish it from the later Secondary *Qaṣīdah*. We need not, indeed cannot, adopt Lewis's criteria of classification and view the distinction between the two as purely chronological; despite superficial resemblances, the Secondary *Qaṣīdah* is a very different type of thing from the Primary, alike in its nature, its function and indeed in its *raison d'être*.

EARLY ISLAMIC AND UMAYYAD POETRY

The change, of course, was not immediate. On the contrary, because it related to people's sensibility and their world outlook, it was slow to make itself felt. The view once widely held that Muḥammad and Islam discouraged poetry and poets is now generally discredited, and, according to the early biographies, the Prophet enlisted the help of several poets, such as Ḥassān b. Thābit, in his struggle against his pagan opponents. However, there is nothing specifically Islamic in any significant way in the poetry ascribed to Muḥammad's followers: it praises him for traditional values

[5] Hamori, *The Art*, ch. 1.

[6] *A Preface to Paradise Lost*, Oxford, 1946, 12; Lewis distinguishes between the Primary Epic such as Homer's and the Secondary Epic of poets like Milton.

such as munificence, courage in battle, etc. (and Ḥassān b. Thābit still praises wine even in eulogies of the Prophet of God); though it is true that, in the early Islamic period, *hijāʾ* (satire) seemed to suffer, and Islam seemed to moderate, at least for a while, the tone of *fakhr* (boasting poetry): for instance, the author of a poem known as *al-Yatīmah*, Suwayd b. Abī Kāhil (d. 65/684), gratefully attributes his tribe's virtues to God's work.[7] There seems to have been, also, a relative decline in poetic output in the early years of Islam, attributed by some medieval theorists to the Arabs' being engaged in the wars of conquest; however, recent research has shown evidence that a considerable amount of poetry was in fact composed by men who fought in these wars.[8] The poems, of whose absolute authenticity we can never be certain, tend to be short passages, the polythematic *qaṣīdah* giving place to the *qiṭʿah* with a single theme, that of urging on the warriors or celebrating their courage. There are also elegies on those fallen in battle and poems of longing for the homeland. Instead of the stately language of the traditional *qaṣīdah*, the vocabulary of these poems – some of which are composed in the *rajaz* metre, which at this period still connoted extemporization and simplicity – tends to be simple and straightforward, with occasional Quranic allusions. Many of the authors of such poems remained obscure; a few, such as Abū Miḥjan al-Thaqafī, Abū Dhuʾayb al-Hudhalī and al-Nābighah al-Jaʿdī,[9] had established a reputation before Islam, but very few of those who first distinguished themselves during the conquests attained the reputation of al-Qaʿqāʿ b. ʿAmr al-Tamīmī. Yet their work is important in that it signalled the onset of a new stage in the development of Arabic poetry, one in which the Primary *Qaṣīdah* had obviously ceased to be relevant to the new social, intellectual and spiritual reality.

This lack of relevance of the *qaṣīdah* is accentuated in the poetry of the Khārijīs.[10] Al-Ṭirimmāḥ b. Ḥakīm is probably the only Khārijī poet to open a poem *qaṣīdah*-fashion with a *nasīb* (amatory prelude), but in this, as in some other respects such as his eulogy of Umayyad rulers, he is very much the exception. Generally Khārijī poets seemed to confine themselves to poems of the *qiṭʿah* type, short pieces of great simplicity and immediacy; at times, as in the case of ʿImrān b. Ḥiṭṭān, Qaṭarī b. al-Fujāʾah and Mālik al-Mazmūm, the poetry acquires a markedly subjective character, expressing a high degree of emotional intensity. All these poets gave expression to an attitude towards death entirely different from that which characterizes pre-Islamic poetry, where the fear and awareness of inevitable death seems to dominate the perception of life. In Khārijī poetry, there is a positive and indeed gleeful welcoming of dying, since to die for one's religion was an act of

7 Lyall, *Mufaḍḍalīyāt*, I, 381ff. 8 See e.g. al-Qāḍī, *Shiʿr al-futūḥ*.
9 Cf. *CHALUP*, ch. 2. On Abū Miḥjan, cf. 223, below. 10 See pp. 186–8.

martyrdom believed to bring about a certain reward in heaven. Like the pre-Islamic poet, the Khārijī tends to boast of his prowess and physical courage, but here the similarity between them ends, for, although the Khārijī poet is still his own hero, he is serving a cause greater than that of self or tribe; he is God's soldier, fighting for God's cause, his death testifying to God's glory. Hence the ontological irrelevance of the *qaṣīdah* to him: he no longer needs its ritual function, Islam having provided him with a more meaningful alternative.

But the selfsame religion that made the dissident Khārijī a warrior–hero inevitably reduced the social status of the conformist poet. The Khārijī poet was, spiritually, the Muslim descendant of the pre-Islamic brigand–poet, the *ṣuᶜlūk* outsider;[11] but the Muslim counterpart of the pre-Islamic tribal poet became, in the course of time, the panegyric poet who sang the praises of a patron. Whatever spiritual and edifying or socially cohesive functions the *qaṣīdah* might have had were taken over by the Qurʾān and the new religion; and the tribe which needed its own spokesman was submerged, for a period at least, to re-emerge only within the context of a state in which certain tribes or tribal groupings achieved dominance and the holders of high office needed to have their praises sung by poets of proven distinction, but not necessarily related to them by ties of blood or tribal kinship. It was as a result of this fundamental change in the position of poets under the Umayyads that the Secondary *Qaṣīdah* was born.

Primary and Secondary Qaṣīdah

It is time now to consider the main differences between the Primary and Secondary *Qaṣīdah*. In the first place the Primary *Qaṣīdah* was not just a poem in the familiar modern sense of the word; it had more than a literary function. As we have seen, it was akin to ancient Greek tragedy in that it was a re-enactment of the common values of the tribe, with a similar ritual function, asserting life-impulses and enabling the tribe to face with greater fortitude the forces of death in a hostile world. This does not mean that in some respects the *qaṣīdah* had not already become a literary convention, or had not acquired such conventions, in pre-Islamic Arabia: in the very opening of his *Muᶜallaqah*, ᶜAntarah wonders if previous poets had left anything unsaid or unsung – a sentiment also expressed by a poet as early as Imruʾ al-Qays – while ᶜAdī b. Zayd, who was a Christian, could still begin a *qaṣīdah* with weeping over the ruins of the encampment of the beloved, although presumably his religious faith was in theory capable of providing

[11] Cf. *CHALUP*, 32.

him with an answer to the riddle of life which would render the emotional need for the *qaṣīdah* less urgent. Nevertheless, it is safe to assert that whereas the Primary *Qaṣīdah* was predominantly ritual in character, the Secondary *Qaṣīdah* was predominantly literary and craftsmanly. The fifth/eleventh-century critic Ibn Rashīq once likened ancient and "modern" (i.e. post-Umayyad) Arab poets to builders and decorators respectively: after the ancients had erected the edifice, the moderns came and embellished it. The analogy underlines a basic difference in both function and style, which emerged even earlier than Ibn Rashīq believed: the ancient poet was concerned with a building which served an immediately useful purpose, for his was a functional role in his society; the poet of the Islamic era, on the other hand, was not trying to create another building – he worked within the framework of the old *qaṣīdah* – but performed a secondary, aesthetic role, insofar as his task was chiefly one of refinement and his concern with detail, not broad outlines. (Nevertheless, such "details" and "embellishments" could, on occasion, take on a significant and structural role.)

Secondly, the Secondary *Qaṣīdah* is generally the product of literary rather than primary experience. It is full of allusions to Primary *Qaṣīdah*s which it consciously sets out to imitate (a fact which was responsible for the eventual development of a peculiarly Arabic branch of literary criticism, the study of plagiarisms).[12] Thus when, in a famous eulogy of the caliph ᶜAbd al-Malik, the Umayyad poet al-Akhṭal compares his patron to the Euphrates, the audience is immediately aware that he is drawing upon the same comparison made by an earlier poet, al-Nābighah al-Dhubyānī, in his eulogy of al-Nuᶜmān, king of Ḥīrah, and can appreciate the degree of elaboration and refinement wrought by the later poet. This Horation conception of "imitation" was maintained throughout the subsequent history of Arabic poetry (and indeed until comparatively recent times): just as al-Mutanabbī echoes the pre-Islamic al-Aᶜshā, so al-Maᶜarrī imitates al-Mutanabbī, and so on.

Thirdly, the Secondary *Qaṣīdah* is chiefly a poem of panegyric, however polythematic it may outwardly appear to be. In the Primary *Qaṣīdah* the poet usually identifies himself with his tribe, so that in boasting of his virtues he is making more than an individual assertion; but in the Secondary *Qaṣīdah* the element of self-praise is generally reduced to a minimum: instead, the poet sings the praises of his patron, who may or may not be of his tribe. He is therefore selling his poetic wares to the highest bidder, and is prepared to change his patron if this proves more profitable and even, if his patron disappoints him, to reverse his attitude completely and satirize him.

[12] See p. 351.

To an extent unknown in the Primary *Qaṣīdah*, even where the poet was a court-poet, the concept of sincerity therefore is not, nor should it be, of much relevance to the Secondary *Qaṣīdah*. On the whole, then, the author of the Secondary *Qaṣīdah* is at the opposite pole from the Khārijī poet, and it is not surprising to find the Khārijī ᶜImrān b. Ḥiṭṭān bitterly criticizing the Umayyad poet al-Farazdaq for his "false" panegyrics. Seen against this background, the growing dominance of hyperbole ceases to be a puzzle. In addition, the poet's need to secure a living drives the author of the Secondary *Qaṣīdah* not only to write panegyrics, but also to act as an entertainer to please his patron and his patron's court. To a large extent, the *naqāʾiḍ* or poetic slanging-matches in which the Umayyad trio, Jarīr, al-Farazdaq and al-Akhṭal, were involved[13] were motivated less by any wish to uphold the honour of their tribes than by the desire to entertain their patrons and their audience; Jarīr and al-Farazdaq in fact belonged to the same tribe, Tamīm, and, in his elegy on al-Farazdaq, Jarīr describes him as "the support of the whole tribe of Tamīm, its tongue and proud spokesman everywhere". Poets often became their patrons' boon-companions as well as their entertainers, particularly when a patron developed a real interest in poetry rather than merely commissioning it for propaganda purposes.

Finally, the former sharp distinction between *rajaz*, the metre used in earlier times for such lowly forms of verse as the shanty, and the grander metres (*ṭawīl*, *kāmil*, *basīṭ*, etc.) used in the polythematic *qaṣīdah*, now disappeared; *rajaz* was henceforth to be used for serious purposes as much as any other metre – indeed it eventually became the medium of didactic poetry – and, though a distinction was still made between *urjūzah* (a piece written in *rajaz*) and *qaṣīdah* (a piece written in the other metres), the distinction was no more than formal; the term *qaṣīdah* itself, by ᶜAbbasid times, was no longer reserved for polythematic poems of some length, but could simply mean "a poem" of any kind.

The recipe for the Islamic panegyric was basically the same as for the pre-Islamic, but with some Islamic ingredients added. The patron's courage and martial valour are there, together with his hospitality and munificence, which are more strongly emphasized, for obvious reasons. The ruler is not only just and resolute but the Guardian of the Faith and God's favourite, ruling by a special mandate from Him according to His dictates; the poet also sees to it that there are some Quranic allusions in his language. These are the common themes encountered, for instance, in Jarīr's eulogies of Umayyad rulers, governors and generals, and, as has been noted, many of the ideas which occur in them subsequently became regular features of the

[13] *CHALUP*, 410–12.

Secondary *Qaṣīdah*, to be used later on by ᶜAbbasid poets such as Bashshār, Abū Nuwās, Abū Tammām and al-Buḥturī.[14] Yet within the limitations, technical, thematic and social, of the Secondary *Qaṣīdah*, poets even as early as the Umayyad period had been able to express their individuality and give shape to their own insights into reality. In his panegyric on Sulaymān b. ᶜAbd al-Malik, despite its conventional *qaṣīdah* structure, al-Farazdaq produced a poem deeply rooted in the social and political reality of the time with a wealth of allusions to the malpractices of tax-collectors and the brutality and repression of al-Ḥajjāj, governor of Iraq; in one of the *naqāʾiḍ*, the poet slips in a marvellous description of a frosty night in the desert, clearly drawn from experience, not convention,[15] and many other examples could be cited in his poetry. His contemporary Dhū ʾl-Rummah often makes descriptions of his feelings for his beloved, Mayy, form part of his *qaṣīdah*s and makes nature share his sorrows, investing even the conventional theme of the deserted encampment with such moments of direct vision as his justly praised description of himself sitting making and unmaking patterns in the dust while the crows circle overhead; indeed, it often seems that to describe nature is the chief object of his *qaṣīdah*s.[16] The potential of the *qaṣīdah* for conveying an individual poetic vision was to be still further developed by a number of ᶜAbbasid poets.

Development of the qiṭᶜah

The two areas in which dramatic changes took place in the *qiṭᶜah* in early Islamic and Umayyad times were love poetry (*ghazal*) and the wine-poem (*khamriyyah*), no doubt in large part thanks to the spectacular development of singing during the same period, which saw the rise in Mecca and Medina of a wealthy class of Arabs whom the Umayyads paid to discourage them from seeking political power, and who developed a passion for entertainment, particularly the art of singing in which captive slave-girls from the conquered lands excelled. Poems were now composed specifically in order to be sung, with the result that their vocabulary had to be considerably simplified to accommodate their musical setting and to enable foreign girls not well versed in the Arabic language to perform them, and for the same reasons there was a preference for shorter metrical forms such as *ramal*, *khafīf*, *sarīᶜ* and *mutaqārib*. Instead of the tribal *qaṣīdah* celebrating communal values, we now have poems dealing with the various aspects of love, which centre on the poet's "individual" psyche. These are best exemplified by the work of ᶜUmar b. Abī Rabīᶜah, whose bulky *Dīwān* is

[14] Ḍayf, *Taṭawwur*, 161. [15] *Dīwān*, I, 324ff, II, 551ff. [16] Cf. *CHALUP*, 427–31.

devoted to the subject of love. Even when he uses the props of the *qaṣīdah*, he clearly does so as an excuse to introduce love as the real subject of the poem, and the women he writes about belong to a totally different world from that of the *qaṣīdah*; they are sophisticated and literate and enjoy the wit of the literary salon. Different too are the situations he creates for the lover and his mistress: in many an elegant poem he depicts himself as the helpless victim of unreciprocated passion; at times love is set against a beautiful natural landscape, with nature, as it were, ennobling his passion, and, anticipating one of the features of "courtly" Arabic love poetry, the poet may pray to God not for salvation but for fulfilment of his love. Finally, despite the freshness and directness of his love poetry, its playfulness and lively dialogues, its dealing with concrete experience and its strikingly sensuous elements, it already contains the beginnings of what was later to become the conventional love "situation" in ᶜAbbasid poetry, with its apparatus of messengers, spies, slanderers, etc.

"Courtly" love poetry proper developed at much the same time, but against the much simpler background of desert life; ᶜUdhrī poetry, so called from the tribe of ᶜUdhrah with which it is chiefly associated, takes as its theme hopeless and unfulfilled passion. Composed in a tremulous language of unusual transparency, revealing great emotional intensity, it shows the lover yearning for a highly idealized woman placed far beyond his grasp, who inspires in him a love which may lead to madness or death. Often the lover's feelings attain an unmistakable degree of spirituality, ranging from the use of religious terms to an almost Platonic concept of the pairing of the lovers' souls, and in much ᶜUdhrī poetry nature figures quite prominently, as the lovers address birds, the wind, clouds and rain, and even hills and mountains which seem to call out to them in sympathy. This tradition of idealized love was to continue, albeit in somewhat diluted form, in the poetry of the ᶜAbbasid period in the work of such poets as al-ᶜAbbās b. al-Aḥnaf,[17] and indeed left its mark on all subsequent love poetry, even of the most sensual variety. With the rise of mysticism it also influenced the work of Sufi poets who, instead of endowing human love with a quasi-religious dimension, employed it as a metaphor for divine love. ᶜUdhrī poetry also contributed to a tradition of prose writing in which love is studied and sacred or profane theories of love propounded.[18]

It was in the affluent and sophisticated world of the Umayyad princes that the wine-song was developed as an independent genre, and the poet who is regarded, with some justice, by the fourth/tenth-century author of *Kitāb al-Aghānī*, as the originator of the *khamriyyah*, and who provided the model for

17 See ch. 12, nn. 6–8. 18 Cf. pp. 91–2, 210.

all his successors, including Abū Nuwās, is al-Walīd b. Yazīd.[19] This prince was himself a poet, musician and singer all in one, and this may explain why in his poetry a remarkable degree of lyricism is achieved. Though only a small amount of his poetry has survived, there is enough to suggest that his originality lay not in his treating wine as an independent theme and in his use of new, short metres, but in the attitude of adoration he adopts towards wine, complicated by the awareness of breaking a religious taboo; this adds a spiritual dimension to his poems which was profoundly to influence Abū Nuwās. Al-Walīd, in fact, paves the way for ᶜAbbasid poetry in many ways. His wine-poems sometimes express a defiant attitude to the certainties of religion, an attitude of doubt and even rejection, which is clearly the product of a clash of ideas and of the intellectual sophistication which marked the latter part of the Umayyad era and is the hallmark of the ᶜAbbasid. It has been claimed that al-Walīd absorbed his cynicism from his teacher ᶜAbd al-Ṣamad b. ᶜAbd al-Aᶜlāʾ, who was thought by some to be a *zindīq* (free-thinker).[20] However, some Umayyad poets had already shown an interest in the intellectual life and debates of their time: al-Farazdaq is said to have attended the sessions of the ascetic Ḥasan al-Baṣrī,[21] while Jarīr went to those of the theologian Ibn Sīrīn. But with the leading ᶜAbbasid poets we find not only a keener interest in intellectual debates, but that the quality of philosophical thinking had immeasurably deepened and its range widened as a result of the expansion of Arabic culture. Most, if not all, of these poets were involved in the intellectual and theological controversies of their day: Bashshār, Abū Nuwās, Ibn al-Rūmī and Abū Tammām were all influenced by the Muᶜtazilah, the rationalist theologians of Islam, and what is no less important is that the patrons they sought to please, particularly the caliphs, were themselves well-educated and intellectually sophisticated, their intellectual tastes often being closely linked to their political objectives, as in the case of the caliph al-Maʾmūn's adoption of Muᶜtazilism.

"MODERN" POETRY

It is clear, from the foregoing remarks, that the major changes in post-Islamic poetry, which decisively influenced its course throughout the ᶜAbbasid era, actually took place in the Umayyad period, and that both the growth of the Secondary *Qaṣīdah* and the stylistic and thematic development of the *qiṭᶜah* were due to a process of gradual transition. It is no

19 Abū ʾl-Faraj al-Iṣfahānī, *Aghānī*, VI, 110.
20 Ḍayf, *Taṭawwur*, 293; on the *zindīqs*, cf. pp. 41–2, above.
21 Cf. pp. 267–8, 273.

accident that the poet described by many medieval critics as the first of the moderns (*muḥdathūn*) was Bashshār b. Burd (*c.* 95–167/713–83), who straddled both the Umayyad and ᶜAbbasid periods. Yet, like some European literatures, Arabic literature had its own battle of the Ancients and Moderns, and in this battle it was assumed that the moderns were really the ᶜAbbasids and not the Umayyads. What then, one may ask, led ᶜAbbasid critics to hold this view; what are the developments in ᶜAbbasid poetry that might be regarded as new, even though some of them may have had their germ in the preceding period?

Ethnic diversity

By ᶜAbbasid times, the composition of Arabic poetry was no longer the prerogative of Arabs: major contributions were made by poets of non-Arab origin (known in Arabic as *muwalladūn*), such as Bashshār and Abū Nuwās, both Persian by origin, and Ibn al-Rūmī, who had Byzantine blood in him. The Arabic language and literary traditions had now become easily accessible to the conquered peoples, who were not slow to realize that to distinguish themselves in Arabic culture was, apart from other considerations, a likely means to attain wealth or high office. While it is hazardous to attribute specific stylistic features to particular races, there is no doubt that ethnic variety must have contributed considerably, alike in themes and in attitudes and techniques, to the varied richness of poetic production under the ᶜAbbasid empire, which stretched over an enormous area and covered a multiplicity of cultures, and the implications of this process of cultural assimilation and diversification were not lost on early ᶜAbbasid critics.

Diversification of poetic language

Patrons, particularly from early ᶜAbbasid times, were often well versed in literary Arabic and in poetry, many having received a thorough training from the philologists who assumed an increasing importance in Arabic literary life. For obvious religious and political reasons, many ᶜAbbasid caliphs were anxious to appear as defenders of the faith and consequently to encourage the learning of Arabic, the language of the Qurʾān; they had their children educated in the Islamic and relevant ancillary sciences, including the study of ancient poetry, and encouraged philologists and transmitters (*rāwī*s) to compile collections of pre-Islamic poetry (the best-known example is the *Mufaḍḍaliyyāt* compiled by al-Mufaḍḍal al-Ḍabbī for al-Mahdī while the future caliph was still a boy). As a result, a generally conservative attitude to language prevailed, and in order to please their patrons, poets had to write panegyrics that satisfied their criteria of excellence by showing a mastery of the language and of the pre-Islamic poetic tradition through the use of literary and historical allusion and of obscure and archaic words (*gharīb*). It was inevitable that poets should seek to outdo, and be measured against, their pre-Islamic models. Although it has been suggested that the role and authority of the philologists were exaggerated by subsequent medieval critics and literary historians,[22] there is no doubt that a powerful section of contemporary literary opinion rejected the work of the "moderns", who either failed to measure up to, or deviated from, their predecessors; the testimony of men such as al-Jāḥiẓ and Ibn Qutaybah cannot be lightly brushed aside.

In the face of such pressure, poets tended to take one of three main courses. One is typified by Bashshār, who, although he sometimes wrote poems and *urjūzah*s brimful of archaisms to prove his command of *gharīb*, in the main chose a medium halfway between the language of pre-Islam and the contemporary idiom, the language of modern sophisticated living. This type of language is often, but by no means always, what critics have in mind when they speak of the language of the *muwalladūn* and the *muḥdathūn* (at other times it is *badīᶜ* which critics refer to under these labels, a subject we shall turn to later). Another solution was that of utter simplicity of language, the style which is the indirect descendant of the medium not of the *qaṣīdah* but of the *qiṭᶜah*, and which became associated with the name of Abū ᵓl-ᶜAtāhiyah, whose output consisted chiefly of *zuhdiyyāt* (ascetic poems). Although this medium was used by some, including Abū ᵓl-ᶜAtāhiyah himself, in panegyrics, it was not regarded as best suited for the *qaṣīdah*, for, as Abū ᵓl-ᶜAtāhiyah is reputed to have said, it did not appeal "to kings, *rāwī*s or those in search of *gharīb*", and hence was unlikely to prove remunerative (though it should be noted in this connection that the panegyric *qaṣīdah* was not the only type of poetry to receive patronage; there is evidence that the *qiṭᶜah* too might on occasion earn its practitioner a comfortable living).[23] A last solution, arising either out of personal choice or from the philologists' insistence, was to opt for a predominantly archaic, formal and high-sounding mode of expression; this is best illustrated by the poetry of Muslim b. al-Walīd and, later, by Abū Tammām (see below).

It is not without significance that it was the last course that was destined to dominate subsequent *qaṣīdah* poetry in the long run. No doubt the great success of the formal style, with its sonorous phrases, in expressing "epic" themes in the poetry of Abū Tammām and al-Mutanabbī, contributed in no small measure to its ultimate victory. At his best Mutanabbī's imagination

[22] Gibb, "Arab poet and Arabic philologist"; Bonebakker, "Poets and critics"; cf. also p. 21, above. [23] See p. 290.

conceived everything on a grand scale for which only the grand style was appropriate. The Byzantine army which Sayf al-Dawlah vanquished stretched from the eastern corner of the globe to its western limit and the clamour it caused reached Gemini. Sayf al-Dawlah "is the sea: when it is calm, you should dive in it for pearls, but beware of it when it is rough." In a panegyric on Badr b. ᶜAmmār al-Kharshanī in which he describes his patron's successful fight against a lion, Mutanabbī gives only enough details to render the incident plausible, but the antagonist no less than the protagonist is conceived in gigantic proportions. The lion is no ordinary lion: when it drinks from the lake of Tiberias, its roar can be heard from the banks of the Euphrates and the Nile; its mane looks like a forest. As for the hero, every pigeon sings his praises (as if he were the Lord of Creation). Such images are clearly the product of something akin to the mythological imagination, for which Abū ʾl-ᶜAtāhiyah's homely style would have been singularly inappropriate.

Thematic innovations in the qaṣīdah

The third element which led critics to identify modernism with ᶜAbbasid poetry was thematic. Although the basic themes of the Secondary *Qaṣīdah* of the Umayyad poets were retained, particularly as regards the attributes of the person eulogized, ᶜAbbasid poets occasionally allowed themselves the freedom to innovate in the opening part of the poem. Sometimes this was an expression of their critical attitude to the conventions of the Arabic tradition, often coupled with anti-Arab sentiment, rife in Shuᶜūbī poets such as Abū Nuwās and Bashshār, who never tired of asserting the inferiority of Arab culture to Persian. Abū Nuwās mocks the irrelevance of such hackneyed motifs as the description of the ruined encampment of the beloved to an urban poet living in the height of luxury in sophisticated surroundings, addressing a patron who himself lives in great splendour. Bashshār, Muslim b. al-Walīd and Abū ʾl-ᶜAtāhiyah wrote several panegyrics with bacchic openings; likewise, Abū Tammām might begin a *qaṣīdah* with a highly sensitive description of nature in spring, and Ibn al-Muᶜtazz starts his eulogy of the caliph al-Muᶜtaḍid with a description of lightning and a rainstorm. Abū Tammām, too, began some of his panegyrics with gnomic verses, lamenting the fickleness of fate and the vicissitudes of time, thereby setting an example which Mutanabbī was to follow with memorable results. On certain occasions, as in his celebrated Amorium *qaṣīdah* (discussed below), he might dispense with the prelude altogether and plunge directly into his main theme with powerful immediacy and dramatic effect (although for several reasons it is questionable if this particular poem can still be regarded as a typical *qaṣīdah*; it is, in fact, more akin to epic poetry rendered in a suitably magniloquent style). Finally, a poet might, like Ibn al-Rūmī, open a poem with a description of his beloved or manage to insert into his panegyric detailed and loving descriptions of aspects of contemporary life, such as Ibn al-Rūmī's famous account of slave-girls playing their musical instruments.

Badīʿ

However, because in its essential features the subject of the Secondary *Qaṣīdah* remained the same – an ideal type of the addressee with certain stock virtues and attributes – the task of the ʿAbbasid poet became one of providing variations on a main theme. Hence the need to elaborate and ingeniously to diversify verbal expression, using all the devices and resources made available by the lively intellectual life of ʿAbbasid civilization. It is against this background that the birth of *badīʿ* (the "new style") must be seen. This highly rhetorical and ornate style, abounding in "conceits", is commonly assumed to have become the dominant fashion in the third/ninth century, but in fact it already appears, in an incipient form, in the work of Bashshār, in whose poetry later critics and writers on rhetoric find examples to illustrate many of the figures of speech constituting *badīʿ*, and Jāḥiẓ certainly regards Bashshār, perhaps with some exaggeration, as the leader of the *badīʿ* school, whom poets like al-ʿAttābī (d. early third/ninth century) and Muslim b. al-Walīd (d. 208/823) followed.[24] Ibn al-Muʿtazz (d. 296/908) wrote the first treatise on *badīʿ*, *Kitāb al-Badīʿ*, in the late third/ninth century; as his theory of *badīʿ*, his classification of the rhetorical figures which characterize it, and the critical traditions on which he drew are analyzed at length elsewhere in this volume,[25] we will confine ourselves here to discussing examples of the "new" style. Perhaps its most striking exponents were Muslim b. al-Walīd and Abū Tammām, who as a result provoked a controversy that was to rage among critics for a long time to come, but there is hardly a single ʿAbbasid poet who managed to escape its influence altogether. *Badīʿ* is, no doubt, the product of conscious craftsmanship (often too conscious), but it does not preclude genuine feeling, as we can see from the manner in which poets used it even in their elegies. Abū Tammām's well-known elegy on his son is a poem charged with deep emotion, revealed, among other things, in the detailed and moving description of the final stages of the boy's illness, and, though its language is perhaps the simplest to be found in the whole of Abū Tammām's poetry, it is not entirely free of *badīʿ* devices;[26] nor did Ibn al-

[24] *Bayān*, I, 51. [25] See pp. 346–8, and ch. 21. [26] *Dīwān*, IV, 577.

Rūmī's grief at the death of his middle son prevent him using *badīᶜ* in his elegy on him. *Badīᶜ* is to be found in such impassioned utterances as Mutanabbī's elegy on his grandmother, the pleas of Abū Firās al-Ḥamdānī from prison among the Byzantines, his pathetic address to his mother or his complaint to his cousin, Sayf al-Dawlah, who had failed to ransom him. Later, Ibn al-Fāriḍ was said to have composed some of his mystical verses in a state of trance sometimes lasting several days; yet his poetry abounds in *badīᶜ*; while al-Maᶜarrī's elegy on a Ḥanafī man of learning, one of the most justly praised poems in the Arabic language, is, to cite but another example, full of *badīᶜ*, but the various figures of speech in it are so well integrated, and the relationship between them and the general tenor of the work is so close, that no sensitive reading of the poem will yield an impression of artificiality.[27] Abū Tammām's great Amorium poem shows how a particular rhetorical device can at once be a structural principle and a clue to the overall meaning of the poem, and how in the finest examples of ᶜAbbasid poetry *badīᶜ* is more than a rhetorical embellishment or mere outward trapping.

The following translation quotes the first forty of the poem's seventy-one lines:

Sword tells more truth than books; its edge is parting wisdom from vanity:
In gleaming blades, not lines of dusky tomes, are texts to dispel uncertainty and doubt.[28]
Knowledge is found in the sparkle of lances, glittering between opposing ranks, not in the seven sparkling lights of heaven.
What use is such lore, what use the stars themselves, and men's specious inventions about them? All lies,
Mere falsity and patched-up fables, neither tough oak (if reckoned right) nor pliant sapling.[29]
Strange things they declared time would reveal in direful summer months,
To scare men with dread disasters, on the appearance of the star in the west with its comet-tail;[30]
They claim to see in the lofty zodiac an ordered precedence, of signs "reversed" and signs not so,
Judging events thereby – but the stars are heedless, whether moving the full circle of the firmament or close to the pole.
Were it true that they had ever plainly forecast a coming event, they would not have concealed this, stamped as it is in stocks and stones.
Victory of victories! too lofty to be compassed by poet's verse or orator's speech,
A victory at which heaven's gates are thrown open and earth struts in her freshest garments.[31]

27 *Shurūḥ Saqṭ al-zand*, bk. 2, III, 981–1005.

28 The Byzantine astrologers declared that Amorium would never be taken in winter; al-Muᶜtaṣim mounted his campaign in winter.

29 A proverbial expression.

30 A comet had recently appeared, believed to presage the overthrow of nations.

31 The Muslim victory took place in spring.

Day of Amorium fight! our hopes have come away from you with udders full of honeysweet milk;[32]
You have left the fortunes of Islam's children at the height, heathens and heathendom at lowest ebb.
She [Amorium] was a mother to them: had they had any hope of ransoming her, they would have paid as ransom every kindly mother among them and father too.
She's now a maiden unveiled and humbled, though Chosroes had been impotent to master her, and Abukarib she had spurned[33]
– virgin unravished by the hand of disaster, greedy Fate's blows could never hope to reach her –
From the age of Alexander, or before then, time's locks have grown gray while she remained untouched by age;
God's purpose, working in her year after year (a thrifty housewife's churning) made her at last cream of ages.[34]
But black grief, blindly striking, came upon her, her who had before been called the dispeller of griefs.
It was an ill omen for her, that day when Ankara fell[35] and was left deserted, with empty squares and streets:
When she saw her sister of yesterday laid waste, it was a worse contagion for her than the mange.
Within her walls lie numberless heroic cavaliers, locks reddened with hot flowing gore,
By practice of the sword (henna of their own blood), not in accord with practice of faith and Islam.[36]
Commander of the Faithful! you have given over to the fire a day of hers, whereon stone and wood alike were brought low;
When you departed, night's gloom there was as noonday, dispelled in her midst by dayspring of flame,
As if the robes of darkness had renounced their colour, or sun never set:
Radiance of fire while darkness still lasted, murk of smoke in a noontide smirched,
Sun seeming to rise here though it had sunk, sun seeming to depart there although it had not.
Fate, like clouds rolling away, had revealed for her a day both fair and foul
(Sun did not rise that day on any bridegroom, nor set on any man unwed):
Dwelling of Mayyah, not yet deserted, haunted by her lover Ghaylān,[37] was a scene not more sweet to look on than Amorium's deserted dwelling,
Nor were Mayyah's cheeks, blood-red with modest shame, more charming to beholder than Amorium's cheek all grimed
By disfigurement with which our eyes are better pleased than with any beauty that has ever appeared, or any wondrous sight.

[32] Bedouin imagery: sweet pastures yield sweet milk.
[33] A legendary pre-Islamic conqueror.
[34] Al-Tibrīzī observes, "This metaphor had never been used before."
[35] Conquered by the Muslims on their way to Amorium.
[36] The Prophet dyed his hair and beard with henna.
[37] The allusion is to Dhū ʾl-Rummah (Ghaylān b. ʿUqbah) and his beloved.

A fine event! its effects seen plainly, joyfulness the outcome of evil event.
Would that heathendom could have known for how many ages past Fate had been holding in store for her the spears and lances!
This is the wise design of al-Muᶜtaṣim, God's avenger, expectant and yearning for God.[38]
Full-fed with victory, his spearheads have never been blunted not parried in defence of a life inviolate;
Never did he make war on a folk, or assault a town, without an army of terrors going before him;
Had he not led a mighty host on the day of battle, he would yet have had a clamorous host in himself alone . . .[39]

The lines quoted are built on antitheses: between truth and falsehood, victory and defeat, light and dark, virginity and violation; and the poem culminates in two parallel passages (not quoted) in which the ravishing and dishonour of the city and its womenfolk are contrasted with the caliph's vision of the heavenly reward he has won by upholding the honour of Islam: for the conquest of Amorium was supposedly inspired by his vow to avenge a Muslim woman who had called upon his name when widowed by the Byzantines, and he had sworn not to enjoy his own wives until she was avenged; hence the poem's overall mingling of masculine and feminine imagery.[40]

One particular element of *badīᶜ* in Ibn al-Muᶜtazz's analysis deserves special consideration, in the light of the above example, because more than any other it was the specific product of the intellectual climate of the ᶜAbbasid age (rather than the kind of common tropes of which scattered examples could be found in much earlier poetry, as the ᶜAbbasid critics argued); and as such it was often at the root of Arab critics' rejection of Modern poetry. This is *al-madhhab al-kalāmī*, translated by Kratchkovsky as "dialectical mannerism".[41] It denotes a type of rational argumentation, an ability to produce subtle and ingenious ideas, a way of evolving images and conceits akin to Donne's "wit" and the appellation "metaphysical" used by Dryden to describe it. A comparison between these phenomena in the two poetic traditions is illuminating. In a famous passage in his *Discourse Concerning Satire*, Dryden complains that Donne "perplexes the minds of the fair sex with nice speculations of philosophy, where he should engage their hearts and entertain them with the softness of love". Similarly, *al-madhhab al-kalāmī* is a term which Ibn al-Muᶜtazz took over from Jāḥiẓ, who, himself a Muᶜtazilī, was aware that underlying some of the poetry of the moderns

[38] *Tadbīru muᶜtaṣimin bi ʾllāhi muntaqimin/li ʾllāhi murtaqibin fī ʾllāhi murtaghibī*: a prolonged play on the caliph's regnal title, al-Muᶜtaṣim bi ʾllāh, "he who takes refuge in God".

[39] *Dīwān*, I, 40–59, trans. A.F.L. B.

[40] For a more detailed analysis of the poem, see Badawi, "The function of rhetoric"; cf. Stetkevych, "The ᶜAbbasid poet interprets history".

[41] Cf. ch. 21.

was a cerebral type of activity not unlike that which marks the rationalist theology known as *kalām*; and, as we have noted, Abū Tammām, who made *badīᶜ* his own, was a Muᶜtazilī, not unacquainted with the work and methods of *kalām* thinkers, and his poetry abounds in philosophical terms.

In the case both of the Metaphysical and the *badīᶜ* poets, rigorous argumentative logic results in witty comparisons, surprising conceits and far-fetched images. Just as Dr Johnson complains, in his essay on Abraham Cowley, that in the work of the Metaphysicals there is "a combination of dissimilar images or discovery of occult resemblances in things apparently unlike" and that "the most heterogeneous ideas are yoked by violence together; nature and art are ransacked for illustrations, comparisons and allusions", so the ᶜAbbasid critic al-Āmidī complains of Abū Tammām and his unfamiliar and far-fetched metaphors.[42] Of course earlier Arabic poetry was not devoid of tropes or even sustained "conceits"; but these are solitary occurrences, and it is the cumulative force of conceits backed by ingenious and subtle thinking, the product of the logical argumentation of the time, that gives the *badīᶜ* of ᶜAbbasid poetry its peculiar flavour. A poet of a less philosophical turn of mind, such as Abū Tammām's younger contemporary and pupil, al-Buḥturī, who was relatively free from the influence of contemporary thinkers, was driven to complain of the current fashion for infusing logic into poetry, protesting that poetry surely has nothing to do with truth and logic.

Humour and irony: tradition transformed

The results of this intellectual sophistication were particularly striking in the *qiṭᶜah*. At the hands of the ᶜAbbasid poets, the occasional poem acquired an unprecedented degree of complexity of sentiment and attitude, and an ironic tone hitherto unknown, and their humour reveals not only a comprehensive view of life where nothing deserves to be taken too seriously, but also an urbane and cultured spirit reflected in the very allusiveness of the style of humour. Likewise the *mujūn* (buffoonery and gaiety) of love poetry addressed to women and boys was not always the product of simple hedonism, but generally carried a degree of awareness of the expense of spirit in a waste of shame which renders their tone at once more convincing and moving. It is this awareness of ultimate issues in life and death, this religious feeling (for lack of a better term), which gives some of Abū Nuwās's wine poetry a spiritual quality which had been beyond the reach of al-Walīd b. Yazīd, whose mind had been formed in an intellectually

[42] See pp. 372–5.

less developed and adventurous age. In one poem,[43] Abū Nuwās chides for his facile certainty and cocksureness the would-be philosopher who assumes that a drunkard is bound to be denied God's forgiveness: "You who claim to be a learned philosopher, you have learned only one thing, while a great many others have eluded you." This scepticism, this obsession with obstinate questionings, is an expression of the spiritual restlessness of the times, which also witnessed the emergence of mystical poetry, and it also helps to explain the work of Abū ʾl-ᶜAtāhiyah, whose devotional verse, often expressed in movingly simple language, at times attains a high degree of profundity.

Humour is evinced, too, in the creative manner in which poets used poetic tradition, either turning a convention upside down in order to poke fun at it while at the same time exploiting it, or manipulating it for their own purposes, for example, in order to provide a contrast with their own experiences. In both cases, poets managed to produce poetry of supreme irony. Two conventions will suffice to illustrate the point: the ᶜUdhrī tradition, and the motif of weeping over the deserted campsite. Bashshār often writes seriously in the ᶜUdhrī vein; but at the opposite extreme he will relate how his jackass died of a desperate passion for a she-ass.[44] Between these two extremes come the poems in which he falls in love with a woman whom he sets out by idealizing and who tells him to behave like true lovers of old and die of love for her, but whom he successfully seduces in the end: here the poet relates himself to convention only to rise above it. A similar ironic relation is created towards the "deserted encampment" tradition by Abū Nuwās when he turns it upside down: it is not that the poet's beloved has deserted the campsite which now lies in ruins before the lamenting poet; it is he himself who has deserted the place, which is far from having been destroyed. The irony is enriched when we learn that what the poet is deserting is a mosque, a place of piety, the implication being that the poet has turned his back on religion (and sought his solace in wine). The light-hearted opening brings out more fully the metaphysical implications of the poem: it is the poet's grief at the transitoriness of human relationships and the departure and death of friends that has made him desert religion and turn to wine, a theme reinforced by the religious imagery, both Muslim and Christian, as well as by imagery derived from death, time and mutability.[45] Another, and quite different, creative use of this convention occurs in the poem on the Arch of Ctesiphon (Īwān Kisrā) by al-Buḥturī, a poet whose attitude to tradition is usually much more conformist. Starting from a mood of dejection at his impecuniousness, the poet rides out on his camel to

[43] Cf. ch. 16, n. 62. [44] See p. 211. [45] Trans. Monteil, *Abû-Nuwâs*, 79–80.

the ruined remains of the Persian palace in search of diversion. There ensues a lively and sensitive description of the ruins, in which the poet recreates in his imagination court scenes from the glorious Persian past – a masterpiece of descriptive writing, interspersed with the poet's meditations on time and mutability, life and death. Yet the whole is ironically related to the *qaṣīdah*-tradition, where the pre-Islamic poet, musing on the ruined encampment of a past mistress, set off on a camel-journey to shake off his melancholy. Al-Buḥturī's dejection is real, not a literary device pinned on an imaginary love, and the glory that was Persia, he is careful to point out, is not the insignificant remains of a desert encampment.

Description (waṣf)

Al-Buḥturī's descriptive power, whether in this poem or in other works such as his celebrated description of the pool in one of the caliph al-Mutawakkil's palaces, was recognized from the start. He is generally regarded as among the most skilful descriptive poets in an age which witnessed remarkable developments in the descriptive genre. Yet on the whole his treatment of *waṣf* is much more straightforward than the subtler and more cerebral descriptions of his contemporary Ibn al-Rūmī (d. *c.* 283/896), whose work contains many more surprising "conceits" (not that he was incapable of writing more simply, as witness his magnificent description of the voice and manner of his beloved singing-girl Waḥīd, or his vivid and amusing portrayal of scenes from everyday life in the market-place, such as the making of pastry and sweetmeats; while in his satirical poems – a genre made sharper and more personal in the ʿAbbasid age – his eye was very much fixed on the object of his attack, thus providing several satirical portraits or caricatures in which he makes full use of his victims' physical deformities – although the scathing details in such attacks are not without "wit").

It is in the work of Ibn al-Rūmī that we find some of the most famous instances of far-fetched images and metaphors in the whole of ʿAbbasid *waṣf* poetry. In one poem he compares singing-girls bending over their musical instruments to women nursing their babies; the comparison is carried over six lines in which points of analogy are pursued to their extremes, with a subtle hint at the miraculous healing power of music in the allusion to the Virgin Mary and the infant Jesus. In the amatory prelude to another poem (his panegyric on Ismāʿīl b. Bulbul), the woman's individual features and parts of her body, no fewer than nine in number, are likened to different items from the vegetable kingdom, her figure to a bough, her buttocks to a hillock, her cheeks to apples, her breasts to pomegranates, her hair to dark vines, her eyes to narcissi, etc. Although it has been argued by a recent scholar that Ibn al-Rūmī is the only ᶜAbbasid poet to endow nature with a life of its own and to make it a source of spiritual solace,[46] his descriptive nature poetry is clearly the work of an urban poet who sees nature in an essentially civilized context. To him the earth is proudly decked out like a maiden in embroidered garments, boughs "whisper" to one another, birds and boughs look "intoxicated", the rainbow looks like "many layers of women's clothes, each of a different colour and length". After rain the earth comes out in bloom, displaying its beauty like a once modest female accosting a male in order to ensnare him.

The last stage in the "mannerist" style in descriptive verse is to be found by the time we reach Ibn al-Muᶜtazz and al-Ṣanawbarī (d. 334/945). It was called "phantastic" by von Grunebaum, and is perhaps an offshoot rather than a continuation of *badīᶜ*; to borrow again Dr Johnson's words about the later Metaphysicals, these poets "left not only reason but fancy behind them" and "produced combinations . . . that not only could not be credited, but could not be imagined". Ibn al-Muᶜtazz's energies were directed towards the discovery of new and startling comparisons: the star in the dark night is likened to an eye looking stealthily while the attention of those watching is distracted; the crescent moon is like a silver boat weighed down with a load of amber. Likewise al-Ṣanawbarī writes of "red anemones rising and falling like banners of ruby unfurled on spears of chrysolite". In fact, in al-Ṣanawbarī's poetry, we witness a fascinating phenomenon in which art and nature have become so inextricably intertwined that nature has become art and art nature, and reality and convention have exchanged places. "The likening of gardens to lovers" he writes in one poem "has increased the lovers' love for gardens." "How many a girl's supple and delicate figure there is in the branches of trees / How many a cheek with a black mole in its pure red / How many a captivating, fragrant mouth, how many a winning eye." Here, no doubt, is the ultimate apotheosis of a literary convention which has itself become a mode of apprehending reality, a perfect illustration of the thesis that man's apprehension of nature is determined by his art. Now instead of women being likened to boughs it is boughs that are likened to women, and apples look like cheeks. Roses, too, resemble cheeks, and narcissi eyes, and cypress trees look like courtesans who have lifted their skirts. Al-Sarī al-Raffāʾ (d. 361/972) compares roses to cheeks flushed from blushing. This attitude to nature is, of course, not an entirely new departure but the culmination of several earlier strands, some of which are to be found even in Ibn al-Rūmī. However, to see nature purely in terms

[46] Schoeler, *Naturdichtung*, 234, 369.

of art is full of damaging implications both for art and for the perception of nature. It points to the stagnation which was eventually to set in in Arab culture, in which convention would take over completely, to the exclusion of the possibility of any fresh vision of reality, as amply illustrated by the excessive artificiality and verbal acrobatics to which poetry was to be reduced in the course of time.

Yet Ṣanawbarī makes effective use of this attitude when he indulges in pure fantasy in such poems as those in which he imagines a dramatic war between flowers or a debate between the rose and narcissus.[47] Here the conception of poetry as mimesis becomes totally irrelevant, and indeed there is in them more than the mere absence of verisimilitude. Untrammelled by the slightest hint that the poet is making a comment on life, directly or indirectly – for the poems are neither allegorical nor symbolic – these delightful works are frankly artificial creations of a whimsical and playful imagination, in which nature plays the human role assigned to it – a role which man in his search for his own identity had originally found in nature itself. This tradition was kept alive by other poets, many of whom, like al-Shābb al-Ẓarīf (661–88/1262–89), merely produced insipid imitations, but occasionally it was given elegant and charming expression, as in some of the work of Ṣafī al-Dīn al-Ḥillī (676–740/1277–1339).

[47] *Dīwān*, 77–9, 498.

CHAPTER 10

HUNTING POETRY (*ṬARDIYYĀT*)

Perhaps one of the first types of poetry to have emerged from the framework of the polythematic *qaṣīdah* as an independent genre – a process often held to mark the beginnings of the development of "modern" poetry – was the hunting-poem or *ṭardiyyah*. There can be no doubt that the peoples of the Arabic-speaking world have practised hunting in some form or another as far back into the past as our records go. Pre-Islamic poetry, stereotyped as it undoubtedly is, nevertheless records ample vivid descriptions of the oryx hunt, and it is in such poetry that we must look in order to find the origins of the hunting-poems of the late Umayyad and ᶜAbbasid eras, although the poetry of the chase of these later periods is vastly different from the compositions of the Arab poets of pre-Islamic days. It was not only the poetic revolution of the late Umayyad and early ᶜAbbasid periods which brought about this change. The "moderns" (*muḥdathūn*) felt no qualms in depicting quarry and hunter which could play no part in the strictly limited area in which the pre-Islamic poet was forced by convention to operate; in addition, the oryx, the Jāhilī hunter's traditional quarry, from an early date was over-hunted and by the time of the ᶜAbbasid assumption of the caliphate the animal's numbers must have been seriously depleted. The moderns were thus in part forced, though in part also perfectly willing, to broaden the scope of their poetic descriptions of hunting. Now, too, the Islamic borders were far and away beyond the desert confines of the Arabian peninsula proper. Mountainous and even wooded areas, terrain of relatively high rainfall and dense vegetation, were within the ken of the poet, as was the varied game of such areas, which had to be hunted by much more sophisticated methods than those employed by the pre-Islamic bedouin.

In pre-Islamic poetic descriptions of the oryx hunt, victory went frequently to the huntsman and his faithful accomplices, his saluki (Ar. *salūqī*) hounds. The oryx might, however, free itself from the hounds and make good its escape. Tradition indeed dictated that in odes of elegy (*marthiyah*) and exhortation (*mawᶜiẓah*) the hounds must triumph over the hapless oryx; whereas in odes of eulogy (*madīḥ*), when the poet, for example, in an extended simile comprising a depiction of the hunt, compares his riding beast with the oryx, it is the latter which must escape from the salukis.[1] These descriptions were of course merely parts of the longer ode (*qaṣīdah*), and this traditional account of the oryx hunt continued along with the *qaṣīdah* itself into Umayyad times. Although only the oryx hunt is depicted in this early poetry, it must be assumed that the bedouin of the peninsula at this time would also have hunted the gazelle, and the hare too would have been a welcome change of diet. If we are to be guided by the relative silence of early poetry and *ḥadīth* literature, falconry can be said to have been known, but by no means widespread. It undoubtedly gained great popularity under the Umayyad caliphs.

THE MAJOR POETS IN THE GENRE

It is necessary to go back into the Umayyad era in order to find the true beginnings of the *ṭardiyyāt*, short poems (*qiṭᶜah*s) devoted to the single theme of hunting. Abū ʾl-Najm al-ᶜIjlī, who died towards the end of the Umayyad period, is the first poet in chronological order worthy of mention. We have no extant *dīwān* in his name, though a number of relatively short pieces is to be found in different literary compilations. The majority of his poetry is composed in the *rajaz* metre and there are pieces on several different types of hunt, including one on coursing with cheetahs.[2] The latter is, however, only part of a longer poem which in fact begins with the traditional pre-Islamic amatory prelude (*nasīb*). We remain within the Umayyad period with al-Shamardal b. Shurayk (or Sharīk) al-Yarbūᶜī who died after 109/727 and is the most interesting of the early *ṭardiyyāt* composers. He wrote poetry in the pre-Islamic mould, as well as at least one poem in the *rajaz* metre which has all the hallmarks of the later *ṭardiyyāt*.[3]There are two editions of his fragmentary *Dīwān*, reconstructed from various sources.

Abū Nuwās (d. *c.* 200/815) is undoubtedly the major figure in ᶜAbbasid hunting poetry. His complete *Dīwān* is extant and is the earliest to contain a section specially devoted to the chase. His hunting poetry consists of pieces in both *rajaz* and the other metres. ᶜAbd al-Ṣamad b. al-Muᶜadhdhal died in 240/854. Though of less importance for our study, Ibn al-Muᶜadhdhal has nevertheless left a long *urjūzah* (poem in *rajaz* metre; for a fuller definition

1 Jāḥiẓ, *Ḥayawān*, II, 20, spells out clearly how the main subject of the ode dictates the outcome of the hunt.
2 Abū ʾl-Faraj al-Iṣfahānī, *Aghānī*, IX, 82; on Abū ʾl-Najm al-ᶜIjlī's *rajaz* poetry, see *CHALUP*, 416–18.
3 *Gedichte*, no. 20.

of this poetic form, see below) concerning the cheetah and some pieces from more lengthy poems no longer extant. Only a passing mention needs to be made here of Ibn Abī Karīmah, a contemporary of Jāḥiẓ, who has left to posterity a thirty-three line poem on the cheetah. Al-Nāshiʾ al-Akbar (d. 293/905) is credited with twenty-four *ṭardiyyāt* in all, mainly *urjūzahs*, but also composed in the *ṭawīl* and *mutaqārib* metres. His poems cover the whole range of mammals and birds of prey employed by medieval Arab huntsmen. Ibn al-Muʿtazz, the "caliph of one day", who was assassinated in 296/908, is the second major figure, after Abū Nuwās, in the field of *ṭardiyyāt*. He has a complete and published *Dīwān* of which the first section of the fourth part is devoted entirely to the genre. His *urjūzah*s are not classed separately, as in the *Dīwān* of Abū Nuwās, but merely appear in order of the rhyming letter along with hunting-poems composed in other metres. The latter are in the main in the *sarīʿ* and *mutaqārib* metres. To this list must be added the names of Abū Firās al-Ḥamdānī (d. 357/968) and Kushājim (d. *c.* 350/961). The former's *Dīwān* includes a lengthy *urjūzah*, perhaps the longest on this subject in Arabic, which makes mention of a number of different hunters and quarry. Kushājim is reputed to have composed about twenty hunting poems which find a place in his *Kitāb al-Maṣāyid wa-ʾl-maṭārid* (a book which deals with the instruments of hunting, including animals) as well as in his *Dīwān*.

THE HUNTERS AND THE HUNTED

Ṭardiyyāt show such a predilection for metonymy, the omission of the noun and substitution of a characteristic adjective or descriptive phrase (a favourite device in pre-Islamic poetry), that it is sometimes not immediately obvious to the reader what mammal or bird of prey is engaged in the hunt and what exactly the quarry is. Dealing with the hunters first, the following all figure in the *ṭardiyyāt* with greater or lesser prominence.

The great favourite as hunter among the poets is the hound. Although called only rarely *salūqī* or so identified in any way, it is certainly the saluki which is in question, both in this poetry and also in that of the pre-Islamic and Umayyad poets. The saluki is of medium-size, belonging to the gazehound family, that is the hounds which hunt entirely by sight. The saluki has long and pendulous ears, to which reference is frequently made in the poetry, and also possesses great stamina. The only other mammal used as a hunter in the Umayyad and ʿAbbasid periods and described frequently by the *ṭardiyyāt* poets is the cheetah (Ar. *fahd*, Lat. *Acinonyx jubatus*). We can assume with some confidence that the cheetah played little or no part in the chase in pre-Islamic Arabia, for the poetry of that period fails to mention him. It is probable that this member of the cat family became a popular hunter under the hunt-loving Umayyads. It certainly figures prominently in lists recorded by historians of gifts passed between rulers, subordinates and rulers, etc., from Umayyad times onwards. It is a spectacular performer, particularly in dealing with gazelle, and, perhaps less commonly, hare. Undoubtedly the swiftest mammal, the cheetah, in common with his cousins in the cat family, is, however, lacking in stamina and relies on a quick kill.

Falconry – strictly speaking hunting with long-winged falcons – and hawking – hunting with short-winged hawks – also, to a large extent, owe their popularity in the Islamic world to the Umayyad caliphs. The *ṭardiyyāt*-poets portray hunting with both falcons and hawks. Of the latter, short-winged hawks with yellow irises, the goshawk (Ar. *bāz* or *bāzī*, Lat. *Accipter gentilis*) is most popular in this genre of poetry. Indeed, she forms the subject of the *ṭardiyyah* more frequently than any other bird of prey and takes second place after the saluki in the relevant sections of the *dīwān*s. The hawks in general are fierce and aggressive and less easily manned and trained for the hunt than the falcons. The gos is capable of tremendous short bursts of speed, and prefers a wooded environment in which to hunt both bird and hare quarry and in which she steers herself deftly with her large tail feathers. The male, smaller than the female by approximately one-third and hence called the tiercel (Ar. *zurraq*), is also specifically mentioned in the poems. The other hawk to be listed here is the sparrow-hawk (Ar. *bāshaq/bāshiq*, Lat. *Accipiter nisus*), which is much smaller than the gos and a hunter of small birds, generally by stealth and in short, quick dashes.

Of the falcons, long-winged birds with black irises, hunting particularly in open terrain and often attaching the quarry by stooping from above, the saker (Ar. *ṣaqr*, Lat. *Falco cherrug*) should take pride of place. This is a true desert bird, extremely hardy and inured to the rigours of desert life, as well as less demanding with her food than other birds of prey. She is an expert performer against the houbara (Ar. *ḥubārā*, Lat. *Chlamydotis undulata Macqueenii*) and may be employed on occasions to tackle the desert hare. She was sometimes used together with the saluki in the hunting of the gazelle (see below). The peregrine (Ar. *shāhīn*, Lat. *Falco peregrinus*) is a delicate bird to keep for falconry, although her ringing-up and spectacular stoop from above on to the quarry make her popular with the Arab hunter. She is particularly good at hunting water birds, her quarry in the wild. The list of true falcons which form the subject of our hunting-poems can be brought to an end with the merlin (Ar. *yuʾyuʾ*, Lat. *Falco columbarius*). This tiny falcon, much loved, incidentally, by Mary Queen of Scots during her long years in captivity, is an excellent performer against the lark and it is in this role that she is described by our Arab poets.

It might perhaps be added here that the poet sometimes speaks at length about his other companion in the chase, his faithful horse. Such passages belong rather to the extensive equine literature that exists in Arabic, than to this discussion of the *ṭardiyyāt*. On rare occasions too the poets sing of hunting with nets and spears.

A variety of game, both mammal and bird, was hunted by the hounds, cheetahs and birds of prey described above. It is not possible to deal here with every species found in the poetry: the addiction of some of the poets to metonymy has already been mentioned, and even when the quarry's name is precisely given, in some cases it is not sufficient to make a positive identification possible. A *ṭuwwal*, for example, is clearly a long-legged wader, presumably quite small, since it is hunted in the poetry by the tiercel goshawk. Sometimes, too, the poet is not precise enough; "wild geese" could indicate any one of four or five species. Only the more common types of quarry need be mentioned here therefore, and it would seem best to begin with the mammals.

The oryx (Ar. *baqar waḥshī* or *mahā*, Lat. *Oryx leucoryx*), the largest Middle Eastern antelope, just qualifies for a place in the list, for this handsome creature had almost been hunted to extinction by the time our poets were composing their hunting-poems. The pre-Islamic oryx hunt has been briefly referred to above and the practice continued into Islamic times. The oryx stands at about forty inches at the shoulder and its long, straight, spear-like horns were particularly dangerous, bringing death and injury to the hounds engaged in the chase. The gazelle (Ar. invariably *ẓaby*, Lat. *Gazella gazella*) is the most popular mammal quarry in the poems. There are numerous species of this antelope, of varying size and colour. It can be said in general terms that the gazelle stands about the same size as the saluki and is equally swift, as well as showing itself a match for its stamina. This outwardly delicate creature is therefore a formidable adversary and, although this does not occur in the poems, it is generally recognized that the gazelle is best hunted by both hounds and falcons. The hare must always have been a popular quarry. In relative abundance until quite recent times, it would be readily taken by hound, cheetah, goshawk and possibly saker alike as an acceptable substitute for the gazelle. The Arabian hare is small and a fast and tricky opponent in the chase. Although the fox appears on occasions in the *ṭardiyyāt*, as if the principal quarry hunted by salukis, it would seem doubtful that the huntsman would have set out to hunt with the fox specifically in mind. He certainly could not have eaten the quarry and it is doubtful that the fox would provide thrilling sport when coursed by hounds. Naturally the latter would pursue a fleeing fox, as indeed they would pursue anything moving, and it appears safer to assume that the pursuit of the fox where it does occur in the poetry would have resulted from a chance encounter.

Of the bird quarry introduced by the hunting-poets, mention might be made of the following. The houbara (MacQueen's bustard), a desert bird, is usually the speciality of the saker. A large bird, larger than the saker, it is a powerful quarry, kicking viciously when held by the talons of the falcon. Smaller game which features in the poems includes the francolin (Ar. *durrāj*, Lat. *Francolinus francolinus*), the lark (Ar. *mukkā*ᵓ, Lat. *Alaemon alaudipes*), hunted by the merlin, and one of the sandgrouse family (Ar. *qaṭāh*, *qaṭā* or collective *ghaṭāṭ*). The crane (Ar. *kurkī*, Lat. *Grus grus*) appears also, usually hunted by the goshawk. This latter event is surprising, for the crane is a high-flying bird and best hunted by a cast of peregrines in order to match the bird's high aerial skills. It should be said, however, that the goshawk is depicted in other Arabic hunting literature as the worthy hunter of the crane.

THE STRUCTURE OF THE *ṬARDIYYĀT*

There is nothing complicated about the structure of the hunting-poems of the period. It can be said in general terms that every *ṭardiyyah* from the structural point of view falls into one of two categories: (a) the more common, "early-morning expedition" category and (b) the "descriptive". It seems likely that the first must have its origins in such pre-Islamic stereotypes as the first hemistich of a line of the *Muᶜallaqah* of Imruᵓ al-Qays: "Oft I go forth in the early morning, while the birds are still in their nests."[4] In hunting-poems of this type, the poet devotes his first, possibly also his second, line to a reference to his early departure for the hunt, and usually, though not always, employs an expression similar to that quoted above, "Oft I go forth in the early morning". Phase two of the poem begins with the preposition "with" (*bi-*), plus the hunting-animal or bird of prey the poet decides to take out with him on this outing. On occasions the poet does not introduce the usual name of the hunter (hound, cheetah, goshawk, etc.), but prefers metonymy, referring to the animal or bird by one of its distinctive features. The way is now open for the poet to launch into a physical description of his hunting-animal, its prowess on the hunting-field and the dread it inspires in the quarry, etc. He may devote some space to an actual happening at the hunt, e.g. the kill, which may be presented in very graphic, not to say bloody, terms, and he may end this second phase of the poem with a mention of the number of the quarry taken. There may then be

[4] Tibrīzī, *Sharḥ*, 21, l. 53.

a brief third phase, which, if it is included at all, is a reference to the preparation and cooking of the meat after a successful day in the field. Again, a pre-Islamic inspiration for these culinary references is suggested by Imruʾ al-Qays's line: "The cooks continued [their work], some cooking well the grilled meat, others preparing a hasty stew."[5] Alternatively the poem may terminate with an exclamation concerning the fine qualities of the huntsman's hound or bird of prey. He may even praise God for its very existence. This "early-morning expedition" type poem can be illustrated as follows, in extracts from a piece by Abū Nuwās:[6]

phase one

Oft I go forth in the early morning, with the birds still in their nests and their voices not yet joined to the dawn chorus,

phase two

With hounds in a cheerful mood, their collars on, [all] reckoning the oryx as part of their rations.

Their sunken eyes have taken the place of plump ones . . .

[All this] to separate the hare from its life. The hound's life lies in the death of the hare . . .

phase three

So that you can see the cooking-pot in its place, [surrounded by] numerous guests.

The second category of *ṭardiyyah*, the descriptive hunting-poem, can scarcely be divided into phases at all. The poet moves straight into his physical description of his favourite hunting-animal with the expression, "I will sing the praises of . . ." (*anʿatu*). He may then bring the poem to an end, as in the first category, by proclaiming the excellent qualities of this animal.

Examples of the descriptive category are: "I will sing the praises of a hound whose owners' good fortune is assured by his tremendous effort . . .", ending as follows: "Hunting them down, twenty [of them], in his headlong course!/What a fine hound you are, without equal!" and: "O my gos! I will sing your praises and sing them again, both in *rajaz* and in *qaṣīdah*s" (both by Abū Nuwās);[7] and: "I will sing the praises of [a hound], bouncy of step, digging [into the ground] as he courses desert quarry, swiftly wreaking havoc", and: "I will sing the praises of [cheetahs] like [arrows], well and truly feathered, sharpened by the long course" (both by Ibn al-Muʿtazz).[8]

The popular "early-morning expedition" category is found throughout the whole historical range of the genre, from Umayyad times well into the fourth/tenth century. The second, "descriptive" category may have

[5] Ibid., 25, l. 68. [6] *Dīwān*, II, 194. [7] Ibid., 179, 211. [8] *Dīwān*, IV, 14, 20.

appeared on the scene at a later date and perhaps was the invention of Abū Nuwās. From that time on, however, it occurs from time to time, and the lengthy *urjūzah* of Abū Firās, who died in 357/968, comprising 137 lines, should be counted in this type. Line 5 reads: "I will describe (*anᶜatu*) a day which I spent in Syria, the most pleasant day that I ever spent".[9]

METRES AND RHYME

In a verse already quoted above ("O my gos!"), Abū Nuwās, the unquestioned doyen of hunting-poets, clearly distinguishes two types of *ṭardiyyah*. He says he will sing the praises of his goshawk over and over again, "both in *rajaz* and in *qaṣīdah*s". This division is maintained by the compilers of his *Dīwān* and is a convenient one to employ here. The two terms, *urjūzah* and *qaṣīdah* indicate only the metre used and nothing more (indeed in the context of the poems of the ᶜAbbasid era in general the *qaṣīdah* is often a piece written in a metre other than *rajaz*). Throughout the whole of the historical range of the poems under discussion, the *urjūzah* is in the overwhelming majority. From our first exponent, Abū ᵓl-Najm al-ᶜIjlī, who died before 132/750, right through into the late fourth/tenth century the *rajaz* metre is closely associated with the *ṭardiyyāt*. Indeed in the lengthy *Dīwān*s of Abū Nuwās and Ibn al-Muᶜtazz, for example, with one or two minor exceptions in the latter, *rajaz* is kept exclusively for the hunting-poems. Shamardal, who, it has already been remarked, produced pre-Islamic style verse and one surviving true *ṭardiyyah*, appears to have written *qaṣīdah*s for the former and an *urjūzah* for the latter, and fragments of otherwise lost hunting-poems by Shamardal are also in *rajaz*.[10] It should be admitted that Ibn Abī Karīmah's one extant *ṭardiyyah* is a *qaṣīdah*, and al-Nāshiᵓ has a higher percentage of *qaṣīdah*s (approximately forty) than any other poet of the genre. This, however, does not alter the overall picture of the great preponderance of *urjūzah*s. As for the metres of the *qaṣīdah*s, those most commonly found are *mutaqārib*, *ṭawīl* and *sarīᶜ*. In all *urjūzah*s the two hemistichs of each line rhyme with each other, overwhelmingly on the pattern *aa aa aa*, etc. (i.e. every single hemistich has the same rhyme throughout the poem). A notable exception is the hunting-*urjūzah* of Abū Firās, which has an *aa bb cc*, etc., rhyme-pattern.

LANGUAGE AND STYLE OF THE *ṬARDIYYĀT*

There are no particularly difficult problems of syntax for the reader of the hunting-poems. The "early morning" poems usually begin with, "Oft I go

[9] *Dīwān*, III, 435–48; see p. 318, below, for the background of this poem.
[10] See *Gedichte*, nos. 19, 21–9.

forth in the early morning . . ." (*qad aghtadī* . . .), or some such formula, immediately followed by a circumstantial clause, e.g. ". . . while the birds are still in . . ." (*wa-ʾl-ṭayru fī* . . .). Once we arrive at the hunting-animal – the hound, cheetah or bird of prey, which is invariably an indefinite noun or adjective, e.g. "with a hound" (*bi-kalbin*), or, in poems of the "descriptive" category, after "I will sing the praises of", "a hound" (*kalban*) – there may be verbs expressed dependent on the indefinite noun, but much more likely is a whole series of adjectives, compound adjectives and other epithets, perhaps running for several lines, again all dependent on the indefinite noun, the hunting-animal. This being so, the major difficulty encountered in the reading of the *ṭardiyyāt* is the lexical one, and this difficulty presents itself in two forms. We are in any case dealing here with a subject possessing its own technical vocabulary; and we are also discussing a literary genre, elaborated by individual contributors. Thus, many of the poems, particularly, it would seem, those portraying hounds, have a distinct desert, bedouin flavour with its accompanying rich vocabulary, greatly reminiscent of that of pre-Islamic poetry. However, in the specific case of Abū Nuwās, who offers us the most and the best *ṭardiyyāt*, we find a plethora of Persian vocabulary. This cannot be the place for a discussion of whether Abū Nuwās was a Shuʿūbī – Persian vocabulary is found in his other poetry too – but as far as his hunting-poems are concerned, his wide use of Persian words and expressions may well reflect a continuing powerful influence from the east of the Islamic empire on hunting in general, and on hawking in particular. The goshawk, for example, in the Middle Eastern context, was from early times thought of as the Persian bird of prey, much suited as she was to the eastern terrain. In short, then, the vocabulary of the *ṭardiyyāt* is at the same time rich, extensive and, in parts, technical, and, in Abū Nuwās's *ṭardiyyāt*, it is heavily laced with words of Persian origin.

Little needs to be said of the style of the hunting-poems; it is in any case extremely difficult to try to categorize the style of a whole genre of poetry, composed by numerous different poets. One point should be stressed, however. The majority of both categories of *ṭardiyyah* comprises a description of the hunting-animal, and this is always a vital passage which retains our interest throughout; we feel that the hunting-field is never far away and, with the constant interjection of vivid similes and a not infrequent description of the kill, the pace too is never allowed to slacken.

POETIC DEVICES OF THE *ṬARDIYYĀT*

The reader of the hunting-poems of this period can expect to encounter the full range of the poetic devices usually employed in Arabic. Three in particular, however, require special mention: simile, metaphor and metonymy, while a fourth, hyperbole, is also worthy of remark.

Simile

The profusion of similes scattered throughout is a remarkable feature of the poetry and one which strikes the reader immediately. Most are extremely apt and easily understood, though some may appear obscure without a complete understanding of the technicalities of the hunt, of climatic phenomena, of zoology, of botany, etc. The following are examples:

"... a hare, jinking and obstinate, like a lad of the tribe
chasing around, playing the game of *dabbūq*." (Abū Nuwās, *Dīwān*, II, 180) (From the available evidence, it is impossible to identify this children's game exactly. It may be something to do with catching birds – *dabbaqa* means "to catch with bird-lime" – or it may simply be a ball-game, since the same root is sometimes found linked with the game of polo.)

"... a hound pulling to and fro on his tether, like a madman fleeing
from having medicine introduced up his nose ..." (Ibid. 181)

The stars, heavenly bodies or natural phenomena figure commonly in these similes:

"[A hound] like the brightly shining star as it appears ..." (Ibid., 181)

"[A hound] like a flash of lightning, throwing up white stones,
as he gathers up the ground like something fried flying out [of the pan] ..." (Ibid., 182)

"[A hound] like a saker stooping on her sandgrouse prey." (Ibid., 183)

"Many's the pot too, grumbling like a refractory stallion ..." (Ibid., 200.) (This refers to the cooking of the game.)

"The sides of the mouth [of the goshawk], when she screams out in hunger, are like two split pieces of a juniper tree." (Ibid., 206)

"[The gos's] eyes when they stare are like two identical stones of carnelian,
[Set] in a broad head which guides her beak, this latter like the curve of a letter *jīm* [written] by someone left-handed" (Ibid., 207)

"[The saluki's] tail is raised like a brown scorpion's ...
Like a *maddah* [the sign ~] from a pen with black ink ..." (Ibn al-Muʿtazz, *Dīwān*, IV, 2)

"[A saluki] with ears hanging down each side like the flower of a purple iris." (Ibid., 3)

Metaphor

Metaphors are distinctly less in number, though no less effective. Some examples are as follows:

"... and [the saluki's] flanks, when he stretches forward to move,

You suggested, are two sandal straps, excellently fashioned, cut of Ṭāʾif leather and slit length-ways." (Abū Nuwās, *Dīwān*, II, 185)
"[The quarry] finds [the hound] an unjust judge . . ." (Ibid.)
"[The saker] is a stone, hurling down on other stones." (Ibid., 219) (This is a reference to the great distance of the flight, when both the hunter, the saker, and its quarry appear as small stones in the sky.)
"[The hound] is our store-house during a barren year, when it comes round; such as he is stored up as treasure for lean times." (Ibid., 246)
"[My horse] is a blazing fire, burning brightly . . ." (Ibn al-Muᶜtazz, *Dīwān*, IV, 8)

Metonymy

Metonymy is commonest at the beginning of phase two of the "early morning" category of *ṭardiyyah*, or after "I will sing the praises of" (*anᶜatu*) in the "descriptive" category with the first mention of the hunted, the hound, cheetah or bird of prey. Examples are:

". . . and with a well-made [saker], under control as a result of her training." (Ibid., 8)
"Oft I go forth early as morning appears, with a joyful [goshawk], greedy for game." (Ibid., 16)
"I will sing the praises of [a hound] bouncy of step . . ." (Ibid., 14)

On occasion metonymy is used in other situations, e.g.:

"[The hound] advances on three speedy, lean [gazelles] . . ." (Ibid.)

Hyperbole

Brief mention must now be made, with examples, of the role of hyperbole in the *ṭardiyyāt*. It is most apparent in the tally of game at the end of the day, usually fifty, in most cases an impossible total for any one creature. But again huntsmen everywhere like to exaggerate! Examples are:

"What [the gos] hunts will never escape; before the violent dust-carrying wind she had hunted down
Fifty wild geese and francolins . . ." (Abū Nuwās, *Dīwān*, II, 204)
". . . [the tiercel gos] accounted for
Fifty [*ṭuwwal* birds] [previously] spared the slaughter!" (Ibid., 216)
". . . [the saker] has hunted
Fifty, like slaughtered victims . . ." (Ibid., 221)

Other examples are:

"Even if the quarry were to pass beyond the ᶜAyyūq star [Capella]
[The hound] would bring it down . . ." (Ibid., 180)
". . . . the plain buzzes with the speed [of the hound], as he runs hard; he does not touch the surface of the ground as he flies along" (Ibid., 188)

THE *ṬARDIYYĀT*

It is now proposed to allow the hunting-poems to speak for themselves. Examples below are given under the heading of the hunting-animal in the order in which each appears in the *Dīwān* of Abū Nuwās, from which, with the exception of numbers 6 and 15, all the poems are taken. Where applicable, the first line is also quoted in Arabic, to give some idea of stylistic features which it has not been possible to render into English.

Hunting with hounds

1 *anᶜatu kalban ahluhu fī kiddihi qad saᶜidat jud$\bar{u}$duhum bi-jaddihi*
I will sing the praises of a hound whose owners' good fortune is assured by his tremendous effort.
All the good things they have come from him; all the assistance they have come from him.
His master is always like a slave to him; at night he brings him nearest to his bed.
If he is uncovered, his master puts on him his own coat.
He has a blaze and his legs are white.
His excellent conformation is pleasing to the eye; also the receding corners of his mouth and his long muzzle.
Gazelles are really in trouble when he is hunting; he relishes his hard-running attacks on them,
Hunting them down, twenty [of them], in his headlong course!
What a fine hound you are, without equal! (Abū Nuwās, *Dīwān*, II, 179)

2 *anᶜatu kalban laysa bi ʾl-masbūqi mutahhaman yajrī ᶜalā ʾl-ᶜurūqi*
I will sing the praises of a hound who cannot be outstripped, of perfect conformation, he courses over all types of terrain.
He was brought by kings from Salūq, as if on a long, flexible leash.
When he charges forward like someone who cannot be deterred, coursing over plain and wide, wind-blown deserts
A hare, jinking and obstinate, like a lad of the tribe chasing around playing the game of *dabbūq*;
And curing by his hunting the passion of him afflicted by it.
Even if the quarry were to pass beyond the ᶜAyyūq star,
He would bring it down, bloody at the throat; this is his most solemn duty
Towards every man of the chase sustained by him. (Ibid., 180)

(In line 2, the reference to "kings from Salūq" reflects the traditional view of the Arab geographers and lexicographers that the *salūqī* hound comes from a place named Salūq or Salūqiyyah. The word can be taken to refer to the Seleucid dynasty which controlled vast areas of the Near and Middle East in the fourth century BC. For some reason the Arabs regarded the hound as "Seleucid".)[11]

[11] See Smith, "The Arabian hound".

A brief quotation of the final two lines of a *ṭardiyyah*:

3 Some roast what can be roasted of [the game], while the cook cooks the offal,
Until the smell of its cooking rises high in the air, like smoking naphtha from a machine of war. (Ibid., 181)

4 *aᶜdattu kalban li ʾl-ṭirādi salṭā* *idhā ghadā man nahama ashaṭṭā*
I prepared a hound for the chase, long in body (when he comes forth in the morning, the hungry lick their lips),
Bedecked in collars and hemp ropes.
He is like a saker when she stoops, or the flame of a fire fed with naphtha.
He is beauty [itself], noble of pedigree; you can see his jaws marked out in a line;
Also cheeks with little flesh and soft whiskers; all this and his flanks when he stretches forward to move,
You suggested, are two sandal straps, excellently fashioned, cut of Ṭāʾif leather and slit length-ways.
When slipped suddenly, he rips his hairless, stony-black paws.
With his claws he tears his ears to pieces; you would imagine they drew no blood from their incisions.
[The paws] hit the ground only at times.
He speeds away from the cry of a sandgrouse, taking the measure of the mottled desert jack hares.
They find him an unjust judge, breaking bones and rending skin
(As the manufacturer tears *sābir* and *qubṭ* garments) when good, wholesome food is mixed with the dust.
Praise be to God for what He has provided! (Ibid., 185)

(The picture of hounds tearing their ears with their claws is frequently painted by the *ṭardiyyāt*-poets. It is in fact another example of hyperbole; it is a physical impossibility for a saluki to injure itself in this way. In the penultimate line, *sābir* and *qubṭ* ("Coptics") are types of cloth.)

5 *idhā ʾl-shayāṭīnu raʾat zunbūrā* *qad qullida ʾl-ḥalqata wa ʾl-suyūrā*
When the jinn see Zunbūr with his collar and leash on,
They call out perdition to the desert jack hares. He is long in the neck and his jaw wide.
When you come across him with his mouth open, you can see his daggers cultivated in rows;
Closing together, they reach right through to the ribs [of the hare]; he was well trained as a pup,
Until he was a full six months old and had reached the age of cocking his leg.
He knows how to read signals and whistles, also to hold off if you make signs to him.
He gives his utmost in his coursing, stored up as treasure; as he runs into the attack you can see his claws,
Tearing strips from his ears; he goes on lapping up the blood of a fox which he has left wounded or a hare brought down.

May God allow my lord the prince to enjoy him long! May he continue happy with [his hound],
Revered in exultation, gladdened, as he embellishes the *minbar* and the throne! (Ibid., 196)

(Zanbūr, literally "hornet", is the name of the hound. For the image of the hound throwing himself so eagerly into the chase that he rips his ears with his claws, see the note to poem 4. In the last line, the *minbar* or "pulpit" is, like the throne, a symbol of rulership.)

Hunting with cheetahs

6 *lā ṣayda illā bi-waththābatin taṭīru ᶜalā arbaᶜin ka ᵓl-ᶜadhab*

There can be no hunting without a bounding [cheetah], flying like motes on four [gazelles].
When she is slipped from her collar, the dust flies up and the chase is joined in earnest,
Like a whirlwind, one of the daughters of the winds, she will show you something amazing over the ground . . .
If the quarry sees her running behind it, its conscience whispers perdition in its ear.
Ah! Many's the day when she cannot be blamed! She pours forth blood and relieves us from hunger.
She has her seat behind the rider like a Turkish woman captured by Arabs.
Her eye runs with kohl . . .
She goes forth early, confident that she can provision a mighty army.
The meat of the desert gazelle is constantly on the coals, quickly snatched away;
'Tis as if their knives disperse dyed meat above the plentiful supply of firewood. (Ibn al-Muᶜtazz, *Dīwān*, IV, 12)

(The comparison of the cheetah to "a Turkish woman captured" is based on the fact that the cheetah – here a female hunting-animal, hence "she" – lacks stamina and is invariably carried to the hunt, either by cart, or, as here, on the crupper of the horse behind the rider. The eyes of the cheetah are usually surrounded by black fur, hence the reference to kohl.)

Hunting with the goshawk

7 *qad aghtadī wa ᵓl-laylu fī maswaddihi wardun yuraqqī ᵓl-ṭayra fī munqaddihi*

Oft I go forth in the early morning, while night is still black, a dark-bay colour, sending the birds flying as it breaks up.
[It is] the morn of one desiring the hunt . . .
With a [hawk] ruddy in colour or light-bay with a blaze on her cheek.
The Maker has fashioned her with the finest body; she is the same before and after the hunt.
She has a blaze; whomsoever she sees, she menaces noisily, in a tunic sewn
Of pure brocade or silk.
She gazes hard, if game show itself far off, with an eye which fixes on it before the strenuous flight . . .

We only had to set her down from her bow-perch
And slip her with her jesses; off she went over the land at great speed.
She wheeled round and the quarry then behind her; 'tis as if it then sought refuge from her punishment.
[All the birds] collect together when they see the hawk's persistent endeavour, the family of Chosroes on the day when [they gather to play] *dastaband*.
She hunted for us, before giving her full measure of effort, fifty birds counted by both hands of the reckoner.
We are granted gifts and favours by her; [she is] the father of a family, having provided them with food by her exertion.
All good things they have come from her; what a fine hawk you are, without equal! (Abū Nuwās, *Dīwān* II, 202)

(A ruddy colour would indicate the goshawk's youth. The blaze is a feature of the markings of a horse, possibly a hound, and scarcely appropriate here: the poet presumably refers to a light patch of feathers on the cheek. *Dastaband*, a Persian word, is a game played by numerous participants holding hands.)

8 . . . When shining morn appears
From dark obscurity over the mountain passes, I untie her jesses, as a hopeful austringer does.
Then I call in a whisper to her and she is off like lightning, without deviating.
What she hunts will never escape; before the violent dust-carrying wind she had hunted down
Fifty wild geese and francolins which I reckoned up myself without commotion.
What a fine companion for a needy young man! (Ibid., 204)

Hunting with a tiercel goshawk

9 *qad aghtadī bi-zurraqin jurāzi* *maḥḍin raqīqi ʾl-riffi wa ʾl-ṭirāzi*
Oft I go forth in the early morning with a sharp-set tiercel gos, pure, with fine feathers and feather shafts.
He was trapped and taken from Naʿmān Shuradāz [a place-name] and now hunts for us, darting forth [into the attack] straight from the fist.
He is an intrepid fighter and called Abū Khurrāz, frequently into the attack, swift of movement.
He is the adornment of the fist and of the glove of him who carries him; how many quick-walking *ṭuwwal*,
As long as they settle in their watery habitat, does he bind to in hard, open terrain!
He foots them with a swift prick of his talons which thrust in hard,
Like the awl of a master cobbler; he selects his quarry individually without [need of] a scout.
Nor by scanning at the hover; with a thrust he breaks the back right in the middle
Like the [true] son of a hawk and with the skill of a hawk; what a fine friend in time of need! (Ibid., 216)

(The word "Khurrāz" is clearly to be associated with the moult; the bird's name, Abū Khurrāz, indicates that he is an intermewed hawk, i.e. one which has been retained from a previous season and moulted in the mews.)

10 . . . How many *ṭuwwal*s there are, constantly raising their eyes, whose aerial jinks do not save them
From the sudden, swift and unremitting [attacks of the gos], tossed hither and thither by the wind,
And from a blow with a poisoned javelin! Before becoming tired and troubled, he accounted for
Fifty [previously] spared the slaughter. (Ibid., 216)

Hunting with the saker

11 . . . The flock [is divided], some petrified with fear, some escaping; 'tis as if she, when she climbs high like someone lying in wait, has
inverted eyes, always on the watch, swift in pursuit of their panicking flock,
A stone hurling down on other stones, which suffer either from imminent death cantering on,
Or from a torn back, ripped to pieces . . . (Ibid., 219)

12 *lā ṣayda illā bi ʾl-ṣuqūri ʾl-lummaḥi* *kulli qaṭāmiyyin baʿīdi ʾl-miṭraḥi*
There can be no hunting without sharp-sighted sakers, each one greedy for meat, far-sighted,
Displaying the bone of the eye which has no injury; she had not been fed on milk mixed with water
By her mother, nor was she born on the flat plain, rather in the lofty mountains.
She takes the jinking desert jacks, attacking them with head raised high,
With a long [talon] like a short poisoned spear and a beak hooked like a spoon.
. . . She is spotted between the back and the throat, her primaries little distinguished one from another at the extremities, nimble.
Before she becomes completely exhausted and before the distant herder returns in the evening, she hunted
Fifty, like slaughtered victims (Ibid., 221)

(The saker is to this day regarded as having the keenest sight of all the birds of prey. She is always employed to scan the terrain to seek out game for her falconer. The "bone of the eye" is the supra-orbital ridge, the prominent bone which protects the eyes in most birds of prey. The image in lines 2–3 might be more appropriate for a mammal: the poet means simply that the bird has not had a soft upbringing. The primaries are the feathers at the end of the wings, the main flying feathers; on the saker they are found close together, though in some birds of prey they can be spaced out with clear gaps between them.)

Hunting with the peregrine

13 *qad aghtadī qabla ʾl-ṣabāḥi ʾl-ablaji* *wa-qabla naqnāqi ʾl-dajāji ʾl-dujjaji*

Oft I go forth early before morning is clear and before the slowly advancing hens cluck,
With a [peregrine] ruddy and whitish in colour, sitting up on the fist like a little eagle,
With garments tucked up away from her feet, which seem to have been dyed with indigo . . .
My companions continue with their *dolce vita*, eating the meat of their quarry and drinking wine.
You can see some of them quick [to eat], and others thoroughly cooking their meat; some actually lighting a fire, others not bothering to do so. (Ibid., 227)

(The legs of a peregrine are of a distinct blue colour, hence the image of line 3.)

Hunting with the merlin

14 *qad aghtadī waʾl-ṣubḥu fī dujāhu* *ka-ṭurrati ʾl-burdi ʿalā mathnāhu*

Oft I go forth early, while morning is still dark, [but] like the hem of a robe folded over,
With a merlin admired by all who see her and whose falconer has brought her up from the nest.
There is no merlin like her; [she is admired] for the blackish patches with which her cheeks are streaked.
She has black eyes which never deceive her; if a falconer could see what she can see
Because of her far sight, he would sacrifice his mother – and one actually did!
Its shoulders cannot save the lark, nor its wings protect it
From her; when the lark flies up, with her in pursuit, its lungs will be snatched away from its intestines.
Even if it were to invoke constantly God's protection, it would not deliver the lark which God has granted to us.
God who made us a present of the merlin is ever blessed! (Ibid., 230)

Hunting with the sparrowhawk

15 *yā kaffi mā khubbibti idh ghadawti* *bi-bāshiqin yuʿṭīki mā ʾbtghayti*

O my fist! You were not deceived when you went forth early with a sparrowhawk which gives you all you desire.
Only quarry escaping her grasp fear her; she is an arrow which hits the mark whenever you [the fist] shoot it.
Well trained, she hastens in when you summon her; she has no fault save a passion for death. (Ibn al-Muʿtazz, *Dīwān*, IV, 14)

Out of the sections devoted to the oryx hunt in longer pre-Islamic poems came the encouragement to the "moderns" of the Umayyad and ʿAbbasid periods to commit their hunting experiences to poetry. That the goal at the end of the day was a banquet of fresh meat is undeniable, though the excitement of the chase and the immense pride in the animals and birds which carried it out shine through equally strongly. In addition, this was excellent training, and a substitute, for battle. Thus despite the stereotyped openings and finales of the *ṭardiyyāt*, with few exceptions it seems clear that the poets involved were not armchair observers of the hunt. Certainly the major exponents, Abū Nuwās and Ibn al-Muᶜtazz, must have gained wide practical experience on the hunting-field, for technical faults are negligible and their works utterly convincing. On the other hand, the formulaic structure of the *ṭardiyyāt* not only reflects the unvarying technicalities of the hunt; in the opportunities it affords for coining similes etc., there are clear links with the new vistas opened up by these same poets in descriptive poetry (*waṣf*) in other genres.

We can only speculate in this context on why the genre appears to have run out of steam with Kushājim (d. *c.* 360/971),[12] whose compositions, in his *Kitāb al-Maṣāyid wa ᵓl-maṭārid* (an *adab* work concerned with the etiquette of hunting rather than a scientific work on the chase), represent the last examples of the genre worthy of a place beside the verses of the giants, Abū Nuwās and Ibn al-Muᶜtazz. With Kushājim, in the late fourth/tenth century, the *ṭardiyyah* loses its importance as a genre and passes into relative obscurity.

[12] See Giese, *Waṣf*.

CHAPTER 11

POLITICAL POETRY

If poetry in which the beliefs or acts of the leaders of a particular socio-political system are supported or opposed can be defined as political poetry, then there is no doubt that this type of verse flourished in Arabia well before Islam. Indeed, whatever the subject treated, the ultimate aim of the sizeable surviving body of pre-Islamic poetry was the glorification or criticism of the tribe, the nucleus of the system on which the contemporary social structure was based. In an earlier volume, the political verse, tribal or otherwise, of Jāhilī Arabia and of Arab society in the early Islamic period, has been treated in broad outline.[1] It is, however, necessary to retrace some steps in order fully to comprehend the background of the later political verse covered in the present chapter. In ancient bedouin poetry, self-glorification (*fakhr*) celebrated tribal exploits, and satire (*hijāʾ*) rebuked the tribe or individuals for unworthy behaviour. Poetry of a quasi-revolutionary type was composed by the *ṣaʿālīk*, the so-called brigand–poets, who attacked not this tribe or that, but the entire social order.[2] The advent of Islam impelled a change in these types of political poetry. The Prophet recognized the important political function of poetry, and employed poets to respond in kind to the attacks of the pagan poets of Quraysh; the weapons were still those of *fakhr* and *hijāʾ*, but the new way of life gave far greater prominence to the religious element than had been found in old bedouin verse. This was the beginning of a process by which political themes, in the theocratic Islamic states which evolved later, came to be conceived and expressed in confessional terms. However, with the death of Muḥammad and the temporary consolidation of the internal order of Islam under the first caliphs, political and religious poetry alike seemed to stagnate, and were replaced by a genre which C. A. Nallino has called "the poetry of conquest";[3] for, when the tribal soldiers of Islam thrust beyond the Arabian peninsula, their verse again resumed the ancient themes of battle, hardship, valour and lands traversed. But this stasis was of

[1] *CHALUP*, 67–85, 368–73, 413–16, 419. [2] Ibid., 32.
[3] *La Littérature arabe*, 81; cf. also ch. 9, n. 8, above.

brief duration. Fresh impetus was given to politico–religious poetry by the murder of the third caliph, ᶜUthmān (35/656), which inaugurated a series of internecine wars. The origins – sometimes obscure or controversial – of these factions may be briefly described, together with the types of poetry to which they gave rise.

After the Prophet's death, leadership of the Muslim community devolved, by election, on his Companions; but the murder of ᶜUthmān and election of ᶜAlī b. Abī Ṭālib, cousin and son-in-law of the Prophet, resulted in a fresh outbreak of the rivalry between the Meccan families – both of Quraysh – of Banū Hāshim (to which the Prophet had belonged) and Banū Umayyah, which had initially opposed Muḥammad. ᶜUthmān's Umayyad kinsman, Muᶜāwiyah, governor of Syria, demanded vengeance on his cousin's murderers; this ᶜAlī was unable to effect, and not a few Medinans considered him implicated in the murder and refused him their allegiance. So two parties came to dominate the political scene: the ᶜUthmāniyyah, partisans of the murdered caliph, whose most powerful supporter was Muᶜāwiyah in Damascus, and the Party of ᶜAlī (*shīᶜat ᶜAlī*), based on Iraq, where ᶜAlī had his headquarters. However, there were still further divisions within and in addition to these larger groupings, all of which turned their divergent political stances into articles of faith and used poetry, among other weapons, to defend them. (Only the Zubayrīs, supporters of the Meccan anti-caliph ᶜAbdullāh b. al-Zubayr who was defeated by the Umayyads in 73/692, seem to have produced no poetry which fused political and religious creeds, for the Zubayrī movement was motivated by Muᶜāwiyah's violation of the elective principle by appointing his son as his successor, and did not rest on a theoretical religious foundation that would have assured its continuation after the death of its leader. The sole objective of the rare Zubayrī poets whose names tradition has preserved was to celebrate the valour of their most famous captain, Muṣᶜab b. al-Zubayr.)

THE KHĀRIJĪS

The Khārijī movement was a schism which arose in ᶜAlī's camp after the battle of Ṣiffīn (37/657) as a result of his acceptance of arbitration over the murder of ᶜUthmān and his own succession to the caliphate. A minority in ᶜAlī's army refused to accept human intervention, proclaiming that "judgement belongs to God alone" (*lā ḥukma illā li ᵓllāh*) and quitted (*kharajū*) ᶜAlī's ranks. Khārijī intransigence was soon further manifested in affirmations of principle and, in extreme cases, in acts of terrorism. In the eyes of the Khārijīs, anyone who committed a serious offence became an infidel (*kāfir*) and was to be combated as such; accordingly ᶜUthmān was condemned for his behaviour when caliph and considered unworthy of vengeance, while ᶜAlī, whom the Khārijīs held to have been in the right at the battle of Ṣiffīn, was condemned as an infidel for accepting arbitration, and Muᶜāwiyah was considered a usurper. In the light of these criteria, the Khārijīs maintained – in sharp contradistinction to the legitimism of the Shīᶜīs and the quietism of the Murjiᵓīs, which will discussed below – that any worthy Muslim, "even a black slave", might be elected imam. This conception of the caliphate is reminiscent of the bedouin concept of the *sayyid*, who becomes chief by the free choice of the men of the tribe. Such factors may explain the success that the movement won among the bedouin, despite its links with urban settlements, and also the fact that while the literary sources have bequeathed us specimens of Khārijī poetry that are typically bedouin in form and diction, the historical sources describe a faith and devotional practices more typical of urban culture. The Khārijī movement in the east was at its most active in the period roughly coinciding with Umayyad rule; the poetry which it produced served both as a stimulus to action and as a commentary on contemporary events, on which it casts a vivid light. Medieval Muslim sources are known to have devoted anthologies and monographs to Khārijī verse, which was admired for its simplicity and vigour,[4] but little has survived beyond brief fragments, mainly retailed in historical sources dealing with the Umayyad period. The approximately 340 verses published by Gabrieli in 1943 include those of only two professional poets, the moderate ᶜImrān b. Ḥiṭṭān al-Sadūsi (d. 84/703), and al-Ṭirimmāḥ b. Ḥakīm (d. *c*. 105/723), who held extremist beliefs.[5] The latter's *Dīwān* is extant, but only some dozen or so verses can be considered of Khārijī inspiration; the following two pieces seem faithfully to reflect the austere life of prayer and struggle of the Khārijī militant, the *shārī* (pl. *shurāh*), who has "sold" his life to God:

How splendid the *shurāh*, for when heads droop with drowsiness, they keep vigil,
Groaning from time to time; and when overwhelmed with groans, they break into choking sobs.
For fear of God they pass the livelong night with throbbing hearts which almost rend their breasts.

Lord, if the hour of my death be near, let me not be carried on a bier draped in green silk;[6]
Let my tomb be the crop of a vulture hovering ever with its fellows in the depths of the sky.[7]

[4] See e.g. the list of Khārijī orators, poets and jurists drawn up by Jāḥiẓ, Pellat, "Djāḥiẓ et les Khāridjites". [5] *CHALUP*, 414, 326, 340.

[6] I.e. let me die in battle.

[7] Gabrieli, "La poesia ḫārigita", L, LII; the flocking of the vultures to the battlefield to gorge themselves on the slain is often alluded to in early Arabian poetry.

Repression of the Khārijī movement by ᶜAlī at the battle of Nahrawān (38/658), and then by Muᶜāwiyah, who inherited the full odium of the movement, was duly lamented in verse, but despite the lengthening toll of martyrs, Kharijism continued to flourish, and was only destroyed in Arabia, after years of struggle, in the reign of ᶜAbd al-Malik, while a revolt which erupted in the upper Tigris districts in 76/695, threatening the unity of the re-established Umayyad empire, ended only with the death in battle a few years later of Qaṭarī b. al-Fujāʾah. In the poetry attributed to him, he appeared as the very personification of the ideal *shārī*:

I say to my soul dismayed –
"Courage! Thou canst not achieve,
With praying, an hour of life
Beyond the appointed term.
Then courage on death's dark field,
Courage! Impossible 'tis
To live for ever and aye . . ."[8]

Despite these reverses, the movement gained a second wind with the decline of the Umayyads, and the anarchy caused by Khārijī revolts aided the rise of the ᶜAbbasids. But the Khārijīs were equally opposed to ᶜAbbasid rule, and remained for some time a thorn in the flesh of the new dynasty, not so much in the East, where their frequent revolts lacked broad support, but in North Africa, where on two occasions, from 141/758 to 144/761 and in 156–7/772–3, Khārijī forces checked the advance of the caliph's troops. But the times when an ᶜImrān b. Ḥiṭṭān or a Qaṭarī b. al-Fujāʾah could rouse the ardour of their coreligionists with their verse had passed, and, as Charles Pellat notes, there is no surviving report of any Khārijī poet during the ᶜAbbasid era (though the movement survived, notably in eastern Arabia and in North Africa, where it produced a noted school of theologians, the Ibāḍiyyah).[9]

SHĪᶜĪ POETRY UNDER THE UMAYYADS

Like the poetry of the Khārijīs, Shīᶜī poetry drew its first inspiration from the events of the Umayyad period, but Shiᶜism, unlike Kharijism, continued to be a disruptive element and to generate a poetic literature throughout the ᶜAbbasid caliphate. Forced into relative clandestinity after Muᶜāwiyah's triumph over ᶜAlī and the renunciation of the caliphate by ᶜAlī's elder son, al-Ḥasan, ᶜAlid partisans nevertheless occasionally broke cover. The slaying at Karbalāʾ, on 10 Muḥarram 61/10 October 680, of al-Ḥusayn, ᶜAlī's younger son, by the troops of the Umayyad caliph Yazīd,

[8] Ibid., XXVII; trans. Nicholson, *Literary History*, 213.

[9] Pellat, *Le Milieu basrien*, 175.

was the crowning act of the tragedy of the House of ʿAlī. The ʿAlid party drew fresh inspiration from the martyrdom of al-Ḥusayn and gained ground, particularly in southern Iraq and in Persia, both because dynastic legitimacy was traditional there, and because the ʿAlids supported the claim of new converts to Islam, the *mawālī*, to be treated equally with Arabs. Meanwhile, support of the family of ʿAlī was being transformed from a simple dynastic issue into a new religious outlook of sometimes only marginal othodoxy. This transformation was initiated by al-Mukhtār b. Abī ʿUbayd, an adventurer who, proclaiming himself the avenger of al-Ḥusayn, led an uprising against the Umayyads in 66/685–6 in the name of the imamate of Muḥammad b. al-Ḥanafiyyah, ʿAlī's son not by Fāṭimah, the Prophet's daughter, but by a woman of the Banū Ḥanīfah. Though the new imam greeted his champion with passivity, the uprising spread, gaining the adhesion of the *mawālī* and posing a considerable threat to the Umayyads until its suppression some two years later. The success of the movement was due to the distinctly religious character of al-Mukhtār's propaganda; aspects of this were his presentation of himself as an inspired prophet, the cult of the vacant throne, and the theory of the mutability of divine decrees according to circumstances (*badāʾ*);[10] but most significant was the concept of the *Mahdī*, the coming saviour of the world, a borrowed concept which al-Mukhtār vigorously promoted, claiming that the *Mahdī* was embodied in the person of Muḥammad b. al-Ḥanafiyyah. The name most generally given to al-Mukhtār's movement is that of Kaysāniyyah, after a *mawlā* who played a prominent part in al-Mukhtār's revolt, but, after the death of Muḥammad b. al-Ḥanafiyyah in 81/700, the Kaysānīs split into several groups. The Kuraybiyyah maintained that Muḥammad b. al-Ḥanafiyyah was still alive, hidden in a cave on Mount Raḍwā, west of Medina, where he conversed with the angels while awaiting the moment of his return to liberate humanity. (Other concepts that seem to emerge among this group are *ḥulūl* (reincarnation), *tanāsukh* (metempsychosis) and, in part linked to them, *rajʿah*, the idea that upon the Prophet's death his prophetic mission passed to ʿAlī, and thence to ʿAlī's eldest son, and so on.) Another group, on the contrary, recognized that Muḥammad b. al-Ḥanafiyyah was dead and recognized as imam his son Abū Hāshim; hence there arose a group of sects called Hāshimiyyah, the most important of which was involved in the beginning of the ʿAbbasid propaganda in Khurāsān and in Iraq. (This propaganda was based on the teaching that at the time of his death in *c*. 96–7/715–17 Abū Hāshim bequeathed the imamate to Muḥammad b. ʿAlī b.

10 See Moscati, "Per una storia", 257; interpretations of the religious content of al-Mukhtār's movement and of the role played in it by the *mawālī* are summarized in Hawting, *The First Dynasty*, 51–2.

ᶜAbdullāh b. al-ᶜAbbās – whose ancestor al-ᶜAbbās was the uncle of the Prophet – who in turn transmitted it to his son Ibrāhīm, who finally transmitted it to his brother Abū ʾl-ᶜAbbās ᶜAbdullāh al-Saffāḥ who, in 132/750, became the first ᶜAbbasid caliph.)

Tradition has it that the Shīᶜī poet, Kuthayyir b. ᶜAbd al-Raḥmān al-Khuzāᶜī (d. 105/723–4), known as Kuthayyir ᶜAzzah after the love-poems he wrote for ᶜAzzah al-Ḍamriyyah, contributed to a large extent to spreading the Kaysānī dogma of the hidden imam, and so to rekindling opposition to the Umayyad regime.[11] The passages devoted to the poet by Abū ʾl-Faraj al-Iṣfahānī in the fourth/tenth-century *Kitāb al-Aghānī* also state that he publicly professed belief in *tanāsukh* and *rajᶜah*, though in a fragment cited by H. Pérès, Kuthayyir seems, on the contrary, to espouse the beliefs of the Hāshimiyyah, who recognized Abū Hāshim as imam, for he eulogizes the later Umayyads by associating them with Abū Hāshim.[12] However, it seems more probable that the verses about the hidden imam, though attributed to Kuthayyir by two sources, are in fact by another celebrated Shīᶜī poet, whose life straddled both the Umayyad and ᶜAbbasid dynasties, Abū Hāshim Ismāᶜīl b. Muḥammad, known as al-Sayyid al-Ḥimyarī (d. 171/787–8): the same verses are found, without significant variation, in the famous *qaṣīdah* which the author of *Kitāb al-Aghānī* himself elsewhere attributes to al-Sayyid al-Ḥimyarī. That al-Sayyid al-Ḥimyarī believed in the return of Muḥammad b. al-Ḥanafiyyah is also attested by verses attributed to him by the fourth/tenth century historian al-Masᶜūdī.[13] Originally a Khārijī, al-Sayyid al-Ḥimyarī embraced the Kaysānī doctrine – "by the grace of God", as he is reported to have said – during the crucial years of the transition of power from the Umayyad to the ᶜAbbasid dynasty. For about forty years, in innumerable poems, he celebrated the House of ᶜAlī with an enthusiasm attributable only to genuine zeal, and with a talent which moved even his adversaries to admiration. In around 150/767–8, weary of awaiting the return of Muḥammad b. al-Ḥanafiyyah, he abandoned Kaysānī beliefs and, as he put it, "Jaᶜfarized" himself, recognizing as imam the fifth in the line of ᶜAlī's descendants, Jaᶜfar b. Muḥammad al-Ṣādiq (d. 148/765).

Kuthayyir and al-Sayyid al-Ḥimyarī, as members of the Kaysāniyyah, were both followers of a movement with a particularly heterodox religious content. A no less celebrated poet, al-Kumayt b. Zayd al-Asadī (60–126/679–743), on the contrary, supported the Shīᶜī claim to the sole dynastic legitimacy of the descendants of ᶜAlī by Fāṭimah. The *Hāshimiyyāt*,[14] in

[11] *CHALUP*, 419; see Nagel, *Untersuchungen*, 73ff. [12] *Dīwān*, I, 268.
[13] Abū ʾl-Faraj al-Iṣfahānī, *Aghānī*, VII, 9; trans. Barbier de Meynard, "Le Séid Himyarite", 247–9; Masᶜūdī, *Murūj*, V, 182–3. [14] See *CHALUP*, 414–15.

which he eulogizes the Prophet's House, the Banū Hāshim, present perhaps the oldest testimony to this Shīʿī doctrine. Though al-Kumayt failed to take part in the rebellion of Zayd b. ʿAlī Zayn al-ʿĀbidīn, grandson of al-Ḥusayn, against the Umayyads in 122/740, a fact for which he bitterly reproached himself, he continued to direct his diatribes against both the Umayyads and the Yemenis, their staunchest supporters, and these lampoons – of which the most famous is the long *Qaṣīdah Mudhabhabah* ("Golden Ode") – eventually led to his murder by Yemeni soldiers. But Shīʿī poetry lacked the pugnacity and aggressiveness of contemporary Khārijī verse, and, even in the heat of polemic, the dolorous fate of the House of ʿAlī gave rise to elegy rather than hard-line protest. To quote an earlier volume in this series: "In al-Kumayt's poetry and in that of other Shīʿī poets of this period, three important traditions were established . . . the poem of mourning, which was to become a most important part of Shīʿī literature . . . the religious eulogy which enumerates the great qualities (*manāqib*) of the Hāshimites, which, even at this stage of its history had become highly ritualized[15] . . . the guilt poem, its importance stemming from the fact that guilt had never before been a vital element in Arabic poetry . . . Personal regret and private sorrow mingle with a general guilt and shame which Shīʿī Muslims feel at the death and persecution of the Prophet's family . . . it is the translation of this general feeling into a personal sense of guilt and failure that . . . introduces . . . new horizons of meaning and attitude."[16]

SHĪʿĪS AND MURJIʾĪS

The accession of the ʿAbbasids – who, having seized power with the aid of the Shīʿī sects, had disappointed their expectations by opting, once in power, for the continuation of Sunnism – further stimulated Shīʿī polemic. Al-Sayyid al-Ḥimyarī opposed the new regime until his death: the greeting which he extended to al-Saffāḥ on his accession[17] should probably be regarded as a piece of *taqiyyah* (tactical dissimulation of his true beliefs), and he shortly afterwards reaffirmed his loyalties. The equally famous pro-Shīʿī, Diʿbil (Abū ʿAlī Muḥammad b. Razīn al-Khuzāʿī, 148–246/765–860), who did not share al-Sayyid al-Ḥimyarī's Kaysānī beliefs but, like al-Kumayt, was an exponent only of the principle of dynastic legitimacy, sang the praises of ʿAlī al-Riḍā, eighth imam of the Twelver Shīʿīs (d. *c.* 203/818), and in not a few other compositions attacked the ʿAbbasid caliphs generally, from Hārūn al-Rashīd (reigned 170–93/786–809) to al-Mutawakkil

15 For later examples of the genre, cf. pp. 107–8. 16 *CHALUP*, 415–16.
17 Trans. Barbier de Meynard, "Le Séid Himyarite".

(reigned 232–47/847–61); the lampoon which he directed against the eighth ᶜAbbasid caliph, al-Muᶜtaṣim (reigned 218–27/833–42), is particularly caustic.[18] Shīᶜī contempt was not reserved for the newly successful ᶜAbbasids, but included those movements which had been prepared, under certain circumstances, to accommodate themselves to established authority if not actively to support it. One such was the Murjiʾah; exponents of *irjāʾ* (deferment) – a principle derived from the Qurʾān according to which judgement of a man's inner life is removed from human criteria, subjected to God's judgement alone, and thereby deferred to the Hereafter[19] – held, in sharp contrast to the Khārijīs, that no judgement could be made of ᶜUthmān, ᶜAlī and their partisans, and that it was therefore legitimate to support the Umayyads and combat those who rebelled against them. (Some verses by Thābit Quṭnah, a poet of pronounced Murjiʾī tendencies who also fought bravely on the borders of Khurāsān and was governor of one of its provinces, contain valuable testimony to this political and religious creed, dating back as they do to the first half of the first/seventh–eighth century.)[20] The Shīᶜīs, obviously, opposed the stance of the Murjiʾīs, and the verses in which al-Sayyid al-Ḥimyarī calls upon them to renounce it are famous:

[Once, when the infants] Ḥasan and al-Ḥusayn visited the Prophet, there the two of them sat and played . . .
Then the two rode upon his two shoulders – a goodly steed, goodly its riders twain!
Two infants of a pious mother [Fāṭimah], a pure, chaste spouse,
Two embodiments of ᶜAlī b. Abī Ṭālib – two goodly offspring, goodly the parents twain!
Then, my friends twain,[21] suspend not judgement: you must know the true path is not what you twain maintain,
That blind doubt after certainty, weak insight after seeing face to face
Are sinful erring – so persist not in them, for by your lives, they are wicked.
Is judgement to be suspended upon ᶜAlī, imam of the true path, and ᶜUthmān? – how perverse are the Murjiʾīs!
And on Muᶜāwiyah and his partisans, and the Khārijīs, rash to the point of folly at Nahrawān?
Their imam, on Judgement Day, will be one of evil inclination, a believer in al-Shayṣabān.[22]

That the Shīᶜīs were more irritated by the Murjiʾīs' suspension of judgement on ᶜAlī's actions, than were the Sunnīs by their parallel refusal to judge the conduct of ᶜUthmān, comes through in two short poems which

18 *CHALUP*, 332. 19 Ibid., 221.
20 Abū ʾl-Faraj al-Iṣfahānī, *Aghānī*, XIII, 52; see Nallino, *La Littérature arabe*, 201–2.
21 The conventional address to two anonymous companions adapted to theological argument.
22 Abū ʾl-Faraj al-Iṣfahānī, *Aghānī*, VII, 16; al-Shayṣabān is said to be the name of the Devil or of a tribe of the jinn.

al-Masᶜūdī attributes respectively to the ᶜAbbasid caliph al-Maʾmūn (reigned 198–217/813–33), well known for his partiality to the Shīᶜah, and to his uncle Ibrāhīm, whose Sunnī convictions were unshakeable:

If you would like to see a Murjiʾī expire instantly before his time,
Just repeat before him the praises of ᶜAlī, and bless the Prophet and his House.

If a Shīᶜī mutters when he speaks and you would like to reveal his secret thoughts,
Just bless the Prophet and his two Companions, his viziers and neighbours by his tomb.[23]

However, the neutrality of the Murjiʾīs was not unconditional, and when they felt that the Umayyad government, which they neither openly opposed nor supported, was not acting in conformity with "the Book of God and the *sunnah* of the Prophet", they rebelled; thus, for more than a decade (116–28/734–46) a bloody revolt was waged in Khurāsān under the leadership of al-Ḥārith b. Surayj al-Murjiʾī, with Jahm b. Ṣafwān as the theorist of his movement, which favoured the Persian *mawālī*, the new converts to whom the Umayyads had denied the rights they ought to have acquired on conversion.[24] (It could be said that some *mawālī* themselves began to participate to some extent in the political poetry of this period, if we grant political status to the literary movement which authors of the next two centuries were to call *Shuᶜūbiyyah*, the reaction to the flaunting of Arab claims to superiority, whose pioneer was probably the Umayyad poet, Ismāᶜīl b. Yasār.)[25] This revolt, in which al-Ḥārith was said to have adopted "the black banners" (a foreshadowing of the "black banners" of the ᶜAbbasids whose significance has not been explained), ended with his own death in 128/743; but by this time the province of Khurāsān had become a minefield.

ᶜABBASID PROPAGANDA POETRY

It was from their base in Khurāsān that the ᶜAbbasids had set on foot an intensive propaganda campaign against the Umayyads; that the nascent religious branch of the Muᶜtazilah may have participated in this propaganda can be presumed from a poem by the Muᶜtazilī poet Ṣafwān al-Anṣārī, a contemporary of the founder of the Muᶜtazilī school of theology, Wāṣil b. ᶜAṭāʾ, whom the poem describes as commanding emissaries thoughout the Muslim world.[26] At all events, with or without Muᶜtazilī support, and whatever the truth of their claim to have been bequeathed the imamate by

[23] Masᶜūdī, *Murūj*, v, 4. The first two caliphs, Abū Bakr and ᶜUmar, were buried beside the Prophet's tomb. [24] For this new orientation of *irjāʾ*, see Nallino, *La Littérature arabe*, 209–10.
[25] See pp. 33–4. [26] Jāḥiẓ, *Bayān*, I, 36–8; trans. Pellat, *Le Milieu basrien*, 175.

Abū Hāshim, the ᶜAbbasids began to show their hand immediately after Abū Hāshim's death and some thirty years later open insurrection broke out in Khurāsān under the command of one Abū Muslim, a *mawlā* of probably Persian origin. The insurrectionary forces of the ᶜAbbasids included both Persian *mawālī* and Iraqi Shīᶜīs, but the revolt was not, as has sometimes been argued, a revolt of Persians against Arabs:[27] it paraded under religious colours, upholding the demand that the rights of the ᶜAlids be honoured. Once in power, the ᶜAbbasids required propagandists to uphold their own claim to the caliphate against those of the ᶜAlids. This claim was based on their descent from the Prophet's uncle al-ᶜAbbās, and was championed in verse by Abān b. ᶜAbd al-Ḥamīd al-Lāḥiqī (d. 200/815–16);[28] the lines which he declaimed before the caliph Hārūn al-Rashīd at the urging of his Barmecide patrons are famous:

Which is more closely related to the Prophet of God, his uncle or his nephew?
Which of them has more claim on him and his legacy; who is his rightful heir?
If ᶜAbbās has the sounder claim, then despite ᶜAlī's claim,
The sons of ᶜAbbās are his heirs, just as an uncle's claim on an inheritance debars a nephew's.[29]

Some time later the caliph al-Mutawakkil, for a fee of 10,000 dirhams, had the satisfaction of listening to another edifying lesson in hereditary rights, composed by Marwān b. ᶜAlī al-Janūb:

Yours is the inheritance of Muḥammed, and by your justice is injustice banned,
The daughter's children desire the rights of the caliphate but theirs is not even that which can be put under a nail;
The daughter's husband is no heir, and the daughter does not inherit the Imamate;
And those who claim your inheritance will inherit only repentance.[30]

Legitimacy, righteousness, etc. are standard themes in the panegyric *qaṣīdah*s dedicated to the ᶜAbbasids, their administrators and generals, most of which thus contain elements which could be described as "political"; while it should be noted that both sides in the polemic between Shīᶜīs and ᶜAbbasids employed weapons more insidious than verse, such as fabricated *ḥadīth* and accusations of tampering with the text of the Qurʾān. Nor were the weapons of the new dynasty directed against the Shīᶜīs alone. Claiming to have inaugurated a regime modelled upon that of the Prophet and the

[27] Interpretations of the role and character of these Persian *mawālī* are summarized in Hawting, *The First Dynasty*, 112–13.

[28] A favourite of the Barmecides, the Iranian family of *kuttāb* (secretaries) and viziers, for whom he made a verse translation of *Kalīlah wa-Dimnah*; see Ullman, *Untersuchungen*, 54, and Gimaret, *Le Livre de Bilawhar*, 35–6.

[29] Abū ʾl-Faraj al-Iṣfahānī, *Aghānī*, xx, 76; Goldziher, *Muslim Studies*, ii, 100.

[30] Trans. Goldziher, *Muslim Studies*, ii, 100–1.

first caliphs, the ʿAbbasid rulers, especially al-Mahdī (reigned 158–69/775–85), mercilessly persecuted both heresy and the resurgence of un-Islamic beliefs which went under the broad appellation of *zandaqah*.[31] Thus the poet Marwān b. Abī Ḥafṣah (d. 181/797–8), who later also won the favour of Hārūn al-Rashīd by composing verses against the Shīʿīs, ingratiated himself with the caliph al-Mahdī by means of the following compliment:

The Commander of the Faithful Muḥammad [al-Mahdī] has revived the *sunnah* of the Prophet regarding what is unlawful (*ḥarām*) and what is lawful (*ḥalāl*)![32]

Conversely, it was in the name of the *sunnah*, because he understood the danger to the state of ideas contrary to Sunnism, that al-Mahdī ordered the deaths of Bashshār b. Burd and Ṣāliḥ b. ʿAbd al-Quddūs: Bashshār did not conceal his sympathy for the Persian *mawālī* and was said to have professed a heterogeneous doctrine that appeared to include Manichaean beliefs tinged with Zoroastrianism; Ṣāliḥ b. ʿAbd al-Quddūs, a poet of a similar stamp to Abū ʾl-ʿAtāhiyah, was accused of dualism (*thanawiyyah*), and it is said sealed his fate by confessing to al-Mahdī that he was the author of the lines:

The greybeard will not leave what in the bone is bred
Until the dark tomb covers him with earth o'erspread;
For, tho' deterred awhile, he soon returns again
To his folly, as the sick man to his pain.[33]

THE ZANJ REVOLT

Zandaqah, whose recruits came primarily from the ambient Persian cults, was in essence a reaction against Arab political supremacy and cultural pretensions, and, though it might be perceived as a threat to the established order, it is doubtful whether its adherents, a mixed bag, had clear political objectives. But the authority of the ʿAbbasid caliphs in the provinces was now declining, and the decline was accompanied by a gradual erosion of their power even in Baghdad, where the Turkish military caste, whose recruitment had begun in the reign of al-Muʿtaṣim (218–27/833–42), held real power. Anarchy had followed al-Mutawakkil's attempt to curb the military, and in 255/869 revolt broke out among the Zanj, the black slaves who worked the lands around Basra. Their leader was an agitator, ʿAlī b. Muḥammad, who claimed to be an ʿAlid and called himself *Mahdī*. Displaying brilliant military qualities, he rapidly defeated several armies and established effective control over most of southern Iraq and south-

[31] See pp. 41–2. [32] Abū ʾl-Faraj al-Iṣfahānī, *Aghānī*, IX, 45.
[33] Trans. Nicholson, *Literary History*, 374; see Goldziher, "Salih b. ʿAbd al-Kuddûs".

western Persia. If, as seems likely, the hundred-odd verses attributed to him are authentic, they enable us to understand the origins of the movement and to follow its phases, in outline at least. ʿAlī b. Muḥammad claimed kinship with the ʿAbbasids and made no attempt to conceal his fears for the fate of the empire in Turkish hands:

Cousins mine, kindle not the fire of civil war, slow to subside with passing time;
Cousins mine, we and you are the fingers which the joints of the palms close together;
Cousins mine, you have entrusted command of us, first and last, to the Turks, as we bear witness.[34]

Indignant at the lax and corrupt life led in the palaces of Baghdad, he felt it his duty to protest and take action, and urged the poor and disinherited to insurrection:

How my soul grieves over palaces in Baghdad and what they contain – every kind of sinner –
And for wines openly drunk there, and for men lusting after sins.
I am no son of the noble Fāṭimahs if I do not hurl my horsemen into those courts . . .

Submissively to adopt a moderate stance is humiliation for God's servant
When the spark will not catch, I fan it;
When some leave the sharp blade in its sheath on the day of battle, others will draw theirs![35]

In a foretaste of the struggle to come, he cried:

When our swords are drawn on the bloody day of battle, our palms will be their pulpits, their sheaths the heads of kings.[36]

Grave defeats only sharpened his appetite for vengeance:

May my noble steeds be taken from me if I do not lead them, mounted by brave mail-clad men, commanders!
Does ʿUryān reckon I would forget my knights, fallen on the morning they dismounted their camels to fight on horseback at the barrier, death looming over them?
Do ʿAbd al-Qays reckon I have forgotten them? Never will I forget them, never will I renounce my vengeance![37]

A sense of destiny spurred him on:

When my soul disputes with me I say: Decide! Death that grants rest, or to mount the pulpit [as caliph]!

[34] Ḥuṣrī, *Dhayl Zahr*, 192.
[35] Ibn Abī ʾl-Ḥadīd, *Sharḥ Nahj*, VIII, 127; Fāṭimahs: Fāṭimah, daughter of the Prophet and her ancestresses. [36] Ibid.; pulpits: the sword will preach the message of the rebels.
[37] Masʿūdī, *Tanbīh*, 393; ʿUryān and ʿAbd al-Qays: the enemy general and his tribe.

What has been decreed must be; bear with it, and you will be safe from what
has not yet been decreed.[38]

Plainly these verses are informed not by the resignation of the Shīʿī but by the bellicose ardour of the Khārijī militant, and though he presented himself as a Shīʿī, it was as a Khārijī that the leader of the Zanj appeared to his contemporaries,[39] as is confirmed by the testimony of al-Masʿūdī.

THE CARMATHIANS

The Zanj revolt, a serious threat to the Empire for some fifteen years, was suppressed by 270/883, but this did not spell the beginning of a period of tranquil rule for the ʿAbbasids. In 277/890, a new and far more dangerous revolt erupted in the very same regions of lower Iraq, its instigator taking advantage of the prevailing economic and social disorder. Ḥamdān Qarmaṭ was an Iraqi peasant who claimed to be an ʿAlid and was recognized as such by many. He had joined the nascent Ismāʿīlī movement, to which the majority of those Shīʿīs who professed esoteric doctrines had adhered when the accession of the ʿAbbasids had brought about the disappearance of the line of Ḥanafiyyah pretenders; however, the exact relationship between the Carmathians (Qarāmiṭah), as the followers of Ḥamdān Qarmaṭ are usually called, and the wider Ismāʿīlī movement is still problematic. The Carmathians taught that the line of ʿAlid imams ended with the seventh imam, who would reappear as the *Mahdī*, that his advent was at hand, and that it would bring the era of Muḥammad to a close, revealing the truth of previous religions. In reality Carmathianism, like other insurrectionary Shīʿī movements before it, was basically the expression, in a theocratic environment, of the revolt of the lower classes, Persian and Arab alike, against the establishment. (The class character of such heresies is clearly suggested by the following verses of mid-fourth/tenth century:

My wife reproaches me for not praying; I replied: Get out of my sight! I
divorce you!
By God, I will not pray to God so long as I am poor; let . . . the general of the
Army of the East and West pray
Whose cellars are stuffed with treasure . . .
Why should *I* pray? Where is *my* garden and *my* mansion?
Where are *my* horses, *my* jewels and *my* gold-and-silver-embroidered belts?
Where are *my* slaves with faces lovely as new moons?
Where are *my* beautiful, nubile serving-girls?
Should *I* pray when I own not span of land? I should be a hypocrite indeed.
(Of course, if God makes me rich I'll never stop praying to him as long as the
lightning-flashes brighten the sky)[40]

[38] Ibn Abī ʾl-Ḥadīd, *Sharḥ Nahj*, VIII, 311.
[39] For the tendency to brand insurrectionaries as Khārijīs, cf. ch. 23, n. 67.
[40] Barbier de Meynard, "Tableau littéraire", 329–31, 358–9.

After the death of Ḥamdān Qarmaṭ, the revolt was brought under control in Iraq in 294/907, but the movment had already spread along the Arabian coast of the Gulf in the territories called al-Baḥrayn, so that by 286/899 the entire region was controlled by a Carmathian state powerful enough to carry out devastating incursions in Iraq in the first half of the following century, and even to seize Mecca during the Pilgrimage of 317/930 and to carry off the Black Stone from the Kaᶜbah. One of the chiefs of the Carmathian state, Abū Ṭāhir al-Jannābī, is credited with composing the following famous verses on the occasion:

Were this indeed the House of God our Lord, he would have poured down a stream of fire upon us,
For we have made a venerable pagan pilgrimage that no longer existed in East or West,
And we have left, between Zamzam and al-Ṣafāᵓ, corpses that desired no Lord but the Lord of the Kaᶜbah.[41]

The allusions to pagan pilgrimage and to the desecration of the holy sites of the well of Zamzam and the mound of al-Ṣafāᵓ show that the Carmathians wished to demonstrate that the Muslim era was at an end. Abū Ṭāhir now decided to deliver the *coup de grâce* to the caliph of Baghdad, and in 319/931, from his capital of al-Ḥajar, threatened the inhabitants of Iraq in these terms:

My return to Ḥajar has deceived you, but it will not be long before you hear of me;
When Mars ascends from the land of Babylon and Saturn is in conjunction with it, then – beware, beware!
I shall send my armies against Egypt and Cyrenaica, against the armies of the Turks, Byzantines and the Khazar.[42]

But events took a different course. In the same year (probably chosen because it corresponded to the fifteen hundredth anniversary of Zarathustra), Abū Ṭāhir is believed to have recognized a young Persian boy from Isfahan as *Mahdī*. However, he soon admitted that he had been deceived, whereupon he had the boy executed. Demoralization set in among the Carmathians, many of whom went over to the ᶜAbbasids. The Carmathian state nevertheless survived, and for more than a century continued to be admired, even by non-Carmathians, as a paragon of order and social justice.

THE FATIMIDS

At the same time as the Carmathians were establishing themselves in Arabia, another branch of the Ismāᶜīlī sect, the Fatimids, had founded an anti-caliphate in Tunisia. In 358/969, they took Egypt and soon threatened

[41] De Goeje, *Mémoire*, 110. [42] Ibid., 113–15.

Syria. Their political and military power was based less on the strength of their armies than on a highly organized religious hierarchy commanding numerous agents, propagandists and sympathizers in the ʿAbbasid provinces. As ever, a favourite medium of propaganda was poetry, and, while still heir-apparent, the Fatimid caliph al-Qāʾim himself (reigned 322–34/934–46) made the following admonition to the Egyptians and, indirectly, to the ʿAbbasid caliphs, while leading an expedition against Egypt:

O people of God's eastern lands, have you lost your wits, or are you led astray by weak understanding and ignorance?
Who leads your prayers? Who heads your pilgrimage? With whom do you campaign? Answer, and no lies!
Your prayer, your pilgrimage and your campaigns, misguided wretches, are with wine-bibbers and men given over to vice.
Stir yourselves: the sword's edge is the best remedy for the sick, the weapon most fitting to bring about justice.
Do you not see that I have exchanged ease for night sorties, that I have risen in the cause of God,[43] as is my duty? . . .
I called out to the people of the West with the summons of one trusting in a Generous Lord: nor can there fail whomsoever He taketh under His charge,
And swiftly they flocked to [me] . . .
And I advanced with the knights of God towards your land, and amid the veils of dust loomed forth the face of death.[44]

Like the ʿAbbasids, the Fatimids were served by professional poets. The Andalusian, Ibn Hāniʾ (d. 362/973) was a sincere admirer of al-Muʿizz, the fourth Fatimid caliph and conqueror of Egypt (reigned 341–65/953–75); a convinced adherent of the Fatimid sect, he upheld the legitimacy of the Fatimid caliphate in poetry noted for its lyric quality. A frequent theme is the caliph's ancestry: "He [al-Muʿizz] is heir to the Earth through two ancestors, one Chosen [*Muṣṭafā*, i.e. the Prophet], one pleasing to God [*Murtaḍā*, i.e. ʿAlī]."[45] In accordance with the Ismāʿīlī doctrine that the imam was a reflection of the Divine Light, he depicted the sovereign as a supernatural being, the predestined Lord of the World:

They come at morn, their gaze lowered before a Caliph gnostic of God's mystery though untaught,
Of guidance the very spirit, in light incorporate, whom rays from the sublime world incorporeal sustain,
Whom firm, unseverable bonds link to the Deity.[46]

Other recurrent motifs in Ibn Hāniʾ's poetry are fierce attacks on the two rival caliphates: the ʿAbbasid, which he considered a usurper now bound by

[43] An allusion to his later regnal title, al-Qāʾim bi-amri ʾllāh, and to *al-qāʾim* as an Ismāʿīlī designation of the *Mahdī*.
[44] Canard, "L'Impérialisme", 172–3.
[45] *Dīwān*, I, 782; Canard, "L'Impérialisme", 159.
[46] *Dīwān*, I, 665; Canard, "L'Impérialisme".

its "senility" to yield to the youthful and worthier energies of the "virgin dynasty", and the Umayyad caliphate of Cordoba, which he disparaged as vigorously as he extolled the Fatimids. But the poet who above all others dedicated his energies to the propagation and glorification of the Fatimid creed was Abū Naṣr Hibat Allāh, known by the nickname al-Muʾayyad fī ʾl-Dīn (d. 469/1077). His *Dīwān*, containing sixty-three *qaṣīdah*s, is certainly one of the most remarkable of efforts to make poetry serve politico–religious ends.[47]

"CONSERVATIVE" SHĪʿĪS

Alongside the Carmathians and Fatimids there were those whom Massignon has dubbed "conservative" Shīʿīs, like the Hamdanids of Syria and Mesopotamia, who never attempted to implement their legitimist aspirations and were happy, in return for lucrative sinecures, to serve the Sunnī ʿAbbasids.[48] The names of Abū Firās, a Hamdanid prince and poet, and of al-Mutanabbī, the greatest Arab poet of the fourth/tenth century, are among the many associated with the outstanding works of literature produced in Mosul and Aleppo under Hamdanid patronage. Abū Firās, who was a cousin of Sayf al-Dawlah, ruler of Aleppo, wrote poetic commentaries on his own exploits and those of his forebears, and though he occasionally attacked the ʿAbbasids in his verse, this was more to defend the political interests of his own family than because of the difference in creed; nevertheless, generalized expressions of ʿAlid sentiment ("Forever do I love him who loves the Prophet and his family, and anyone who hates him, I hate") are occasionally given a sharper edge:

Dead is the faith, justice not done its due,
The booty due to the family of God's Prophet is shared out among others.
The Sons of ʿAlī are become subjects in their own lands
While womenfolk and menials hold power.
Let not the godless dominion (*mulk*) of the Sons of al-ʿAbbās tempt them into excess:
The Sons of ʿAlī are their Lords, despite their pretensions.[49]

It cannot be claimed that Abū Firās's contemporary and rival, al-Mutanabbī, shared his dedication to the ʿAlids; there are few concrete references or allusions to Shīʿī beliefs in his *Dīwān*, with the exception of such Carmathian elements as his allusion to Abū Ṭāhir's massacre of the pilgrims at Mecca, and it is probable, as Gabrieli maintains, that such

[47] See Rizzitano, *Letteratura araba*, 82–3, and *EI*[1], "al-Muʾaiyad fī ʾil-Dīn", for his activities as a general, *dāʿī* (propagandist), his correspondence with al-Maʿarrī and other literary works, which include an autobiography. [48] Massignon, *Opera Minora*, I, 402. [49] Gabrieli, "Note", 328.

elements were simply picked up in his youth and played no significant part in his thought or poetry.[50]

While the Hamdanids were asserting their rule in Syria during the fourth/tenth century, another Shīʿī family, the Buwayhids, founded a dynasty in Iran which soon took power in Baghdad itself. The triumph of Shiʿism seemed irreversible, but in fact the Sunnī caliphate was not abolished, and Sunnism remained the majority creed. Contemporary ʿAlid poets, such as the statesman al-Ṣāḥib Ibn ʿAbbād or the only Shīʿī poet of real distinction during this period, al-Sharīf al-Raḍī (d. 406/1016), represent "conservative" Shiʿism, rather than the militant and self-assertive Shiʿism of the Fatimid poet-propagandists.

[50] See pp. 305–6; and Gabrieli, "Imamisme", 111.

CHAPTER 12

LOVE POETRY (*GHAZAL*)

No independent love lyrics survive from the pre-Islamic period, but love remembered is frequently the first of the themes through which the archaic *qaṣīdah* ranges. In the introductory section of the *qaṣīdah*, the *nasīb*, the poet conjures up lost love through a variety of conventional motifs: the recognition in a deserted encampment of the place where he and a loved woman once enjoyed days of friendship; a dream haunted by the woman's phantom; or the evocation of the morning when her tribe, neighbours for a season, made ready to leave. At times, the poet's grey hair has caused the woman to deny her favours; less often, the poet has tired of waiting for them. Some poets – al-Aᶜshā for example – describe the lady in sensuous detail. The names vary but it is, from top to toe, always the same woman: all pampered softness, languor, plenitude.

The poet may suffer and weep, but he lets us know that he can bear it. By the conventions of the poem, the loss of intimacy with a gentle, sweet and indolent creature of luxury leads him to proclaim his intimacy with hardship and danger in the desert. The poet al-Muthaqqib al-ᶜAbdī tells in three lines of Hind's change of heart, then continues:

Dost thou then mean it so? Shall I tell thee how many a land, what time in the summer days the Sun stood still thereon
And the singing cicadas shrilled in the sunshine, and the shining sun-mist, with its white sheets folded and its striped veils, showed its side to me,
I have traversed on a she-camel with well-knit fore-legs . . .[1]

In the ancient Arabian poems paired memories of good and bad often express stoical endurance in the face of the world's changes. The contrast between the *nasīb* and the journey scene that commonly follows it also makes for a stoical tone, and, while the narrative link between the two scenes is flimsy, the ethical one is strong and essential. Its place in the ethos of the heroic poetry sets apart the *nasīb* from the love lyrics of later times, which succeeded to much of the stock: capricious hearts, partings, the visit of the phantom of the beloved to the sleeping poet and the rest.

The *nasīb* is not usually, in the old poets, an erotic idyll. Scenes of

[1] Trans. Lyall, *Mufaḍḍalīyāt*, no. 28.

tenderness (as distinct from tender descriptions) tend to be sketchy, or by way of hint. The following passage – the leisurely, simile-laden dwelling over the evocative landscape and the plain, brief flashback to the rendezvous – is fairly representative:

Suwaiqah of Balbal, as far as its runnels flow and the plain of dwarf tamarisk,
filled my eyes with tears at the memory of my trysts with Salma –
Places of meeting where now feed only the black troops of ostriches, dark of
hue like Indians taking short steps as though they were sore-footed;
They feed together, in the raviny ground, in the company of a male ostrich,
small-headed and long-necked, looking like a gatherer of acacia pods in
Dhu-t-Talh, who culls them without lopping the tree.
She stood towards the side of the tent-curtain – and the passion that was in her,
but for the eyes of men, had overwhelmed me;
And she said – "Wilt thou not stay and satisfy a desire, O father of Hasan,
among us, and fulfil what thou has promised to me?"[2]

(The *Muʿallaqah* of Imruʾ al-Qays, with its moments of farcical ribaldry, is not in the mainstream.)[3]

As J.-C. Vadet has shown, the *nasīb* does not reflect a single, coherent social reality.[4] Some of the women are very much their own mistresses; others obey a code dictated by men, and are carefully watched. The conservative formulas of poetry may reflect archaic customs: partings after temporary marriages between members of tribes that occupied adjacent encampments for a season; perhaps even, from a more distant past, woman's matriarchal right to receive in her tent whomever she wished. Only some such sedimentation can explain the diversity of scenarios, in some of which the lover's visits are unproblematic, while in others the poet can speak of:

The nights when I paid no heed to him that would hold me back, and my
waist-wrapper flowed down over my ankles,

And I disobeyed him that chid me, and I achieved delight, and vexed, by my
visits, one stirred by jealousy[5]

or (as in Imruʾ al-Qays's *Muʿallaqah*), recall a visit to a camp where the men would be only too happy to kill him. There is every reason to believe that already in the sixth century AD this poetry was not merely conventional, but, having derived its conventions from successive periods of Arabian life, was a mixture of stylized representations of what might occur and what, by then, could only be fiction. This situation continued in the century after Islam.

[2] Muzarrid b. Ḍirār al-Dhubyānī, trans. Lyall, ibid., no. 15 (emended sequence of verses).
[3] Cf. *CHALUP*, 61–2.
[4] *L'Esprit courtois*, 48ff; for a dissenting view, see Wagner, *Grundzüge*, 31–2.
[5] Bishr b. Abī Khāzim, trans. Lyall, *Mufaḍḍalīyāt*, no. 98.

In that century, after the power of the Umayyad house had been established and the political centre of gravity had moved to Syria, the cities of Mecca and Medina enjoyed a life of wealth and ease, and there was in them a high society that nurtured wit, gallantry and style in the place of political ambition. Here the love-poem made itself independent and *ghazal* emerged as a distinct genre, in the verse of such men as ᶜUmar b. Abī Rabīᶜah (d. *c.* 103/721) – the foremost poet of this Hijazi school – Waḍḍāḥ al-Yaman, al-ᶜArjī, and others.[6] Some of their poetry takes the form of *nasīb* without *qaṣīdah*; but much of it breathes a light-hearted atmosphere of easy adventures (for which the pilgrimage often serves as occasion), lovers' quarrels and secret messages. Even where the poet chooses to boast of the danger of his visits to a woman, there may be a touch of humour – as when ᶜUmar slinks out of the camp at dawn dressed in women's clothes and flanked by his lady's sisters. ᶜUmar can also put on the persona of the humble lover abasing himself before the cruel Beauty who commands his heart – a persona that rules the love poetry of the ᶜAbbasid age. For example, he writes a verse letter from "an afflicted lover who admits his sin, who has suffered punishment though he has done no wrong". "It is for you to command" (*anti ᵓl-amīratu*) he tells the lady. Making free with Quranic references, he goes so far as to say "I offer you my repentance" and "I take refuge with you from your wrath".[7] His wit too anticipates later patterns:

> My hearing and sight are both her allies against my person: how could I have the fortitude to do without hearing and sight?[8]

But ᶜUmar is most in his element when he inverts the traditional roles and makes the poet the rakish object of the ladies' yearning and delight. One of them addresses him so:

> You get bored with those who love you; ever running after new loves, you are a man of fickle desires, disbursing false tokens of affection and trivial favors.[9]

Whether the Hijazi love-poems are chaste (ᶜUmar: "I did not obtain anything forbidden . . ."), or licentious (Waḍḍāḥ al-Yaman: "I went to her after her husband had fallen asleep, his head pillowed on her hand. By now the night had grown chill. She gave me a glance as if to say: 'Welcome; you will have what you desire, despite the envious')"[10] has less to do perhaps with the poet's experiences than with the audience's expectations. The *Kitāb al-Aghānī*, a fourth/tenth century compilation, reports that great ladies of early Islamic times were pleased to receive homage in the form of

[6] Cf. *CHALUP*, 422–4, 448. [7] *Dīwān*, nos. 1, 91. [8] Ibid., no. 8. [9] Ibid., no. 3
[10] Ibid., no. 233; Abū ᵓl-Farajal-Iṣfahānī, *Aghānī*, VI, 45, cited Kinany, *Development of Gazal*, 206.

love-poems.[11] Such poems must have had obvious limits. But these ladies' literary salons were not the only places for the gathering of the wealthy and the clever, and less exalted occasions must have called for a freer sense of fun. We may note a line by Waḍḍāḥ al-Yaman which suggests that in some cases the love-poem is not so much homage as fair exchange: "I am Waḍḍāḥ. If you are kind to me, I will write you fine love-poems and describe your beauty.")[12]

In the Hijazi love-poem, language is incomparably simpler than in pre-Islamic verse. Dialogues between the actors – lover, lady, her companions, the messenger – quicken the pace. New, light metres are frequently used: it is not clear how much this has to do with the musical fashions of the time.[13]

There is a second kind of love poetry traditionally ascribed to poets of the first/seventh century. This is the poetry of ʿUdhrī love: a poetry of faithful, chaste and debilitating passion for unattainable objects. The legends have it that these bedouin lovers (Jamīl, Majnūn, etc. – not all of them of the tribe of ʿUdhrah) endured passions that led to deep melancholy and often to death. The poets of ʿUdhrī love are shadowy characters, their biographies full of conventional narrative motifs. It seems quite impossible to separate history from fiction. It has been suggested that ʿUdhrī poetry is the product not of bedouin Arabia, but of Empire sophistication; that it is the romantic creation of the early ʿAbbasid age, projected backwards in history at a time when biographies of bedouin poet-lovers were a popular form of entertainment literature in Baghdad.[14] But already the earliest ʿAbbasid poets know of these ʿUdhrī poets, and it is hardly likely that their romance–biographies (for which the *Kitāb al-Aghānī* is now our principal source) did not from the first contain a core of poetry. In the ʿUdhrī *ghazal* all the equilibrium which alternations of sweet and bitter give to the pre-Islamic *qaṣīdah* is thrown aside: the long view becomes one of permanent obsession. Not so much the memory of past joys, as consummation forever deferred, is at the heart of these poems. Love is a cherished disaster into which one is hurled by fate and which one nurtures with a somewhat ostentatious chastity, as in the line, "My ardour dies when we meet and revives when we part",[15] described by some medieval literary men as, "the most perfect verse of *ghazal* ever uttered by an Arab." The medieval biographies supply in each case reasons for the impossibility (or, in one case, forced dissolution) of that much too prosaic relief, marriage. Love is thus a durable fire:

[11] Vadet, *L'Esprit courtois*, 110f.
[12] Ibid., 44. [13] Cf. *CHALUP*, chs. 20, 21.
[14] *EI*², "Ghazal"; for arguments for a cautious but less sceptical view, see Kratchkovsky, "Frühgeschichte". [15] Jamīl, *Dīwān*, 67.

Love, I have found, is a blaze with lovers' hearts for fuel.
If only they perished in the flame! But as soon as they are burned they must burn again
Like the people of hell, for whose greater torment the roasted skin is endlessly renewed.[16]

The ᶜUdhrī lover's romantic tragedy, willed and fated, strikes one as a plangent attenuation of the readiness, in the heroic verse of the pre-Islamic age, to throw away wealth and life, of the need to reject counsels of sane, commonplace self-interest. Islam had put an end to the pagan ethos; perhaps, as in the Old French courtly romances, love emerged "as a substitute for other possibilities of motivation".[17] The poaching on religious language, which is in fun in ᶜUmar and the poets of his school, is meant in the ᶜUdhrī lyric to express the extent of this dangerous devotion. Thus for Jamīl those who die of love are martyrs, no less than those who fall in the *jihād* (Holy War), and Majnūn at prayer faces towards the place where Laylā lives.[18] Play with such language is frequent in later poets.

In the second/eighth century, the "new poets" or "moderns" (*muḥdathūn*) of the cities of Iraq developed a rhetorically sophisticated style which, beginning with Bashshār ibn Burd (d. *c.* 167/783), also came to dominate the love lyric. For the scholars who believe that ᶜUdhrī poetry is, on the whole, a product of ᶜAbbasid times, Bashshār represents even more of a turning point: in their view, he brought into fashion poems in which "love is from the first known to be hopeless and draws its lasting character from this certainty".[19] Bashshār, in any event, was not all ethereal sentiment: he wrote many poems in the *nasīb* style as well, and was not above boasting of fun he had had, in a sly and humorous manner.[20]

The ethereal found its most devoted poet in al-ᶜAbbās b. al-Aḥnaf (d. after 193/808), who wrote nothing but love-poems. About his life relatively little is known, except that he enjoyed the favour of Hārūn al-Rashīd and several important persons at court. Even in al-ᶜAbbās's poetry, it is true, love is not all despair. There are many passages that speak of mutual, if thwarted, love. In some passages the lovers are together, in scenes known from earlier poets: as in ᶜUmar b. Abī Rabīᶜah, the young lover is disguised in women's clothes; as in the ᶜUdhrī tradition, love began in the shared days of first youth; there is even room for the elegiac, and decently vague, recollection of a long-past night.[21] Nonetheless, the dominant mood is of hopeless, one-

16 Majnūn Laylā, *Dīwān*, no. 83.

17 E. Auerbach, *Mimesis* (New York, 1957), 123.

18 Jamīl, *Dīwān*, 64; Majnūn Laylā, *Dīwān*, no. 299.

19 *EI*², "Ghazal".

20 Cf. e.g. ch. 16, n. 22 for the "Kufan" tradition of love poetry in which he sometimes indulged.

21 *Dīwān*, 117, 191.

way, all-wasting, yet indefatigable love. Al-ᶜAbbās has been described as the inventor of the "courtly *ghazal*".[22] He had certainly much to do with promoting the boast, repeated by him and many subsequent poets, that "there is no good in those who do not feel love's passion".[23] Apart from this, it is hard to see from any one poem what he invented. His motifs are those of his age (many are illustrated in Joseph Hell's "Al-ᶜAbbās ibn al-Aḥnaf"); but none of these – worrying about messengers, misleading the spies who try to thwart the lovers, declaring one's submission to the lady, etc. – is unique. It is true that the lover's happy abjection has an uncommon intensity ("I laid my face in the dust for you; to me that is an enormous gain"),[24] but much the same hopeless, submissive lover, never unsteadied by the lady's pitiless whims, agonizes in many poems by his contemporary, Abū Nuwās, no standard-bearer of courtly love. The difference lies in the overall tone of al-ᶜAbbās's poetry. He achieved it by subtraction: especially in his shorter poems, which tend to be free of narrative incident, and are, as the old anthologies attest, his chief title to fame, feeling is rarely troubled by seductive shapes and never by humour. His language is plain and shows little interest in the play of rhetoric. This and the uniformly dedicated tone have conveyed to some readers a profundity of emotion. In Vadet's view, this poetry springs from "an ideal apprehended if not actually experienced", and in it dim stirrings of "absolute love" may be perceived.[25] By contrast, a strong sense of form, wit, and the sparkle of language distinguish the poetry of Abū Nuwās, who was equally at home with the sighs of refined love, the ironic twist and the belly-laughs of ribaldry.

By the third/ninth century, the pomp of panegyric claimed the attention of the most celebrated poets. Their *qaṣīdah*s often open with *nasīb*s in which pre-Islamic themes are treated with the "new" rhetoric (*badīᶜ*), as in these lines by al-Buḥturī:

Your tears, as the howdahs of the ladies of the tribe were moving off into the distance, showed you what lay beyond tears:
Tears filling the eye, sprung by the fiery pain of separation filling the breast . . .[26]

Non-declamatory verse occupied a less prominent place. Perhaps when the new lyrical style had become a familiar skill it no longer shone with the same lustre, or earned the same rewards at court or at the soirées of the rich. (This is not, however, to say that famous poets no longer bothered to write *ghazal*s or that these were without beauty; examples from such poets of the

[22] Gibb, *Arabic Literature*, 60f. [23] *Dīwān*, 190. [24] Ibid., 244.
[25] *L'Esprit courtois*, 193, 207, 227–32. [26] *Dīwān*, II, 1279.

third–fourth/ninth–tenth centuries as Abū Tammām, Ibn al-Rūmī, al-Sharīf al-Raḍī and Abū Firās may be found in or at the end of this chapter.) The chief exception to this trend was Ibn al-Muᶜtazz (d. 296/908). In him the wit of the "new poets" endured along with their delicacy of touch. Bahāᵓ al-Dīn Zuhayr (d. 656/1258) has also been admired, both by Arab and by European readers, as much perhaps for writing intelligibly in an age of rank rhetorical affectation as for the charm of his poetry. Mystical poetry too found continuing inspiration in the themes of secular love poetry.

The "moderns" more or less completed the tonal range and set the rhetorical orientation of the *ghazal*. After the end of the second/eighth century, conventions and techniques – outside Andalusia, at any rate – do not show much change, except, in the direction of least resistance, towards a certain involution of conceits. The waning of innovation did not, however, mean a loss of polish or popularity, as is clear from the many *ghazal*s by greater and lesser poets in the medieval anthologies. Chief among these, as far as poets of the eastern empire are concerned, are the *Kitāb al-Aghānī* ("Book of Songs") by Abū ᵓl-Faraj al-Iṣfahānī (d. 356/967), and the *Yatīmat al-dahr* of al-Thaᶜālibī (d. 467/1038), continued by the *Dumyat al-qaṣr* of al-Bākharzī (d. 429/1075).

A great variety of themes and attitudes continued to exist: there are erotic moments, humorous moments, descriptive passages and full catalogues of charms; there is tender elegiac recollection of mutual love; and there are also outright imitations of older forms: the *Najdiyyāt* of al-Ābiwardī (d. 507/1113) imitate the ᶜUdhrī style, for example. *Ghazal*s celebrating the love of women and of boys had become equally acceptable. (The pronouns employed do not always tell us whether the poem is heterosexual or homosexual: in the *ghazal* the masculine may refer to either gender. It is thought that the grammatically legitimate use of the masculine in certain constructions, e.g., "the one whom I love", may have made this practice possible. It helps the poet "keep the secret"; it also helps the poet broadcast the secret, since the masculine pronoun is metrically more versatile than the feminine.) For all the variety, however, it is safe to say that refined yearning, with its double rhetoric of emotions and phrases, had become the paramount mode of love poetry. In the work of the "moderns", an elegant social game and an elegant rhetorical game made a happy marriage, and the political and social upheavals of the succeeding centuries did not dissolve it.

Refined love and its poetry became part of refined life. Al-Washshāᵓ (d. *c.* 325/936), who in his *Kitāb al-Muwashshā* sets himself up as an arbiter of elegance, gives us a delightful record of that life. We learn what fabrics and perfumes elegant men and women may wear, how they behave in public places (they do not roll about on the hot flagstones in the bath-house; they do not haggle in shops); how they observe good form in their dealings with friends and acquaintances (they do not enjoy backbiting; they do not show off), and so on. A large part of this book is devoted to lovers and their ways, and another, illuminatingly, to verses of love poetry engraved on signet-rings, embroidered on pillows, or written in gold wash on apples. Being prone to falling in love is, al-Washshāʾ says in so many words, one of the fine traits of elegant men and women; love is the best evidence for a finely constituted temperament; it is a badge of sensibility.

Love poetry was at once an expression and confirmation of a soul with style. An endless *frisson* was ensured by the lover's fidelity, hopeless yearning and humble devotion; by the beloved's pitiless heart and quick tendency to boredom; by the malign ambience in which spies would prevent and gossips blight, the lovers' pleasure. The *wāshī* is an interloper, like the Provençal *lauzengier*, who, as the Andalusian Ibn Ḥazm tells us in his *Ṭawq al-ḥamāmah* (translated by A. R. Nykl in 1931 as *The Dove's Neck-Ring*, and since translated several times into English and other European languages), "acts mostly on the beloved" by insinuating that "the lover is not keeping the secret", that his love is "not exclusive", or that his declarations of love are false. The *raqīb*, "watcher" or "spy", may be the "guardian of the beloved" (*custos*, *gardador*), but often he is simply a nuisance who intrudes on the lovers' privacy out of envy or a desire to force on them the cold wisdom of his own disillusionment. The "fault-finder" who promotes dull good sense and the "envious one" are other stock figures. What, though, was the pleasure of love at the best of times? In the world al-Washshāʾ draws for us, the romantic figure of the chaste bedouin lover had become a model for the imagination: "To love is to kiss, to touch hand or arm / or to send letters whose spells are stronger than witchcraft. / Love is nothing but this; when lovers sleep together, love perishes. / The unchaste are only interested in having children"; and verses attributed to Jamīl are quoted, in which the poet disclaims all knowledge of his mistress's body and assures the reader that he sought only to speak with her and look upon her face.[27] This sexual brinkmanship had already been expressed by al-ʿAbbās b. al-Aḥnaf: "Will you permit a lover to visit you? He craves to see and hear. / If he stays long, he does nothing ill: he has a chaste heart, though sinful eyes."[28] Such is the love of the gentle heart, *ʿishq al-muruwwah*. Some poets and some theorists draw more elastic boundaries, as does Bashshār on occasion, or Jāḥiẓ in his *Risālat al-Qiyān*).

The sensible assumption seems today that such poems were in their own

[27] *Muwashshā*, 70–1. [28] Ibid.; al-ʿAbbās b. al-Aḥnaf, *Dīwān*, 147.

time understood to be stylized gestures. "Homage to woman cast in the form of personal experience" is Joseph Hell's view of the poetry of al-ᶜAbbās b. al-Aḥnaf. But the extensive literature on the psychology and ethics of love that grew up in the medieval Islamic world (English-speaking readers will find an introduction to this literature in Bell's *Love Theory in Later Hanbalite Islam* and Giffen's *Theory of Profane Love Among the Arabs*) took these gestures seriously; perhaps because art shapes life, perhaps because the scholars meant to reach realities behind the stylized gestures. Among other things, they discussed the elevating power of love. Love, al-Washshāᵓ says, lends courage to the cowardly, makes the avaricious liberal, gives resolve to the feckless. One of the first theorists of love, Ibn Dāwūd (d. 294/909), abhors the idea that the lover's noble actions may be a vulgar means of ingratiation: "If a man is prompted to do fine things by his desire of reward, once he obtains his wish or despairs of having it, he will be prompted to leave off doing them." Ibn Dāwūd's dedication of his book also intimates that the lover's virtues have their origin in the loved person: "How could one in whom there is no virtue but is traced to you pretend to have virtues superior to yours?"[29] The value of yearning could not be shrugged off even by religious moralists of a tougher cast of mind. Even the Ḥanbalī scholar, Ibn Qayyim al-Jawziyyah (d. 751/1350), who rejected the distinction between the permissible glance and the prohibited embrace, who believed the story that Ibn Dāwūd had died for the chaste love of a boy but saw nothing elevating about such a death, who began his list of good loves with love of God and His word and of the virtues – even Ibn Qayyim al-Jawziyyah concluded his list of good loves with love of a lawful but unattainable object such as an absent wife or dead concubine. In his no-nonsense theology, this unsatisfiable yearning is a good thing because patient suffering earns rewards in the next life.[30]

All this is of interest for comparisons with the European poetry and theory of *fin' amors*, but it is most important to remember that the poets themselves do not have much to say about the virtues (*makārim*) produced by their yearning. They do not, to be sure, wholly ignore the subject: "There is nothing shameful about love, love is a noble quality (*makrumah*)", writes al-ᶜAbbās ibn al-Aḥnaf; "Only lovers count as people."[31] In the *Thousand and One Nights* a character quotes: "Love never repairs to an ignoble heart."[32] There are such statements, but it seems that in the poetry (whose traditions should be distinguished from those of the theory of love) the virtue bred by love is the sensibility itself, and not so much an awakening to a kind of spring-time of the soul. A theorist like the poet,

[29] *Zahrah*, 1. [30] *Rawḍat al-muḥibbīn*, 130, 180f, 202. [31] *Dīwān*, 119, 197.
[32] *Alf laylah wa-laylah*, 1, 237.

theologian and philosopher Ibn Ḥazm (d. 456/1064) may go so far as to say that love renders a man of coarse temperament capable of being deeply moved (of experiencing *ṭarab*), but even this is a different matter from Bernart de Ventadorn's claim that the *joy* of love augments his worth (and improves his writing).[33] Hell's observation of the absence in al-ᶜAbbās b. al-Aḥnaf of the troubadours' jubilation holds true of medieval Arab love-poets in general, and, while the joy of love is a tricky thing (Bernart can begin a poem with "my heart is so full of joy" and end it with a message of the "pain and martyrdom I endure because of her"), these differences must be kept in mind if a typological comparison, or any attribution of affinity, is attempted.

The books on love and on *elegantiae* know that refined love is something of a construct and limited to high society. Al-Washshāᵓ warns that love is not for the poor: its proprieties – especially the presents – cost too much; and in his discussion of the lover's humility, Ibn Ḥazm reassures us that in love (and in love alone) humbling oneself is no disgrace, for, after all, the beloved is the lover's social inferior.[34] The very boast by al-ᶜAbbās ibn al-Aḥnaf, "I am not the kind that loves slave-girls; the love of slave-girls is for slaves",[35] must mean that Ibn Ḥazm's observation applied to most cases. In an anecdote that either reports, or, if fictitious, grasps and projects, the coexistence of charade and reality, a boy propositioned by the ruler of Saragossa sends back some verses rejecting his advances, and an attached letter inviting his friendly affection, explaining that the verses merely complied with the rules of love poetry.[36] The objects even of the "libertine glance" must as a rule have been slave-women and boys. Perhaps an awkward lopsidedness in such relations promoted balancing fictions. The poets at times poked a bit of fun at the exalted claims of elegant love. Bashshār's joke about his love-sick donkey's refined language is often quoted: "Her cheek" (had said the donkey of his donkey lady-love, according to Bashshār) "is as smooth as that of a *shayfurān*." "What's a *shayfurān*?" (Bashshār is asked). "How should I know?" (replies Bashshār), "it's a frightfully rare word (*gharīb*) used only by donkeys; if ever you happen to meet mine, ask him!"[37] In one of the poems at the end of the present chapter (no. 4, by Abū ᵓl-ᶜAtāhiyah) the poet is at death's door, but if the lady cannot be kind to him this year, he will manage to hang on until the next. Abū Nuwās on occasion blended the language of refined love with *double entendres*, or led with it into scenes of debauchery. Ibn al-Ḥajjāj (d. 391/

33 Ibn Ḥazm, *Ṭawq al-ḥamāmah*, 13; R. T. Hill and T. G. Bergin, *Anthology of the Provençal Troubadours* (New Haven, 1941), 46. 34 *Muwashshā*, 158; *Ṭawq al-ḥamāmah*, 43.

35 *Dīwān*, 86. 36 García Gómez, "Convencionalismo e insinceridad", 42.

37 Abū ᵓl-Faraj al-Iṣfahānī, *Aghānī*, III, 64.

1001), an extravagantly foul-mouthed poet, followed this practice and turned parody into one of his conventional devices; in one poem, for example, the line, "My heart belongs to the Banū ʿUdhrah; love has ever made my body thin and drenched my eyes with tears", introduces a string of scatological obscenities.[38] The great poet of Hispano-Arabic colloquial verse (*zajal*), Ibn Quzmān (d. 555/1160) in one poem turns his back on elegant love altogether:

> As for refined love (*ʿishq al-muruwwah*) – let others claim it.
> May God, instead, give me contentment:
> Kisses, embraces, and the rest.
> (If you ask any further, you prove yourself nosey.)[39]

As with so much European love-poetry (for example, Petrarch's *Pace non trovo e non ho da far guerra; / E temo, e spero; et ardo, e son un ghiaccio*), the basic mode of ʿAbbasid love poetry is paradox. Apart from reflecting the confusion of feelings we experience when in love, paradox makes for a dramatic quality in the poem, and invites rhetorical organization of its text. The principal paradoxes – the lover's choice of pain over indifference, and his submission to a person weaker and of humbler rank – are clearly stated. Ibn Dāwūd quotes a verse attributed to an anonymous early poet of the tribe of Hudhayl: "A wounded heart is dearer to me than a calm mind without you".[40] A verse attributed to the ʿAbbasid princess ʿUlayyah goes further and lays down the first rule of rapt flirtation: "Love is founded on injustice. If the beloved were just, love would become foul."[41] A whole complex of paradoxes is neatly summed up in the line (of uncertain attribution): "By Him who made masters, in love, into servants of slaves and put the leashes of lions into the hands of gazelles, the rose is no more beautiful than a blushing cheek . . ."[42]

The fine love may begin with the slightest of accidents and lead to the gravest disasters: "Many a man has, with a single glance, opened the gate of misfortune and gained sorrow without end."[43] One impending disaster is gravest of all: the lover in his obsession loses sight of the final accounting. Bashshār describes himself as a man who, before falling in love, had lived like a monk, worrying through sleepless nights about what end he would come to, "but was then turned away from his devotions by passion for a full-breasted maiden, / who with love of herself drove the Great Judge's reckoning out of his mind".[44] Nor is it a balanced relationship. The lover's darling would try a sane man's patience. Promises put off, and accusations founded on fancy, torture the poor aspirant; he is forever in suspense: "Can

[38] Thaʿālibī, *Yatīmah*, III, 66. [39] *Todo Ben Quzman*, II, 642. [40] *Zahrah*, 27.
[41] Ṣūlī, *Ashʿār awlād al-khulafāʾ*, 66; Vadet, *L'Esprit courtois*, 259. [42] Thaʿālibī, *Yatīmah*, I, 73.
[43] Al-ʿAbbās b. al-Aḥnaf, *Dīwān*, 141. [44] Trans. Beeston, *Selections*, no. 10.

I find a way to you, or else a way to despair?", asks the Hispano-Arab poet known as the Blind Man of Tudela (al-Aʿmā ʾl-Tuṭīlī, d. 525/1130–1).[45] Even when seen in a dream, the lady is true to form: "A phantom that visited me kept sleep from my eyes. When I said 'Grant me a favour', it went out in silence, saying neither yes nor no."[46] If it is not the lady's cruelty or whim that frustrates the lover, it is the difficulty of arranging a rendezvous: "God knows I only left off visiting you for fear of my enemies and those who keep an eye on me. / If I could come I would – crawling on my face or walking on my head!" writes Abū Nuwās. Charming difficulties keep the willing lady from the lover in another poem (no. 16, p. 218). If by chance the lovers do manage to meet, wit may transfer the essential imbalance of the situation to the perception of time: "I accuse my nights (and this is no mere lover's quarrel) of being either too long or too short: long when you avoid me, short when you are with me – we never meet for the right time. / But O that one night! Evening and daybreak were so close they nearly stumbled over one another."[47]

When the lady is cruel, the lover, humble though he is, cannot help resorting to occasional argument. A paradoxical argument of course: to further a love affair that can receive no religious approval, he warns her of divine punishment for killing him. Ibn al-Rūmī (d. *c.* 283/896) gives this motif a sentimental twist: "How can it have happened that she is a sword held over me though I found my love when I entered her door? / Lord, if there must be retribution, make me her shield; let me suffer for her sins."[48] Love is rough on soul and flesh: "Just see how love has mistreated his body! But for his wandering glances, people would bury him." "In her beauty she is like a pearl the sea has tossed on the shore. / Her mouth, her eyes seem inhabited by the sorceresses of Babylon. / All that love for her has left of me is a last gasp in a gaunt body."[49] Love must remain a secret: "I know that in keeping my distance and concealing my feelings there is a truer union of our hearts than in my being near and causing shame."[50] To conceal the identity of their ladies (an endeavour that renders a fictional lady more real and a real lady more comfortably fictional), the poets frequently invent allusive names for them, rather like the Provençal *senhal*. Al-ʿAbbās b. al-Aḥnaf, for example, writes to *Fawz* ("Good Fortune") and *Ẓalūm* ("Tyrant"). But if the lady is captious, she may accuse the lover of having brought her into notoriety; and, even if the lover has the best of intentions, his tears may give it all away. The secret no doubt has social realities behind it, but it is also an

[45] *Dīwān*, 253. [46] Bashshār, in Beeston, *Selections*, no. 2.
[47] Abū Nuwās, *Dīwān*, IV, 74; al- Sharīf al-Raḍī, *Dīwān*, I, 398. [48] *Dīwān*, I, 315.
[49] Al-ʿAbbās b. al-Aḥnaf, *Dīwān*, 284; Abū ʾl-ʿAtāhiyah, *Ashʿāruh*, 618.
[50] Al-ʿAbbās b. al-Aḥnaf, *Dīwān*, 74.

element in the rhetoric of paradox in love poetry; providing for contrast between inside and outside, feeling and behaviour. "He who loves passionately, remains chaste, conceals his love, and dies is a martyr", the often-recalled (and often-impugned) tradition runs:[51] concealment is indeed an essential part of the martyrdom of love.

Since so much of what happens, happens at a distance, the eyes get starring roles. The lady's eyes shoot fatal arrows: the lover's eyes drown in tears. (This is a piece of rhetorical luck, for inwardly he is on fire.) The eyes, at least, have a chance: "May I be your ransom! All I obtained of you was a glance – and all the rest of me envies my eyes!" Some poets are more modest: "The eye that yearns to see you is much too ambitious. / Is it not a fair portion for an eye to see someone who has seen you? / Or to see someone who has seen someone who has seen someone who has?" Where love is mutual, but surrounded by spies, eye must speak to eye: "As our signals of love we used the most subtle glances, more secret than magic. / A soft glance would tell me of union, an oblique one of coldness."[52]

Apart from the tensions that define the basic dramatic shape of the love-poem, there is also a predilection for oxymoron and antithesis in the weave of details: "His kindness is avoidance and reproof, his favour is harsh withholding. / If for a short while I cannot see him, it is death; when I do meet him – the throes of agony", writes Abū Nuwās. The situation of the moment may contain contradictory elements: "I write, and my tears erase my writing."[53] Paradox inhabits the lover's reactions, and emotions: "You whose eyes hurt and soothe . . ." "Whenever a day with you vexed me to tears, I wept for that day after it had passed." "When I come to her, she bashfully turns her face from me, and I delight in an avoidance sweeter than union . . . / When she passes judgment, she wrongs me – a wrongfulness sweeter than justice."[54] The asymmetry is characteristic in, "My glance brought the blood to her cheeks, and her glance bloodied my heart",[55] where parallel and antithesis (the lover's passion and the beloved's blushing reluctance) are worked into one verse. These elements give rise to more and more involved rhetorical surfaces: "If I wanted to find solace and forget you, O delight of my eye, I would be as criminal as those who took part in killing Ḥusayn. / You assault my heart with your spear-slim figure as ᶜAlī assaulted the enemy at Badr and Ḥunayn." "Since you separated from me, my eyelids have remained separated: they only touch through the stream of

[51] E.g. Ibn Dāwūd, *Zahrah*, 66; Ibn Qayyim al-Jawziyyah, *Rawḍat al-muḥibbīn*, 180ff.

[52] Abū Nuwās, *Dīwān*, IV, 92; Ibrāhīm b. al-ᶜAbbās, cited Ibn Dāwūd, *Zahrah*, 101; Muslim b. al-Walīd, ibid., 92. [53] Abū Nuwās, ed. Ghazālī, 395; Al-ᶜAbbās b. al-Aḥnaf, *Dīwān*, 6.

[54] Ibn ᶜAbd Rabbih, cited Thaᶜālibī, *Yatīmah*, II, 71; al-ᶜAbbās b. al-Aḥnaf (attrib.), cited Bārūdī, *Mukhtārāt*, III, 198; Ibn ᶜAbd Rabbih, cited Thaᶜālibī, *Yatīmah*, II, 70.

[55] Aḥmad Kayghalagh, cited ibid., I, 77.

tears." "You who are like the moon when it is full, take pity on a man who is like the moon when it is worn to a sliver."[56] "Desire does to endurance what repentance does to sin." "Were you to set a millstone to my tears, their stream would make it turn." "She and I spent the night, the wine-skin making a third. Till morning we gave each other to drink; / As if the dark bunches of her curls were grapes whose wine was on her lips."[57]

In its manner of composition the love-poem lends itself to great variety. The narration of anecdotes and vivid scenes, common in ᶜUmar b. Abī Rabīᶜah, is less frequent in later poets, in whose work the witty and delicate manipulation of conventional postures and phrases becomes most important. Several of the poems given below show – even, it is hoped, in prose translation – the subtle and intricate (and at times humorous) weave that can compose these conventions into an enticing intellectual music. First, three poems by Abū Nuwās (d. 200/815):

1 I shall give you contentment: I shall die of grief, silent, not grieving you with reproaches.
I knew you once when you wished us to be together, but today you wish to avoid me.
Time has changed you – everything tends towards change and passing away.
If the right thing, as you see it, is to leave me, may God blind you to the right thing.

2 I love the north wind because it passes where my lover is now said to live.
No doubt he feels the same when the south wind goes to meet him.
Brief is the contentment, long the grief, when we welcome the wind with what is in our hearts.

3 God is Danānīr's master and mine. He sees what I suffer on her account morning and night.
For love of her, I am scorched by two fires: I burn in mind and in heart [literally: heart and bowels].
I have forbidden my tongue clear speech; only my feeble signs express what I feel.
Alas, before my own kinsfolk I fade away on my bed, and they do not know my sickness.
If with the whole world you were the ascetic you are with me, you could no doubt walk on water.[58]

Next, two love-poems from Abū ʾl-ᶜAtāhiyah's (d. *c.* 210/825) earlier period, before he devoted himself to the wholesale production of ascetic poetry (*zuhdiyyāt*):[59]

56 "Al-Khabbāz al-baladī" ("the Common Baker"), cited ibid., II, 190; the vizier al-Muhallabī, ibid., 216; Abū ʾl-Faraj al-Babbaghāʾ, cited ibid., I, 223.

57 Ibn al-Rūmī, *Dīwān*, I, 316; al-Waʾwāʾ al-Dimashqī, cited Thaᶜālibī, *Yatīmah*, I, 236; Abū Firās al-Ḥamdānī, ibid., 44.

58 *Dīwān*, IV, 26, 176–7, 11.

59 See pp. 286–7, 268–9.

4 O my friends, love is killing me. Get my shroud ready, quick!
Do not scold me for following my passion – I am too preoccupied to hear.
A stream of tears for ᶜUtbah falls from my eyes.
Who ever saw a victim weeping with passion for the killer?
I stretch my hand towards you in entreaty. How do you answer a suppliant?
If you have nothing to give him, let him have a kind word instead of a gift;
Or, if you are caught short this year, make him yet wish for the next.[60]

5 How often I try, in shame, to hide my tears from some friend!
When he looks at me closely, he scolds. Then I say: "I am not crying,
The cloak grazed my eye as I was putting it on."[61]

Three poems by al-ᶜAbbās b. al-Aḥnaf (d. after 193/808) follow:

6 I buried my passion for you in the tomb of my heart.
I struggled to hide my love; I guarded your secret by staying away.
I was contented with less than contents a lover from his beloved.
But yes, do suppose that I have wronged you, so that you may forgive me those wrongs.

7 She left you [the poet addresses himself] – not for any wrong you have done her, but mankind has little fidelity.
The passing nights had bent her from mindfulness of our love; the term of our friendship had arrived.
A king's robes, for all their splendour, wear out once they have been put on.
After a quarrel there is yet hope of tenderness, but wearying of a love is incurable.
I have seen despair clothe me in lowliness – but then I hope for her, and in that hope exceed all bounds.

("Exceed all bounds" (*yutghīnī l-rajāʾ*): in the Qurʾān there is a recurrent phrase in which the verb *ṭaghā* is used of Pharaoh, a model of tyranny; there is perhaps a cross-reference here to "a king's robes", etc. in line 3.)

8 If you wish to fashion a thing that will amaze and delight,
And to know what a beloved is like who has sipped the cup of love,
Paint here a picture of Fawz and there of ᶜAbbās.
Measure out a span between them; or if more, no matter.
If they do not move towards each other until the two heads seem one,
Give her suffering the lie; give the lie to his.[62]

The next poem is ascribed to Muslim b. al-Walīd (d. 208/823):

9 In the night of her masses of hair, the moon above a thin sapling upon a soft sandhill [moon, sapling, sandhill: face, waist, hips].
Her breath is purer than musk; the bloom of her beauty is more delicate than breath.

[60] Abū ʾl-ᶜAtāhiyah, *Ashᶜāruh*, 616–18.
[61] Cited Ibn Khallikān, *Biographical Dictionary*, s.v. Abū ʾl-ᶜAtāhiyah.
[62] *Dīwān*, 45, 4, 164.

When she walks proudly swaying, my heart is like her jewelled sashes; her heart is silent as her bracelet.
Her love courses through her lover's heart as health through the limbs of a relapsed patient.[63]

(The jewelled sash (*wishāḥ*) goes diagonally from shoulder to waist; its looseness is a conventional reference to a slender waist, and a swaying walk makes its ornaments jingle. The conventional beauty has plump arms, therefore the bracelet is tight. The poet's heart races noisily; hers is unimpressed.)

Abū Tammām (d. 232/846), chiefly known as a panegyrist, also wrote a small number of love-poems of much more accessible diction than his grand public pieces:

10 You have taken me past the limits of pain. Because of you my tears of blood never cease.
Alas my heart . . . and the spy all but keeps me from saying even this, "alas my heart . . ."
I do not, O loveliest of mankind, blame in the envious that they as one man envy me:
How could I blame them when you are the cause? They saw the new moon from the sky obey my hand![64]

A poem by Ibn al-Rūmī (d. *c.* 283/896):

11 She is in my embrace but my soul desires her still. Is there a closeness beyond embrace?
I kiss her mouth that my fever might end, but my mad thirst only grows.
The lovesickness in me is not of the kind healed by kisses.
Nothing, it seems, can cure my heart's thirst except to see our souls mingle.[65]

Two poems by Ibn al-Muʿtazz (d. 296/908):

12 O eyes that gave love into my heart's safekeeping! Your turning away branded me inwardly; I burn.
O tender sapling on a hill, that felt the breeze, bent and straightened!
Have mercy on an erring lover who relapsed after it was said of him that he had sobered up and seen the light of reason.
Tears have inscribed upon my cheek: "This man is the prisoner of love."
I have had no gift from him but this: my sleeve brushed his, then he turned away.

13 You are the one who made me submissive to others, and multiplied the sorrows of a dread-filled heart.
You made my eyes forth a their stream of tears and taught them glances of doubt and fear.

63 *Dīwān*, 325; Muslim b. al-Walīd is considered one of the pioneers of *badīʿ*, cf. p. 158 above.
64 *Dīwān*, IV, 188.
65 *Dīwān*, 27. On Ibn al-Rūmī's descriptive poetry, see pp. 164–5, above.

I did not use to give love and tears meekly, but from now on, O eyes, do what you will.
Bearing up bravely, I see, offers no intercession with one who is no beloved of tears – so intercede, O eyes.
Do you not see [the poet addresses himself] that star rising above you? It is good for lovers;
Perhaps my glance and his will meet at heaven's arc and it will bring us together, for nothing will on earth.[66]

A brief poem by Abū Firās (d. 357/968):

14 My daily lot from you is reproof – I will use it as my plea.
I have endured your cruelty. It is not that I am so tough: I had no choice but to wait on your free-will.[67]

An erotic passage from a poem by Abū Firās, the main topic of which is the recalling of the past glories of his kin:

15 . . . She who had long put it off paid me her debt, and my heart that had flown returned.
All night I drank the wine of her mouth – it leaves you drunk but not hung over –
Until the cloak of night grew too sheer and she said: "Get up, my bracelet has grown cold."
She walked away stealing glances at me, timorously as oryxes turn their heads . . .[68]

From *Alf laylah wa-laylah* (*The Thousand and One Nights*):

16 Afraid of spies and the wrath of the envious, she is by three things kept from visiting:
The light of her forehead, her jewels' whisper, and the amber scent in her clothes.
Suppose with a broad sleeve she hides her forehead; suppose she takes off her jewels. What can be done about the drops of sweat?[69]

[66] *Dīwān*, 26, 306. [67] *Dīwān*, II, 191. [68] Ibid., 173. [69] *Alf laylah wa-laylah*, I, 351.

CHAPTER 13

WINE POETRY (*KHAMRIYYĀT*)

Wine poetry is found in all periods of Arabic literature, though with fluctuating frequency, and variation between incidental references and pieces devoted wholly to wine; in some periods, the theme of wine dominated poetic production. Prose works devoted to wine are also found, but far less frequently; two typical examples may be cited. In North Africa, at the turn of the fourth–fifth/tenth–eleventh centuries, Abū Isḥāq Ibrāhīm b. al-Qāsim, known as al-Raqīq al-Nadīm, wrote *Quṭb al-surūr fī awṣāf al-khumūr* ("The Acme of Joy in Praise of Wine"), an encyclopaedic work discussing the etiquette of wine and wine-parties, wine's remedial qualities, how to profit from its blends, textual citations dealing with it, legal arguments centred on it, entertaining stories about it, and an appendix of poetical references. In the East, at the beginning of the ninth/fifteenth century, Muḥammad b. Ḥasan b. ʿUthmān al-Nawājī wrote *Ḥalbat al-Kumayt* ("The Bay's Racetrack"; a punning allusion to the fact that *kumayt*, "bay-coloured", is a conventional epithet for both horses and wine), which discusses the origins of wine, its names, appearance, advantages and properties according to learned writers, tales about persons accused of addiction to it, its qualities, both material and moral, the correct behaviour for a drinking-partner or boon-companion (*nadīm*), how to offer wine and issue an invitation to a wine-party, and description of the wine-party and all its appurtenances – drinking-vessels, singing, instrumental music, candles, flowers and gardens.

PRE-ISLAMIC WINE POETRY

The Arabs came to know wine at an early period, probably from their Mediterranean, Mesopotamian and Persian neighbours. Wine drinking was current among all classes in pre-Islamic Arabia, but it was the particular boast of chieftains (*sayyid*s), because wine was rare and costly. References to wine in pre-Islamic poetry are in accordance with the bedouin life-style and the position occupied by *sayyid*s, which required conspicuous displays of extravagance and hospitality. Thus Ṭarafah b. al-ʿAbd boasts:

Unceasingly I tippled the wine and took my joy, unceasingly sold and squandered my hoard and my patrimony,
Till all my family deserted me, every one of them, and I sat alone like a lonely camel, scabby with mange.[1]

Similarly, Labīd b. Rabīʿah brags to the woman who has rejected him:

Ah, but you do not know how many a night (mild of air and sweet in laughter and revelling)
I have passed chatting away the dark hours; how often a trader's sign has been my goal, when it is hoisted to proclaim costly wine –
I pay high prices for its purchase, all stored in ancient dark skin or jar, broached by breaking of its seal.[2]

ʿAlqamah b. ʿAbadah's description of wine includes a reference to the cupbearer:

Wine of ʿĀnah, strong enough to make you shiver, not seen for a year, hidden in a clay-stoppered vessel,
Always sparkling in the cup as it is poured by a Persian boy, mouth masked with linen.[3]

(The server wore a mask to prevent himself being overcome by the fumes of the wine.) Both the wine's age and concealment, in this and the preceding example, and the cupbearer, are themes often used in ʿAbbasid *khamriyyāt*. Similarly, in his *Muʿallaqah*, the pre-Islamic ʿAmr b. Kulthūm infringes the convention of beginning a *qaṣīdah* with the "amatory prelude" (*nasīb*) by devoting his exordium to wine, on which he confers the aura normally reserved for the deserted encampment of the beloved, a precedent followed by some ʿAbbasid poets, notably Abū Nuwās (though it has been argued that this bacchic prelude does not belong originally to ʿAmr's *Muʿallaqah*, but was an independent fragment grafted on to it simply because of the identity of rhyme and metre). Typically, though, pre-Islamic wine description focuses on the wine's material properties, those which impinge directly on the poet's outward senses. The wine's colour is usually red, as in the image coined by al-Aʿshā Maymūn b. Qays, "Wine have I often bought, red as the blood of the sacrifice", an image copied by Ḥassān b. Thābit.[4] Elsewhere, al-Aʿshā likens the colour of wine to saffron, rubies or the crimson dye of the dragon's-blood tree. Pre-Islamic poets were fond of comparing the fragrance of wine to musk, as with Ḥassān b. Thābit's "like musk which you mingle with the pure rain of heaven", an image often used by al-Aʿshā too, while Ṭarafah notices the same scent on the breath of his drinking-partners.

[1] Trans. Arberry, *The Seven Odes*, 86. [2] Trans. Beeston, "An experiment", 5.
[3] *Dīwān*, 69–70. This and following translations by A. F. L. Beeston unless otherwise indicated.
[4] Al-Aʿshā, *Dīwān*, no. 3; Ḥassān b. Thābit, *Dīwān*, I, 29.

Incidental and not very detailed references to wine-parties are also common in pre-Islamic poetry, as in ᶜAlqamah's line, "I often attend a drinking, where the guitar is strummed and the company is laid prostrate by strong ruddy wine", and Ḥassān b. Thābit's fleeting allusion to a gathering filled with topers, which he prefers to wealth and flocks.[5] More elaborate descriptions may be devoted to the wine-jug, as in ᶜAlqamah's lines: "Their wine-jug, slender-necked as a gazelle on a hill-top, with linen strainer veiling its mouth – / Shining silver when brought out to the light by its keeper, garlanded with sprigs of myrtle wafting their odour."[6] A similar description is found in ᶜAntarah b. Shaddād: "And often I have drunk good wine, after noon's sweltering calm, from a bright figured bowl / In a glittering golden glass scored with lines, partnered to a lustrous filtered flask on its left."[7]

Such images, though purely sensuous, are vivid and pulsating with life. Descriptions of the *nadīm* are similarly couched in terms of the external senses. A favourite description of him is as pale-complexioned, probably alluding to his being upper-class: "My boon-companions are white as stars, and a singing-wench comes to us in striped gown or saffron robe," says Ṭarafah;[8] in al-Aᶜshā, a similar description is developed by the addition of non-physical qualities:

Among youths as brilliant as candles in the dark, radiant with well-being and joyfulness,
Good tempers reigning in their assembly, no matter how some cur of a man may yelp.[9]

The effects of wine are a frequent motif, and again they are usually depicted purely in physical terms: "It makes a weakness creep through the limbs; the hair of one's temples covers its throbbing heat"; "You see the drinkers lying prone with drunkenness, like spread out monkey-skin rugs, / Some quite overcome with cheek in the dust, some (though no cripples) with no use of their legs."[10] Sometimes, however, wine's after-effects are stated in paradoxical terms: "One cup I drank for pleasure's sake, the second I took to cure the first"; "It cures the headache, and the strongest sort does you no harm; no swimming in the head goes with it";[11] "We drink it, and it leaves us kings, and lions undismayed by the conflict."[12] Less frequent are references to the censure incurred by drunkenness, though Ṭarafah's kinsfolk shunned him like a mangy camel for squandering his inheritance on drink.

Al-Aᶜshā Maymūn, unquestionably the greatest wine-poet of the

[5] *Dīwān*, I, 316. [6] *Dīwān*, 70–1. [7] Trans. Arberry, *The Seven Odes*, 181. [8] Ibid., 85.
[9] *Dīwān*, no. 36. [10] Ibid., nos. 64, 36. [11] Ibid., no. 22; ᶜAlqamah, *Dīwān*, 69.
[12] Ḥassān b. Thābit, *Dīwān*, I, 17.

Jāhiliyyah, is virtually the only major pre-Islamic poet to devote whole poems exclusively to wine (though it seems that the poets of al-Ḥīrah were already beginning to develop the wine-song as an independent genre).[13] He also sowed the seeds of narrative wine poetry, an example being a piece couched in a pleasant story-telling style, combining narrative with conversation like a stage dialogue, in which the poet and his companion start on a drinking-bout before cock-crow and bargain with the wine-seller over the price of the wine. There follows a description of the wine and the serving-boy; finally, the poet sells his white she-camel and some of his flock to buy wine, which the wine-merchant pours for them, and its intoxication steals through their limbs.[14] Al-Aᶜshā, again by contrast with other pre-Islamic poets, devotes long incidental passages to descriptions of wine-parties and the beauties of the gardens in which they are held:

We are witnessed by the rose, the jasmine, the singers with their accompanying flutists –
Our flute is constantly in use – and for which of these can I be blamed?[15]

EARLY ISLAMIC WINE POETRY

Islam thus found wine-drinking deeply rooted in the habits of the Jāhiliyyah, and proceeded towards its prohibition only by gradual steps. The first revelation on the subject was given in Qurʾān, *sūrah* xvi.67: "From the fruits of the date-palm and the vine you get intoxication (*sakar*) and goodly nourishment"; but there is a divergence of views on the meaning of *sakar*. Wine was then described, in *sūrah* ii.219, as "involving great sin", and *sūrah* iv.43 forbids Muslims to pray while intoxicated. At last wine was explicitly prohibited in *sūrah* v.90–1: "You who believe: wine and gambling and idols and divination by arrows are a defilement of the Devil, so avoid it." Yet, despite the plain prohibition in Qurʾān and *sunnah*, there was acute controversy among exegetes and legists, apparently arising from disagreement about what is meant by "wine" – whether it is only wine made from grapes or whether it also includes date and raisin wine, etc.[16] Abū Ḥanifah (d. 150/767) interpreted the prohibited wine as meaning only that made from grape juice and regarded *nabīdh* (made by boiling dates or raisins) as permitted, provided the quantity drunk was not enough to cause intoxication, in which he was probably following ᶜAbdullāh b. Masᶜūd al-Hudhalī, leader of the Iraqi school of law, whose views were widely adopted in Kufah; a Kufan poet says:

[13] See pp. 282, 291. [14] *Dīwān*, no. 8. [15] Ibid., no. 22.
[16] Cf. p. 86 for examples of the prose literature on the subject.

Over there, they forbid pure water mingled with juice of grape-clusters in the belly of a jar,
But I hate the severity of such expositors, and favour the saying of Ibn Masᶜūd.[17]

The legal controversy over wine provides frequent matter for *jeux d'esprit* in ᶜAbbasid poetry, as in Ibn al-Rūmī's lines:

The Iraqi holds *nabīdh* to be permitted, and the drinking of it, but says that grape-wine and intoxication are both forbidden;
The Hijazi says both drinks are alike. The two dicta together license wine –
I'll take one half from each and drink wine – let the burden of guilt rest on him who imposes it.[18]

Early Islamic poetry and the anecdotes surrounding it show a picture of poets openly disregarding the Islamic prohibition of wine, despite repeated floggings. Abū Miḥjan al-Thaqafī, also famous as a warrior–poet, was flogged several times and banished by the caliph ᶜUmar for drinking wine:

When I die, bury me beneath a vine, that its roots may give drink to my bones
(Do not bury me in the desert, for I fear lest I never taste wine after death),
That my flesh may be refreshed by saffron wine, and I'll be its captive who once used to lead it captive.[19]

Even more blatantly, al-Ḥārithah b. Badr al-Ghudānī (d. 64/684) declares:

I'll drink it openly, alone or with anyone who'll bear me company, so long as any pilgrims ride to Mecca

and:

If you are my drinking partner, take wine and give me some; pay no heed to him who sees you quaffing deep.
I'm no man to drink under the cover of darkness; I sip my *nabīdh*
In all submission to God – He knows what we are about whether in secret or openly.[20]

It was during this period that the free-standing wine-poem, the *khamriyyah*, emerged into the mainstream of Arabic poetry; but the themes associated with wine-drinking follow the same lines as in pre-Islam, as in the following descriptions of flamboyant excess and of drinking-companions: "I'll drink it, ruddy in colour and musk-scented, drink it in every company and every place"; "In distress and evil times I've shared my cup with companions whose faces are as bright as gold coins"; "I aid my companions while I satisfy my own desire, and I'm freely spendthrift of all that I own"

17 Ibn ᶜAbd Rabbih, *ᶜIqd*, VI, 368. 18 Al-Rāghib al-Iṣfahānī, *Muḥāḍarāt al-udabāʾ*, I, 670.
19 Abū ʾl-Faraj al-Iṣfahānī, *Aghānī*, XXI, 210. 20 Ibid., XXI, 32, 33.

(al-Ḥārithah b. Badr);[21] "We drink wine until it makes us reel, like one sleeper's head tumbling against another's" (Ibn Arṭaʾah).[22]

UMAYYAD WINE POETRY

Umayyad society achieved a higher peak than ever before of luxury, and with the general relaxation of mores came a tolerance of wine-drinking and wine-songs which was aided by the attitude of the Umayyad caliphs towards drinking; they are said to have set aside days for drinking, and to have sat with a curtain between themselves and their drinking-companions, so that the latter could not see how they behaved; al-Jāḥiẓ tells us that some Umayyad caliphs were not ashamed to dance or to appear undressed before their boon-companions and singers. Umayyad descriptions of wine conform to the earlier models of concrete imagery. Al-Akhṭal (d. 92/710) uses a simile comparable to al-Aᶜshā's likening of wine to the sun: "They poured out wine looking to the eye of the beholder like a firebrand being consumed";[23] the Umayyad prince al-Walīd b. Yazīd, in the view of some the most influential writer of *khamriyyāt* before Abū Nuwās, uses a similar image: "The wine in its glass seems a firebrand, blazing as a light in the eye of the watcher."[24] Al-Akhṭal, like earlier poets, compares the scent of wine to musk: "As though musk were a booty brought to our homes, by reason of the scent wafting from the new-broached wine as it flows out";[25] again, al-Walīd b. Yazīd employs the traditional term of comparison: "Surely it's musk in the goblet, or in the hand of my cupbearer."[26]

The effects of wine are also described in terms that develop earlier imagery: "It creeps through the frame like ants crawling through drifted sand" (al-Akhṭal);[27] "The heady wine in the goblet creeps up from my feet to my tongue" (al-Walīd b. Yazīd).[28] But a thematic innovation, to be encountered again in ᶜAbbasid times, is al-Akhṭal's metaphor of wine as a virgin freshly revealed to men's sight: "A virgin whose beauty was never revealed to suitors, until my servants revealed her – at the price of a gold coin".[29] Moreover, the bravado and defiance of wine-drinking are accentuated:

Among men of Umayyah's stock, folk of glory, mighty exploits and high renown:
In all mankind there's none like them, and none like me among them, and none can claim an ancestry like mine,[30]

21 Ibid. 22 Ibid., II, 86. 23 *Shiᶜr al-Akhṭal*, I, 19. 24 *Dīwān*, 35.
25 *Shiᶜr al-Akhṭal*, I, 71. 26 *Dīwān*, 35. 27 *Shiᶜr al-Akhṭal*, I, 19. 28 *Dīwān*, 57.
29 *Shiᶜr al-Akhṭal* I, 170. 30 Al-Walīd b. Yazīd, *Dīwān*, 25.

boasts al-Walīd b. Yazīd, himself "of Umayyah's stock", while Ibn Harmah al-Qurashī (d. *c.* 176/792) develops the idea further by envisaging a code of conduct for drinkers which carries echoes of a more respectable code of honour:

My fellow-drinker surely has honour in my eyes, and shall have from me whatever boon he desires;
When he leaves something in the goblet, I'll not say to him "Drink up", if he declines,
But I give him "Good health" and respect him; I'll drink what he leaves, and make him drink only as much as he wishes.[31]

The blatant flouting of religious teaching is also accentuated, and this not only in the case of a Christian like al-Akhṭal ("We drank, and died like pagans who never knew what Muḥammad is"),[32] but also in that of a prince and later caliph, al-Walīd b. Yazīd, notorious for his disgraceful behaviour, who is reputed to have travelled from Damascus to Ḥīrah merely because he had heard tell of a superlatively excellent vintner there. The following lines typify his attitude:

I call to witness God and the pure angels and all pious folk
That I yearn for music, and quaffing the goblet, and planting kisses on beauteous cheeks,
And a noble drinking partner, and a Persian servant to bring me the wine bowls.[33]

Al-Uqayshir al-Asadī (d. 80/700) projects his own cynicism into this caricature of his drinking-companion:

I told him to stand up and pray, but he prayed sitting, overcome by the fever of intoxication;
He tied the noon-prayer to the afternoon one, as a young she-camel is tied to her brother-foal;
He omitted the dawn-prayer, and did not recite it, but included the *sūrah* "Kawthar" in his recitation.[34]

(Qurʾān, *sūrah* cviii, gets its title from its first verse, "We have given thee abundance (*al-kawthar*)"; in popular tradition, the word was supposed to be the name of one of the rivers of Paradise, which would particularly recommend the verse to a drinker.) The conflict between religion and pleasure appears in verses written by Ibn Harmah when the amir of Medina had threatened to have him flogged for drunkenness, but is stated, this time, in terms of paradox:

31 *Shiʿr Ibn Harmah*, 63. 32 *Shiʿr al-Akhṭal*, II, 732. 33 *Dīwān*, 38.
34 Abū ʾl-Faraj al-Iṣfahānī, *Aghānī*, x, 93.

The Prophet's descendant forbids me wine, and gives me noble teaching;
He says, "Abstain from it and leave it alone, for fear of God, not for fear of man."
Yet how can I abstain from it, when my love for it is a love which has gained control over my frame?
For me, the comfort of what is lawful is an evil, and my soul's comfort lies in the evil of what is forbidden.[35]

Paradox and playfulness are found, again, in Abū ᵓl-Hindī (Ghālib b. ᶜAbd al-Quddūs), perhaps the foremost of the Umayyad wine-poets (though he died in ᶜAbbasid times), who gives a new twist to Abū Miḥjan al-Thaqafī's prayer:

When I come to die, make vine-leaves my winding-sheet, with the wine-press as my grave;
I hope in future to have from God the boon of pardon, after all the wine I've drunk.

The same casuistry is apparent in lines also attributed to Abū ᵓl-Hindī:

If I pray five times a day, God will pardon my offences;
My faith is pure; I am sure of salvation.[36]

Abū ᵓl-Hindī also continued the narrative mode of wine poetry, initiated by al-Aᶜshā, in a poem beginning, "Drinking-companions met together after three days, lured by wine to Mount Zayān", in which he describes how he got drunk at Zayān in Sīstān; he introduces a conversation between a group of topers and the vintner; the topers see Abū ᵓl-Hindī drunk, ask who he is, and are told by the vintner that he is a toper. They beg to drink in order to get as drunk as he is; Abū ᵓl-Hindī sobers up, puts the same question to the vintner, is told they are topers, and begs to get as drunk as them, with the result that the drinking goes on for three days.[37] With Abū ᵓl-Hindī, wine poetry, which beside features hardly differing from those of earlier times had shown some developments in concepts and phraseology and in the adoption of elegant, tripping metres, also extended its geographical horizons beyond the Arab lands, for Abū ᵓl-Hindī migrated to Khurāsān, and there devoted his poetic productivity to wine. He gives a faithful representation of the life-style of a class of Islamic society given over to luxury and pleasure; and thereafter there was to be a merging of Arab and non-Arab taste in bacchic imagery.

[35] Al-Raqīq al-Nadīm, *Quṭb al-surūr*, 120.
[36] Abū ᵓl-Faraj al-Iṣfahānī, *Aghānī*, XXI, 279, 280.
[37] Ibid., 278.

ᶜABBASID WINE POETRY

The change of dynasty brought far-reaching changes to life and society, and the spirit of the new age was reflected in wine poetry. We find both occasional pieces and longer poems devoted to wine, and the names of some ᶜAbbasid poets are indissolubly associated with the theme, above all that of Abū Nuwās (al-Ḥasan b. Hāniᵓ al-Ḥakamī, d. 200/815). Some cultural developments which had already begun to make themselves felt in the Umayyad age now became a characteristic mark of the period. Palaces were adorned in the Persian style, filled with flowers, gardens and fountains, forming a suitable setting for parties of wine and pleasure; the vocabulary of wine poetry extended in consequence of this development in refinement, luxury and dissipation. At the same time, a diversity of theological and philosophical schools were disseminating their teaching, and translations from Greek and Persian were being circulated; these found an echo in poetic allusions and gave further development to the paradoxical and witty side of the *khamriyyah* genre. "In the way that I exalt [wine] I am like a Qaᶜadī exalting the *taḥkīm*," writes Abū Nuwās: the *taḥkīm* (*lā ḥukma illā li ᵓllāh*, "judgement belongs to God alone") was the battle-slogan of the Khārijīs,[38] while a Qaᶜadī (stay-at-home) was one who, though sympathizing with the cause, was debarred by age or physical incapacity from taking part in the fighting; in another allusion to Kharijism, Muslim b. al-Walīd speaks of "Wine well-matured, with no complaint of the feet that trod the grapes, a Ḥarūrī in whose belly the blood boils":[39] Ḥarūrī, derived from the name of the Syrian town Ḥarūrah, was an alternative name for Khārijī. Abū Nuwās begins a poem, "Cease blaming me, for blame is merely an incitement; give me as remedy that which was itself the malady",[40] and draws in a number of philosophical ideas and images in connection with wine, as well as principles of law. Not only ethical or religious but also Shuᶜūbī subversiveness – antagonism to the Arab exclusiveness that had characterized the Umayyad regime – served the turn of ᶜAbbasid wine-poets. Abū Nuwās uses the themes of wine to mock Arab classicism; he debunks the "romantic preface" (*nasīb*) of the conventional *qaṣīdah*, with its theme of the deserted encampment (". . . a stupid kind of eloquence: devote your descriptions to the daughter of the vine"), and, in casting scorn on the evocative use of the bedouin women's names, Laylā and Hind (he proposes instead dedications to "matured ruddy wine"), disparages the haughty Arab tribes of Tamīm and Qays. Throughout his *khamriyyāt*, he loses no

[38] *Dīwān*, 29; on the Khārijīs, see pp. 186ff, above. [39] *Sharḥ Dīwān*, 37. [40] See p. 293.

chance of decrying the Arabs and extolling the Persians, as in a piece he composed on a visit to Sabaṭ, a Persian village near Ctesiphon:

Wine is passed round among us in a silver jug, adorned by a Persian craftsman
with a variety of designs,
Chosroes on its base, and round its side oryxes which horsemen hunt with
bows.
Wine's place is where tunics are buttoned; water's place is where the Persian
cap (*qalansuwah*) is worn,[41]

a passage showing the evolution of poetic taste and the blending of cultures, symbolically expressed by the mingling of wine and water in the cup, and the way in which water is poured on top of wine. One modern critic suggests that this prevalence of Persian imagery and vocabulary corresponds to the prevalence of the Persian language in everyday ᶜAbbasid life and among the dissolute Zoroastrian youths with whom the poet associated (Zoroastrians, like Jews and Christians, were allowed to make wine, and Christian monasteries, which turned remote spots into oases of fruit trees and vines, were favourite resorts for pleasure parties, and their names are frequently encountered in poetry). Abū Nuwās's Shuᶜūbī tendencies have given rise to varied comment by modern writers. Ṭāhā Ḥusayn believes that "his attitude towards wine is not simply a poetic one, but both poetic and political; he blames the older style not because it is old but because it is also Arab, and praises the newer one not because it is new but because it is also Persian". By contrast, Shawqī Ḍayf claims that the attack on the *nasīb* is only a somewhat overdone joke, since Abū Nuwās himself often uses the motif without mockery. ᶜAbbās Maḥmūd al-ᶜAqqād gives a psychological explanation based on the poet's narcissistic personality which "attracts him towards unconventional habits, in an age of contending claims to prestige of birth, so that he can find solace in drinking-parties where there was no boast of ancestry, among people for whom he felt an affinity, people who made no boast of ancestry". This explanation is not dissimilar to one which has been advanced to explain the development of modern (*muḥdath*) poetry generally.[42]

ᶜAbbasid writers re-used earlier techniques of describing wine's colour, scent, etc., in material terms; but they also developed a wide range of new imagery. The following examples will give some idea of the interaction of old and new. Abū Nuwās describes wine as "Golden-yellow before mixing, pale thereafter, as though haloed in the rays of the sun", Ibn al-Muᶜtazz (d. 296/908) as "Ruddy before mixing, golden-yellow thereafter, coming

[41] *Dīwān*, 37; see Ritter, "Trinkschale".
[42] Ḥusayn, *Ḥadīth al-arbiᶜāʾ*, II, 113–14; Ḍayf, *al-ᶜAṣr al-ᶜabbāsī*, 231; ᶜAqqād, *Abū Nuwās*, 137–53.

dressed in the garb of both narcissus and poppy";[43] for Abū Nuwās it is also like a flame or pure gold. Its scent reminds poets of musk, apples or attar: "Perfume of aloes would be made more redolent by its scent; noontide is filled by its allure" (Abū ᵓl-Shīṣ b. Razīn al-Khuzāᶜī, d. *c.* 200/815).[44] Though references to the age of the wine, as indicating its excellence, are traditional, Abū Nuwās works them up into striking new hyperboles: "wine that recalls the days of Noah, when he built the ark"; and sometimes depicts it as "old as time" or "having seen all nations' history"; "It was stored up for Adam before his creation, and preceded him by one step in antiquity."[45] Wine is a virgin, and the drinker courts it as his bride: this is so frequent in Abū Nuwās that one modern critic describes his love of wine as sexual, since he calls it virgin, unravished, maid, while the water poured into it "looses its girdle" and so forth. Yet the metaphor of virginity is also found in earlier poets such as al-Akhṭal, and in contemporaries of Abū Nuwās such as Muslim b. al-Walīd:

We sent one of our number as spokesman to seek her espousal, and he brought her back, coming with slow and stately step;
He charmed her master until he won her, but paid a high price for his treasured lady, heedless of kith and kin;
And he bestowed her, still virgin, on some generous fellow, lavish with his gifts, of no mean or worthless quality.[46]

Abū ᵓl-Shīṣ also wrote a poem describing wine as a virgin who fears men yet hastens to them when the goblet reveals her. Can all these poets have had a "sexual" love of wine? The fact is, the description of wine as a virgin is a poetic commonplace, especially among the contemporaries of Abū Nuwās.

ᶜAbbasid developments in the description of the accompaniments of wine are especially noticeable in the description of the cupbearer (*sāqī*). The cupbearer of Abū Nuwās, among other characteristics, is beautiful, with curling forelocks; Muslim b. al-Walīd changes the note, and makes his cupbearer a slender girl like an antelope. The cupbearer may be as much a focus of the drinkers' attention as the wine:

In an assembly where the goblets circulated, and the company were reeling or stretched flat,
While the wine was handed round to them by a fawn-like figure, well-approved by heart and eye;
The gazing eyes, when he appears, are likely to make a modest blush suffuse his cheek.[47]

A major innovation in ᶜAbbasid wine-drinking was its association with pederasty, due to the fact that the monasteries and wine-shops usually

[43] Al-Raqīq al-Nadīm, *Quṭb al-surūr*, 651. [44] Ibn al-Muᶜtazz, *Ṭabaqāt*, 85. [45] *Dīwān*, 42.
[46] *Dīwān*, 31–2. [47] Ibn al-Muᶜtazz quoted al-Raqīq al-Nadīm, *Quṭb al-surūr*, 670.

employed a boy to serve the wine; the customers did not hesitate to abuse either him or the underservants sexually, as Abū Nuwās explicitly declares:

Give me wine to drink in public; clasp me tight and play the whore with me.[48]

The poem beginning, "Come on, give me wine, and say 'It's wine'; don't do it secretly when openness is possible", contains a conversation with the proprietress of a tavern, and ends with her bringing the drinkers a boy to bugger.[49] The drinker's attitude to his fellow-drinkers is less casual, and Abū Nuwās, like Ibn Harmah, describes it in detail:

I do not say to my true friend, when his eye shows sign of his being overcome with drink,
"Take it, or I'll not taste a drop", so that he goes on when it is too much for him;
Instead, I pass the goblet away from him, when he asks with a lift of the eyebrow to be excused;
When he disposes his pillow to sleep off his cups, I pass him my pillow as well:
That is my way of saying "Good health" to him, and thereby am I kindlier to him than his parents.[50]

Rules for a wine-party are listed by the early third/ninth-century poet, Muḥammad b. ᶜAbd al-Raḥmān al-ᶜAṭawī, in a poem beginning, "The laws of the goblet and the drinking-partner are five: the first is to be graced by dignity of bearing", the remaining four being mutual forbearance, avoidance of boasting, not talking too much, and forgetting what others have said in their cups.[51]

ᶜAbbasid poets expatiate at greater length than earlier poets on the open drinking of wine and disregard of religion; Abū Nuwās begs his companion, "Sing to me, Sulayman, and give me wine to drink; serve me a goblet to distract me from the muezzin's call", while his companion demands more to drink and carries on through the time of prayer. Muslim b. al-Walīd prefers as a drinking-partner someone who cannot distinguish between the noon-prayer time and the afternoon one when in his cups; Abū Nuwās is much distressed by Ramaḍān, and if only he could find a drinking-partner during that month he would break the fast and enjoy forbidden pleasures; he argues that the Quranic prohibition of wine cannot restrain him because it is permitted in the Torah and Gospel. Similarly, the magical effects of drinking are amplified; for Muslim b. al-Walīd, "It diverts a man's spirit from that which grieves him, and makes miserly tongues give expression to kindliness";[52] for Abū Nuwās, it drives away care, puts an end to sorrow and brings joyfulness; and an innovatory note is struck by his

[48] *Dīwān*, 33. [49] Ibid., 28. [50] Al-Rāghib al-Iṣfahānī, *Muḥāḍarāt al-udabāʾ*, II, 695.
[51] Al-Raqīq al-Nadīm, *Quṭb al-surūr*, 299–300. [52] *Dīwān*, 36.

declarations, "Drink at dawn; it will bring youth back to the old man, and you will see him both lively and happy", and:

> Wine is called *mudām* ["perpetual"], so drink it perpetually;
> Take goblet after goblet: it will turn the old man into a boy.[53]

If the pun on *mudām* in the line just quoted is typically "modern", so too is his description of wine's physical effects in the line, "It flows through their limbs like healing through a sick body", which owes its originality to the combination of a material description with an abstract simile.[54]

The narrative wine-poem had been developed earlier by Abū ʾl-Hindī, but it was Abū Nuwās who brought it to full fruition, and there are many examples in his *Dīwān*. An instance is the piece beginning: "At night I have often made my camels, exhausted by travel, kneel at a wine-seller's door." He wakes the wine-seller from sleep, and the latter can hardly believe his eyes, saying: "Tell me how you came to my secluded home." The plot thickens: the poet answers by asking for entertainment because he had been guided there by the dawn light shining from his tent; the other grasps the situation and says that there is no dawn and no light except the light of wine. He goes to the jars and covers them up, and immediately it is as dark as ever. Denouement: he pours out a goblet of wine for the visitor.[55] Here we have a dramatic dialogue such as Abū Nuwās was much enamoured of, in which he displays his skill at sketching, with a few words, a situation in its entirety. Dramatic irony is an obvious component in the conversations which he was so good at representing.

DEVELOPMENTS OF THE *KHAMRIYYAH*

Abū Nuwās's was the decisive influence on the subsequent development of the genre. Thus when wine poetry was carried over into Muslim Spain, the ideas of Abū Nuwās came as well. The Andalusians were fervent followers of material pleasures, and great wine-drinkers; their poetry on the subject was traditional in content, but innovatory in manner, and one outstanding innovation consisted in the poetic forms they developed side by side with the traditional types of composition brought from the East. These poetic forms (which were used for other genres besides the *khamriyyah*) were the *muwashshaḥ*, a multi-rhymed, strophic verse-form written in classical Arabic with the final line (*kharjah*), usually in colloquial Arabic or another vernacular, being in direct speech and acting as a punch-line, and the *zajal*,

[53] Al-Raqīq al-Nadīm, *Quṭb al-surūr*, 559; al-Rāghib al-Iṣfahānī, *Muḥāḍarāt al-udabāʾ*, II, 704.
[54] Abū Nuwās, *Dīwān*, 41. [55] *Dīwān*, 77. For another example, see p. 292, below.

the colloquial Arabic counterpart of the *muwashshaḥ*. Both *zajal* and *muwashshaḥ* were especially adapted to singing, and singing was a normal accompaniment of drinking-parties. As an example we may quote part of a *muwashshaḥ* by Ibn Zuhr (Muḥammad b. ʿAbd al-Malik, d. 595/1198):

ayyuhā ʾl-sāqī ilayka ʾl-mushtakā *qad daʿawnaka wa-in lam tasmaʿi*
wa-nadīmin himtu fī ghurratih
wa-sharibtu ʾl-rāḥa min rāḥatih
kullamā ʾstayqaẓa min sakratih
jadhaba ʾl-ziqqa ilayhi wa ʾttakā *wa-saqānī arbaʿan fī arbaʿi*[56]

Cupbearer, to you we make our complaint: we have called you though you did not respond.
I've a companion whom I love for his excellence;
I've shared wine with him,
And as soon as he sobers
He draws the wine-skin to him, sits up again, and makes me drink "four times four".

In Mamlūk Egypt and Syria too, stanzaic verse-forms were applied to the *khamriyyah*. Since the age was one highly favourable to the *badīʿ* style, descriptions of wine are replete with tournures involving *double entendre* and allusive references; the poets introduced rules embodying that studied artificiality in which the taste of the age delighted, while at the same time adhering to the conventions of describing wine as sun, virgin, bride, etc. An innovation characteristic of the period was the use in wine poetry of *taḍmīn*, a device in which lines are constructed around quotations, as in this example, taken from the Egyptian poet Ibn Nubātah (Abū Bakr Jamāl al-Dīn Ibn Nubātah, 686–768/1287–1366), which incorporates Quranic phrases (italicized in the translation):

ḥammālatu ʾl-ḥalyī wa ʾl-dībāji qāmatuhu *tabbat ghuṣūnu ʾl-rubā ḥammālatu ʾl-ḥaṭabi*
in kāna jismī Abā Dharrin bihī saqiman *fa-inna qalbī bi-khaddayhi Abū Lahabi*

Bearer of jewelry and satin is his tall frame, beside which each wooded hill, *bearer of brushwood*, *is as nothing* (*tabbat*);
While love-sickness for him, O Abū Dharr, has wasted my body, my heart is made by his cheeks a "*Father of Flame*".

(Cf. Qurʾān, *sūrah* cxi: "*Perish* (*tabbat*) the hands of *Abū Lahab* ["father of flame"] and *perish* he . . . he shall roast in a *flaming* fire, he and his wife, the *bearer of brushwood* . . .")[57]

Beside such internal developments as these must be set the use by the Sufi mystics of the wine-poem as a medium for propagating their spiritual

[56] Ibn Saʿīd, *Mughrib*, I, 272. [57] Nawājī, *Halbat al-kumayt*, 107.

beliefs. While their physical descriptions of wine conform to traditional models, wholly different meanings are implied, centred on the love of and union with God. It has been suggested by L. Massignon and P. Kraus that Sufi poets first began to employ bacchic imagery in the third/ninth century, on the basis of verses attributed to the Sufi martyr, Manṣūr b. Ḥusayn al-Ḥallāj:

> My friend is not chargeable with any injustice;
> He invited me, and welcomed me as a host does a guest;
> But when the cup circulated, he called for the sword and block:
> So it is with one who drinks wine with the dragon in summer.[58]

However, the lines are also attributed to Abū Nuwās and to his slightly later contemporary al-Ḥusayn b. al-Khalīᶜ, with some variations; it may be that al-Ḥallāj, on his way to his execution, simply quoted them as appropriate to his own situation. In the early fourth/tenth century, however, Shuᶜayb b. al-Ḥasan al-Andalusī, known as Abū Madyan al-Tilimsānī, wrote several long poems which refer to wine in mystical terms, for example:

> Hand it to us pure; let's have no mixing; we are those who have known nothing of mixing since we came into being;
> It is true wine that does not know any vine of its own, was never revealed by mortal hand and does not know the jar.[59]

The most famous of all Sufi wine-songs is that by ᶜUmar b. ᶜAlī Ibn al-Fāriḍ (576–632/1181–1235), throughout which wine terminology is used with reference to the technicalities of Muslim mysticism, and which begins, *sharibnā ᶜalā dhikri ʾl-ḥabībi mudāmatan*:

> We have drunk, in contemplation of the Friend, a draught by which we were intoxicated before the creation of the vine;
> To that wine the full moon is a cup, the wine is a sun handed round by a crescent; a multitude appears, when it is mixed, of stars.

A fuller English version of the poem appears on pp. 255–6. The whole poem should be read with an elaborate code in mind: the "Friend" is God, the "wine" His spirit irradiating mankind, the "vine" is the material creation, the "full moon" the spirit of the Prophet Muḥammad, the "crescent" a semicircle of mystics, the "stars" flashes of illumination experienced by the ecstatic mystic when infused ("mixed") with the divine, and so forth. Yet Sufi wine poetry does not merely take over the traditional imagery of the *khamriyyah* and imprint it with a mystical meaning; as has been remarked, the use in Sufi poetry of wine as a symbol of ecstasy goes

58 *Akhbār al-Ḥallāj*, no. 16. 59 Naṣr, *Ramz*, 359.

back to the tradition of earlier Christian and non-Christian mystics, who also spoke of ecstasy in terms of intoxication, rather than to the tradition of Abū Nuwās, whose imagery had hinted at the miraculous properties of wine and, with mock portentousness, at ancient mysteries surrounding it. Hence such passages as line 34 of Ibn al-Fāriḍ's poem: "I salute the folk of the Christian convents, who have often got drunk on it, though they never imbibed it, but only hoped to do so", which the commentator al-Nābulusī explains in these terms: "The monks were mystics who inherited a Christian spirituality; they cherished this metaphorical wine in their hearts, whereby they came to the brink of the purely spiritual world, and it drove them in the direction of the light of Muḥammad, though they did not actually reach it."[60]

[60] Ibid., 373; Nicholson, *Studies*, 184–8.

CHAPTER 14

MYSTICAL POETRY

GENERAL NOTIONS

The word *ṣūfī* – usually derived from *ṣūf* (wool), supposedly in reference to the coarse woollen garments of the early Muslim mystics – does not appear to have been yet in use at the outset of the ʿAbbasid period, but for the sake of uniformity it will be used here throughout – if need be retrospectively – in the sense of "Muslim mystic". The mystic has by definition one interest only; Sufi poetry is thus centred, explicitly or implicitly, on the eternal and infinite source from which the soul of the poet originated and to which it seeks to return. There is no difficulty in understanding this; but, before we go on to a separate consideration of individual authors, it is imperative to comment on two general points which are often misunderstood. One of these is the state of spiritual expectancy, poised between longing and patience, a state epitomized in the following distich attributed by Sufis to the Baghdadi mystic Abū Bakr al-Shiblī, (d. 334/945), though in fact al-Shiblī is probably quoting from the second /eighth-century poet Bashshār b. Burd, or possibly from ʿAbd al-Ṣamad al-Raqāshī (d. *c.* 200/815–16) to whom the lines, with some variants, are also attributed:[1]

> One day a cloud from Thee o'ershadowed us,
> dazzled us with its lightning, but held back its rain;
> And its darkness cleareth not away, for the eager to despair,
> nor cometh the downpour for the thirsty to drink.[2]

The same characteristic state is described in the first two lines of a poem by Abū ʾl-ʿAbbās Aḥmad Ibn ʿAṭāʾ (d. 309/922):

> Truly I tell Thee, in excess hast Thou burdened me,
> With longing for Thee and with patience – it is wondrous strange!
> Thou hast joined two things in my heart to its peril,
> Two kinds, two opposites, one a chilling, one a burning.[3]

1 Sarrāj, *Lumaʿ*, 251, 403; Shiblī, *Dīwān*, 143.

2 "For the eager to despair": throughout the Qurʾān, the rain-cloud stands for the promise of divine bounty (panegyric poetry (*madīḥ*) uses the same image for the patron's munificence). In metre, the above and subsequent translations attempt to follow very roughly the rhythm of the Arabic, when they do not conform to the rhythms of English verse.

3 Sarrāj, *Lumaʿ*, 254. For Ibn ʿAṭāʾ, a friend of al-Ḥallāj, see Kalābādhī, *Taʿarruf*, trans. Arberry, *The Doctrine of the Ṣūfīs*.

It would be a grave mistake – and this is the point which calls for clarification – to suppose that these and other such plaints could have been uttered only at an intermediary stage upon the spiritual path. Mystical systems are in agreement that for one who reaches the end of the path itself in this life, the divine presence, which constitutes that end, is a framework that admits of temporary "absences" of the Beloved, although these are relative and illusory. The consciousness of the saint is by definition a duality of soul and spirit, inasmuch as he may be said to have two natures, human and divine, each opening as it were on to the other. The lower nature is not effaced by the higher except in union, wherein the temporal condition is effaced by eternity. But when the soul resumes its earthly life it has a sense of separation, while remaining none the less aware of the supreme presence which it has not left and cannot leave. A Sufi of recent times, but altogether in line with tradition, speaks of the divinity "taking one of His slaves to Himself and bringing him into His presence where sometimes He reveals Himself to him and sometimes withdraws from him".[4] Shiblī makes a parallel observation, this time in lines of his own, where having mentioned one of these "withdrawals" he adds:

Yet absent He is not, that I might take
To memory for my consolement's sake,
Nor turned away, that I might absent be.[5]

The reactions to these "separations" within the framework of union cover a wide range, as expressed in Sufi poetry, from serene acceptance to unrestrained lamentation, and it is evident that the trial is experienced in an endless variety of degrees, both as regards duration and intensity, from one mystic to another. The question is made more complex by the fact that some mystics, on principle, are not prepared to write about separations since they are illusory: the supreme identity, being eternal, cannot in truth be lost once it has been realized; the following anonymous line is continually quoted in affirmation of this:

Since they reached their destination they have not returned;
And since they prostrated themselves they have not risen.

There is thus a permanent and, as it were, absolute difference between the fully realized mystic, whatever his momentary state, and all other men. The poems, for example, of ʿAbd al-Qādir al-Jīlānī (d. 561/1166)[6], in so far as

[4] Aḥmad b. Muṣṭafā Ibn ʿAlawī (Ibn ʿAlīwah, d. 1943), *Minaḥ*, 20; see also Massignon, *Essai* [314], and for a more general consideration of this question Lings, *A Sufi Saint*, ch. 8.

[5] Sarrāj, *Lumaʿ*, 252–3.

[6] Ḥanbalī theologian, preacher and saint; of Iranian origin, he lived and taught in Baghdad; an important Sufi order (*ṭarīqah*) is named after him, see EI², "ʿAbd al-Ḳādir al-Djīlānī", "Ḳādirīya".

they relate to his own spiritual degree, are concerned exclusively with this difference, that is, with his realization of his essential identity of God.[7] The same applies, as we shall see, in all that concerns the end of the path, to the famous "Poem of the Way" or "Great *Tāʾiyyah*" by ʿUmar b. ʿAlī b. al-Fāriḍ (d. 632/1235), a poem written more objectively than his other odes, with a view to the instruction of disciples. But many of Ibn al-Fāriḍ's shorter poems spring directly from sorrow caused by an "absence", and it is clear that he takes the alternation in question altogether for granted:

What ease came *to* me when she[8] *to* me came.
What ease turned *from* me when she *from* me turned.[9]

and:

A year when she is with me is a moment;
An hour of absence is a year to me[10]

The adept none the less has the certainty that what appears to have gone will return, and he reasons with himself along such lines. Manṣūr b. Ḥusayn al-Ḥallāj (d. 309/922), for example, affirms that he can always console himself with joyful expectations and remembrances:

The night of separation, be it long or short,
Mine intimate friend is hope of Thee, memory of Thee.

But this reasoned patience does not prevent the same poet from crying out elsewhere:

O surfeit of sadness, that I should forever
Be calling upon Thee as if I were far
Or as if Thou wert absent![11]

We may also quote in this context a poignant couplet attributed to his older contempory and fellow-Baghdadi Abū ʾl-Ḥusayn al-Nūrī (d. 295/907):

Be unto me as Thou wast when I was not,
O Thou for whom I am beset by calamity and sorrow![12]

The words "when I was not" could be glossed "when my consciousness of being a separate entity was overwhelmed and obliterated in union with the one reality". It would be possible to go on almost indefinitely quoting examples of sorrow at interruptions of the state of union, since this is one of the main themes of Sufi poetry. If called to question about these

[7] See e.g. Jīlānī, *Fuyūḍāt*, 46, 52, 62.
[8] The divinity is frequently referred to in Sufi poetry by a woman's name, most often Laylā, the beloved of Majnūn (see ch. 8, n. 3), or by the feminine pronoun.
[9] Arberry ed., *Mystical Poems*, XIV, 95. [10] Ibid., XI, 30. [11] *Le Dîwân d'al-Ḥallâj*, 59; 44.
[12] Ibid., 118.

lamentations, the Sufi would no doubt answer that the "absolute" has its rights, and that the passage from the absolute to the relative, even if it is known to be temporary and illusory, warrants and even demands an "absolute" expression of loss: awareness that the loss is temporary is outweighed by the absolute worth of that which is lost.

The other general consideration which calls for mention here has to do with the relationship between mysticism and asceticism. It is obvious that if every mystic is subordinately or virtually an ascetic, by no means every ascetic is a mystic. Always allowing for borderline cases, it could be said that in the ascetic outlook the stress lies objectively on the vanity of the world and its pleasures, and subjectively on repentance for sins, avoidance of further temptations, preparation for death and the Last Judgement, and hope of salvation and Paradise. In the Sufi conception of asceticism, the stress falls on none of these. The Sufi is expected to take them all, as it were, in his stride, and to dwell in concentration on the positive finality where object and subject meet in a beatitude which infinitely transcends salvation in the ordinary sense of the term. In the words of Shiblī, asceticism (*ẓuhd*) is "the turning away of the heart from things unto the Lord of things".[13]

It must be remembered, however, that if the Sufi is bound to keep himself detached from earthly things he is also bound to love them because they are symbols or manifestations of the Beloved. The *ḥadīth qudsī*,[14] "I was a hidden treasure and I wished to be known, and so I created the world", is one of the most often-quoted traditions in Sufi literature, just as "Wheresoever ye turn, there is the Face of God" is one of the most often-quoted verses of the Qurʾān.[15] The twofold attitude in question – fidelity to the Beloved in Himself and recognition of Him in His outward signs – is expressed in the lines:

> I will weep for Thee with eyes that are sore for Thee,
> And look in delight with glances that point to Thee.[16]

The last sentence is expressive of the realization of the truth which that verse of the Qurʾān discloses, the ability to see through phenomena to the divine face which they both veil and reveal. This sense of the transparency of things is a fundamental aspect of the standpoint of gnosis which dominates the perspective of Sufism; the Sufis refer to themselves as "the gnostics" just as readily as they claim to be "the lovers".

13 Sulamī, *Ṭabaqāt*, ed. Shuraybah, 314/ed. Pedersen, 343.
14 Holy tradition, so called because in it God speaks in the first person on the tongue of the Prophet.
15 Qurʾān, ii.115.
16 Ibn al-Zayyāt, *Tashawwuf*, 171, where the lines are quoted without attribution.

EARLY SUFI POETS

Proceeding now to a more chronological treatment of our subject, it may be noted that as early as the fourth/tenth century the Sufi biographer Jaᶜfar al-Khuldī (d. 348/959) claimed to know by heart the collected poems of over 130 Sufis,[17] and it is evident from the context that his claim was not exhaustive. Much of this poetry appears to have been lost, though it is not unreasonable to hope that what has survived includes what is best. One of the earliest great Sufi poems that has come down to us is the well-known quatrain generally ascribed to Rābiᶜah al-ᶜAdawiyyah of Basra, who died in 185/801 when she was about eighty-five.[18] Nicholson's translation is well-known,[19] but the words "selfishly" and "selfish" introduce an idea which is alien to the poem, and "my adoring gaze" makes explicit an idea which in the original is deliberately left implicit. The following more literal if less pleasing version shows the poem to be a profoundly sober expression of the already explained "ebb and flow" which every great mystic is bound to experience during earthly life:

> Two loves I give Thee, love that yearns,
> And love because Thy due is love.
> My yearning my remembrance turns
> To Thee, nor lets it from Thee rove.
> Thou hast Thy due whene'er it please Thee
> To lift the veils for me to see Thee.
> Praise is not mine in this, nor yet
> In that, but Thine in this and that.[20]

In commenting on these lines Nicholson speaks of "their mixture of devotion and speculation", and adds: "The author distinguishes the illuminative from the comtemplative life, and manifestly regards the latter as the more excellent way." I confess to finding these remarks quite incomprehensible, since there is no question here of making a distinction or choice between two mystical paths. The poem is a record of what lies beyond the poet's control, a record of the two alternating states within the divine presence – veiledness and unveiling, or separation and union. Seldom can things of such profound significance have been recorded with such simplicity and so restrained an economy. These qualities serve to convey the truth that the things in question constituted the everyday life of the speaker – a life lived at so high a level as to exclude all else. To Rābiᶜah are attributed also some poetical prose discourses with God (*munājāt*), and

[17] Sulamī, *Ṭabaqāt*, ed. Shuraybah, 434/ed. Pedersen, 454.

[18] For a general consideration of her life, see Smith, *Rābiᶜa the Mystic*, and Badawī, *Shahīdat al-ᶜishq al-ilāhī*.

[19] *Literary History*, 234.

[20] Makkī, *Qūt al-qulūb*, II, 57.

also some poems of thanksgiving and praise, of which the following – seven lines in the original – is representative; the first two lines are also quoted in the original, as conveying more fully than can a translation how close is the fusion of mystical experience and the poetic recording of that experience (the metre is *ramal*):

rāḥatī yā ikhwatī fī khalwatī *wa-ḥabībī dāʾiman fī ḥaḍratī*
lam ajid lī ʿan hawāhu ʿiwaḍā *wa-hawāhu fī ʾl-barāyā miḥnatī*

Brethren, my rest is in my solitude,
And my Beloved is ever in my presence.
Nothing for me will do but love of Him;
By love of Him I am tested in this world.
Whereso I be I contemplate His beauty;
He is my prayer-niche; He mine orient is.
Died I of love and found not His acceptance,
Of mankind I most wretched, woe were me!

Heart's mediciner, Thou All of longing, grant
Union with Thee; 'twill cure me to the depth.
O Thou, ever my joy, my life, from Thee
Is mine existence and mine ecstasy.
From all creation I have turned away
For union with Thee – mine utmost end.[21]

As may be inferred from what has already been said, the "inward sickness" that is mentioned so often by the great Sufis in their poems is nothing other than the "contradictory" condition of the relative that has been touched by the absolute, of the finite that has been opened to the infinite. The only cure is another touch, another opening. It is this "sickness" which sets the adept apart from other men, and it is by its very nature a secret, since none can understand it except those who are smitten by it. Dhū ʾl-Nūn Thawbān b. Ibrāhīm al-Miṣrī,[22] Rābiʿah's much younger, Egyptian contemporary (d. 246/861), the most outstanding Sufi poet of the first half of the third/ninth century, complains of his sickness as follows:

I die, but my passion for Thee dieth not.
Unfulfilled are my longings to drink deep Thy love.
My desires are the essence of all desire; Thou art they;
And Thou art riches, all riches, for me in my beggary.
Thou art the goal of my quest, the full scope of my wish,
The theme of my plaint,[23] the hidden depth of my consciousness.

[21] Al-Ḥurayfish al-Makkī, *al-Rawḍ al-fāʾiq*, 214. [22] See pp. 415–16.
[23] Or, reading *āmālī* for *shakwāya*, "the place where my hopes are set".

Burdened through Thee is my heart with what I tell not,
Howso long be my ailing for Thee and my constraint.
And from Thee, between my ribs [in my heart] is what clearly Thou seest,
Though its clarity is not clear unto kinsman or neighbour;
And within me a spreading sickness hath weakened my frame,[24]
And my secret confiding unto Thee is poured forth.

Art Thou not guide to lost travellers in bewilderment,
And saviour from the brink of the crumbling precipice?
Whom Thou guidest, Thou lightest their way, when themselves
They have not one tenth of one tenth of the light.
Vouchsafe me then favour, that in its nearness I may live.
Help me with ease from Thee, my hardship to repel.[25]

Elsewhere Dhū ʾl-Nūn expresses the positive aspect of the same state. The two poems must be taken, not as contradictory, but as complementary. With regard to both it is relevant to remember that "nearness" denotes the end of the path; the technical term *muqarrab*, "brought near" (by God to God), is only used of the archangels, the prophets and the highest saints:

The haunt of the hearts of the gnostics is a mead
Celestial – beyond it are the veils of the Lord,
His nearness their sole boundary from the world of the Secret –
Melt they would with love if their moment had come.
For their thirst is a cup purely filled from His love,
And the cool of a breeze beyond words to describe.
Hearts near to the Lord of the Throne[26] – they had sought to be near –
With what blessings the King in their nearness hath graced them!
Pleased with them, He hath pleased them unto ultimate pleasure:
The Beloved's welcome is the abode wherein they dwell,
Most penetrant their resolve; by it they have travelled,
By it their thoughts pierce to what is hidden by the Veils.
Their secret ever goeth between the Beloved and themselves,
From other than nearness by nearness made safe.[27]

The same standpoint is expressed in one of the few poems attributed to the author of one of the first mystical commentaries on the Qurʾān, Sahl b. ʿAbdullāh al-Tustarī (b. 203/818, d. Basra 283/896), Dhū ʾl-Nūn's younger contemporary and like him one of the greatest of the early Sufis:

The gnostics' hearts with eyes are blest
That see what other see-ers see not;

24 The theme of the lover weakened by love and misunderstood by those around him is a commonplace of secular love poetry.

25 Sulamī, *Ṭabaqāt*, ed. Shuraybah, 28–9/ed. Pedersen, 21; Sarrāj, *Lumaʿ*, 368.

26 Cf. Qurʾān, ii.255.

27 Abū Nuʿaym al-Iṣfahānī, *Ḥilyat al-awliyāʾ*, IX, 369 and 391 (variants).

And tongues whose discourse is of secrets
Beyond the recording angels'[28] ken,
And wings that all unfeathered fly
To His dominion, Lord of the Worlds.

We have inherited the draught,
Sciences of hidden secret,
Rarer than all lore of old.
Their samples[29] speak for them as signs
And nullify impostors' claims.[30]

Mention has already been made of Sahl's contemporary, Abū ᵓl-Ḥusayn al-Nūrī (the last part of his name – not strictly a name but a style – could be rendered "the Man of Light"). Several short poems are attributed to him, and the richest source for these is the *Kitāb al-Taᶜarruf* by the Sufi Abū Bakr Muḥammad al-Kalābādhī (d. 308/920), translated by Arberry under the title *The Doctrine of the Ṣūfīs*. Most of the poems are concerned with the inward states of the contemplative. The following – three lines in the original – is less abstruse than some others which would need to be annotated:

From time I'm veiled; my veil is my concern for Him,
My wonder at His Infinite worth transcending mine.
That I am absent from its grasp time seeth not,
And I perceive not time's events, how they flow on,
Since I am all attendance to fulfil His due,
Nor care I, all my life long, for the hand of time.[31]

Of the following, in the same metre – *ṭawīl* – as the above, Arberry's spirited translation is admittedly very free, nor do I find his note on "nearness" and "farness" convincing. The poem leads up to the mention of the supreme state, namely "nearness". Henceforth the mystic is solely preoccupied by that, and by the inevitable temporary "withdrawals" of the Beloved which seem relatively like "farness". Here is a more literal version:

I would, so overflowing is my love for Him,
Remember Him perpetually, yet my remembrance –
Wondrous to tell – is vanished into ecstasy,
And wonder upon wonder, even ecstasy,
With memory's self, in nearness–farness vanished is.[32]

[28] Cf. Qurᵓān, lxxxii.11–12.

[29] *Shawāhid* (witnesses, proofs): each particular example of knowledge derived from these sciences is not only an eloquent sign that the knower in question is a true gnostic, but also a criterion for judging false claims to gnosis.

[30] Abū Nuᶜaym al-Iṣfahānī, *Ḥilyat al-awliyā*ᵓ, x, 200, seems to attribute the poem to Sahl, but gives only the first line. Sahl may however have been quoting from an earlier poet (see Nīsābūrī, *ᶜUqalāᵓ al-majānīn*, 129–30). The above translation is from the recension given by Massignon, who considers the poem to be by Sahl (see *Le Dîwân d'al-Ḥallâj*, 115).

[31] *Taᶜarruf*, ch. 56.

[32] Ibid., ch. 47.

There is a considerable contrast between the poems of Nūrī and those of his contemporary Sumnūn b. Ḥamzah al-Baṣrī (d. 303/915). Moreover Sumnūn is surnamed *al-Muḥibb* ("the Lover"); but it would be as erroneous to draw any far-reaching conclusions from this as from the title *Sulṭān al-ʿĀshiqīn* ("Sultan of the Lovers") which is given to the highly intellectual Ibn al-Fāriḍ, whose poems are discussed in the last section of this chapter. Both these "lovers" are typically Sufi in their perspective and the closing line of one of Sumnūn's poems is no less than a masterly formulation of what might be described as love in the framework of gnosis, which is, as we have seen, the Sufi norm:

> Thou hast thrown me to swim in the ocean of Thy holiness,
> And inexistent, without trace, I desire Thee from within Thee.[33]

A dozen or more short poems are attributed to Sumnūn – enough for us to form a sense of his particular style, which is marked by a touching directness and simplicity. The following is very characteristic (the metre is *basīṭ*):

> Thou'rt the Beloved – no doubt is in my breast.
> My soul, were it to lose Thee, would not live.
> Thou who hast made me thirst so longingly
> For union which Thou hast power to give,
> Were there for me in Thee a place of rest,
> If "Ah, my thirst, my thirst!" I cried to Thee?[34]

The following, which is known to have been recited by Ḥallāj on one occasion, is considered by Massignon – and I am inclined to agree with him – to be the work of Sumnūn:

> If ever once mine eye a vigil kept,
> For other than Thyself, or if it wept,
> Be it ne'er given the gift it was inspired
> To long for, and so longingly desired!
> If e'er it did deliberately gaze
> On other than Thyself, may it ne'er graze
> Upon the Meadows of Felicity,
> Thy Countenance! May its sight darkened be![35]

This could well have been written by the poet who wrote the following lines – in the same metre, *ṭawīl* – which are attributed to Sumnūn on good authority:

> Empty I was within me ere Thy love I found,
> Idly on men and things I thought, oft merry-making,

33 Sarrāj, *Lumaʿ*, 250.

34 Sulamī, *Ṭabaqāt*, ed. Shuraybah, 197/ed. Pedersen, 188. It is difficult to convey in English the effect of his final cry *wā ʿaṭashī* ("Ah, my thirst!").

35 *Recueil*, 72; Ḥallāj, *Le Dīwân d'al-Ḥallâj*, 117.

But when Thy love summoned my heart, it did respond,
Nor can I see it ever now Thy court forsaking.
May I be smitten with severance from Thee if I lie.
If in this world I ever joy in aught but Thee,
If any thing in any land ever to me
Seem beautiful, if Thou art absent from mine eye!
So take me *to* Thee, if Thou wilt, or say me no,
Whiche'er it be, for none but Thee my heart will do.[36]

The idea that love calls and the mystic answers occurs also in Sumnūn's most often-quoted poem, again in *ṭawīl*:

With yearning at each dawn and dusk I long,
And when at night love calls I answer her.
More our days vanish, more my love grows strong,
Even as if love's time unvanishing were.[37]

Abū Bakr al-Shiblī must have known Sumnūn, and perhaps known him well. They moved in the same circles, and he was already over fifty when Sumnūn died; and he may have had the above lines in mind when he himself based two lines, in *ṭawīl*, on the idea that love for the divinity has power not only to escape from time but also to draw with it the lover into eternity:

Strange is my case, in strangeness I am all alone,
Unique amongst mankind, peer have I none.
My time, in Thee eternized, is Eternity,
And from myself Thou has extinguished me.
So am I from createdness withdrawn, set free.[38]

On another occasion Shiblī condensed two lines of Sumnūn into one (two in translation):

If "Step into fire" Thou saidst, I eagerly
T'wards it would haste, in joy that Thou hadst thought on me.[39]

Shiblī is known to have been one of the most spiritually intoxicated of Sufis, and one has the impression that he lived as it were on the verge of poetry – whence the many single lines and couplets, both brilliant and profound, which flashed forth from him so spontaneously. Here are two more examples of single lines (*mafārid*):

Not one heart didst Thou captive make in me;
Mine every limb a heart is unto Thee.

[36] Sulamī, *Ṭabaqāt*, ed. Shuraybah, 198/ed. Pedersen, 189.
[37] Ibid., ed. Shuraybah, 198/ed. Pedersen, 191; Abū Nuʿaym al-Iṣfahānī, *Ḥilyat al-awliyāʾ*, x, 311; Ibn al-Zayyāt, *Tashawwuf*, 110 (anonymously).
[38] Ibn al-Zayyāt, *Tashawwuf*, 108 (anonymously); Sarrāj, *Lumaʿ*, 365.
[39] See Abū Nuʿaym al-Iṣfahānī, *Ḥilyat al-awliyāʾ*, x, 210; 373.

They said: "Thou art mad [with love] for Laylā."[40] I said:
"Madmen know only the easier part of love."[41]

The following lines (two in the original) are also characteristic:

Said my friend: "How now is Thy patience with them?"[42]
So I said: "Is there patience, to be asked of, how it is?

Fiercer than fire is love's heat in my heart,
Sweeter than piety, and sharper than the sword."[43]

He expresses much the same state of soul in the following poem:

To access they[44] inured me – union is sweet!
Then barred my way – how hard, barriers to meet!
They, my reprovers,[45] my excess reproved
Of love for the beloved – no sin there!
By beauty of humility at tryst, I swear
The lover's meed is not that he should not be loved![46]

Complementary to both these last is a serene expression of the permanent consciousness which the great mystic retains over and above any vicissitudes he may have to undergo:

Let the moons set or still be bright,
Ours is a full moon: in its sight
Full moons are humbled; for us its light
A splendour is by day and night.
No change of time can alter it.[47]

More than one brief extract has already been quoted from Manṣūr b. Ḥusayn al-Ḥallāj, but, since he is the greatest Sufi poet of all this earlier period, he must be considered in more detail. He is reported to have been in his youth a disciple of Tustarī, one of whose poems we quoted earlier, and also of Abū ʾl-Qāsim b. Muḥammad al-Junayd (d. 298/910),[48] and he was the friend of Shiblī, who was three years younger but outlived him by over twenty years. At the age of about sixty-five, Ḥallāj was cruelly put to death (in 309/922) on a charge of blasphemy – for having said *anā ʾl-ḥaqq*, "I am the Truth" (*al-Ḥaqq* meaning God). These words occur in fact in one of his poems, though this may not be the actual source against which the

[40] See n. 8.
[41] Abū Nuʿaym al-Iṣfahānī, *Ḥilyat al-awliyāʾ*, x, 373; 372; see also Shiblī, *Dīwān*, 170.
[42] When the object of love is plural in Sufi poetry, the reference is to the divine qualities; see Ibn ʿArabī, *Tarjumán al-Ashwáq*, I. [43] Shiblī, *Dīwān*, 112. [44] See n. 42.
[45] A conventional character in Arabic love poetry, the "reproacher" or "railer" reproves the lover for extravagance, thus enabling him to retort.
[46] See Abū Nuʿaym al-Iṣfahānī, *Ḥilyat al-awliyāʾ*, x, 367. [47] Ibid., 372.
[48] Accounted, together with his contemporary al-Muḥāsibī, "the greatest orthodox exponent of the 'sober' type of Ṣūfism" and as having "laid the foundations on which the later systems of Ṣūfism were built", *EI*², "al-Djunayd".

accusation was levelled. He – or any other great mystic – might well have made the formulation more than once. The same consciousness is expressed – somewhat less dangerously – in what is perhaps his best-known line (two in translation), though the poem which it opens is seldom quoted in full:

I saw my Lord with the eye of the heart.
I said: "Who art thou?" He answered: "Thou."
Thus where no where hath, as from Thee,
Nor is there, as to Thee, a where.
Thou givst imagining no image
For it to imagine where Thou art.
He art Thou who hath filled all where –
Beyond where too. Where art Thou then?[49]

The poems of Ḥallāj have a relatively wide range, from more simple but none the less profound affirmations of pious devotion – far more than pious in the ordinary sense – to veiled expressions of truths which are mainly ineffable. But, in either case, one is conscious of a striking spontaneity suggestive of an inward cause too powerful for the lines in question to have remained unwritten. The following is representative of his simpler writing:

Diverse longings had my soul,
But seeing Thee hath made them one.
Mine envied now mine envier is,
And lord of men I have become
Since Thou becamest Lord of me.
They chided me because of Thee,[50]
My friends and foes, in ignorance
How grievously I had been tried.
Their world and their religion I
Have left to men, for Thy love's sake,
O my religion and my world.

Here is another example which belongs to the same category and is in the same metre, *basīṭ*:

I swear by God, sun riseth not nor setteth,
But in each breath I breathe my love for Thee,
Nor go I e'er apart with friends for discourse
But Thou, as I sit with them, art my theme;
Nor dwell my thoughts on Thee, sadly or gladly,
But Thou art in my heart, I murmur Thee.
Nor have I mind to drink of water in thirst,
But I behold Thine image in the cup.
And could I come to Thee, then speed I would
Upon my face, or walking on my head.[51]

[49] *Le Dîwân d'al-Ḥallâj*, 46.
[50] Because of what they deemed to be my extravagant behaviour with regard to Thee – see n. 45.
[51] *Le Dîwân d'al-Ḥallâj*, 38–9; 67.

At the opposite pole to these two poems are three lines which express the profoundest of realities, the immanence of the divinity in the depth of every being. It is this immanence which makes possible the beatific vision, for only the divine can see the divine:

For the Lights of religion's Light are Lights in men,
For the Secret, Secrets in secret depths of souls,
And for Being, in beings, is a Being that saith "Be".
Reserved for it my heart is, guided, and chosen.
O ponder what I say with the Intellect's eye.
Keen is the Intellect of hearing and of insight.[52]

Close to this in theme – at any rate in its opening – but very different in mood is a poem which has already been quoted from at the beginning of this chapter:

Within my heart Thou dwellst; therein, of Thee, are secrets.
Good be that house for Thee, nay, good Whom there Thou findest!
Therein no secret is but Thee, none that I know of.
Look with Thine Eye; doth any other tenant dwell there?
The night of separation, be it long or short,
Mine intimate friend is hope of Thee, memory of Thee.
Well pleased am I if it should please Thee to destroy me,
For what Thy choice is, O my Slayer, that I choose.[53]

The second line reads, literally: "May the house suit Thee, nay, rather, may the neighbour suit Thee!" The reference is to the proverb, "the neighbour first, then the house", that is, "in choosing a home, inspect the neighbours first, then the dwelling". Rābiʿah has characteristically quoted this proverb in the sense of, "Put God before Paradise". No less inspired is the profoundly ingenious inversion by which Ḥallāj here addresses the divinity, merging the idea of "neighbour" into that of "tenant". To the same context – that of the divine immanence – belongs another poem of which the first two lines (four in the translation) are frequently quoted throughout Sufi literature, often without mention of an author:

O Secret of my secret, so subtle, Thou art veiled
From all imaginations of all beings that have life,
Yet outwardly, inwardly, Thou manifestest
Thyself in every thing to every thing.
Ignorance it were that I should proffer Thee my pleas,
Enormity of doubt, excess of impotence!
Sum of Totality, other than me Thou art not:
How then shall I plead for myself unto myself?[54]

[52] Ibid., 58. Cf. Qurʾān, ii.117, etc.: "When He decreeth a thing, He only saith unto it, Be, and it is."
[53] *Le Dîwân d'al-Ḥallâj*, 59. [54] Ibid., 1.

Centred upon the same mystery, seen from another angle, and again very different in mood, is a poem which, especially in its last line (two in translation) has been much commented by Sufis of subsequent generations:

Is it I or Thou? These twain! Two gods!
Far be it, far be it from me to affirm two!
Selfhood is Thine in my nothingness forever:
Mine all, over all, casts illusion twofold:
For where is Thine Essence, where from me, for me to see,
When mine hath no where, as already is plain?
And Thy Countenance, where with my two sights may I seek it,
In the seeing of my heart, or the seeing of mine eye?
Twixt Thee and me an "I am" is, o'ercrowding me:
Take, by Thine own "I am", mine from between us.[55]

All the verse quoted so far was clearly written for a spiritual élite. Most of what it expresses would be beyond the aspirations, let alone the experience, of the majority of believers. But in addition to its exclusive aspect Sufism, like other mysticisms, has also an inclusive aspect – witness the thousands of men and women who are at the fringe of all the great Sufi brotherhoods, spiritually dependent upon them, yet not fully integrated into them; and there is a certain type of religious verse which may be called mystical and which in Islam is classed as Sufi poetry, but which expresses ideas which everyone can understand, and which can awaken an echo in every believing soul. This "openness" does not however make it any the less profound, and it is in fact mystical precisely in virtue of the depth from which it springs. Let us take, by way of example, three often-quoted lines ascribed to Ḥallāj's younger contemporary, Abū ʾl-Qāsim al-Sayyārī of Marv (d. 342/953):

Patiently pleasures I shunned till they shunned me.
I made my soul[56] forsake them; steadfast she stood.
The soul's for man to make her as he would:
If fed, she seeks more; else, resigned she'll be.
Mine was an arrogant soul; but when she knew
Me resolute for humbleness, humble she grew.[57]

The typical dry sobriety of the content of these lines, which does not make them any the less melodious in the original, is to be found in an even starker degree in three lines attributed to the North African ʿAbd al-ʿAziz al-Tūnisī (d. 486/1093), which, rhythmically,– the metre is *ramal* – have a distinctly martial quality which serves as a reminder that one of Sufism's definitions of itself is "the greater Holy War" (*al-jihād al-akbar*):

55 Ibid., 90. 56 Feminine in Arabic.

57 Sulamī, *Ṭabaqāt*, ed. Shuraybah, 444/ed. Pedersen, 464–5; Ibn al-Zayyāt, *Tashawwuf*, 242 (less complete, and unattributed).

inna li ᵓllāhi ᶜibādan fuṭunā — *ṭallaqū ᵓl-dunyā wa-khāfū ᵓl-fitanā*
fakkarū fīhā fa-lammā ᶜalimū — *annahā laysat li ᵓl-ḥayyi waṭanā*
jaᶜalūhā lujjatan wa ᵓttakhadhū — *ṣāliḥa ᵓl-aᶜmāli fīhā sufunā*

God hath slaves of insight: they
The world divorced have, lest she tempt them.
They thought on her, and when they knew her
To be no homeland for the living,
They took her as a sea, embarking
On best of deeds as boats to cross her.[58]

No less profound and equally open to the generality of pious souls is the elegy which is said to have been composed by the great theologian Abū Ḥāmid al-Ghazālī (d. 505/1111) on himself shortly before his death. Of its twenty-seven lines, we will translate the first eight:

Say unto brethren when they see me dead,
And weep for me, lamenting me in sadness:
"Think ye I am this corpse ye are to bury?
I swear by God, this dead one is not I.
I in the Spirit am, and this my body
My dwelling was, my garment for a time.
I am a treasure: hidden I was beneath
This talisman of dust, wherein I suffered.
I am a pearl; a shell imprisoned me,
But leaving it, all trials I have left.
I am a bird, and this was once my cage;
But I have flown, leaving it as a token.
I praise God who hath set me free, and made
for me a dwelling in the heavenly heights.
Ere now I was a dead man in your midst,
But I have come to life, and doffed my shroud."[59]

The Sufi poets of all this earlier period, even as far as the beginning of the sixth/twelfth century, have this in common, that they are little concerned with literary conventions. They say what they have to with relative directness and simplicity. When they are obscure, the obscurity results mainly from the abstruseness of the theme itself, from the fact that they are seeking to express the inexpressible. They are not given to using allegory, and there is no great profusion of symbols.

58 Ibid., 69; the "best of deeds" is remembrance of God (*dhikr Allāh*).

59 Nābulusī, *Kawkab* (see Pedersen, "Ein Gedicht al-Ġazālī's"); there is a full translation in Smith, *Al-Ghazālī the Mystic*, evidently from a different recension. Although the poem is also attributed to others, in particular to Abū Ḥamīd's brother, Aḥmad al-Ghazālī (d. 520/1126), and to Abū ᵓl-Ḥasan ᶜAlī al-Sibtī (d. 600/1203), Pedersen remarks ("Ein Gedicht") that the weight of manuscript authority is strongly in favour of the attribution to Abū Ḥamīd.

POETS OF THE LATER ᶜABBASID PERIOD

By the end of the fifth/eleventh century, a change was beginning to take place. The symbolism used by ᶜAbdullāh al-Shahrazūrī (d. 511/1117) in his best-known poem[60] is an anticipation of what was to follow; and a little more than a century later, within the last fifty years of ᶜAbbasid rule, we find that the two greatest Sufi poets of this period make full use of conventions which had come to prevail in literary circles, in particular of the formal love-poem which had been developed from elements of the pre-Islamic ode.[61] Thus, in certain outward respects, both Ibn al-ᶜArabī and Ibn al-Fāriḍ have less in common with their own spiritual ancestors, such as Shiblī and Ḥallāj, than with the poets of the caliphal and princely courts. But as regards ultimate content, Sufi poetry remains, needless to say, unchanged – as it still does to this day. The four poets just mentioned, despite stylistic differences, are identical in their outlook.

Muḥyī ʾl-Dīn Muḥammad b. ᶜAlī Ibn al-ᶜArabī, or, less correctly but more commonly, Ibn ᶜArabī (d. 638/1240), was born in Murcia in Spain, and brought up mainly in Seville; but he went to the East in his early thirties, and finally settled in Damascus, where he died at the age of seventy-five. He was the most prolific of Sufi writers in verse as well as in prose. In this connection it must be remembered that mystical poets are first of all mystics and then poets. This does not mean that they are not capable of poetry in the highest and fullest sense of the term, but they recognize that verse can serve certain practical purposes. As mystics they are potentially, if not always actually, spiritual instructors; and verse can sharpen the expression of formulations which the master may need to "shoot like arrows into the heart" of a disciple. It can also serve dialectical and other purposes: it can be the medium through which concepts are developed; and in the case of Ibn al-ᶜArabī another factor which is perhaps relevant is his extraordinary facility for verse. His prose writings, such as *al-Futūḥāt al-makkiyyah* and *Fuṣūṣ al-ḥikam*, and some of his shorter doctrinal treatises, abound in verses which cannot all be said, strictly speaking, to belong to the domain of art. The same applies to much of his voluminous *Dīwān*, which is one of the unquestionably authentic works ascribed to him. Its themes are many and various – questions of doctrine and practical theology, comments on single Quranic verses or longer passages, with at least one poem on each of the 114 *sūrah*s of the Qurʾān. There are also comments on traditions of the Prophet, reflections on all the obligatory ritual practices of Islam and on many of its voluntary practices, and on a number of other subjects, some personal and

[60] For Arabic text and English translation of this forty-four line poem, see Nadeem, *Critical Appreciation*, 112–15.
[61] See chs. 9, 12.

others general. The whole is a rich and largely unexplored field which deserves a well-annotated edition. But the full flowering of Ibn ʿArabī's poetical gifts is rather to be found in his *Tarjumān al-ashwāq* ("The Interpreter of Desires"), where the great Sufi consciously invests himself, as it were, with the apparel and insignia of the bard, as one bent on writing in the grand style and on exploiting all the beauty of the Arabic language and all the resources of its poetic art. The sixty-one odes in question were written, Nicholson convincingly argues in the preface to his edition of *Tarjumān*, in 611/1215, when he was about fifty years old. He tells us in his commentary – written to explain that they are purely mystical – that the different women's names mentioned all refer, as regards their earthly starting point, to the beautiful daughter of a Sufi friend whose house he had frequented during his visit to Mecca some twelve years previously. The poems, he tells us, convey only a small part of the longing that he felt, even in restrospect, for the 14-year-old beauty, wise and accomplished far beyond her age, who personified for him "harmony of union with God" – for so he interpreted her name, Niẓām (poem XXIV, 14). That, we may conclude, is her central significance in these poems; but, being for him as a semi-transparent veil between this world and the next, her beauty was also his means of beholding the various divine aspects, whence the frequent references to a plurality of loved ones.

The most current theme in the poems is, as usual, grief at parting with the beloved – the lament of the visionary for the loss of the beatific vision, expressed in terms of the stock elements of the *nasīb* (amatory prelude). Thus the conventional lamentation over the ruined and now deserted dwellings is a reference to the poet's own heart. The departing beauties in the camel howdahs are spiritual mysteries, aspects of gnosis, and the camel-driver, whom the poet begs to delay departure or to stop, once departed, is the voice of God who has summoned back to Himself these divine manifestations. The white tents in which the departed ones halt at noon are the veils of light which cover the splendours of the divine countenance.

These few simple examples may serve to give a general impression, but in fact the symbolism is very detailed and complex. Nicholson speaks of "the obscurity of the style and the strangeness of its imagery", and no one can deny that many of the poems contain abstruse passages calling for explanations which only the author's commentary can give. But this must not be allowed to overshadow the majesty of the verses and their compelling melodious flow which is such an eloquent reminder of the author's general claim never to have written anything except under the pressure of inspiration. Moreover many of the poems are simple enough to be enjoyed without any recourse to the commentary, which can be replaced by the general knowledge that, for the mystic, the divinity is always the ultimate object of love. Here is an example in translation:

Endurance went, and patience went, when they went.
Gone, even they, tenants of mine inmost heart!
I asked where the riders rest at noon, was answered:
"They rest where the *shīh* and *bān* tree spread their fragrance."
So said I to the wind: "Go and o'ertake them,
For they, even now, in the shade of the grove are biding,
And give them greetings of peace from a sorrowful man,
Whose heart sorroweth at severance from his folk."[62]

The following *qaṣīdah* expresses the idea that the earthly beloved is a symbol of that which lies beyond all plurality:

There rose for me twixt Adhriᶜāt and Busrah
A maiden of fourteen like a full moon.
Higher than time she stood in majesty,
Transcendent over it in pride and glory.
Each moon when it hath reached its plenitude
A waning suffereth to fulfil the month,
Save this: no movements hath she through the Signs [of the Zodiac],
Nor maketh, being repeated, two of One.[63]

Treasury, thou, of blended fragrances,
Meadow that putteth forth spring herbs and flowers,
Beauty hath reached in thee her utmost end.
For others like to thee there is no room
In all the scope of what is possible.[64]

The arresting content of the most famous lines of the *Tarjumān* has certainly distracted attention from their poetical excellence, and for this reason they are given here not only in translation but also in Arabic (metre: *ṭawīl*):

la-qad ṣāra qalbī qābilan kulla ṣūratin
fa-marᶜan li-ghizlānin wa-dayrun li-ruhbānī
wa-baytun li-awthānin wa-kaᶜbatu ṭāʾifin
wa-alwāḥu tawrātin wa-muṣḥafu qurʾānī
adīnu bi-dīni ʾl-ḥubbi annā tawajjahat
rakāʾibuhā fa ʾl-dīnuy dīnī wa-īmānī

My heart is capable of every form:
Pasture for deer, a monastery for monks,
Temple for idols, pilgrim's Kaᶜbah,
Tables of Torah and book of Qurʾān.
My religion is love's religion: where turn
Her camels, that religion my religion is, my faith.[65]

62 *Tarjumán*, VI. 63 I.e. as each new moon does in relation to the old moon. 64 *Tarjumán*, XL.
65 Ibid., XI.

In the mystical poetry of most religions – and Islamic mysticism is no exception – there is a category of poems which are obscure by intention because the author is bent on emphasizing the mysterial aspect of what he is expressing. A much-quoted example is to be found in three lines generally attributed to Ibn ᶜArabī:

> Make thine ablution with the waters of the Unseen,[66]
> If hast the secret; else, with earth or stone;[67]
> And take as leader one whose leader thou'rt become,
> And pray the dawn prayer in mid afternoon.[68]
> This is the gnostics' prayer; if of them thou be,
> Then flood the land with waters of the sea.[69]

ᶜUmar b. ᶜAlī, called Ibn al-Fāriḍ (d. 632/1235), an Egyptian whose father's family came from Hama in Syria, was the slightly younger contemporary of Ibn ᶜArabī, who outlived him by about five years. In the main lines of their destinies the two men have much in common. Each was revered as a saint in his lifetime, and the tomb of each is a shrine of pilgrimage to this day. Their spiritual outlook was the same, and the writings of both have been copiously commented. Their poetry also has many features in common, as might be expected. But, unlike the exceedingly versatile Ibn ᶜArabī, Ibn al-Fāriḍ was, as regards his writings, exclusively a poet; and even in this respect he wrote far less than his Andalusian brother. His poems consist of one long *qaṣīdah* of 761 verses, and some nineteen shorter odes ranging from 151 to seven verses.

Ibn al-Fāriḍ is thought by some to be the greatest of all Arab poets. Nicholson, in his *Literary History of the Arabs*, speaks of "the fervid rapture and almost etherial exaltation" which has won for his poetry "a unique place in Arabic literature". But the examples with which he seeks to illustrate these remarks are too freely translated to give a close enough impression of their originals. Here is a more literal translation of the first of the two poems in question:

> Give me excess of love and so increase me
> In marvelling at Thee; and mercy have
> Upon a heart for Thee by passion seared.
> And when I ask of Thee that I may see Thee

66 With the infinite reality of God, of which water is the symbol; so also in the final line of the poem.

67 The ritual ablution may be performed with sand, etc., in the absence of water; the allusion in this and the following line is to those who have not achieved gnosis.

68 Combine illumination (the escape from darkness, i.e. dawn) with readiness to receive it, spiritual maturity (mid-afternoon).

69 Shaᶜrānī, *al-Ṭabaqāt al-kubrā*, II (s.v. Muḥammad Abū ʾl-Mawāhib al-Shādhilī, who quotes and interprets the lines); see also Shādhilī, *Qawānīn*, trans. Jurjī, *Illumination*, 80–1.

Even as Thou art, in Thy reality,
Say not: *Thou shalt not see*,[70] but let me see.

Heart, thou didst promise patience in love of them.
Take heed, and be not troubled, be not anguished.
Verily love is life, so die in love,
And claim thy right to die, all sins forgiven.
Tell those before me and those after me,
And whoso witness of my sorrow was:
Learn from me, my example take, and hear me,
And tell mankind the story of my love.

Alone with the Belovèd I have been:
A secret subtler than wind's lightest breath,
When on the night it steals, between us passed;
He granted to my gaze a longed for sight,
Whence I, till then unknown, illustrious am.
Between His Beauty and His Majesty
I marvelled, and my state of marvelling
Was like an eloquent tongue that spake of me.
Turn then thy looks unto His Countenance,
To find the whole of beauty lineate there.
All beauty, if it gathered were and made
One perfect form, beholding Him, would say;
There is no god but God; God is most great.[71]

Ibn al-Fāriḍ's poems have received lavish attention from western scholars; and finally, in 1952, they were re-edited by Arberry from the oldest extant manuscript, which however omits five odes, including the one just quoted, which are to be found in the next oldest collection, said to have been made by the poet's grandson from an autograph manuscript. The poems in Arberry's edition were subsequently translated by him and extensively annotated. With remarkable scholarship, he has noted a wealth of single lines and longer passages from previous poets, some of them pre-Islamic, which Ibn al-Fāriḍ may have been echoing, consciously or unconsciously. It must be admitted however – and Arberry would have been among the first to do so – that the result of such "echoing" is never an effect of triteness. The following is an example of opening lines in a poem which express "newly" an idea that is not new, and use conventional rhetorical devices, such as *tajnīs* (paronomasia), to suggest mystical correspondences:

Did lightning (*barq*) flash on the slopes of Ubayriq,
Or see I a lantern in the hills of Najd?

[70] God's reply to Moses when he asked the same favour, Qurʾān, vii.139; see n. 90 below.
[71] *Dīwān*, 99.

> Or hath Laylā, even she, the ᶜĀmiriyyah, unveiled
> Her face in the night (*laylan*), changing darkness to daybreak?[72]

Another comparable example of what has, without being altogether new, all the freshness of originality, is the opening of his famous "wine-song" (*khamriyyah*). Arberry quotes passages from previous poets – Fakhr al-Dīn al-Rāzī, Abū Nuwās, al-Thaᶜālibī and Ibn al-Muᶜtazz – which contain ideas and images expressed in the first two lines alone; and there follow other parallel quotations for later passages. But Ibn al-Fāriḍ's poem has not only the last word, in virtue of the mystical dimension which he adds, but also in a sense "the first word" inasmuch as that dimension is itself the very track of inspiration. The poem has been translated in full by Nicholson in his *Studies in Islamic Mysticism*, as well as by Arberry, not to mention others. I will therefore translate only its opening and closing passages here.

> Remembering the Belovèd, wine we drink
> Which drunk had made us ere the vine's creation.
> A sun it is; the full moon is its cup;
> A crescent hands it round; how many stars
> Shine forth from it the moment it be mixed!
> But for its fragrance ne'er had I been guided
> Unto its tavern; but for its resplendence
> Imagining could no image make of it.
> Time its mere gasp hath left; its vanishing
> Like hiding is of secrets pent in the mind.
> Yet if it be but mentioned in the tribe,
> All become drunk – no shame on them nor sin . . .
> So in the tavern seek it; bid it unveil
> To strains of music – they offset its worth,
> For wine and care dwelt never in one place,
> Even as woe with music cannot dwell.
> Be drunk one hour with it, and thou shalt see
> Time's whole age as thy slave, at thy command.
> He hath not lived here, who hath sober lived,
> And he that dieth not drunk, hath missed his mark.
> With tears then let him mourn himself, whose life
> Hath passed, and he no share of it hath had.[73]

Immediately before the closing passage given here is a line of great importance not only for the poem as a whole but also for Ibn al-Fāriḍ's other poems, and Sufi poetry in general. It can be paraphrased: "You should drink the wine pure; but if you wish to dilute it, then it would be

[72] *Mystical Poems*, III. "Did lightning flash . . . or a lantern": cf. Imruʾ al-Qays, *Muᶜallaqah* (*CHALUP*, 94); Laylā of the tribe of ᶜĀmir: the beloved of Majnūn, see n. 8 above.

[73] *Mystical Poems*, x.

wrong to do so with anything other than the water of the Beloved's mouth" (as the kiss is conventionally called in Arabic love poetry). It is well known that throughout the ancient world saliva was considered as one of the great potential vehicles of theurgic power. In Sufi symbolism the "saliva of God", which is not fully separate from Him yet none the less virtually separate, is the Logos or the divine spirit, known in Islam as *al-rūḥ al-Muḥammadī* (the spirit of Muḥammad). The pure wine is the Beloved in Himself, the divinity, or the divine essence. But if, the poet tells us, you cannot take it at the supreme level, only dilute it with that water which is nearest to its nature and which is the first created thing to proceed from it. At this lower degree of concentration, the wine mixed with the water is the divinity manifesting Himself in His word. The stars (line 4) which result immediately from the addition of water to the wine (a conventional image in secular wine poetry), that is, from the appearance of the spirit of Muḥammad, are the spirits of the Companions of the Prophet, whom he likened to stars in a well-known tradition: "My Companions are even as the stars: whichever of them ye follow, ye shall be rightly guided"; by extension the stars must be taken to include the subsequent saints of Islam. In some of Ibn al-Fāriḍ's other poems, there is no question of anything other than "diluted wine": the object of love is the divine beauty as manifested in its first creation. As regards the following passage, which will serve as an example, let it be mentioned in passing that the first line (two in the translation), given here in the original, is often chanted by the Sufis at their sessions, especially during the sacred dance:

law asmaʿū Yaʿqūba dhikrā malāḥatin
fī wajhihī nasiya ʾl-jamāla ʾl-yūsufī

Had they recalled his face's loveliness to Jacob,
From his remembrance Joseph's beauty would have vanished;[74]
Or if Job even in his sleep had seen him come
A visitant, the sooner had his plague been cured.
To him when he is manifest and face to face
Every full moon and every lesser form do lean.
His virtues are perfections: had he given his light
To the full moon, it never would have been eclipsed.
Said I "all love for thee is in me", he would say:
"Loveliness is mine; the whole of beauty is in me."
For all the art of those who would describe his beauty,
Time shall run out, and never he be full described.[75]

It goes without saying that such passages as this may be taken to refer to the Prophet at every degree in the hierarchy of existence, cosmological,

[74] Although Muḥammad is after Jacob in time, his spirit is the starting-point of creation and therefore needs to be "remembered" by Jacob.

[75] *Mystical Poems*, VII, ll.38–42.

historical, etc., from the spirit of Muḥammad to the Arab of Abrahamic descent who brought the religion of Islam to mankind. On the other hand, it must not be forgotten that the spirit has an uncreated aspect which, as it were, opens on to the divinity. In some of these poems where the Prophet is addressed, the feelings expressed are so absolute and the dedication so total that the poet could scarcely be called a monotheist if the object in question were not conceived as being mysteriously identical with the divinity. But in all the poems, other than the five already noted, the Beloved is God in Himself, as indeed we might expect, for the poet has said, "Drink it pure", and has only accepted dilution as a second best. Moreover it is normal for the Sufis, as for every Muslim, to address God directly; and in Sufi love-poems, it is normal to refer to the divine essence (*dhāt*, a feminine word) by the name of a woman. I, therefore, can see no reason why we should suppose, as Arberry would have us do, that Nuᶜm in ode IX, for example, and the unnamed maiden in ode XIII represent the spirit of Muḥammad or indeed anything other than the divinity. This applies also, predominantly, to the "She" of his longest and most celebrated work, *Naẓm al-sulūk* ("Poem of the Way"). This poem is equally well known as *al-Tāʾiyyah al-kubrā* ("The Great *Tāʾiyyah*"), so-called to distinguish it from "The Lesser *Tāʾiyyah*", his shorter ode rhyming in *tāʾ*. About three-quarters of it were translated by Nicholson into prose in *Studies in Islamic Mysticism*, and the whole of it by Arberry into verse (*The Poem of the Way*). Its 761 lines of *ṭawīl* amount to 2,363 lines of Arberry's blank verse, which does not however mean that his translation is unduly wordy, since an average line of *ṭawīl* has twenty-eight syllables. The few passages translated below are done into blank alexandrines.

The poem differs in more than one way from Ibn al-Fāriḍ's other odes, and one of the main differences, its instructive intention, has already been noted at the beginning of this chapter. It would be a simplification to say that the poems of a mystic are written either for God or for men, the truth being that all are written for both; but it is none the less possible to speak of a predominance, and this poem sets out to be for the enlightenment of disciples. In consequence, it has none of those intimate complaints, for God's ear alone or for the ears of fellow-adepts, about the relative absences and severances that the fully realized mystic has to endure in this life within the framework of the great presence. The expressions of woe near the outset are those of one who has received only a fleeting foretaste of the not-yet-reached end, for the poem, as its title suggests, concerns the whole path. These sufferings are related objectively and as a thing of the past, but the manner of expression makes it clear that the experience, though incomplete, was none the less related to the Absolute:

Even as my lamenting tears was Noah's flood,
The blazing fires lit for God's Friend[76] were as my passion.
But for my sighs my weeping would have drownèd me;
But for my tears, my sighs had me to ashes burned,
All the distress of Jacob was my smallest woe,
And all the suffering of Job but part of mine.
Last agonies of those who loved and died of love
A fragment were of what as novice I endured.

But when the end is reached the final drunkenness is followed by a sobriety which is quite different from the loss of rapture referred to in the above lines. The poet says that he was able to embrace the object of vision and to retain that embrace and his effacement in it even in his subsequent sobriety. It is this retention of the essential which is the mystic's guarantee that the end has been reached. The stress of the poem is on this and on the total and absolute oneness of lover and Beloved. The fact that the earthly aspect of the mystic is not immune from fluctuations is implicitly admitted here and there, but it is never a matter for complaint, as it is in most of Ibn al-Fāriḍ's other poems. The following translation quotes lines 210–18 according to the manuscript of the poet's grandson; the order of the lines differs slightly in the manuscript used by Arberry:

Showing Herself, She showed forth Being to mine eye
So that I saw Her in my seeing's every sight.
Her showing made me witness mine own hidden deep:
There, once my secret was displayed, I found me Her.
So mine existence in my seeing vanishèd,
Seeing's existence I sloughed off, effacing it,
And I embraced the Object I did contemplate,
With seeing effaced in what it saw. This state I kept
For my sobriety after my drunkenness.
Thus once effaced, ev'n sober I am none but She:
Her shining forth my robing was of self with self.
Since that not two is, I must be described as She,
And Her appearance, since we are but one, is mine.
Thus I, if She be summoned, am the answerer,
And She my summoner answereth with "here am I",
And if She maketh utterance it is I that speak,
And She, whene'er I tell a tale, the teller is.
Gone from between us is the one-to-other's "Thou";
Gone, at its going, I from separation's sect.

The poem follows a somewhat undulating course, for there are backward glances, as one would expect from the title, to different stages upon the

[76] *Khalīl Allāh*: Abraham, the first Muslim, whose heathen enemies tried to destroy him by burning, Qurʾān, xxi.68–70; xxvii.97–8.

path. But such reminiscences are as a hand held back to the disciple, whose powers of conception are then quickly drawn forward once more to the finality, seen from a slightly different angle. Thus, for example, the last-quoted lines are followed by an assumption that the disciple has been prevented, by a secret polytheism, from fully understanding what is meant. He is told to abandon his belief in outward appearances, that is, in a multiplicity of separate entities:

From separation's error separate thyself,
Seek to be joined, reap joining's fruit, the guidance
Of that good company that vied for union.
Beauty is absolute: declare it; count it not
Relative, lured by glitter of some ornament.
Every fair youth, every fair maid their beauty have
On loan from Hers: She was it that Qays loved
In Lubnā,[77] every yearning lover loved but Her.

The poet goes on to mention some of the most famous lovers of Arab history as being all nothing other than manifestations of the divine beauty. The inevitable shortcomings of a translation are here increased by the fact that these lovers' names, melodious and charged with significance for the Arab, are unfamiliar to both ear and tongue of the English reader. We will however translate the concluding part of this superb passage:

In every guise to yearning lovers She appeared,
Arrayed in forms most marvellous in their loveliness.
Thus on a time by name of Lubnā She is called,
And now Buthaynah, now again the longed-for ʿAzzah.[78]
Other than She they are not, no, nor ever were,
For in Her beauty She without a sharer is.
Even so, as She in others unto me appeared,
Clad in their forms, so I, united with Her beauty,
Appeared to Her in every lover thralled by love
Of youth or maid of wonder-striking loveliness.
Although before me, other than I these lovers were not,
Since them I had preceded in the Eternal Nights.
Other than I men are not in their love for Her,
I manifest myself in them in every guise.
I have been Qays, then as Kuthayyir I was seen,
Then yet again I was Jamīl who loved Buthaynah,
Outwardly manifest in them, yet veiled by them –
O marvel how I show a thing by hiding it!
Beyond delusion, they and they, women and men,
Theophanies are, where love and beauty We display.

[77] Qays and Lubnā: a proverbial pair of lovers, cf. *CHALUP*, 421, 426.
[78] Buthaynah was the beloved of Jamīl, and ʿAzzah of Kuthayyir, see ibid., 421, 424–7.

Thus every loved one's man am I, She every man's
Belovèd, and each one a name is of disguise,
Names wherewith I the namèd was in very truth;
For I to Me appeared in them, with Self concealed.
I ever She am, and She I hath ever been –
No difference, but it was Myself that loved Myself,
And there is nothing with Me in the world but I,
No thoughts of with-ness trespass mine intelligence.

The poem as a whole might be described as an objective exposition of metaphysical doctrine inextricably combined with a profound and subtle disclosing of the secrets of the mystic path – a disclosing which convinces us that it is drawn from supreme personal experience. (In this connection it is perhaps worth mentioning that, according to an eyewitness, the poet's states of ecstasy would sometimes last for ten days or more, during which time he would remain motionless, without speaking, eating or drinking.)

Doctrinally the exposition would not be complete if there were no reference to the Logos, and in fact the spirit of Muḥammad subsequently figures in the poem in the way that is the norm for Sufi poetry and for Sufi doctrine, not as the Beloved but as the ideal lover, with whom the mystic must be identified before he can attain to union with the Beloved. It becomes subsequently clear that the oneness expressed in the last-quoted passage owes its absoluteness to the poet's identification with the highest aspect of the spirit, the uncreated aspect which opens on to the infinite.

Though Ibn al-Fāriḍ's verses are chanted by the Sufis at their sessions, they were not written specifically for this purpose, with the possible exception of one or two short poems. But his younger contemporary, Abū ʾl-Ḥasan ʿAlī b. ʿAbdullāh al-Shushtarī (d. 668/1268–9), was a singer and a musician as well as a poet, and he wrote most of his poems with a view to their being chanted. Like Ibn ʿArabī, Shushtarī was born and brought up in Andalusia, and like him also he went to North Africa, and finally to Egypt, Syria and Lebanon, with many pilgrimages to Mecca. He too was venerated as a saint in his lifetime, and is still considered as one of the great mystics of Islam, but his place of burial, near Damietta, has been lost sight of. He was a learned man, well versed in jurisprudence and other Islamic sciences. In particular he had a considerable knowledge of Sufi literature and was himself the author of several treatises, mainly on Sufism. Only three of these appear to have survived.[79] It was in Bijāyah (Bougie, now ʿAnnābah), Algeria, in 648/1248, that he met Ibn Sabʿīn,[80] whose disciple he became, and whose successor he was to be; and, although before and after this he

[79] See Shushtarī, *Dīwān*, 13–14.

[80] Sufi and Aristotelian; for this controversial but compelling figure, see EI², "Ibn Sabʿīn".

received teaching from other Sufis, especially from followers of Abū Madyan and Abū ʾl-Ḥasan al-Shādhilī,[81] Ibn Sabᶜīn must be considered as his chief and, as it were, central Shaykh. One day the master told his disciple to stroll through the market-place chanting: "With mention of the Beloved I begin, and life for me is good." For two days he wandered, chanting these words again and again, unable to add anything to them. On the third day however he made them the basis of a complete poem.[82] Since he was already thirty-six, this significant event probably did not mark the outset of his poetical career. His Shaykh may have simply wished to encourage or confirm a mode of spirituality which was already strongly developed in him. However that may be, his life from then on – though possibly also before – appears to have been a semi-nomadic one; and he would often chant his lyrics as he walked along or rode, sometimes accompanying himself on a stringed instrument. He would interrupt his travels with shorter or longer visits to Sufi *zāwiyahs*;[83] and sometimes in his later years, after the death of his Shaykh, whose successor he had become, he would camp at the outskirts of towns and villages with as many as 400 disciples. He also had contacts with Christian monks, who invited him to stay in their monasteries.

Ibn ᶜArabī is said to have been the first to write Sufi poetry in the form of the *muwashshaḥ* – the lyric in stanzas with a change of rhyme and sometimes a refrain; his *Dīwān* contains many examples. Shushtarī also wrote many *muwashshaḥāt*, and he was the first Sufi poet to write the *zajal* which differs from the *muwashshaḥ* only by being in colloquial Arabic. Many of his *azjāl* are borderline cases, verging on classical Arabic. Some others are in the broadest dialect. In the later part of his life his native Andalusian–Moroccan parlance became influenced by the spoken language of Egypt and Syria. He must have spent some earlier years in Meknes in Morocco, since one of his best known *azjāl* begins:

> A shaykhling from the land of Meknes
> In the market's midst is singing:
> What care I about the people?
> What care the people about me?[84]

These last two lines are repeated as a refrain throughout. The poems of Shushtarī became quickly known in both East and West, in Sufi circles and beyond them. According to Massignon this particular lyric was a source of inspiration for the Catalan mystic, Raymond Lull, who adapted it for a

[81] See EI², "Abū Madyan"; EI¹, "Shādhilīya", and p. 233, above.
[82] Shushtarī, *Dīwān*, 339; see also ibid., 9.
[83] A *zāwiyah*, literally "corner", is a place where the Sufis meet and where many of them live.
[84] Shushtarī, *Dīwān*, 272.

poem of his own.[85] Another very characteristic *zajal* begins, and has for refrain:

qūlu li ᵓl-faqīh ᶜannī
ᶜishqu dhā ᵓl-malīḥ fannī

Tell of me the man of law:[86]
Love for the Beautiful is my doctrine,[87]
My drinking with Him from the cup,
My presence in the midst of friends,
Wise friends who sit with me and take
All my cares away from me.
Tell of me the man of law . . . .[88]

Of all his poems, the one most often chanted at Sufi gatherings is no doubt the *muwashshaḥ* on the letters of the divine name, which begins: "*Alif* before double *lām* and *hāᵓ* [Allāh] – coolness of the eyes [delight]."[89]

Shushtarī had much admiration for his two great older contemporaries, Ibn ᶜArabī and Ibn al-Fāriḍ, and one of his best and most often-quoted *azjāl* recalls certain already quoted lines from "Poem of the Way", while being very different in style. It is here translated in full, in a rhythm close to that of the original:

Truly I am a wondrous thing
For him who sees me:
Lover and Beloved, both am I,
There is no second.
O seeker of the essential Truth,
Thine eye's film hides it.
Return unto thyself, take note:
None is but thee.
All good, all knowledge springs from thee;
In thee's the Secret.
Stored up in thee is what's poured forth
from all the vessels.
Hear my word and drink it in,
If thou canst grasp it:
Thy treasure naked is, not hid
Neath riddling spell.
There Speaker, Spoken-to[90] are on

[85] "Investigaciones", 30.
[86] The word *faqīh* denotes one who is an authority on all the more outward aspects of religion.
[87] Or "my art", "my expertise", "my occupation".
[88] Shushtarī, *Dīwān*, 276.
[89] Ibid., 243; French translation with commentary of Ibn ᶜAjībah, Michon, *Le Soufi marocain Aḥmad ibn ᶜAjîba*, 124–31.
[90] *Al-kalīm*: Moses, in the Qurᵓān the forerunner of Muḥammad and the only mortal to whom God has spoken "except by inspiration or from behind a veil" (Qurᵓān, xlii.50–1) or through an angelic intermediary: "He said, O Lord, shew me thy glory, that I may behold thee. God answered, Thou shalt in no wise behold me; but look towards the mountain, and if it stands firm in its place, then shalt

The mount of knowledge.
Hearken to my call from near,
Not with thine ears.
My self's sun setteth ne'er from vision
Face to face.
Behold my beauty, witness of me
In every man,
Like the water flowing through
The sap of branches.
One water drink they, yet they flower
In many hues.

In awe of Majesty prostrate thee
As thou approachest.
Perfection's verses, oft repeated,
Recite, the seven.[91]

Shushtarī also wrote classical Arabic odes (*qaṣāʾid*) in the traditional metres of Arabic poetry. One of the most celebrated of these reflects his visits to monasteries. In it he imagines himself asking the priest to give him the wine of the Eucharist to drink. On being refused he remonstrates and offers various gifts in exchange. Finally the priest agrees to barter the wine for his sacred mantle (*khirqah*, the mystic's coarse robe). But when offered the wine in a chalice he tells him that it is the reality he wants, not the symbol.[92]

Another of his odes is said to have been written in Libya after he had been called a madman for rejecting the post of *qāḍī* (judge) offered him by the authorities of Tripoli:

The slave to love well pleased is with his madness.
Let him wear out his life even as he will.
Reprove him not; your blame will nothing serve:
Forsaking love is not in his religion.

I swear by Him for whom ʿAqīq[93] was mentioned –
A lover's oath by his belovèd – none
But ye[94] are mine; yet have I to repent me
Remissnesses in loving, waveringness.

Why, when I hear the dove coo in the glade,
Why yearn I ever at his sorrowing?

thou see me. But when his Lord appeared in glory in the mount, he reduced it to dust . . . God said unto him, O Moses, I have chosen thee above all men . . . by speaking unto thee." Qurʾān, vii.143–4, trans. Sale, *The Korân*.

[91] i.e. *Sūrat al-Fātiḥah*, the first chapter of the Qurʾān; it has seven verses. Shushtarī, *Dīwān*, 267.

[92] Ibid., 59. The poem is modelled on secular narrative, *khamriyyāt*, cf. pp. 222, 231, above.

[93] A valley near Medina through which the route to Mecca passes. An angel told the Prophet that ʿAqīq was especially blessed by God. [94] See n. 42.

And though his way is weeping without tears,
When lover weeps, the tears pour from his eyes.[95]

In this summary survey of Sufi poetry in the ʿAbbasid period, literary interests have taken precedence over other considerations. Nonetheless, the passages quoted tell us not a little about Sufism itself; and they serve to demonstrate once again that the poetry of the mystics reveals certain aspects of their spirituality more clearly than any other source is capable of doing.

[95] Shushtarī, *Dīwān*, 77.

CHAPTER 15

ASCETIC POETRY (*ZUHDIYYĀT*)

PRECURSORS OF THE *ZUHDIYYAH*

"To renounce", "to withdraw", "to abstain from gratification" – these are the senses of the verb *zahada*. The verbal noun *zuhd* came in Islam to mean a life of self-denial and devotional exercises. The master-themes of the poems that medieval Arab anthologists and editors placed in the category of *zuhdiyyāt* are, accordingly, the cold look at the allurements of the world in which fortune is capricious and life frail, and the need for repentance before time runs out and the accounts are closed. Many *zuhdiyyāt* are built on motifs of the first kind alone, dwelling on mortality and the vanity of human wishes.

The literary history of many of these motifs goes back to the pre-Islamic age. This was obvious to the authors of medieval literary studies and *adab* works (treasuries of prose anecdote and verse, intended for the pleasant teaching of practical wisdom and polite culture). Verses on the inevitability of death, or the succession of feeble old age on vigorous youth, are quoted from pagans and Muslims alike in the *zuhd* chapters of such books as al-Jāḥiẓ's *Kitāb al-Bayān wa ʾl-tabyīn* or Ibn Qutaybah's *ʿUyūn al-akhbār*. Pagans and Muslims both used such motifs as premises, but to different results. Al-Jāḥiẓ, for example, quotes the pagan poet ʿAntarah: "I answered her: death is a watering stop where, no doubt, I will have to drink." This, a convention of the pre-Islamic poetry, is the warrior's reply to a scold who disapproves of his reckless ways with his money and his blood.[1] A man should take what pleasures he could, and stand his ground in battle, for only a good name escaped the general ruin: this was, on the pagan view, the sensible conclusion from the premise of mortality. Life, in pre-Islamic poetry, has its bitterness, but the world is not in any moral sense evil. The Muslim *zuhdiyyah* inherited but rethought the old preoccupation with death and mutability. The preoccupation itself became a pious exercise. In a tradition the Prophet is asked: "Who does most truly renounce the world?"

[1] *Bayān*, III, 183. For the stock figure of the scold, see ch. 16, n. 64, below.

He replies: "He who is ever mindful of decay in the tomb, who prizes the enduring above the transitory, and who numbers himself among the dead."

It is possible to observe the infusion, in early Islamic times, of new content into the old attitudes. Of the poems ascribed to Khārijī warriors – fierce puritans of the Umayyad age who loathed compromise with sin or politics and did not shrink from assassination to save the world, or martyrdom to save themselves – some are well in the pre-Islamic mould. A Khārijī leader, Qaṭarī b. al-Fujāʾah (d. *c.* 79/698), urges himself to be of good courage: "Soul, no entreaty will gain you as much as a day beyond the appointed term. Bear yourself with fortitude then in the arena of death..."[2] Some of these poems make new connections. In a piece attributed to ᶜImrān b. Ḥiṭṭān (d. 84/703), we find reflections on the approaching judgement and on the mind's frivolous attention to this life, then come to the argument, at once old and new: "Why does the soul crave this life in which, once it has lasted a while, death catches up with it?"[3] The world begins to turn malignant. Al-Ṭirimmāḥ b. Ḥakīm (d. *c.* 105/723) foresees, with the relish of a pagan warrior, that vultures will eat his flesh and that his disjointed bones will lie strewn over the desert, but his companions "are joined in the guidance of God", and "when they leave this world, it is an injurious thing they leave".[4]

The prehistory of the *zuhdiyyah* also includes a pre-Islamic poet of the sixth century who devoted entire poems to meditation on the fugitive nature of life and human achievement. This was ᶜAdī b. Zayd (d. *c.* 600 AD) a Christian Arab from al-Ḥīrah, the vassal principality near the Euphrates, who served the Persian emperors in various capacities at court and abroad, and who secured for Nuᶜmān III the succession to the Ḥīran throne. Nuᶜmān later had him imprisoned and eventually killed. The poems ᶜAdī is thought to have written in prison served in some respects as models for *zuhdiyyāt*. His poems speak of great men swept away like so many withered leaves, of palaces where the owl hoots and at dusk the reedpipe answers. He recalls the lord of the castle of al-Khawarnaq, the Sasanian king, Yazdigird I, who gazed on his possessions with delight and suddenly knew that there was no joy in a life that must come to death.[5] He recalls, too, a grimmer emblem of the strokes of fate: the blood-spattered braids of the pampered princess of al-Ḥaḍir, whom the Persian emperor Shāpūr, uneasy at the love that had prompted her betrayal to him of her father and her father's stronghold, had tied to a horse's tail and dragged to her death.[6] ᶜAdī's verse owes much to the rhetorical tradition of the homilies of the Eastern Church.

[2] See p. 188 for Nicholson's translation of this poem and pp. 148f, 186f on Kharijism and Khārijī poets.
[3] ᶜAbbās, *Shiᶜr al-Khawārij*, 39f.
[4] Ibn ᶜAbd Rabbih, *ᶜIqd*, III, 245.
[5] See *CHALUP*, 92, and Nicholson, *Literary History*, 40–1.
[6] ᶜAdī b. Zayd, *Dīwān*, nos. 16, 5.

As C. H. Becker has shown, his elaborations of the *ubi sunt* motif are reminiscent of ideas and phrases in the Syriac of Saint Ephraim and, farther back, the Greek of Cyril of Alexandria.[7] The melancholy "Where are they?" is repeated in many Islamic *zuhdiyyāt*.

The *zuhdiyyah*, however, is most profoundly rooted in the Qurʾān. The Qurʾān proclaims to people that they will die and live again to be judged. It summons to repentance and speaks of the evil end of those who prefer this world over the next. Its reports of peoples annihilated by the wrath of God give a cautionary air to the passing of the happy and the great: ". . . those before you, who were more powerful than you, and richer in possessions and in children. They enjoyed their portion and you have enjoyed yours . . ." (ix.69). Or: "Does it not give them guidance how many generations We have destroyed before them, in whose habitations they now walk?" (xx.129). The Qurʾān teaches that greed for the goods of this world goes with moral irresponsibility and a bad end: "Those who hoard up silver and gold and do not spend it in the way of God" will be branded in Hell with their own treasures (ix.34–5). "As for those who wish for the life of this world and its glitter, We will give them in this life the wages of their works in full, and they shall not be shortchanged in it. These are the ones who in the next world have nothing but fire" (xi.16–17). But, despite the stress on the transitory nature of this life, despite the ascetic mood of many passages, the Qurʾān, so the Muslim could feel, did not represent the world as an altogether evil place. The bloom, to be sure, withers:

This life may be likened to water We send down from heaven: the vegetation of the earth, that men and cattle eat, absorbs it, until when the earth has put on its finery and has been made beautiful, and its people think they have mastery over it, Our command comes to it, by night or day, and We leave it as cut grain, as if it had not flourished the day before. Thus We expound the signs for those who think. (x.25)

Nevertheless it is bloom:

The dead earth is a sign for them. We bring it back to life and bring forth grain from it, so that they may eat. We have placed in it gardens of datepalms and grapes, and caused springs to flow, so that they may eat of its fruits, although it is not of their hands' work. Will they not give thanks? (xxxvi.34–6)

The *zuhdiyyah*, as it emerges in the early Islamic age, tends to see in the bloom of this world only evil, a baited snare. In this it resembles the literature of pious admonition. By the time al-Ḥasan al-Baṣrī (d. 110/728) writes his famous epistle to the Umayyad caliph ʿUmar II, he not only advises the caliph to beware of the world, for life in it is short and full of reverses, but he can say:

[7] "Ubi sunt".

as I have been told, God has created nothing more hateful to Him than this world, and from the day He created it He has not looked upon it, so much He hates it. It was offered to our Prophet with all its keys and treasures and that would not have lessened him in God's sight by so much as the wing of a gnat, but he refused it.[8]

Ḥasan's bleak view of the world was shared by many pious Muslims of the age. Islam had always had room for asceticism; several of the Prophet's Companions are known for their self-denying ways. In the age of conquest and empire, when wealth and power were fiercely and often viciously pursued, and the wheel of fortune spun fast, many pious people saw no safety for their souls except in flight from the world. The *zuhdiyyah* is, by and large, a reflection of this mood.

EARLY DEVELOPMENT OF THE *ZUHDIYYAH*

The genre is not well-defined. It overlaps with gnomic verse (e.g., the two-line poem by Jarīr cited below)[9] and with poems of contemplation. For example, in a long poem by Ṣāliḥ b. ʿAbd al-Quddūs (executed 167/783–4),[10] which labels itself as *naṣīḥah* (sincere advice), the poet, conventionally spurned by a lady on account of his grey hair, resolves that it is time to give up the world, reminds himself of the Recording Angels and the impermanence of all things on earth, but then proceeds to blend *zuhd* with maxims of general piety and practical wisdom (on dealing with enemies, flatterers, etc.).[11] It does appear, however, that by the time of Abū ʾl-ʿAtāhiyah (d. *c.* 210/825) the poetry of *zuhd* was recognized as a distinct literary activity. According to an anecdote, this poet urged Abū Nuwās to stick to pleasure poetry and warned him off *zuhd*, which Abū ʾl-ʿAtāhiyah – the only major poet, in fact, who owes his fame to *zuhdiyyāt* – regarded as his private preserve. *Zuhdiyyāt* had of course been written before they were thought of as a genre. A poet of the Umayyad age, Sābiq b. ʿAbdullāh al-Barbarī (late first/early eighth century), is the earliest Muslim writer to whom a significant body of *zuhdiyyāt* is ascribed. One of these is a sermon in verse, said to have been addressed to the pious caliph ʿUmar II.[12]

Two important figures in the early history of the *zuhdiyyah* – Ṣāliḥ b. ʿAbd al-Quddūs and Abū ʾl-ʿAtāhiyah – were suspected of tainted religious beliefs. Abū ʾl-ʿAtāhiyah is reported to have incorporated Manichaean tenets into his Islam, and Ṣāliḥ ibn ʿAbd al-Quddūs was executed on the charge of Manichaeism.[13] Their poems offer no evidence for these charges, which may have been slanderous. There is a chance, however, that

[8] Trans. Arberry, *Sufism*, 33f. [9] Cf. *CHALUP*, 90–3. [10] Cf. p. 195.
[11] Khaṭīb, *Ṣāliḥ b. ʿAbd al-Quddūs*, 123–7. [12] Kannūn, *Sābiq al-Barbarī*, 6–8.
[13] See ch. 11, n. 33, and Vajda, "Les zindiqs".

Manichaean notions about the evil nature of this world and of the accumulation of wealth were channelled into the poetry of these men, or perhaps that their *zuhdiyyāt* were directed against a worldly social order that retaliated by calling into question the purity of its critics' faith. On the other hand, it is clear that, if the story of his warning to Abū Nuwās is genuine, Abū ᵓl-ᶜAtāhiyah's gloomy ascetic preaching, much respected by the common people of Baghdad, was at least in part a deliberately chosen literary attitude and, if the poetry attributed to Sābiq al-Barbarī is genuine, some of Abū ᵓl-ᶜAtāhiyah's verses owe more to convention, and less to particular circumstances, than has sometimes been argued.[14] In any event, once the *zuhdiyyah* had become a distinct type of poem with its own conventions, a poet might determine to write one just to try his hand at it. There is no textual evidence for deciding whether particular *zuhdiyyāt* by Abū Nuwās, for example, are flourishes of poetic versatility, or expressions of religious anguish from a man better known for his devotion to the senses.

There is no question about the authenticity of the voice of a much greater poet than Abū ᵓl-ᶜAtāhiyah: Abū ᵓl-ᶜAlāᵓ al-Maᶜarrī (363–449/973–1058). Acknowledgment of a divinely ordained fate, puzzlement at the meaning of life, and despair of all happiness shape this poet's work. It uses many motifs common in *zuhdiyyāt*, but, contemplative rather than homiletic – thinking of death, for one thing, more as a source of release than a passage to dreadful judgement – it does not readily fit into the *zuhd* category. Many historians of literature have, however, stretched the limits of the *zuhdiyyah* to include Maᶜarrī's pessimistic verse.

CHARACTERISTICS OF THE GENRE

On the whole, *zuhdiyyāt* tend to be extremely conventional in theme and simple in language. Links in form and substance to sermons and homiletic writings, and perhaps a feeling that pomp of any sort was ill-suited to the subject, account for this. There are frequent echoes of phrases from Qurᵓān and *ḥadīth*. In construction, *zuhdiyyāt* range from strings of pious maxims, through simple sequences of argument, to pointed epigrams. Al-Jāḥiẓ remarked that poems of the first type – he refers to the works of Sābiq al-Barbarī and Ṣāliḥ b. ᶜAbd al-Quddūs – did not, despite the excellence of the individual verses, create a forceful effect.[15]

Since the conventions of the *zuhdiyyah* do not change much with time, its chief motifs may be illustrated without reference to chronology. The old

[14] E.g. by Kafrawy and Latham, "Perspective". [15] *Bayān*, I, 206.

cry, "Where have they all gone?", is much heard. "Where are the kings who never heeded their true concern until the cup of death was passed to them?" asks Sābiq al-Barbarī.[16] The living should contemplate the dead: "Those that are gone are a lesson to us as we shall be a lesson to ponder tomorrow."[17] "The silent graves have admonished you; your death has been announced by speechless ages."[18] Earthly glory is vanity: "How many haughty, ambitious kings, wearers of crowns, who burned for war, who reclined on silk brocades, secluded in royal pavilions, have been left by death – stripped of their arms, hurled to the ground, their faces strewn with dust . . ."[19] Abū Nuwās casts an ironic glance at the boast of noble origins: "Every living man is mortal, the son of a mortal. Every last one is descended from a long line of purebred mortals."[20] "You who are proud of your share of this world and its splendour," Abū ʾl-ʿAtāhiyah exclaims, "there is no cause for pride in exalting clay with clay." Human endeavour would strike us as altogether derisory if we did not insist on ignoring our state: "Man strives for glory while giving off the stench of decay."[21]

Mortality is made the more bitter by the casual speed with which bonds of feeling, once all-important, are cast off: "People will turn from my memory. Their love for me will be forgotten; I will be dead and my friends will find new friends." The living have more urgent concerns than to think of the dead: "They have grown tired of weeping; no more tears will be shed for you. Gossip about the estate is so much more absorbing!"[22] If mortality makes human striving laughable or pitiful, fate – which in Islamic poetry means the divine will – makes it foolish. There might be, in early Islamic times, intellectual debates about whether the moral choices of men are determined by God. There might be *ḥadīth* and proverbs in support of the view that God helps those who help themselves. In popular piety there was no question but that God foreordains whether a man will live or die, whether he will be rich or destitute. "Seeking his fortune," al-Maʿarrī writes, "man strives with sword and spear, mounted on horse or camel. If he stayed put, he would still receive the much or little that fate has allotted him."[23] Such striving implies an element of distrust in God. A minor *zuhd*-poet, Maḥmūd al-Warrāq (d. early third/mid-ninth century) writes: "Is it not odd that when a man offers himself as guarantor for another, the claimant accepts him, but when God, who keeps His promises, offers his guarantee, man is not content?"[24] *Tawakkul* (trust in God) was a master concept of early Muslim asceticism and mysticism. In its extreme form, it

[16] Kannūn, *Sābiq al-Barbarī*, 5.
[17] Abū Nuwās, *Dīwān*, ed. Wagner, II, 165.
[18] Abū ʾl-ʿAtāhiyah, *Ashʿāruh*, 78.
[19] Kannūn, *Sābiq al-Barbarī*, 7.
[20] *Dīwān*, ed. Wagner, II, 159.
[21] *Ashʿāruh*, 392, 222.
[22] Ibid., 317, 310.
[23] *Luzūm mā lā yalzam*, IV, 79.
[24] *Dīwān*, 42.

could mean the dismissal of all concern in one's livelihood (a sound conclusion, but hard on society, and, indeed, there are traditions in which the Prophet censures this degree of *tawakkul*). It could mean limiting oneself to mere sufficiency. Thus, in an anecdote, when two men of great piety discuss which manner of life is best for man, one wishes for a plot of land that will just free him of dependence on others; the other calls that man happy who finds his breakfast without knowing how he will eat in the evening. Abū ʾl-ʿAtāhiyah writes: "If you look for the man most worthy of honour, look for the king in beggar's clothes." But the less extreme view is also represented: "He who is not satisfied with mere sufficiency (*kafāf*) will find the whole world, spacious as it is, too narrow."[25]

Trust in God will lead a man to slough off ambition, but contemplation of this world may do so as well. A quiet life spares one the misfortunes of the great. One should not be like one whom "his appetites lead without a halter; whom you see now on a cushioned saddle, now naked under the whip", warns Ibn ʿAbd Rabbih (d. 328/940).[26] A contemporary of Abū ʾl-ʿAtāhiyah, al-ʿAttābī, recalls the famous, fallen favourites of Hārūn al-Rashīd, the Barmecides: "This woman of Bāhilah [the stock figure of the scold, referred to at the beginning of this chapter] rebukes me for indifference to wealth ... All around her she sees women flouncing about in fine clothes, their necks clasped with necklaces. / Would it please you to think that I came to Jaʿfar's and Yaḥyā's fate? ... / Let my death, when it comes, be tranquil; I would not seek such horrors."[27]

By and large, however, love of this world is incurable. Oddly so: "A man, if he serves others ill, draws their hatred on himself. The world ever hurts us, yet keeps our passionate love."[28] The warnings of religion and the wisdom of experience are alike lost on most people, for whom the real object of worship is money: "People make a show of religion, but their Kaʿbah is the dinar."[29] Corrupt and corrupting, people are best left alone: "Be content with God for a companion, and turn your back on mankind. / Look at them closely from every side – you will find people so many scorpions."[30] Or: "Be humble towards God, not your fellow men. Be content with giving up worldly hope – that is where nobility lies. / Learn to do without kin and connections – he is wealthy who can do without others."[31] This melancholy view of mankind also has parallels in the prose writings of pious ascetics: "Beware of the people of thy time: it is not good to live with any that men today think well of, nor with any they think ill of

[25] Goldziher, *Introduction*, 122; Abū ʾl-ʿAtāhiyah, *Ashʿāruh*, 392, 54. [26] ʿ*Iqd*, III, 202.
[27] Cited ibid., 208. [28] Maʿarrī, *Luzūm mā lā yalzam*, III, 193. [29] Maḥmūd al-Warrāq, *Dīwān*, 72.
[30] Ibn ʿAbd Rabbih, ʿ*Iqd*, III, 213, attrib. Ibrāhīm b. Adham, an early Sufi.
[31] Ibn Abī Ḥāzim, cited ʿ*Iqd*, III, 207.

either. It is better to die alone, then to live . . . If thou givest them power over thee, they will incite thee to sin, and if thou avoidest them, they will lay a snare for thee," writes Bishr b. al-Ḥārith (d. 227/841).[32]

The heedlessness of man is an all-important religious theme. The Qurʾān repeatedly warns those for whom death and judgement are out of mind while out of sight: "Those who took their religion for a frivolous game, those whom life in the lower world deluded – today We shall forget them just as they forgot that they would come to this Day" (vii.52). The deluded sinner is lulled by a complacent belief in his safety: "Are the people of the towns secure from the calamity We may send upon them by night as they sleep? Are the people of the towns secure from the calamity We may send upon them in the daytime while they are at play? Are they secure from God's stratagem? No one believes himself to be secure from God's stratagem except those who are to perish" (vii.98–100). There is no time to procrastinate; punishment catches up suddenly with the sinner: "We seized them all at once, before they knew what was happening to them" (vii.96). These matters – the forgetfulness, the perverse feeling of security – are among the dominant themes in homiletic literature, and in the *zuhdiyyah* as well. Worldly desires shut man's eyes to reality: "You rejoice in what passes away and delight in wishes, as a dreamer is fooled by the pleasures he dreams."[33] "People are heedless, while the mill of death grinds."[34] "Funeral processions strike fear into us as they approach, but once they are past, we are soon distracted. / We are like a grazing herd that takes fright when a wild beast attacks, and again falls to grazing when it is gone."[35] "He who feels safe from the world is like one who would hold a fistful of water and is betrayed by the spaces between his fingers." "Many a man goes to bed and gets up in the morning thinking himself safe when his shroud has already been woven."[36] The deceptive hopes of earthly happiness and longlife may be personified: "Hopes frequent him, till at length they lay him in the dust next to all the others they have made their prey."[37] So too may death: "How long will you trifle and play, while death, its mouth gaping, is leaping to seize you?"[38]

Already ʿAdī b. Zayd had used travel and the call to make ready to depart as metaphors of mortality. These metaphors become Islamic. In Abū ʾl-ʿAtāhiyah's verse, "The crier of mortality calls; take your provisions and tie on the saddles!" "provisions" (*zād*) means, of course, fear of God and good

32 Arberry, *Sufism*, 40f. 33 Attrib. ʿUmar II; cited Ibn Qutaybah, *ʿUyūn al-akhbār*, II, 309.
34 Abū ʾl-ʿAtāhiyah, *Ashʿāruh*, 381.
35 Jarīr (d. *c*. 112/730; see *CHALUP*, 401–13), quoted Ibn ʿAbd Rabbih, *ʿIqd*, III, 186.
36 Anon., ibid., 177, 199. 37 Ibn al-Muʿtazz, *Dīwān*, 264.
38 Abū ʾl-ʿAtāhiyah, *Ashʿāruh*, 419.

works (cf. Qurʾān, ii.197).[39] Paraphrasing a *ḥadīth* about those who at the age of forty have not repented, a poet writes: "When Iblīs [the devil] glimpses his face, he salutes him and says: 'How dear to me is a man whose soul will never prosper'."[40] In one *zuhdiyyah*, fragmentary syntax reminds the reader of the uncertainty of life and the abrupt stroke of death: "Be with God, He will be for you. / Fear God, perhaps you . . . / Make sure you are prepared to die, as if you . . ."[41] Indeed, one should regard oneself as already dead: "If you must wail for anyone, wail for yourself." "It is as if the earth had already closed over me and I had been taken from my possessions."[42]

Finally, the *zuhdiyyah* deals with the emotions with which man looks to the Last Judgement: fear, and hope in God's mercy. The former predominates, as pious self-awareness acknowledges that it should. As Ḥasan al-Baṣrī is reported to have said: "Fear should be stronger than hope, for when hope has the upper hand, the heart is corrupted." The twin emotions of fear and hope are summed up in a *ḥadīth*: "God has prohibited hellfire from touching anyone who weeps for fear of God."[42a] Maḥmūd al-Warrāq reminds the reader of the other side of the coin: "You commit sin after sin, but hope to enter Paradise and obtain the reward of the pious. / You have forgotten that God cast Adam out of Paradise and into the world for a single sin."[43] If judgement were a matter of justice untempered by mercy, the result would be sad indeed: "Alas for us who will stand in a court where nothing can be more terrifying than that the judge should act justly!"[44] For that day in court, the only preparation is repentance: "Let others bring excuses and arguments before you. My excuse is the confession that I have none."[45] Each theme of the *zuhdiyyah* implies the fearful judgement and urges repentance. But hope is not abandoned: "O you whose sins are great! God's mercy is greater."[46] In a descriptive poem, Ibn al-Rūmī (d. *c.* 283/896) speaks of ascetics "between fear and hope" who, with tears streaming from their eyes, call upon God to forgive their sins: "And they were answered, by a voice heard in no human ear: 'What you do, my holy ones (*awliyāʾī*) does not go to waste. Give up your souls to me; they will be in my safe-keeping'."[47] Eschatological elements are used less than one might expect, but we do hear of the Book, the Scales, the Fire, "the Bridge from whose knife's-edge, those who fall, fall to lasting ignominy and pain".[48] A less-common form of eschatological prompting is offered by Abū Nuwās: "Raise your eyes to the women whose bride-price is paid in

39 Ibid., 41. 40 Cited Ibn ʿAbd Rabbih, *ʿIqd*, III, 185.
41 Maḥmūd al-Warrāq, *Dīwān*, 100 (sometimes attrib. Abū Nuwās).
42 Abū ʾl-ʿAtāhiyah, *Ashʿāruh*, 99, 442. 42a Cited *ʿIqd*, III, 178, 199. 43 *Dīwān*, 61.
44 Ibn ʿAbd Rabbih, *ʿIqd*, III, 182. 45 Abū Nuwās, *Dīwān*, ed. Ghazālī, 579.
46 *Dīwān*, ed. Wagner, II, 166. 47 *Dīwān*, IV, 1482. 48 Abū ʾl-ʿAtāhiyah, *Ashʿāruh*, 30.

good works. The black-eyed houri is displayed only before the man whose scales tip in his favour."[49]

Perhaps the *zuhdiyyah* probes most deeply when it questions the speaker's own steadiness of purpose. Already Sābiq al-Barbarī knows the problem: "If only the thought of the lasting world kept my eyes from sleep as much as this fleeting world does!"[50] So too does Abū ᵓl-ᶜAtāhiyah: "I have renounced the world, and yet crave it."[51]

[49] *Dīwān*, ed. Wagner, II, 158. [50] Kannūn, *Sābiq al-Barbarī*, 7. [51] *Ashᶜāruh*, 71.

CHAPTER 16

BASHSHĀR B. BURD, ABŪ ʾL-ʿATĀHIYAH AND ABŪ NUWĀS

Abū Muʿādh Bashshār b. Burd al-Muraʿʿath (*c.* 95–167/*c.* 714–83), Abū Isḥāq Ismāʿīl b. al-Qāsim, nicknamed Abū ʾl-ʿAtāhiyah (130–*c.* 210/748–*c.* 825) and al-Ḥasan b. Hāniʾ al-Ḥakamī, known as Abū Nuwās (*c.* 140–200/*c.* 757–815) are among the earliest and most important representatives of a group of poets whom medieval Arab critics describe as "moderns" (*muḥdathūn*). In this context, "modern" simply means that these poets belong to the "modern", that is ʿAbbasid, period, or, to be precise, that their poetic activity falls mainly within this period. However, these three poets can be grouped together not only because they lived at much the same time, but also because they came from the same region and belonged to the same ethnic stock or to the same social class. All three were from Iraq or the neighbouring part of Persia: Bashshār from Basra, Abū ʾl-ʿAtāhiyah either from Kufa or ʿAyn al-Tamr, and Abū Nuwās from a village near Ahwāz. The first two passed the formative years of their lives in their native towns; Abū Nuwās spent his youth first in Basra, then in Kufa. All three poets were decisively influenced by the social and cultural life of Basra or Kufa respectively before they came into contact with the newly founded capital of the ʿAbbasid empire, Baghdad, and its court. Abū ʾl-ʿAtāhiyah and Abū Nuwās settled permanently in the new centre; it is not quite clear whether Bashshār did so too, although we often find him there, and for extended periods. Bashshār died near Basra, Abū ʾl-ʿAtāhiyah and Abū Nuwās in Baghdad. None of the three poets was of Arab stock; all three were Persians or of Persian descent. They were clients (*mawālī*, sing. *mawlā*), standing under the protection (*walāʾ*) of an Arab bedouin tribe; for the inhabitants of the garrison towns in Iraq consisted mainly of two groups, pure Arabs on the one hand (bedouin settlers of north or south Arabian origin), and their clients, mostly of Persian origin, on the other. We shall see that the time at which the three poets lived, where they lived, and their ethnic or class affinities are of decisive importance for an understanding of their art.

BASHSHĀR B. BURD

Bashshār b. Burd, the eldest of the three poets, was born blind (and his biographers state that he was also exceptionally ugly). Doubt has always been cast on his religious orthodoxy, but his *Dīwān* contains no evidence that he in fact had leanings towards *zandaqah* (a blanket-term used for Manichaeism or suspect orthodoxy), a charge sometimes brought against him. However, Bashshār was certainly a Shuᶜūbī: in his poems he very frequently plays off the glorious past of the Persians against the bedouins' alleged lack of culture. He died at the age of nearly seventy, after the caliph al-Mahdī had ordered him to be flogged, apparently in retaliation for a lampoon which Bashshār had composed against him.

Bashshār had already distinguished himself as a poet in the time of the Umayyads; for this reason some Arab critics classify him as "straddling both dynasties" (*mukhaḍram al-dawlatayn*); many consider him the first modern poet: Bashshār, says the literary theorist Ibn Rashīq (390–*c.* 456/1000–*c.* 1063), "has been compared to Imruᵓ al-Qays, because he was the most outstanding (and earliest) of those poets who are not of pure Arabian blood (*li-taqaddumih ᶜalā ᵓl-muwalladīn*) – just as Imruᵓ al-Qays was the most outstanding Arab poet – and because they borrowed from him; Bashshār is called the Father of the Moderns".[1]

It is sometimes claimed that it was an achievement of the moderns to have introduced new genres into Arabic poetry; they started a process, so it is said, which can be described as the splitting up of the old Arabic *qaṣīdah*, cultivating for the first time in independent forms and more extensively themes such as love, drinking and hunting that had earlier been treated predominantly in the context of the larger unit, the polythematic ode. However, this is true neither of Bashshār nor of other early moderns; in Bashshār's case in particular it can be shown that, on the whole, the poet took over and developed further the genres that had traditionally been cultivated in his time and in his city.

Madīḥ (eulogy)

The long praise-poem or panegyric *qaṣīdah* was able to preserve its importance and popularity in Basra principally because there were governors in the city who modelled their courts on those of the Umayyads of Damascus or the ᶜAbbasids of Baghdad, and one of the main aspects of courtly ceremonial was the glorification of the ruler by the recitation of

[1] Ibn Rashīq, *ᶜUmdah*, I, 131.

panegyrics at the Great Audience (*majlis ᶜāmm*). Striking innovations in this genre cannot be expected from Bashshār, for in public poetry the poet must always conform to the taste of the addressee; and the dominant political powers operated, as in all traditionalist milieux, not only towards maintaining the political status quo, but also towards preserving with as few changes as possible the traditional artistic forms. However, other factors must also be taken into account to explain why *madīḥ*, and the other "classical" genres, retained more or less their traditional outline in the Basra of Bashshār's time. One of the most important of these may well have been the activity of the philologists who at this time, in Basra and Kufa, were systematically collecting and editing the poems of pre-Islamic and early Islamic poets from oral transmitters (*ruwāh*, sing. *rāwī*), or from written versions made by these same transmitters, thus favouring a revival of the old Arabic *qaṣīdah*. Another factor may have been the influence of the two famous "classical" (*faḥl*) poets of the Umayyad period, Jarīr (d. *c.* 112/730) and al-Farazdaq (d. *c.* 110/728),[2] who frequently stayed in Basra and published some of their most famous poems there.

Bashshār addressed his panegyrics to the Umayyad and ᶜAbbasid governors of Basra; he also celebrated princes and caliphs, including the last Umayyad, Marwān, and the ᶜAbbasid, al-Mahdī. In form, most of his *qaṣīdah*s are traditional (i.e. they consist of two or three sections) or variations on tradition; the example given below, addressed to Marwān, is eighty-five lines long in the original and has the following succession of themes, which may be compared with the scheme outlined by the theorist Ibn Qutaybah (213–76/828–89):[3] amatory prelude (*nasīb*), lines 1–6; gnomic aphorisms (*ḥikmah*), lines 7–10; description of a night-ride through the desert (*raḥīl*), lines 11–14; praise (*madīḥ*) of the Qays ᶜAylān tribe, to which the poet was attached as a client and to which the caliph Marwān was indebted for a decisive victory (the passage includes a description of the battle); eulogy of the caliph.[4] This *qaṣīdah* also conforms to the "rules" in so far as the *raḥīl* has a bedouin background, while in the *nasīb*, adopting an innovation used by such Umayyad poets as Dhū ᵓl-Rummah, Bashshār refers, not to a fictitious bedouin maiden, but to his beloved, ᶜAbdah, to whom he dedicated the major part of his love-poems. The following is a translation of the first three sections of the poem:

[2] *CHALUP*, 401–13.

[3] Amatory prelude, designed to catch the attention of the listeners; description, to the addressee, of the hardships the poet has passed through to reach him; praise of the addressee and request for generous recompense, *Introduction au Livre de la poésie*, 13–14; cf. p. 343 below. On the validity of Ibn Qutaybah's description of the *qaṣīdah*, see Jacobi, "The camel-section of the panegyrical ode".

[4] For examples of how Bashshār adapts such "classical" patterns to new encomiastic themes, see Meisami, "Uses of the *qaṣīda*".

Have springs of kindness dried, its course gone crooked, or is the partner [i.e. the poet] tedious and scorned, to be so chidden still?
My friends, do not deny love's sting, do not refuse a smitten, sorrowful heart its consolation:
Soul's cure is sight of ʿAbdah, and the healing that my spirit used to find;
But stout heart is now subdued – it's touch of love that brings me low with its assaults.

If your brother is an oft-taster of passion, the steeds of his inclinations hither and thither turned,
Then leave open for him the way of parting, and do not be the mount of a rider whose goings are all too frequent.
Your true friend is he who, when you give him cause for suspicion, says, "It was I that did so" and when you upbraid him receives it mildly.
If you are inclined to reproach your friend for everything, you'll never find anyone whom you never have cause to reproach.
So live in solitude, or be at amity with your brother; sometimes he may avoid a fault, but sometimes cling to it:
If you do not at times drink a bitter cup and endure it, you must go thirsty; what man is there whose drink is always limpid?

Many's the gloomy night (when boys and girls sleep through its dreariness, and the whole household too)
I have denied the boon of sleep to eyes of self and steed until the troops of darkness dispersed;
Often at a water-hole with sandgrouse feather floating there,[5] a hidden well, its markstones unseen,
Bordering the trackless waste, far from men's homes – there has my hard night's travelling brought me to drink . . .[6]

Hijāʾ (lampoon)

Bashshār's lampoons are also constructed in a traditional way. The lampoon had always had two possible forms: it could be a short, often improvised, occasional poem, or it could be a long *qaṣīdah* the formal structure of which had more or less adapted itself to that of the panegyric *qaṣīdah*. In the Umayyad period the traditional lampoon had remained alive thanks especially to the rivalries that were always liable to break out between the Arabian tribes;[7] it throve particularly in Basra, where Jarīr and al-Farazdaq, surrounded by a large audience, used to settle their literary feuds on the Mirbad, the famous caravan-halt by the city gate. Their polemic poems (*naqāʾiḍ*) are often complex in structure; besides the amatory

[5] I.e. at earliest dawn: the sandgrouse, proverbially early risers, have only just left the water-hole.

[6] *Dīwān*, I, 306–23; trans. A. F. L. Beeston (hereafter A.F.L.B.). With the exception of the panegyric poem on p. 296, this and all other translations in this chapter have been supplied by the editors; their interpretations do not necessarily reflect those of the author of this chapter.

[7] Cf. *CHALUP*, 409–13.

prelude (often omitted by al-Farazdaq) and lampoon proper, they frequently contain self-praise (*fakhr*) and the eulogy of a patron. In his multi-part lampoons, Bashshār continues the tradition of Jarīr and al-Farazdaq, whom he had heard in the flesh. An abusive poem of thirty-seven lines on his fellow-poet Ḥammād ʿAjrad is constructed as follows: amatory prelude; eulogy of an unnamed comrade; lampoon on Ḥammād:

O Salmā, will your guardian tarry;
  if I hasten, will you stay?
My love is utter and complete;
  reverses make my ardour grow:
O Salmā! Passion's laid me low
  in weariness of piercing-glancing blows . . .
I have a comrade like a sword in hand –
  vainly to gild it might its maker seek –
Who is the death of every mortal care,
  whose goodness is a charter for abuse,
Who does not worship lucre, but pursues
  the foe unflaggingly, unswervingly,
Who's been with me through wealth and pauperdom,
  his love for me untinctured, unforsworn . . .
But ʿAjrad the Flasher jumps on his mother –
  a sow giving suck to a hog –
Though any appeal to his purse is met
  with a leonine baring of fangs.
What good to anyone is a man
  who won't even pray, the scum?
You son of a rutting beast, you are
  a pustulous, foul, filthy bum! . . .[8]

Fakhr (self-praise)

Bashshār also follows his predecessors in the formal structure of his poems of self-praise, often combining it with lampoon in one poem. Thus he casts the following *fakhr*-poem in the form of a message, as the old Arab poets frequently did, though the content of the message is anything but Arabian: addressing all the Arabs, Bashshār makes known to them the fame of the old Persian rulers, whose descendant he proclaims himself, while at the same time pouring ridicule on the bedouin and their primitive mode of life:

Is there a messenger who will carry my message to all the Arabs,
To him among them who is alive and to him that lies hid in dust?
To say that I am a man of lineage, lofty above any other one of lineage:
The grandfather in whom I glory was Chosroes, and Sāsān was my father,

[8] *Dīwān*, II, 61–9; trans. J. Ashtiany (hereafter J.A.).

Caesar was my uncle, if ever you reckon my ancestry.
How many, how many a forebear I have whose brow was encircled by his diadem,
Haughty in his court, to whom knees were bowed,
Coming in the morning to his court, clothed in blazing gems,
Splendidly attired in ermine, standing within curtains,[9]
The servitors hastening to him with golden vessels:
He was not given to drink the thin milk of goatskins, or to sup it in leather vessels;
Never did my father sing a camel-song, trailing along behind a scabby camel,
Nor approach the colocynth, to pierce it for very hunger,
Nor the mimosa, to beat down its fruits with a stave;[10]
Nor did we roast a skink, with its quivering tail,
Nor did I dig for and eat the lizard of the stony ground,[11]
Nor did my father warm himself standing astraddle a flame;[12]
No, nor did my father use to ride the twin supports of a camel-saddle.
We are kings, who have always been so through long ages past;
We brought the horsemen from Balkh, with no lie,
Until we watered them (for we are not to be taken by surprise by the enemy) in the twin streams[13] of Aleppo;
Then, when they had trampled on the hard earth of Syria,
We marched them to Egypt, in a noisy host,
Seizing that realm in place of our own, plundered realm,
And the horses brought us past Tangier, place of wonder,
So that we restored the sovereignty into the family of the Arabian Prophet.[14]
Who is there that has fought against guidance and religion without being stripped?
Who, O who, has rebelled against it without being plundered?
For the sake of God and Islam we are wrathful with a most noble wrath;
We are the possessors of crowns and of disdainful, stiff-necked kingship.[15]

Ghazal (love poetry)

We must now turn to the genre in which Bashshār produced perhaps his best work and which makes up a large part of his *Dīwān*, love poetry. Some Arab critics distinguish two classes of poetic genres, one serving public, the other private purposes. While in genres of the first class – eulogy, "official" lampoons, elegy (*rithāʾ*), etc. – poets were bound by more or less strict rules, in genres of the second class – love poetry, drinking-poems (*khamriyyāt*),

[9] I.e. veiled from the vulgar gaze.
[10] Both colocynth and mimosa are extremely bitter fruits.
[11] The bedouin relish for foods viewed by their more cultured neighbours as disgusting was a standard theme of anti-Arab abuse, cf. pp. 46, 88, 108.
[12] An indecent posture in anyone wearing the short bedouin kilt.
[13] Poetic licence.
[14] Bashshār claims that the Iranians, not the Arabs, are the true upholders of Islam; he credits them with overthrowing the Umayyads of Syria and giving the caliphate to the ʿAbbasids, the "family of the Prophet". The reference to Tangier is probably hyperbolic.
[15] *Dīwān*, I, 377–80; trans. A.F.L.B.

etc. – they were fairly free. We may therefore expect Bashshār's love-poems to differ perceptibly from the poems belonging to the genres so far discussed.[16] In the Jāhiliyyah, independent love-poems scarcely existed; the subject was dealt with almost exclusively in the *nasīb* of the *qaṣīdah*. In the Umayyad period or even earlier the *nasīb* developed into the independent love-poem (*ghazal*),[17] but also continued to function as a prelude to the various types of *qaṣīdah*, a tradition continued by Bashshār and illustrated in the first two poems quoted in this chapter. Apart from these *qaṣīdah*-preludes, in the Umayyad period, three different trends or kinds of love poetry can be distinguished, though, since they rarely occur in their "pure" form, the following categories should be regarded as ideal types.[18] The Hijazi *ghazal*, best exemplified in the work of ʿUmar b. Abī Rabīʿah, usually presupposes an urban background, though bedouin reminiscences are still very frequent; it is written in simple language, recounts gallant adventures and reproduces conversations and correspondence between the lover and his beloved. The lover is a seducer and irresistible breaker of hearts, while the maiden – who is always a free-born woman – is compliant, although capricious and jealous. The ʿUdhrī *ghazal*, associated with such poets as Jamīl, is, on the other hand, still set against a bedouin background; it sings of a love that may have begun even before birth and lasts until death or beyond, a love that makes the lover ill, sometimes drives him mad, and inevitably leads to his death. The lover subjects himself to the beloved and humbles himself before her; she is a bedouin maiden of noble birth who marries another man and appears, through the worship given to her by the poet, in a stylized form already suggesting the Lady of the Provençal troubadours. These first two *ghazal* types are well-known and have been discussed at some length in chapters 9 and 12, but the existence of a third type, the Kufan *ghazal*, is generally overlooked.[19] The Kufan *ghazal* is decidedly more urban than the Hijazi variety. It reflects the interests and activities of certain elements of Kufan society which would today be described as bohemian. Here we find for the first time independent poems on female slaves,[20] often singers, whose charms are described in detail, and also poems on boys. Unlike the other two types of *ghazal*, the Kufan love-poem is often obscene: *ghazal* becomes *mujūniyyah* (licentious verse). Alongside love poetry, and often connected with it, the drinking-song – a poetic genre only poorly represented in the cities of the Hijaz and among ʿUdhrī poets – flourished in Kufa. This was certainly due to the influence of

[16] For the relationship between Bashshār's "public" and "private" verse, see Beeston, *Selections*, 3–4.
[17] See Jacobi, "Die Anfänge der arabischen Ġazalpoesie".
[18] Cf. the typology recently established ibid., 226.
[19] It was first noted by Nallino, *La Littérature arabe*, 85–6, 223–31.
[20] For earlier descriptions of singing slave-girls in the context of the *qaṣīdah*, see *CHALUP*, 438–9.

the city of al-Ḥīrah, only a few miles distant from Kufa, where the wine-trade and drinking-songs already flourished in pre-Islamic times.

It should be emphasized once again that Hijazi, ᶜUdhrī and Kufan love poetry – especially the first two – frequently overlap in their motifs. In addition it should be noted that some scholars are inclined to regard ᶜUdhrism as a later phenomenon projected back into the work of the nevertheless by and large historical ᶜUdhrī poets, in the second/eighth and third/ninth centuries.[21] However, for Bashshār (as also for Abū Nuwās), the existence of ᶜUdhrī poetry was already a *fait accompli*, as references to ᶜUdhrī lovers in their poetry show. In his own poetry Bashshār, the native of Basra, works with all three varieties of *ghazal*. The Hijazi and ᶜUdhrī traditions seem to have reached Basra by way of the migration of singer-composers from the peninsula to Iraq in the first quarter of the second/eighth century. The Ḳufan tradition had also found entry to Basra long before Bashshār's time, as is evidenced by the love- and drinking-songs and obscene poetry written in the Kufan style by Ḥārithah b. Badr al-Ghudānī in Umayyad times.[22] The only group of Bashshār's love-poems with which it is possible to deal here in detail is that which continues the ᶜUdhrī tradition, and this is, in any case, both the largest and in every way the most important group. These poems sing of a lady whom the poet usually calls ᶜAbdah, though she is also addressed by other names; she is supposedly the wife of a Basran notable. Bashshār offers her a love which, rightly or wrongly, has been dubbed "courtly",[23] a passion without much hope of fulfilment, but none the less – or perhaps all the more – lasting. The ᶜAbdah of Bashshār's poems is an ideal figure who certainly bears no relation to the "real" ᶜAbdah: she is designed by the poet as a contrast to all the women whom he had known and associated with.[24] It has been pointed out that the surroundings in which Bashshār wrote were highly favourable to such "emotional exaltation"; in the Basra of his time, "mystical experiences were particularly to be observed among women" (the most famous example being Rābiᶜah al-ᶜAdawiyyah), while in Basra, as in Kufa, "a giddy society, free-thinking and morally lax" was addicted to light-hearted pleasures which must sometimes have given rise to a longing for purer and more genuine joys.[25]

At the centre of Bashshār's ᶜAbdah poems stands the phenomenon of love itself. We learn far more about the state of the lover than about that of the beloved; the latter is described chiefly in terms of her character-traits,

[21] See p. 205.

[22] See p. 223; a poem by Bashshār showing elements of Kufan *ghazal* is translated by Beeston in *Selections*, XVII.

[23] Cf. Vadet, *L'Esprit courtois*.

[24] Blachère, *Analecta*, 589–90.

[25] *EI*², "Ghazal".

actions and reactions, to which the poet alludes or which he recites in detail; descriptions of her physical charms are much rarer. Occasionally Bashshār makes use of the conventional motifs of the bedouin *nasīb*, such as the morning of parting, the long night, the abandoned dwelling; the stock figures of the slanderer (*wāshī* or *nāmī*) and the jealous watcher (*raqīb*) – old Arabian, Hijazi and ʿUdhrī traditions – also appear.[26] Less common themes are a letter to his beloved, a device familiar from Hijazi poetry, and the description of visits to a fortune-teller, who foresees the poet's death, and to a witch, who promises to prepare him a love-spell:

"Seer in the great city, as you peer into the inky depths,
Is it revealed to you that I shall live to see ʿAbdah under my roof?"
"Draw near! – I see only death and a path leading to death."
But a girl well-known in fame said to me,
"Do you bemoan the passing of love, and not bemoan your own passing?
I'll cast a spell on her and she shall come to you, even from the sea-monster's dwelling."
Then I cried, "Come straight to me, by virtue of your fastings and prayers!
(How delightful is what you say, the good news you bring, the hopes you raise.)
If she cares at all for me, you will foster that care and will have brought fulfilment;
But if forgetfulness sways her, you will remind her and call on her name,
And my life will be rejoiced by her, through her goodness and yours.
Accept my affection, for what you have favoured me with and what you bring about –
If only the hidden future may be as she and you have shown!"
But she replied, "In what we have uttered to you lies surcease from doubting hopes."[27]

Perhaps surprising, yet characteristic of Bashshār's personality as a poet, is the fact that he did not feel "sublime" love was sacred enough to keep from parodying it from time to time, as in the occasional poem in which his dead donkey appears to him in a dream, declaring that he died of unrequited love for a beautiful she-ass.[28]

The question arises in what Bashshār's "modernity" consists. He did not introduce new genres, and the thematic innovations which could be adduced are anything but striking. The simple diction, close to the spoken language, which he uses particularly in his love-poems but also, for example, in elegies on members of his family, is already familiar from Hijazi poetry. What is really new in Bashshār and his modern successors is a stylistic peculiarity, the frequent and conscious use of *badīʿ* (literally, what is new, unprecedented), i.e. of rhetorical figures and images. Nearly all *badīʿ*

[26] See Roman, "Thèmes", for a fuller listing of motifs.
[27] *Dīwān*, II, 16–18; trans. A.F.L.B. [28] Cf. p. 211.

devices already occur in old Arabian poetry; but, as the first literary theorist to give a systematic analysis of *badīʿ*, Ibn al-Muʿtazz (d. 296/908), observes, modern poets employ them much more frequently and with greater awareness. *Badīʿ*, in modern poetry, increasingly becomes an artistic principle rather than merely an artistic instrument. It has been suggested that the rhetorical colouring thus given to poetic language, its "rhetoricization" – a process said to begin with Bashshār – should be seen as a reaction to the traditionalism of Arabic poetry in point of content: since thematic innovations, especially in the *qaṣīdah*, were difficult to introduce, so the argument runs, poets were driven to focus their attention exclusively on form. There is certainly some truth in this, but it does not suffice to explain the phenomenon completely; for why did poets abandon the traditional treatment of prescribed themes for a new one at a particular time and not before? The conscious use and accumulation of *badīʿ* devices is rather, it may be argued, primarily a socio-psychological phenomenon, which can only be understood by reference to the specific circumstances of Bashshār and the early moderns.[29] Most modern poets were clients (*mawālī*), who did not at first find it easy to gain recognition as valid representatives of Arabic poetry in the eyes of the guardians of bedouin tradition (nor indeed did poets of Arab stock who wrote in the modern idiom). The point is illustrated in several anecdotes about Bashshār himself. It is said that a bedouin who had learned that Bashshār was a client exclaimed, "What have clients to do with poetry?" – a remark which naturally inspired Bashshār to produce a lampoon on the bedouin and their way of life; and there are three versions of a story which tells how, at the beginning of his career, Bashshār walked up to Jarīr and lampooned him, simply in the hope of being thought worthy of a reply by the great poet. However, Jarīr considered it beneath his dignity to react. "Had he lampooned me," Bashshār is said to have commented, "I should have become the best poet in the world."[30] This feeling of inferiority *vis-à-vis* the Arabs and their poetry, for which Bashshār sought to compensate by emphasizing his own, allegedly glorious Persian origin, also led him to compete with the "classics" and, wherever possible, to outdo them, and this on their very own ground: the *qaṣīdah*, *rajaz*-poems, the use of rare Arabic vocabulary (*gharīb*), and the coining of striking similes; thus after hearing a famous verse by the pre-Islamic poet Imruʾ al-Qays which contains a double simile, Bashshār is said to have been unable to rest until he produced an even more ingenious double simile.[31] The compulsion which Bashshār and the early moderns seem continually to

[29] See Schoeler, "Ein Wendepunkt".
[30] Abū ʾl-Faraj al-Iṣfahānī, *Aghānī*, III, 33–4, 23–4.
[31] Ibid., 47–8.

have felt to emulate and outdo the classics must also be adduced in explanation of their interest in rhetorical figures. This was another area where they could outdo the classics on their own ground: "When . . . the moderns . . . observed the striking effects achieved by the uniqueness and beauty of those [ancient] verses [which contained rhetorical figures] and felt their superiority over the others in elegance and charm, they strove to imitate them, and called the result *badīᶜ*."[32] But the rhetoricization of language also has an audience-related aspect. This becomes clear when we note which figures of speech the early moderns are most often said by Arab critics to have preferred, pun (*tajnīs*) and antithesis (*ṭibāq*, *muṭābaqah*).[33] In this connection a side-glance at depth-psychology may prove interesting. Freud sees the pun as a kind of joke motivated by an ambitious urge to show off one's own cleverness, to display oneself, its aim being to gain acceptance with the listener;[34] and this was precisely the situation of the early moderns. Antithesis could be similarly interpreted; the striving to parade contrasts and to create them in speech, even where they do not genuinely exist, is intended to arouse or arrest the audience's attention. Another favourite figure in modern poetry is hyperbole, which creates amazement by evoking images that surpass reality; a similar end is served by metaphor (*istiᶜārah*) of the more far-fetched kinds.

A few examples will illustrate something of Bashshār's style. A verse which Bashshār wrote in his youth and later rejected – apparently even his contemporaries found it tasteless – nevertheless gives a clear indication of some of the characteristics of *badīᶜ* poetry:

> If you put onions close to Salmā
> the musk scent overpowers the onion stench;[35]

and the following metaphor, because it is so far-fetched, exposes something of the mechanism of the figure:

> O thou liver [heart], half of which longing has roasted
> while the other half roasts on the fire of passionate love . . .[36]

More characteristically, perhaps, pun and antithesis are combined in a motif to which Bashshār often returns:

> Suᶜdā's saliva [kiss] . . . is a healing fluid,
> so give it me to drink! Every malady (*dāᵓ*) has a remedy (*dawāᵓ*);[37]

[32] Al-Qāḍī ᵓl-Jurjānī, *Wasāṭah*, 33–4.

[33] For these and other rhetorical terms, see chs. 20, 21.

[34] *Der Witz und seine Beziehung zum Unbewussten* (Frankfurt, 2nd. edn., 1970), 134, 91, 98.

[35] *Dīwān*, IV, 129. [36] Ibid., II, 95. [37] Ibid., I, 113; full trans. Beeston, *Selections*, XI.

and melodic and conceptual patterning are typically combined[38] in the following piece (of which the first three lines are also quoted in Arabic; metre: *khafīf*):

ayyuhā ʾl-sāqiyāni ṣubbā sharābī
wa ʾsqiyānī min rīqi bayḍāʾa rūdī
inna dāʾī ʾl-ẓamā wa-inna dawāʾī
shurbatun min ruḍābi thaghrin barūdī
wa-lahā maḍḥakun ka-ghurri ʾl-aqāḥī
wa-ḥadīthun ka ʾl-washyi washyi ʾl-burūdī . . .

You pages, pour me out a potion,
pour me to drink her soft, sweet kiss:
I suffer drought; its healing draught
is drinking from her moist, fresh lips.
The smiling corners of her mouth are brilliant as camomile;
her speech is like embroidery, a mantle with embroidery.
Lodged in the core and kernel of
my heart, she is insatiable.
She said to me: "I'll meet with you a few nights hence."
But night and day will wear away, and nothing new will come my way.
She is content without me; my
portion is sighs to gnaw a heart of steel.[39]

From Bashshār's time onwards, despite occasional setbacks, the "rhetorical" style was to dominate most Arabic poetry and, soon, Arabic prose as well, though its original function of self-advertisement gradually changed, and *badīʿ* might be employed simply to advertise its user's culture, his membership of the social and intellectual élite.

ABŪ ʾL-ʿATĀHIYAH

Abū ʾl-ʿAtāhiyah is said to have been a potter in his youth, together with his brother, but soon his talent for poetry gained him a certain celebrity; following the Kufan style referred to above, and passing his time with a group that had formed round the notorious bohemian Wālibah b. al-Ḥubāb (d. *c.* 170/786),[40] he at first produced mainly love-songs and drinking-songs. In the reign of the caliph al-Mahdī he moved to Baghdad; there he fell in love with a slave-girl called ʿUtbah, to whom he dedicated numerous poems without her reciprocating his love.[41] Under Hārūn al-Rashīd he suddenly decided to give up life at court and indeed in the world, and to become an ascetic. It is tempting to see Abū ʾl-ʿAtāhiyah's renunciation of a life of

[38] Cf. Meisami, "Uses of the *qaṣīda*", 48–9.
[39] Beeston, *Selections*, VIII; *Dīwān*, II, 272–3; trans. J.A.
[40] See Wagner, *Abū Nuwās*, 24–5. [41] For examples, see ch. 12, nos. 4, 5.

pleasure that in the last analysis failed to bring fulfilment, as a similar, though more drastic reaction to that displayed by Bashshār when he took refuge in "sublime" love.[42] This, though possible, is by no means certain; doubts have sometimes been expressed as to the sincerity of Abū ᵓl-ᶜAtāhiyah's conversion; he is represented as jealous of what he regarded as his own, very profitable, literary preserve, and the "pious" poet, like the "irreligious" Bashshār, was even suspected of sympathizing with the views of the *zindīqs*.[43] Whatever the case may be, he henceforth wrote nothing but ascetic poems (*zuhdiyyāt*), and even an imprisonment by the caliph designed to induce him to write love-poems again was of no avail. So famous did Abū ᵓl-ᶜAtāhiyah become thanks to his *zuhdiyyāt* that even the Byzantine emperor is said to have tried, without success, to lure him to his court.

The Arabs regard Abū ᵓl-ᶜAtāhiyah as the poet of renunciation *par excellence*. Although his poetry certainly marks a climax in the development of the genre, he did not create it any more than Bashshār created the love-lyric or Abū Nuwās the drinking-song. Some of the motifs employed by Abū ᵓl-ᶜAtāhiyah can already be seen in the gnomic sections of old Arabian *qaṣīdah*s; in particular, bedouin poets would often begin an elegy (*rithāᵓ*) with a consideration of the transitory nature of all things earthly. There are also pre-Islamic poems devoted exclusively to expressions of gnomic wisdom (*ḥikmah*), for example a poem by the Christian ᶜAdī b. Zayd of Ḥīrah in which the *ubi sunt* (*ayna*) scheme is already developed – a theme that was later to become part of the stock-in-trade of the *zuhdiyyah*. Such poems as ᶜAdī's naturally lack any specifically Islamic ideas; the first *zuhdiyyāt* in the true, Islamic, sense of the word would seem to belong to the Umayyad period, when Sābiq b. ᶜAbdullāh al-Barbarī (d. first quarter second/eighth century), imam and *qāḍī* under the caliph ᶜUmar II in the Syrian town of Raqqah, was the outstanding practitioner of the genre.[44] It is possible that Abū ᵓl-ᶜAtāhiyah was directly influenced by Sābiq al-Barbarī, though it is possible too that the *zuhdiyyah* tradition had already undergone further development in Ḥīrah and neighbouring Kufa.

Ascetic poetry cannot readily be assigned to either of the two categories referred to earlier in this chapter, poetry serving either private or public ends, and, according to the *Kitāb al-Aghānī*, Abū ᵓl-ᶜAtāhiyah himself once characterized the style and public of the *zuhdiyyah* in the following terms: "[Good] poetry should either be like the poems of the classics (*fuḥūl*) of old, or like that of Bashshār and Ibn Harmah.[45] Failing this, the poet's words

[42] Blachère, *Analecta*, 588.

[43] See Martin, "Religious beliefs", and pp. 195, 268, above.

[44] See pp. 268–9.

[45] D. *c.* 176/792; regarded by medieval critics both as linguistically authoritative and as an outstanding practitioner of *badīᶜ*.

should at least be so chosen that they are understood by the masses – as with my poetry – and this is especially true of *zuhd* poetry, for *zuhd* does not appeal to kings, nor to transmitters of poetry, nor to students of lexical rarities; the people who really delight in it are ascetics, students of *ḥadīth*, scholars of religious law, people who make a show of piety, and the common people, who most admire what they can understand."[46]

Abū ʾl-ʿAtāhiyah's *zuhdiyyāt* deal with the transitoriness and vanity of earthly things – the *ubi sunt* motif is of frequent occurrence – and with the uselessness of wealth and futility of worldly pleasures; they preach the need to perform good works in this life with a view to the life to come, and warn of men's heedlessness in this respect; they criticize love of pleasure and covetousness, calling on men to fear God, renounce the world and practice patience in the face of tribulation; they lament the rarity of true friendship, and describe with peculiar insistence the grave and its denizens, death and its horrors, though they also speak of the resurrection and what awaits man in the hereafter, thank God for his blessings and beg for forgiveness of sins (O. Rescher's German translation of the *Dīwān*, which provides the poems with titles, gives a good general view of their thematic content). The language of these poems, though simple, is by no means artless. A frequent device is the re-use or reinterpretation of classical motifs borrowed from the *qaṣīdah*; for example a motif characteristic of the *nasīb* (amatory prelude), that of weeping over the ruins of the dwellings where the poet's beloved and her tribe used to live, is adapted by Abū ʾl-ʿAtāhiyah to man's dwelling in this world: "It is as if I stood by houses already in ruins and beheld the many tears that are shed . . ."[47] Where the bedouin poet despaired because the ruined encampment could not answer him and tell him where his beloved had gone, Abū ʾl-ʿAtāhiyah wonders at the muteness of the grave: "Why do graves not answer when the afflicted call on them?"[48] He also draws inspiration from contemporary life; he was, for example, said to have been prompted, by watching a fuller at work, to write a poem which imitated the rhythm of the fulling-stick; the first verse speaks of the blows dealt by death (metre: *ramal*):

al-manūnu mufniyātun wāḥidan fa-wāḥidā
Death annihilates us one by one.[49]

A favourite device is anaphora (*takrār*), the repetition of a word or phrase at the beginning of a line, intended to hammer home the ideas expressed; as an example, the first six lines of one *zuhdiyyah* begin, "I want to bewail . . .", the next two, "O house, O house", lines 10 and 11, "O eye", and lines 21 and 22, "O soul".[50] Such repetitions or echoes occur not only at the

[46] Abū ʾl-Faraj al-Iṣfahānī, *Aghānī*, III, 161. [47] *Ashʿāruh*, 54. [48] Ibid., 35.
[49] Ibid., 523. [50] Ibid., 453–7.

beginnings of lines, but in a variety of positions within the lines; they can be subtle as well as insistent, and occur so frequently as to produce a positively mannered effect; Abū ʾl-ʿAtāhiyah too is a *badīʿ* poet

satarā baʿda mā tarā *ghayra hādhā ʾlladhī tarā*
satarā mā baqīta mā *yamnaʿu ʾl-nāʾima ʾl-karā*
satarā man yaṣīru baʿ *-da naʿīmin ilā ʾl-tharā*
satarā kulla ḥādithin *kayfa yajrī idhā jarā*

(metre: *khafīf*):

Hereafter thou shalt see, shalt see
things hidden now from thee, from thee:
In fullness of time thou shalt see
what makes rest from the sleeper flee;
The rich and happy thou shalt see
depart from hence to dust and dearth;
In all that happens, thou shalt see
the course of things eternally.[51]

For the rest, of the stylistic devices generally associated with modern poetry, pun and striking metaphor are of less frequent occurrence in Abū ʾl-ʿAtāhiyah's verse than antithesis. In the following extracts from a twenty-two line poem, anaphora, pun and metaphor all function as components of antithesis; as the combined effect cannot be reproduced in English, the first two lines are also quoted in Arabic (metre: *kāmil*):

inna ʾl-fanāʾa mina ʾl-baqāʾi qarību
inna ʾl-zamāna idhā ramā la-muṣību
inna ʾl-zamāna li-ahlihī la-muʾaddibun
law kāna yanfaʿu fīhimu ʾl-taʾdību . . .

Living's so close to dying; Time's aim is so unfailing;
Time chastens mortals so, could they be chastened.
Wise and eloquent is Time; Time's a poet and a preacher . . .
Often Time speaks to you in tongues of Arabic: I see you mute;
Could you but understand Time's words, you would be seized with grief and tears . . .
Born were you to reason, yet I see no sign of reason in you;
Long have you sought your object, but I see no sign of your succeeding . . .[52]

One long poem deserves special mention, the *urjūzah* (poem written in the *rajaz* metre) nicknamed *Dhāt al-amthāl* ("The Proverb-Poem").[53] As this suggests, it contains proverbs, aphorisms and exhortations, and in point of content is of a piece with the poet's other *zuhdiyyāt*. What differentiates it from the rest of his output is its length – 320 verses are extant, but it is said originally to have run to several thousand lines – and the fact that it is written not in monorhyme but in rhyming couplets (*aa*, *bb*, *cc*, etc.);

[51] Ibid., 150; trans. J.A. [52] Ibid., 27–8; trans. J.A. [53] Ibid., 444–65.

Bashshār is also said to have written *muzdawij* verse of this kind, but none has survived. This form later served for very long poems, mainly with didactic content; Abū ᵓl-ᶜAtāhiyah's *urjūzah muzdawijah* may thus perhaps be regarded as a forerunner of the didactic poem in Arabic.

ABŪ NUWĀS

In his youth Abū Nuwās received a thorough grounding in the religious sciences and secular learning in both Basra and Kufa. Of all his teachers, those who most influenced the development of his character and work were the Kufan bohemian and poet, Wālibah b. al-Ḥubāb, whose contacts with Abū ᵓl-ᶜAtāhiyah have already been referred to, and the Basran philologist, *rāwī* and poet, Khalaf al-Aḥmar (d. 180/796). In Basra, Abū Nuwās fell in love with the singing slave-girl Janān, the only woman ever to have played any role in his life. In 170/786 he moved to Baghdad, and attracted some patronage from the vizieral Barmakī (Barmecide) family; after their fall, he withdrew to Egypt, but was soon able to return to the capital. The high point of his career was the period during which he was the close confidant and boon-companion (*nadīm*) of the caliph al-Amīn; the caliph died in 198/813 and Abū Nuwās himself soon after.

Abū Nuwās is undoubtedly one of the most versatile of the early moderns, indeed one of the most versatile of all ᶜAbbasid poets, as can be seen from the chapter-headings of his *Dīwān*, the first extant *dīwān* to have been classified according to subject-matter (most earlier *dīwān*s were arranged alphabetically according to rhyming-letter). In the redaction of Abū Bakr al-Ṣūlī (d. *c.* 335/946),[54] it comprises ten sections: drinking-songs; hunting-poems; panegyrics; lampoons; love of boys; love of women; licentious verse; poems of reproach; elegies; ascetic verse.[55] Genres serving private ends occupy a striking amount of space, but, while this may reflect the poet's own temperament, inclinations and background, it should be borne in mind that his patrons at the court of Baghdad, especially the caliph al-Amīn, were by no means averse to the kind of pleasures such poetry celebrates and liked to have poems of an appropriate kind recited to them at their social gatherings (*majālis al-uns*). Thus "public" poetry was not the only kind to receive official patronage, as is evidenced earlier by the caliph Hārūn al-Rashīd's having made a favourite of al-ᶜAbbās b. al-Aḥnaf, who wrote only love poetry in the ᶜUdhrī style; similarly, after Abū Nuwās's time, though drinking-poems and hunting-poems did not command the same universal esteem as poetry serving public ends, they appear in the

[54] See ch. 4, n. 4. [55] For sources and editions, see Wagner, *Abū Nuwās*, 1–9.

*dīwān*s of several poets in separate chapters, side by side with those containing poems in the "official" genres.

Abū Nuwās's hunting-poems (*ṭardiyyāt*) are dealt with extensively in chapter 10, and specimens of his *zuhd* poetry are referred to in chapter 15. In this chapter we shall treat exclusively the drinking-songs, panegyrics (in brief), and love poetry.

Khamriyyāt (drinking-songs)

Abū Nuwās is the most celebrated and heavily imitated writer of *khamriyyāt* in Arabic; however, the genre had already passed through a long process of development before his time. This process is described in some detail in chapter 13, but the points of more immediate relevance to Abū Nuwās's handling of the genre merit separate discussion. The role played in the development of the *khamriyyah* by pre-Islamic Ḥīrah has already been referred to; in Ḥīrah it was cultivated as an independent genre, but most of the early poets who continued to treat it within the framework of the polythematic *qaṣīdah* also had links with Ḥīrah. In the Islamic era, after the founding of Kufa in the immediate vicinity of Ḥīrah, Kufan poets showed particular enthusiasm for the independent *khamriyyah*; the *Kitāb al-Aghānī* contains the biographies of many minor poets of the new era who wrote such *khamriyyāt* together with love-songs and obscene verse, notably ᶜAmmār b. ᶜAmr Dhū Kināz (early second/eighth century). According to tradition, the Umayyad caliph al-Walīd b. Yazīd (d. 126/744), probably the most important writer of *khamriyyāt* before Abū Nuwās, thought highly of this poet, and it seems likely that al-Walīd himself wrote in the Hiran–Kufan tradition.[56] The first wine-poet of the modern school was Muṭīᶜ b. Iyās (d. 169/785), a drinking-companion of ᶜAmmār Dhū Kināz, and apparently it was mainly he, and, later, another Kufan, Muslim b. al-Walīd (d. 208/823), who brought the genre to Baghdad and made it popular there. Abū Nuwās's own teacher in the genre was Wālibah b. al-Ḥubāb, yet another Kufan, who also introduced him to *ghazal* and obscene verse and to whom belongs the credit of "discovering" the poet. Abū Nuwās's *khamriyyāt* seem to have been influenced by those of al-Walīd b. Yazīd and are sometimes difficult to distinguish from them, as is shown by an early misattribution. However, according to Arab tradition, the chief influence on Abū Nuwās as a wine-poet was Abū ᵓl-Hindī, in all probability yet another Kufan, though his later life was spent in the eastern part of the Islamic empire.[57]

[56] Ibid., 290. [57] See p. 226.

Abū Nuwās's wine-songs are relatively free in their subject-matter. In many *khamriyyāt* the main theme is naturally the description of wine, its age, strength and effect on the drinkers. However, much space is often devoted to descriptions of the boy or girl who pours the wine, of the drinkers, of the male or female singer who entertains the revellers, or of the Jewish, Christian or Zoroastrian innkeeper (members of all these religions being permitted to make wine). Some poems take the form of quite realistic narratives describing how the poet and his companions set off for the tavern in the dark of the night, waken the innkeeper and persuade him or her to sell them wine:

Behold an ostleress in whom remained a trace of youthful bloom,
towards the hostelry of whom we three set out one eve.
The night upon us and around did hang, as though it were a gown,
and neither man nor jinn
rode with us, but that in the sky the stars were pendant upon high
to guide us to our goal.
At last we beat upon her door (first taking pause to have a snore);
"Who knocks?" she cried. "Us," we replied,
"A group of youths who, met by chance,
before your door, by happenstance benighted wandered hither.
Refuse us and our band must scatter;
unite us and we're friends forever."
"Come in," she said, "a welcome visit;
you're fine young blades, and brainy with it."
"Pour by the book," said we to her, "full bottles bring, no less, no more."
She brought wine like the sun, with rays like stars, fair wine, in glass ablaze.
"Your name, your price," said I, "pray let
us know the price, and you will get
our custom here forever."
"Ḥanūn's the name," she said, "the price
nine dirhams, three times three a glass,
and that's my going rate."
When night was nearly on the turn, she came with scales to test our coin;
I said, "We didn't bring a lot of money with us; could you not
take one of us in pawn?"
"You be the pawn," she said to me, "and if with cash you're not set free
I'll keep you prisoner with me
forever."[58]

In another, much-admired poem, Abū Nuwās describes a gold Sasanian drinking-cup, engraved with old Persian figured motifs.[59] Since taverns were often decorated with flowers, and since wine-parties often also took place in gardens, extensive descriptions of flowers and gardens are frequently found.[60] Some poems are melancholy in tone, recalling the

[58] *Dīwān*, ed. Ghazālī, 49; trans. J.A.; other examples trans. p. 230–1, above, and Monteil, *Abû Nuwâs*, 66–8. [59] Cf. p. 228. [60] E.g. trans. Schoeler, *Naturdichtung*, 60–85.

pleasures of the poet's long-lost youth.[61] Abū Nuwās's *khamriyyāt* are also diverse in terms of structure. Often they begin with a prelude, sometimes modelled on that of the classical *qaṣīdah*, as in one poem which begins with a *nasīb* and a ride through the desert.[62] But a much more frequent motif is the invitation to turn to the joys of wine instead of weeping over deserted ruins, a mockery of classicizing attitudes in which Abū Nuwās, like Bashshār before him, sometimes pokes fun at the uncouth habits of the real, unromanticized bedouin. Another favourite opening theme is the rebuttal of criticism of his scandalous way of life, the most famous example being the poem beginning:

daʿ ʿanka lawmī fa-inna ʾl-lawma ighrāʾū
wa-dāwinī bi ʾllatī kānat hiya ʾl-dāʾū

Cease blaming me, for blame is merely an incitement;
give me as remedy that which was itself the malady [i.e. the hair of the dog].[63]

The simultaneous pun on and antithesis between *dāʾ* (malady) and *dawāʾ* (remedy) are already familiar from the poetry of Bashshār. In the additional antithesis between "blame" and "incitement", Abū Nuwās is teasing his right-minded critics. The following poem elaborates this theme:

Cease, scold;[64] my face is not besmirched;
I do not sell my honour cheap;
A gentleman of peerless fame,
I draw no censure, deal no blame:
Scold! Tattered though my raiment be,
beneath it beats a lordly heart:
I'm sire to folly, and folly's scion
as sure as grapes grow on the vine.[65]
I do not put my pleasures off
from day to day, like creditors,
Nor push the cup away until
my fellow-drinkers twist my arm.
– I've a comrade of high intent,
no stranger he to noble deeds,
To whom I cried "Go get it, lad!"
when stars shone in the firmament,
Swearing my humblest love in terms

[61] E.g. trans. Monteil, *Abû Nuwâs*, 79–80. [62] Trans. Schoeler, *Naturdichtung*, 76–7.

[63] *Dīwān*, ed. Ghazālī, 6–7; full trans. Monteil, *Abû Nuwâs*, 80–1.

[64] A stock figure of bedouin poetry whose role, as the representative of moderation, is to let the poet give vent to a bout of self-praise in which he expresses his contempt for small-minded values.

[65] The line is almost impossible to translate literally; the following is an approximation: "I was rent asunder (*shuqiqtu*) by the folly of youth, and it came from/is derived from me (*wa-shtuqqa minnī*) as grapes (*kurūm*) come from/are derived etymologically from generosity (*karam*)" – (and/or . . . "come from the vine (*karm*)").

that kith and kin to blazes sent.
He rose, I rose, two brothers bent
on pleasure, in the dead of night:
I drag the wineskin, he his feet,
which sleep has suborned, straightens course:
Ask him (the toper) what good she
(the wine, his bride) has done to him;
ask her how the fine fellow did;
By law, both parties can expect
the right to satisfaction;[66] she's
fulfilled herself, and made him – sick.[67]

A possible explanation for the frequency with which Abū Nuwās prefaces his drinking-songs with preludes might be that he wanted to raise this genre, which he had made his own, to the rank of the *qaṣīdah* – though it should be borne in mind that many of the *khamriyyāt* are improvisatory in manner and do not aspire either to the linguistic or to the structural complexity of the panegyric *qaṣīdah*. Another suggestion is that, in inverting classical themes, Abū Nuwās was casting himself in the role of an anti-hero, at a time of uncertain values, when heroic pagan values were no longer tenable and Islamic ones did not always fill the gap left by them;[68] other scholars view the procedure as an expression of *Shuᶜūbiyyah* (although it is by no means certain that Abū Nuwās was a Shuᶜūbī).

The wine imagery draws heavily on simile (*tashbīh*), the drink being compared in particular to precious stones, light or the heavenly bodies. Metaphorical description is rarer, though actions may be described metaphorically, as when the unstopping of the wine is presented in terms of the unveiling of a bride or deflowering of a virgin; and elaborate figures sometimes occur, as in the figure known as phantastic aetiology (*ḥusn al-taᶜlīl*), through which Abū Nuwās explains the little bubbles that form when wine and water are mixed as the expression of elemental repugnancy, of wine's "hatred" of water.[69] With the description of the cupbearer an element of *ghazal* – and with it the specific imagery of this genre – enters the wine-song. The description of the boy in the opening lines of the following poem consists of a series of antitheses the components of which are in some cases expressed by metaphor:

A boy of beckoning glances and chaste tongue,
neck bowed enticingly, who scorns the rein,
Proffers me wine of hope mixed with despair,
distant in word and deed, yet ever-near.

66 Islamic law recognizes both marriage partners' right to physical satisfaction.
67 *Dīwān*, ed. Ghazālī, 55; trans. J.A.
68 Hamori, *The Art*, ch. 2.
69 Trans. Wagner, *Abū Nuwās*, 411, 416.

When sense has serious talks with me about him,
hope's discourse gives the lie to common sense;
So I will write as fantasy inspires me,
belie the evidence of my own eyes,
And make a virtuoso composition
of simple words and many-sided sense,
So deep-rooted in my imagination
that I reach out, to find it isn't there,
As though drawn onward by a loveliness
in front of me, that just eludes my sight.
– I cheered myself with vintage, unmixed wine
that grew up in the lap of ages past,
Ancient as Time itself to practised eyes,
two milk-sisters who sucked at the same breast
(Oblivious of them, night and day rolled on,
tripling the wine's strength as its substance shrank).
What I deflowered, then, was a tart brew,
brisk as a virgin, yielding as a drab . . .
I weep for the red wine that's all been drunk;
let poets weep for classic mistresses![70]

Madīḥ (panegyric)

Part of Abū Nuwās's panegyric poems consists of *qaṣīdah*s made up of a prelude and a main section (the eulogy proper), the other part being longer or shorter monothematic poems. The *qaṣīdah*s may be constructed in a thoroughly traditional way, and some of them even feign a bedouin setting. Sometimes we find the following sequence of themes: *nasīb*, occasionally with a description of the ruined encampment of the beloved; camel-ride through the desert; eulogy. This scheme, which corresponds strictly to Ibn Qutaybah's description, is, however, rather rare; frequently the desert-ride or, occasionally, the *nasīb* is omitted, the result being a two-part *qaṣīdah*. Thus the famous *qaṣīdah* in the metre *rajaz* known as *al-Manhūkah*, which became the object of a long and learned commentary by the grammarian Ibn Jinnī (d. 392/1002), consists simply of camel-ride and eulogy.[71] In another group of poems, the traditional amatory prelude gives place to other themes; frequently, as in the *khamriyyāt*, Abū Nuwās mocks the classical theme of weeping over ruins and contrasts the bedouin way of life with the comforts of urban living.[72] Still further removed from classical models are those poems in which the *nasīb* is replaced with descriptions of revelry or hunting.[73] That, even in Abū Nuwās's day, such alterations to the framework of the *qaṣīdah* were considered daring innovations is suggested

[70] *Dīwān*, ed. Ghazālī, 18–19; trans. J.A.
[71] Trans. Monteil, *Abû Nuwâs*, 125–7.
[72] E.g. trans. Wagner, *Abū Nuwās*, 244–6.
[73] Ibid., 252–7.

by the fact that he thought it advisable, in a panegyric of the caliph al-Amīn beginning with a description of wine, to prefix the recitation with a few words "excusing"[74] his procedure. Finally, some poems dispense with introductory matter altogether.

The main theme of panegyric is the virtues of the addressee, and these differ according to his rank. In the case of a caliph, the virtues of the old Arabian *sayyid* are adduced: generosity, judicious mildness, bravery, noble birth and so on, though the caliph's severity towards his enemies is also emphasized, as is his piety (an important factor in the ʿAbbasids' claim to legitimacy). Viziers, on the other hand, are praised as good advisers to the caliph, as showing resolve in difficult situations, etc. Unusual themes, which occur in shorter poems in praise of al-Amīn, are descriptions of a dome which the caliph had restored, and of boats shaped like various animals which he had built for pleasure-trips on the Tigris. The following poem is an example:

The "full moon" [i.e. the caliph] in the dark night was astride the "dolphin" [i.e. a boat shaped like this animal].
Dashing into the waves, it reached the fathomless depths of the river.
The Tigris was illuminated by its light; the river banks shone and were delighted.
Never had my eyes beheld a boat more beautiful in motion or in repose.
Goaded by the oars, it dashes over the waves or idles along.
God has distinguished with it al-Amīn, who wears the crown of the realm.[75]

Ghazal (love poetry)

Perhaps the most immediately striking feature of Abū Nuwās's love-poems is that they are divided into poems about girls (*muʾannathāt*) and poems about boys (*mudhakkarāt*), the latter, as already mentioned, being a genre which had already existed in Kufa as early as Umayyad times. However, though Wālibah b. al-Ḥubāb, Abū Nuwās's teacher, had written *mudhakkarāt*, the genre had previously been cultivated only by minor poets; Abū Nuwās was the first to give it full literary status, and in fact wrote about twice as many *mudhakkarāt* as he did *muʾannathāt*. In his poems to women Abū Nuwās also, very often, continues the Kufan tradition, many of them being addressed to singing slave-girls. The ʿUdhrī tradition, though mostly not in its completely pure form, is mainly represented by a smaller group of poems in which Abū Nuwās celebrates his beloved Janān. Notwithstanding, the *mudhakkarāt* and *muʾannathāt* may be treated as a single group, for in essentials they do not differ; so much so that the various redactors of the

[74] Ibid., 253–4. [75] *Dīwān*, I, 266.

Dīwān of Abū Nuwās sometimes disagree as to whether a given poem refers to a girl or a boy. (There is also a kind of transitional form, *ghulāmiyyāt*, addressed to girls who dress and look like boys.) The following brief survey attempts, wherever possible, to assign themes to the particular tradition to which they are related, though it should once again be noted that these traditions frequently overlap.

Many of the love-poems consist exclusively of physical descriptions of the beloved, in the Kufan tradition;[76] the ʿUdhrī tradition is represented by musings on love itself, the unhappiness of the lover, his tears, emaciation, sleeplessness and submissiveness to the beloved.[77] Other poems centre on the joy of reunion, in the Hijazi tradition. Yet other themes are the blamer, the slanderer, the jealous watcher (old Arabian, Hijazi and ʿUdhrī traditions), love-letters (Hijazi tradition), go-betweens, procuresses, the poet's reproach to his eye for revealing the beloved to him, and descriptions of the apple which serves as the messenger of love. Less usual subjects are a love-poem addressed to the caliph al-Amīn, a conjuration of the devil, in which Abū Nuwās threatens to turn pious if the devil does not make his beloved come to him, and an arithmetical problem in which the poet gives up trying to count how many parts of his heart belong to Janān, how many to other loves and the cupbearer respectively, and a description of a boat-trip to Basra to see the beloved.[78] But reminiscences of old Arabian love poetry also occur – descriptions of the interminable night through which the lover struggles, of the visit of the phantasm of the beloved to the poet's bedside, etc., and on one occasion Abū Nuwās describes Janān's departure from Baghdad in the same terms as bedouin poets used to describe women riding off in howdahs.

In the imagery of the love-poems, the physical charms of the beloved seem to be more frequently expressed through metaphor than was the appearance of wine in drinking-songs (which was described mainly in terms of simile). A famous example of accumulated metaphors occurs in the two opening lines of a poem describing a weeping girl: "O moon, whom I glimpsed at a funeral, lamenting amid her companions, weeping, and shedding pearls [tears] from narcissi [eyes] and striking roses [cheeks] with jujubes [henna-tinted fingers]."[79] One of the redactors of the *Dīwān* (unpublished section) of Abū Nuwās, Ḥamzah al-Iṣfahānī (d. after 350/961), gave a special place to lines and poems – nearly always love-poems – which contain what he considered to be exaggerated *badīʿ* of this kind; interestingly enough, they nearly always exemplify a particular kind of

[76] See Monteil, *Abû Nuwâs*, 91–2, 101. [77] See ch. 12, nos. 1–3.

[78] *Dīwān*, IV, 195; trans. Wagner, *Abū Nuwās*, 60; *Dīwān*, IV, 216–17, 83–4 (trans. ibid., 48), 184–5.

[79] *Dīwān*, IV, 15.

metaphor, based on the genitive of identification,[80] which has already been encountered in the poetry of Bashshār (". . . roasts on the fire of passionate love"), e.g. "You wanted to slay me with the lance of your glances" and "The crescent-moon of union rose, and the cloud of rejection was dissipated".

Examples of complete poems will give a fuller idea of Abū Nuwās's technique:

On every path Love waits to ambush me,
a sword of passion and a spear in hand;
I cannot flee it and am sore afraid
of it, for every lover is a coward.
My hearth affords no amnesty, and I
have no safe-conduct if I stir outside.[81]

His face, a goblet next his lip,
looks like a moon lit with a lamp;
Armed with love's weaponry, he rides
on beauty's steed, squares up eye's steel –
Which is his smile, the bow his brow,
the shafts his eyes, his lashes lances.[82]

As in Abū Nuwās's *khamriyyāt*, semi-narrative may also be employed:

I caught sight of someone who
no longer seemed to care for me,
Sitting on a prayer-mat
with a group of schoolboy-slaves;
He darted a glance at me –
that's the way he hunts his prey.
(All this was at Ḥafṣ's ac-
ademy; lucky old Ḥafṣ!)
Ḥafṣ exclaimed, "Away with him!
The boy's nothing but a dunce;
Ever since he's been at school
he hasn't paid attention once."
One by one and layer by layer
they stripped his clothes and laid him bare,
Threatening to fetch a strap
(limp and flaccid) to his back;
Whereat my beloved yelled,
"Teacher, teacher, I'll behave!"
"Please, Ḥafṣ, let him off," said I,
"he'll be a good little boy,
Learn his book off pat and do
anything you want him to."[83]

80 See Heinrichs, "Istiᶜārah and badīᶜ". 81 *Dīwān*, IV, 131; trans. J.A.
82 Ibid., 188; trans. J.A. The last two half-lines use the figure *taqsīm* (distributio).
83 Ibid., 194; trans. J.A.

Abū Nuwās was noted for his love of teasing and shocking, as numerous anecdotes attest, and this characteristic finally led to his passing into legend as a jokester; he appears in some of the stories of the *Thousand and One Nights* as the court jester of Hārūn al-Rashīd. This love of mockery, which as we have seen found expression in the ridicule of classical themes, is also applied to himself; his elegies include a number of poems in which he sardonically describes the decay of his own body shortly before death. Most such poems occur, however, in the sections of his *Dīwān* entitled "lampoons" and "licentious verse", examples from the latter being a humorous depiction of an unhappy love-affair with a boy, and a "Testament of Libertines" in which the poet, apparently in all seriousness, though really of course just to shock, invites his readers to commit every conceivable infamy.[84]

Finally a word should be said about the poetic forms used by Abū Nuwās. By far the commonest, as one would expect, is verse written in standard monorhyme, but, exceptionally, strophic forms are employed, examples being a poem in rhymed couplets (*muzdawijah*) on the game of chess, and a poem rhyming in blocks of five lines (*mukhammasah*): *aaaaa/bbbbb*, etc., which warns against marriage and advises masturbation.[85] Of particular interest is a wine-poem which can be read both as a *qaṣīdah* written in regular monorhyme and as a strophic poem with recurring rhyme (*musammaṭah*) on the pattern *aaaa bbba ccca*, etc.[86] It has rightly been described as a pre-*muwashshah*, for there is much evidence to suggest that the strophic, multi-rhymed Andalusian–Arabic *muwashshaḥ* (in classical Arabic), and *zajal* (in colloquial Arabic) stemmed from this or a similar type of *musammaṭ*.[87]

[84] Trans. Wagner, *Abū Nuwās*, 104–6. [85] Trans. Monteil, *Abû Nuwâs*, 134–40.
[86] Text and trans. Monteil, *Abû Nuwâs*, 72–4. [87] Schoeler, "Strophendichtung".

CHAPTER 17

AL-MUTANABBĪ

LIFE

Abū ʾl-Ṭayyib Aḥmad b. al-Ḥusayn, known as al-Mutanabbī, was born in 303/915 into a poor Kufan family. He took up the career of professional panegyrist while still a boy, and early began his travels in search of patrons. For years he had to content himself with offering hyperboles to men of modest distinction. In 322/933 we find him in prison in Ḥimṣ (Homs): according to most Arabic sources, he had attempted to lead a bedouin revolt in the Syrian desert. The religious tincture of his call (of which his collected verse may retain some samples) earned him, according to this tradition, the name al-Mutanabbī, "He who sets up as a prophet." This appears to have been his only try at advancement by extraliterary means. Gradually he grew in fame, and his patrons in rank. The nine years he spent, from 337/948 to 346/957, at the court of the Hamdanid prince Sayf al-Dawlah[1] in Aleppo were his longest stay with any one patron, and must have been the most satisfying. Sayf al-Dawlah was an Arab prince – a matter of great importance to Mutanabbī – and he truly possessed the virtues – generosity and courage – that are the twin pillars of the Arabic panegyric. It was not an altogether easy relationship: Sayf al-Dawlah was quick to anger, and Mutanabbī had more pride than pliancy. But respect appears to have been mutual. Sayf al-Dawlah accepted Mutanabbī's conditions for the ceremonial recitals: the poet would not have to kiss the ground before the prince, and would not stand to recite.[2] At court, literary rivals and other enemies intrigued against Mutanabbī, at length with success. He fled to Egypt, dedicating his praises to Kāfūr, a former slave and now ruler of the country. Mutanabbī appears to have entertained hopes of a high government post. This was denied him; he fled once more and made Kāfūr a theme of venomous satire. His next journeys took him to Baghdad, then to Iran. After a stay with the Buwayhid amir ʿAḍud al-Dawlah in Shiraz, he returned to Iraq in 354/965. On the road bedouins attacked his party and killed him.

[1] Cf. pp. 318–19. [2] Badīʿī, *Ṣubḥ*, 71.

POETRY AND PERSONALITY

"His verse," we read in al-Thaᶜālibī's (d. 429/1038) survey of the poetry of the fourth Islamic century, *Yatīmat al-dahr*, "flourishes alike where scholars meet for study and where friends join for pleasant conversation. It is upon the pens of epistolarians and the tongues of orators. It is sung by singers and chanted by wandering preachers (*qawwālūn*). It fills the books of writers and anthologists . . ." He has ardent partisans and ardent detractors, "and this is the chief indication of the abundance of his gift, of his superior achievement, and of his peerlessness in his age". Abū ᵓl-ᶜAlāᵓ al-Maᶜarrī (d. 449/1057) referred to Mutanabbī as "the Poet";according to a plausible report, he would head a quote with "Abū Nuwās says", "Abū Tammām says", "the Poet says".[3] Abū Tammām, al-Buḥturī and al-Mutanabbī were thought of as the panegyrists *par excellence*; they invited comparison. For al-Sharīf al-Raḍī (d. 406/1016), Abū Tammām was an orator, Buḥturī a delicate painter in words, Mutanabbī a leader of armies. For Ḍiyāᵓ al-Dīn Ibn al-Athīr (d. 637/1239), Abū Tammām was the supreme inventor of conceits, Buḥturī was pre-eminent in the graceful nobility and music of language, Mutanabbī "wished to follow in the path of Abū Tammām, could not equal him . . . but excelled in his aphoristic verses and showed particular invention in the descriptions of battle". Of all the poets, Ibn al-Athīr found Abū Tammām and Mutanabbī richest in original conceits, and he writes: "the fortunes of the man were more brilliant than his poetry, for in truth he is the seal of the poets."[4] Mutanabbī's particular glory, on this view, is that, the last in a line of great panegyrists, he stands at the summit of a tradition. In a similar appraisal of Mutanabbī's place in the history of Arabic verse, Ṭāhā Ḥusayn, a critical but sympathetic reader, judges that Mutanabbī, the model for his successors (*imām li ᵓl-shuyᶜarāᵓ*), must bear the blame for the vices – laboured conceits the chief among them – that they adopted.[5]

The medieval critics' lists of vices and virtues are useful to the reader who would place Mutanabbī in his age. The handiest of these are Thaᶜālibī's; for the European reader, the main lines of attack and defence are detailed in Blachère's *Un Poète arabe du IVᵉ siècle*. Such lists are, it is true, largely predictable, generated by conventional do's and don't's. On the debit side, instances of substandard or bizarre words, arbitrary grammar, and obscurity of expression are offered, along with such breaches of decorum as the employment of ill-omened phrases at the beginning of poems, and the like. There are pages after pages of quotations to substantiate the charge of

[3] Ibid., 72. [4] Ibid., 177–9. [5] *Maᶜa ᵓl-Mutanabbī*, I, 203.

plagiarism. This is a conventional line of attack;[6] still, no subsequent poet invited such a storm about his use of received material. Mutanabbī was indeed the seal of those poets who tended the efflorescence of the panegyric in the grand neo-classical style, which linked a "modern" rhetoric of conceits, antitheses, syntactic symmetries, etc., to themes and a lexicon which hark back to the "classical" poets of pre-Islamic and early Islamic times. Some of the quotations used to prove Mutanabbī's plagiarism are of verses merely reshuffled to suit metre and rhyme; some are of lines in which an earlier conceit is refined, as where the second/eighth-century love-poet al-ᶜAbbās ibn al-Aḥnaf's, "She wept, unaccustomed to weeping; the tears in her eyes looked like strangers", yields Mutanabbī's description of girls weeping for Sayf al-Dawlah's mother: "Calamity struck when they little expected it, and tears of grief stood where tears of coquetry had."[7] In either case, such verses remind us of the degree to which, even in reading a medieval Arab poet as distinctive as Mutanabbī, we are reading a tradition that delighted in tying, by imitation or innovation, text to text.

On the credit side of their balance sheets, the critics quote brilliant conceits and metaphors, striking maxims, rhetorical felicities. Some remarks, however, draw attention to aspects of Mutanabbī's poetry that they considered peculiar to him. Thaᶜālibī lists among the virtues Mutanabbī's invention of "addressing the patron as one addresses one's beloved", and "using expressions proper to love poetry in the description of war".[8] Such breaching of the boundaries between the different domains of poetry must have struck contemporaries as extremely bold; al-Wāḥidī (d. 468/1075) objects at one point to Mutanabbī's use (not infrequent in his practice) of grim gnomic verses to introduce a panegyric: "This kind of thing is considered proper in laments for the dead, not in panegyrics."[9]

Perhaps more than any other Arab poet of the Islamic age, Mutanabbī has tempted readers to see his poems in the light of the biographical anecdotes about him. This is true especially of his early work. Much of it consists in wholly conventional (if on occasion blasphemously hyperbolic) *qaṣīdah*s, introduced by the conventional elegiac love theme (*nasīb*) – though, as Blachère notes, in line with a practice which had developed over the previous half-century, the old theme of the poet's desert-journey (*raḥīl*) in quest of the patron is of rarer occurrence.[10] There are also about a dozen pieces of self-praise (*fakhr*) blending contempt for mankind and the world with promises of great and violent deeds. Most of these pieces are relatively

[6] Cf. p. 351 [7] Al-Qāḍī ʾl-Jurjānī, *Wasāṭah*, 228. [8] *Yatīmah*, I, 163, 165.
[9] Gabrieli, *Studi*, 55.
[10] *Un Poète arabe*, 47. On Mutanabbī's use of the conventional divisions of the *qaṣīdah*, see Gabrieli, *Studi*, 53–5.

short. Two are done in *qaṣīdah* style, with *nasīb* (Y, I, 112, 135/W, 26, 52).[11] Some of the panegyrics use passages of gloomy *sententiae* or scorn for the world as overtures (Y, I, 124, 231/W, 38, 160). A few use self-praise built into the *nasīb* (Y, I, 200/W, 128); a few a combination of gnomic verse and self-praise (Y, I, 208, 326/W, 137, 245). Blachère and Ṭāhā Ḥusayn, in their thoughtful large-scale studies, try to find the fit between poems and anecdotes. Life is not, for them, far from these texts, in which they see wild exultation, inflammatory harangues and reflections of bitterly disappointed hopes. They may be right. Their readings require them to suit the chronology of texts to the tale, but since the received chronological order (as in Wāḥidī's commentary) is rough, rearrangements are certainly possible. Blachère writes of the poems he dates from 318–24/930–6 (the period, in his view, of Mutanabbī's agitation and revolt in Syria) that, although the *qaṣīdah*s and occasional poems Mutanabbī produced during these years are scattered throughout the *Dīwān*, they are similar enough in form and content to be easily identified by their mounting vehemence, which dictates the chronological sequence in which Blachère sets them. But it is not certain that likeness of form and substance must spring from unitary experience. In another place, Blachère himself suggests that a melancholy *ubi sunt* passage in a panegyric may owe as much to Mutanabbī's wish to vary the plan of the *qaṣīdah* as to his pondering of mutability (although he is still tempted to see it as an attempt by the poet to inject his personality into an impersonal verse-form). The case may be the same with the passages of self-praise in panegyrics, in the *fakhr* in which the poet, as Blachère notes, reached back to the old tradition of heroic verse. Blachère also believes, however, that these passages of Mutanabbī's reintroduced life into what had, in a "century of drawing-room poetry", become mere school exercises.[12] But other interpretations are possible and perhaps more probable. In a panegyric to a member of the Tanūkhī family, which befriended the poet in Latakia, the heroic spirit works as a neat overture to expressions of gratitude:

> My resolve guarantees that in desert and town
> the Khaṭṭī lances will be running with blood.
>
> How much more of this hanging back? How much more
> of this delay after delay?
>
> Of letting the sale of verses in a sluggish market
> keep my soul from the paths of glory?

[11] Y = *Dīwān* with the commentary of al-Yāzijī; W = *Dīwān* with the commentary of al-Wāḥidī.
[12] *Un Poète arabe*, 58, 85.

> What has passed of youth will not return. A day once gone cannot be brought back.
>
> When my eye glimpsed the white in my hair, it was [like a painful object] in the black of my eye.
>
> After the perfection of youth, each added day diminishes me.
>
> Shall I be content to live and not offer just recompense for the Prince's liberality?[13]

To take the line about the sale of verses out of context, as an expression of Romantic discontent, is very likely to increase the distance between us and the poet. It is the panegyric itself that puts an end to "delay after delay" and guarantees "the Prince's liberality". Later in his life, when the adventures that had led to the prison in Ḥimṣ were long past, *fakhr* – as in the *qaṣīdah*s dedicated to Sayf al-Dawlah – still played an important part in the texture of themes in Mutanabbī's panegyrics. To vary this texture; to create a signature, or even to conquer, as it were, a province of writing (as a century and a half earlier Abū ʾl-ʿAtāhiyah had claimed, according to the story, the *zuhdiyyah* as his preserve),[14] or indeed to gain followers for some wild, dubious enterprise – any of these motives may have drawn the young poet's interest to *fakhr*. They may have overlapped. Perhaps he thought there might be a market for pure *fakhr*: one short poem (Y, I, 132/W, 48) is glossed, "to be spoken by one of the Tanūkhīs" (*qāla ʿalā lisān baʿḍ al-Tanūkhiyyīn*).

Several anecdotes jeer at Mutanabbī the man. At a moment of princely magnificence he makes a show of standing aloof, only to end up scrambling after dirhams on the floor. He rides with Sayf al-Dawlah's army, but panics when his turban is caught on a branch.[15] These stories have a prototypal air. Perhaps they were sparked – not unlike our modern biographical curiosity – by the strident foregrounding of the panegyrist's ego; perhaps they are gestures pointing at the literariness of the poetry. There are, to be sure, admiring remarks as well. Ibn al-Athīr finds it worth mentioning that Mutanabbī saw battle with his own eyes; Ibn Khallikān (d. 681/1282) calls him "a man of high soul and lofty thought". In the story of his death, Mutanabbī is attacked by a band of bedouins, and turns to flee. A servant's remark – "Where is your verse 'I am known to horse, night and desert, to sword and lance, to parchment and to pen'?" – causes him to turn again and fight until he is killed.[16] The last anecdote cancels the embarrassment of literariness.

[13] Y, I, 208–9/W, 138. Khaṭṭī (from Khaṭṭ in Arabia): a conventional epithet of lances.

[14] See p. 268. [15] Badīʿī, *Ṣubḥ*, 92, 78–9.

[16] Ibid., 175, 178; Ibn Khallikān, *Biographical Dictionary*, I, 106–7.

Massignon thought that Mutanabbī's Qarmaṭī (Carmathian) convictions accounted for his "bitter and combative thought,"[17] for such verses as these:

What station shall I attain! What power shall I fear
When all that God has created and all that he has not
Is of no greater account to my high resolve (*himmah*) than one hair of my head?[18]

or as these, with the strange echo of the Qarmaṭī attack on the pilgrims returning from Mecca:

In me the sword will have a companion like its own sharp edge;
my fame will be that of the boldest of the bold.

I have exhausted the utmost measure of patience. I will
now hurl myself into the perils of war, to the utmost measure . . .

With men of resolve who have long awaited that I should
turn over to them the power I took from the hands of slaves,

[With] a shaykh who regards the five prayers as supererogatory,
and permits shedding the blood of pilgrims in the sacred enclosure . . .

Tomorrow is the rendez-vous between the slender blades
and the kings – Arab or non-Arab – who do not submit . . .[19]

But how much can we know of Mutanabbī's convictions? Some medieval commentators attempt to play down Mutanabbī's more scandalous utterances; others throw them in relief. In a famous anecdote, Mutanabbī reveals to a certain Abū ᶜAbdullāh Muᶜādh b. Ismāᶜīl al-Lādhiqī that he has been sent "to this erring community" as a prophet. "To do what?" the man asks. "To fill the world with righteousness, as it has been filled with iniquity," Mutanabbī replies.[20] Supposing that Mutanabbī kindled a religiously tinged uprising in the Syrian desert, are we to take these words seriously? The phrase is traditional, therefore he may have spoken it; or therefore it may be a tag in a stylized narrative. A short poem of pure warlike *fakhr* follows, but neither in this nor in any of the rest of the *Dīwān* is there anything that goes beyond the bitter and the combative. If there is no evidence in Mutanabbī's poems to prove he was a rebel, there is still less to suggest he was a would-be reformer, as Ṭāhā Ḥusayn would have it. All accounts agree that Mutanabbī was not a devout man, and he occasionally wrote lines to which a devout reader could object. But what he thought of man and God we do not know. Unlike Maᶜarrī's *Luzūmiyyāt*, for Mutanabbī's poetry human perplexity and off-stage suffering are not essential topics. The biographical anecdotes do not permit us to look

[17] "Mutanabbī", 13; for the Carmathians and the events alluded to in the verses which follow, see pp. 197–8, above. [18] Y, I, 141/W, 60. [19] Y, I, 137–8/W, 56–7. [20] Badīᶜī, *Ṣubḥ*, 52; Y, I, 158.

behind the texts, and even the texts are ambiguous. Gabrieli cites a large selection of verses in which readers have seen signs of religious nihilism or philosophical interests, but he is probably right in believing these to be instances of rhetorical hyperbole and *sententiae*. Blachère sees no merit in medieval comparisons of apophthegms by Mutanabbī and Aristotle; he does however discern an intellectual and spiritual kinship between Mutanabbī and Maᶜarrī.[21]

The poetic persona of the early *fakhr* may tempt the reader to see the stamp of personality elsewhere in Mutanabbī's poetry. In his sensitive but deeply Romantic work, Ṭāhā Ḥusayn writes of the panegyric to Badr al-Kharshanī, whose centre-piece is this man's fight with a lion: "It has a nobility of spirit and a power which I cannot but think the poet borrowed from himself for the adornment of his patron."[22] It is indeed difficult not to think of the exuberant power of some of the celebrations of Sayf al-Dawlah's border wars as the work of a poet who has found a hero worthy of him. We note how Mutanabbī applies to Sayf al-Dawlah certain images that he previously used in self-praise:

> Only he mentions his ancestors who stands before defeat
> [in a contest for superior honours] and has no other resource left

and:

> The nights have not attained their wish: they did not,
> as they passed, have me on their lead-rope,[23]

over against:

> Praise belongs to Ibn Abī ᵓl-Hayjāᵓ [Sayf al-Dawlah] himself. To have to
> bring his Jāhilī ancestors to his aid is to be tongue-tied and feeble-minded

and:

> The visitations of time upon the people follow his [Sayf's]
> bidding; he holds in his hand the lead-rope of time.[24]

But then one looks at the tables, compiled by medieval critics, of the many instances in which Mutanabbī repeats a poetic idea, and the curtain between word and motive comes down once again.

PANEGYRIC (*MADĪḤ*)

Poems in the big, public genres – panegyrics mainly, along with some elegies and satires – make up the greatest part of Mutanabbī's *Dīwān*. Such

[21] Gabrieli, *Studi*, 68–78; Blachère, *Un Poète arabe*, 30, 72, 278.
[22] *Maᶜa ᵓl-Mutanabbī*, I, 239; for a brief analysis of this poem, see p. 157, above.
[23] Y, I, 456, 159/W, 364, 85.
[24] Y, II, 132, 211/W, 490, 556.

poetry had a job to do, but once the job was done, its second, longer life would begin. It would enter circulation and become, more often than not in the form of single lines or brief passages, the cash of the literate life. From scholarly worrying-bone and rhetorical stiffener, its uses stretched to literary re-casting – Thaʿālibī has a section on conceits by Mutanabbī elegantly done into prose and used in epistles (*rasāʾil*) by al-Ṣāḥib Ibn ʿAbbād, the vizier and littérateur who nursed a grudge against Mutanabbī, but knew a good phrase when he saw one[25] – and to playful allusion (known as *talmīḥ*) in social intercourse.[26] Mutanabbī is certainly quotable. His aphorisms are forceful:

> Rage against Time is like a fire in the belly,
> but it is the captive's rage against the thongs

or:

> A mindless ignoramus needs polite learning (*adab*) as
> a headless donkey needs a halter.[27]

His images can be astonishingly bold and, within a mannerist system of perception, beautifully precise:

> Their hair blackened the trees on the mountain-side;
> it was as if low-flying crows flitted among the trees.
>
> Crimson blood ran upon the leaves, seeming oranges
> among the boughs

or:

> Above the clashing waves the birds are like
> riders of dappled horses, who have lost hold of the reins.[28]

For its first job, however – for its *use* as a panegyric or the like – a *qaṣīdah* needed to work as a piece. It might be a suite on a succession of themes, but as a piece it had to hold the attention of the audience and enhance the impact of its message. This is not to say that poems were recited in the respectful silence of the concert-hall. In an anecdote of Mutanabbī's recital of the *qaṣīdah* written to thaw a chill between himself and Sayf al-Dawlah, Abū Firās (the prince's kinsman, rival poet, and Mutanabbī's enemy) throws, line after line, accusations of plagiarism and ill-decorum at the poet. The prince himself interrupts the performance when the verse,

> If you are gladdened by my envier's tales [it is
> well]; no wound that gives you pleasure causes pain

[25] *Yatīmah*, I, 101; for Mutanabbī's relations with Ibn ʿAbbād, see pp. 105–6, above.
[26] See e.g. Badīʿī, *Ṣubḥ*, 313–37.
[27] Thaʿālibī, *Yatīmah*, I, 173; Y, II, 438/W, 752; Y, I, 337/W, 254.
[28] Y, II, 258/W, 599; Y, I, 224/W, 153.

moves him to embrace Mutanabbī.[29] The anecdote may be stylized, but it presents a scene thought conceivable. Nor is there reason to think that all the poems are constructed with equal care. It is clear, however, that in many cases Mutanabbī takes pains to keep the poem moving and to give to the whole text, or to certain passages in it, effective form. A few examples may be offered.

The Sayf al-Dawlah period, with its endless border war against the Byzantines, supplied the poet with stories of brave doings – the handiest means of pulling a panegyric together. To be sure, a panegyrist wants to persuade the audience not so much of the mere fact that his patron did thus and so, but rather of his affinity for doing thus and so. A passage relating specific events will usually be framed in general statements about the patron's valour and munificence. Nor does the panegyrist write history. In a poem about a military expedition, place-names may provide a kind of armature; outstanding details may be briefly recalled; but the fibre of the narrative comes from its images – of burning cities and wild mountains, of armed might, danger, endurance, violence and death – and from great set-pieces of marching and clashing armies, and the decisive intervention of the hero. Such elements are combined in the poem celebrating the battle for the fort of al-Ḥadath. The reader will note how the poet gradually moves from compact reference to detail and then to broad canvas, giving the poem a sense of movement. After the opening maxims and their application to the patron, the poem moves through several, increasingly specific, compact references to the event that occasioned it. Then, with the verb of motion ("they came . . ."), a detailed if stylized chronicle begins. These are frequent patterns of composition in Mutanabbī, as is the subsequent narrowing of focus on to the hero. The theme of the fledgelings is perhaps intended to frame the passage (metre: *ṭawīl*):

ʿalā qadri ahli ʾl-ʿaẓmi taʾtī ʾl-ʿaẓāʾimu   *wa-taʾtī ʿalā qadri ʾl-kirāmi ʾl-makārimu*
wa-taʿẓumu fī ʿayni ʾl-ṣaghīri ṣighāruhā   *wa-taṣghuru fī ʿayni ʾl-ʿaẓīmi ʾl-ʿaẓāʾimu*

According to the degree of the people of resolve come the resolutions, and according to the degree of noble men come the noble actions.

Small deeds are great in the eyes of the small, and great deeds are small in the eyes of the great.

Saif al-Daula charges the army with the burden of his own zeal, which numerous [enemy] armies have proved incapable of bearing,

And he demands of men what he has in himself – and that is something which (even) lions do not claim.

[29] Badīʿī, *Ṣubḥ*, 89–91.

The longest-living of birds, even eagles of the desert, the young ones and the old ones of them, offer (themselves as) ransom[30] for his armoury;

It would not harm them that they were created without talons, seeing that his swords and hilts have been created.

Does al-Ḥadath the red recognise its[31] own colour, and does it know which of the two wine-bearers was the clouds?

The white [rain-] clouds watered it before he descended, then when he drew near it the skulls watered it (again) [with blood].

He built it, and built it high, whilst lances were clashing against lances and the waves of the fates surged around it;[32]

The like of madness possessed it, then amulets consisting of the corpses of the slain thereafter bedecked it.[33]

(It was) an exile driven away by destiny, then you restored it to the (true) religion with Khaṭṭi lances in destiny's despite.

You cause the nights [fate] to lose (forever) anything that you take (from them), whereas they are debtors repaying what they take from you.

When what you intend is a future verb (act), it becomes past tense before any conditional particles can be prefixed to it;

And how can the Byzantines and Russians[34] hope to destroy it (al-Ḥadath), seeing that that thrust (of yours) is for it foundations and pillars?

They had summoned it to justice, and the fates were the arbiters; and no wronged man died, nor did any wronger live.

They came against you trailing their steel,[35] as though they travelled by night on horses that had no feet.

When they flashed, their swords could not be distinguished – and their garments and headgear were of the like (steel);

An army that marched slowly from the east of the earth and the west, confused noises proceeding from it (echoing) in the ears of the Gemini;

Gathered together in it was every tongue and nation, and only interpreters could make the speakers understand.

What a time, the time whose fire melted away the counterfeit, and all that remained was a sharp (sword) or a sturdy warrior (lion)!

Broken to pieces was all that could not break through armour and lances, and of the champions there fled whoever did not strike against (the enemy).

30 I.e. "salute" (the expression is a polite form of address to superiors, equivalent to "your humble servant"). The birds are vultures, which do not have powerful claws.

31 Or "her": the city is feminine; cf. Abū Tammām's personification of the city of Amorium, pp. 159–61, above.

32 The Byzantines had earlier taken the fortress and razed it; the Muslims were rebuilding it as the attack came.

33 Madness: the city's possession by the Byzantines, which the Muslims "cure" with amulets.

34 Byzantine mercenaries. 35 Long chain-mail reaching almost to the ground.

You stood firm, when there was no doubt that any who stood must die, as though you were in the very eyelid of death, and death was asleep,

The champions passing you by, wounded and in flight, whilst your face shone brightly and your mouth was smiling.

You surpassed the bounds of courage and reason, so that people said you had knowledge of the unseen.

You pressed their two wings[36] tightly upon the heart, so that the under-feathers and wing-tips died under the squeezing,

With a blow that struck the crania while victory was still absent, and proceeded (forthwith) to the upper breasts as victory advanced.

You despised the Rudaini[37] spears so that you flung them away, and so that it was as though the sword was reviling the lance;[38]

Whoever seeks a great victory, its keys are only the light, cutting white swords.

You scattered them over all [the hill of] al-Uḥaydib, just as dirhams are scattered over a bride,

Your horses trampling with you the nests [of the eagles] on the mountain-tops, and many dishes of food lay about the nests.

The eagles' chicks thought you visited them with their mothers, whilst they were (in reality) sturdy, noble steeds;

When they [the horses] slipped you made them go on their bellies, as snakes crawl along on the earth's surface . . .[39]

We see why al-Sharīf al-Raḍī called Mutanabbī a leader of armies. Blachère, who is a Romantic reader with little use for mannerist brilliancies, and who writes of the poetry of the Sayf al-Dawlah period that it seldom achieves the vibrancy of the poetry from before Mutanabbī's imprisonment, nevertheless agrees with this opinion, and concedes that the praise of Sayf al-Dawlah sometimes calls forth an epic grandeur unexampled in earlier Arabic poetry.[40]

One text, in which Mutanabbī gives his version of a check to a planned raid into Byzantine territory, is an instructive example of poetic power as a means of managing the news. In the section quoted below, the large-scale composition is not unlike that in the last example. The poem moves from the broadest view – "Byzantium", "the land" – closer, through distinctions

[36] The pun ("wings of an army"/"wings of a bird") is the same in Arabic as in English.

[37] An antique poetic term of uncertain origin.

[38] The sword (*sayf*, a play on Sayf al-Dawlah's title) is the weapon of a braver man than the lance, because it is used in close combat.

[39] Y, II, 202–8/W, 548–54; trans. Arberry, *Arabic Poetry*, 84–8. For further analyses, see Latham, "Toward a better understanding", and Hamori, "Reading al-Mutanabbī's ode".

[40] *Un Poète arabe*, 187.

of mountain and cave and then the names of particular places, to focus on the hero; then it broadens to the general again, to Sayf al-Dawlah's habit of being a hero, after which it seems ready to seal the matter with an aphorism, but, refusing to let performer and audience catch their breath, contradicts itself and only then, with a second gnomic verse, comes to a cadence. The poet uses this compositional scheme of focusing and broadening, and then of the false before the true cadence, to catch us up in a powerful current. The propagandist uses the current to announce, and yet conceal as the mere exception that proves the heroic habit, the setback – "except when the Sayḥān freezes over":

. . . Do not be amazed: there are many swords, but today there is only the one Sword of Dynasty [Sayf al-Dawlah].

His noble nature unsheathes him in war, and the habit of benevolence and mercy sheathes him.

When I saw that mankind were beneath his station, I knew that Fate [*dahr*] tries mankind and separates the true coin:

Most worthy of the sword is he who smites men's necks, and of secure peace he who takes hardships lightly.

Most wretched of lands is, thus, the land of Byzantium; none in it can deny your glory.

You have poured out your horsemen upon it, so that even beyond Faranjah [i.e., at the farthest end of the Byzantine empire] all eyes were sleepless.

The land is daubed with the saffron dye of blood; the people, although not at prayer, are prostrate on the ground; the land is like so many painted mosques.

You overthrow them though they take to the mountains – those are now their fast horses – and you thrust at them the lances of your stratagems.

You hew them to pieces though they hide beneath rocks as snakes hide in the belly of the dust;

And the lofty strongholds on the mountaintops are encircled by your horsemen, a necklace around their necks.

They [your horsemen] annihilated them [the Byzantines] on the day of the Luqan, and drove them at Hinzīṭ, till Āmid was white with captives;

They made [the fort of] Safsāf join in the fate of [the fort of] Sābūr and it fell; their people, their very stones, tasted destruction.

In the wadi there marched with them [with your horsemen] in the night a man of courage, of blessed face, devout,

A man [*fatā*] who desires that the land be broad and time long, for time is too narrow for him, and no goal is far enough,

A man of raids whose swords are never absent from their necks unless [the river] Sayḥān freezes over,[41]

So that not one of them is left except those whom their dark lips and high breasts protect from the sword [i.e. the women] –

The patricians weep over them in the gloom, while among us they are unwanted goods cast aside on the market.

This is what fate [*al-ayyām*] has decreed for those it rules: a disaster to one people is a benefit to another.

But, because of the nobility of your valour, you, though their killer, are loved like a benefactor among them,

And the blood you shed is proud of you, and the heart in which you strike fear sings your praise,

For everyone sees the ways of courage and generosity, but the mind is governed by its temper . . .[42]

Poems of pure, general praise may rely on degrees of formal organization. The following seems a plausible breakdown of such a text (Y, I, 326–32/W, 245–51):

A Introduction: gnomic verses leading into self-praise; eleven verses (of which the last is the hinge-line, *takhalluṣ*, included here because it depends syntactically on verse 10).

B Patron praised in the third person; six verses.

C His kin praised; eight verses.

D Patron praised, addressed in the second person; six verses.

E Poet and patron (in which it is explained why the poet has only now come to praise him); four verses.

F Patron praised in cosmic and religious terms (Time would obey his bidding, God is his guide, etc.); six verses. (Grouping such terms of praise near the end of a poem is frequent practice with Mutanabbī.)

G Poet and patron: some poetry is trash but this patron deserves (and gets) the best; two verses, end.

The recurrence of sixes may well be an accident, but the alternation of passages, and the rough proportions, are very likely planned (Blachère observes that as the young Mutanabbī's craft matures, the parts of the *qaṣīdah* – *nasīb* and the panegyric proper – achieve a certain equilibrium).[43] Besides supplying an armature, such organization allows the poet to move, as it were, in a spiral, re-working the same limited stock of virtues on level after level. Rhetoric may also organize smaller regions. A plain example is

[41] It was the freezing weather that had checked Sayf al-Dawlah's campaign.

[42] Y, II, 99–105/W, 460–7. [43] *Un Poète arabe*, 93.

passage B of the same poem. The six lines quoted below illustrate how the poet orders his matter and manipulates syntax and sentence rhythms to give the passage shape:

Polished in learning (*adīb*), refined in manners, grave, a man of deeds,
intelligent, magnanimous, noble, a hero,

The vicissitudes of time are among his captives, among those jealous of his
hands are the rainclouds [symbols of liberality].

He cures his riches by impoverishing himself through generosity, as if wealth
were an illness.

He is beautiful, but in the eyes of his enemies he is more abhorrent than a guest
is to his cattle.[44]

If anything protected a noble chief from death, death's veneration and
exaltation of him would protect him,

Along with gleaming naked swords, whose religion is to permit all, although
they are bare as pilgrims observing the sacred prohibitions.[45]

The design is built on asymmetries and symmetries. The passage starts with the choppiest, most percussive kind of syntax and winds down with a leisurely, but syntactically complex, two-line period.[46] After the catchall chain of adjectives in the first verse, two lines are devoted to the addressee's generosity, then a turn-line ingeniously combines generosity and valour into a single conceit; then two lines follow about valour alone. The symmetry is pointed up by the chiastic arrangement, around the turn-line, of the verbs in the couplets about generosity and valour. The most arresting conceit is placed at the end, making the formal break there also into a pause for thought.

In the following passage grammatical parallelism, and the like, are somewhat obscured in translation, but the shaping by imagery remains:

He has two armies: his cavalry and his birds of prey [which scavenge after the
battle].
When he hurls them against the enemy, only skulls remain.

Their horse-cloths are the clothes of every impious
ruler; their hooves trample the face of every unjust usurper.

The light of morning is weary because of the jealousy
you excite in it; the black of night is weary because you press it hard.

The spears are weary from your breaking their points;
the Indian steel is weary from your striking it against steel.

44 Because the guests will eat the cattle.

45 In the sacred enclosure no blood may be shed and the pilgrims, although not bare, may not wear sewn garments.

46 Cf. Scheindlin, *Form and Structure*, 102, 125.

A cloud of vultures beneath which a cloud marches . . .
If they ask for a drink, their swords offer it to them.[47]

The last line ties it up neatly: it resumes the opening metaphor, the antithesis between light and dark from the third verse, and the clashing weapons from the fourth (for the swords are lightning in the dust of battle, promising a certain rain). The sense that a circle is being closed is strengthened by the symmetry in the metaphorical extensions: *army* from cavalry to birds, *cloud* from birds (its primary metaphorical referent) to cavalry. The rhetoric delights in shifting relations: bright weapons against the light, a dark mass of soldiers against the dark; then weapon against weapon; then bright weapon against dark cloud. Or: above and below, on and under, and the strange inversion where the cloud that brings rain is beneath the cloud that absorbs it.

TRANSMISSION OF MUTANABBĪ'S POETRY

Mutanabbī himself oversaw a recension of the poems he wished preserved and helped his scholarly admirers on difficult points; a commentary (partially preserved) by the grammarian Ibn Jinnī, who followed Mutanabbī on his journeys after the departure from Aleppo, was heavily used by later commentators. The best-known medieval commentaries are by al-Wāḥidī (d. 468/1075), and al-ᶜUkbarī (d. 616/1219); Wāḥidī is regarded by Blachère, and indeed generally, as the best medieval commentator; ᶜUkbarī lacks his finesse, but his commentary quotes from several other scholars. Among modern commentaries, pride of place belongs to the extremely clear work of Nāṣīf al-Yāzijī, first published in Beirut in 1882 and reprinted many times since then.[48] Among scholarly works, the ones by Blachère and Gabrieli, quoted in this chapter, are indispensable. Ṭāhā Ḥusayn's *Maᶜa ᵓl-Mutanabbī*, not intended as an academic book, is a thoughtful reading with a most learned and sensitive eye for the nuances of Arabic poetry. A selection of poems in English translation was published by A.J. Arberry (*Poems of al-Mutanabbī*) in 1967. A bibliography of studies in Arabic and in European languages is *Rāᵓid al-dirāsah ᶜan al-Mutanabbī*, edited by G. and M. ᶜAwwād (Baghdad, 1979).

[47] Y, II, 20/W, 380–1.
[48] Yāzijī omits several lines from two poems, see Blachère, *Un Poète arabe*, 303.

CHAPTER 18

ABŪ FIRĀS AL-ḤAMDĀNĪ

BACKGROUND AND UPBRINGING

Abū Firās al-Ḥārith b. Saᶜīd was a grandson of Abū ᵓl-ᶜAbbās Ḥamdān b. Ḥamdūn al-Taghlibī, founder of the Hamdanid dynasty. The Banū Ḥamdān were a distinguished Arab family of bedouin origin and Shīᶜī inclination which played a leading role in the affairs of the declining ᶜAbbasid caliphate from near the end of the third/ninth century until about the end of the following century; al-Thaᶜālibī, in his *Yatīmat al-dahr* (written sometime before the close of the fourth/tenth century), calls them "kings and princes, comely of face, eloquent of tongue, liberal of hand, weighty of mind", describing the amir Sayf al-Dawlah as "the centre-jewel of their necklace".[1] Into this princely and distinguished line Abū Firās was born in the year 320/932 or 321/933, at the time when the fortunes of his family were approaching their zenith; when he died in 357/968 their hour of glory had already passed. His mother was of Greek origin, and, although she would have been classed as *umm walad* (a slave freed on giving birth to her master's son), yet Abū Firās speaks of himself as the son of a free-born woman, *ibn ḥurrah*,[2] showing his pride in his mother's origin in defiance of taunts and innuendoes from other kinsmen. In one of his earliest poems he remarks:

> I see that my people and I are different in our ways, in spite of the bonds of parentage which should tie us;
> The furthest in kinship are the furthest from injuring me, the nearest kin are the closest to harming me.[3]

Later, in one of his *Rūmiyyāt*, the collection of poems written while he was a captive in Byzantium (Rūm), he bitterly says: "Should I fear a single wrong from my Byzantine maternal uncles, then also must I fear fourfold from my paternal uncles."[4]

Ibn Khālawayh, the famous grammarian, who taught Abū Firās as a boy, and was the transmitter and commentator of his poetry after his death, and

[1] *Yatīmah*, I, 15. [2] *Dīwān*, 81.
[3] Ibid., 20; this and all following translations by A. F. L. B. [4] Ibid., 134.

the witness of many events of the fourth/tenth century both in Iraq and in Syria, tells us that the poet's father, Abū ʾl-ʿAlāʾ Saʿīd b. Ḥamdān, had "merits more than can be described", and that he was permanently on duty at the court of the ʿAbbasid caliph al-Muqtadir, "was fully trusted by him, and most of his heroic actions were performed before him and at his very gate" (this suggests that Abū Firās's birthplace was most probably Baghdad).[5] A series of power struggles for the amirate of Mosul between Abū Firās's cousin Nāṣir al-Dawlah and his father Abū ʾl-ʿAlāʾ Saʿīd ended with the latter's death in 323/935, when Abū Firās was a child of two or three. His mother took refuge with her son-in-law Sayf al-Dawlah, who had not yet established himself as an independent prince, but was still his elder brother's vassal, with a shaky hold over some areas in the vicinity of Wāsiṭ in Mesopotamia. In 330/942 both he and his brother played a decisive part in crushing a rebellion against the caliph, whereupon they received the titles respectively of Sayf al-Dawlah ("Sword of the Realm") and Nāṣir al-Dawlah ("Supporter of the Realm"). Of this honour Abū Firās speaks in the *Ḥamdāniyyah* (a poem of 225 lines treating of the annals and noble deeds of the Hamdanids; metre: *ṭawīl*):

wa fīnā li-dīni ʾllāhi ʿizzun wa-munʿatun   *wa-fīnā li-dīni ʾllāhi sayfun wa-nāṣiru*
humā wa-amīru ʾl-muʾminīna musharradun   *ajārāhu lammā lam yajid man yujāwiru*
wa raddāhu ḥattā mallakāhu sarīrahū   *bi-ʿishrīna alfan baynahā ʾl-mawtu sāfiru*

Among us is a glory and a defence of God's religion, among us a *sword* and *supporter* of God's religion:
These two, when the Commander of the Faithful was but a fugitive, gave shelter to him when there was no other to do so,
and brought him back to his throne, so that he was again able to campaign with twenty thousand death-dealing troops under him.[6]

In 333/945 Sayf al-Dawlah took possession of Aleppo and Ḥimṣ, and extended his territory over the larger part of Syria and Diarbakr, and became henceforth an independent amir. Abū Firās was taken by his mother to his court, where he received the attention and care of Sayf al-Dawlah as a growing boy. He says of this period, in a poem addressed to one of his literary contemporaries:

I lost my father as a child, but afterwards I found a father in one whose nature among men is of evergreen nobility;
He is my cousin as to blood-kinship, but also my revered elder and my master whom I do not disobey.

[5] Ibid., 245. [6] Ibid., 114.

He has been my shelter to escape from whatever I have feared; may he forever find shelter and escape from whatever he fears;
May the wiles of fate spare his abode, and we shall not care whose abode they strike.[7]

Sayf al-Dawlah gained renown throughout the world of Islam not only because he appeared to be the sole defender of Islam against its enemies and ensured peace and safety for travellers and pilgrims against bedouin marauders, but also because he was a cultured patron of letters. Nothing like the splendour of his court had been seen since the days of the early ʿAbbasid caliphate, for it was enriched by the great scholars, poets, masters of *belles-lettres* and philosophers of his day, among them such men as the preacher Ibn Nubātah, the philosopher and musician al-Fārābī, and above all the poet al-Mutanabbī, who joined his court in 337/948 and was associated with it for nine years afterwards. Growing up in this cultured atmosphere, Abū Firās distinguished himself in early youth in his literary studies as well as in the practice of war. Sayf al-Dawlah recognized his merit, and in 336/948, when he was only sixteen, made him amir of the rich province of Manbij in appreciation of his valour and brilliance. Later the town of Ḥarrān was added to Abū Firās's governorship, and he continued to serve with honour until one day in 351/962 he was taken captive by a Byzantine army near his headquarters at Manbij. The Crusades were to be launched in earnest more than a century later, but the ferocious campaigns of the emperor Nicephorus II Phocas at this time seem to have foreshadowed them. (Ibn Khallikān, writing in the seventh/thirteenth century, speaks also of an earlier occasion in 348/959 when Abū Firās was captured by the Byzantines but escaped by jumping on horseback from the summit of the castle of Kharshanah;[8] but this romantic feat is dismissed as a mere legend by some of the poet's recent biographers.) It is to the well-documented captivity of 351/962, lasting for four years, that we owe the group of *qaṣīdah*s called *al-Rūmiyyāt*, in which is to be found some of Abū Firās's finest poetry. Sayf al-Dawlah was now beginning to suffer some serious reverses in his contests with the Byzantines; on one occasion, he was forced out of his main capital Aleppo and had to make his headquarters at Mayyāfarīqīn in Diarbakr, and with defeat came sickness and financial hardship. Abū Firās sent Sayf al-Dawlah letter after letter requesting to be ransomed in exchange for the captured nephew of the Byzantine emperor, but Sayf al-Dawlah appears to have felt that he could not secure the release of his kinsman alone, leaving another 6,000 Muslims in captivity. Four

[7] Ibid., 184. [8] *Biographical Dictionary*, I, 367.

years passed before Sayf al-Dawlah was finally able to secure the release of Abū Firās and all the other prisoners, after the payment of a large ransom which he was only able to raise by means of a legacy. Abū Firās, however, was only concerned about his own plight in captivity, and whether or not his absence had affected his political standing with his patron. Fluctuating between hope and despair, tormented by grief, loneliness and frustration in his ignorance of the true situation, he sought consolation in poetry.

THE INFLUENCE OF AL-MUTANABBĪ

Long before his captivity, he had shown himself to be a highly accomplished poet in the *qaṣīdah*s addressed to Sayf al-Dawlah in praise of his victories over both the rebellious bedouin tribes of the Syrian desert and the Byzantines. The *Ḥamdāniyyah* by its sheer length testifies to his mastery of metre and rhyme, though it may appear to us now as rather tedious and prosaic; like the long *rajaz*-poem in which the ᶜAbbasid poet-prince Ibn al-Muᶜtazz (d. 296/908) chronicles the times of his uncle the caliph al-Muwaffaq, the *Ḥamdāniyyah* sacrifices the classical bedouin ideal of pith and economy (*jazālah*) to the voluble bragging proverbially associated with the *Muᶜallaqah* of Abū Firās's distant tribal ancestor, the Taghlibi ᶜAmr b. Kulthūm.[9] To this period also belong some of Abū Firās's love-poems on boys and women, wine-songs, hunting poetry and verse on similar courtly and light-hearted themes.[10]

The early poetry of Abū Firās and most of the *Rūmiyyāt* carry strong echoes of al-Mutanabbī, by whom he could not have escaped being influenced as he was still very young when al-Mutanabbī first appeared at the court of Sayf al-Dawlah and only in his middle twenties when he left it. Al-Thaᶜālibī tells us that al-Mutanabbī showed some deference towards Abū Firās and avoided any conflict with him;[11] no doubt, for all his arrogance, he did not dare to ignore the close ties of blood between Abū Firās and his patron Sayf al-Dawlah. Nevertheless, there is evidence that Abū Firās took part in the hostile criticism of a poem which al-Mutanabbī recited in front of Sayf al-Dawlah, together with his teacher Ibn Khālawayh who was an open enemy of al-Mutanabbī.[12] This may indicate some kind of early rivalry, due perhaps to the secret instigation and machinations of Ibn Khālawayh and others who took advantage of Abū Firās's princely pride; it is said that al-Mutanabbī's taunt, in the same poem:

Let not your keen eyes, I beseech you, be deceived by the appearance of fat
where there is really nothing but a bloated body

[9] See *CHALUP*, 34, 38. [10] Cf. pp. 169, 174, and ch. 12, nos. 14, 15. [11] *Yatīmah*, I, 35.
[12] Mutanabbī, *Dīwān* with commentary of Yāzijī (= Y), II, 120; cf. pp. 307–8, above.

was meant for Abū Firās, though more probably it was intended for Ibn Khālawayh, whose obsessive competitiveness with al-Mutanabbī lasted long after the latter's death.

Abū Firās's early imitations of al-Mutanabbī take the form of crude echoes of his words, ideas and epigrams, as in this description of raiders' horses:

wa-jāwazna ʾl-budayyata ṣādiyātin *yulāḥizna ʾl-sarāba wa-lā sarābā*
And they crossed the desert of al-Budayyah thirsting, their gaze fixed on phantom water where there was not even mirage[13]

which recalls Mutanabbī's

wa-khaylan taghtadhī rīḥa ʾl-mawāmī *wa-yakfīhā mina ʾl-māʾi ʾl-sarābu*
Horses feeding on the wind of the sands, satisfied by mirage in the absence of water[14]

both being in the metre *wāfir*. Similarly, the conceit:

kaʾanna ʾl-ḥijā wa ʾl-ṣawna wa ʾl-ʿaqla wa ʾl-tuqā *ladayya li-rabbāti ʾl-khudūri ḍarāʾiru*
It is as if my forethought, continence, wisdom and piety were my rivals for the love of fair ladies[15]

imitates Mutanabbī's

Every fair woman sees as a rival for her love of me, my chivalry, honour and pride;
These prevent me from taking advantage of pleasure when there is privacy, and not only fear of consequences.[16]

Many more such instances are to be found in Abū Firās's youthful poetry. Later, in the *Rūmiyyāt*, he had no need to place himself in competition with al-Mutanabbī, for he had a rich emotional reserve from which to draw his own ideas, and themes, but the *qaṣīdah*s of al-Mutanabbī still served him as artistic models. Unlike his teacher Ibn Khālawayh, Abū Firās seems to have developed during the period of his captivity a more genuine understanding of al-Mutanabbī and a more sympathetic admiration for his poetry, judging from the spontaneous way in which he quotes from his *qaṣīdah*s and borrows from his expressions and stylistic techniques, a type of stylistic imitation called by the Arab critics "calque" (*ḥadhw*). Illustration of the calque process appears in one of the *Rūmiyyāt*, beginning *a-mā li-jamīlin ʿindakunna thawābun*,[17] which is modelled on a poem in the same metre (*ṭawīl*) and rhyme addressed by al-Mutanabbī to Kāfūr, the governor of Egypt, with whom he took employment after leaving Sayf al-Dawlah.[18] In

[13] *Dīwān*, 14. [14] Y, II, 200. [15] *Dīwān*, 105.
[16] *Dīwān* with commentary of Barqūqī, I, 349. [17] *Dīwān*, 21–5. [18] Y, II, 352–8.

his own piece al-Mutanabbī starts with a satirical treatment of the frailty of amorous youth and fickle love, a variation on a beautiful and humorous erotic prelude (*nasīb*) by the pre-Islamic poet ʿAlqamah, and then proceeds, after a poignant passage of self-praise and self-justification, to put his case before Kāfūr, now eulogizing, now protesting and blaming, now uttering words of wisdom, now giving vent to reckless and bitter expressions of disappointment. This scheme is faithfully followed by Abū Firās, to the extent of borrowing whole lines or hemistichs with very slight alteration. He begins:

Is there no reward among you for a good action? Nor any mercy to be shown when a mistake is made?
Indeed, he is gone astray who is beguiled by a woman, and weak is he who is under the spell of a maiden.
Praise be to God, my heart is whole, and when other necks are bent and humbled by women, mine is raised up.
No beautiful woman possesses my heart entirely, even though she be as a blossom in her youth;
I run the course of love without fully yielding my reins to it; I may err, but am not blind to what is right.

Then, taking up the theme of yearning for the homeland, he continues:

If a friend drifts away from you for no other reason than weariness, then the only remedy is to let him go.
If I fail to get my desire in one land, I seek another with strong will and ready mount.
I do my utmost to avoid separation, but if it happens there will be no return for me.
I am patient and enduring even when exhaustion is extreme, fearless in speech and eloquent even when faced with naked swords,
Imperturbable when struck by the darts of fate and when death is coming and going all around me;
I gaze at the changes and chances of time with an eye that perceives the truth and distinguishes it from falsehood.
In whom shall a man confide when misfortune befalls him? Whence can the generous free-spirited man find his peers?
All men – save a very few – are but wolves clothed in men's garments.
I overlook the folly of my folk and they think it is folly in me; but which of us is more foolish? Dust and ashes be on *his* head.
If they knew me as well as I know them, they would understand that I am the one with vision and they are far removed from it.
Many words fall on my ears, but are like buzzing of flies in the midday glare.
To God I complain of being in a place where lions are ruled by dogs.
I am everyone's neighbour, my hospitality unhesitatingly extended to them, and my door never closed to hoard my wealth in times of need.
I do not seek out their faults to taunt them with, myself without blemish that could be attacked by the envious.

I wield influence, and love of me is implanted in people's hearts; I am gentle towards the ignorant, and am revered.

This may be compared with the following lines from al-Mutanabbī's poem:

I used to long that white could be a dye, so that by whitening my locks I could hide my youth,
In the time when the hair of my temples was an enchantment for women and something to boast of, though that boast was for me a shame . . .
Within my body is a soul which will not grow old as the body does, even though the white hairs were to pierce my cheeks like spears;
Time may change whatever else in me it pleases, but my soul it will not change; however long I live that will remain young.
I am guiding star for my companions when dark clouds obscure the stars;
I have no need of homeland, not fretted by desire to return to a land from which I have once departed . . .
I suffer thirst without disclosing need for water, when the sun casts shimmering haze over the trotting camels . . .
A fair woman has but an hour from me, to be followed by a desert leading to no meeting.
Love is nothing but being taken unawares, and overcome with desire: a heart exposes itself and is smitten.
But it is not my heart that is a target for fair women, nor are my fingers made to hold the wine-glass . . .
The noblest place in the world is the saddle of a charger, and the best companion is a book.

The similarity in the satirical treatment of love and nostalgia is unmistakable; the likening of men to wolves is also found in a *qaṣīdah* of al-Mutanabbī where Kāfūr's rivals are compared to dogs and wolves. Then comes Abū Firās's main theme, his grief, the bitterness of captivity, his shattered hopes and conflicting feelings of doubt, anger and loyalty for Sayf al-Dawlah. First he addresses his Hamdanid cousins:

banī ᶜamminā ma yaṣnaᶜu ʾl-sayfu fī ʾl-waghā *idhā fulla minhu maḍribun wa-dhubābu*
banī ᶜamminā lā tunkirū ʾl-wudda innanā *shidādun ᶜalā ghayri ʾl-hawāni ṣilābu*
banī ᶜamminā naḥnu ʾl-sawāᶜidu wa ʾl-ẓubā *wa-yūshiku yawman an yakūna ḍirābu*

Cousins, what can a sword do in battle if its edge and tip are blunted?
Cousins, do not gainsay our mutual love; we are firm and steadfast against humiliation.
Cousins, we are both the sword-arms and the blades they wield: soon there will be fighting to be done.

Then he chides his cousins for refusing to come to his aid while the Byzantine ruler was ready to help his nephew, and goes on to address his complaint directly to Sayf al-Dawlah, his erstwhile benefactor, his brother-in-law and closest cousin, in lines which owe much to the passage in which al-Mutanabbī addresses his patron, Kāfūr:

I do not claim to say what God knows is untrue: the dwellings of ʿAlī [i.e. Sayf al-Dawlah] are wide open for the destitute;
His deeds are generous and noble, his wealth a gift for seekers of bounty.
Yet he, that was a sharp sword in my hand, has failed me; before my eyes his bright star has darkened.
He has been slow to help me, while the Fates are swift, and death is at hand with tooth and claw.
Even had there not been between us long-standing friendship and the family ties which bind men,
Still for the sake of Islam he should not desert me, for I am a defender of it and a fighter on its behalf.
Nevertheless, I am content in any event, so it be known on which side appearances are deceitful.
I have always been contented with a small measure of love from him, though there would have been no bar to much being given.
I would wish to remain in his land for friendship's sake, though my fame is sought as a boon elsewhere.
Pure friendship is thus: no reward is expected for it, no torment feared while it endures;
I do not desire to be bribed into loving, for weak is the passion for which reward is desired.
I used to fear parting, when prosperity brought us together and we met and talked daily;
But how is it now, with Caesar's lands between us, and I am encompassed by the surging frothy sea?
Why, when I have sacrificed myself for your sake, is the only reward I get bitter reproach?
I could have wished that you had been sweet when life was bitter, satisfied with me when others were angry,
And that between me and you there should have been a flourishing field of friendship, between me and all the world besides a desolation.
If I secure your friendship, all else is worthless, all that is upon the face of the earth mere dust.

Abū Firās's mother died before his return from captivity, and he wrote an elegy for her in which he borrowed many ideas and themes from al-Mutanabbī, particularly from the latter's elegies on his grandmother and on Khawlah, the sister of Sayf al-Dawlah. In the elegy on his grandmother, al-Mutanabbī tells us that he wrote announcing his approaching return after a long absence, and that she died from excess of joy; in the lament of Khawlah he speaks of her piety and liberality.[19] Reversing the former theme and elaborating the latter, Abū Firās writes:

[19] Ibid., 19–25, 280–6.

ayā umma ʾl-asīri saqāki ghaythun *bi-karhin minki mā laqiya ʾl-asīru . . .*

Mother of the captive (may your grave be refreshed by rain), the fate which the captive has met was in despite of you.
Mother of the captive (may your grave be refreshed by rain), he is perplexed, unable to stay or go,
Mother of the captive (may your grave be refreshed by rain), to whom can the bearer of the good news of the ransom go?
Mother of the captive, now that you are dead, for whom will his locks and hair be grown?
When your son travels by land or sea, who will pray for him and seek God's protection for him? . . .
You have faced the calamities of Fate with no child or companion at your side;
The darling of your heart was absent from the place where the heavenly angels were present.
May you be mourned by every day that you fasted patiently through the noontide heat;
May you be mourned by every night you remained wakeful until bright dawn broke;
May you be mourned by everyone oppressed and fearful to whom you gave shelter when there were few indeed to do so;
May you be mourned by every destitute and poverty-stricken man whom you made rich when there was little marrow left in his bones.
Mother, how many a long care have you suffered with no-one to help you . . .
Mother, how often did good news of my approach come to you, but was forestalled by your untimely death;
To whom can I complain, in whom confide, when my heart is overwhelmed by its sorrows?
By what prayer of woman shall I be shielded? By the light of what face shall I gain comfort?[20]

The fatherless Abū Firās's attachment to his mother is understandable and is further illustrated in a poem he wrote on hearing how she had implored Sayf al-Dawlah to raise his ransom and had fallen ill from disappointment at receiving an unfavourable answer. This poem, again, contains many stylistic and rhythmic echoes from al-Mutanabbī:

What excuse have you for turning away a broken-hearted woman who relies on you above all mortals else?
She came to you pleading for the return of her only son, and men were all expectant – how could you shut the door to her?
By sacrificing me you have sacrificed a noble soul, whose hope, in face of despair, lies in you.[21]

This poem, together with the elegy on his mother, has recently met with considerable appreciation from some Arab critics who appear to have been influenced in this respect by the early nineteenth-century German scholar

[20] *Dīwān*, 215. [21] Ibid., 332.

Freytag. But the style of both poems falls markedly short of the dignity of spirit and purity of diction found in most of the *Rūmiyyāt*, and with their undisciplined flow of emotion they verge somewhat on the prosaic.

OTHER INFLUENCES

The influence of that other great exponent of *badīʿ*, the third/ninth-century Abū Tammām, is also discernible in the *Rūmiyyāt*. Borrowing the technique whereby Abū Tammām weaves strands of historical allusion into his poems to increase the grandeur and significance of their subject-matter,[22] Abū Firās displays his familiarity with the early history of Islam, showing an unmistakable Shiʿī bias, as in the famous line:

wa-lā khayra fī dafʿi ʾl-radā bi-madhallatin *kamā raddahū yawman bi-sūʾatihī ʿAmrū*

No good can come of seeking to avoid death by an ignoble action, as did ʿAmr in exposing his nakedness.[23]

which alludes to the encounter between ʿAlī b. Abī Ṭālib and ʿAmr b. al-ʿĀṣ in single combat at the battle of Ṣiffīn. Another example is his reference to the desertion of ʿAlī by his brother ʿAqīl, who defected to join his opponent Muʿāwiyah:

Of old treachery has been one of the common traits of man, and there have been complaints of fate's adversity and friends proving false:
ʿAmr b. al-Zubayr deserted his brother and ʿAqīl abandoned the Commander of the Faithful.[24]

We may also note a poignant allusion to the Khārijī Shabīb:

wa qad ʿalimat ummī bi-anna maniyyatī *bi-ḥaddi sinānin aw bi-ḥaddi qaḍībi*
kamā ʿalimat min qablu an yaghraqa ʾbnuhā *bi-mahlakihī fī ʾl-māʾi ummu Shabībi*

My mother knows that my death will be by blade of sword or spear,
As Shabīb's mother knew beforehand that her son would die by water.[25]

Shabīb's mother allegedly had this premonition in a dream, but fortunately for Abū Firās's mother, she did not live to see her apprehensions fulfilled.

Abū Tammām's younger contemporary, al-Buḥturī (d. 284/897), whose panegyrics were greatly admired for their purity of diction, superb cadence and relative simplicity, was a lesser influence on Abū Firās, yet some aspects of his verse reflect the same kind of lucidity, and it is from al-Buḥturī that Abū Firās seems to have learned how to look back to the pre-Islamic bards

22 See Stetkevych, "The ʿAbbasid poet interprets history". 23 *Dīwān*, 209.
24 Ibid., 315; for Shīʿī themes in Abū Firās's poetry, cf. also p. 200, above. 25 *Dīwān*, 35.

for the purpose of achieving a sort of new, urbanized bedouinity; thus he seems to have been particularly influenced by ʿAntarah, the model "knight–poet",[26] and by his own tribal ancestor, the Taghlibi al-Muhalhil.[27] The latter employed the device – known as *takrār* – of repeating the first hemistich of some lines several times for rhythmic and artistic effect; Abū Firās uses the device in the *Rūmiyyāt* (as illustrated in some of the quotations above) in a way that singles it out as one of his most distinctive stylistic characteristics. One short poem by Abū Firās, inspired by his hearing the cooing of a dove in his captivity, almost approaches the rhythmic elegance of al-Buḥturī (the metre is *ṭawīl*):

aqūlu wa-qad nāḥat bi-qurbī ḥamāmatun   *ayā jāratā hal bāta ḥāluki ḥālī*
maʿādha ʾl-hawā mā dhuqti ṭāriqata ʾl-nawā   *wa-lā khaṭarat minki ʾl-humūmu bi-bāli*
a-taḥmilu maḥzūna ʾl-fuʾādi qawādimun   *ʿalā ghusunin nāʾī ʾl-masāfati ʿāli*
ayā jāratā mā anṣafa ʾl-dahru baynanā   *taʿālay uqāsimki ʾl-humūma taʿlī*
taʿālay tarā rūḥan ladayya ḍaʿīfatan   *taraddadu fī jismin tuʿadhdhabu bālī*
a-yaḍḥaku maʾsūrun wa-tabkī ṭalīqatun   *wa-yaskutu maḥzūnun wa-yandubu sāli*
la-qad kuntu awlā minki bi ʾl-damʿi muqlatan   *wa-lākinna damʿī fī ʾl-ḥawādithi ghāli*

I say to a dove, mournfully cooing nearby, Neighbour, is your condition indeed mine?
Love forbid! You've not tasted the pang of separation, anxieties have never entered your mind.
Can a burdened heart be borne aloft by your pinions, or to a topmost distant branch?
Neighbour, fate has not dealt justly between us; come, let me give you a share of my distresses.
Come, see my feeble soul which haunts a body worn out with torment.
Can a prisoner laugh and a free bird weep? Can a sorrowful man hold his peace and one at his ease lament aloud?
Indeed I have a better right to a tearful eye than you; but my tears in these troubles are too costly.[28]

The best-known today of the *Rūmiyyāt* is a piece beginning *arāka ʿaṣiyya ʾl-damʿi*, selections from which have been popularized by the famous modern singer Umm Kulthūm. The following lines too are often quoted (the metre is again *ṭawīl*):

usirtu wa-mā ṣaḥbī bi ʿuzlin ladā ʾl-waghā   *wa-lā farasī muhrun wa-lā rabbuhū ghamru*
wa-lākin idhā ḥumma ʾl-qaḍāʾu ʿalā ʾmriʾin   *fa-laysa lahū barrun yaqīhi wa-lā baḥru*
wa-qāla uṣayḥābī ʾl-firāru awi ʾl-radā   *fa-qultu humā amrāni aḥlāhumā murru*
wa-lākinnanī amḍī li-mā lā yaʿībunī   *wa-ḥasbuka min amrayni khayruhmā ʾl-asru*

[26] Cf. *CHALUP*, 46, 64, 82, and pp. 141–2, above.
[27] *CHALUP*, 49.
[28] *Dīwān*, 325; cf. the use of repetition in the *zuhdiyyāt* of Abū ʾl-ʿAtāhiyah, p. 289, above.

I was taken prisoner, though my companions were not unarmed in the battle, my horse no untrained colt and its master not inexperienced;
but when a man's allotted day comes, no land or sea can shelter him.
My craven companions said, "It's flight or death," but I answered, "Two things of which the sweeter is itself bitter;
Yet I'll press on to a goal which will not disgrace me – it's bad enough to have two choices, the better of which is captivity."[29]

After four years of captivity, Abū Firās was ransomed; but his joy was short-lived. Though he was restored to his former amirate and political status with his patron, Sayf al-Dawlah died only a year after his release, in 356/967. This was soon followed by the disintegration of the Hamdanid dynasty. Sayf al-Dawlah's brother Nāṣir al-Dawlah began to show signs of mental derangement after his brother's death, and was placed under arrest by his own son. In Aleppo there was an estrangement between Abū Firās and his 15-year-old nephew Abū ʾl-Maʿālī, son of Sayf al-Dawlah by the poet's sister Sakhīnah. Abū Firās, overestimating his popularity among the bedouin of the Syrian desert, and extending his largesse in the hope of winning support for his own claim to the succession, made a rash attempt to capture Ḥimṣ as a prelude to taking Aleppo. Abū ʾl-Maʿālī sent his able general Farghawayh[30] to deal with his uncle's rebellion; the poet's troops and allies failed him at the crucial moment, and he was put to death by Farghawayh, acting either independently or on orders from Abū ʾl-Maʿālī (historical reports are conflicting on this issue). Before meeting his tragic end, Abū Firās is said to have addressed these lines to his young daughter, herself a widow (metre: *kāmil*):

a-bunayyatī lā taḥzanī kullu ʾl-anāmi ilā dhahābi
a-bunayyatī ṣabran jamīlan li ʾl-jalīli mina ʾl-muṣābi
nūḥī ʿalayya bi-ḥasratin min khalfi sitriki wa ʾl-ḥijābi
qūlī idhā nādaytinī wa-ʿayītu mina ʾl-jawābi
zaynu ʾl-shabābi Abū Firāsi lam yumattaʿ bi ʾl-shabābi

Dear daughter, do not grieve: all men must depart;
Dear daughter, show the virtue of patience under heavy misfortune.[31]
Mourn me with true sorrow, but in your secret chamber.
Say, when you call to me and I have no power to answer,
Abū Firās, adornment of youth, had little joy of his own youth.[32]

Thus on Jumādā II 357/April 968 ended the short and crowded life of Abū Firās. His sister was allegedly so grief-stricken that she plucked out one of her eyes.

[29] *Dīwān*, 213.
[30] There is some uncertainty about the initial letter of this name.
[31] Alluding to Jacob's steadfastness at the loss of Joseph, Qurʾān, xii.18, 83.
[32] *Dīwān*, 47.

The memory of Abū Firās has outlived that of both his own and his father's vanquishers; his *Rūmiyyāt*, inspired by the sufferings of captivity, have won him a secure place in the forum of Arabic poetry. He may not rank as high as such masters as Abū Tammām, al-Buḥturī, al-Mutanabbī and al-Maᶜarrī, but surely it is not merely because of his kinship to Sayf al-Dawlah (as is suggested by Ibn Rashīq)[33] that he was not totally eclipsed by al-Mutanabbī. For the *Rūmiyyāt* are remarkable in the combination they offer of pathos, dignity and pride with real artistic accomplishment. His near contemporary al-Thaᶜālibī summed him up as:

singular in his time, a shining sun of his day in manners, excellence, generosity, nobility, celebrity, eloquence, brilliance and courage, and his poetry is famous and noted for its beauty and polish . . . and princely lustre; qualities such as were never found before in any poet except Ibn al-Muᶜtazz, to whom, however, Abū Firās is considered superior by professional poets and by the critics. The Ṣāḥib Ibn ᶜAbbād used to say, "Poetry began with a prince and ended with a prince" (meaning Imruᵓ al-Qays and Abū Firās).[34]

[33] Quoted ibid., 465. [34] Ibid., 462.

CHAPTER 19

ABŪ ʾL-ʿALĀʾ AL-MAʿARRĪ

In the early decades of this century, the poet and prose-writer al-Maʿarrī was an object of particular interest to western scholars as one of a number of possible links between medieval Christian and Muslim literature. More recent studies have investigated his writings in the light of a wider range of concerns, literary, historical and philosophical. A more general approach is attempted in the present chapter; many aspects of al-Maʿarrī's thought are of great contemporary appeal, and it is these that it is proposed to address here.

LIFE

Abū ʾl-ʿAlāʾ Aḥmad b. ʿAbdullāh b. Sulaymān al-Maʿarrī (363–449/973–1058) was of Arab stock, a member of the tribe of Tanūkh, and was born into a learned and distinguished family at Maʿarrat al-Nuʿmān, a town near Aleppo which had long been a resort of eminent *qāḍī*s, scholars and poets; from the first he was trained up to assume his rightful place as a member of this social and cultural élite.[1] At the age of four, however, he contracted smallpox, which left him not only disfigured but blind; his education nevertheless continued to follow a conventional course, but his blindness ultimately transformed both his personal and his artistic development. His father supervised his studies; he was taught the Qurʾān by some of the leading shaykhs of Maʿarrah, and *ḥadīth* by his father, grandparents and the local traditionists, and proved so proficient at the Islamic sciences and at Arabic that he was sent to his mother's family in Aleppo to continue studying Arabic under the leading scholar of the city. All this while, he refused to make concessions to his disability, played chess and backgammon with his sighted companions and joined in their games; his learning he viewed not merely as a compensation but as a weapon, and his early poetry bears witness to his ambition and fierce pride (metre: *ṭawīl*):

[1] For biographical sources, see Margoliouth, ed. and trans., *Letters of Abū ʾl-ʿAlāʾ*, preface, and al-Jundī, *Jāmiʿ*.

wa-qad sāra dhikrī fī ᵓl-bilādi fa-man lahum
bi-ikhfāᵓi shamsin ḍawᵓuha mutakāmilu
yahummu ᵓl-layālī baᶜḍu mā annā muḍmirun
wa-yathqulu Raḍwā *dūna mā anā ḥāmilu*
wa-innī wa-in kuntu ᵓl-akhīra zamānuhu
la-ātin bi-mā lam tastaṭiᶜhu ᵓl-awāᵓilu
wa-aghdū wa-law anna ᵓl-ṣabāḥa ṣawārimu
wa-asrī wa-law anna ᵓl-ẓalāma jaḥāfilu

My fame has gone out into all lands; who is there that can douse the sun's all-embracing ray?
The Fates themselves would be overwhelmed by a small part of what is in my heart, and Raḍwā's mountain[2] would find less than I bear too heavy a load.
Though I come late in time, I will achieve what men of old could not;
I'll face the morning though it were to dawn sharp swords, and the evening's gloom though it be menacing hosts.

Another poem in the metre *wāfir*:

liya ᵓl-sharafu ᵓlladhī yaṭaᵓu ᵓl-thurayyā
maᶜa ᵓl-faḍli ᵓladhī bahara ᵓl-ᶜibādā . . .
ufillu nawāᵓiba ᵓl-ayyāmi waḥdī
idhā jamaᶜat katāᵓibahā ᵓḥtishādā

Mine is a nobility that sets the Pleiades beneath its foot, mine a grandeur to dazzle mankind; . . .
I'll parry fate's assaults by my sole effort, when its squadrons are massed in battle array.[3]

For a while he enjoyed his status as a local celebrity, a wit, scholar, poet and social lion; in his early poetry, with a fine disregard for his personal circumstances, he describes his yearnings for love, depicts night as a dusky-skinned bride, and in the *dīwān* entitled *al-Dirᶜiyyāt* (see below) sings of weapons and war and celebrates the heroism of the champions in the wars between Arabs and Byzantium. But even in the most bombastic of the youthful odes there are flashes which reveal the psychological strain of the conflict between al-Maᶜarrī's ambitions and his handicap, his will to live and his sense of life's futility and consequent impulse towards resignation. This struggle reached a crisis with the death of his father in 395/1005, when al-Maᶜarrī was thirty-two. The blow had deprived him of a friend, teacher and guide; the long elegy which he wrote on the occasion is a portrait not only of his father but of his own inner state and of the development which his feelings of anguish and impotence forced on his poetry. His already acute sense of human tragedy deepened, and, when a beloved relative of his died,

[2] Mount Raḍwā: a mountain near Mecca. This and subsequent verse translations by A. F. L. B.
[3] *Saqṭ al-zand*, Bk. 2, II, 522–5; 567, 570.

he mourned him in a poem which is really an elegy for all mankind (metre: *khafīf*):

ṣāḥi hādhī qubūrunā tamlaʾu ʾl-raḥba fa-ayna ʾl-qubūru min ᶜahdi ᶜĀdi
khaffifi ʾl-waṭʾa mā aẓunnu adīma ʾl-arḍi illā min hādhihī ʾl-ajsādi. . . .
sir ini ʾstaṭaᶜta fī ʾl-hawāʾi ruwaydan lā ʾkhtiyālan ᶜalā rufāti ʾl-ᶜibādi
rubba laḥdin qad ṣāra laḥdan mirāran ḍāḥikin min tazāḥumi ʾl-aḍdādi
wa-dafīnin ᶜalā baqāyā dafīnin fī ṭawīli ʾl-azmāni wa ʾl-ābādi . . .
taᶜabun kulluhā ʾl-ḥayātu fa-mā aᶜjabu illā min rāghibin fī ʾzdiyādi

My friend, these are our graves filling the plain; but where are they all from antique time on?
Tread softly; the whole face of the earth seems to me nothing but the dead . . .
So, if you can, step gently through the living air, and do not roughly trample the bones of the departed.
Many a grave space has served time and time again, so as to rejoice in the piling up of so many different men;
Body is buried on top of remains of body, as the long ages roll on . . .
All life is a wearisome thing; the wonder is that any should wish to spin it out.[4]

In the first shock of his father's death, al-Maᶜarrī had thought of going to Baghdad; in fact it took him three more years to make up his mind to leave his mother and two brothers and chance his luck in cosmopolitan society. We can only speculate as to the reasons which prompted him, blind and helpless as he was, to undertake such a hazardous move; equally open to conjecture is the nature of the experiences he underwent in Baghdad, the effect of which was to make him choose a life of permanent retirement and seclusion. Ostensibly, having charmed provincial Aleppo and Damascus with his literary gifts, he was drawn to the capital by "its library facilities", as he says in his "Epistle to the people of Maᶜarrah";[5] but in all probability he had deeper motives. Events had sharpened his self-awareness while showing him how futile was his boast of "parrying fate's assaults", but he refused to give way to despair and decided to put his powers of endurance to the test by travelling to Baghdad. His hopes were staked on the gamble that the reputation he had won in Damascus and Aleppo for almost legendary sharp-wittedness, prodigious learning and astounding literary talent would survive transplantation to the capital. He arrived in Baghdad modestly provided for and took a house by the Tigris; his provincial fame had preceded him, and the Baghdadis flocked to try him out. He passed the test with flying colours and was universally conceded to be "the marvel of the age for his memory and his attainments in Arabic". His poetic gifts were acknowledged also, and he lectured to packed audiences on his own poetic

[4] Ibid., III, 974–7. [5] Trans. Margoliouth, *Letters of Abū ʾl-ᶜAlāʾ*, VIII, 42–4.

dīwān entitled *Saqṭ al-zand* (see below). But it was not long before the capital revealed its rules and standards and forced him to reassess his ability to survive there. Literature was profitless unless it gratified those in power and abjectly flattered the placemen; high society seemed to have more regard for mountebanks than for men of genuine learning; integrity was little in demand in a market ruled by sharp practice. He resolved to withdraw without waiting for the outcome of the fight, recognizing that he was poorly armed to combat sycophancy and humbug, incapacitated as he was by his blindness, guilelessness and a character which made him uncomfortably conspicuous in a world of time-servers. His withdrawal, as he declares in his "Epistle to the People of Maʿarrah", began before ever he left Baghdad. He left no richer than he came, though the Baghdadis made him "lavish offers" to stay and flocked around him lamenting his departure. He too was bitterly disappointed and, as he says in his "Farewell Ode" in *Saqṭ al-zand*, went into mourning for his crushed hopes, observing that he wished he could at least turn to drink to drown his worldly sorrows.

He set off for Maʿarrat al-Nuʿmān at the end of Ramaḍān 400/1010, his feelings a mixture of apprehension for his own situation, for his mother's health – word had reached him that she was ill – and for the dangers of the road, which he recorded in a *qaṣīdah*. He was preceded by his "Epistle" to his fellow-townsmen, which tells them of his fixed resolve to live in seclusion, and begs them not to visit him in his cell at home so as to spare him the trouble of turning them away. On reaching home, he found his mother already dead. Writing of her to his uncle, her brother, he refers to her as his "only comfort": "We shall meet again on Resurrection Day; alas! how distant is that day!" "My grief for her loss is no sooner exhausted than renewed; to tell it would weary the hearer and wear out Time itself."[6] With his mother's death came a feeling of rootlessness, and, when his two brothers also died, he wondered how it was that the loss of parents and brothers had not destroyed him utterly, and how he could call himself loyal to his departed kin while he still ate, drank, dressed and sheltered within the family home.[7] From his return to Maʿarrah until the end of his life he kept to his room, doubly a prisoner to his blindness and seclusion. At first only his servants were admitted to see him; later he relented, and received a constant stream of scholars and students. Otherwise his regime remained unaltered for forty-nine years: his time was shared between teaching, dictating his compositions, religious duties and meditation; he never married or had children, fasted continually, was a vegetarian, dressed in the coarsest cotton and slept on his prayer-mat. He had a small income from a charitable trust,

[6] Ibid., VII, 34–6. [7] *al-Fuṣūl wa ʾl-ghāyāt*.

amounting to twenty-odd dinars a month, of which half was spent on the salaries of his servant and amanuensis and the other half on personal necessities and the support of indigent pupils. He would never accept any remuneration for his scholarship, and refused to supplement his income in any way, turning down the offer of a government pension paid from local taxes.

Not surprisingly, it was popularly believed that he had achieved an other-worldly serenity, but this was far from being the case. He was still torn between a deep-seated love of the things of this world and a passionate rejection of them; to the end of his days, he groaned over his inability to turn his back completely on the world and achieve the peace of disillusionment. His writings reveal the agony of the struggle and confirm that only by fleeing the world was he able to triumph over it:

ayyuhā ʾl-dunyā laḥāki ʾllāhu min rabbati dalli
mā tasallā khaladī ¦ ᶜanki wa-in ẓanna ʾl-tasallī
Curse you, World, for a coy mistress!
I cannot dismiss you from my mind, however much I think to do so.

muhjatī ḍiddun yuḥāribunī anā minnī kayfa aḥtarisu
My own soul is my adversary; yet it is part of myself, and what defence have I against myself?

wa-qāla ʾl-fārisūna ḥalīfu ẓuhdin wa-akhṭaʾati ʾl-ẓunūnu bi-mā farasnah
wa-lam uᶜriḍ ᶜani ʾl-ladhdhāti illā li-anna khiyārahā ᶜannī khanasnah
They scan my face and say, "A thorough ascetic!", but their guess is wrong;
I have not turned my back on pleasures, it is they that have shunned me.

law anna ᶜishqaka li ʾl-dunyā lahū shabaḥun ṣawwartahū la-malaʾta ʾl-sahla wa ʾl-jabalā
If your passion for the world possessed a bodily form for you to fashion, you would fill plain and mountains with it.[8]

But if al-Maᶜarrī never found peace from wild hopes nor was able to stop his mind dwelling on the pleasures denied him by his disabilities – and these are crucial factors for the understanding of the literary works he produced in the course of nearly half a century – he was nevertheless able to adapt to deprivation as the price of freedom of thought and speech. His withdrawal from society and from careerism was a rejection of an age whose values he considered false and distorted. For his blindness, solitude and intellect gave him a heightened insight into the practical issues of the outside world. With rare simplicity, he countered tyranny with outspokenness and declared war on those who exploited popular ignorance, politics, religion and learning for their own ends. The masses, stultified by their long subjection and the

[8] *Luzūmiyyāt*, II, 239; 10; 352–3; 193.

numbing effects of constant misguidance, got no exoneration from al-Maʿarrī while they were content to hug their chains in sleepy irresponsibility (*qad ẓalamatnā ʾl-mulūku wa-naḥnu ʿalā ḍuʿfinā aẓlamu*, "We are oppressed by kings, yet it is we who do the greater wrong, for all our weakness").[9]

In contemporary opinion, al-Maʿarrī was a rebel against society, revolting in word and deed against the established order. Naturally, his enemies wished to gag him and, since it was impossible to seduce him by bribery, frighten him with imprisonment or threaten him through wife or child, they threatened him instead by impugning his religious orthodoxy. Al-Maʿarrī's conduct was at variance with that of the generality of Muslims. He shunned the good things of life which God, according to the Qurʾān, has placed at mankind's disposal; he was unmarried, in defiance of the Prophet's dictum that there should be "no monkery in Islam"; he unreservedly uttered expressions of doubt and perplexity, some of which, indeed, directly challenged the zealots. One might have expected his asceticism to shield him from slander, but his very austerity seemed suspect:

la-ʿamrī la-qad ʿazza ʾl-mubāḥu ʿalaykumu *wa-hāna bi-jahlin mā yuṣānu wa-yuḥẓaru*

For you, licensed indulgence is a precious thing, while you ignorantly belittle what should be protected and shielded.[10]

As an example, he aroused the antagonism of the chief *dāʿī* (propagandist) of the Fatimids, the Shīʿī rulers of Egypt and Syria; al-Maʿarrī, as noted above, was a vegetarian, although meat is licit in Islam; did he, the *dāʿī* enquired, mean to be kinder to animals than his Creator was? The issue developed from an examination of the conduct of an individual ascetic into an acute scholastic debate about the wisdom of God, the ordering of the universe, the problem of good and evil and the categories of licit and illicit (*ḥalāl* and *ḥarām*).[11] The *dāʿī* may well have succeeded in vexing al-Maʿarrī (now a man of eighty-five), but neither he nor his colleagues ever managed to induce him to change his ways; he simply regarded trials of this nature as a sort of tax payable by those who defy custom. Nevertheless, he was frequently subjected to false accusations, his sayings were distorted and his verses misrepresented, and, despite his patent self-denial and the personal testimony to his piety given by those who knew him, his deviation from the community at large would always present the rabble-rousers with a weapon they could hope to turn against him.

Al-Maʿarrī died at the beginning of Rabīʿ I 449/1058, leaving

9 Ibid., 277. 10 Ibid., 311.

11 Trans. Margoliouth, "Abū ʾl-ʿAlāʾ al-Maʿarrī's correspondence on vegetarianism"; cf. ch. 11, n. 47 above.

instructions that these words should be written on his tomb: "This trespass did my father commit against me; I never trespassed so against any man." Crowds followed his funeral; eighty-four poets recited elegies and for seven days afterwards the Qurʾān was recited over his grave.

THE WORKS OF AL-MAᶜARRĪ – A CHARACTERIZATION

Al-Maᶜarrī's seventh/thirteenth-century biographers record nearly seventy works by him, including four *dīwān*s of verse. The following have survived and it is to be hoped that manuscripts of others may yet be discovered:[12]

Poetry: two *dīwān*s: *Saqṭ al-zand* ("Spark from the Fire-Stick"), which comprises pieces composed up until *c.* 411/1020 and has a subsection (sometimes treated as a separate *dīwān*), *al-Dirᶜiyyāt*, on arms and war;[13] and *Luzūm mā lā yalzam*, often known for short as *al-Luzūmiyyāt* (the full title, "Assuming of Unnecessary Obligations", refers to the rhyme-scheme, described below).[14]

Prose: the "Epistles" (*Rasāʾil*); *al-Fuṣūl wa ʾl-ghāyāt* ("Paragraphs and Periods", discussed below); *Mulqā ʾl-sabīl* ("Met on the Road", see below); *Risālat al-Ṣāhil wa ʾl-shāḥij* ("The Neigher and the Brayer", see below); *Risālat al-Malāʾikah* ("Epistle of the Angels"), which debates questions about Heaven and Hell;[15] *Risālat al-Ghufrān* ("Epistle of Forgiveness", see below); *Kitāb al-Ilghāz* ("The Book of Riddling", see below); and *ᶜAbath al-Walīd* ("Child's Play"), a commentary on the *Dīwān* of the poet al-Buḥturī (206–84/821–97), the title of which is a pun on the poet's name, Abū ᶜUbādah *al-Walīd* b. ᶜUbayd al-Buḥturī.

Up until the present century, literary historians have been concerned with al-Maᶜarrī's beliefs virtually to the exclusion of his writings – a fate which other writers of more suspect orthodoxy, such as Bashshār, Abū Nuwās and al-Mutanabbī have nevertheless escaped – and have been puzzled whether to class him as a literary figure or as a philosopher. The beginning of the twentieth century saw a revival of interest in al-Maᶜarrī as a writer, pioneered by R. A. Nicholson, whose study of a manuscript of *Risālat al-Ghufrān* appeared in 1900–2. European scholars thereafter became engrossed in the question of whether there was any justification for M. Asín Palacios's hypothesis, advanced in 1919, that this work influenced Dante's

[12] Cf. Smoor, *Kings and Bedouins*, 205, 217; for the most recent bibliography, *see* EI^2, "al-Maᶜarrī
[13] Discussed, with some translations, in Cachia, "Dramatic monologues".
[14] Discussed, with translations, in Verity, "Two poems"; Nicholson, *Studies*, 43–289.
[15] See Smoor, *Kings and Bedouins*, 214.

Divine Comedy. In 1898, D. S. Margoliouth had published the first critical edition of a work by al-Maʿarrī, the "Epistles" (*The Letters of Abūʾl-ʿAlāʾ of Maʿarrat al-Nuʿmān*), which drew the attention of Arab scholars, and in 1915 the Egyptian scholar Ṭāhā Ḥusayn produced his "Memorial" (*Dhikrā Abī ʾl-ʿAlāʾ*); in 1938 appeared the first oriental critical edition of any of al-Maʿarrī's works, the first part of *al-Fuṣūl wa ʾl-ghāyāt*, edited by Ḥasan Zanātī, still a valuable contribution to literary studies; and in 1944 a celebration of al-Maʿarrī's millennium was held in Cairo which further stimulated research.

The chief characteristic of al-Maʿarrī's works is an unusually passionate sincerity, embracing all aspects of his personality, as a very human writer, as a thinker and as a scholar deeply imbued with a feeling for the Arabic language. He was a poet who had found himself, and expressed his inmost feelings with the utmost frankness; a controversial thinker who knew his mission and declared his position in relation to the world and mankind boldly and unashamedly. This is quite contrary to the notion entertained by many students of his works, that he "concealed the secret of his personality" by employing symbolic language to wrap up his meaning in riddles. In fact his works are characterized by a remarkable candour, and his passion and sincerity are transparent in such features as the emotional bond he felt with his works. Just as no father would let his children be deprived of distinctive names, so al-Maʿarrī was unwilling to allow his various works to go out into the world without titles and merely distinguished by the author's name, as had been the practice of many earlier poets and prose-writers alike, whose works were often merely given – whether by the author himself, by the pupils to whom those works were dictated or by the editors who collated them – descriptive titles such as *dīwān* (for poetry), *amālī* ("dictations"), *majālis* ("sessions") or "epistles", etc., for prose. Each child of al-Maʿarrī, whether prose or poetry, had its own distinctive title, and the independent commentaries which he wrote on these works were also given their own titles, such as *Ḍawʾ al-Saqṭ* ("Light of the Spark"), *Rāḥat al-Luzūm* ("Repose from the Obligatoriness"), *Iqlīd al-Ghāyāt* ("Key of the Periods"), *Lisān al-Ṣāhil wa ʾl-shāḥij* ("Tongue of the Neigher and the Brayer"). Nor would al-Maʿarrī allow his offspring into the world without their birthdays' being recorded; each of his works, prose or poetry, carries indications of the date of its conception, either in explicit terms or by reference to historical events and personages, so that the date of composition is easily identifiable.

All this allows us clear insights into his mental and emotional world and the technical stages by which his art developed. He gives us unmistakable glimpses of his personality and circumstances – as, of course, do other writers; but what is unique to al-Maʿarrī is that it is his literary works themselves, rather than secondary biographical material, that provide us with a convincing record of his life and development. Secondary sources are of far less value in establishing a picture either of the writer or of the man; his verse and prose give us an artistic appraisal of his worldly circumstances, of the events and personalities that he witnessed and of the details of the phases through which he passed from childhood almost until his death, while the sincerity of his writings suggests a congruity of feeling, thought and action which emphasizes the close connection of the writer with his works, the thinker with his words.

In his younger days al-Maʿarrī made no attempt to assume, prematurely, the role of the scholar, despite being equipped for it by his superior attainments in Arabic and Islamic learning. This phase produced no such demonstrations of literary and linguistic virtuosity as the later "Epistles", but only the *dīwān* of an ambitious and gifted poet engaged in a defiant struggle, truthfully delineated in the lines of *Saqṭ al-zand*, directed by the spark of ambition and accompanied by revelatory flashes of his sensitivity to his personal tragedy. The lines are instinct with youthful vigour unfettered by anything except the normal conventions of the *qaṣīdah*, with single-consonant monorhyme at the end of each line. Later, in the *Luzūmiyyāt*, he adopted a double-consonant rhyme scheme not observed by any previous poet, and every letter of the alphabet is exemplified; an artifice which parallels his code of conduct in the latter part of his life, when he fettered himself with an abnormal code of retirement and self-abnegation.

Along with the *Luzūmiyyāt*, there come in his phase of retirement all the prose works, cast in highly original moulds. They combine the elements of his personality as littérateur, scholar, critic and controversialist and are characterized by extreme freedom of speech in the interests of truth and beauty. In *al-Fuṣūl wa ʾl-ghāyāt*, begun after his withdrawal from Baghdad, he formulated his griefs in a kind of poetic prose, where the last letters of all the clauses form an alphabetic acrostic (there is some parallel here with the procedure of the *Luzūmiyyāt*). In *Mulqā ʾl-sabīl*, written at the beginning of his retirement, we find a collection of moral *sententiae*, similarly arranged alphabetically, with each one formulated first in literary prose and then in verse. The "Book of Riddling" is a collection of versified conundrums, to each of which is appended an explanation of its vocabulary and the point of its *double entendre*. In "The Neigher and the Brayer", composed around 410/1019 when he was close on fifty, we have a uniquely formulated historico–literary document. It is put into the mouths of a horse and a mule, and also brings on to the stage a dove, a camel, a hyena and a fox. Yet it is no way like the *Kalīlah wa-Dimnah* stories,[16] which are intended to give instruction by way of fables unconnected with any temporal events or geographical setting, simply using animals to point a moral for mankind. "The Neigher and the Brayer", on the contrary, is a connected narrative in a series of scenes (not leading on to any "moral"), told by the author in a dramatically representational way; we seem to be watching a play with animal actors, written, produced and directed by al-Maʿarrī. The beasts' conversations turn on real events in the history of Syria and Egypt at the time of composition; the names which occur in the conversations are those of actual personalities in the political and literary world of the time. The author was not inventing a world of animals and composing moral fables; he was observing important events of the time and analyzing the trends and covert motives underlying those events. He then presents his own interpretation and evaluation of them in the speeches put dramatically into the mouths of the beasts.[17]

This very original literary form was developed further in the "Epistle of Forgiveness", composed around 424/1033 when he was in his sixties, in reply to an epistle he had received from a scholar of Aleppo, ʿAlī b. Manṣūr Ibn al-Qāriḥ.[18] But his reply to that epistle begins only after he has taken Ibn al-Qāriḥ on a visit to Paradise and Hell, remarkably vividly presented. Students of al-Maʿarrī have always tended to be puzzled about how to classify the work: is it narrative (*qaṣaṣ*), or a written account of learned discussions (*amālī*) such as would normally be classified as *adab*, or a *maqāmah*, or the epistle form extended to book length? Literary historians have been accustomed to insist that there was no pre-modern dramatic writing in Arabic, apart from the shadow-plays of Ibn Dāniyāl;[19] but the "Epistle of Forgiveness", to an even more striking degree than "The Neigher and the Brayer", has features markedly reminiscent of deliberately "dramatic" orchestration.[20] The text begins with an introduction full of references to various kinds of snakes and their common names in peasant dialect; this functions like the musical overture to a play, and is intended by the author as an allegory for the hypocrisy and malice of Ibn al-Qāriḥ, preparatory to his appearance on the stage. Then follow three acts, the first two set in Paradise and Hell, the last portraying the return to Paradise. The author does not appear in person on the stage but is present in the background, directing the action, changing the scene, moving the characters around and teaching them their lines. The tricky – perhaps

16 See pp. 50–3. 17 ʿAbd al-Raḥmān, *Madkhal*; see also Smoor, "Enigmatic allusion".
18 For which see Monteil, trans., *L'Epître du pardon*.
19 D. 710/1310; see Badawi, "Medieval Arabic drama". 20 ʿAbd al-Raḥmān, *Qirāʾah jadīdah*.

crucial – balance in the play is that it has to express the personality of the author while at the same time adapting itself to that of its "hero", Ibn al-Qāriḥ, although the two are at opposite poles, outwardly and inwardly, in life, morals and conduct. There is no simple line of demarcation. The character of the author – noble, chaste, truthful and valiant – appears in his vision of the world to come, as imagined by a man learned, refined, blind and helpless: there he would find relief from the repression of his natural desires and fulfilment of his dreams and yearnings. When, however, he expatiates on sensual satisfactions, the embodiment of material lusts, then it is the greedy, dissolute and false Ibn al-Qāriḥ who inspires his elaborate description of desires satiated – as Ibn al-Qāriḥ would wish them to be. The "Epistle of Forgiveness", with its depictions of life to come, has often been cited as an attack on Islam on the part of the author. This is perhaps a rather naïve view; the "Epistle" is an artistic vision in which the doubly imprisoned captive surveys his private world, as he envisages it in his hopes and dreams, shadowed, throughout the composition, by Ibn al-Qāriḥ's evil presence.

In both the "Epistle of Forgiveness" and "The Neigher and the Brayer", there is an obvious spirit of irony and sarcasm. In thus laying bare the world of men and the spirit of the age, al-Maᶜarrī uses the evidence he has exposed to summon up the courage needed in his struggle to conquer his innate attachment to a world which he has rejected. Both works also display features common to all his writings: a love of rhyming, punning, symbolism, allusion and conundrums; al-Maᶜarrī's work was based on his rich fund of Arabic lore, so that his compositions are full of rare proverbs and unusual vocabulary, metrical and linguistic conceits, and critical comments on language, literature and history. These are the building-blocks; but most importantly, al-Maᶜarrī's works demonstrate the validity of the notion of a writer's being a recluse whose isolation and imprisonment allow him to battle for human freedom more effectively than those competing on the world stage. His stance and technique show the difference between the self-imposed bondage of responsibility, integrity and freedom of thought, and the externally conditioned bondage of writers forced to exercise their craft according to the directives of sectaries and censors. Freedom, though the antithesis of bondage, is nevertheless, as al-Maᶜarri realized, a heavy burden of trust.

CHAPTER 20

LITERARY CRITICISM

BASIC ISSUES AND PRINCIPLES

Writing in 274/887, the ᶜAbbasid poet and literary theorist Ibn al-Muᶜtazz expressed the feeling that he was exploring a new territory of literary enquiry by identifying a new "poetics" which had emerged with the "modern" poets (*muḥdathūn*) of the second and third centuries of Islam. The term *al-badīᶜ* by which he characterized this poetics had been used before by al-Jāḥiẓ in a brief reference attributing the actual coinage of the term to the transmitters (*rāwīs*) of poetry.[1] The time gap between the first appearance of the term and its usage to designate a distinct trend in Arabic poetry might well span a whole century. Yet when Ibn al-Muᶜtazz wrote, delimiting its boundaries and identifying its constituents, he did so with an obvious degree of tentativeness. His work, he said, represented a personal choice and allowed for the possibility of others defining the new poetics and identifying its elements in different ways.[2] A few decades later, another critic of a very different temperament and education, Qudāmah b. Jaᶜfar, wrote on poetry with an equal feeling of being a pioneer, asserting that, despite much work on various aspects of poetry, nobody had produced a book on its critical evaluation.[3] Moreover, Qudāmah felt that his was a new territory unmapped by critics and thus lacking a specialized terminology which could furnish the necessary background for his discussion. He had to invent terms to designate the concepts which he had undertaken to define; terms (*asmāʾ*) were signs over which there should be no dispute, for should anybody dissatisfied with Qudāmah's terms wish to coin different ones, he would not be in disagreement with them. This indeed was to happen later on, although many of Qudāmah's terms became well-established in Arabic poetics and literary criticism. The pioneering spirit running through the works of both writers emerged round the last quarter of the third/ninth century and the first quarter of the fourth/tenth; Qudāmah died in 337/948. The Arabs had then been producing poetry for about five centuries,

[1] *Bayān*, IV, 55–6. [2] *Badīᶜ*, 57–8; see summary, ch. 21, below. [3] *Naqd al-shiᶜr*, 1.

according to the conservative estimate of al-Jāḥiẓ, and possibly for much longer. Thinking about poetry – and thinking critically – had been in evidence at least since the late pre-Islamic poet al-Nābighah al-Dhubyānī is reported to have judged poets at ᶜUkāẓ.[4] As Qudāmah himself observed, works had since been written on four aspects of poetry: its metres and prosody, its rhymes, its language (and "strange", archaic or abstruse vocabulary, *gharīb*) and its themes or subjects and "the intention behind them". A fifth aspect about which he had now undertaken to write was the knowledge of good and bad poetry. Meanwhile, debates over "modern" poetry had raged for at least a century, its great representative Abū Tammām, who proved a focal point for such debate, having died in 231/846. If anything, these facts point to the late emergence of systematic, specialized analyses of poetry as an independent field of enquiry, though interest in and enthusiasm for poetry had long been dominant features of cultural life.

All known previous works had sprung from two motives. The first, and more powerful, was an extension of the pre-Islamic and early Islamic impulse of "vying" between poets and the placing of them in classes on the basis of very elementary and fragmented aspects of their works (sometimes one poem or one line); the second was theorization on the nature of language and eloquence (*balāghah*) which originated, as will be suggested later, in disputes over the theological rather than the literary aspects of the Qurʾān. It is true that some titles of early books reportedly dealing with the critical evaluation of poetry have been preserved in late biographical works,[5] but the exact nature of such books is difficult to determine. Al-Nāshiʾ al-Akbar (d. 293/905), for instance, himself a poet, is reported to have written a "Book of Poetry" (*Kitāb al-Shiᶜr*), but what little is known of it shows no sign of its being the type of work that Qudāmah had in mind when he proclaimed the uniqueness of his own work. Writing on aspects of language and *balāghah* in general was, however, very much in evidence from the end of the second/eighth century; but the works produced were either outside the domain of poetry (e.g. *Majāz al-Qurʾān* by Abū ᶜUbaydah, discussed later in this chapter), or treated of poetry externally, in ways which had little bearing on the development of poetics, literary theory or literary criticism. The major exception to this is Ibn Sallām al-Jumaḥī's *Ṭabaqāt fuḥūl al-shuᶜarāʾ* which merits a brief discussion.

[4] See *CHALUP*, 30. On pre-ᶜAbbasid critical anecdotes, see ᶜAbbās, *Tārīkh al-naqd*, 43–59.
[5] Cf. ibid., 63–76.

The "classification" of poets

Ibn Sallām (d. *c.* 232/847) gave the first reasonably methodic articulation to the old impulse of comparing and classifying poets, extending the application of this impulse to cover every poet of note up to the middle of the second/eighth century. The idea of a systematic classification of poets can potentially form the basis for a fruitful critical analysis, if the works of various poets are subjected to methodic enquiry based on clearly defined theoretical principles and an in-depth analysis of the poetry of each individual poet. But Ibn Sallām was probably writing too early to be expected to perform such a task. He uses no definite criteria for classification, with the exception of the implicit criterion which necessarily forms the very basis of his work, namely, the "goodness" (*jawdah*) of poetry, as all the poets he includes in his work are, by definition, good poets, *fuḥūl*. Beyond this, only the number of excellent poems a certain poet has produced functions as a definite criterion for placement within a given class. Since excellence is not defined, the value of the latter criterion becomes questionable. A third criterion was the multiplicity of themes in a poet's work. A fourth was the similarities and interconnections between poets, applied as a basis for the grouping of poets in one given class. But such interconnections are often difficult to detect, and the author does not identify them; it is not easy to see interconnections between al-Aᶜshā, Zuhayr and al-Nābighah. The similarities obviously used as criteria are those of theme (e.g. elegy) or place (e.g. urban environment) or ethnic or religious (e.g. Jewish) origin, or genre (e.g. writers of *rajaz*, the least prestigious of the classical metres). It is interesting to note that he places three of the *Muᶜallaqāt* poets (whom he calls "poets of a single poem") in the sixth class, one in the third, one in the second and one in the fourth. But his scheme is blurred by several factors. At the outset, he states that he groups poets in ten pre-Islamic and ten Islamic classes, with four poets in each. Yet at the end of the first ten he adds three new categories, but only the first is designated a "class" (*ṭabaqah*)[6] and explicitly annexed to the preceding ten (it groups four elegiac poets). The other two groups (poets of Arab towns, and Jewish poets) do not contain the regulation four. After this he goes back to his original scheme, giving ten Islamic classes with four poets in each, without any appendix. Secondly, his choice of four poets in each class seems arbitrary, as he himself recognizes. He puts Aws b. Ḥajar[7] in the second class but says that he is equal to the poets of the first class although he is obliged by his scheme to put him in the second; conversely, he admits

[6] The modern editor, however, gives the rubric *ṭabaqah* to all three.

[7] See *CHALUP*, 89, 95.

that the fourth poet in the first Islamic class is "below" the other three. Thirdly, as the classes of Islamic poets approach the tenth, the names of the poets become less familiar and less prominent, and a total absence of commentary makes it difficult to see what justifies grouping them together (this is especially the case with class 8).

Ibn Sallām's work was, according to Iḥsān ᶜAbbās, a collection of ideas developed by his teacher al-Aṣmaᶜī (d. 213/825),[8] which may well be true. Yet it is of undeniable importance that he laid the foundations for two aspects of literary study: the specialization and independence of criticism; and the authority of the critic as ultimate judge. He also devoted an entire work (possibly two) to one single theoretical problem which had been of central interest to the culture. His contribution is significant for his articulation of the problem of authenticity and forgery (*naḥl*), and his attempt to develop ways of discriminating between genuine and forged poetry. His treatment of the subject is unbiased, unhesitating and displays a remarkable lack of any sense of the sacredness of tradition – a quality rare in his age. Of interest in his discussion of *naḥl* is his remark that it was fairly easy to detect in modern poetry, but extremely difficult to uncover in the case of poetry forged by the bedouin themselves. Finally, some of Ibn Sallām's observations on the disposition of a poem, on rhyme and metre, on the qualities of certain poets, and his relating the work of some poets to their cultural environment (ᶜAdī b. Zayd as a city poet, and differences between urban and bedouin poets), are interesting though embryonic in nature. He also offers some of the earliest remarks on defects of metre and rhyme, quoting examples from the "great" tradition.[9]

The principle of classification continued, at least as a general notion, to occupy a place in critical thinking. It formed the basis for two works by immediate successors of Ibn Sallām, Ibn Qutaybah and Ibn al-Muᶜtazz. But a new type of purely theoretical interest in poetry, approaching the concept of "poetics", begins to emerge almost simultaneously with the interest in classification. It seems that the notion of specialized writing on poetry was by now well-established: a number of writers or poets are reported to have written *on* poetry, some surviving in quotations by encyclopaedic writers of later periods (such as al-Tawḥīdī), others now lost. Famous among these are the poet Diᶜbil's *Kitāb al-Shiᶜr* and al-Nāshiᵓ al-Akbar's similarly entitled work mentioned above. Concurrent with this there was developing a specialized type of analysis of the Qurᵓān from a literary point of view, a trend reported to have begun with a (lost) book by al-Jāḥiẓ entitled *Naẓm al-Qurᵓān*, Abū ᶜUbaydah's work mentioned above, and others including

[8] *Tārīkh al-naqd*, 80–2. [9] *Ṭabaqāt al-shuᶜarāᵓ*, 46–9, 66–81.

Ibn Qutaybah's *Taʾwīl mushkil al-Qurʾān* ("Interpretation of Difficult Expressions in the Qurʾān"). A background to these developments is the great force represented by the work of al-Jāḥiẓ, encyclopaedic and unspecialized as it was, but full of insights from which a considerable amount of material was to run into the mainstream of critical writing. Of a similar nature, but much less influential, was the work of al-Mubarrad (d. *c.* 285/898), one of the very earliest writers to comment favourably on modern poetry and to relate its differences from ancient poetry to the process of evolution on the social and cultural levels.[10] He also compiled an anthology of the work of modern poets.

If Ibn Sallām's work represented the canons of poetry as defined by the "establishment" of linguists, *rāwīs* and collectors (of traditions and language), the next two *ṭabaqāt* works, by Ibn Qutaybah d. (276/889) and Ibn al-Muʿtazz (d. 296/908), seem to have come as a rejection of his strictly conventional views. Ibn Qutaybah sets out in his introduction (the most interesting part of the book, available to European readers in Gaudefroy-Desmombynes' French translation, *Introduction au Livre de la poésie et des poètes*) with the explicit aim of refuting the conventional view which judged poetry purely on the basis of the period in which its author lived. This, Ibn Qutaybah intimates, was preference for the poets rather than for the poetry, and he does his best to shift the balance the other way round. In the course of his endeavour he makes some important points, five being of particular significance:

1 Poetry should be judged according to intrinsic qualities and criteria, not by chronological standards.
2 His description of the structure of the *qaṣīdah* and its movement from one theme to another discerns behind the multiplicity of themes an inner logic – a psychological drive to keep the hearer's attention alive and render the poem more effective. Although he attributed this description to "some knowledgeable people", he can be credited with this first attempt to go beyond the individual text and the surface composition to reach a basically structural account of the movements of the poem.
3 He emphasizes that later poets were unable to make a break with the themes and images of the traditional structure, by substituting scenes of modern life for the desert ones (inhabited buildings instead of deserted encampments, fields of roses and narcissus instead of the thorny plants of the desert, running streams of pure water instead of muddy water-holes). His views here hardly contradict principle 1

[10] Cf. p. 21.

above, for what seems to be the case is that he is fully aware of the inner logic of development of the poem, and the power of this logic to elicit the right response: ruined encampments, then the ordeals of the journey (thorny plants and muddy waters), have a powerful function as they heighten the sense of crisis and deprivation suffered by the poet before he comes ultimately to his patron, an arrival which is in total contrast to what went before; the patron is hope against despair, affluence against deprivation, and so on. In other words, the *qaṣīdah* structure has a symbolic dimension, akin to ritual. If we change the functions, in the sense used by Vladimir Propp, within this structure, we shall destroy its power and effectiveness, since for a poet to say, "I live in a marvellous place, travel comfortably, and my road is strewn with roses", and then to say, "yet you are my hope and saviour", would be nonsense. Ibn Qutaybah evidently recognizes this fundamental symbolic dimension and function of the *qaṣīdah*'s structure; however, his views here have no bearing on, but are rather simply unrelated to, his views about the ancient and the modern.

4 In his attempt to explore the psychological basis for poetic composition, he gathers together most of what was considered by the commentators on poetry to represent its motives and the difference between the dispositions of poets and the roles of the qualities of *ṭab*ᶜ and *ṣan*ᶜ*ah*; of these two fundamental terms, the former can be approximately evaluated as "innate", "unforced", and the latter as "conscious artistry" (a poet or poem predominantly characterized by one or the other is respectively *maṭbū*ᶜ or *maṣnū*ᶜ). He further asserts the relationship between true feeling or experience and good poetry – though he seems to disregard this link when he talks about the Umayyad poet Jarīr's love poetry (*ghazal*) compared with that of al-Farazdaq.[11]

5 He tries to distinguish "good" poetry from "bad" by dividing poetry into four types – good meaning expressed in good words; good meaning in bad words; bad meaning in good words; bad meaning in bad words. But the duality of meanings and words in his work is so sharply defined that it destroys the wholeness of the poetic text. His divisions, though influential in some circles, were to be strongly rejected by major figures during the next two centuries.

The second book on *ṭabaqāt* is Ibn al-Muᶜtazz's *Ṭabaqāt al-shu*ᶜ*arā*ᵓ [*al-muḥdathīn*], devoted entirely to modern poets. While not explicitly taking a stand against Ibn Sallām, it represents a strong reaction against his views in

[11] Cf. a modern evaluation of these poets, *CHALUP*, 404–5, 408–9.

its scope, and in the author's refusal to write about ancient poets because "many have written about them and they have become boring", and because "everything new is enjoyable".[12] He deals both with poets ignored by Ibn Sallām and with those who came after his time. The starting point of the book is Ibn Harmah (d. *c.* 176/792), who was declared by traditional linguists and *rāwī*s to be the "seal" placed on poetry, meaning that he was the last of the "authentic" poets (yet one manuscript of the work, the fullest one, does not start with him but with Bashshār b. Burd, the first of the major exponents of modernism). The book's range of poets demonstrates a genuine shift in ideas both on the nature and on the function of poetry. Here, for the first time, we witness the involvement of poetry in everyday life, in experiences which by older standards were mundane and outside the domain of poetry. Here also we see the dominance of a modern sensibility. But, perhaps more significantly, we also see an excellent representation of the work and lives of poets who were genuine rebels and total outsiders. We even have a selection of "mad" poets who receive high praise from the author for the quality of their poetry.[13] Altogether, the book is a good embodiment of the poetry of conflict in Arab culture and society – conflict social, moral (sex, wine, homosexuality), political, religious, racial, partisan and, above all, literary. It is the *œuvre* of dislocation and displacement. Although brief and restricted to a limited number of poets, Ibn al-Muᶜtazz's comments are often full of insights into poetry and the changes in its language and diction. He enthuses over a couple of poets writing in the traditional style, but his major attention is given to the poets of modern sensibility. His comments on them and lavish praise for their achievement are unparalleled in his time. He clearly views them differently from other critics, who on the whole had identified *ṭab*ᶜ with the ancients and *ṣan*ᶜ*ah* with the moderns. Ibn al-Muᶜtazz rejects this, describing poets like Bashshār and Salam al-Khāsir, pillars of modernism, as *maṭbū*ᶜ.[14] His concept of *ṭab*ᶜ is different from that of Ibn Sallām or Ibn Qutaybah; indeed, he describes four poets as being the most *maṭbū*ᶜ of any, and all four are moderns.

Another deviation from the course Ibn Sallām had taken is evident in the fact that Ibn al-Muᶜtazz, like Ibn Qutaybah, concentrates on individual poets rather than on grouping poets into classes. The whole notion of hierarchic structure is absent from their works, which are more in the nature of biographical notes on selected poets, whose merits are determined by their achievements in their own time rather than by their place in a given hierarchy. With all these points in mind, one can perhaps accept Iḥsān

12 *Ṭabaqāt al-shu*ᶜ*arā*ʾ, 86. 13 Ibid., 384–6. 14 Ibid., 100, 24.

ᶜAbbās's remark that the *ṭabaqāt* scheme was a difficult one to operate, and hence abandoned by critics after Ibn Sallām, notwithstanding the number of works with titles containing the word (apparently *ṭabaqāt* had undergone a major semantic change and ceased to designate, at least in the literary tradition, preference, and had acquired the general sense of "poets of note").

Badīᶜ

Ibn al-Muᶜtazz's interest in the modern poets was such that, in addition to devoting a whole work to them considered as individual poets, he also explored the properties of their poetry as a collective trend with its own distinctive character. Thus, he produced the first theoretical treatment of "ornamentation", *al-badīᶜ*, which lay at the heart of the modernists' work, identifying its elements and placing it within the historical development of Arabic poetry. The genesis of this work, *Kitāb al-Badīᶜ*, is discussed in detail in chapter 21. The significance of this book has hardly been fully realized. His epoch-making delimitation of *al-badīᶜ* as "the new, creative, beautiful" opens up some interesting possibilities for the contemplation of the nature of the modern as a stage in the process of development of poetry. The actual breakthrough is represented by the very conceptual act of identifying a distinct space within the poetic corpus and thinking of certain linguistic and intellectual processes as belonging within this space, and placing other processes outside it. One must ask, why these processes and no other? What do such processes have in common? Are they interrelated or are they just a group of isolated features? These questions will be considered after a brief summary of Ibn al-Muᶜtazz's analysis.

He states, in the briefest possible manner, that *badīᶜ* consists of five elements:[15] *istiᶜārah* (roughly, metaphor); *tajnīs* (paronomasia); *ṭibāq* (antithesis); *radd aᶜjāz al-kalām ᶜalā ṣudūrih* (internal repetition); and *al-madhhab al-kalāmī* (the "dialectical" manner). For each element he quotes, after a concise definition, good and bad examples. His basic argument is that *badīᶜ* existed in the discourse of the Arabs before the modern poets, but that the latter made it into a doctrine and sought to make extensive use of it in their poetry. The only exception is the last element, which, he says, is not in the Qurʾān. Significantly, this element is said to be *mutakallaf* (artificial, affected, forced) – a quality impossible to associate with the Qurʾān on doctrinal grounds.

Roman Jakobson and other modern linguists have provided a descrip-

[15] Cf. also pp. 393–4.

tion of language in terms of two elements, the message and the code.[16] This binary opposition can be used in the present context to illuminate *badīʿ* as defined by Ibn al-Muʿtazz, and to offer possible answers to the questions posed above concerning the identification of its elements. If we conceive of *badīʿ*, as described by Ibn al-Muʿtazz, as forming a structure, a system within which the elements are not isolated but interrelated, we can see that the basic property of the structure is that it is formed on the level of the code, rather than the message of discourse; it explores relations of opposition and similarity, of oneness and multiplicity, between the linguistic constituents of poetry. *Istiʿārah* is a process which involves a double-relationship, a linguistic and semantic similarity-in-difference; the signifieds are similar but different, their signifiers, originally different, are now to be made one. *Tajnīs* is based on similarity (or identity) of signifiers with difference in the signifieds. *Ṭibāq* is based on total opposition between the signifieds and no relationship of signifiers. *Radd* involves identity of signifiers together with identity of significance. The fifth element, *al-madhhab al-kalāmī*, deserves special attention, since it appears to be of a different nature. Having defined it as "artificiality and laboured deliberation", Ibn al-Muʿtazz gives examples which reveal that it consists in the relating of two distinct, unrelated thought-processes, ideas or experiences, in an effort to establish the validity of the first (felt initially to be invalid or illogical) by linking it with the second (which is clearly valid and logical). The first is usually an abstract or theoretical statement, the second a physical image. No direct similarity is usually pointed out in such a process, but, by putting two things next to each other, an implied similarity becomes the operative force in linking the signifieds, whereas the signifiers are in no way related to each other. Such a method of validation is based on a degree of what ʿAbd al-Qāhir al-Jurjānī (see below) was later to call "self-deception", and is a process which may be identified with the notion of the conceit in seventeenth-century English poetry.[17] Because of its inherent properties, this device, unlike the first four, cannot be said to exist in the Qurʾān; it was the product of a new cultural environment in which *kalām*, the art of argumentation and polemics over religious issues, generated this power of persuasion, of showing that things can be what they seem not to be.

The extremes of Ibn al-Muʿtazz's system are thus *radd* and *ṭibāq*, the first representing total oneness on the level of both signifier and signified, the second total difference on both levels. Mediating between them are *tajnīs* (oneness of signifiers with difference of signifieds) and *al-madhhab al-kalāmī*

16 Roman Jakobson and Morris Halle, *The Fundamentals of Language* (The Hague, 1971).

17 Abu Deeb, *Al-Jurjānī's Theory*, 11–14. For a contrasting interpretation of Ibn al-Muʿtazz's understanding of *badīʿ*, see Stetkevych, "Toward a redefinition".

(difference of signifiers with oneness of signifieds). *Istiᶜārah* combines all these elements: total difference of signifiers becomes oneness (substitution), similarity and difference of signifieds become identification, yet preserving a certain degree of tension between them. *Badīᶜ* thus represents a system of relations, a type of poetry which explores the complex network of relationships between signifier and signified, creating a high degree of intensity and fullness on the level of the code, rather than that of the message conveyed. Ibn al-Muᶜtazz's perception of it can thus be seen as a first criterion of modernism: that modernism shifts the emphasis in the text from the level of the message to the level of the code.

The authority of the critic

One definite sign of early maturity in literary criticism was the claim critics made to specialization and authoritative knowledge. From the early ᶜAbbasid Khalaf al-Aḥmar, we learn that the authority of a knowledgeable judge overrules the subjective response to poetry (or, for that matter, to any other "product") of the non-specialist.[18] The critic was seen as a special kind of agent, performing an act which required a special kind of knowledge, not within the reach of an ordinary recipient. As early as Ibn Sallām, we witness this confidence in the critic's role, which he compares to the role of any other professional master in any other profession or craft (*ṣināᶜah*). The comparison was to acquire great currency in following centuries. In the fourth/tenth century, for instance, al-Āmidī, in *al-Muwāzanah*, goes further, restricting knowledge of poetry to the specialists and saying that ordinary people ought to leave the matter of judgement to them altogether.[19] The principle was reiterated in similar terms in the following century by Ibn Rashīq, who collected the views of a number of prominent writers in support of his argument in his *al-ᶜUmdah*.[20]

Criticism thus began and continued to be a specialized knowledge, and it is interesting to note that emphasis was almost always placed on acquired knowledge (*ᶜilm*) and understanding rather than evaluation – an emphasis which denies the value of the subjective response, whether positive or negative, and asserts that knowledge requires long training added to a special type of disposition or innate preparedness. This special knowledge cannot be arrogated to oneself; it must be demonstrated through analysis and justification of judgement by the discovery of the qualities of a given work of art. Al-Āmidī, in the passage referred to above, advises his

[18] Quoted Ibn Sallām, *Ṭabaqāt al-shuᶜarāʾ*, 7. [19] *Muwāzanah*, I, 410–19. [20] *ᶜUmdah*, 113–19.

opponent to test his degree of knowledge by looking at the choices of the masters of this craft and trying to discover the reasons for their preferences. Despite the fact that the nature of this knowledge is not explored in analytical terms (more often than not it is defined negatively, by asserting what it is not rather than what it is), the conditions pertaining to its acquisition are clearly stated. According to al-Āmidī, knowledge of poetry is an "experience" of countless individual instances and the power to abstract from them; it is the product of long "looking" at poetry, long intimacy and long training; it is a natural disposition nurtured by experience, knowledge of the literary traditions of the Arabs, coupled with refined taste and linguistic competence plus that undefined and undefinable quality, the mysterious "power of recognition and discrimination". Nevertheless, in spite of its crucial importance, this special power of discrimination is not a sufficient condition: there remains an area of inexplicability in poetry, as much as in other areas of human activity. Two things may possess the same definable conditions of goodness, yet one may still prefer one to the other. Here one reaches the limits of explanation; the ultimate criterion is indefinable. Both al-Āmidī and, at around the same time, al-Qāḍī ʾl-Jurjānī (see below), put this very effectively, but it had been stated in a less definitive form as early as Ibn Sallām.

The whole notion of "authoritative knowledge" and the authority of the specialist ought perhaps to be seen in the wider context of the emergence of religious authority, especially that type of authority claimed by the *fuqahāʾ* (jurisconsults) in connection with the interpretation of the Qurʾān, religious doctrine and its legal principles. It is not a coincidence that many of the leading critics were at the same time steeped in *kalām*, theology and religious studies in general; some of them were even professional judges.

Poetics and practical criticism

By the first quarter of the fourth/tenth century many important questions about poetry, its nature, function and structure had been asked; and some interesting answers given. The issues which were to dominate the thinking of Arab critics for centuries to come had been identified and discussed in varying degrees of comprehensiveness and depth. The one major dimension to emerge after this period derived from the increasing influence of Aristotle's *Rhetoric* and *Poetics* and the commentaries on them in philosophical circles. Poetry began now to be defined in terms of mimesis (so much so that by the seventh/thirteenth century, Ḥāzim al-Qarṭājannī was to refuse to describe as poetry metrical and rhymed discourse in which the mimesis (*muḥākāh*) was unappealing),[21] and as an imaginative (*takhyīlī*) type of discourse which stood in direct opposition to prose (*khaṭābah*) on the level of function. The distinction between poetry and prose acquired greater importance, and the study of poeticality generated new ideas in sharp contrast with ideas derived originally from considering poetry just another form of discourse, distinguished by purely formal constraints such as metre and rhyme. Criticism, on the theoretical level, shifted now from rhetoric to poetics, and from the study of discourse in general to the study of those properties specific to poetry as a distinct and different activity.

The fourth/tenth century was, however, also distinguished by the strong development of practical criticism, since most of the major theoretical issues had, as was suggested earlier, been defined by the first two decades of that century. This powerful new impulse found its scope in the disputes over ancient and modern, or over the merits and demerits of the work of one particular poet or the comparative achievements of two poets. It issued from the strong sense of dislocation generated in the previous century, and attempted to bring back into equilibrium both Arabic poetry and critical theory. This is well reflected in the titles of the two major works of this age: *al-Muwāzanah* ("The Counterbalancing") of al-Āmidī and *al-Wasāṭah* ("The Mediation") by al-Qāḍī ʾl-Jurjānī (d. 392/1002). Outwardly, the former was an attempt to analyze the achievements of two major poets of the previous century, Abū Tammām and al-Buḥturī, through detailed comparison of their work, without reaching a judgement on which was the better poet; the latter was an attempt to mediate between the opponents and supporters of a single poet, al-Mutanabbī. On a much deeper level, each was seeking in its own way to re-establish a lost equilibrium and a sense of continuity within the great tradition. Al-Āmidī soon deserted his "balancing out" effort to reaffirm the supremacy of the ancient notions of poetry which preceded the new school and to establish, in their most rigid form, the "traditional" criteria. Similarly, al-Qāḍī ʾl-Jurjānī could not but desert his mediatory effort to seek a sense of equilibrium, in asserting not so much the newness and freshness of the poetry of the controversial poet he was studying, as his equality with the great poets of the past: if he had made mistakes, well, they too had made mistakes; if he achieved anything good, he must be accorded recognition for it – good being defined in moderate terms which mediated between the old and the relatively and reasonably new. The excessively new was rejected, because it was difficult to assimilate within a system possessing its inner equilibrium.

In the light of this search for equilibrium, we can begin to understand the

[21] See ʿUṣfūr, *al-Ṣūrah al-fanniyyah*, 88–9; see ibid., for a discussion of the influence of philosophy on Arabic poetics; cf. ch. 21, nn. 45, 46, below.

critics' preoccupation with the otherwise rather puzzling issue of plagiarism (*sariqah*). The literature devoted to this problem far exceeds that devoted to any other single problem in Arabic literary history. This entails a striking paradox; for the whole notion of plagiarism, the search for the minutest form of one poet's "stealing" something from another, is tenable only in a cultural context where originality is a highly valued aspect of poetic creativity. Yet this search takes place in a culture which has often been described as traditional, in which creativity and originality are generally ruled out in favour of emulation and continuity. The paradox is unresolvable unless we understand the obsession with plagiarism not as a manifestation of an underlying preoccupation with originality, but as a keen search for equilibrium, for the affirmation of the continuity of the classical model, of the deep-rootedness of the new in the old, in the structure of the poetic world which preceded the dislocation. This is immediately evident in the first work on the "new", Ibn al-Muᶜtazz's *Kitāb al-Badīᶜ*, the premise of which, as we have already seen, was that *badīᶜ* was not new in kind, since it all existed in the classical model; its novelty was one of degree. It is also evident in the domain most affected by the interest in plagiarism: the poets whose plagiarisms were hunted out most keenly were the poets of the "new" school, who generated or contributed to the process of dislocation, rather than those poets who continued to write within the established tradition (although, of course, it is in their work, almost by definition, that one would be more likely to find plagiarisms of all types). Whereas the critics of the time often found plagiarism a peculiar problem, superficial and extraneous to the study of poetry, we can see it now in a new light as being functional within the total structure of critical and cultural activity, as having in fact a kind of therapeutic effect, since it helped to reveal the survival of the classical model in the new poetry and to regain the lost equilibrium. Another factor underlying the interest in the phenomenon, and it is an important one, relates to the image of the world as finite and explorable in totality, as will be mentioned later.

It is remarkable that, in what is usually presumed to be a strongly religious culture, poetic criticism remained almost entirely secular; major critics argued that poeticality had nothing to do with religiosity. This is undoubtedly paradoxical, for all critical activity ultimately originated in religiosity, yet critics separated poetry from religious faith and morality. Such separation is attributable to two factors: first, the great poetic tradition was pre-Islamic, composed by those who knew nothing of Islam, and included the great Imruᵓ al-Qays himself, an "immoral" poet; secondly, poetry like all forms of writing or composition was split into two dimensions, thought and language – thought could be judged morally only as raw material, as reality, but once it entered the domain of art it ceased to be reality and became "reality-made" (*poiēsis*), and this has no relationship to morality, since the "made" has to be judged in terms of the conditions pertaining to its making rather than to any moral, social or religious values. Thus critical activity had to concern itself with the factors and processes whereby an object of art becomes what it is. This is reflected most expressively in the comparison dominant in all Arabic criticism between poetry and other forms of "making". The poet was fundamentally a "maker" (just as the Greek *poiētēs* was). This view was ultimately responsible for isolating poetry, as conceived of and discussed by the critics, from its cultural, political and economic conditions and turning it into a body of "knowledge" (*ᶜilm*) superimposed on those conditions. It also ultimately turned most literary criticism into rhetoric and poetics, excluding any possibility of critical trends which would have concentrated on the "vision" of a poet, or the social, political or moral conflicts in the corpus of poetry.

This same view of poetry formed also the conceptual basis responsible for making literary criticism the worldly activity it was, an activity preoccupied with the *here* and never with the *there* (to use modern critical terminology only for the purpose of illustration).[22] This preoccupation found its best manifestation in the following three forms:

1 Total concentration on the text as a physical reality of genuine material weight. The materiality of the text and its immediacy are conspicuously present in the work of all Arab critics. The text is viewed as a well-defined, well-shaped, well-conveyed and well-received material object. It said everything and left nothing beyond its power of articulation. The few instances in which, in the view of some critics, it failed to do this were harshly criticized.

2 Preoccupation with the text as an article of exchange, taking place to express a specific, definable intention and to serve a specific, definable purpose. The conditions governing this exchange between the producer and recipient were present in the mind of almost every critic and writer on poetry.

3 Concentration on the type of poetry which was part and parcel of the life of the establishment; poets writing outside the establishment were rarely the subject of discussion or enquiry.

Yet paradoxically this concentration on the code, on the nature of poetic language and treatment of an already recognized or definable experience, embodied a religious conception of the world and man's role in and

22 Cf. Thomas MacFarlane, "Poetry and the poem", *Literary Theory and Structure: Essays in Honor of William K. Wimsatt*, eds. F. Brady et al. (New Haven and London, 1973), 83–113.

relationship to it. According to this conception, the world was created, perfected and revealed in its totality by God. Hence it was fixed, unchanging, ahistorical; man's role in it was that of witness to its creation and perfection and to the manifestations of God in it. The world was finite and totally comprehensible; indeed it had been comprehended once and for all by a bygone generation; hence one poet differed from another not in terms of his individual comprehension of the world, but in his ability to reformulate the inherited comprehension in more (or less) effective and eloquent modes of expression. Experience as an individual confrontation with, and an independent exploration of, reality was never central to the discussion of poetry; only craftsmanship was.[23] It is this conception that was responsible for the attempts to produce a typology of meanings, which was put in an extreme form by the early ᶜAbbasid poet al-Qiṣāfi, who argued that all poetry could be subsumed in the words, "You are [thus]: eulogy; you were [thus]: elegy; you are not [thus]: satire", a dictum which survived in the fifth/eleventh century in the work of Ibn Rashīq (d. *c.* 456/1064).[24] Such efforts culminated in the work of Ḥāzim al-Qarṭājannī in the seventh/thirteenth century, having begun with the endeavours to define the sections of the poem and its motifs which we encountered for the first time in Ibn Qutaybah's work.

The finite nature of the world was closely linked to a fundamental preoccupation of all Arabic literary criticism: the relationship of meanings to words. From the earliest phases, we witness the crystallization of a view of poetry, indeed of all discourse, as consisting of the dual elements *maᶜnā* (meaning) and *lafẓ* (expression). The amount of material devoted to the study of this duality even so early as al-Jāḥiẓ, is rather astonishing; the whole notion of *balāghah* (rhetoric) was defined in terms of it. On many occasions, words and meanings seem to represent not merely a duality but even a binary opposition, as if words were not the very constituents which generate meaning. We face this conception as early as a paper (*ṣaḥīfah*) attributed to Bishr b. al-Muᶜtamir (d. 210/825) and quoted by al-Jāḥiẓ,[25] and also in the latter's own formulations. It appears too in an acute form in the divisions of poetry described by Ibn Qutaybah, in which words and meanings can be qualified as good or bad in total isolation from each other. From these studies to Ibn Sinān al-Khafājī's (d. 466/1072) "measurement" of words and meanings and their coincidence ("if this is as long as that"),[26] the duality often determines the outcome of critical activity on the one hand, and restricts its scope on the other. The restriction results from the

[23] For an important discussion of this, see the modern poet and critic Adūnīs, *al-Thābit waʾl-mutaḥawwil*, II.
[24] Quoted Ibn al-Jarrāḥ (d. 296/908), *Waraqah*, 9; Ibn Rashīq, *ᶜUmdah*, I, 123.
[25] *Bayān*, I, 135–9. [26] *Sirr al-faṣāḥah*, 199–206.

practical need to select units of expression of a manageable length for the purpose of discussion. Such a unit will also have to be complete in what it states in order for one to be able to judge the degree of suitability of its words to its meanings. Behind this notion lies a concept of meaning as an independent, complete, solid entity which it is possible to isolate, describe and express in differing ways of precision, concision and eloquence. Meaning as a vague, undefinable, evolving presence in the text, inseparable from the language used to embody it, was hardly ever conceived of by Arab critics. It was generally believed that it was possible to restate a meaning of a line of poetry and then compare this restatement with the way in which the poet formulated it, and thence judge his ability as a poet. The one major exception is ᶜAbd al-Qāhir al-Jurjānī, who rejects the "heresy of paraphrase" (in Cleanth Brooks' phrase), as will be seen later.

The problem was accentuated by the fact that discussions of this duality took place in the total absence of a properly worked-out theory of meaning. From the *ṣaḥīfah* of Bishr b. al-Muᶜtamir and al-Jāḥiẓ, meaning is discussed from many angles, but is taken completely for granted, as if it were the most obvious thing to comprehend. Yet in fact, a great many of the misconceptions and shortcomings of literary criticism arose precisely from the fact that meaning is a vague entity; different writers were talking about different things, though they were all in superficial appearances discussing the relationship of meaning to words. In al-Jāḥiẓ, a preliminary examination has revealed four different ways of using the term "meaning", and each way generated independent critical statements resulting in real contradiction between some of his views. His famous statement that "meanings are to be found in the highways and byways", and that "poetry is a type of formulation and casting",[27] offers an example of the confusion caused by the ambiguity of the concept of meaning. Many critics asserted that al-Jāḥiẓ gave priority to words over meaning; ᶜAbd al-Qāhir al-Jurjānī rejected this interpretation, saying that al-Jāḥiẓ's passage reveals the importance of construction rather than words, and adding that construction was a process of constructing meanings, not words. But in so speaking, he was clearly referring to meaning in a sense altogether different from that which it had in the works of his opponents. It is highly significant that the two writers who made the finest contribution to the study of construction – al-Khaṭṭābī (d. 388/988) in his *Bayān iᶜjāz al-Qurʾān* ("Exposition of the Qurʾān's Inimitability"), and ᶜAbd al-Qāhir al-Jurjānī himself – made the cornerstone of their work a close analysis of the nature of meaning, giving it definitions consistent with their own theoretical constructs. Most other

[27] *Ḥayawān*, III, 131–2.

writers dealt with questions of poetics in the absence of such definitions; al-Āmidī, for instance, who lays great stress on the study of meaning in his comparison of Abū Tammām and al-Buḥturī, at times describes two general notions as being "meanings" and at other times distinguishes between very close statements on the basis that the meanings in them are not the same. The confusion between the two designations of "meaning" is evident in most discussions of the subject. Underlying the application of the first designation there is a reductive view of meaning, for in order to identify two meanings as being one, it ignores language, syntactic structure and other elements of discourse and seeks behind all these a general notion, an idea, a conception, which is common to the two formulations. In this fashion, Ibn Ṭabāṭabā (d. 322/934) considers four pieces of writing, widely different in their language, imagery, tone, details and so forth, two being in verse and two in prose, as conveying the same "meaning", because they all revolve around the idea of lamenting the death of one ruler and congratulating his successor.[28]

The concentration on writing as a craft, on the "secrets" of the superiority of the Qurʾān, and on the function of discourse both in secular writing and in religious life, resulted in a current of critical enquiry which perhaps represents the central achievement of Arabic literary criticism, namely the exploration of the nature and structure of literary, especially poetic, language. From such remarkable studies as al-Āmidī's analysis of certain instances of metaphorical language (e.g. his discussion of Abū Tammām's metaphor of the "width" of time),[29] to the subtle and penetrating analysis by ʿAbd al-Qāhir al-Jurjānī of the way metaphor operates within the syntactic structure[30] and the refined discussions of the power of expression embodied in certain Quranic verses, we witness the analytical vigour of minds enchanted with the beauty and power of language and yet rigorous enough to try to describe the mechanism by which the beauty and power are achieved. Qudāmah's discussion of the interconnections between the semantic units of a line or group of lines, defined not as single words but as complete thought processes, and his search for harmony and balance, are extended in Ibn Ṭabāṭabā's work to apply to the entire poem.[31] Similarly, al-Jāḥiẓ's comments on the significance of syntactic relations on the level of a single sentence are enlarged by ʿAbd al-Qāhir al-Jurjānī to form a critical principle which explores the power of expression and the semantic properties of syntactic relations on the level of an entire line or a larger unit of composition, sometimes even a whole, though short, poem. The purely phonetic

[28] *ʿIyār al-shiʿr*, 78–80. [29] *Muwāzanah*, I, 196–203. [30] E.g. *Asrār al-balāghah*, 21–4.
[31] Qudāmah b. Jaʿfar, *Naqd al-shiʿr*, 199ff; Ibn Ṭabāṭabā, *ʿIyār al-shiʿr*, 5–7, 43–4, 124–8.

properties of literary composition were discussed at length: Ibn Sinān al-Khafājī devoted an entire work (*Sirr al-faṣāḥah*, "The Secret of Eloquence") to such properties, developing observations originally made by, amongst others, al-Jāḥiẓ. Although such studies suffered from a major defect – the acoustic level of literary language being discussed in almost total isolation from the semantic structure – some observations are undoubtedly of genuine critical significance.

This current of critical thought, which concentrated on the linguistic structure of poetic composition, runs parallel right from the start to another, theoretically oriented, current which was preoccupied with the structural properties of Arabic poetry and, ultimately, with "poetics", with the general rules and conditions controlling not particular texts but the *meta*-text. Foremost amongst the representatives of this trend is Ibn Qutaybah, discussed above. Into this category fall a number of other works such as *Qawāʿid al-shiʿr* ("The Bases of Poetry") by Thaʿlab (d. 291/904), which divides poetry into four types, these being in fact four semantic categories, imperative, prohibition, statement and interrogation, with poetic quotations to illustrate each type. Thaʿlab also describes the "arts" of poetry, identifying them as themes such as praise, elegy, satire and "similizing" (comparison). The book's bearing on literary theory and criticism is very limited,[32] but it offers an example of the kind of thinking about poetry current in the circles of traditional linguists. The two most important works in this tradition up to the fifth/eleventh century are undoubtedly Qudāmah's and Ibn Ṭabāṭabā's, both of which will receive further attention below. Almost all the ideas and most of the material known up to the end of the fourth/tenth century was collected in Abū Hilāl al-ʿAskarī's (d. 395/1005) work *Kitāb al-Ṣināʿatayn* ("The Two Arts", i.e. poetry and prose), a famous handbook on the craft of writing which, however, makes very little – if any – personal contribution except for the occasional comment on some detail; the book may have played a role in the development of the science of *balāghah*, but its role in the development of literary criticism is negligible.

Poetry as a craft is the cornerstone of Qudāmah's entire work. Starting from the premises that "poetry has a craft to it", and that the intention behind every craft is to carry what is made and done by it to the ultimate degree of perfection, Quadāmah believes the craft of poetry to have two poles, extreme goodness and extreme badness; all poetry belongs to one of these poles or falls between them. He then illustrates these extremes and the factors which produce each of them, constructing a logical model in terms

[32] Cf. pp. 403–4.

of which all poetry can be described and evalutated. The basic elements of the model are words, meaning, metre and rhyme. These four constituents can be joined in six permutations, with some modifications resulting from the role of rhyme. His final model yields four modes of conjunction: words with meaning, words with metre, meaning with metre, meaning with rhyme. Thus the types of poetry become eight: the four simple types generated by the basic constituents, and the four generated by their conjunction. Each type can be good or bad, and all poetry can be described by describing how the goodness or badness is achieved. If all types of conjunction are good in one poem, it reaches the ultimate degree of goodness; and vice versa. The rest of poetry falls between these two extremes. The remainder of the book is a detailed study of the eight types, starting with "properties of words" and ending with "defective conjugation of meaning with rhyme"; thus offering a unique model of logical organization with some real insights into poetry and the conditions of its appeal or "goodness" as Qudāmah puts it.

Ibn Ṭabāṭabā carries this trend a step further by identifying some of the basic constituents of what he calls, "the customs and traditions of the Arabs in composing poetry",[33] not merely with reference to the structure of the poem, but also in so far as detailed aspects of poetic composition are concerned. His analysis of the traditions governing simile, for instance, is of interest in revealing the obscurity which underlies a large number of instances of simile; he explains them by placing them in the wider cultural context in which they were constructed. Throughout his discussion he relates poetry to its geographical, cultural and linguistic environment, viewing its conventions as being necessarily generated by the conditions of its production (a view which he does not readily apply to modernist poetry). Yet despite this reverence for tradition, Ibn Ṭabāṭabā praises the subtlety and variety of modes used by the modern poets to link the opening section of the panegyric poem to its main part, claiming that the ancients were limited and lacked subtlety on this particular level.[34]

A further degree of refinement in the description of poetic structure was achieved in the fourth/tenth century by al-Āmidī in the course of his detailed comparison of Abū Tammām with al-Buḥturī (see below). This current of critical enquiry culminated in the fifth/eleventh century in the work of al-Marzūqī (d. 421/1030), best known for his final formulation of what has been called the theory of *ᶜamūd al-shiᶜr* (constituents of [traditional, good] poetry). Al-Marzūqī's work represents a shift in interest from the structure of the poem to the structure of poetry. The question he

[33] *ᶜIyār al-shiᶜr*, 32–40. [34] Ibid., 111–19.

tries to answer is not, how is a poem constructed? but, how is good poetry constituted? The answer he gives represents, as Iḥsān ʿAbbās has shown, a fusion into one theoretical framework of criteria and concepts proposed and developed by his predecessors, especially Qudāmah, al-Qāḍī ʾl-Jurjānī and al-Āmidī. The constituents, in the final form given them by al-Marzūqī, are:

1 Nobility and correctness of meaning
2 Tautness or strength of words (*jazālah*), and their "uprightness" (*istiqāmah*)
3 Correctness and precision of description
4 Closeness of similarity
5 Tightness of construction and fusion of its parts, coupled with the choice of enjoyable metre
6 Suitability of the extremes of metaphor to each other
7 Homogeneity of words and meaning and the demands made on them by the rhyme, so that no discordance may exist between them.[35]

ʿAmūd al-shiʿr serves a definite purpose for al-Marzūqī: it is not simply a study of poetry in the absolute, but a descriptive statement on the properties of "classical" poetry. Its purpose is "to distinguish old art (*ṣanʿah*) from new, and the ancient system of poetry from the modern". But it is also an aesthetic evaluative scheme, with a clear historical dimension as the basis for evaluation. The last phrase of the passage just quoted runs, "so that the difference between *maṣnūʿ* and *maṭbūʿ* may be known". Placed in the context of al-Marzūqī's definition of these two terms, both of which he views as emanating from the same impulse yet differing in the degree of conscious application of a critical, selective faculty to the original impulse on the level of composition, it becomes evident that *ʿamūd al-shiʿr* has an aesthetic and critical function rather than being a merely descriptive one. *Maṭbūʿ*, al-Marzūqī believes, is the poetry of the ancients *par excellence*; whereas the moderns vary in their degree of *ṭabʿ* and the degree of *ṣanʿah* to which they subject their compositions.

As part of the growing interest in poetics, a definite trend is observable, the search for a definition of poetry itself: what it is, what function it has, how it relates to other artistic activities, and to morality and religion. It is often said that the Arabs defined poetry in terms of metrical composition and rhyme; but this is a false impression resulting from generalizing on the basis of one famous instance, Qudāmah's definition of poetry as "metrical, rhymed and expressive of meaning".[36] In fact, two distinct viewpoints on the nature of poetry are evident in the culture. The first defines poetry in

35 ʿAbbās, *Tārīkh al-naqd*, 404–5. 36 *Naqd al-shiʿr*, 2.

terms which exclude other forms of writing by identifying formal conditions which are exclusive to poetry; the second attempts to define poetry in terms of the nature of the imaginative activity generating it as well as its formal properties, placing more emphasis on the first where divergence between the imaginative and the formal criteria is in evidence.

The strictest example of the first tendency was not in fact Qudāmah's definition, but the one offered in an almost unknown text by Abū ʾl-Jaysh al-Anṣārī, who saw rhyme itself as the most distinctive and essential feature of poetry, thus reducing the constituents of a definition from three to one.[37] Qudāmah's definition stated that poetry was metrical, rhymed and significant discourse; yet even he refused to consider merely metred discourse, devoid of other properties of poeticality, as poetry. All significant critics shared this view with him; no critic is known to have described as poetry the metrical compositions of grammarians or philosophers, or even verse composed by known poets but lacking in such other almost indefinable qualities as *ṭab*ᶜ, *rawnaq* (charm), *ṭalāwah* (elegance) and *badīhah* (spontaneity), which most critics believed to be essential constituents of poeticality. So early and conservative a critic as Ibn Sallām al-Jumaḥī distinguished poetry from what he called "constructed, textured discourse, based on rhyme".[38] Similarly, Abū Ḥātim al-Rāzī (d. *c.* 322/933–4), who asserted that poetry could *only* be metrical, hastened to add that *shi*ᶜ*r* (which is indeed related to the verb *sha*ᶜ*ara* "to feel, to know intuitively") is so called because it is "intuitive apprehension of things not immediately obvious".[39]

The second trend related poetry to creativity, to the power of emotional and intellectual apprehension, to intuition and imaginative creation. One of the best instances of this view is provided by Ibn Wahb (whose *al-Burhān fī wujūh al-bayān* was once mistakenly attributed to Qudāmah) and he says, "*shā*ᶜ*ir* (poet) derives from *sha*ᶜ*ara* (to feel); he does not deserve this name until he produces what nobody else than he can feel. Therefore, whoever is devoid of this quality is not a poet, even if he composes metrical and rhymed discourse". Going even beyond this definition, writers within philosophical circles identified poetry with imagination (*takhyīl*) and mimesis (*muḥākāh*) first and foremost. This new, distinctive mark of poetry was soon to be incorporated in critical writings, and to find its finest expression in the work of ᶜAbd al-Qāhir al-Jurjānī in the fifth/eleventh century. But as early as the first part of the fourth/tenth century, Ibn Abī ᶜAwn had confined poetry to three types of activity which are in essence three modes of imagery: rare and accurate simile; striking (*gharīb*)

[37] British Library Ms. Add. 23, f. 446. [38] *Ṭabaqāt al-shu*ᶜ*arā*ʾ, 8. [39] *Zīnāh*, 130.

metaphor; and *amthāl* ("proverbial" sayings – though the scope of this Arabic term is much wider than that of English "proverb"). In this formulation metre and rhyme find no place.[40]

However, the finest achievement within this current of thought is undoubtedly that of the philosopher al-Fārābī (d. 339/950), who not only lays greater stress on the imaginative aspect of poetry, but goes further, to distinguish between poetry and poeticality.[41] This was the first such distinction in Arabic writing, and would only be grasped and elaborated much later in the works of Ḥāzim al-Qarṭājannī and al-Sijilmāsī.[42] For al-Fārābī, discourse can be poetic without being "poetry". Its poeticality is a property derived from its power of mimesis, but in order to be poetry it has to be divided into parts and organized metrically. As mentioned above, this new emphasis on the imaginative activity involved in poetry came essentially from the new major influence on literary studies, the commentaries on Aristotle's *Poetics* and *Rhetoric*, although its roots in Arabic literary traditions go much deeper than is generally recognized. They originate in the concept of poetry as magic, demonic, spiritual and *different*. This deeply rooted conception appears in the fact that contemporaries of the Prophet first reacted to the Qurʾān by saying that it was poetry and magic, meaning that it had qualities which were identical with certain properties of poetry as they conceived it, albeit on a totally different level. The full significance of this early response to the Qurʾān deserves further analysis in a more specialized context.

Criticism and Quranic studies

As was suggested earlier, thinking critically about poetry dates back at least to the age of the great pre-Islamic poets. The rise of Islam generated sharper critical thinking, particularly about the function of poetry, when Islam attempted, as does any revolution with a total vision of society, to subject poetry to its overall vision of social order and religious values. The really important questions concerning literary language and eloquence (*balāghah*) were no longer asked with reference to poetry, but rather to the new text which superseded it as the high point of literary achievement within the culture: the Qurʾān. Such questions were generated from within the text itself, not only as a literary, but as a religious text raising issues of vital importance to the very existence of man, his conception of God, and his relationship to Him. Although such questions were not in essence of a literary nature, they were language-based not simply because no conception

[40] *Tashbīhāt*, 1–2. [41] See ʿUṣfūr, *al-Ṣūrah al-fanniyyah*, 166.

[42] Ḥāzim al-Qarṭājannī, *Minhāj al-bulaghāʾ*, 70–3; Sijilmāsī, *Manziʿ*, 218–61.

of God or the universe can be formulated outside language, but also because the language of the Qurʾān was on certain issues ambiguous and open to more than one interpretation. Of the many possibilities in such a language, two became of crucial importance: the first centred on the nature of the divine being, the second on man's relationship to Him in so far as man's freedom of action and responsibility for his acts were concerned (free will against predestination). On a very different but no less important level for the development of critical thinking, a third issue acquired great significance, the question of the inimitability (*iʿjāz*) of the Qurʾān. The first two will be considered briefly, before closer examination is given to the third, which was to acquire increasing relevance to the development of literary criticism in the following centuries.

Of central importance to the development of critical enquiry into the nature of poetry is undoubtedly the awareness of the dual nature of language itself, as a literal statement of meaning and as a non-literal statement. In Arabic culture this awareness first crystallized in theological circles and with reference to questions of free will versus predestination and of anthropomorphism; in both matters two currents of thought dominated the culture. With respect to the former question, the Jabriyyah held that the only true agent and creator of actions is God, and that man is not such an agent; the Qadariyyah asserted man's freedom of action. With regard to anthropomorphism, the first group believed that God was "in the image of man" and had the psychological and physical attributes of man; the second negated all divine attributes and all likeness to man. Each group found evidence in the Qurʾān to support its claims; and, in the course of the disputes, each resorted to "interpreting" those Quranic verses which were antagonistic to its own views; this interpretation involved the notion that such passages did not mean what they seemed on the surface to mean, but something beyond that. This "something beyond" came to be called *majāz* and thence evolved the concept of language as being "literal" or "non-literal": verses such as *sūrah* xx.5, "God is seated on the throne", were said to have a literal (*ḥaqīqī*) meaning, and a non-literal (*majāzī*) one, according to which the meaning would not be a physical act of "being seated" with the physical attributes that presupposes, but rather God's power and total control. Similar interpretations were offered for other verses, such as *sūrah* xlvii.10, "God's hand is above their hand". The domains in which the concepts of *ḥaqīqī* and *majāzī* were exploited were many, but the most interesting for our purpose is that of literary studies. Here, al-Jāḥiẓ (a leading Muʿtazilī as well as pioneering littérateur) played a key role in secularizing these concepts and beginning to use them in the study of poetry. He identified figures such as *istiʿārah* (metaphor) and made use of his theological notions in discussing it as it appears in poetry; he was also the first to record the usage of the term *badīʿ*, which in his example seems to relate closely to a particular way of using *istiʿārah*. Significantly, Ibn al-Muʿtazz was later on to consider *istiʿārah* the first element of *badīʿ*.[43] Study of the metaphorical nature of language opened totally new horizons to critical enquiry.

Within this trend came the first work on the *majāzī* nature of an entire – and considerable – text in any major critical tradition: *Majāz al-Qurʾān* by Abū ʿUbaydah (d. 209/824–5), in which *majāz* does not mean simply "transference" or "metaphorical usage", but in fact any kind of deviation from the norm, the norm being understood not only in terms of common usage but also in terms of the shape the text would have taken had it been constructed in a manner showing the fullest possible form a given meaning can take. Deviation here is almost identical with what Michael Riffaterre has recently called "destruction of mimesis".[44] Abū ʿUbaydah is, in this sense, the founder of the deviationist approach to literary language; the significance of his work has not yet been fully realized, and it deserves much greater attention than it has received. Within the same tradition come two books by the Shīʿī poet al-Sharīf al-Raḍī (d. 406/1016), *Talkhīṣ al-bayān fī majāzāt al-Qurʾān* ("Summary Exposition of Quranic *Majāz*") and *al-Majāzāt al-nabawiyyah* ("*Majāz* Usages of the Prophet"), as well as, earlier, Ibn Qutaybah's *Taʾwīl mushkil al-Qurʾān* ("Interpretation of Difficult Expressions in the qurʾān"), all of them highly specialized studies with revealing insights into the language of the Qurʾān and, by implication and extension, the language of literature generally.

The issue of the inimitability (*iʿjāz*) of the Qurʾān, which was to be of central importance for literary criticism, was not an external one, since *iʿjāz* was proclaimed by the Book itself, and in such a forceful manner that it staked its very authenticity as the word of God on its uniqueness and the inability of men or jinn to produce anything "like it". The challenge thus posed, however, was ambiguous as it specified no particular qualities which those who were challenged were to match. But it was just this ambiguity which was to enrich literary enquiry perhaps more than any purely literary issue up to the fifth/eleventh century, as scholars began to examine the multitude of possibilities which might have rendered the Qurʾān inimitable. Of such possibilities only those which relate to linguistic or literary aspects concern us here, and central among these is the view that the inimitability resided in the language of the Qurʾān. Initially, two positions seem to have been taken, one attributing inimitability to the "meanings"

[43] See ch. 21. [44] *Semiotics of Poetry* (Bloomington/London, 1978), 1–10.

and the other to the words. In the fourth/tenth century however al-Khaṭṭābī, in the short but important treatise on *iʿjāz* referred to earlier, advanced the new thesis that the *iʿjāz* resided in three elements: words, meanings, and a link between those two, this link being represented by the "construction" (*naẓm*) of the text. The notion was perhaps not absolutely new, because, as noted at the beginning of this chapter, al-Jāḥiẓ is reported to have written a whole book on the *naẓm* of the Qurʾān. But al-Khaṭṭābī's treatment of the subject is the first mature attempt to go beyond the duality of words and meanings in search of a higher, more fundamental principle determining the nature of literary expression. Underlying his notion of construction was the concept of meaning as a well-defined element, namely the significance of a single word which could be conveyed by no other word. His criterion for the distinction between two apparently synonymous words was the context in which they occur. By showing the differences between the set of syntactic and grammatical relations each word effects, studied through the word's contextual meaning, he established that two constructions could not express the same idea. There is a mutual effect between the context and the word, and eloquence was said to be "putting the right word in its most suitable place", where it could not be replaced by another without changing the meaning or corrupting the expressive power of the construction. This was his most valuable contribution to the theory of construction, and it was, in its historical setting, a remarkable one indeed.

Of the many writers on the inimitability of the Qurʾān after al-Khaṭṭābī, two in particular contributed significantly to the analysis of its literary qualities, al-Bāqillānī (d. 403/1013) and the Muʿtazilī *qāḍī* ʿAbd al-Jabbār al-Asadī (d. 415/1025).[45] The latter applied the term *faṣāḥah* to literary superiority, and to this aspect of the Qurʾān, and defined it in terms of "the joining together of words in a particular way".[46] *Faṣāḥah*, he argues, does not appear in single words but in an expression, and it derives from convention (*muwāḍaʿah*), the vocalization of the word, or its position. These elements are all related to the "joining together". He also argues that meanings, despite their importance, are not a factor contributing to the *faṣāḥah* of the expression. Two writers, therefore, may express the same meaning with varying degrees of *faṣāḥah*; a nobler meaning may also be expressed with less *faṣāḥah* than a less noble one. His most important view is that the word may have more *faṣāḥah* in one context than in another, which was to be a fundamental idea in ʿAbd al-Qāhir al-Jurjānī's theory of construction. ʿAbd al-Jabbār discusses the problem of *ḥaqīqah* and *majāz*

[45] For whom see ch. 5.

[46] *Mughnī*, XVI, 199.

(literal versus non-literal) as part of his concept of *faṣāḥah* and "joining"; he declares that the fluency of the expression and its rhythm or musical appeal do not add any extra distinction to the *faṣāḥah*, and that "there is no difference between *majāz* and *ḥaqīqah* as far as what we are discussing is concerned: indeed, *majāz* may be more a part of *faṣāḥah* than *ḥaqīqah*". According to him, the conditions of the *faṣāḥah* of a literal expression apply equally to a non-literal one, although the latter may have some inherent qualities which contribute to its *faṣāḥah*. Finally, it is significant that he employs the comparison between discourse and other arts which depend on "joining", or the composition of interrelated parts.[47]

Al-Bāqillānī's endeavour was to demonstrate Quranic inimitability by comparing it with the best poetry produced by the Arabs; he selected for his purpose the famous *Muᶜallaqah* of Imruᵓ al-Qays and a poem of al-Buḥturī, trying in each of these to reveal instances of internal weakness, lack of coherence, imprecision of expression, defective use of language and discordance in texture. (This section of his *Iᶜjāz al-Qurᵓān* is available in von Grunebaum's English translation, *A Tenth-Century Document of Arabic Literary Theory and Criticism*.) Contrary to this, he argues, the Qurᵓān's construction and composition are invariable: each and every part of it possesses the same degree of eloquence regardless of the theme with which it deals. In this way, he established clear-cut criteria for literary achievement, deriving them from a consideration of the entire text rather than a line or group of lines. His was the first attempt in Arabic criticism to examine a whole text and make judgements which related one part of the text to another, but he failed to develop this into a fully-fledged critical method. This has prompted Iḥsān ᶜAbbās to dismiss his enterprise on this level, arguing that he offered nothing of significance when it came to revealing the positive properties of the Quranic verses he dealt with, and had ultimately to fall back on the Qurᵓān's psychological effect on the recipient, just as his predecessors had done, as the cause of its power and inimitability.[48] Al-Bāqillānī's work reveals the shortcomings of a critical method based on a view of the text as a "grouping" of elements, features and rhetorical categories. In refuting the views of those of his predecessors like al-Rummānī (d. 386/996), who held that the inimitability of the Qurᵓān is due to the *badīᶜ* it contains,[49] al-Bāqillānī based himself on an extraliterary position, arguing that *badīᶜ* can be produced by learning, acquired skill and training; and that anything that can be learned in this fashion cannot possibly be an aspect of the inimitability of the Qurᵓān. Underlying this refutation is a view of *badīᶜ* as consisting of rhetorical categories

[47] Ibid., 227. [48] *Tārīkh al-naqd*, 353–4. [49] *Thalāth rasāᵓil*, 75–6.

independent of any particular linguistic structure or any particular context. Only according to such a view can he argue that use of metaphor or antithesis or any other elements of *badīʿ* is not part of the properties that render the Qurʾān inimitable. As if he senses the implication of this argument, he quickly retracts his position and states that what he refuses to accept is that any single element of *badīʿ* independently of its position or usage can be an element of the inimitability; but, "if it is claimed that a verse which contains a simile (for instance) is inimitable because of its words, construction and composition, I will not declare this wrong, but I will not attribute the inimitability of the verse to the occurrence of the simile". Further, the very notion that *badīʿ* can be learned, and skilful use of its elements acquired by practice, shows the extent to which the belief that writing was merely a craft had developed. It is as if using a metaphor, or antithesis or paronomasia, was a process totally independent of the nature of the experience or the vision of reality, of emotion and thought, which generates the poetic text. One can understand how, in such an intellectual environment, the poetry of Abū Tammām was never studied except as an exercise in language, a play with words and rhetorical categories.

In his determination to demonstrate the uniqueness of the Qurʾān, al-Bāqillānī makes one or two points of real interest. One of his major principles is that the construction of the Qurʾān differs from the genres, or types of discourse, known to the Arabs: poetry (metrical, rhymed discourse), various types of *sajʿ* (balanced and rhymed discourse without strict metre), balanced prose which does not rhyme, and other kinds of uncontrolled or free discourse. Yet he, like others before him, recognizes that the Qurʾān has rhyming verses and verses which can be analyzed prosodically and seem to fit into Arabic metres. Faced with this fact, he searches for definitions of poetry which will make it possible to reconcile its being metrical with the dogma of the seemingly metrical parts of the Qurʾān not being poetry. He finds this possible by negating an established view which defined poetry in terms of metre; he argues that being metrical is not sufficient to make a piece of discourse poetry, and that two other conditions must be satisfied – intention of metricality and length of composition.[50] The Quranic text lacks both conditions and is therefore not poetry. In itself, the argument is important, though it was not used either by him or others to the ultimate point of ridding poetry of the condition of metrical organization. Strangely, no critic took the step of applying to non-metrical discourse criteria which were established for the assessment of the quality of "poeticality"; and this in spite of the fact that quite a number of non-

[50] *Iʿjāz*, 35, 55.

metrical texts satisfy those criteria to a high degree. A second point of interest in al-Bāqillānī's work, as has been pointed out by Iḥsān ʿAbbās, is the statement that poetry is "the depiction of what is in the composer's soul and mind to others", which lies (admittedly in a much more sophisticated form) at the root of all romantic, creative concepts of poetry. But again, he fails to make the fullest use of this seminal notion.

Literary studies of the Qurʾān were of major importance for the development of some specialized aspects of critical analysis, most significantly in the domain of metaphorical language. Starting perhaps with the work of al-Rummānī, with his definition of *balāghah* and its constituents and his insights into the nature of the "point of similarity" in simile and metaphor, especially his identification of a psychological (*nafsī*) type of similarity,[51] and ending with the remarkable work of al-Sharīf al-Raḍī, this trend made a great contribution to the development of the study of *balāghah* and poetic imagery, as well as to methodological analysis itself.

FIVE MAJOR CRITICS

Having described the basic issues with which Arabic criticism was preoccupied and the critical principles it developed, we will now deal (necessarily in a condensed fashion) with specific aspects of the work of five major figures, placing emphasis on features which constitute each one's individual contribution.

Ibn Ṭabāṭabā

Ibn Ṭabāṭabā's critical approach is largely determined by his conception of the domain of poetry. In a chapter of *ʿIyār al-shiʿr* ("The Gauge of Poetry") entitled, "The suitability of the meanings of poetry to its structures", he argues that poetry cannot be anything except:

1 Poems which "narrate" things already present in men's souls and minds (*al-nufūs wa ʾl-ʿ-uqūl*), expressing them well and revealing what is hidden in the heart. The recipient delights in receiving such poems because he receives what his disposition had already known and his understanding had accepted; thus what had been buried is brought to light.

2 Poems endowed with a "wisdom" with which souls feel familiar, so that they contentedly accept its truthfulness.

3 Poems which contain truthful descriptions, suitable similes and

[51] *Thalāth rasāʾil*, 80–1.

illuminating *amthāl* (perhaps in this context best rendered as "parables"), in which "the distant is brought closer and what is close distanced, for fear of repetition engendering boredom."

Beneath this view lie three basic conceptions:

1 That thought is pre-linguistic, well-formed and delimited; poetry expresses thought well or badly.
2 That the domain of poetry is restricted and finite, hence it can easily end up in repetition; this necessitates skill and awareness in handling meanings, so that new elements can be added for the sake of variety and avoidance of repetition.
3 That what poetry offers is already known by the recipient, since it derives from a store of common knowledge and shared experiences; its virtue is to reveal this covert knowledge and present it in a manner attractive to the hearer.

Concomitant with this conception of the domain of poetry is Ibn Ṭabāṭabā's view that poetry should be governed by principles of "perfect rationality" (*kamāl al-ʿaql*) and "well-formedness" (*iʿtidāl*);[52] the outcome of this being that the ultimate criterion of good poetry is that it should be as lucidly, tightly and regularly structured as prose. Behind this is the belief that poetry, because of the demands of metre and rhyme, imposes greater constraints on the poet; and the really fine poet is he who contrives to meet those demands without having recourse to linguistic constructions which deviate from the natural lucid prosaic alternative. Ibn Ṭabāṭabā concedes that poets often do deviate from the norm, but condemns such deviation. In this way, his views are diametrically opposed to modern deviationist theory. The same conceptual basis determines his views on poetic meaning, on the norm and the exaggerated in conveying meaning; following the passage quoted above, he devotes a longish section to "exaggeration" (*ighrāq*), which does not appeal to him. Among things that also do not appeal to him are some fine-drawn metaphors and comparisons which would hardly strike us now as exaggerated.

The shortcomings of his approach are reflected in the metaphor through which he conceives of meanings, a metaphor reflecting the ubiquitous antithesis of substance or essence versus accidents or attributes. He regards meaning as an essence isolable from language, just as gold, silver or colour is an essence regardless of the shape or pattern in which it occurs; a poet is thus like a craftsman – a goldsmith or silversmith who can take a piece of gold or silver in one shape, melt it and refashion it better than before; or a weaver who can create a variety of patterns out of his raw material. Ibn

[52] *ʿIyār al-shiʿr*, 5, 15.

Ṭabāṭabā uses this concept in assessing the poet's handling of old themes, whether expressed originally in poetry or prose, and his representation of them; and it naturally determines his whole attitude towards plagiarism.[53]

There is a wide gap between Ibn Ṭabāṭabā's attitude to meaning, as here expounded, and some genuinely fresh theoretical pronouncements he makes on poetry, which could have opened a new path for critical study. None of these is more remarkable than his statement on the power of poetry to express the hidden depths of man's soul and "the truthful ideas which pulsate there", and "to articulate and make explicit what had been kept secret within". Comparable with this view of poetry as "revelation of the hidden self" is the view of it as "magic" to the same degree as the verbiage of sorcery or shamanism; a view expressed in a saying which had already become a proverb of long standing, that poetry is "white magic" (*siḥr ḥalāl*).[54]

Unfortunately, in his practical criticism, Ibn Ṭabāṭabā's obsession with meaning and the suitability of construction to it, and the tightness of its composition and texture, overrides his interest in the structure of the poem as a totality. His practical analysis is at times of considerable subtlety and sophistication, but it remains localized, concentrating on details of textual coherence and the suitability of the poetry to status or genre, hardly ever going beyond this to produce the sort of criticism that his theoretical remarks encourage us to expect. Similarly his insight into the structure of the poem in ancient and modern poetry, where he finds the moderns superior, would have acquired an added dimension had it been applied analytically. The ancients, he said, knew only one manner of thematic bridging (*takhalluṣ*); compared with them, the moderns were more creative, inventing new methods of *takhalluṣ*.[55] These remarks have a nice structuralist bent, but he fails to make much use of them.

However, Ibn Ṭabāṭabā's main achievement remains his conception of the compositional aspect of the poem; virtually for the first time, we find a critic transcending the limited notion of the composition of a line or group of lines, to concentrate on the composition of a poem as a totality. In doing this, and despite the constraints imposed by the lack of a well-defined terminology, he formulates principles that even today possess a certain degree of relevance. Of special interest is his statement:

The best poetry is that in which discourse is organized in a fashion which harmonizes its beginning with its end . . . so that if one line is replaced by another it is dislocated . . . its composition will not be good if it is put together like segments, such as can stand by themselves, of epistles and orations, or like gnomic dicta which are self-sufficient, or proverbs which are distinguished by their concision. The

[53] Ibid., 76–9. [54] Ibid., 16–17. [55] Ibid., 11–19.

poem must be in its entirety like one word in the harmony and homogeneity (*ishtibāh*) of its beginning with its end, in texture, beauty, eloquence, compactness and strength of words, precision of meanings, and accuracy of composition, . . . so that each word will presuppose what follows it, and what follows will be related to and dependent on it.[56]

In the analogy he makes between "understanding" and the other faculties, Ibn Ṭabāṭabā established what approaches a naturalistic and determinist theory of poetry, looking at it solely from the recipient's viewpoint. His thesis is that each of the faculties "accepts what is proper to it and what it is prepared for by its own nature, if that comes upon it in a gentle, unobtrusive, just manner, in a way which is agreeable and arouses no opposition. Thus the eye feels at home with a pleasant sight, but is hurt by an ugly one; the nose . . ., etc." These faculties respond in a determinist, natural fashion, and "understanding" responds to poetry in exactly the same way; since the properties of objects which appeal to the physical senses are fixed, determined by their own inherent qualities, so too the properties of poetry that appeal to the understanding are of the same nature. The understanding feels at home with "just, fair, truthful, known, probable discourse", and dislikes discourse which is "unjust, untruthful, improbable, unknown, unfamiliar". The conditions in which discourse of the former kind is produced are when it is "purified of ineloquence, free of the weakness of error and linguistic impropriety (*laḥn*), free of inequability of composition, balanced out in the scales of correctness in words, meanings and constructions". The ultimate cause of beauty and acceptability is well-formedness and harmony (*iʿtidāl*), and the cause of ugliness is discordance and absence of harmony. In a further elaboration, he defines the elements of appeal and well-formedness as "the well-formedness of prosodic rhythm, the correctness and accuracy of meaning and the beauty of words". If these conditions are met, "the audible and comprehensible dimensions of poetry will be pure of any discordance and it will be perfect". If, on the other hand, poetry lacks any of these conditions, its imperfection will be proportionate to the lack. When it possesses the qualities mentioned plus (as the author adds a little further on) "completeness of revelation", its power is like the power of magic: "it commingles with the soul and suits the understanding, it penetrates more powerfully than the spells of magic, more subtly than the sorcerer's charm, more enchantingly than singing . . . it is like wine in the gentleness of its mysterious spreading, its enchantment, thrill and excitement."[57]

The weakness of this view of poetry is that it rules out difficulty,

[56] Ibid., 126–7. [57] Ibid., 14–16.

unfamiliarity and allusiveness by appealing not to an explicit subjective response but to a universal innate disposition. The recipient is not a particular individual, but (very much as he is in modern reader-oriented criticism) the critic himself masquerading as "the universal man". The tyranny of subjectivism is evident here, and manifests itself in the rejection of any "unfamiliar" or "untruthful" linguistic usage. Ibn Ṭabāṭabā ends up by advocating a type of poetry devoid of any power of suggestion, of shading, ambiguity or multiplicity of implication. He wants poetry to reveal itself totally and completely, failing to realize that poetry does not simply express the already-formed and wholly definable, but is often an attempt to explore the ambiguity and undefinable nature of human experience itself.

Qudāmah b. Jaʿfar

At the heart of Qudāmah's permutation of the elements of poetry and their combinations lies "the conjoining (*iʾtilāf*) of words with meanings",[58] which is the central process in poetic composition as he sees it. His formalistic logical classification has obscured the importance of this and another aspect of his work, the study of the properties of prosodic organization (*naʿt al-wazn*).

The most significant aspect of his discussion of the first of these topics is that it is based on a relational concept of the process. His is a study of the semantic complexity of modes of expression in poetry and the mechanism by which meaning is generated; it is concerned with the questions: How does language acquire meaning? What is the nature of the signification of which words are capable, and how does this ultimately form meaning? Put differently, the analysis is an attempt to reveal the mechanism by which poetic language communicates meaning. The mechanism is of two types: one a process of unfolding meaning in which, to use modern terminology, the signifier embodies its own signified; the other a process of double or multiple signification, where the signifier–signified relationship itself forms a new signifier whose signified is a totally new entity in relation to the first signified. The former type has only one manifestation, equality (*musāwāh*), whereas the second has a variety of different manifestations according to the manner in which the first signifier–signified relates to the new signified. Among these manifestations Qudāmah distinguishes between, on the one hand, the case of two meanings sharing the same word, which he terms "correspondence" (*muṭābaqah*); and, on the other hand, the case of two

[58] *Naqd al-shiʿr*, 81; for the technical terms discussed below, see ibid., index.

meanings expressed by two words sharing the same derivational base, which he terms "mutual resemblance" (*tajānus*). Both varieties were indifferently termed by Ibn al-Muᶜtazz "paronomasia" (*tajnīs*); Qudāmah's attitude was and remained unique in Arabic studies, since other writers took as their starting point the linguistic sign as phonetic entity and viewed it as having two meanings, rather than working in the opposite direction and seeing two meanings as sharing the same phonetic representation. Qudāmah's analysis is a system consisting of *musāwāh* as a base, and a number of processes which move away from the base in various directions.

In discussing the properties of metrical organization, Qudāmah uses the criterion of "ease of prosody" (which most likely refers to the smoothness and fluency of the rhythmic structures), quoting examples based on metres other than those dominant in ancient poetry, such as *sarīᶜ*.[59] Most significant, however, is his identification and analysis of a feature which he calls *tarṣīᶜ*; this, he says, is "when there is an effort to make the endings of the sections of a line either rhyming (or near rhyming), or exhibiting the same type of morphological structure (*taṣrīf*)". So what he means by *tarṣīᶜ* is both morphological and metrical harmony and internal rhyming; it can occur in single words or in phrases. He says that the most successful poets, ancients and moderns, have aimed at this process. Such a feature is obviously a structural property belonging to the level of organization and symmetry, considered by Roman Jakobson to be a distinctive feature of poetic language. Qudāmah's contribution to its analysis takes the form of appreciating it if it occurs not haphazardly but in a position "suitable" for it. He argues that it loses all appeal if it becomes dominant in a poem, because it is then a product of "artificial deliberation". Even more significantly, he quotes sayings of the Prophet based on this deliberate form of organization, and then concludes, "as they are at times deliberately aimed at in prose, their use in metrical discourse is more attractive and more worthwhile", thus regarding this form of organization a natural property of poetic language. His theoretical explanation is that poets "aim in this respect at achieving closeness in discourse between similar elements". This is a fundamental principle of modern critical theory, as evident in Jakobson's analysis of equivalent patterning and organization in general.[60] A few pages later, describing rhyme, Qudāmah goes back to the same process as manifested in one particular way, the principle, enshrined in tradition, that both hemistichs of the first line of a *qaṣīdah* should have the same rhyme as the whole poem. His study expands from one line to the whole poem, and concludes with a remarkable statement: "Naturally-gifted

[59] On such metres, which gained prominence in Umayyad poetry, cf. p. 152, above.
[60] See e.g. "Poetry of grammar and grammar of poetry", *Lingua*, XXI, 1968, 597–609.

and good poets seek to achieve this because the structure of poetry lies in internal rhyming and end rhyming; the more that a poem includes this, the closer it is to the essence of poetry and the more distant from the art of prose." As in Jakobson, this identifies poetic language as a structure of rhyming and repetition which distances it from prose.

Of the many relations of meanings that Qudāmah describes, none is more remarkable than *takāfu*ʾ, which he defines as a relation of tension between meanings, in the form of either contrast and opposition, or equivalence, or *taqābul* (complementarity?). It subsists not only between words but also between phrasal meanings (e.g. black versus white and black versus not black). It is noticeable that he identifies this phenomenon mainly with the modernist school, explaining this by the fact that "it has more affinity with the natures of those whose poetry results from forethought and reflection, and who consciously strive for structural organization (*tajnīs*), than it has with the natures of those who, like the bedouin compose spontaneously just as things come into their minds; nevertheless, even the latter, with their own natures, have also produced a lot of it". This use of the term *tajnīs* deserves notice, because it is quite different from the normal later use in the sense of paronomasia of various kinds.

Al-Āmidī

Al-Muwāzanah, al-Āmidī's chief critical work, is one of the high points of achievement in the history of Arabic criticism. Conceptually, it is an articulation of the ancient impulse of comparing two major poets; but in its scope, methodology, analytical power and care for detail, it is a massive development of this simple impulse. Right from its inception, it purports to be different: its aim is to analyze and compare, but not to reach a definitive value-judgement between the two poets with whom it is concerned, Abū Tammām and al-Buḥturī.[61] It devotes a large introductory section to statements by the supporters of each poet, in which is contained the body of ideas and preferences known to the culture on many issues of literary creation: the old and the new, poetry and science (linguistics as well as philosophy and logic), meaning and form, poetic imagery, prosody, rhyme, texture and construction, plagiarism, etc. It then compares in exhaustive detail, the merits and defects of the two, by listing what they said on each of the numerous themes which al-Āmidī conceives of as forming the groundwork of the Arabic poem from pre-Islamic times down to the age of the two poets. It devotes special chapters to the constituents of the new

[61] *Muwāzanah*, I, 6.

poetry, and how each poet made use of them (e.g. metaphor, antithesis, paronomasia, etc.). However, underneath this impressive design lies, not totally concealed, the temperament of a critic with strong likes and dislikes, who undoubtedly and unequivocally considers the ways of the ancient Arabs, their conception of poetry and methods of composing it, and their judgements on it, to be almost sacred, inviolable, non-historical. For al-Āmidī, language itself, especially in its metaphorical, non-literal usage, is fixed and permanent; no modern poets are permitted to create a single figurative expression unknown to the tradition, or if a new usage is made, it must copy or mirror to a perfect degree one existing in the tradition. In al-Āmidī's eyes, it seems, the world was conceived once and for all, and expressed once and for all, by the ancient Arabs; nothing new or different can be even thought possible. Still, his considerable achievement lies in his ability to sound serious and fair as he repeatedly asserts that he is not saying who is the better poet, even as he enthuses over an image, a phrase or an idea of Abū Tammām's (his *bête noire*). He does not hesitate, however, to describe him at times as deluded (*muwaswas*), ignorant, etc.

In his act of balancing out the merits and defects of the two poets, he sets out a clear-cut binary opposition which gives greater substance to the notions of old and new. The first pole of this opposition is what is "delicate of meaning" (*laṭīf al-maᶜnā* or *daqīq al-maᶜnā*), and he gives the impression, while describing the poetry of Imruᵓ al-Qays and Abū Tammām, that he regards this as the very essence of great achievement; he argues that if we accept the view of some of al-Buḥturī's supporters, who concede that Abū Tammām is a poet of "delicate meanings", then we are "yielding to him that which has always been the topmost ambition of poets"; it is these qualities that have made Imruᵓ al-Qays the greatest of poets. Yet a little later, we find al-Āmidī retracting and arguing that "delicate meanings" are available to all people and exist in all types of language, whereas poetry is nothing but "niceness of approaching a subject, familiarity and ease of handling it, the selection of words and the placing of them in their proper positions, and that the sense be conveyed in the words usually employed to express it . . . and that the metaphors (*istiᶜārāt*) and similes (*tamthīlāt*) be suitable to the ideas which they express".[62] This contradiction runs through al-Āmidī's entire enterprise, and seems to be due to the very nature of the opposition he identifies. For delicacy of meaning cannot be placed in dichotomy with "ease of handling, selection of words", etc., without turning poetry into a formulation of the common and trite. What he seems unable to appreciate is the dominance of an intellectual force in poetry, a

[62] Ibid., 420, 423.

force which generates difficulty and ambiguity and relates poetry to philosophy and intellectual exploration. It is here that he becomes the perfect representative of traditional thought: incapable of coping with multiplicity, ambiguity and open possibilities, searching constantly for a single and only meaning.

It is this, rather than any one other problem, that seems to have troubled him in his treatment of Abū Tammām's poetry. Traditional approaches tend to settle and become one-dimensional, or "automatized" to use the key term of Russian formalist critics,[63] allowing only one possibility of interpretation and response. A fresh approach is unsettling, because it demands a new response and allows for more than one interpretation, for other ways of seeing the world, language and experience. Faced with such an approach, an image or a "meaning", al-Āmidī reacts with a degree of animosity and anger incongruous with the nature of the problem in hand. Nowhere is this clearer than in his reaction to two lines of Abū Tammām's, the first of which conceives a traditional theme or response in a totally new way, while the second extends the application of an old metaphor beyond the "accepted" limits. Al-Āmidī thus denies the poet the right to feel differently from traditional ways, or to explore individual experience. He rejects Abū Tammām's whole attitude to women because the poet shows signs of defiance *vis-à-vis* a woman, is prepared to forget a woman he has loved, and describes a woman's tears over him.[64] No less restrictive is al-Āmidī's negation of individual experience not simply because it deviates from the traditional usage, but because it deviates from, or does not absolutely correspond to, social habits or social reality. Abū Tammām describes a woman and her friends as being "beyond-human and unique", and then says that they went out "wearing a greenness like the greenness of spring gardens", to which al-Āmidī responds by asserting that bedouin women do not wear green, nor (except rarely) do urban ones; Abū Tammām's usage is correct but unfamiliar, and by unfamiliar al-Āmidī undoubtedly means bad. In all this, al-Āmidī discusses the instances with which he is preoccupied in isolation from the text as a whole; at times he describes one half of a line as bad and the other half as reaching the ultimate degree of skill and beauty. Conceptually his atomism far exceeds that of any other fourth/tenth century critic.

Of particular interest in his scheme for the comparison of two poets is the chapter he devotes to the way each of them linked the *nasīb* section to the panegyric section. Detailing the ways each poet followed to achieve this movement (termed *khurūj* or *takhalluṣ*), he comes close to identifying a

[63] Cf. Tony Bennet, *Formalism and Marxism* (London, 1979).

[64] *Muwāzanah*, I, 143, 261; II, 37.

fundamental principle of structuralist analysis: the search for changing contents but invariable forms. A poet might describe a journey on camel-back, another a journey on a ship, but the one is only a substitute for the other. The identity of different terms in the structure is an identity of function, to use the terminology of Vladimir Propp in his analysis of the morphology of the folk-tale. Al-Āmidī, in a more restricted way, is in fact trying to describe the morphology of the panegyric poem. In the course of his discussion, he makes detailed comparisons between the ways of ancient and modern poets in the *takhalluṣ*, and for once the ways of the latter seem to appeal to him more; in this, he follows in the footsteps of Ibn Ṭabāṭabā.

Ultimately, al-Āmidī's enterprise in his detailed act of balancing out seems to rest on a theoretical notion of the morphology of the poem – more specifically of the panegyric; since the divisions he uses for his comparative effort represent a strict division of the poem into functions, beginning with "the effacement of the ruins of the campsite by the wind", and ending (in the incomplete, printed edition) with the completion of the panegyric movement, having covered a number of functions and a number of different ways of moving from the *nasīb* to the praise section. Each division represents a fixed function which can, however, have differing manifestations. Without such a theoretical conception of the poems, the act of "balancing" would have been impossible, for there would have been no common grounds of comparison between the two poets. The fact that such a conception exists in *al-Muwāzanah* in itself shows to what extent the structure of the panegyric poem had become a traditional one by the third/ninth century, and certainly by the time al-Āmidī was writing.

Al-Qāḍī ʾl-Jurjānī

The sense of dislocation caused by the poetry of *badīʿ* in the second/eighth and third/ninth centuries was deepened in the fourth/tenth century by the poetry of al-Mutanabbī. Disputes over his poetry acquired an added personal dimension which had been lacking in the disputes over Abū Tammām. Though of interest for the study of al-Mutanabbī's life and works, this personal dimension is of little significance in the present context; of greater relevance are those aspects of the works written about him which contributed directly to the development of literary criticism and theory. In this respect, the works of al-Ḥātimī (d. 388/998) and al-Ṣāḥib Ibn ʿAbbād offer no more than critical observations on minute details of al-Mutanabbī's poetry: defective uses of language, grammatical deviations, "inaccuracies" of meaning, and so forth.[65] The controversy over al-

[65] On al-Ḥātimī, cf. van Gelder, *Beyond the Line*, 82–9.

Mutanabbī did, however, produce one major work of literary criticism, *al-Wasāṭah bayna ʾl-Mutanabbī wa-khuṣūmih* by al-Qāḍī ʿAlī b. ʿAbd al-ʿAzīz al-Jurjānī (d. 392/1002). A professional judge, of a balanced temperament and with a clear ability for mediation, this critic attempts to offer a fair judgement on al-Mutanabbī transcending both the attacks on him by his adversaries and the extravagant enthusiasm of his admirers. He concedes a lot of points made by the former, but proceeds to suggest that no poet has ever been perfect. Defects are common in the work of the great poets of the past, and just as this does not undermine their achievements so it should not undermine that of al-Mutanabbī. On the other hand, he is a poet of undeniable qualities and talent; this should be acknowledged by his adversaries, but without submitting to the extravagant claims of his supporters. This was a genuine work of mediation which succeeded at the same time in formulating coherently many of the critical principles which had been evolving, to varying degrees of maturity, in the works of al-Qāḍī ʾl-Jurjānī's predecessors.

The first striking feature of his approach is its ability to transcend the dislocation, not by rejecting the modernist achievement, but by establishing that its distinctive features are no more than analogical extensions of features present to a lesser degree in the classical tradition. If these are defects, then they must be so considered wherever they are found, in classical as well as in modern poetry. In this way, both parties are to blame, and, as the blame is shared, the modern is acquitted of any serious offence. On the other hand, if those features are tolerated, then they must be tolerated in the works of the modernists including those of al-Mutanabbī. This critic thus resolves the opposition between modern and ancient, and speaks of common defects rather than a perfect tradition and a defective modernity. Underlying this attitude is a feeling that modern poets are judged with unjust harshness for any errors they make, whereas ancient poets were treated differently. Grammarians and scholars had pointed out many defects in words, composition and meanings in ancient poetry, but then proceeded to offer excuses for defects and explain them away, the spirit behind their work being one of reverence for the ancients. What our critic advocates is a similar stance *vis-à-vis* the moderns, including al-Mutanabbī, a stance which acknowledges virtues and overlooks defects. Once positive achievements establish a certain writer as a good poet, his defects should no longer matter.

A modernist in philosophical outlook, al-Qāḍī ʾl-Jurjānī offered perhaps the first theoretical view of modernity not simply as situated on a time scale but as a process of change. Modernity for him is the climax of a historical process whereby increasing refinement of urban life is reflected first and foremost in a more refined mental, psychological and linguistic state in man.[66] The modern is by definition the opposite of the bedouin, who is rough in temperament, habits, speech and even the acoustic quality of his utterance. This modern spirit becomes a new *ṭabᶜ*, inherent sensibility, just as the ancients had their own, different, *ṭabᶜ*. Deviation from one's own *ṭabᶜ*, any conscious effort to suppress it and imitate the ancients, is a betrayal of authenticity which produces only clumsiness and ugliness. For the first time we see here not only a rejection of the ancient tradition as a model to be emulated, but the overt distinction between ancient and modern as two modes of feeling, observing, behaving and writing poetry – as two conflicting sensibilities. Each is embodied in its poetic and linguistic expression as well as in its way of feeling. The modern cannot emulate the ancient without losing his own self, his sweetness, smoothness and eloquence, and ending up discordant, lacking in eloquence and appeal, and with ragged texture (*ikhlāq al-dībāj*). As an example of this is cited the poet who had come to be seen as the most modern of all moderns, Abū Tammām: he tried in many of his linguistic usages to emulate the ancients and ended up with ugliness in more than one place in his corpus. In the same context, al-Qāḍī ᵓl-Jurjānī identifies what seems to him to be the worst thing a poet can do: to mix the very ancient with the very modern. Abū Tammām has done just this, using the difficult, laboured language of the ancients and adding to it *badīᶜ*, together with obscure meanings and hidden implications. This type of poetry is the most exhausting and least appealing. Yet at the same time, al-Qāḍī ᵓl-Jurjānī is not willing to denigrate Abū Tammām: "Alas, how can I do so, when I esteem him so highly, glorify him and consider him to be the Kaᶜbah of poets of meaning and *badīᶜ*." His adherence to his principle, however, is such that he criticizes modern poets who are betrayed, in the course of a poem embodying their modern sensibility, into introducing a line or even a phrase which, in his view, "disrupts your joy and ruins your pleasure". He wants modern poets to allow their modern spirit to flow uninterrupted, smooth and easy, but without falling to the level of the mundane.

His modernist spirit is reflected in his attitude to the poetry of his own age and the immediately preceding centuries, as is clear in his comments on al-Buḥturī, whom he regards as a prime example of the *maṭbūᶜ* poet. He selects al-Buḥturī, he says, because "he is closer in time to us, and we are more at home with him, his discourse is more suited to our disposition and more similar to our habits. The soul feels at home with what is homogeneous with it (*mā jānasahā*), and readily accepts what comes ever

[66] *Wasāṭah*, 18–22.

closer to it."[67] In this passage, he almost reverses the old equation of ancient poetry with spontaneity, *ṭab*ᶜ, absence of artificiality and labouring of an idea or phrase; he suggests that smoothness and fluency are marks of the modern age. When he does deal with ancient poetry, he chooses that type which is most in harmony with his modern sensibility. In all this, his criteria are harmony of the lines of a poem and of its parts, suitability of one section to the others, absence of artificiality, purity of texture; and when this is coupled with creativity, delicate *ṣan*ᶜ*ah*, fine metaphors and other types of *badī*ᶜ, then poetry reaches a degree of effectiveness which induces in the hearer a state of pure delight (*aryaḥiyyah*). Ultimately he summarizes the values of achievement in ancient Arabic culture in a manner which was to prepare the way for the final formulation of ᶜ*amūd al-shi*ᶜ*r*. He then offers the most detailed analysis of elements of *badī*ᶜ in poetry up to the end of the fourth/tenth century, taking three of Ibn al-Muᶜtazz's elements, *isti*ᶜ*ārah*, *tajnīs* and *muṭābaqah*, and adding the elements of *taṣḥīf* (visual punning between words distinguished only by their diacritical dots), *taqsīm* (distributio)[68] and *jam*ᶜ *al-awṣāf* (cumulation of epithets); and further allowing the possibility of considering procedures such as *iltifāt* (change of person, e.g. when a poet switches from speaking in the first person to addressing himself in the second) as types of *badī*ᶜ.

In the course of his discussion of current attitudes to poetry, he establishes, perhaps for the first time in Arabic criticism, a dividing line between modernist poets based on the criteria of pure *ṣan*ᶜ*ah*, *ṣan*ᶜ*ah* mixed with *ṭab*ᶜ, and predominating *ṭab*ᶜ. The poets of pure *ṣan*ᶜ*ah* are headed by Abū Tammām, those with predominating *ṭab*ᶜ by al-Buḥturī, those of *ṣan*ᶜ*ah* mixed with *ṭab*ᶜ by Muslim b. al-Walīd. On the basis of these criteria, he divides al-Mutanabbī's poetry into two phases, an earlier one in which he belongs to the school of Abū Tammām, and the later phase in which he belongs to that of Muslim.[69] Carrying the observations of his predecessors a step further, he defines the constituents of ᶜ*amūd al-shi*ᶜ*r* in a more comprehensive way, without explicitly formulating the problem theoretically. He argues, like al-Āmidī, that the ancient Arabs did not care for the adornments of *badī*ᶜ, provided that they achieved ᶜ*amūd al-shi*ᶜ*r* and the systematic composition (*niẓām al-qarīḍ*) inspired by native genius. The constituents of this system are:

1 Nobility and correctness of meaning
2 Strength or tautness (*jazālah*) and correctness of words
3 Precision of description
4 Closeness of comparisons

[67] Ibid., 29. [68] For an example of this figure, see p. 298. [69] *Wasāṭah*, 27–33, 41–50.

5 Richness of spontaneous response (or the spontaneous flow of composition)
6 Abundance of pointful expressions and quotable lines[70]

His formulation was the basis for the more rigid account of *ᶜamūd al-shiᶜr* presented by al-Marzūqī, which has been briefly considered earlier in this chapter.

ᶜAbd al-Qāhir al-Jurjānī

The numerous questions relating to the Quranic text as well as to prose and poetry which had been formulated and considered up to the fifth/eleventh century came to fruition in the work of this second al-Jurjānī (d. 471/1079), who assimilated the diverse currents of thought in his background and developed a new approach to literary expression. Basing his approach on a view of language as a system of relations, and of the text as totality, he argues that single elements have no value, semantic or aesthetic, in themselves and independently of an actual linguistic context. The text is a body of interacting elements which acquires shape only as a totality. All semantic, phonetic and syntactic features of the text are subject to the same rule and are all governed by the same principle, which can be called structural inasmuch as it relates individual features of the text to an overall structural force which determines their function and operation. Figurative language, such as metaphor, is part of this process and has no independent value of its own. Going even further, he assigns literary analysis the role of discovering the properties of the artistic text, emphasizing that, although grammatical in nature, his approach is not concerned with correctness or grammaticality but with texts as literary products in which language transcends the mere state of correctness in order to fulfil an artistic function.[71] His exploration of "superiority" focuses entirely on the body of language present in the text, viewing the text as a network of relationships determined by the structure of experience itself; poetry expresses by embodying the structure of thought and emotion, and the structure of reality in all its complexity, by using a set of linguistic relations. Within this set, poetic imagery plays a fundamental role, as it functions through a principle different from that at work in literal language, forming a double-layered process which moves from meaning to the meaning of meaning, as will be seen later.

By assimilating poetic imagery in all its forms into the totality of his system, he made a major contribution to textual analysis. Imagery is no

[70] Ibid., 33–4.

[71] See *Dalāʾil al-iᶜjāz*, 306; cf. Abu Deeb, *Al-Jurjānī's Theory*, 39–40.

longer viewed either as ornament or as a substitute for literal statement. Imagery in his view exists at times without there being any possibility of its having a literal origin or equivalent. This is the core of religious language which attributes human traits to God, where the admission of a literal counterpart would lead to "error" (*ḍalālah*).[72] He thus introduces a totally new notion, creating a new possibility for exploring human thought, the possibility of actually thinking in images or metaphor. As such, poetic language could be analyzed on a different level from non-poetic language, rather than as deviation from it.

At the heart of his system is his detailed re-examination of such basic concepts as "meaning" and "words", and his rigorous definition of both.[73] He devotes much energy to the refutation of imprecise notions prevalent in the works of certain writers, and demonstrates the dangers inherent in them. Meaning is no longer separable from language; semantics and syntax become two dimensions of the same creative process, meaning being a function of the syntactic structure within which semantic units appear. Hence two sentences cannot mean the same thing unless the one repeats the structure of the other using identical semantic units – in which case the two would be identical replications of the same utterance. The slightest change in linguistic, especially syntactic, usage creates a new "meaning" altogether; so a sentence based on an image cannot express the same meaning as one not based on that image. In this fashion, the dynamics of literal and figurative usages of language are shown to be different. Literal usage works through a process that generates "meaning", figurative usage through one which generates "the meaning of meaning" ("I met a lion" intended literally contrasts with figurative usage in which "man" and "lion" are subsumed under the common attribute of courage).[74]

The inseparability of meaning, imagery and syntactic structure from each other is demonstrated in abundant instances in al-Jurjānī's work. One such is his study of al-Muzarrid's hemistich *wa-sālat bi-aʿnāqi ʾl-maṭiyyi ʾl-abāṭiḥu* in which he attributes the beauty of the image, "and the valleys were flooded with the necks of the riding-beasts", not only to "the highest degree of precision possible in comparison", but to the fact that the image appears in this particular syntactic structure and in the context of the experience of performing the pilgrimage. The "dominant emotion" (to use Coleridge's phrase) is of such a richly overflowing kind that nature and man are fused together in a moment of total harmony and joy, so that the valleys themselves "overflow" with the camels' necks. The dominant emotion

72 *Asrār al-balāghah*, 47.

73 E.g. *Dalāʾil al-iʿjāz*, 194–203.

74 See Abu Deeb, *Al-Jurjānī's Theory*, 75–81.

spreads through all elements of the linguistic structure, and no other structure would be capable of embodying the same experience.[75]

Another instance is his analysis of the Quranic phrase (*sūrah* xix.4) *wa-ʾshtaʿala ʾl-raʾsu shayban*, "the head was lit up, all hoary", where he argues that the beauty and expressive power are not due merely to the metaphor (similarity of the spreading of fire and the spreading of hoariness), but to the very structure in which the image is presented. Construct the sentence as *wa-ʾshtaʿala raʾsī bi ʾl-shaybi*, "my head was lit up by reason of hoariness", he says, and it will lose its beauty and effectiveness.[76] In such an analysis, thought (or meaning) is no longer conceived as an isolable essence capable of expression first in a linguistic structure without imagery, and secondly by the use of an added image to improve or decorate it. Language and thought or experience, and the linguistic embodiment, are not even two items brought together; they are much more than this, they are a structure in which all elements function as part of a totality inconceivable in any other way. Imagery thus becomes a thought process expressible in one, and only one, linguistic structure.

As he transcends the duality of meaning and words, and searches for means of designating the oneness and wholeness of literary expression, he coins the term "form [*ṣūrah*, here in the philosophical sense antithetic to "matter, substance"] of meaning".[77] This term remains even today one of the most precise notions to designate the unity and inseparability of experience and language, content and form. He uses, he says, the term *ṣūrah* "to express an intellectual concept by analogy with a visual object", e.g. the way one individual of the species man differs from another individual; similarly, as we realize intellectually that the meaning in a line of poetry has distinctive features not present in another line, we indicate the difference by saying that the meaning has a *ṣūrah* in the first line different from the *ṣūrah* in the second.

Having positioned imagery within his total theoretical system, he embarks on a detailed enquiry into poetic imagery for its own sake, exploring its nature, function, forms and its relationship to its creator and impact on the recipient; thus constructing a theoretical universe which deservedly earned him the epithet "founder of the sciences of *bayān* and *balāghah*" (both terms have been translated as "rhetoric", and the differentiation between them, if any, is hardly perceptible). The following brief sketch of his ideas on imagery cannot adequately depict the vitality and subtlety of his work, and in particular his remarkable powers of textual

[75] *Asrār al-balāghah*, 21–4; see Abu Deeb, *Al-Jurjānī's Theory*, 75–81.
[76] *Dalāʾil al-iʿjāz*, 309, 300–1. [77] Ibid., 388–9.

analysis. A central feature is the distinction he makes between two types of relationship through which one thing may be seen in terms of another: similarity and contiguity.[78] Similarity is the basis of simile, metaphor, etc.; contiguity produces figures like allusiveness (*kināyah*) and tropes not based on similarity such as part/whole, cause/effect relationships, etc. Failure to recognize these basic distinctions results in a serious misunderstanding of the nature and function of figurative language, and – significantly – religious language in some of its fundamental aspects. The differences he discovers between similarity and contiguity go beyond classification of similes, as he explores the structural differences between statements containing these types. Similarity, for instance, can be expressed in terms of direct identification using the subject–predicate structure, or direct substitution, as in one type of *istiᶜārah*; or complex analogy as in another type of this figure; or in *tamthīl*, the coining of a "parable" (using this word in the sense of the New Testament parable, introduced in the New English Bible by the form, "The kingdom of heaven is like this: a man . . ."). Contiguity can only be expressed in the form of simple substitution, and here, no real difference exists between the suppressed statement and the overt one replacing it, as in the phrase *laka ᶜalayya yad*, "I am indebted to you for a hand", where *yad*, "hand", is substituted for *niᶜmah*, "favour". Similarity receives greater attention in al-Jurjānī's work because it forms the basis for the major types of poetic imagery. He elaborates a classification into various types, each generating one distinct form of the image and involving different imaginative and linguistic processes. The most important of his divisions is based on the identification of two kinds of similarity. The first occurs "in the attribute itself", as with, "her hair is the night", blackness being an attribute of both hair and night; the second occurs in a corollary or consequence presupposed by the attribute, as in, "her words are like honey", since sweetness is actually present in honey, but can only be attributed to words in respect of the psychological effect on the recipient.[79]

Making extensive use of these basic divisions, al-Jurjānī identifies different forms of imagery and studies them as imaginative and linguistic processes. He rejects the notion that a subject–predicate statement of the type, "ᶜAlī is a lion", is a metaphor (*istiᶜārah*), firstly because it involves no transference, and secondly because it fails to achieve the fusion between "ᶜAlī" and "lion" characteristic of the *istiᶜārah*; it lacks the tension generated in true *istiᶜārah* by the latter's being a double unit in which both elements must be present imaginatively, but only one of them expressed

[78] See Abu Deeb, *Al-Jurjānī's Theory*, 184–8, 190–3.

[79] Ibid., 104–8, 123–42.

overtly in the linguistic form. He also rejects the dominant view that simile (*tashbīh*) and metaphor are interchangeable, and the latter only a concise equivalent of the former (a view expressed by Aristotle and by a number of Arab critics); he shows that simile cannot always be reformulated as metaphor, and explores the conditions which govern their interchangeability in certain circumstances only.[80] His classification of *isti^cārah* is the first of its type in Arabic and the basis for practically all subsequent work on the subject. It is here that the major difference between this work and that of his predecessors – including both Aristotle's analysis and the studies written by commentators on it – is best displayed.[81]

As a religious thinker, a *mutakallim* (scholastic) in the Ash^carī tradition, he starts from the same conception of the world as finite and revealed, as possessing an objective existence, from which other critics started. This is most evident in his search for the roots of similarity: does it lie hidden in the world until a searching mind manages to discover or reveal it, or is it something connected immediately with the act of perceiving it? At times, he seems to move strongly in the direction of the latter possibility, especially in his enthusiasm for the power of the image to strike us with fresh, unfamiliar links between various seemingly unrelated objects or aspects of experience. In such contexts, he borders on the language of creativity, invention, total individuality. But then he faces the deep paradox emanating from the contradiction between this view of man (as a poet), and the central religious view that only God creates out of nothing, and that the world is finite, delimited, objectively present, possessed of all its attributes so that nothing can be "added" to it. This sense of paradox emerges in his work in a modified form, almost an aesthetic one: if we emphasize the creative aspect of the discovery of similarity in dissimilar objects, where is the limit to be placed on this process of discovery (a problem similar to that faced by Coleridge in the course of articulating his "theory" of imagination and its unifying power, e.g. in *Biographia Literaria*)? Is *any* image revealing similarity acceptable? Answering this question positively would open totally new doors for poetry, for criticism and for man; but this goes against the very core of the enshrined religious conception of the world which dominated the culture and al-Jurjānī's thinking alike. Hence, he answers it negatively, asserting that not every act of linking objects through similarity is justified; the similarity has to be "there already", the poet merely "revealing" it through an act of penetration and an unusual power of perception:

[80] Ibid., 178–89, and ch. 4.
[81] See *Asrār al-balāghah*, 40–80, and Abu Deeb, "Al-Jurjānī's classification of *isti^cāra*".

one must find a correct and comprehensible similarity between them . . . I do not mean that one can invent a similarity which has no origin in the intellect. What I mean is that there are hidden similarities which have very subtle paths to them. If one's mind penetrates and comprehends them, then one deserves honour . . . for you to find something where it has not previously been found is equal, in exciting the sense of wonder and great enjoyment in him who feels that wonder, to the creation of something which did not exist and whose substance and qualities were not known.[82]

The deep paradox he faces underlies al-Jurjānī's analysis of another extremely important aspect of literary creation: the nature of meaning itself and the role of imagination, as opposed to reason, in it. He recognizes two distinct kinds of meaning – in fact, of processes of seeing, thinking and feeling – in discourse, an intellectual (*ᶜaqlī*) type and an imaginative (*takhyīlī*) one, reaching areas of enquiry not touched upon by his predecessors.[83] But as he describes those types and states his own position on their appeal and importance for literary creation, the tension generated by the paradox becomes evident.

His concentration on the differences between the various forms of imagery permitted him to produce hypotheses which, although in embryonic fashion, constitute the basis for a better understanding of his notion of modernity. In one such formulation, having described the difference between *tashbīh* and *tamthīl*, he states that one can describe the poetry of Ibn al-Muᶜtazz as abundant in *tashbīh* and that of Ṣāliḥ b. ᶜAbd al-Quddūs, the *zuhd*-poet, as abundant in *tamthīl*. He also hints at a possible link between *tamthīl* and the imagery of the modernist poets.[84] Concise though this formulation is, it can form the basis for a closer analysis of Abū Tammām and the modernist poets in Arabic, and for classical and modern poetry in general. The point of similarity in classical poetry tends to be predominantly of a physical nature, whereas modern poetry tends to exploit similarities of a non-physical nature between objects or domains of experience. When he develops his analysis of *tamthīl* to cover the type of image displayed in, for example, Abū Tammām's "Don't be surprised to find a generous man devoid of wealth, for flood-water is in constant war against the highest of peaks",[85] he identifies and describes in a very detailed fashion the type of image which came to be considered central for an entire school of poetry in seventeenth-century England: the conceit. His analysis of this type is of interest even within the context of modern European studies of its nature and function. Using his discussion of it as the groundwork for the study of Arabic *badīᶜ* offers a new approach to the

[82] *Asrār al-balāghah*, 139–40, 136. [83] Ibid., 241–5. [84] Ibid., 85–8, 244–96. [85] Ibid., 245.

latter, totally different from the way critics like al-Āmidī approached it. Through al-Jurjānī's analysis of *tamthīl*, we can perhaps reach a better understanding also of the perplexing fact that Ibn al-Muᶜtazz considered *al-madhhab al-kalāmī* ("the manner of dialectics") an element of *badīᶜ* but denied its existence in the Qurᵓān. Al-Jurjānī's analysis of this type of *tamthīl*, taking the form of imaginative explanation or justification (*taᶜlīl takhyīlī*) brings out the element of self-deception at its roots. An illogical, untruthful statement is rendered logical and truthful through the relation of similarity, explicit or implicit, on which *taᶜlīl takhyīlī* is based. As such, its function is to present as valid a statement which is recognized initially as being invalid. This being so, *al-madhhab al-kalāmī* cannot, from a religious point of view, exist in the Qurᵓān, which is the word of God, the All-Truthful.

Al-Jurjānī's discussion of *takhyīl* must be seen in its proper context. He is not concerned here with the problems of truthfulness and falsehood in the crude form which they take in most discussions of the matter, but with the nature of poetic statement. He defines *takhyīl* as that in which a poet "affirms something which is not certain at the outset, and makes a claim which cannot be verified, and says something by which he deceives himself and makes himself see what he sees not". He then distinguishes grades of *takhyīl*, some of which are close to truth, while others are more remote and are clearly "deception of the mind and a kind of ornamentation". In the light of this, he deals with the famous contradictory sayings, "The best of poetry is that which lies most", and "The best of poetry is the most truthful", and interprets them in a manner placing them outside the sphere of crude lying or crude faithfulness to reality; he demonstrates that each of them refers to a particular mode of poetic expression, the first involving artistic treatment, craftsmanship, intelligence, and so forth. As for the second dictum, he views the truthfulness of poetry not as faithfulness to objective reality, such as when a poet praises a man for certain qualities only when it is known that he in fact does possess them, but as making statements which express a "wisdom" acceptable to reason, or a sermon which tames uncontrolled emotion and urges piety, or reveals the seat of beauty and ugliness in human action, or separates praiseworthy from bad qualities. It is to be noted that in distinguishing these two types of meaning, al-Jurjānī is not rejecting one and accepting the other; he considers them both proper modes of poetic creation. His concern is to assert that, although it may be thought that the *takhyīlī* type allows a greater freedom and creativity, the *ᶜaqlī* type allows such creativity also.[86] He denies that the

[86] Ibid., 253, 249–52.

latter type is a static stock which leaves no room for the poet's individual perception of things or inventive powers and ability to add new truths to what has already been discovered. While his admiration for the various types of *takhyīlī* meanings reaches the highest degree of enthusiasm that he shows for any aspect of poetry whatever, the fact that he identifies *takhyīl* with non-verifiability remains a descriptive analytical operation and never turns into a moralistic attitude favouring rationality, common sense, or crude faithfulness to reality.

His approach to literary expression is essentially structural, in that he sees every single element of the text in terms of its relationship to the totality of the experience underlying it, and to the linguistic structure of which this element is a constituent. In terms of application, however, the unit to which he applies his critical principle varies according to the nature of the particular point under consideration.[87] Theoretically, he does not refer to "text" as the totality subjected to analysis; but in practice the units of composition he deals with can be an image within a poem (in which case he views the image in terms of its position within the poem), or a line or group of lines forming one short poem or, in one case at least, an entire longish poem. With this in mind, we can see his approach as a theoretical apparatus which can be applied to small units of composition but can also be extended to cover any unit no matter how large. Conceived of in this way, his work can be justifiably related to much that has happened in modern critical theory on the level of the structural analysis of the text as a total closed entity which forms a system of relationships, an interactive body within which a total organizing structural principle operates. His five fundamental concepts are:

1 That language is a convention.
2 That the linguistic sign is arbitrary; there is no inherent relationship between its "meaning" (more accurately *signifié*) and its phonetic shape; thus no one of two words can be, in isolation, better or worse than the other.
3 That a poem (or for that matter a piece of prose) is first and foremost a linguistic body of material which functions as a system of relationships, a structure formed by the interrelationships between its linguistic components.
4 That literal and figurative usages of language represent two modes of comprehension and two modes of generating meaning: the former generates "meaning", the latter the "meaning of meaning".
5 That the second process has two main categories, that of similarity

[87] See Abu Deeb, "Studies in Arabic literary criticism".

(*istiʿārah*), and that of contiguity (synecdoche, *kināyah*, and other types of *majāz*).

These five points have been at the heart of some of the most important currents of thought in modern studies of language and literary analysis from Ferdinand de Saussure to Roman Jakobson. There can be no finer tribute to al-Jurjānī's genius than to acknowledge this fact.

CHAPTER 21

IBN AL-MUᶜTAZZ AND *KITĀB AL-BADĪᶜ*

The foregoing chapter offered a general survey of ᶜAbbasid literary theory and criticism, described some of their basic concerns and discussed a number of major critics. It must always be remembered, however, that the background to much ᶜAbbasid criticism is still far from having been exhaustively researched, and this must be borne in mind in any attempts at interpretation. A case in point is one of the most notable works of Arabic criticism, Ibn al-Muᶜtazz's (d. 296/908) *Kitāb al-Badīᶜ*. This chapter will discuss some of the technical problems surrounding the use of this text.

MODERN STUDIES OF *KITĀB AL-BADĪᶜ*

At the time of its appearance in 1935, the edition by I. Kratchkovsky of *Kitāb al-Badīᶜ* did not receive the attention it deserved. Only in the years following the Second World War have scholars become fully aware of the importance of this publication, which brought to light one of the first, and certainly the most fundamental, work of a genre that was to be amongst the most brilliant achievements of medieval Muslim scholarship. In the introduction to his edition, Kratchkovsky made a significant attempt to shed light on the early history of Arabic rhetoric. A further contribution by Kratchkovsky dealing with the terminology of Ibn al-Muᶜtazz and the history of Arabic rhetoric in general was published posthumously in 1960 in the edition of his collected works, and appeared in a French translation in 1962. In addition to reviews published in the late thirties, there were some incidental observations on the book in the fifties by G. von Grunebaum, H. Ritter, and the present writer; more thorough studies were conducted in the next two decades, notably by W. Heinrichs.

Any attempt to outline the history of Arabic rhetoric, both in its earlier and its later stages, meets with considerable difficulties. The work published as early as 1853 by A. F. Mehren under the title *Die Rhetorik der Araber* was aimed at providing a key to the understanding of medieval Arabic literature. Though it still stands out as a major achievement, it was essentially a summary of compendia dating from the late Middle Ages. Mehren may have felt that the time was not yet ripe for a study of Arabic rhetoric as a genre. He must have been aware of the fact that most medieval authors depend heavily on their predecessors; often definitions and even examples are borrowed by one author from another without acknowledgement, and few authors feel themselves called upon to give their readers an insight into the history of Arabic literary theory and criticism (a notable exception is Ibn Abī ᵓl-Iṣbaᶜ, d. 654/1256, whose observations will be examined below). Moreover, the number of texts available to Mehren may have been limited and probably did not supply sufficient data to enable him to attempt a detailed investigation into the history of Arabic literary theory, especially its early stages. The quotations which Mehren found in the later medieval handbooks he used prompted him to add a "Literaturgeschichtlicher Anhang" to his book. Though this is no more than an alphabetically arranged list of scholars and poets, it nevertheless gives the names of all those who played an important role in the evolution of the genre. Since medieval authors are unanimous in considering Ibn al-Muᶜtazz (Abū ᵓl-ᶜAbbās ᶜAbdullāh b. al-Muᶜtazz) and Qudāmah b. Jaᶜfar (d. 337/948) as the first scholars to deal with Arabic literary theory, Mehren, following their example, described Ibn al-Muᶜtazz as the scholar who was the first to offer, in his *Kitāb al-Badīᶜ*, an analysis of the "various rhetorical devices of Arabic poetry". Mehren gave some details about Ibn al-Muᶜtazz's career, but found himself apparently unable to give details about Abū ᵓl-Faraj Qudāmah b. Jaᶜfar al-Baghdādī, whom he describes merely as a contemporary of Ibn al-Muᶜtazz and the author of a work on rhetoric entitled *Naqd al-shiᶜr* ("Poetic Criticism").

Some twenty years earlier G.W. Freytag, in his *Darstellung der arabischen Verskunst*, had drawn attention to Ibn al-Muᶜtazz's work and had correctly enumerated the five categories of *badīᶜ* distinguished by Ibn al-Muᶜtazz. The history of the numerous other, mostly erroneous, references to the book in Arabic and European sources has been outlined in detail by Kratchkovsky in the introduction to his edition of *Kitāb al-Badīᶜ*. As had happened so often in the history of Arabic literature, the existence of quotations as well as unacknowledged borrowings, often incorporated in more detailed and systematic treatises on the same subject, had eliminated the need for the original text, which was given over to oblivion. Only a single manuscript of *Kitāb al-Badīᶜ* is known to have survived, even though the book had had, in Kratchkovsky's words, "a vivid and effective influence over the development of that branch of knowledge to which it is devoted" and "few books in this field . . . can compare with it in their legacy to the thought of succeeding ages". There is no exaggeration when Kratchkovsky observes that one cannot find any book in which an organic tie cannot be traced with the work of Ibn al-Muʿtazz, which had led the way in a new direction. Yet Kratchkovsky himself admitted that the influence of Qudāmah's *Naqd al-shiʿr* was at least equal to that of *Kitāb al-Badīʿ* and that the early history of Arabic literary theory cannot be studied without also including the works of Thaʿlab (d. 291/904) and Jāḥiẓ (d. 255/868–9).

Recent studies have not substantially altered this view. Even though a detailed study of the connections between Ibn al-Muʿtazz, Qudāmah and their predecessors and followers has still to be made, there can be no doubt that (a) possible models and sources of inspiration of these two authors were, with rare exceptions, unknown to or overlooked by later critics; that (b) Ibn al-Muʿtazz was the first author to consider the frequency of the occurrence of certain figures of speech from the point of view of the literary historian; that (c) the title of Ibn al-Muʿtazz's book, which was taken from the collective term for the first five rhetorical devices which Ibn al-Muʿtazz enumerates, was adopted as a collective term for rhetorical devices in general; and that (d) his treatise, for better or worse, became the archetype of a long series of writings, the sole purpose of which was to define, analyze and illustrate figures of speech and stylistic devices and even some questions that were closer to grammar than to literary theory. The following pages will focus on the motives that prompted Ibn al-Muʿtazz to write *Kitāb al-Badīʿ*, and will try to identify some of the older texts or traditions that could have been known to him and from which he could have borrowed terms, definitions, or examples. There will be no attempt to offer an analysis of the figures of speech themselves; such an analysis could hardly stand on its own and would necessarily involve the interpretations which Ibn al-Muʿtazz's successors gave of his definitions and examples. Though there was never complete agreement on these examples, there emerged from many centuries of discussion a "school version" of Arabic rhetoric, which then became the basis of Mehren's book. No doubt much could be learned by tracing a given term or concept through the entire source material, not only for the sake of establishing the exact connotation of a term, but also to determine, by establishing the dependence of one author on another, what artistic, dogmatic-exegetic, or philosophical views may have influenced individual interpretations; however, such a task would go beyond the limited scope of this study.

TEXTUAL PROBLEMS

In the third chapter of the introduction to his edition of *Kitāb al-Badīʿ*, Kratchkovsky expresses his feeling that, at least on the basis of the material at his disposal, the attribution of *Kitāb al-Badīᶜ* to Ibn al-Muᶜtazz could not be questioned; nor did he find good reasons to doubt the authenticity of the text found in the unique Escorial manuscript of the work, with the possible exception of some examples which might have been added or deleted by a copyist. A different opinion was expressed by M. Guidi in his review of Kratchkovsky's edition.[1] Guidi doubted that a passage, which in Kratchkovsky's edition appears as the introduction of the book, was in its proper place. This introduction begins as follows: *Qad qaddamnā fī abwābi kitābinā hādhā baᶜḍa mā wajadnā fī ᵓl-Qurᵓāni . . . wa-ashᶜāri ᵓl-mutaqaddimīna mina ᵓl-kalāmi ᵓlladhī sammāhu ᵓl-muḥdathūna ᵓl-badīᶜa*, "In the chapters which make up this book of ours we have put first (*qaddamnā*) some examples we found in the Qurᵓān . . . and the poetry of the ancient [poets] of the style of composition which the new generation [of poets] calls *badīᶜ*". Guidi found the translation of *qaddamnā* by "we have put first" difficult to accept since there is no mention in the same passage of a second section. Other translations, such as "we have submitted" or "we have offered", he felt, were unusual and awkward in this context. He also observed that the *basmalah* ("In the name of God . . .", the conventional opening formula for a book or chapter) on page 2 of Kratchkovsky's text suggested that the text originally began at this point, and that a passage on pages 2–3 repeated the introduction on pages 1–2. He thought it possible that two versions had existed of a passage on pages 57–8, both beginning with *qad qaddamnā*. A copyist, he argued, might well have found both versions in his original and have decided to move the old version to the beginning of the book. The survival of the *basmalah* on page 2 would support this assumption. The problem became even more complicated when it was found that part of the passage now on pages 57–8 of Kratchkovsky's edition was, according to Ibn Abī ᵓl-Iṣbaᶜ, part of the beginning (*ṣadr*) of the book.[2]

The whole question may, at first sight, appear somewhat trivial, the more so since the authenticity of the passage now on pages 1–2 of Kratchkovsky's edition (according to Guidi the "old version" of pages 57–8 misplaced at the beginning of the book) is supported by a quotation in Abū ᵓl-Qāsim al-Ḥasan b. Bishr al-Āmidī's (d. 370/980–1) *al-Muwāzanah bayna shiᶜr Abī Tammām wa-ᵓl-Buḥturī* ("The Counterbalancing of the Poetry of Abū Tammām and al-Buḥturī").[3] It becomes important, however, if one keeps in mind that it has some bearing on the question of the distinction between *badīᶜ* devices and *maḥāsin*, "beauties" (Kratchkovsky's translation of the term), i.e. distinctive marks of good style, stylistic and rhetorical devices. This distinction is part of Ibn al-Muᶜtazz's thesis and, in

[1] *Rivista degli Studi Orientali*, XVI, 1936, 409–15.
[2] Bonebakker, "Ibn Abī ᵓl-Iṣbaᶜ's text", 86; Ibn Abī ᵓl-Iṣbaᶜ, *Taḥrīr*, 84.
[3] *Muwāzānah*, I, 16–17. On this work, see pp. 372–5, above.

Kratchkovsky's opinion, suggests that the second half of the book dealing with these *maḥāsin* may not have been part of the work as it was originally planned (it occupies a little more than a quarter of the text) and may even have been written at a later date. The question, therefore, deserves some attention, even in the context of an introductory survey. To facilitate the discussion it is necessary to give a summary of the introduction as it now stands in Kratchkovsky's edition, and of the passage on pages 57–8 which connects the *badīᶜ* section with the section on *maḥāsin*. At the same time this summary will serve as a useful outline of Ibn al-Muᶜtazz's views on the position of *badīᶜ* in the history of Arabic poetry and the origin of the debate on the figures of speech. As indicated earlier, not much is to be learned at this stage from an analysis of the individual figures that make up the two sections. They are divided by headings each introducing a particular figure of speech. First, though not always, there is a definition of the term as it appears in this heading. This definition is immediately followed by a series of examples, which are sometimes accompanied by brief explanations or comments. In the *badīᶜ* section, the order observed in presenting these examples is always: quotations from the Qurʾān, the sayings of Muḥammad and his Companions and other fragments of ancient prose; quotations from poets belonging to the pre-Islamic, early Islamic, and Umayyad periods; quotations in prose and poetry from the "new generation" (*muḥdathūn*), i.e. the authors who lived in the early ᶜAbbasid period; examples of the infelicitous use of the figure under discussion. In the *maḥāsin* section we find that a distinction is made between ancient and modern authors in one chapter only, and that the lists of examples demonstrating the "wrong" use of the figures are dropped. Neither section offers any further elucidations on such questions as the consistency of the examples with the terms and definitions, the choice of the terms, or the function of *badīᶜ* in different periods of Arabic literature. The resulting difficulties of interpretation, though they are strictly speaking outside the scope of this chapter, cannot be entirely disregarded, and two of them will be mentioned later. The content of the passages (pages 1–3 and 57–8) may be summarized as follows:

Page 1

1 In the chapters which make up his book, Ibn al-Muᶜtazz intends to present examples of what the poets of the new generation call the "new" (or "innovated", *badīᶜ*) style of composition (*qad qaddamnā fī abwābi kitābinā hādhā*, etc.). These examples have been taken from the Qurʾān, the *lughah* (uncommon, idiomatic expressions), tradition, sayings of the Companions of the Prophet and "others", as well as

from the poems of the ancients, in order that it be known that
2 Bashshār, Muslim b. al-Walīd, Abū Nuwās, and those resembling these three poets and following in their footsteps were not the first to engage in this art (*fann*, i.e. the use of *badīᶜ*).
3 What did happen, however, was that it appeared frequently in their poetry and attracted so much attention that eventually this term (*al-badīᶜ*) was adopted as an appropriate means of referring to the new fashion.
4 In the next generation we find Abū Tammām being so much attracted to *badīᶜ* that it became a dominant feature in his work; sometimes this enhanced its quality, but at other times he spoiled his poetry by exaggerating the use of *badīᶜ*.
5 [Abū Tammām's failures cannot be attributed to *badīᶜ* as such.] Earlier, *badīᶜ* would appear only once or twice in a *qaṣīdah*, or not at all. Whenever it was used sparingly it would improve a poem or prose composition.

Pages 1–2

6 Ibn al-Muᶜtazz quotes an unnamed scholar as saying that Abū Tammām's exaggerated use of *badīᶜ* could be compared to the *zuhd*-poet Ṣāliḥ b. ᶜAbd al-Quddūs's (d. 167/783) excessive use of proverbs (*amthāl*) in his poetry. If Ṣāliḥ had brought in these proverbs less frequently he would have been an outstanding poet.
7 *Basmalah* (opening formula) followed by examples of *badīᶜ* in prose and poetry. These examples are identified as illustrations of the use of *istiᶜārah* (metaphor), which is briefly defined.
8 The figures of *tajnīs* (paronomasia) and *muṭābaqah* (antithesis) also belong to *badīᶜ*. Ibn al-Muᶜtazz repeats that the ancients were the first to use these figures and that they were not invented by the new generation. The same can be said of the fourth and fifth chapter of *badīᶜ* [identified on pages 47 and 53 respectively as *radd aᶜjāz al-kalām ᶜalā mā taqaddamahā* and *madhhab kalāmī*].[4]
9 In quoting traditions from the Prophet and his Companions he will omit chains of transmitters and will limit himself to well-known traditions.

Pages 2–3

10 Ibn al-Muᶜtazz's originality in composing a treatise of this kind may prompt others, who hope for a share of the fame it has earned him, to

[4] See pp. 346–8.

suggest a different terminology, or to add examples or explanations which Ibn al-Muʿtazz himself found unsuitable or unnecessary.

11 This can happen to any book (i.e. this kind of criticism can be directed against every book; or every book can be replaced by another book on this basis).

12 Even if his book did not offer as much as it does, he would still achieve his aim which is to make clear that the new generation were not the first to use any of the categories of *badīʿ*.

Page 57

13 He has presented the five categories of *badīʿ* and therewith the subject, in his opinion, has been dealt with in full (*qad qaddamnā abwāba ʾl-badīʿi al-khamsata wa-kamula ʿindanā*).

14 People who are inclined to engage in disputations and to detract from the merits of others may argue that there are more *badīʿ* categories, or that *badīʿ* consists of only one or two of the five devices he has presented (*al-funūn al-khamsah allatī qaddamnāhā*).

Pages 57–8

15 Few, however, are entitled to an opinion on such matters, because

16 *badīʿ* is a term adopted for certain devices in poetry (*funūn min al-shiʿr*) discussed by poets and the educated critics among the poets (*nuqqād al-mutaʾaddibīn minhum*). As for

17 philologists and scholars [engaged in the study] of ancient poetry (*ʿulamāʾ al-lughah wa-ʾl-shiʿr al-qadīm*), they do not know this term and what it stands for.

18 Nobody before him has made a catalogue of *badīʿ* devices [according to Ibn Abī ʾl-Iṣbaʿ this statement appears at the beginning of the book].

19 He composed the book in 274/887 [according to Ibn Abī ʾl-Iṣbaʿ this statement comes at the beginning of the book].

20 ʿAlī b. Hārūn [b. ʿAlī] b. Yaḥyā b. Abī Manṣūr al-Munajjim (born 276 or 277, i.e. two or three years after *Kitāb al-Badīʿ* was completed!) was the first to make a copy of his autograph [Ibn Abī ʾl-Iṣbaʿ, who places the passage at the beginning of the book, gives the name of the scholar as ʿAlī b. Yaḥyā b. [Abī] Manṣūr al-Munajjim; ʿAlī b. Yaḥyā died in 275].

21 He will now mention a number of *maḥāsin* (ornaments, rhetorical devices) of [prose] compositions and poetry.

22 These *maḥāsin* are numerous; nobody can enumerate, let alone be acquainted, with all of them.

23 (a) He hopes that thereby the book will be more useful to students of literature (*al-mutaᵓaddibūn*). (b) In stating the number of *badīᶜ* devices to be five he is making a choice based on experience [*ikhtibāran*, or: is making a deliberate choice, *ikhtiyāran*, if we follow the reading of Ibn Abī ᵓl-Iṣbaᶜ],[5] and is not ignorant of the existence of these other *maḥāsin*.

24 One can follow him in this and limit *badīᶜ* to these five devices; or one can adopt a different viewpoint and count some of the *maḥāsin*, even *maḥāsin* which he, Ibn al-Muᶜtazz, does not mention, among the *badīᶜ* [devices].

At this point we may propose a solution to the problem raised by Guidi's review and the passage in Ibn Abī ᵓl-Iṣbāᶜ's *Taḥrīr*. Guidi questioned the position at the beginning of the book of pages 1–2 of Kratchkovsky's edition (1)–(6) of summary, and its claim to be part of the final version of *Kitāb al-Badīᶜ*. Once the existence of two different versions of a particular passage is assumed and the correct position of this passage is uncertain, the number of emendations that can be suggested sometimes appears almost unlimited. Without excluding other and perhaps better solutions, we might suggest that Ibn al-Muᶜtazz did indeed substitute a new version for part of the original text. For reasons outlined elsewhere,[6] it may be argued that (10)–(12) of the summary (pages 2–3 of Kratchkovsky's text) were later replaced by (13)–(20) (pages 57–8 of Kratchkovsky's text). The two sections are both directed against Ibn al-Muᶜtazz's critics, but (13)–(20) is more specific than (10)–(12). A later copyist finding both versions in his original may have decided that it would be more appropriate to have (13)–(20) *after* the discussion of *badīᶜ* figures, not only because the mention of a transcript suggests that part of the book was already in existence, but also because (13)–(20) would fit well in the context where it stands now.

One of several objections that could be raised against this emendation is that it does not solve the problem of how to interpret the words *qad qaddamnā* with which the treatise begins. Guidi does not rule out the possibility that one could translate *qaddamnā* by "we have presented" or "we have put first", but feels that since the book was written in two parts, the second dating from a later period, this last solution is difficult to accept. If, however, one removes the reference to the transcript from where it stands now and assumes that the introduction was written only after the book had been completed, it is possible to consider *Kitāb al-Badīᶜ* as intended from the beginning to consist of two sections, one comprising five

[5] Quoting (21)–(24), Ibn Abī ᵓl-Iṣbaᶜ states that this passage occurs between the end of the *badīᶜ* section and the beginning of the *maḥāṣin* section (*Taḥrīr*, 84).

[6] Bonebakker, "Ibn Abī ᵓl-Iṣbaᶜ's text", 84–9.

categories of *badīᶜ*, and the second dealing with *maḥāsin*, and it then makes sense to translate *qad qaddamnā fī abwābi kitābinā hādhā* . . . by "In the chapters which make up this book of ours we have put first . . .".

BACKGROUND TO THE COMPOSITION OF *KITĀB AL-BADĪᶜ*

We may now address the more fundamental question of the motives which prompted Ibn al-Muᶜtazz to write his *Kitāb al-Badīᶜ* and the various claims he makes in the two introductory sections of his book. The above summary may serve as an outline for our discussion. According to Ibn al-Muᶜtazz, *badīᶜ* devices do not appear for the first time in the work of the early ᶜAbbasid poets such as Bashshār, Muslim b. al-Walīd and Abū Nuwās; still they are more frequently found in their work than in the poems of the ancients. This claim is twice repeated ((8) and (12) of summary) and seems to be the central theme of *Kitāb al-Badīᶜ*. The first part of this claim is supported by the examples Ibn al-Muᶜtazz gives in the five chapters of the *badīᶜ* section, even though, as Kratchkovsky observes, the number of instances in the two last chapters is somewhat less. No study seems to have been made, in medieval or in modern times, of the frequency of the occurrence of *badīᶜ* devices in the early ᶜAbbasid period as compared to the pre-Islamic, early Islamic and Umayyad periods; E. Wagner has studied the rhetorical devices in the poetry of Abū Nuwās, but has made no attempt to compare Abū Nuwās's use of rhetorical devices to that of any of the older poets.[7] We therefore have, as things stand, to accept Ibn al-Muᶜtazz's word for the accuracy of the second part of his claim. His statement (3) on the appearance of the term *badīᶜ* in the early ᶜAbbasid period, particularly in reference to the "new generation of poets" (*al-muḥdathūn*), is amply supported by other evidence. The word *badīᶜ* occurs in an elegy on Abū Nuwās (d. *c.* 200/815), but is perhaps used there of the poet, not of his poetry, and therefore not in a technical sense.[8] The same may be true of a passage in the *Muwashshaḥ* of al-Marzubānī and the *Kitāb al-Aghānī* of Abū ʾl-Faraj al-Iṣfahānī, works dating from the fourth/tenth century: Aṣmaᶜī (d. 213/828) is asked to compare the two early ᶜAbbasid poets, Bashshār (d. *c.* 167/783) and Marwān b. Abī Ḥafṣah (alive during the reign of Hārūn al-Rashīd, 170–93/786–809); he supports his preference for Bashshār by observing that Bashshār trod a new path on which he travelled alone, so that he became unique and outstanding, while Marwān followed the methods of the ancients. Bashshār's poetry is more diversified; he manages to be more versatile, more productive, and more original (*akthar badīᶜan*).[9]

[7] *Abū Nuwās*, 384–441. [8] Mihzamī, *Akhbār Abī Nuwās*, 36; Wagner, *Abū Nuwās*, 97.
[9] Marzubānī, *Muwashshaḥ*, 251; Abū ʾl-Faraj al-Iṣfahānī, *Aghānī*, III, 25.

It is far from certain that the term *badīᶜ* in this passage has to be understood in a technical sense; however it definitely must be taken as a technical term in a saying by a certain Ḥudhayfah b. Muḥammad, apparently a pupil of Aṣmaᶜī, who speaks of Abū Tammām (d. 231/845 or 232/846) as a poet who "intends *badīᶜ* but ends up with absurdities" (*yurīdu ᵓl-badīᶜa fa-yakhruju ilā ᵓl-muḥāl*).[10] If we may believe the *Kitāb al-Aghānī*, Muslim b. al-Walīd (d. 208/823) was the first poet "to have composed the poetry known as *badīᶜ* [and] to have styled this type of poetry the *badīᶜ* and the subtle" (... *laqqaba hādhā ᵓl-jinsa ᵓl-badīᶜ a wa-ᵓl-laṭīf*).[11] The author of *Kitāb al-Aghānī* goes on to say that the best-known among Muslim's followers was Abū Tammām, because he "made all his poetry follow the style of *badīᶜ*, while Muslim had [still] shown diversity and versatility in his work". This statement echoes a tradition about a certain Qāsim b. Mihrawayh (who seems to have lived in the middle of the third/ninth century) which appears on the same page of *Kitāb al-Aghānī* and contains a similar assertion: Qāsim observes that "the first to corrupt poetry was Muslim b. al-Walīd. He introduced the style (*fann*) which people call *badīᶜ*. He was followed by [Abū Tammām] al-Ṭāᵓī who used this style without restraint (?), so that people became confused [and did not understand his poems]". (According to another version of the same tradition: "Abū Tammām admired the method of Muslim and wished no line of his to be without one of these figures (*aṣnāf*). He followed a rough path, strained word and meaning, and thus corrupted his poetry, so that it lost elegance and its sap dried out".)[12] Ibn al-Muᶜtazz himself quotes in his *Ṭabaqāt al-shuᶜarāᵓ* one Ṣāliḥ b. Muḥammad al-ᶜAwfī (who, according to one of the manuscripts, quotes in his turn one Ibrāhīm b. Abī Yaḥyā al-Madanī al-Anṣārī) as saying that "Muslim b. al-Walīd was the first to enlarge the scope of *badīᶜ*. Bashshār had been the first to introduce it, but Muslim filled his poetry with it. Then Abū Tammām came, exaggerated the use of *badīᶜ*, and exceeded the proper limits".[13] Finally the *Muwashshaḥ* has, again in the form of a tradition, a statement by the poet Kulthūm b. ᶜAmr al-ᶜAttābī (d. *c.* 220/835) introducing his contemporary, Abū Nuwās, as a *badīᶜ* poet. Abū Nuwās, he says, is a witty poet who used an exquisite vocabulary, except that he exaggerates in affecting the *badīᶜ* [style] to such an extent that he once said: "When the fox of avoidance appeared to us, I sent the dog of union in pursuit."[14]

From the above it would appear that Ibn al-Muᶜtazz took up the thesis put forward in the tradition of Qāsim b. Mihrawayh, and perhaps also the

[10] Āmidī, *Muwāzanah*, I, 20, 138–9; Marzubānī, *Muwashshaḥ*, 304.

[11] Abū ᵓl-Faraj al-Iṣfahānī, *Aghānī*, XIX (Cairo, 1972), 31.

[12] Āmidī, *Muwāzanah*, I, 17–18.

[13] Ibn al-Muᶜtazz, *Ṭabaqāt*, 235. On this work, see pp. 344–5, above.

[14] Marzubānī, *Muwashshaḥ*, 286. Ibid., 271, offers a different version where the use of *al-badīᶜ* in a technical sense does not appear so clearly.

traditions of Ṣāliḥ b. ᶜAwf and ᶜAttābī. Ibn al-Muᶜtazz seems to modify this thesis in what he says under (1)–(5) of the summary, though one notes that the three poets mentioned by Ibn al-Muᶜtazz are the same as those discussed in the traditions. Unfortunately Ibn al-Muᶜtazz does not refer explicitly to any of these traditions, or to the sharp attack on the poet Abū Tammām by Ḥudhayfah.[15] Nor is any such reference to be found as part of the discussion of the figures of speech. We will see later that Ibn al-Muᶜtazz may have drawn some inspiration from his predecessors in selecting definitions and examples for the *badīᶜ* and *maḥāsin* devices but, with one interesting exception (the mention of Jāḥiẓ as the author of the term *madhhab kalāmī*), found it unnecessary to refer to the numerous traditions which reflect the work of these predecessors. Ibn al-Muᶜtazz's motives and his sources of inspiration are therefore a matter of speculation. It may well be that Ibn al-Muᶜtazz was not as critical of Abū Tammām as his contemporaries and predecessors, though at first sight his introduction may create this impression. He may have felt that the fact that *badīᶜ* devices are also found in the work of the ancients justified a more temperate judgement. For the same reason he may also have felt that the discussion of terminology, definitions and examples of figures of speech should be revived and that the relation of these figures of speech to the work of the early ᶜAbbasid masters should be put in its proper perspective. In dealing with these figures of speech, the philologists of the second/eighth and the first half of the third/ninth centuries had drawn their examples almost invariably from ancient poetry. On the other hand, critics like Qāsim b. Mihrawayh had associated *badīᶜ* with the generation of Bashshār, Muslim b. al-Walīd and Abū Nuwās, a viewpoint which Ibn al-Muᶜtazz was ready to accept only in the case of a limited number of figures and only with the understanding that Bashshār, Muslim, and Abū Nuwās had not "invented" these figures.

That Ibn al-Muᶜtazz may have had good reason to be dissatisfied with the way these questions had been dealt with, not only by earlier critics but also by his immediate predecessors, is shown by some passages from authors of the third/ninth century in which the term *badīᶜ* appears in a technical sense. From these passages it can be seen that no attempt was made to define the term or to associate it with specific categories of examples. Jāḥiẓ (d. 255/868–9) observes that ᶜAttābī followed Bashshār's *badīᶜ* style. ᶜAttābī in his turn was imitated by all post-classical (*muwalladūn*) *badīᶜ* poets, such as his contemporaries, Manṣūr al-Namarī and Muslim b. al-Walīd. Among the post-classical poets the best *badīᶜ* poets were Bashshār and Ibn Harmah (d. between 140/757 and 170/786). A few pages later Jāḥiẓ observes that *badīᶜ* is

15 But Āmidī, *Muwazanah*, I, 138–9, sees a connection between *K. al-Badīᶜ* and the Ḥudhayfah tradition, and probably also the tradition of Qāsim b. Mihrawayh.

limited to the Arabs and that, on account of it, their language is superior to all other languages. The (Umayyad) poet al-Rāᶜī used *badīᶜ* frequently in his poetry; Bashshār's *badīᶜ* was good and with ᶜAttābī *badīᶜ* became a regular pattern (*yadhhabu shiᶜruhū fī ᵓl-badīᶜ*). In the same passage Jāḥiẓ illustrates what he understands by *badīᶜ* by quoting a line from an elegy by al-Ashhab b. Rumaylah, an early Islamic poet: "They are the forearm of Fate by which people defend themselves; what good is there in a hand that is not lifted by a forearm?"[16] In his commentary Jāḥiẓ identifies the expression, "they are the forearm of fate", as a *mathal* (figurative expression),[17] adding that "this is what the *ruwāh* (here: professional reciters?) call *badīᶜ*", an interesting reference to a *badīᶜ* line by an ancient poet and (depending on whom one identifies as the *ruwāh*) an indication that the term *badīᶜ* may be quite old. He further illustrates this type of metaphor by quoting a line from al-Rāᶜī: "They are the base of the neck of Fate by which people defend themselves, etc.," and a *ḥadīth*: "The razor of God is sharper, and the forearm of God is stronger." Jāḥiẓ also knows the term *istiᶜārah* and uses it to explain a line by an anonymous *rajaz*-poet: "The eyes of the clouds shed tears on its [the dwelling's] deserted courtyards." He defines *istiᶜārah*, but curiously enough does not mention it as a *badīᶜ* device.[18] Ibn Qutaybah (d. 276/889) speaks of the subtlety of Muslim's poetry and offers examples of that poet's *badīᶜ*, presumably his metaphors, and according to Ibn Qutaybah the style of Muslim and Abū Nuwās was closely followed by Abū Tammām.[19] Kratchkovsky concludes that in Jāḥiẓ's books the term *badīᶜ* "is felt to be new and as yet unconfirmed". By this Kratchkovsky does not mean to say that the term was not yet used in a technical sense. It seems likely that precisely because Jāḥiẓ, and later, in some contexts, Ibn al-Muᶜtazz, use *badīᶜ* as a common qualification for outstanding, original compositions, they must have assumed that their readers were able to distinguish between the general and the technical sense of the term. On the other hand, it can be seen from the passages quoted from Jāḥiẓ and Ibn Qutaybah, if one may consider them as representative, that there was room for a more precise definition, and Ibn al-Muᶜtazz may have realized that these passages could lead people to believe that metaphor was the only figure to be considered when discussing the "new style". In a more positive vein, one could suggest, on the basis of the examples, that the idea of looking for *badīᶜ* examples in the poetry of older poets was borrowed by Ibn al-Muᶜtazz from Jāḥiẓ, but there is no proof of this.

16 *Bayān*, I, 51; IV, 55–6.
17 On discussions of Jāḥiẓ's use of the term *mathal*, see Heinrichs, *The Hand of the Northwind*, 7–8.
18 *Bayān*, I, 152–3. Similarly, *K. al-Ḥayawān*, II, 57–9, a chapter on *badīᶜ* which offers no definition of the term and no explanation of the examples; cf. Heinrichs, *The Hand of the Northwind*, 10, 26–30.
19 *K. al-Shiᶜr*, 528–9.

As regards Ibn al-Muᶜtazz's elaboration of his own thesis, as set forth in (2) and (4) of the summary, there is no evidence that, in singling out Bashshār, Muslim, and Abū Nuwās in the introduction, he wished to do more than cite typical representatives of the *badīᶜ* school mentioned repeatedly as such by his predecessors; he certainly did not intend to limit his investigations to the work of these three poets: of the 213 examples cited in the *badīᶜ* section, five are from Bashshār, six from Muslim, and fifteen from Abū Nuwās. Nor did he pay particular attention to the poets mentioned by Jāḥiẓ: there are four quotations from ᶜAttābī, and none from Ibn Harmah, Manṣūr al-Namarī and al-Rāᶜī. Limiting ourselves again to the *badīᶜ* section, we find that Ibn al-Muᶜtazz has thirty-one quotations from Abū Tammām (against six in the *maḥāsin* section). Two of the quotations are anonymous (but attributed by Kratchkovsky to Abū Tammām), so that actually only twenty-nine quotations have to be taken into consideration. Of these twenty-nine quotations only six are unfavourable to Abū Tammām. Kratchkovsky's assertion that Abū Tammām is singled out with special frequency in specimens of how people should not write therefore needs some qualification.[20] What Kratchkovsky probably meant was that against a total of twenty-four specimens of infelicitous use of *badīᶜ* in poetry, the number of Abū Tammām quotations is significant. Kratchkovsky also observes that Ibn al-Muᶜtazz quotes fragments from nearly 200 poets, in the majority of cases once only (*Kitāb al-Badīᶜ* contains 312 quotations). These quotations show only a slight majority for the "new", that is ᶜAbbasid, poets. That the principal, or one of the principal, aims of the book was to demonstrate that *badīᶜ* devices were not the exclusive property of the new generation is thus clear, not only from Ibn al-Muᶜtazz's twice-repeated statement, but also from the ratio between quotations from old and new poets.

The rather dominant position of Abū Tammām's work among the quotations from the new generation of poets also makes it likely that in writing *Kitāb al-Badīᶜ*, Ibn al-Muᶜtazz may indeed have drawn inspiration from the second part of the traditions about Qāsim b. Mihrawayh and Ṣāliḥ b. ᶜAwf cited above. The modern critic Muḥammad Mandūr even seems to believe that it was the controversy over the appreciation of Abū Tammām's poetry which was Ibn al-Muᶜtazz's principal motive in composing *Kitāb al-Badīᶜ*.[21] There can be no doubt that this controversy attracted much attention; a whole host of contemporary critics had expressed negative judgements on the poet. The question as to whether this controversy was still alive when Ibn al-Muᶜtazz wrote *Kitāb al-Badīᶜ* in 274/887 should be

[20] Ibn al-Muᶜtazz, *Badīᶜ*, introd., 12.

[21] Cf. *al-Naqd al-manhajī*, 47–63, 75.

answered in the affirmative. Although in the *Kitāb al-Shiᶜr* of Ibn Qutaybah the only reference to Abū Tammām is the brief statement quoted earlier, this could be interpreted to mean that Ibn Qutaybah took no interest in Abū Tammām and had lined up with the critics of the poet, in spite of his strong emphasis on the need for an impartial judgement on poets from all generations.[22] The existence of treatises by Abū Bakr Muḥammad b. Yaḥyā al-Ṣūlī (d. 335/946 or 336/947) (*Akhbār Abī Tammām*), and al-Āmidī (*al-Muwāzanah*) shows how much interest this controversy created even in the next century. A more convincing argument can be derived from the fact that Ibn al-Muᶜtazz himself wrote a treatise on the merits and shortcomings of Abū Tammām's poetry[23] as well as a book on plagiarisms, *Kitāb Sariqāt al-shuᶜarāʾ*, which included quotations from Abū Tammām, and criticized the prejudice which the philologist Ibn al-Aᶜrābī had against the poet.[24] Ibn al-Muᶜtazz's teacher, Mubarrad, also appears to have been interested in the question.[25] But one can also turn this argument around and suggest that the existence of a treatise from Ibn al-Muᶜtazz's own hand made a second work specifically dealing with this subject unnecessary. Most likely Ibn al-Muᶜtazz wrote his *Kitāb al-Badīᶜ* to demonstrate not simply the early existence of the *badīᶜ* devices, but also, implicitly, the poet's right to use them as he sees fit, provided he does not go to extremes. The reference to Abū Tammām therefore seems to be incidental rather than a dominating subject of the thesis, and the predominance of quotations from Abū Tammām may be the result of the author's continued interest in this poet.

In any case, it is highly unlikely that Ibn al-Muᶜtazz's interest in *badīᶜ* has to be associated with the general controversy over the merits of ancient and "modern" poetry, that is, the controversy over the early ᶜAbbasid poets as a category not limited to Abū Tammām. In the first place, this controversy no longer, it seems, attracted much attention in the days of Ibn al-Muᶜtazz. Secondly, there seems to be evidence that not only Ibn al-Muᶜtazz himself, but also some of his immediate predecessors, such as Isḥāq b. Ibrāhīm al-Mawṣilī (d. 235/849–50), Abū Ḥātim al-Sijistānī (d. 252/866), and al-Mubarrad (d. 285/898 or 286/899), felt that the poetry of the new generation did not present a break with tradition.[26] Ibn Qutaybah, the only author who explicitly mentions the existence of a category of scholars who were hostile to modern poetry, would have mentioned *badīᶜ* if the appearance of *badīᶜ* devices had been a reason for rejecting these modern poets.

[22] Cf. p. 343.
[23] Quoted Marzubānī, *Muwashshaḥ*, 307–19 (Ibn al-Muᶜtazz, *Rasāʾil Ibn al-Muᶜtazz*, 19–31).
[24] Āmidī, *Muwāzanah*, I, 77, 278, 304; Ṣūlī, *Akhbār Abī Tammām*, 175–6.
[25] See e.g. Ṣūlī, *Akhbār Abī Tammām*, 96–7, 202–4; Marzubānī, *Muwashshaḥ*, 306, 319–20.
[26] Cf. p. 21, and Bonebakker, 'Poets and critics", 94–6.

ORIGINS OF IBN AL-MUᶜTAZZ'S TERMINOLOGY

It should not surprise us that Ibn al-Muᶜtazz chose to list *istiᶜārah* (metaphor) as the first figure of *badīᶜ*, and even anticipated the more detailed treatment of *istiᶜārah* which follows shortly afterwards in the first chapter by offering examples and a brief definition. We have seen that previous discussions of *badīᶜ*, at least as far as they are known to us, are limited to metaphor. Ibn al-Muᶜtazz may very well have felt that it would be appropriate to draw the attention of his readers to this most familiar category before setting out to list what, in his view, were the other figures characteristic of *badīᶜ*. It is now time to examine the second of the two main subjects of the introduction, Ibn al-Muᶜtazz's reply to real or imaginary critics of his work and his attitude towards, and possible dependence upon, his contemporaries and predecessors. Since (13)–(20) of the summary may be a later version of (10)–(12), it is enough to give attention to (13)–(20) and more specifically (13)–(18) which take up the argument set forth in the earlier passage in a more detailed manner.

Given that Ibn al-Muᶜtazz may have felt that the association of *badīᶜ* with metaphor, as we find it in Jāḥiẓ, was too limited, it is perhaps this that he has in mind when he introduces a critic as saying that *badīᶜ* consists of only one or two of the categories he has enumerated. He also leaves open the possibility (in the earlier passage under (10)) that one may prefer a different terminology. In the seventh/thirteenth century Ibn Abī ᵓl-Iṣbaᶜ observed, in speaking of the five categories of *badīᶜ*, that Ibn al-Muᶜtazz attributes the fifth, *madhhab kalāmī*, to Jāḥiẓ, but that the remaining four categories might have been known under different names among "the Arabs". He suggests that Ibn al-Muᶜtazz had introduced new terms that were more in keeping with his own views.[27] It is not clear whom Ibn Abī ᵓl-Iṣbaᶜ has in mind when he speaks about "the Arabs"; perhaps he is thinking of the professional reciters from whom the earliest generations of Iraqī philologists received their information (cf. Jāḥiẓ's reference to the use of the term *badīᶜ* among the *ruwāh*). We have seen that Jāḥiẓ uses *mathal* in the sense of "figurative expression", and there are other instances of the use of *mathal* for *istiᶜārah*;[28] moreover the term continued in use long after *istiᶜārah* had become the common term used in all handbooks on literary theory. Another early synonym of *istiᶜārah* may have been the term *ishtiqāq*,[29] but there is no way of telling whether these terms went back as far as the ancient Arabs, as Ibn Abī ᵓl-Iṣbaᶜ asserts. There may also have been subtle distinctions between *mathal*, *ishtiqāq* and *istiᶜārah* that some day will be

27 *Taḥrīr*, 84. 28 *EI*², "Istiᶜāra". 29 See Kratchkovsky, "Deux chapitres", 57, 59–60.

elucidated by further research. Similarly, the term *raddāt* was reportedly used in the sense of *tajnīs* by the poet ᶜUmārah (alive during the caliphate of Mutawakkil, 232–47/847–61), a great-grandson of the poet Jarīr, who actually compares the *raddāt* of Abū Tammām to those of his ancestor,[30] and Ibn Rashīq (d. *c.* 456/1063–4) even thinks it possible that the poet Ruᶜbah (d. 145/762) used the term *ᶜaṭf* for *tajnīs* and believes that the term *tajnīs* was first used by Ibn al-Muᶜtazz.[31] This opinion perhaps deserves some credit, since Abū Hilāl al-ᶜAskarī (d. *c.* 400/1009) uses the term *taᶜaṭṭuf* for a form of *tajnīs*.[32]

It is difficult to identify the "scholars of language and of ancient poetry", to whom Ibn al-Muᶜtazz denies any knowledge of the term *badīᶜ* and what it stands for. From the above examples, it is easy to see that figures of speech had been discussed frequently before Ibn al-Muᶜtazz's time, and that Ibn al-Muᶜtazz in all likelihood borrowed examples from early philologists, such as Aṣmaᶜī and Abū ᶜUbaydah. It is also true that these scholars did not use the term *badīᶜ* in the context of their discussions of these rhetorical devices. But what to say of the *Qawāᶜid al-shiᶜr* ("The Bases of Poetry") of Abū ᵓl-ᶜAbbās Aḥmad b. Yaḥyā Thaᶜlab (d. 291/904)? We have to admit that this treatise is an example of a discussion of the figures of speech by a "scholar of language and of ancient poetry" who failed to use the term *badīᶜ*. Yet, in view of the fact that Thaᶜlab is said to have been Ibn al-Muᶜtazz's teacher and that three of Ibn al-Muᶜtazz's *badīᶜ* figures, *istiᶜārah*, *tajnīs* and *muṭābaqah*, show an affinity, if not an actual agreement, with figures discussed by Thaᶜlab, it is strange that Ibn al-Muᶜtazz keeps silent about this treatise.[33] The question of the authenticity of *Qawāᶜid al-shiᶜr* has been raised; it is not mentioned among the works of Thaᶜlab, but a treatise of the same name is listed among the works of Mubarrad whose *kunyah*, Abū ᵓl-ᶜAbbās, is the same as Thaᶜlab's. However, there seems to no good reason to question the attribution of *Qawāᶜid al-shiᶜr* to Thaᶜlab. Moreover, even if the treatise were by Mubarrad, we would still be faced with the same problem, since Mubarrad is also mentioned among Ibn al-Muᶜtazz's teachers. One could suggest the following answers to the question, none of which are entirely satisfactory: (a) Ibn al-Muᶜtazz was not aware of the existence of Thaᶜlab's *Qawāᶜid*; (b) he found no reason to take notice of Thaᶜlab's work because only "poets and educated critics who were also poets were competent to deal with *badīᶜ*, even though others might have dealt with figures of speech"; in other words, philologists such as Thaᶜlab engaged in collecting and interpreting ancient poetry were not aware of the

30 Bonebakker, *Notes*, 36. 31 *ᶜUmdah*, I, 331f. 32 *Ṣināᶜatayn*, 307.

33 See Kratchkovsky, "Deux chapitres", 29, for points of agreement between Ibn al-Muᶜtazz and Thaᶜlab.

significance of the frequent occurrence of *badīʿ* figures in ʿAbbasid poetry; (c) the treatise by Thaʿlab was not yet in existence when Ibn al-Muʿtazz wrote his *Kitāb al-Badīʿ*. Ibn al-Muʿtazz wrote his treatise in 274/887 and Thaʿlab died in 291/904 at the age of ninety-one, but considering that Thaʿlab was born in 200/815 and Ibn al-Muʿtazz in 247/861 there is a considerable likelihood that *Qawāʿid al-shiʿr* was the older of the two treatises. However, it is reasonable to suggest that *Qawāʿid al-shiʿr* never enjoyed much popularity, since it is, apparently, never quoted in other treatises on literary theory. It may conceivably have remained unnoticed, even during the author's lifetime and even among some of his pupils; moreover, it must not be forgotten that, though Ibn al-Muʿtazz met Thaʿlab and studied with him, no close teacher-student relationship may have existed between the two men. If, however, Ibn al-Muʿtazz deliberately ignored *Qawāʿid al-shiʿr*, it can have been for no other reason than that, on the one hand, the scope of *Qawāʿid al-shiʿr* was much wider than that of his own *Kitāb al-Badīʿ* and that, on the other hand, the two main subjects of his book, the enumeration of *badīʿ* devices and the carrying over of these devices from the pre-Islamic days into his own times, were not a matter of concern to Thaʿlab.

This brings us again to the question of the extent to which Ibn al-Muʿtazz's claim that *badīʿ* was a term common among, and only understood by, poets and his claim to have composed the first monograph on the subject can be justified. The only evidence that poets used the term comes from the statement, quoted earlier, by Abū ʾl-Faraj al-Iṣfahānī, who believes that the poet Muslim b. al-Walīd invented it. However, he does not substantiate this assertion with a tradition, as one would expect him to do (the tradition about Qāsim b. Mihrawayh only says that others used the term *badīʿ* in speaking of Muslim's poetry). On the other hand, Jāḥiẓ uses the term *badīʿ* and associates it with metaphor. It may well be, however, that Ibn al-Muʿtazz did not place Jāḥiẓ in the category of "scholars of language and of ancient poetry" and recognized the diversity of objectives and the versatility of Jāḥiẓ's work as well as his qualities as a critic. Being himself a poet of the new school, Ibn al-Muʿtazz could hardly have disagreed with Jāḥiẓ's list of typical *badīʿ* poets.

In an article published in 1973, W. Heinrichs distinguished four stimuli which led to the genesis and development of Arabic literary theory, and which, by their diversity, account for the lack of homogeneity which characterizes this branch of literature. First on his list are the endeavours of the philologists, the collectors and commentators of ancient poetry, among whom he counts Thaʿlab. Another stimulus was the concern with Quranic exegesis, which had to face the problem of how to interpret anthropomorphic passages in the Qurʾān and to demonstrate the stylistic inimitability of the Holy Book. The third stimulus, the one with which we are here concerned, was the challenge of the *badīᶜ* style, the need to define the term *badīᶜ* and to assess the significance of the appearance of this style in early ᶜAbbasid poetry. Lastly, Heinrichs notes the attempts to offer a systematic and coherent presentation of literary theory. This last tendency he sees as the result of "the imprint of philosophy, or to be more precise, logical training". He rightly observes that "the individual works usually consist of a mixture of these different traditions and must be analyzed accordingly."[34] To take these items in a slightly different order, a point could be made of considering the exegetic, or if one prefers the apologetic, endeavours by Ibn al-Muᶜtazz in *Kitāb al-Badīᶜ* to explain the occurrence of Quranic examples of *badīᶜ*. This question needs further investigation; from our present perspective Ibn al-Muᶜtazz's interest in the Qurᵓān appears to be wholly subordinated to his interest in the history of the figures of speech. However, the agreement between the terms and examples used by Ibn al-Muᶜtazz and those used earlier by the philologists deserves to be given some attention. The *Ḥilyat al-muḥāḍarah* of Abū ᶜAlī Muḥammad b. al-Ḥasan al-Ḥātimī (d. 388/998) contains traditions which could have been known to, and used by, Ibn al-Muᶜtazz, Qudāmah and others.[35] Since Ibn al-Muᶜtazz (except in the case of the term *madhhab kalāmī*), does not mention his sources, these parallels offer no proof; in fact the interest of the collection of traditions in *Ḥilyah* should be seen more in that it proves the early existence of discussions of figures of speech among philologists, and to a lesser extent among poets, than that it supplies firm evidence of specific traditions being known to this or that author of a work on literary theory. From these traditions it can be seen that Ibn al-Muᶜtazz used examples, and sometimes terms, that were already familiar to such scholars as Abū ᶜAmr b. al-ᶜAlāᵓ (d. *c.* 154/770), Khalaf al-Aḥmar (d. 180/796), Yūnus b. Ḥabīb (d. 182/798), Aṣmaᶜī, and Thaᶜlab. The lines of poetry quoted are from pre-Islamic, early Islamic, or Umayyad poetry. As noted earlier, the term *badīᶜ* is never used in any of these traditions. Moreover there is hardly any mention of contemporary poets in reports of this kind. This adds weight to the other claim by Ibn al-Muᶜtazz which is less clearly formulated, but undoubtedly implied, namely that philologists were not aware of the frequency of the appearance, much less the significance, of *badīᶜ* figures in the poetry of the new generation. On the other hand, we have no proof either that the term *badīᶜ* was known to poets. It will be remembered from the majority of the examples quoted earlier that when poets discussed poetry, they used isolated terms, not the general technical term *badīᶜ*, and that these were terms, moreover, not reproduced in *Kitāb al-Badīᶜ*; thus the poet ᶜUmārah in

[34] "Literary theory", 30–2.

[35] See Bonebakker, "Materials".

discussing the work of his contemporary, Abū Tammām, compares the latter's *raddāt* to those of his own ancestor Jarīr; Abū Tammām himself, referring to figures of speech, quotes an example of *tardīd* from the work of the pre-Islamic poet Zuhayr b. Abī Sulmā, and discusses *istiṭrād* with his pupil al-Buḥturī.[36] *Raddāt* and *istiṭrād*, however, correspond respectively to *tajnīs* and *ḥusn al-khurūj* (skilful transition) in the chapter on *tajnīs* in *Kitāb al-Badīᶜ*. What is more, two of ᶜUmārah's examples appear in this same chapter. If, therefore, the term *tajnīs* was known to and used by poets, there is some reason to expect we would find it at least in the tradition about ᶜUmārah. Thus this part of Ibn al-Muᶜtazz's claim – that poets understood what was really meant by *badīᶜ* – is still only supported by the statement in *Kitāb al-Aghānī* and the observation on the poetry of Abū Nuwās by the poet ᶜAttābī quoted earlier.

Among those literati belonging to Ibn al-Muᶜtazz's circle, four should be mentioned as authorities from whom Ibn al-Muᶜtazz could have received information on figures of speech. They are: Abū ᵓl-Ḥasan ᶜAlī b. Yaḥyā al-Munajjim, Abū Bakr Muḥammad b. Yaḥyā al-Ṣūlī, Abū ᵓl-Qāsim Jaᶜfar b. Qudāmah b. Ziyād (d. 319/931), and al-Mubarrad. The name of the scholar who was the first to copy the autograph of *Kitāb al-Badīᶜ* (see (20) of summary) should probably read ᶜAlī b. Yaḥyā b. Abī Manṣūr al-Munajjim (not ᶜAlī b. Hārūn b. Yaḥyā b. Abī Manṣūr al-Munajjim).[37] Ḥātimī's *Ḥilyat al-Muḥāḍarah* mentions ᶜAlī b. Yaḥyā in the *isnād* (chain of transmitters) of a tradition about Abū ᶜAmr b. al-ᶜAlāᵓ which Ibn al-Muᶜtazz used in a learned discussion with Abū Bakr al-Ṣūlī reported by a later author. It again mentions him in the *isnād* of a tradition about *iltifāt* (apostrophe), which Ibn al-Muᶜtazz could have used in the *maḥasin* section of *Kitāb al-Badīᶜ*.[38] The same *iltifāt* tradition could have reached Ibn al-Muᶜtazz through al-Ṣūlī who appears as the latest authority in the chain of transmitters. Al-Ṣūlī may also have transmitted to Ibn al-Muᶜtazz a tradition on Bashshār discussing *tashbīh* (simile) in which we find the line quoted on page 69, number 262, of *Kitāb al-Badīᶜ*.[39]

In what seems to be the only detailed biography of ᶜAlī b. Yaḥyā, he is characterized as a literary historian who wrote a *Kitāb al-Shuᶜarāᵓ al-qudamāᵓ wa-ᵓl-islāmiyyīn* on pre-Islamic and Islamic poets and a *Kitāb Akhbār Isḥāq b. Ibrāhīm* [*al-Mawṣilī*], a life of the poet-musician and court companion who died in 235/849–50.[40] As appears from quotations and anecdotes, he was also an accomplished poet, a scholar, and a boon-companion of several caliphs of the ᶜAbbasid House. It is easy to imagine that the interest in ancient and contemporary poetry which the two men had in common

[36] Ibid., 55, 62–3. [37] Bonebakker, "Ibn Abī ᵓl-Iṣbaᶜᵓs text", 90–1.
[38] Bonebakker, "Materials", 33, 58. [39] Ibid., 66. [40] Yāqūt, *Irshād*, v, 459–77.

brought them together, and that Ibn al-Muᶜtazz could have heard some traditions from him. His friendship with Ibn al-Muᶜtazz, though not recorded in any of the biographies, is nevertheless attested in Ibn al-Muᶜtazz's *Dīwān* by several elegies that he composed after the death of his friend. Ibn al-Muᶜtazz wrote *Kitāb al-Badīᶜ* in 274/887 at the age of twenty-seven. In the above-mentioned discussion with al-Ṣūlī, which may have taken place at a much later date (al-Ṣūlī died in 335 or 336/*c*. 947, the date of his birth is not known), he introduces the figure *muqābalah* which does not yet appear in *Kitāb al-Badīᶜ*. Perhaps for this term we have also an antecedent: in Ḥātimī's *Ḥilyah* and the *Kitāb Naḍrat al-ighrīḍ* of Abū ᶜAlī al-Muẓaffar b. al-Faḍl al-Ḥusaynī (d. 642/1244?), the terms appears in a tradition which may go back to Qudāmah b. Jaᶜfar's father, Jaᶜfar b. Qudāmah.[41] If this theory is correct, we may have identified another scholar to whom Ibn al-Muᶜtazz was indebted. For we know of one Abū ʾl-Qāsim Jaᶜfar b. Qudāmah [b. Ziyād] (d. 319/931) who was a close companion of Ibn al-Muᶜtazz, as attested by *Kitāb al-Aghānī*. One might also suggest that the first verse example in *Kitāb al-Badīᶜ* (a line by ᶜAbd al-Raḥmān b. ᶜAlī b. ᶜAlqamah quoted to illustrate *istiᶜārah*) was borrowed from Jaᶜfar b. Qudāmah, for this same example is found in a tradition on Ḥammād b. Isḥāq al-Mawṣilī, who was Jaᶜfar's teacher and himself a pupil of Abū ᶜUbaydah and al-Aṣmaᶜī.[42] One could go even further and speculate that wherever there are agreements between *Kitāb al-Badīᶜ* and Qudāmah's *Naqd al-shiᶜr*, these should be attributed to the fact that Jaᶜfar was the teacher of both Ibn al-Muᶜtazz and his own son, Qudāmah. The same kind of speculation could be applied to Thaᶜlab with whom both Ibn al-Muᶜtazz and Qudāmah were acquainted. Both suggestions, however, depend on scanty evidence; the identification of Abū ʾl-Qāsim Jaᶜfar b. Qudāmah b. Ziyād as the father of Qudāmah remains to be proven, and neither Ibn al-Muᶜtazz nor Qudāmah appears to have been intimately acquainted with Thaᶜlab.

Ibn al-Muᶜtazz's contacts with al-Mubarrad seem to have been more frequent than his contacts with Thaᶜlab. One would expect a comparison between *Kitāb al-Badīᶜ* and the works of Mubarrad, notably *al-Kāmil*, to yield interesting results, but Kratchkovsky found no striking parallels between the two works.[43]

THE QUESTION OF FOREIGN INFLUENCE

A few words remain to be said on the question of a possible foreign origin of some of the early terminology and definitions of figures of speech in

[41] Bonebakker, *Notes*, 16–20, 27–9. [42] Ibid., 19. [43] "Deux chapitres", 40–1.

Arabic. This question was first raised by Ṭāhā Ḥusayn; it has never been answered satisfactorily, and probably cannot be answered as long as the early history of Arabic literary theory is still largely unknown. Comparisons between Greek and Arabic texts therefore lack cogency. The traditions in Ḥātimī's *Ḥilyah* and in the other texts referred to earlier were largely unknown in Ṭāhā Ḥusayn's time. They were also apparently unknown to Kratchkovsky at the time he wrote his introduction to *Kitāb al-Badīᶜ* and the other papers referred to in this chapter. If the traditions transmitted in such texts are genuine, one would have to begin looking for foreign influence as far back as the early days of the ᶜAbbasids. The answer to the question may therefore depend to a large extent on the outcome of further research on these traditions and their authors. Could, for example, early authors such as al-Aṣmaᶜī, Abū ᶜUbaydah, Ḥammād al-Rāwiyah (d. *c.* 156/772), and Abū ᶜAmr b. al-ᶜAlāʾ have discussed *istiᶜārah*, as al-Bāqillānī (d. 403/1013) asserts?[44] Or is this an anachronism in the sense that, even though they analyzed instances of metaphor, they did not use a technical term for it? Let us assume that the term was indeed current in their days, which seems likely, since it would be difficult to eliminate or paraphrase in our texts of the traditions (though the term *mathal* might have served instead): was this due to the influence of a Graeco-Roman tradition that had not died out and found imitators among students of Arabic poetry who then substituted a terminology of their own making? Or did these terms come from a native tradition which went back to the Umayyad or even the pre-Islamic period?

More frequently the suggestion has been made that it was the generation of Ibn al-Muᶜtazz and Qudāmah which first came under the influence of Greek rhetoric, particularly the *Rhetoric* and *Poetics* of Aristotle, translations of which are known to have existed in their days. For various reasons Aristotelian influence is unlikely; on the one hand no reference is made to either work, and on the other hand it is difficult to see how these two works could have been of any use to the Arabic literary theorists who were dealing with categories of literature quite different from those discussed by Aristotle.[45] Still the absence of any traces of Aristotle's *Rhetoric* and *Poetics* in the *Naqd al-shiᶜr* of Qudāmah is surprising, since influence from other philosophical texts can be demonstrated there. The only safe assumption seems to be that influence from the *Rhetoric* and the *Poetics* or any Hellenistic

[44] *Iᶜjāz*, 108. On al-Bāqillānī, see pp. 364–5, above.

[45] This was most clearly demonstrated, in the centuries that followed, by the digests of the *Poetics* by Fārābī, Avicenna and Averroes; see Heinrichs, *Arabische Dichtung und griechische Poetik*, and Bonebakker, "Reflections", 192–3, 196–7.

writings on the subject of literary theory, if it ever existed, remained marginal and did not lead at any time to the integration of Greek rhetoric into the Arabic system.[46] This appears nowhere more clearly than in the terminology; as far as Ibn al-Muᶜtazz is concerned, the only close parallel between his terminology and that of the rhetoricians of the West is the use of the term *iltifāt* which could very well be a literal translation of the term "apostrophe". Since, however, this term is a definition in itself, the agreement is likely to be coincidental.

IBN AL-MUᶜTAZZ AND QUDĀMAH B. JAᶜFAR

Together with *Kitāb al-Badīᶜ*, the *Naqd al-shiᶜr* of Qudāmah b. Jaᶜfar is one of the most frequently quoted texts from the early period. Ibn Abī ᵓl-Iṣbaᶜ considers both works classics and takes as a basis for his own work the terminology of both Ibn al-Muᶜtazz and Qudāmah.[47] It is appropriate, therefore, to conclude with a few observations on Qudāmah. It is at least probable that *Kitāb al-Badīᶜ* is the older of the two treatises; and that Qudāmah must have known *Kitāb al-Badīᶜ* and borrowed from it.[48] Neither of these conclusions is certain; one could argue, for instance, that even if *Naqd al-shiᶜr* is later than *Kitāb al-Badīᶜ*, the two authors might have written their treatises independently using the same texts and traditions as a basis for their terminology and examples. A related question is that of the identity of Abū ᵓl-Qāsim Jaᶜfar b. Qudāmah b. Ziyād, referred to above. If this person was indeed the father of the author of *Naqd al-shiᶜr*, then Qudāmah could hardly have ignored the treatise written by a close friend of his father. One would have to assume that he deliberately chose to omit any mention of the existence of the work of his illustrious predecessor, or that he felt that the scope of his own treatise was so much different that he could conveniently disregard it. Again this hinges on facts which have not been established with certainty. According to Ibn al-Nadīm, Qudāmah wrote a book against Abū Tammām (*Kitāb Diryāq al-fikr fīmā ᶜāba bihī Abā Tammām*), as well as a book against Ibn al-Muᶜtazz (*Kitāb al-Radd ᶜalā Ibn al-Muᶜtazz*). In Yāqūt's biography of Qudāmah, which quotes the titles of Qudāmah's works from Ibn al-Nadīm, the titles appear as *Kitāb al-Diryāq* and *Kitāb al-Radd ᶜalā Ibn al-Muᶜtazz fīmā ᶜāba bihī Abā Tammām*.[49] Which of the two is the correct title of the book? In *Naqd al-shiᶜr*, Qudāmah quotes Abū Tammām only twice, once to show how he imitated the pre-Islamic poet, al-Aᶜshā, and in a second even less complimentary reference to show

46 See Bürgel, "Remarques". 47 *Taḥrīr*, 83. 48 *Naqd al-shiᶜr*, introd., 6–7, 29–30.
49 Ibn al-Nadīm, *Fihrist*, Tajaddud, 144/Dodge, I, 285; Yāqūt, *Irshād*, VI, 204.

how Abū Tammām built a whole verse around a meaningless term in the rhyme.[50] Qudāmah's attitude towards Abū Tammām, as evidenced by these two passages, suggests that he wrote a work against Abū Tammām rather than a work in which he repudiated Ibn al-Muᶜtazz's criticism of Abū Tammām, which would mean that the second work criticized Ibn al-Muᶜtazz in more general terms. But would the existence of such a work (the title of which does not specify that it was a refutation of *Kitāb al-Badīᶜ*) in itself be sufficient to explain one of the most curious facts resulting from a comparison of *Naqd al-shiᶜr* with *Kitāb al-Badīᶜ*, namely the absence of the term *badīᶜ* from the former? The term had been common for half a century, perhaps even longer, and by using it Qudāmah would not necessarily have indicated that he was following in the footsteps of his rival. Yet no other explanation comes to mind. Qudāmah may have felt that his own treatise was vastly superior to that of his predecessor, since it set forth, for the first time, logical and therefore well-founded criteria for distinguishing good from bad poetry. If he had referred, even obliquely, to the work of Ibn al-Muᶜtazz, he would have had to admit that it had sections on the infelicitous use of the figures of speech which would have invalidated part of his own claim to originality. Qudāmah's systematic classification of the figures of speech may be suggested as a second motive. He may have feared that his book would attract less attention if he declared himself a follower of Ibn al-Muᶜtazz or conspicuously agreed with him in matters of terminology (cf. Qudāmah's discussion of the *istiᶜārah*!).[51] Perhaps he hoped that by keeping himself wholly independent of his predecessor, his more systematic approach would secure him a place in the history of Arabic literature as the first critic to deal with literary theory and criticism in all its aspects. It must be admitted that, if these were Qudāmah's intentions, he was to a large extent successful; his *Naqd al-shiᶜr* is quoted hardly less frequently than *Kitāb al-Badīᶜ*.

It is curious that the framework of both treatises was almost forgotten, and that only the terminology, the definitions, and some of the examples continued to be a subject of discussion. In the case of Qudāmah it is easy to see that there were good reasons to disregard the framework of his treatise in future discussions. This framework may have helped him to arrange his material in a logical and orderly fashion, but was too rigid and exclusive to lend itself to further development.[52] In the case of Ibn al-Muᶜtazz, the lack of interest in the book's original purpose has to be explained along somewhat different lines. His book was built around a thesis which, while widely discussed in Ibn al-Muᶜtazz's own days, could not have held the

[50] *Naqd al-shiᶜr*, 46, 141. [51] Ibid., 103–4. [52] Cf. pp. 356ff, 370.

same fascination for future generations even though, as with similar discussions on the relative merits of groups of early poets, the debate was never closed. The fate of the book might have been different if Ibn al-Muᶜtazz had outlined his thesis in greater detail and had dwelt at length on the historical importance of *badīᶜ* as one of the characteristics of a new trend in the poetry of the ᶜAbbasid period.[53] The aims and characteristics of this trend, which often appears to us as marked as it is difficult to define, must have been clear to the author of *Kitāb al-Badīᶜ*, who was not only an authority on ancient poetry, but also a poet of considerable merit peculiarly associated with the development of the modern genre of descriptive poetry (*waṣf*).[54]

53 It may have been Ibn al-Muᶜtazz's very success in isolating the components of *badīᶜ* that pushed a definition of its contribution to the modern movement into the background; cf. Stetkevych, "Toward a redefinition".

54 See pp. 165, 217–18.

CHAPTER 22

REGIONAL LITERATURE: EGYPT

REGIONAL IDENTITY

In common with general historians, most literary historians view the year 656/1258, in which Baghdad fell to the Mongols, as the end of an era, the ensuing period, lasting until modern times, being considered an age of decadence. While the wisdom of such periodization is strongly to be questioned, it may be useful to point out some significant dates in Egyptian history which might serve as more appropriate terms of reference for the discussion of Egyptian literature.

Only eight years before the fall of Baghdad, the Crusaders of Louis IX had suffered a crushing defeat near the Egyptian town of al-Manṣūrah; the fact that the common people had taken part in the campaign added to its importance. The year in which Baghdad fell also witnessed another, less momentous event: an epidemic raged in Cairo, and one of its victims was the old poet Bahāʾ al-Dīn Zuhayr, who had for the first time given expression to the Egyptian character as we now know it. Thus we might accept 656/1258 as approximately marking the end of our period, albeit for other reasons than those posed by the general historian. On the basis of the two events just described, we might characterize this period as witnessing the maturing of the Egyptian national character within a community of Arab entities. The purpose of this chapter[1] is to try to discover some of the main traits of this character as reflected in creative literature, bearing in mind that the increasing role played by Egypt as a meeting-ground for various trends coming from East and West prepared the developing Arab–Egyptian culture to act both as a focus and as a point of diffusion to a wide circle of Arab lands which enjoyed less political stability and ethnic homogeneity.

If it seems plausible to distinguish the middle of the seventh/thirteenth century for the manifestation of a well-defined Egyptian character, thus

[1] This chapter could not have been written without the work carried out over the past thirty-five years by the late M. Kāmil Ḥusayn and by ʿAbd al-ʿAzīz al-Ahwānī and Shawqī Ḍayf.

concluding a stage in the evolution of Arab culture, no such clear-cut demarcation is possible when we try to look for the embryonic stage in the formation of this character. However, it seems certain that the Arabicization of Egypt progressed at a relatively slow pace compared to that of Syria, Iraq or even some of the eastern parts of the Islamic empire. On the other hand, once the Arabicization of Egypt was complete (about the fourth/tenth century), there was no setback. We might compare the famous complaint of al-Mutanabbī in the fourth/tenth century that in Shiʿb Bawwān in Iran an Arab was "alien of countenance, hand and tongue",[2] or the sixth/twelfth-century grammarian al-Zamakhsharī's dismay at the decline of the Arabic language in the eastern provinces of Islam, with the fact that by the fourth Islamic century the Egyptian monk Severus (Sāwīris) Ibn al-Muqaffaʿ had to labour, with his assistants, through Greek and Coptic texts in order to turn them into Arabic for the benefit of his Coptic readers. The difference is all the more striking when we compare the progress of Arabicization and Islamization on both sides. While the peoples of central Asia readily adopted Islam and only temporarily, as well as partially, the Arabic language, reverting afterwards to their national idioms, with Arabic reserved for collateral use only as a literary vehicle, the Copts of Egypt appropriated the Arabic language for all their needs, with the Coptic language gradually disappearing both as a spoken and as a literary language; by contrast, a great number of Copts kept their Christian faith. Arabic, fast developing as a language of culture – with the added advantage of its establishment for official use some sixty years after the Arab conquest – gradually gained sway over Coptic, which was torn between several dialects, with a tenuous, straggling literary heritage that could not hold its own beside the all-pervading Greek. While this was happening in the sphere of language, Islam must have seemed to more conservative Copts a mere revival of the Arian heresy (which denied the divinity of Christ), which the Egyptian patriarchs had been combating for more than two centuries.

For about a century after the Arab conquest, political activity was confined to the ruling Arab community in the garrison town (*miṣr*) of al-Fusṭāṭ. Soon al-Fusṭāṭ grew into a metropolis, while the Arab community itself spread all over Egypt, generally taking up quarters at grazing areas on the outskirts of the arable lands. The Arab community of Egypt was involved in the internal strife in the Arabian peninsula that started during the reign of the third caliph, ʿUthmān; but there are indications that Egyptian interests came to the fore at important junctures, strengthened by

[2] *Dīwān*, II, 452.

the feeling that Egypt was geographically isolated from the mass of the domains of the caliphate.[3] The economic policies which the ᶜAbbasids followed in the province not only bred general discontent and led to frequent armed uprisings among the Coptic population, but also withdrew practically all the privileges the Arab community had enjoyed until then, leaving them no better off than their Coptic neighbours. The separation between the Arab–Egyptians and the central government in Baghdad was clinched by the former's wavering attitude during the civil war that raged after the death of Hārūn al-Rashīd, and led to the consolidation of power in the hands of al-Maᵓmūn and the "Persian" party. Henceforward the demarcation line between Arab–Egyptians (*miṣriyyūn*) and Copts became more and more vague, almost dwindling to a difference between two denominations, especially when most Arabs began to drop their tribal affiliation and use instead a *nisbah* derived from their home town or region.[4]

THE EMERGENCE OF A REGIONAL LITERATURE

Poetry

While it can be shown that Arab–Egyptians acquired a sense of regional identity at a relatively early stage, it is more difficult to trace the beginnings of a regional Arabic literature in Egypt. Most scholars have tended to link its appearance with the emergence of Egypt as an independent state under the Tulunids in the second half of the third/ninth century. However, the successes of Aḥmad b. Ṭūlūn, the founder of the dynasty, were due not only to his own qualities but also to the existence in Egypt of a growing society in the process of establishing its own way of life, of which Ibn Ṭūlūn was rather the expression than the begetter, and some evidence of a distinct cultural identity can be found in Egyptian literature as early as around the beginning of the third/ninth century, some fifty years before the arrival of Ibn Ṭūlūn, at a date which coincides approximately with the ultimate decline of Arab supremacy and the virtual assimilation of Arab elements within Egyptian society. The first such hint of the existence of a genuinely regional literature – apart from poems connected with local political events, which in literary terms show no particular characteristics that would differentiate them from the common tradition of political poetry in the Umayyad and early ᶜAbbasid periods – occurs in one of the classics of Arabic criticism, the fourth/tenth-century *Wasāṭah* by al-Qāḍī ᵓl-Jurjānī. Referring to Abū Tammām (d. 231/846) as the inaugurator of a philosophizing trend in Arabic poetry, which he condemns, al-Qāḍī ᵓl-Jurjānī clinches his point by observing:

[3] Cf. Maqrīzī, *Mawāᶜiẓ*, I, 300–2. [4] Muᵓnis, "Tārīkh", 370.

In this I am only upholding Abū Tammām's own case against Yūsuf al-Sarrāj, Egypt's poet at that time; for Abū Tammām says:

> It's enough to make Zuhayr[5] turn in his grave!
> When did *his* verse ever demand glosses derived from Hippocrates the Physician?
> Poetry should flow sweetly through our hearts like a stream caressed by basil.[6]

We know nothing more about Yūsuf al-Sarrāj, and none of his poetry is to be found in the anthologies now extant (regrettably, the earliest anthology devoted to Egyptian poets, the fourth/tenth-century *Shuʿarāʾ Miṣr* by al-Ṣūlī, is considered lost). However, three important facts are implied in the full text of Abū Tammām's poem as it appears in his *Dīwān*: firstly, that Yūsuf al-Sarrāj actually got his nickname from being a saddler (*sarrāj*), an indication that he was probably Egyptian by origin, since at this time Arabs looked down on manual trades; second, that he was fond of (presumably inept) archaisms, which again suggests that he was not a "pure" Arab; and last, that his poetry defied conventional analysis (according to Abū Tammām and al-Qāḍī ʾl-Jurjānī) because of its pseudo-philosophical content. While this tells us little enough about Yūsuf al-Sarrāj himself, it does suggest that Abū Tammām may have owed the philosophical orientation of his later style to the days of his apprenticeship in al-Fusṭāṭ, his satire of al-Sarrāj revealing only a first reaction to be followed by a gradual assimilation of the new style.

Fortunately, we have more biographical data about another important figure of the same period, the mystic sage Dhū ʾl-Nūn al-Miṣrī (d. 246/861). Dhū ʾl-Nūn, who was of Nubian origin, apparently spent the greater part of his life in the town of his birth, Akhmīm in Upper Egypt, which had managed, from Pharaonic through Graeco–Roman to Arab times, to retain its reputation as a seat of learning and an industrial centre. He was reported to be "versed in the old script", which meant either Greek or Coptic or both. If this is true, and it seems natural enough, he must have acquired such knowledge from the monasteries which spread along the Nile valley both in Upper and Lower Egypt. But he was also a traditionist (*muḥaddith*) generally accepted as trustworthy. He appears to have kept aloof from the dogmatic controversies of his day, notably the thorny question of whether the Qurʾān was created in time or coeternal with God;[7] subjected to the Muʿtazilī inquisition in Baghdad, he seems to have managed to avoid committing himself either way. He was even less inclined to involve himself in public affairs, unlike the early mystics who appeared in Alexandria during the turbulent years of the civil war which followed the death of Hārūn al-Rashīd. His brand of Sufism was of a contemplative,

[5] Zuhayr b. Abī Sulmā, a famous pre-Islamic poet, see *CHALUP*, ch. 2.

[6] *Wasāṭah*, 20; Abū Tammām, *Dīwān*, IV, 315–16. [7] See p. 5.

individualistic character. The authenticity of the sayings attributed to him in *Ḥilyat al-awliyāʾ* by Abū Nuʿaym al-Iṣfahānī (d. 430/1038) and other sources must be critically examined before any conclusions may be drawn from them; however, for their sheer simplicity and crystalline purity we cannot hesitate long in accepting these lines:

Seek your peace of mind
 as I did find:
I've found a haven
 of love requited.
Whenever I stray
 He draws near me;
When I draw near
 He comes closer still.[8]

There is little doubt that Dhū ʾl-Nūn's influence was great, particularly when he moved to al-Fusṭāṭ, where he had many disciples. Several miraculous events were reported to have happened to him during his life and even at his funeral. If we accept the sayings and acts attributed to him as representative of a popular attitude, without regard to their historical truth, we may note a certain disinclination to debate points of doctrine compensated by an emotional faith in the mysterious, unfathomable, all-pervading presence of an omnipotent but bountiful and loving God. The vaguely religious and easy-going attitude of most Egyptians is noted even today; however, nobody should jump to the conclusion that this is a constant trait of the Egyptian character, the heated debates and bloody trials of the Roman and Byzantine periods offering convincing proof of an opposite disposition. Be this as it may, the philosophizing tradition, if the surviving references to Yūsuf al-Sarrāj offer sufficient proof that there was one, was to be set back for some time to come.

Early sīrah literature and jurisprudence

The first two centuries of the Islamic era witnessed the growth of two main literary activities, in which Egypt played an important role: the *sīrah* (biography of the Prophet),[9] and *fiqh* (Islamic jurisprudence). Both depended, as their chief source, on the *sunnah* or sayings and practice of the Prophet. It seems that the father of Islamic historiography, the Medinan Muḥammad b. Isḥāq (*c*. 85–150/704–67), first conceived the idea of writing a biography of the Prophet when he was in Alexandria in 115/733, and met several Egyptian traditionists from whom he got much of his material. ʿAbd

[8] *Ḥilyat al-awliyāʾ*, IX, 344. Further poems by Dhū ʾl-Nūn are quoted pp. 240–1, above.
[9] For a general outline of the *sīrah* genre, see *CHALUP*, ch. 17.

al-Malik b. Hishām, who edited Ibn Isḥāq's *Sīrah* (which as a consequence is commonly known as the *Sīrah* of Ibn Hishām), came to Egypt as a young man from Basra, where he was born, and died at al-Fusṭāṭ in *c.* 218/833. Ibn Hishām, a linguist as well as a historian, described his contribution to the *Sīrah* as mainly a process of refining and condensing and of eliminating digressions and much interpolation. Thus the *sīrah*-form took final shape as a literary genre, to be followed in its main lines by medieval heroic legends,[10] while the material of Ibn Hishām's *Sīrah* became a quarry for countless authors, who drew upon it freely in more popular productions, such as verse panegyrics of the Prophet and rhymed-prose *mawlid*s (celebrations of the Prophet's birthday), two of the most common entertainments not only at religious but also at purely social festivities, characteristic of the Arab and Egyptian way of life until very recently.

Al-Layth b. Saᶜd (d. 197/812), a Persian by origin but Egyptian by birth, was a contemporary of one of the first leading jurists in Islam, Mālik b. Anas,[11] whom al-Layth met and corresponded with. Although al-Layth gave his own *fatwā*s (legal opinions) on matters of public concern, the younger generation of Egyptian jurists were more inclined to follow those of Mālik, since the latter lived in the original seat of Islam, where the traditions of the Prophet were considered to be consolidated in common usage. It seems that al-Layth himself did not contest this preference. At the turn of the century, another leading jurist from the Hijaz, Muḥammad b. Idrīs al-Shāfiᶜī (150–204/767–820), who for many years had been a disciple of Mālik but had also studied in Iraq and become versed in the syllogistic method of the Ḥanafīs,[12] came to live and teach in Egypt, where he perfected his method. Al-Shāfiᶜī's teachings seemed more congenial to the Egyptians, because they effected a delicate balance between Prophetic *sunnah* and local usage. Perhaps, too, al-Shāfiᶜī himself was the type of jurist the Egyptians desired: his emotional temperament can be deduced from the fact that he loved poetry and is supposed occasionally to have composed verses himself; and though he was not actually a Shīᶜī, a story about his involvement in a Shīᶜī conspiracy in Yemen when still a young man made him all the more likeable, for the Egyptians, short of embracing the Shīᶜī cause, had developed a reverence for the descendants of the Prophet which verged, in later times and with simpler souls, on sheer idolatry. It should be mentioned as an instance of the deep-seated conformism – whether it be viewed as group solidarity or as conservatism – of the typical Egyptian that some found even such a slight shift as that from the Mālikī to the Shāfiᶜī school an actual mischief. Thus a certain ᶜĪsā b. al-Munkadir, who was

[10] Cf. ch. 8. [11] Cf. *CHALUP*, 272–3. [12] Cf. *CHALUP*, 477–8.

appointed chief judge of Egypt, used to shout at al-Shāfiʿī: "You! When you came to this town we were of one mind; we were like one man. Now you have sown discord and bred mischief among us!" The words of the Muslim judge bear a striking resemblance to many a phrase in Severus Ibn al-Muqaffaʿ's "Lives of the Patriarchs" relating the discords within the Egyptian church. It is curious how a keen sense of belonging could foster rancours that led to mutual destruction: just as the Egyptian church had witnessed many fierce battles between Orthodox and Monophysite, so the rivalry between Mālikīs and Shāfiʿīs now led to frequent scuffles, one of which was reported to have involved al-Shāfiʿī himself and ultimately to have caused his death.

Chancery prose

Among the many factors which enter into the making of a given literature, those which shape the role of the writer himself are perhaps the most direct and obvious. The Arabic literature of the pre-Islamic period was essentially the product of the tribe's poet or orator, mysteriously inspired, filled with the spirit of the tribe's ancestors; by contrast, the main corpus of the literature of the first two centuries of Islam is clearly the work of men deeply involved in the theological, political and racial issues of the day. The dominant influence of subsequent centuries was undoubtedly that of the *kātib* or secretary. The *kātib* might be a "secretary of state" or minister, or merely the secretary of a governor or local judge, but the difference in rank did not imply a difference of category. The ideals of the profession were the same, and to varying degrees they left their imprint on official and on "creative" prose alike.

The drafting of official documents leaves no room for self-expression; reticence and decorum must be strictly observed and the taste and aims of the ruler fully adopted. However, state documents are rarely composed of mere formalities which leave the zealous scribe with nothing more to do than play with verbal effects. More often they serve practical purposes, and in delicate situations might call for the most refined handling of a difficult subject, and the most expert distribution of effective nuances and balancing of contradictory innuendoes. On such occasions, an official scribe may rise to unusual heights of functional rhetoric. Few specimens of such writing have been preserved by historians; fortunately, some of these are Egyptian. Special mention should be made of the epistle composed by Ibrāhīm b. ʿAbdullāh al-Najīramī for the fourth/tenth-century Egyptian ruler al-Ikhshīd,[13] in reply to one from the Byzantine emperor Romanus Lecapinus.

[13] See p. 12.

The character of al-Ikhshīd, a self-made ruler, was a curious combination of ruthless ambition, affected modesty, cunning and greed. Romanus, as can be gathered from al-Ikhshīd's reply, had approached the latter for an exchange of prisoners and trade, but in a manner calculated to show the Byzantine emperor's superiority. There can be little doubt that al-Ikhshīd rejoiced at receiving Romanus's epistle. He decided to grant his requests, while giving a suitable rebuff to his presumptuous attitude. The reply had to be couched in friendly terms without showing undue cordiality, Romanus's proposals accepted with dignity, and his arrogance met with equal hauteur, for he was an enemy although he was offering peace. Al-Najīramī, whose draft was approved by al-Ikhshīd in preference to several other attempts, was rightly proud of his literary achievement.[14]

EPISTOLOGRAPHY IN THE FATIMID AND AYYUBID PERIODS

As well as the requirements of individual political masters, the changing style of political regimes also influenced literary production and especially official documents. The canonization of rhymed prose (*sajᶜ*) and other verbal tricks and their speedy invasion of most forms of writing, including chancery documents and historiography, throughout the Arab domain including Egypt, is more easily understood when we remember that political power in most regions of the ᶜAbbasid empire from the latter half of the third/ninth century fell gradually into the hands of barbarian mercenaries, mostly manumitted slaves, who might be expected to appreciate a ringing rhyme or an unsuspected pun (even a poor one) above all else. At the same time, local developments in Egypt were to produce some documents of a highly individual stamp.

In more than one respect the Fatimid period (358–567/969–1171) marks a crystallization of the "Egyptian way of life" whose beginnings we noted at about the turn of the third/ninth century. The Ikhshidids, no less than the Tulunids before them, had considered themselves vassals of the caliph in Baghdad, and Baghdad had been looked up to as the source of everything stylish: the Iraqi writer was considered superior to the Egyptian, and masons were brought from Sāmarrā in Iraq to build Ibn Ṭūlūn's famous mosque. Yet it seems that both Ibn Ṭūlūn and al-Ikhshīd after him were holding in check more radical aspirations. The staunch resistance deployed against the invading troops of the caliphate and the ruthless measures taken by those troops to liquidate all supporters of the Tulunid regime prove that

[14] Full text in Ibn Saᶜīd, *Mughrib*, I, 167–72; Qalqashandī, *Ṣubḥ*, VII, 10–18.

the re-establishment of the authority of Baghdad was not just a *coup d'état*, but an attack designed to check the growth of a new, independent society. By comparison, the ease with which the Fatimid troops made their way to al-Fusṭāṭ (the description of the expedition offered by the historians recalls the splendour of a pageant rather than the grimness of war) indicates a well-founded belief on the part of most Egyptians that the new era, which made the new capital, Cairo, the feared rival of Baghdad, was certain to be more propitious to their self-realization.

The Fatimid state came into being as the implementation of a particular branch of Shīʿī ideology, Ismaʿilism, which owed much to Greek philosophy and Christian theology in giving its own solutions to such problems of Islamic dogma as the attributes of God and the metaphysical interpretation of the Qurʾān,[15] as well as to other more practical ones such as the meaning and scope of theocratic government and even the place of women in Islamic society. When the Fatimid theology became the guiding philosophy of the state, the practical considerations of how to govern a country with deeply rooted traditions that had managed to live through many changes of government and religion obliged the ruling class to place greater emphasis on ritual than on dogma. Many Coptic festivals were freely celebrated and were heartily shared in by Muslims, including sometimes the Fatimid caliph himself; the description of the Feast of the Epiphany (*ghiṭās*) in commemoration of the birth of Christ cited by Taqī al-Dīn al-Maqrīzī (d. 845/1442) leaves little doubt that in social life not only Christian but also pagan elements were given free play.[16] While the more abstruse points of Ismāʿīlī doctrine were reserved for initiates, popular practices were looked upon tolerantly by the more philosophically minded, since the doctrine itself gave an "interior" and an "exterior" meaning to almost everything. (This attitude was to have a lasting legacy, for it is clear that it was shared by the Sufis, and when the Ismāʿīlī creed was, to all appearances, completely eradicated in Egypt, Sufism carried on as a powerful institution, disregarding differences of dogma and helping to weld together the disparate elements of society.) However, for all this tolerance, ideological propaganda remained one of the main concerns of the Fatimid state. The caliph was, above all, the Imam of the Age, the infallible leader appointed by God. Since his exterior as imam concealed an interior which was that of the Prime Mover, an imam was not only the seat of all temporal power but also the source of all knowledge. A well-knit system of propaganda, designed to reinforce public acceptance of the Fatimid caliph's sacred character, was carefully devised and put into action with the imam, at

[15] Cf. ch. 23, nn. 12, 71. [16] Maqrīzī, *Mawāʿiẓ*, I, 497–8.

its head, holding special meetings with his closest followers and entering, on more public occasions, into direct contact with the mass of the people. This last procedure was effected through the communal Friday prayers, as well as through caliphal documents.

Official documents

For the historian, S. M. Stern's *Fāṭimid Decrees* provides the English-speaking reader with a detailed general introduction to Fatimid official documents – which differ in a number of significant respects from their ᶜAbbasid counterparts – as well as translations and analyses of ten surviving original specimens. That the Fatimids kept an able and highly organized secretariat seems clear from the guide to chancery practice written by the Fatimid *kātib* Ibn al-Ṣayrafī (d. 542/1147), *Qānūn dīwān al-rasāʾil*; but there is evidence to prove that at least the first, powerful caliphs took it upon themselves to compose some of the more important documents. The Fatimid caliphs considered rhetorical ability a part of the dignity of their high rank, and in the "Biography" of Ustādh Jawdhar (see below), who held something like the post of chamberlain at the Fatimid court at al-Mahdiyyah in North Africa, before the conquest of Egypt, we find several documents and addresses which the author ascribes explicitly to the caliph al-Manṣūr, both before and after his succession to the imamate. It matters little that the wording of these and similar documents may not all have been the caliph's own work, but that of some *kātib*, for some contain ideas and expressions which could not possibly be attributed to a scribe. Among the more interesting passages, the following introduces a theme rarely found in documents other than Fatimid ones; it occurs in an epistle from the caliph al-Mustanṣir (427–87/1036–94) to his representative (*dāᶜī*) in Yemen, ᶜAlī b. Muḥammad al-Ṣulayḥī,[17] conferring certain favours and higher titles on the recipient and his sons (a whole series of such letters has survived, and is published under the title *al-Sijillāt al-mustanṣiriyyah*):

> The Commander of the Faithful is not ignorant of the ways of your noble and pious spouse, Protectress of the Faithful, that zealous, God-fearing, righteous and constant promoter of the faith, a virtuous lady such as ever pursue good works, never failing to relieve the broken and succour the destitute, in never-failing compassion towards the infant and the aged alike. Verily the tree of her hopes shall she find laden with fruits of noble meed, and her deeds shall stand witness for her on Judgement Day.[18]

Into such passages, within the bombastic, flowery language characteristic not only of the chancery documents but of all the prose of the period, a

[17] See pp. 444, 454–60. [18] *Al-Sijillāt al-mustanṣiriyyah*, 36; cf. Hamdānī, "Letters".

more lively spirit is infused. Moreover, the Fatimid imam being, in a sense, inspired, his *obiter dicta* and casual remarks were piously recorded, and the few specimens of these preserved in the "Biography of Ustādh Jawdhar" suffice to indicate the existence of another type of prose, stamped by the same natural, functional rhetoric that was common at the beginning of the Islamic era,[19] with the difference that here the language is of course more modern. There is something startling in the vehemence of some of al-Manṣūr's letters, especially when he complains of the misdemeanours of certain members of his own family; but we need only remember the letters that passed between the second "Orthodox" caliph, ᶜUmar b. al-Khaṭṭāb, and his governor in Egypt, ᶜAmr b. al-ᶜĀṣ, to conclude that there was nothing altogether unprecedented in al-Manṣūr's letters except, perhaps, that they were all too human. However, the theoretically sacred status of the imam in the Ismāᶜīlī creed notwithstanding, the curious blend of worldliness and spirituality found in these letters seems the key not only to the personal behaviour of the Fatimid rulers, but also to the whole outlook of the society they tried to establish.

We do not possess anything like a corpus of literary texts comparable to al-Manṣūr's informal letters, as preserved in the "Biography of Ustādh Jawdhar"; these neither inaugurated a new tradition nor re-established an old one, and if they had any literary influence at all, it was through the historical writings of the period (it might be more apt to treat such ostensibly historical material as a distinct literary genre, giving it the name of narrative prose, under which heading the "Biography" will be discussed below). Meanwhile, the few sparks of realism which appeared in the earlier Fatimid documents were soon smothered by pedantic allusions, irrelevant descriptions and jarring metaphors. The author of this metamorphosis, al-Qāḍī ᶜAbd al-Raḥīm b. ᶜAlī al-Fāḍil (529–96/1135–1200), was a man who managed to straddle comfortably the decline of the Fatimid era and the emergence of the Ayyubid state. Saladin is reported to have said: "I took Egypt not by force of arms but by al-Qāḍī ʾl-Fāḍil's pen." Many of al-Qāḍī ʾl-Fāḍil's contemporaries claimed that he introduced a new style (to which they gave his name); modern scholars deny this, since flowery language was anything but new in ᶜAbbasid poetry or prose generally. However, there are some historical grounds for the claim: the ornate style dominant since the fourth/tenth century was probably held in check for a while in Egypt itself by the example of the Fatimid imams. The fact remains, outside all honours claimed or apologies offered, that "al-Qāḍī ʾl-Fāḍil's manner" was nothing but mannerism.

[19] Cf. *CHALUP*, chs. 3, 5.

The informal epistle

Official documents were not the only literary form to be contaminated by mannerism. The genre of the informal epistle (*al-risālah al-ikhwāniyyah*), in the hands of Jāḥiẓ and Hamadhānī, had proved flexible enough to express the changing moods of sophisticated societies; but now stylized forms consecrated by "al-Qāḍī ᵓl-Fāḍil's manner" replaced what little spontaneity the medium still possessed with a sort of pale, insipid beauty. It is certainly a healthy breeze that blows from the letters of Muḥammad b. Muḥriz al-Wahrānī (d. 574/1178). Little is known about al-Wahrānī's life; the most valuable information is to be found in his own letters. He was born in Wahrān (Oran, in present-day Algeria) but settled in Egypt, where he made his living as a copyist and gave a daughter in marriage to an Egyptian; he travelled occasionally to Syria, where he died. It seems either that he was not satisfied with working as a copyist, or that his eyesight failed with age, so that he had to shift for himself, and sought to ingratiate himself with a number of potential patrons by writing panegyric poetry, in the turbulent days which witnessed the fall of the Fatimids and the rise of the Ayyubids. Whether his satirical prose, on the other hand, was genuinely intended as criticism of his masters, or merely follows the literary convention of buffoonery or the "jocular manner", as described a generation or so later by the Andalusian critic, Ḥāzim al-Qarṭājannī (d. 684/1285),[20] it is difficult to decide. However, one thing is certain: he ridiculed al-Qāḍī ᵓl-Fāḍil's manner, throwing off the yoke of rhyme together with all its paraphernalia of verbal refinements – though when confronting al-Fāḍil himself he was generally on his guard, seeing that the proverbially serene dignity of the Ayyubid sultan's *kātib* would not allow any mockery of his person. The *Manām* ("Dream") – a piece of writing, also in the form of a letter, which was highly praised by the biographer Ibn Khallikān (d. 681/1282)[21] – is a parody of the more famous *Risālat al-Ghufrān* of al-Maᶜarrī. Although the parodic use of quotations from serious literature has always been one of the main devices of the "jocular manner", the parody as an avowed literary genre has hardly been represented in Arabic literature until very recent times. Al-Wahrānī may be considered one of its pioneers.

[20] "The enunciation should lower itself to disreputable qualities, should not stop at the limits of shame nor hesitate to descend to the lowest things", *Minhāj al-bulaghāᵓ*, 331.

[21] Trans. de Slane, *Biographical Dictionary*, III, 95: "This work, copies of which are very common, is a proof of the buoyant humour, acute mind and accomplished wit possessed by the author."

NARRATIVE PROSE FROM THE TULUNIDS TO THE FATIMIDS

Historiography has always been the handmaid of politics, but contains, as well, the two basic elements of all literary production: entertainment and edification. Among the earliest forms of history, genealogy (probably reflecting the still more primitive cult of ancestor-worship) formed an essential part of pre-Islamic culture: one of the assets of the first caliph, Abū Bakr, was that of being a good genealogist. The historical material included in the Qurʾān moved away from genealogy to give a universal conception of history as being essentially a covenant between God and man. The first Umayyad caliph Muʿāwiyah's well-known interest in history[22] seems to furnish a meeting-ground between Islamic and pre-Islamic concepts. When Islam itself started to "make history" in the figurative sense, it also had to make history in the literal one. Precedents attributed to the Prophet and his first successors laid the legal foundation of the new era and had therefore to be recorded. There was no clear dividing-line between tradition (*ḥadīth*) and historical accounts (*akhbār*, sing. *khabar*), except that true traditionists were concerned only with the sayings and acts of the Prophet and observed strict rules to sift the material that was transmitted orally for many generations after his death; the early historians, being less stringent, were severely attacked by the former group. However, historians proved hardly less indispensable than traditionists; in one field at least, their work was of prime importance to the newly established state: namely the accounts of Islamic invasions (*maghāzī*),[23] since the status of the annexed lands and their inhabitants was determined according to whether they were "surrendered by negotiation" or "conquered by force". This question opened up new vistas to regional history, and books on *maghāzī*, such as Ibn ʿAbd al-Ḥakam's *Futūḥ Miṣr*, while supplying necessary information about the proper administration of new territories, also included much legendary material about the ancient history of the lands in question.[24] In the meantime, history had developed as an independent discipline. As a pure science pursued for its own sake, albeit with an eye to contemporary demands, it had to record incidents of common interest with the greatest possible accuracy and thoroughness. Hence the emergence of the annalistic form, used by most historians from Muḥammad b. Jarīr al-Ṭabarī (d. 310/923) to the Egyptian chronicler of the Napoleonic invasion, ʿAbd al-Raḥmān al-Jabartī (d. 1240/1825). Concomitant with the annalistic and regional forms and infiltrating through them was the other, common form of the biography. The biography of the Prophet was soon followed by that

[22] See p. 137. [23] See *CHALUP*, 344–5. [24] Cf. p. 138.

of his Companions; other biographical works were, in most cases, devoted to single categories of subject, e.g. grammarians, men of letters, jurists, etc., thus supplying material for the history of civilization or other subclasses of history. The "Biographical Dictionary" of Aḥmad b. Muḥammad Ibn Khallikān, who lived and worked for much of his life in Egypt, crowned these efforts in the seventh/thirteenth century; it became and has remained a standard reference-work, and ushered in a train of similar, general compilations, although specialized biographical works (*ṭabaqāt*) dealing with single categories of subject continued to appear. Regional history gave birth to a more developed form, that of districts (*khiṭaṭ*, the chief example referred to in this chapter being the Mamlūk historian al-Maqrīzī's *al-Mawāʿiẓ wa'l-iʿtibār fī dhikr al-khiṭaṭ wa'l-āthār*), which apparently began in Egypt as early as the third/ninth century.[25] *Futūḥ Miṣr* ("The Conquest of Egypt"), already referred to, by Ibn ʿAbd al-Ḥakam (d. 257/871) is mainly a book of *maghāzī*, while *al-Wulāh* and *al-Quḍāh* by Muḥammad b. Yūsuf al-Kindī (283–350/895–961) are biographical works dealing with Egyptian governors and judges respectively. Of the voluminous works of the Fatimid historians, Muḥammad b. ʿUbayd Allāh al-Musabbiḥī (366–420/977–1029), ʿAbd al-ʿAzīz b. ʿAbd al-Raḥmān b. Muhadhdhab (see below), Muḥammad b. Saʿd al-Qurṭī and al-Rawḥī, only a few excerpts survive, giving only a faint idea of their literary value.[26] The chief specimens of narrative prose to be discussed below belong, by their authorship as well as by their subjects, to an earlier period. Centred around the Tulunid and Ikhshidid dynasties, they are more than dynastic history, which is often an abridged form of annal: in place of mere tabulations of a ruler's succession and the chief events of his reign, these narratives offer life-pictures which are not without sympathetic insights and do not spurn popular legend, but manage nevertheless to remain sober and realistic.

The great exponent of this genre is Aḥmad b. Yūsuf al-Miṣrī (d. 340/951). His father, Yūsuf b. Ibrāhīm, was a *kātib* in the service of Ibrāhīm b. al-Mahdī, the ʿAbbasid prince who had briefly headed a revolt against the caliph al-Maʾmūn but was better known as a musician. Yūsuf's mother having served as wet-nurse to Ibrāhīm b. al-Mahdī, it seems that relations between the prince and his scribe were more than usually close, hence Yūsuf's nickname of Ibn al-Dāyah ("Son of the Wet-Nurse"), which his son, the historian, inherited and by which he is usually known. On the death of Ibrāhīm, Yūsuf wisely left Iraq for Egypt, where he became a wealthy merchant, keeping at a safe distance from the ʿAbbasid court at al-Fusṭāṭ, though as one of the notables of that city who also had important

[25] Ḥusayn, *Adabunā*, 81. [26] See Fuʾād Sayyid, "Nuṣūṣ ḍāʾiʿah" and "Lumières nouvelles".

connections in the capital, Baghdad, it was both desirable and inevitable that he should come into contact with influential persons around the amir. His son's relations with the Tulunids were equally cautious, for there is no mention that he was ever in their service. Nevertheless he is sometimes called the "Scribe of the Tulunids", probably on account of his biographies of Aḥmad b. Ṭūlūn and his son Khumārawayh. He also wrote a collection of tales to which he gave the title *al-Mukāfaʾah* ("Just Deserts"); only this and fragments of the biography of Ibn Ṭūlūn are extant. *Al-Mukāfaʾah* treats a theme which was popular with Arab story-tellers both before and after Ibn al-Dāyah, that of God's unfailing mercy towards those who bear tribulation with fortitude. ʿAlī b. Muḥammad al-Madāʾinī (135–234/753–849) had written a short book of anecdotes entitled *al-Faraj baʿd al-shiddah* ("Deliverance after Distress") on the same theme, and the subject was taken up again by ʿAbdullāh b. Muḥammad b. Abī ʾl-Dunyā (known as Ibn Abī ʾl-Dunyā, 208–81/823–94) and later by al-Tanūkhī (d. 384/994),[27] both of whom used the same title. Ibn al-Dāyah's originality lies in the morality his tales are made to expound, which is based on utilitarian principles rather than blind faith. Apart from its literary merits, *al-Mukāfaʾah*, besides being partly autobiographical, also helps to establish the text of Ibn al-Dāyah's biography of Ibn Ṭūlūn, which has only survived in a copy incorporated by the Andalusian Abū ʾl-Ḥasan ʿAlī b. Mūsā b. Saʿīd (Ibn Saʿīd, d. 685/1286) in the section of his voluminous history *al-Mughrib* which deals with Egypt. Parts of *al-Mukāfaʾah* draw on the same material as the biography; collation of the relevant passages leaves no doubt as to the authenticity of the text transmitted in *al-Mughrib*, though which of Ibn al-Dāyah's two texts predates the other cannot be ascertained. Ibn al-Dāyah's biography of Ibn Ṭūlūn's son and successor, Khumārawayh, though mentioned by Brockelmann,[28] must be assumed to be lost, if it was ever written: not even excerpts survive. Whatever the case, the two works cannot be spoken of as one book, as does Brockelmann, for the text of the life of Ibn Ṭūlūn incorporated in *al-Mughrib* ends with a clear *finis*.

This biography is sometimes referred to as a *sīrah*, and Ibn al-Dāyah's title is given as "Choicest Accounts of Ibn Ṭūlūn" – clear indications of the author's attitude towards his subject. Ibn Ṭūlūn's character was indeed rich stuff for tragedy. Extremely emotional, highly intelligent, with a relentless will bent solely on achieving his lifelong goal of becoming and remaining a leader of men, he could by turns be tender, ruthless, vicious, cunning; but he was never simple. Under Ibn al-Dāyah's pen he commands our deepest feelings of sympathy and fear. No mere extract from this unique book can do it justice, since much of the writer's art lies in the piecing together of the

[27] See ch. 7, n. 10. [28] *GAL*, I, 149.

numerous episodes collected from eye witnesses. However, one such episode from towards the end of the book will convey something of its flavour:

In that year he entered Tarsus with a mighty host and in great pomp . . . Abū ʾl-ʿAbbās al-Ṭarsūsī (who washed Ibn Ṭūlūn's body after he died), a truthful, clean-living man, said as follows: "There was in Tarsus a ragged Sufi, who had forsaken great wealth and ease to seek God, learned to weave palm-fronds from which he earned his livelihood, and campaigned year after year as a simple foot-soldier. When Ibn Ṭūlūn was in Tarsus, he used to visit him and marvel at his words. One night he said to me: 'Go before me to the house of such a one [i.e the Sufi]; I shall follow hard on your heels. Be sure not to make him feel that deference to my rank requires his compliance, approach him humbly, but tell him how I have been longing to see him and ask him if he is willing to see me.'" Abū ʾl-ʿAbbās said: "I went, found him at home, and said: 'The amir Ibn Ṭūlūn sends you his greetings and says he longs to see you. He is hard on my heels.' The Sufi replied: 'I was angry with him, but your message has won me over.' I repeated Ibn Ṭūlūn's command that the message should be delivered with the utmost courtesy; the Sufi said: 'He can come when he likes.' I hurried back to Ibn Ṭūlūn and found him on his way with only a small entourage; when I told him what had passed he rejoiced and hastened to the meeting. At his approach the Sufi went up to him, saying, 'This duty we owe to our rulers', and Ibn Ṭūlūn wept. When the two of them were alone together, the Sufi said: 'What have you got against God that you run away from him like this? You may shun him, but you cannot escape him. Spare your soul a burden which it cannot bear; do not put your trust in this world, this joyless world; remember that when you return to God, your deeds will go with you.' Ibn Ṭūlūn made no reply, but wept. 'Look,' said the Sufi, turning to me, 'He is quite racked with pain.' Then he looked up at the sky and said: 'Open his eyes; guide him; spare him Your wrath. – Go now in God's keeping, lest you infect me with the love of this world and I yield to my own judgement. God willing, I shall remember you in my prayers.'" When asked by Ibn al-Dāyah how it was that he knew what the hermit had said and could repeat it so exactly, Abū ʾl-ʿAbbās replied that he could not have done so, but that Ibn Ṭūlūn had a confidential secretary who wrote down everything the Sufi said so that the two of them could ponder it afterwards. He added that whenever Ibn Ṭūlūn sent an aide with a verbal message, he had the confidential secretary write it down for reference, and when the messenger came to take leave he would question him to see if he had got the message right; if he had, he was sent on his errand; if not, Ibn Ṭūlūn would throw him in jail and appoint a replacement.[29]

ʿAlī b. Muḥammad al-Balawī al-Madanī (*c.* mid-fourth/tenth century), who wrote another *sīrah* of Ibn Ṭūlūn, followed closely in the footsteps of Ibn al-Dāyah, but his is neither a reshaping nor an imitation of the latter's book; he admits his debt to Ibn al-Dāyah but claims at the same time to be attempting a more detailed and exhaustive work. Comparing the two, it should be noted that al-Balawī not only took more pains with his style than Ibn al-

[29] Ibn Saʿīd, *Mughrib*, I, 117–18.

Dāyah, who is often too unstudied and offhand, but also added many lively touches of his own. For example, Ibn Ṭūlūn took revenge on Shuqayr, the chief of the caliph's intelligence service (*barīd*), for trying to undermine his position as amir by accusing him of fomenting rebellion; this is how Ibn al-Dāyah describes the event:

Aḥmad b. Ṭūlūn had him brought from his house on foot; he was jostled about so severely on the way that he nearly died. Then he was stripped [for flogging] and cried for mercy. When he could cry no more, he was carried out, sent home and put under guard. He died the following day.

This is how al-Balawī describes the same episode:

Aḥmad b. Ṭūlūn had Shuqayr the eunuch brought from his mansion on foot, directing that on the way from his house in Fusṭāṭ to the amir's palace he should be jostled about unmercifully: Shuqayr the eunuch being fat and pampered, Ibn Ṭūlūn designed that he should die of exhaustion; and indeed on arrival he was already half-dead. When at last he was brought before Ibn Ṭūlūn, the latter sent for whips and whipping-posts, had him tied to the posts, and then ignored him. He cried for mercy awhile, till he could cry no more, then collapsed like a dead thing, though not a finger had been laid on him. Ibn Ṭūlūn sent him home, on horseback, and there he died that same evening. Ibn Ṭūlūn then sent certified witnesses to inspect his naked corpse and testify that he had died, not of a beating, but simply because his hour had come.[30]

Al-Ḥasan b. Ibrāhīm b. Zūlāq (306–87/919–98) wrote a life of al-Ikhshīd in imitation of Ibn al-Dāyah's life of Ibn Ṭūlūn and a (lost) life of Khumārawayh; it is quoted by Ibn Saᶜīd and al-Maqrīzī. Ibn Zūlāq has a flair for characterization and follows Ibn al-Dāyah's technique of piecing together episodes heard from eyewitnesses, but is less happy with the general construction, sometimes allowing his narrative to get bogged down by disconnected episodes. One would hesitate to place in the same category another of his works, *Akhbār Sībawayh al-miṣrī* ("The Egyptian Sībawayh"), although it has considerable importance as a social document. "The Egyptian Sībawayh" (his real name was Abū Bakr Muḥammad b. Mūsā al-Kindī al-Ṣayrafī), presumably so nicknamed for his outstanding ability as a grammarian, was also a poet whom al-Thaᶜālibī included in his *Yatīmah*.[31] However, his reputation rested mainly on his eccentricities or, in the eyes of his contemporaries, a kind of madness, which secured for him the rare privilege of blurting out caustic remarks in the faces of the most influential men of his time. Ibn Zūlāq's book consists of a collection of anecdotes (*akhbār*) without any plan, and continues a tradition of books

[30] Ibid., 79; Balawī, *Sīrat Aḥmad b. Ṭūlūn*, 58–9.

[31] Abū Bishr ᶜAmr b. ᶜUthmān Sībawayh (d. 177/793–4) had written the most famous of all Arabic grammars, which was consequently known simply as *al-Kitāb*, ("The Book"). In his *Yatīmah*, Thaᶜālibī cites the men he considers prominent literary figures of his own period.

about "wise fools" already represented in the previous century by such writers as al-Madāʾinī and Ibn Abī ʾl-Dunyā.

Of the rare Fatimid historical texts to have reached us in integral form, special attention must be accorded to *Sīrat al-Ustādh Jawdhar* ("The Life of Ustādh Jawdhar") by his secretary Abū ʿAlī Manṣūr al-ʿAzīzī al-Jawdharī. Jawdhar, the manumitted eunuch slave who held the post of chamberlain to three successive Fatimid caliphs, al-Qāʾim, al-Manṣūr and al-Muʿizz, died when the Fatimid expedition to Egypt had only reached Cyrenaica; but his secretary, Manṣūr, continued in the service of the Fatimid caliphs until the reign of al-Ḥākim (d. 411/1021). While as a historical document the book is of the highest importance, its literary value should not be overlooked. It is a palace history as reported by eyewitnesses, the events being selected by the writer with the aim of showing the confidence his master enjoyed in the eyes of the sacred caliphs. Accounts of revolutions and campaigns are interspersed with money-matters and family vexations, the whole being imbued with a deep veneration which gives the work a peculiar affective unity. Since the narrative records the incidents either as they were imparted to the writer by his master, or on the direct evidence of the caliph's written commands to Jawdhar, the first and second persons gain predominance over the customary third person of biography, a quality which enhances the book's narrative appeal.

Finally, mention must be made of *Sīrat (?Siyar) al-aʾimmah* ("Biographies of the Imams") by ʿAbd al-ʿAzīz b. ʿAbd al-Raḥmān al-Muhadhdhab (after 411/1020), excerpts from which are included in the second part of Ibn Saʿīd's *Mughrib*, and which reveal a writer with an exquisite narrative talent. As against these brief extracts, the emergent popular *sīrah*s (*Sīrat ʿAntar*, etc.),[32] which may also be included in this section, have survived, in later versions, as fully fledged narrative texts of stupendous length. They are, in fact, flagrant deformations of history, but the mere fact that they adopt the historical formula of a recorded narrative is at least symptomatic of the narrators' wish to attach themselves to the genre of the historical *sīrah*. Analytical study of the texts will probably show closer and more significant affinities, due allowance being made for the fact that the folk *sīrah*, ranging widely beyond the facts of history, incorporated more primary mythological structures.

POETRY

From the third/ninth century, four trends combined, with varying emphasis, in shaping the poetic production of Arab Egypt. The same trends

[32] See ch. 8.

were in evidence throughout the Arab world, each associated with the name of one or more exponents whose influence continued in force everywhere for centuries to come. They may be summarized under the following heads: the "licentious" manner (*mujūn*) of Abū Nuwās; the asceticism (*zuhd*) of his contemporary Abū ʾl-ʿAtāhiyah; the descriptive poetry (*waṣf*) of Ibn al-Muʿtazz; the stately and magniloquent idiom, connected especially with panegyric (*madīḥ*), consecrated by Abū Tammām, al-Buḥturī and al-Mutanabbī. In the Egyptian context these trends or genres take on a special, arguably local colouring, and in order to emphasize the particular regional and historical circumstances which fostered their development in Egypt, we shall discuss them in the following order: *mujūn*; *waṣf*; *madīḥ*; and *zuhd*.

The hedonist trend (mujūn)

Rather than speak of a "licentious" or libertine trend (*mujūn*) in Egyptian poetry, it is perhaps more apt to speak of a hedonistic tradition. The rakish but strangely solemn wine-songs of Abū Nuwās, sometimes almost devotional in tone, were perhaps never to be repeated in the whole history of Arabic literature; the true spirit of libertinism, as a long-lived tradition in Arabic poetry, found expression in a careless, cynical, lightly blasphemous attitude; its crystallized form, the "jocular manner" already spoken of in connection with the letters of al-Wahrānī, demanded certain qualifications of its votaries: self-vilification, feigned stupidity, and complete surrender to what normal people consider base instincts – all, in an age of rampant sectarianism, glorified, even raised to the level of a minority cult. Some minor Egyptian poets in the period under discussion were professed "Nuwasists", as boastfully proclaimed by one of them;[33] it seems that the social and cultural climate of the reigns of the Tulunids and Ikhshidids (third–fourth/ninth–tenth centuries) was particularly favourable to this trend: Arabic culture had not yet struck roots deep enough in the Egyptian soil to produce any great poet, and a minor poet could easily compose a few light verses, seasoned with the requisite amount of ribaldry, to gain the favour of a semi-literate amir. The prosperity which characterized this period, after long years of internal strife and unstable economic conditions, made such a trend widely congenial. Thus a certain Saʿīd, known as Qāḍī ʾl-Baqar (either a nickname meaning "Judge of the Kine", or the title of a real judiciary office, "judge to the clan of Baqar"), who acted as a jester of sorts at al-Ikhshīd's court, describes his idea of the good life:

33 ʿImād al-Dīn al-Iṣfahānī, *Kharīdat al-qaṣr*, II, 57.

Wake up to the cup of morn!
heed not good advice, nor scorn!
Grab whatever life may bring;
soon you'll be upon the wing.
Shun the man of paltry mind
to wine and women grossly blind!
Prithee, gracious God, prithee
no redemption grant to me!
Long as I live, I would fain
a toper and a rake remain.[34]

It seems that even during this relatively undeveloped phase, a circle of intimates, most of them *kātib*s and all of them lovers both of poetry and good living, carried on a sort of epistolary conversation in verse. Unfortunately little of this survives, but, from what does, we can picture a group of polished epicureans savouring all the delights life could offer, with as little fuss as possible about what comes or what goes. The Ṣāliḥ of this little elegiac poem by Aḥmad b. Abī ʾl-ʿIṣām is perhaps Ṣāliḥ b. Rashdīn, who was the "lion" of the group. The poem is striking in its simplicity:

Death has undone for Ṣāliḥ
all that Ṣāliḥ has done.
The porter has left his door;
where once he entertained, the mourner cries.
He has been left in the House of Decay,
and in his own house he is bewailed.
What, I wonder, did he say
as he was lowered into the grave?
"Listen to me, O men!
This I tell you out of pity for you:
Seek something better than this world!
The difference is plain to see.
All praise and thanks to God,
every man shall depart and leave his kin."[35]

Later we find another such circle centred round the Fatimid prince Tamīm b. al-Muʿizz (337–74/948–84), who came with his family to Egypt when barely twenty and was soon to find its climate most suitable for his youthful escapades. However, he has been too readily pictured by modern scholars as a prodigal prince, just as he was too simply categorized by tradition as an Egyptian copy of the ʿAbbasid poet-prince Ibn al-Muʿtazz.[36] His *Dīwān*, now available in two editions, calls for the most attentive reading; as a character he is evidently many-sided; as an artist, he has his own way of using the rich tradition of Arabic poetry and the legacy of others besides

[34] Ibn Saʿīd, *Mughrib*, I, 272. [35] Thaʿālibī, *Yatīmah*, I, 361.
[36] Cf. Tamīm b. al-Muʿizz, *Dīwān*, introd., and Ḥusayn, *Fī adab Miṣr al-fāṭimiyyah*, 170–3, 247–52.

Ibn al-Muᶜtazz. On the testimony of his *Dīwān* alone one would hesitate to categorize him as a hedonist, much less a libertine poet.

Ibn Wakīᶜ al-Tinnīsī (d. 393/1003) is a less complicated man, and as a poet he is more committed to the tradition of *mujūn*. He is rather outspoken in his erotic poetry, without, however, falling into the vulgar or clownish; and when he plays the debauchee, it is a light-hearted debauchery even more agreeable than that of his great master, Abū Nuwās. Here are some of his more audacious lines:

. . . Don't tell me to stifle passion –
 life consists of flouting shame.
What a bore to be a stuffed shirt –
 life is a rumbustious game.
Whoever only does what's right
 reaps a crop of scant delight.

. . . On seeing him, I said – my heart
 fluttering with painful delight –
"No beauty in this world – O beauty bright!
 but lacks of your perfection part.
Methinks (I said) that only boors
 prefer a girl's beauty to yours."[37]

ᶜAlī b. al-Ḥusayn b. Ḥaydarah al-Sharīf al-ᶜAqīlī probably lived until 450/1058. Although very little is known about his life, his *Dīwān*, which has been preserved in good shape and is now published, confirms the scanty information we have about his life as a well-to-do gentleman, living comfortably at al-Fusṭāṭ, where he owned some orchards. He is further revealed as a perfect aesthete in both life and art. Not only did he enjoy good food and good wine, he was a fine cook himself; and not only are his verses highly melodious, but he himself set some of them to music and sang them. The hedonist trend in Egyptian literature can have no worthier exponent. His sizeable *Dīwān* is devoted almost entirely to singing the beauties of nature (of which more later), wine, women and young boys. Nevertheless, it contains no trace of either the "dissolute" or the "jocose" traditions. His short poems (he seldom writes at any length) are finely chiselled statuettes, often so complete in their objective conception of beauty as to leave no place either for a gloating smile or a sly chuckle. Here is a vignette of a young boy:

A Persian boy in a smock resplendent
 houris and cherubs did outshine.
As if upon a wasp's waist pendent
 his purses dance all in a line.

[37] Thaᶜālibī, *Yatīmah*, I, 334–5, 333.

Like camphor smudged with a musk streak
the jet tress on his dazzling cheek.[38]

Pictorial charm and epigrammatic wit are combined in this portrait of a young woman:

Bewitching her every limb, maddening her figure,
of the element of darkness her tresses, of light her cheeks.
When my loving complaint runs wild, she grants her sympathy;
if yet ungratified, she assuages it with a promise.
If my eyes upbraid her with their flowing tears,
how wise is she! More of her cruelty must I suffer.[39]

The English reader may notice here a certain amalgamation of feeling and thought that reminds him of the Metaphysical poets. Here are two more cases in point:

Toy of transparent element,
willowy girl with smooth, small fingers,
You have become so very distant
my hand and yours will never clasp.
Then, since your bounty is not wide enough,
let your greetings pass between our outstretched hands.[40]

A thirsty sash of red lips I recall, and a smile,
displaying daisy-teeth tiny as hail,
Her mouth a-kissing, wine meanwhile
and flowers around, fragrant and frail,
I felt the night, for all its realms,
too narrow to hold our embrace.
No sooner had dusk shown its face
than morning rose and seized the place.[41]

This mode of sensibility was by no means restricted to an élite. Let us illustrate it by two more examples, taken this time from a poet from a humble background, chiefly known as a panegyrist. Ẓāfir al-Ḥaddād, originally a blacksmith, as his name indicates, died in 529/1134, which means that he was most probably born and brought up in the years that followed the famine of 450/1058, when terrible stories of that "Great Scourge" were still in the air. This short poem describes a popular beverage made of fermented barley:

A purveyor of fragrant barley-beer (*fuqqāᶜ*)
which warms the cockles with its scent
Is this venerable old man who for many a year
has laboured to this sole intent.

[38] Al-Sharīf al-ᶜAqīlī, *Dīwān*, 155. [39] Ibid., 120. [40] Ibid., 205. [41] Ibid., 102.

He's mixed it up with spices sweet –
of mixers all, there's none so neat –
And steeped green beans in it – a sight
to whet the appetite –
Like a jeweller who's set
chunks of emerald in jet.[42]

It certainly takes a strong appetite to make poetry of such a common thing. In another mood of pensive emotion, Ẓāfir commemorates a night of requited love:

I never shall forget the sweetness of embracing,
especially in the chill of dawn;
We clasped each other so very tight
that our two skins became one,
Like streams running down two slopes of a hill
that flow together into one pool.
Were death to try and seize us singly
it never would succeed.[43]

These and a few similar examples may be considered as high points marking the "spirit of the age" in its truer and deeper sense. Much exists besides that should be treated as sub-literature, emotional rehash or plain burlesque. In this last category we must include the innumerable lampoons composed by a group of poets at the court of Ṭalā᾿iᶜ b. Ruzzīk (496–556/1102–61), one of the military dictators who brought the Fatimid caliphate under their tutelage for more than a century before its ultimate collapse. One of his favourite pastimes was to set his poets against each other, half in earnest and half in jest. Some of their lampooning was not completely devoid of literary merit; the rivalry, by sharpening wits, often produced good epigrammatic verse.

Humour was not lacking in other, more serious spheres. Certain social types were held up to ridicule by al-Sharīf al-ᶜAqīlī, whose few satirical poems offer valuable data for social history. Some occupations, particularly those of physician and barber, were easy targets for sarcasm. Scenes from the daily life of Egyptians in the Middle Ages, such as the public bath, supplied ready themes for most poets. In the field of social satire, which might be considered the obverse of hedonistic poetry, special mention must be made of Dāwūd b. Miqdām al-Maḥallī (*c.* 550/1156), a plebian poet who was bold enough to produce a long poem mercilessly castigating a local administrator no doubt typical of his class.[44]

The sanguine hedonism of the fourth–fifth/tenth–eleventh centuries thinned down during the following two centuries into a sort of easy

[42] Ẓāfir al-Ḥaddād, *Dīwān*, 75. [43] Ibid., 138.
[44] ᶜImād al-Dīn al-Iṣfahānī, *Kharīdat al-qaṣr*, II, 45–51.

affability, or degenerated into an undiscriminating pursuit of purely physical pleasure. A mixture of both, with a grain of humour to sustain the mixture, makes a poet like Bahāʾ al-Dīn Zuhayr (581–656/1185–1258) worth reading, and even worthy of general admiration. Many (among whom is a highly respected professor of Islamic philosophy, the Shaykh Muṣṭafā ʿAbd al-Rāziq) have considered him as the representative of the Egyptian character *par excellence*.[45] E. H. Palmer, who discovered him for the English reader, compared him to the Cavalier poets. He was on sounder ground when he drew his readers' attention to "that peculiar trifling of words and sentiments, of which the English poets of the Restoration were so fond". This observation does not justify describing Zuhayr as "eminently the poet of sentiment",[46] unless it is a light, skipping, pleasure-loving sentiment. Compared to al-Sharīf al-ʿAqīlī, Ẓāfir al-Ḥaddād or even Ibn Wakīʿ al-Tinnīsī, Zuhayr is evidently a trifling lover.

Earlier, Ibn Sanāʾ al-Mulk (545–608/1150–1211) had tried, with little success, to escape into the *muwashshaḥ* or "girdle-poem", a strophic and multi-rhymed form, often of considerable formal complexity, which owed its development to the poets of Spain and North Africa. The *muwashshaḥ*'s high degree of musicality offered a sort of compensation for Ibn Sanāʾ al-Mulk's triviality of feeling, but in overworking this asset he was left with nothing to ply but verbal wit. Zuhayr's facility (some would say felicity) of feeling and expression came as a healthy, rejuvenating experience after such abortive attempts.

Descriptive poetry (waṣf)

The welding together of hedonism and description is characteristic of the manner of Ibn al-Muʿtazz (d. 296/908),[47] who was looked up to as a master by most Egyptian poets, from al-Sharīf al-ʿAqīlī to Ibn Sanāʾ al-Mulk. Description is, of course, a component of all poetry, and the descriptions in pre-Islamic poetry had always provided a source of inspiration and emulation.[48] Among early ʿAbbasid poets, the verse of Abū Nuwās abounds in descriptions of wine: of its colour, odour and effects; of the jars it is stored in, the glasses into which it is poured, and of the cupbearer who carries it round, as well as of those who assemble to drink it: the boon-companions, the singer and their host; but his poems combine description and narrative. To speak of the manner of Ibn al-Muʿtazz as mainly descriptive is to use the word in a special sense: what holds his poems, or for that matter his entire poetic output, together is not the personality that

45 ʿAbd al-Rāziq, *Al-Bahāʾ Zuhayr*. 46 Palmer, ed. and trans., *The Poetical Works*, II, xvii, xxv.
47 Cf. pp. 165, 217f. 48 Cf. *CHALUP*, 93–104.

informs them (although this is an inescapable element), nor the poems' function (panegyric, elegy, etc.), but the thing described for its own sake. Thus it can be said with some justice that Ibn al-Muᶜtazz's poetry constitutes something akin to "pure" art. Similarly, the erotic poems discussed above owe much of their hedonist, as distinct from libertine, character to the fact that they are constructed on the basis of description: that the poet is thinking objectively, rather than emotively, of the person of the beloved or of his own feelings towards him or her. It should be borne in mind that these two attitudes are essentially different, although there is no clear line of division between them and each might easily shade into the other.

Most wine-songs by Egyptian poets are static descriptions of the wine-party in natural settings – a private orchard or garden, a secluded spot on the Nile island or the bank of the canal which joined al-Fusṭāṭ to Cairo, or some similar spot. The influence of Ibn al-Muᶜtazz is strongly felt, with the exception that attachment to particular places is rarely felt in Ibn al-Muᶜtazz. In fact the role of place – not simply "nature" but a particular environment, lovingly personified – is characteristic of much Egyptian poetry of this period. In classical Arabic poetry, the distinguishing marks of place came to the fore only with the remembrance of past, human attachments; nature, as such, was impenetrable, intractable, almost inhuman. Here, by contrast, it is a partner. In longer poems of this sort – pastoral in tone and feeling though not in form – nature, wine and love are often linked by the use of metaphors: roses, the beloved's cheeks and the colour of wine are by turns vehicle and tenor; so are pearls, dew-drops, daisies, wine-bubbles, etc. Often, in an attempt to combine all that is considered beautiful or pleasing, the figurative material becomes so dense as to smother the feeling. Sometimes a descriptive passage or a whole poem lacks any true feeling, so overloaded is it with pure sense-images. This is particularly true of descriptions of different dishes, which became a major theme in Egyptian poetry, almost on a par with wine or nature description. Trivial as this might seem to a modern reader, it acquired a kind of topical importance, thanks to the vogue for epistolary conversation in verse mentioned earlier, and is a reasonable development of a hedonistic attitude towards nature.

Although the amount of nature-description produced by the Egyptian poets of the period is considerable, it is almost uniform in tone. Perhaps the physical environment as well as the annual cycle in Egypt do not inspire that strong feeling of wonder which makes for great nature poetry. The change of seasons, steady, assured and monotonous, provides material only for such an uninteresting poem as Ibn Wakīʿ al-Tinnīsī's on the subject.[49] Egyptian poets rise to vivid descriptions of nature only when they are expressing attachment to their place of origin. Thus Ẓāfir al-Ḥaddād, who left his native Alexandria to seek a better fortune in Cairo, distinguishes himself as a nature-poet when he sends touching songs of yearning and remembrance to his old friends in the "White City".

Panegyric (madīḥ)

Ever since his panegyrics of Sayf al-Dawlah, the field of encomiastic poetry had been dominated by the colossal figure of al-Mutanabbī. There were two major themes in these poems: first, the towering personality of the Hamdanid amir, made more conspicuous by the surrounding decline in moral standards; secondly, the moral greatness of al-Mutanabbī himself, in direct contrast to his actual status as court poet. Later panegyrists were fascinated by and tried to re-enact this unique combination of heroic themes, but could only produce a faint echo of al-Mutanabbī, whose wide-ranging command of the Arabic language was in any case far beyond the ability of most poets. Very little encomiastic poetry from the Fatimid period has been preserved, but what remains suggests the important fact that poetry, no less than official documents, played a sizeable part in the Fatimid propaganda system.[50] For better or worse, poets were treated as a body of professionals in the service of the state. The rank and file received a monthly allowance of five dinars (gold coins), but this could be augmented, and there were also the prizes collected on special occasions.[51] This system, together with the wider opportunities offered by combining the office of poet with that of *kātib* in the chancery (*dīwān al-inshāʾ*) or other departments of the administration, provides a possible explanation for the fact that the type of the itinerant man of letters, then so common in the eastern empire, was almost non-existent in Egypt. His place was taken by the man of letters in government service (a type that prevails to this day). This does not mean that the poet, any more than other government functionaries, had no cause for complaint, and it seems that those holding posts in the countryside were the least fortunate of all (as suggested by Dāwūd b. Miqdām al-Maḥallī's satire, referred to earlier). Ẓāfir al-Ḥaddād had had to leave his native Alexandria to seek his fortune near the court and suffered a great deal before he was able to attract the attention of the caliph and his grand vizier; the juvenilia in al-Qāḍī ʾl-Fāḍil's *Dīwān* contain several bitter complaints which

49 Thaʿālibī, *Yatīmah*, I, 323–8. 50 See p. 199, for examples.

51 See ʿImād al-Dīn al-Iṣfahānī, *Kharīdat al-qaṣr*, II, 83; and Ẓāfir al-Ḥaddād, *Dīwān*, 75.

show what an obscure man of letters was apt to suffer. Nevertheless Fatimid Cairo, while not exactly an intellectual paradise, seems to have been a pleasant place for a poet to live in. It was luxurious, lively and tolerant. This is the impression left by a famous elegy on the downfall of the Fatimids which Ibn Saᶜīd cites in full.[52] The poet and historian ᶜUmārah al-Ḥakamī al-Yamanī (d. 569/1174)[53] came from his native Yemen to live in Cairo and enjoyed high esteem as a prominent court poet although he was not himself an Ismāᶜīlī – some indication of the liberal and cosmopolitan character of the capital. Moreover a court poet's duties could be discharged with little effort. He had only to give expression to the Fatimid ideology to reach heights of panegyric unattainable by other encomiasts.

It seems that the Ayyubid panegyrists' failure to match the glorious deeds of Saladin was due, among other things, to a kind of dislocation in their tools. They were not sure of the right way to deal with their new patron: to treat him as less than a Fatimid imam was logical enough, but not really acceptable. Minor poets fell back on the examples of Abū Tammām and al-Mutanabbī, a course which could not lead to anything better than different degrees of failure. More talented and experienced poets knew better or realized soon enough that both styles were inappropriate. Hence, perhaps, Ibn Sanāʾ al-Mulk's strange silence on the occasion of Saladin's victory at Ḥiṭṭīn and recapture of Jerusalem, noted by the editors of his *Dīwān*. Al-Qāḍī ʾl-Fāḍil's example is even more enlightening. He had already achieved eminence in the last days of the Fatimid caliphate; much of what remains of his encomiastic poetry is devoted to members of the Fatimid house and high-ranking officers of the Fatimid state. But the texts have been corrupted in some places and purged in others, making it impossible to draw any conclusions as to how far or how consistently he upheld the Ismāᶜīlī ideology. What strikes the reader more is the fact that only a few eulogies of Ayyubid princes are included in his *Dīwān*, one of which, dedicated to al-ᶜAzīz ᶜUthmān, is nothing more than a piece of word-play. However, there is one other such poem (presumably dedicated to Saladin, because it mentions his first name as Yūsuf), which follows a completely different technique. It is, in many respects, a new and audacious experiment in the genre. Verbal play, so characteristic of al-Qāḍī ʾl-Fāḍil's writing, is almost absent here. Absent also are the exaggerated encomia which have always infested Arabic eulogies. But for the presence of some of al-Qāḍī ʾl-Fāḍil's idiosyncratic constructions one would be tempted to question the authenticity of the poem. As it is, it may be taken as a proof of his genuine talent, his originality, even his sense of humour. If these gifts

[52] *Mughrib*, II, 98–100. [53] Cf. p. 457, 460.

are elsewhere misused by him, it is because he was also circumspect and practical-minded and had to try to eke out a safe existence amid unforeseeable perils. The poem, as it stands,[54] consists of a hundred hemistichs (fifty *bayt*s or lines). Unfortunately, the only text now extant is so disfigured as to make the poem, in some places, almost impossible to decipher, especially in the case of topical allusions, and we have no idea how it begins, for the opening lines have been lost. These might have consisted of the traditional erotic introduction (*nasīb*), but might equally have used an unconventional theme, probably narrative. The first surviving lines begin: "The corpses of the foe I saw – their heads lopped off – thus did I see them!" The poem continues in the same light vein, describing the scene of the "battle", which we soon discover to be a "battle of wine-jars", Saladin having issued a decree prohibiting wine. Al-Qāḍī ᵓl-Fāḍil describes the act of destroying wine-jars and spilling out wine as a huge conflagration which spreads through "the loftiest mansions" of Cairo, and wonders if the earth, after drinking so much wine, would not yield fiery fruits; whether the stone jars, in the same way as men, had not incurred God's chastisement. Wine had once been treasured like gold; let it vanish as, under its spell, the wits of noble men used once to vanish. Apostrophizing these "noble men", dwellers in "lofty mansions", he warns them that the easy, luxurious life they had led on their estates had ended, for war and victory are not accomplished without due preparation. No more excuses for hanging back will be accepted: neither the fast of Ramaḍān, nor extreme heat and cold (an allusion to one of ᶜAlī b. Abī Ṭālib's famous speeches to his men before battle). The poem concludes with four lines of greeting to the house of the amir.

Ascetic poetry (zuhd)

In such troubled times an encomiast's lot was not a happy one, especially when he was trying to sell his poetry to unwilling patrons. Thus Ẓāfir al-Ḥaddād writes:

> If you wish to be hateful to all men,
> thoroughly shunned, without hope of reconciliation,
> Looked on in the same light as vicious vipers
> as a source of injury and detriment,
> You have only to seek money and honours from them,
> especially if you do so by means of panegyrics.
> So let contentment be your sole gain,
> for it is a free man's trade, not devoid of profit;

[54] Al-Qāḍī ᵓl-Fāḍil, *Dīwān*, I, 285–9.

I give you warning; heed my advice
or leave it and have only yourself to blame.[55]

Resignation was the only course open to a free man; but in order to accept this simple truth, he must wage a relentless war against his own strongest impulses, sustained only by the belief that God was in some mysterious way near to him, giving him much-needed love. This is an attitude common to all phases and forms of Sufism, philosophical as well as practical. Dhū ʾl-Nūn al-Miṣrī had been one of the forerunners of philosophical Sufism in the Arab world, but the fact that no great mystic, in the philosophical sense, appeared in Egypt for almost three centuries after his death has led some modern scholars to believe that the Egyptian mind has no natural aptitude for philosophy – a point which may be left for future research to decide. However, we do witness the appearance, in the latter half of the sixth/twelfth century, of a mystic philosopher-poet, Muḥammad b. Ibrāhīm al-Kīzānī (d. 560/1165), who gained immense popularity. His poetry is devoted to divine love, which reminds the reader of the little that is known about Dhū ʾl-Nūn. As a singer of lost hope, vague yearning and unrequited love, Ibn al-Kīzānī was at one and the same time a typical Sufi poet and a popular bard, the two identities showing a tendency to merge as Sufism developed into a kind of popular religion. Ibn al-Fāriḍ is better known in western circles. He is, in fact, a better poet, more polished and with a wider range of themes. His "Great *Tāʾiyyah*" (poem rhyming in *tāʾ*) is purely didactic in manner; but a fuller presentation of the Sufi inner experience is successfully conveyed in his other poems.[56] His poetry, like that of Ibn al-Kīzānī, might be called symbolic, with one qualification, namely that the relation between the surface meaning and the "deep" one is here expected to be construed more or less clearly (compare the relation between exterior and interior meanings in the Ismāʿīlī creed, referred to above). Thus the meaning is still outside the poem, as in all classical poetry, and not in it. Arab Sufism, in general, absorbed elements of rationalist philosophy as well as of various esoteric cults, a mixture that rendered poetic expressions of it either too simple, as with Ibn al-Kīzānī, or too stylized, as with Ibn al-Fāriḍ.

A rapid summary may be made of some of the more obvious changes that occurred in the language of poetry during this period of approximately four centuries. The key role given to metaphor by such poets as al-ʿAqīlī and Ẓāfir al-Ḥaddād reflects a conscious effort to pin down a fleeting sensation, or, in less happy but more common moments of creation, a gratuitous pleasure in joining together disparate things. The equivoques that

[55] *Dīwān*, 82–3. [56] See pp. 253ff.

predominate in the work of later poets seem to function as verbal fireworks, designed to lure the poet – and the reader – away from their true preoccupations. The euphonic qualities of the Arabic language, exploited with varying degrees of felicity by all Arab poets, became almost the sole aim of the *muwashshaḥ*s to which Ibn Sanāʾ al-Mulk devoted so much of his poetic energy. When depth of feeling or, at the opposite extreme, sheer cerebration gave way to urbanity, the music of words and simplicity of thought and feeling became the guiding principles. Both equivoque and metaphor were now used with an air of natural ease. With the support of rhythm, direct forms of repetition and the occasional pun, poetry could become, as with al-Bahāʾ Zuhayr, a language of statement referring to common sentiments.

The literary and cultural developments outlined above seem to have re-established Egypt as a well-defined entity, which made the common Arabic heritage its own, and discovered new ways to continue elaborating it under different conditions. Important changes occurred, but only a little has been preserved from each successive stage. Radical innovations were not usually welcomed, while the mixed heritage, with all its inherent and newly acquired contradictions, seemed able to survive in an atmosphere of general tolerance, and every problem that emerged proved liable to be blandly forgotten or ingeniously solved by some reconciliatory device. Thus it is, perhaps, that no major work was produced, within the recognized forms of Arabic literature, to commemorate the long, turbulent years of the Crusades and the Tatar invasions. But it must not be forgotten that the same period saw the emergence in Egypt of a popular literature, of the prose romances and Sufi songs which, in diverging from the paths of formal and official literature, had moral and political implications which have yet to be fully explored.

CHAPTER 23

REGIONAL LITERATURE: THE YEMEN

This outline survey of Yemeni literature broadly contemporary with the ʿAbbasid caliphate of Baghdad by the nature of the present situation inevitably has many imperfections. Yemeni civilization is very little known beyond its own borders, and editions of Yemeni texts prepared abroad often misunderstand the background or are inaccurate in other ways; nor are Yemeni editors themselves always beyond reproach. Moreover the bulk of Yemeni literature is still in manuscript, including many major works, so that much of it remains unknown outside the Yemen.[1] A great proportion of the works known by report from such sources as the medieval biographical dictionaries and listed by al-Ḥabshī in his *Maṣādir al-fikr . . . fī ʾl-Yaman* are not known to be extant, though they may yet be discovered in the Yemen, where some texts previously thought to be lost are coming to light, as indeed are documents and writings not noted in the literary sources; but it was only in 1978 that the new catalogue of Ṣanʿāʾ Jāmiʿ Mosque Library appeared, and the four-volume catalogue of documents stored in the *waqf* depository was published as this chapter was being written.[2] Yet if what has been discovered since 1962 is compared with what was known to Brockelmann almost half a century ago, it is clear that the horizon of our knowledge of Yemeni literature is vastly extended.

Only a limited critical investigation of Yemeni literature has so far been essayed, and analysis of movements, trends, fashions and the like is only in the earliest of stages. It follows that the selection of what is significant in the work of individual writers and survey of the literature as a whole is fraught with difficulties and all too open to misjudgements. Our modest task can only be to attempt to reveal the Yemen as a province of Islam in touch with developments in other Islamic centres and with a rich and continuing intellectual activity and literary output of its own, in no way inferior in

[1] For writings of the ʿAbbasid period, see Shāmī, *Tārīkh al-Yaman al-fikrī*.

[2] Ruqayḥī, Ḥabshī and Anisī, *Fihrist makhṭūṭāt al-Jāmiʿ al-Kabīr*. Likewise, in Europe, the important Caprotti collection is still only partly catalogued, cf. Löfgren and Traini, *Arabic Manuscripts in the Biblioteca Ambrosiana*. In the following chapter, MS sources appear in footnotes, editions in the bibliography.

quality to other provinces of the caliphate in the ᶜAbbasid era. If this chapter succeeds in highlighting some of the landmarks of this literature, that is perhaps the most that can be achieved at present.

GENERAL BACKGROUND

Rulers

Yemeni history of the first centuries of the Islamic era is obscure; the sources supply little more than a list of the governors assigned to the region first by the Prophet, then by the four *Rāshidūn* ("Orthodox") caliphs, the Umayyads and the ᶜAbbasids. Most of these governors are unlikely to have exerted much authority beyond the cities. Declining ᶜAbbasid power made the Yemen an attractive field for ᶜAlid ventures, but the early attempt (beginning third/ninth century) by Ibrāhīm, a son of the seventh Shīᶜī imam, Mūsā al-Kāẓim, to gain support there for a Zaydī rising against the ᶜAbbasids in Iraq resulted in struggles without avail until he fled the country.[3] The rule of the ᶜAbbasids, becoming ever more impotent, ended effectively in 247/861, though certain of the succession of petty local dynasties acknowledged them as overlords.

It is not the purpose of this chapter to examine the confused and intricate course of early Yemeni history, but the following table will serve at least to identify dynasties, the main centres of their power and, where known, their politico–religious persuasions. Documentation for the third/ninth century up to the Ayyubid period becomes ampler than for the two preceding centuries:

Ziyadids	Zabīd	204–409/819–1019
Yuᶜfirids	Shibām Kawkabān	225–387/840–997
Najahids	Zabīd	403–555/1013–1161
(These three dynasties recognized the ᶜAbbasid caliphs.)		
Sulayhids	Ṣanᶜāᵓ, Dhū Jiblah	439–532/1048–1138
Zurayᶜids	Aden	480–569/1087–1174
Hatimids	Ṣanᶜāᵓ	494–569/1101–1174
(These three dynasties were Ismāᶜīlī Shīᶜīs.)		
Mahdids	Zabīd	553–69/1159–1174
Ayyubids (Sunnī)	Taᶜizz	569–628/1173–1229
Rasulids (Sunnī)	Taᶜizz	628–858/1229–1454
Zaydī Imams (Shīᶜī)	Ṣaᶜdah, Ṣanᶜāᵓ, Shahārah	284–1382/897–1962

[3] Yaḥyā b. al-Ḥusayn, *Ghāyat al-amānī*, I, 48ff. Verses composed on the occasion are quoted by Hamdānī, *Iklīl*, II (Cairo, 1963), 132ff.

The mid-third/ninth century saw the rise in the north of the Yuᶜfirids, claiming descent from pre-Islamic kings, but more significantly the arrival at Ṣaᶜdah in the year 284/897 of the first Zaydī Imam, Yaḥyā b. al-Ḥusayn al-Hādī ilā ᵓl-Ḥaqq, in the role of mediator between certain Hamdān tribes. That the tribal and country districts of the North were little more than nominally Islamized is patently evident from the social conditions al-Hādī ilā ᵓl-Ḥaqq encountered;[4] there is no reason to think the southern Yemen was any different. In contrast to the tribal districts, the main cities were centres of diffusion of Islam, with traditionists of some note in Ṣanᶜāᵓ and Dhamār. From the outset the Zaydī Imams never relaxed the combat against un-Islamic practices and propagated Islamic orthodoxy of a very moderate Shiᶜism.

The Fatimids, following a Shīᶜī creed of a markedly different complexion, also turned their attention to the Yemen at about this time, and in 268/881 two *dāᶜīs* (Fāṭimī "missionaries"), Ibn Ḥawshab, who became known as Manṣūr al-Yaman, and ᶜAlī b. al-Faḍl al-Qarmaṭī, arrived in the Yemen to win adherents to the Fāṭimī *daᶜwah*, though ᶜAlī b. al-Faḍl subsequently broke with the Fāṭimīs.[5] By the opening years of the fourth/tenth century both men were dead. In the fifth/eleventh century however, a chief in the high Ḥarāz mountains, al-Ṣulayḥī, converted to the Fāṭimī *daᶜwah*. The dynasty he established with its capital at Ṣanᶜāᵓ was in direct contact with the Fatimid caliphate in Cairo; the renowned Sulayhid queen, Arwā, adherent of the infant Fāṭimī imam al-Ṭayyib, moved her capital to Dhū Jiblah, where her tomb may be seen to this day. In the north the Sulayhids were succeeded by three houses of the Hamdān tribe, the Ḥātimīs, who fought among themselves and against the Zaydī Imams of Ṣaᶜdah.

In 569/1173 the Ayyubid sultans who had destroyed the Fatimid rulers of Egypt set out to conquer the Yemen, for a variety of reasons which may have included the design of extirpating a nucleus of the *daᶜwah* potentially dangerous were it left unchallenged.[6] With the departure of the last Ayyubid from Yemen, an amir of the Rasulid house took over and was confirmed as an independent ruler by the ᶜAbbasid caliph in Baghdad in 632/1234–5; Rasulid rule continued until about the mid-ninth/fifteenth century.

[4] See Serjeant, "Interplay", 19ff.

[5] Cf. Geddes, "Apostacy". With the basic sense of "invitation (to accept the faith)", *daᶜwah*, in Ismāᶜīlī usage, comes to mean "in the religio-political sense . . . an invitation to adopt the cause of an individual or family claiming the right to the imamate" and also the council of *dāᶜīs* (missionaries, propagandists) and the hierarchy of ranks within this organization; Poonawala, *Biobibliography*, 375.

[6] For a summary of medieval and modern historians' interpretations of the Ayyubid conquest, see Smith, *Ayyūbids and Early Rasūlids*, II, 32–49.

For some two centuries the political pattern was now to remain more or less constant. The Shīʿī Zaydīs were paid allegiance by northern tribes; the Ismāʿīlīs (Fāṭimī–Ṭayyibīs since the reign of queen Arwā, holder of one of the highest ranks in the Fāṭimī hierarchy)[7] had adherents in various districts of the Hamdān tribe, and the Sunnī Rasulids usually held Ṣanʿāʾ (until the second quarter of the eighth/fourteenth century, when the Zaydīs took it from them), and dominated the south and the coast as far east as Ẓafār. Their capital was at Taʿizz, but they wintered at Zabīd, and their administration was based on the Ayyubid model.[8] They gave much of the Yemen a fairly stable era of peace and prosperity. The Zaydī Imams remained opposed to both the Rasulids and the Ismāʿīlīs, the latter more particularly, and intent on extending their territory when opportunity seemed to offer.

Religious schools and sects

From the third/ninth century onwards three main groupings – minor sects, heresies or splinter groups apart – began to take shape: Sunnīs, Zaydīs and Ismāʿīlīs. The main centres were Ṣanʿāʾ, Janad, Zabīd, but also Lahej and other towns. The people of the Yemen, says the sixth/twelfth-century Sunnī writer Ibn Samurah, either "adhered to a sort of *sharīʿah* or were Ḥanafī, it being the majority, or Mālikī".[9] Perhaps he is to be understood as meaning that their knowledge of the *sharīʿah*, the Islamic legal code, was imperfect. The Shāfiʿī school of law (*madhhab*) he considers as spreading in Janad, Ṣanʿāʾ and elsewhere only in the first half of the fifth/eleventh century; Shafiʿism came to predominate in the south (al-Yaman al-Asfal) and, in a later age, greatly developed in Ḥaḍramawt.

Zaydī writing in the Yemen commences with the first Imam, al-Hādī ilā ʾl-Ḥaqq,[10] while successive Imams produced an extensive literature of *fiqh* (jurisprudence), *tafsīr* (Quranic exegesis), *kalām* (theology), and indeed covered the entire range of the "Islamic sciences"; Zaydī law and theology are permeated by Muʿtazilī thinking. But the Imams were also responsible for much polemical literature supporting the Imamate and attacking political sectarianism. They were men of wide culture, notably the Imam al-Mahdī al-Ḥusayn al-ʿIyānī (d. 404/1013),[11] but the great expansion of their activities actually took place in the post-ʿAbbasid period.

The Ismāʿīlīs, whom the other groups regard as heretical, divide knowledge (*ʿilm*) into exoteric (*ẓāhirī*) and esoteric (*bāṭinī*) and have an

7 For Ṭayyibī Ismaʿilism, see pp. 454-5.

8 See Cahen and Serjeant, "A fiscal survey".

9 *Ṭabaqāt*, 74; for Ibn Samurah, see p. 457, below.

10 His writings are listed in Ḥabshī/Niewöhner–Eberhard, *Muʾallafāt*, 2–14.

11 See p. 454.

elaborate cosmological and philosophical literature, but they also write on *fiqh*, history and related topics, *taʾwīl* and *ḥaqāʾiq* – much of this writing is not of a specifically Yemeni character[12] – and composed polemics against other Ismāʿīlī sects and attacks on the Zaydīs, these being especially virulent.

Whether because their limited power at Ṣaʿdah gave them more leisure to write or because of the necessity to further their cause, the Zaydī Imams' literary activities contrast with those of the Rasulids, secular rulers who cosseted the *ʿulamāʾ* but were themselves preoccupied with administration and the maintenance of their kingdom by peaceful or warlike means; several Rasulids wrote on practical matters, as described on pp. 461–2.

The fourth/tenth and early fifth/eleventh centuries were a period of fierce sectarian conflict between Shāfiʿīs, Zaydīs, Ismāʿīlīs and the Muʿtazilī and Ashʿarī[13] trends (to say nothing of inter-family or tribal clashes). The scholars, writers and poets of these groups are remembered with pride in Yemeni literature, especially in the works, discussed below, of al-Hamdānī, Nashwān b. Saʿīd al-Ḥimyarī and ʿUmārah al-Ḥakamī, in al-Qāsim b. Ibrāhīm's *Ṭabaqāt al-Zaydiyyah*,[14] Ibn Abī ʾl-Rijāl's *Maṭlaʿ al-budūr wa-majmaʿ al-buḥūr*,[15] the *Sīrat al-Hādī ilā ʾl-Ḥaqq* of ʿAlī b. Muḥammad al-ʿAbbāsī al-ʿAlawī and, in our time, in Muḥammad Zabārah's *Aʾimmat al-Yaman*.

Since "literature", as defined in the introduction to the first volume in this series, is held to comprehend "virtually everything that has been recorded in writing", religion, history, science and other topics are not excluded here, but their treatment in this chapter is necessarily schematic and provisional, for it is little more than a decade since the riches of Yemeni writing have begun to be revealed, far less scientifically edited and printed. Not included here are scholars, authors and poets who, while having some connection with the Yemen, were neither born nor lived there for any length of time, or who received their education elsewhere. Nor does this chapter deal with celebrated men of Yemeni descent, or who claimed Yemeni descent, such as the poets Abū Tammām, al-Buḥturī and al-Mutanabbī and the philosopher al-Kindī.

12 For Ismāʿīlīs, *taʾwīl* "became a technical term for the esoterical interpretation and allegorical exposition of the Qurʾān and the *sharīʿah*"; *ḥaqāʾiq* (pl. of *ḥaqīqah*): "truth, reality, a term used for the ultimate cosmological and eschatological system of Ismāʿīlī doctrine" (Poonawala, *Biobibliography*, 380, 376). For the distinctiveness of Ṭayyibī–Ismāʿīlī *fiqh*, cf. Madelung, "Sources".

13 On the two latter, see pp. 5–6.

14 Photocopy of Ṣanʿāʾ MS in Imam Yaḥyā's Library in the Jāmiʿ Mosque, Cairo, Dār al-Kutub, no. 13848, *ḥāʾ*.

15 MS with Sayyid Muḥammad Zabārah; Zabīd photocopy at Cairo, Maʿhad al-Makhṭūṭāt.

LITERATURE TO THE FOURTH/TENTH CENTURY

Verse

The Yemen being a land of tribes unendingly engaged in warfare, verse from the Jāhiliyyah onwards has a heroic quality and reflects the ethics of tribal concepts of honour, as exemplified in the lines attributed to the semi-legendary pre-Islamic poet Qudam b. Qādim:[16]

Act not with bad faith, my sons, in a trust[17] committed to you,
For he who betrays a trust is the loser.
Break not a pact because of [some act of] treachery –
He who does not back out of a pledge alone comes out clean [-handed].
Nor eat when your protégé's children are empty of belly,
Their eyes reaching out to [the food] you are preparing.
Your neighbour/protégé – defend him from all maltreatment,
For there is no worth in a man who defends not one who has sought [his] protection. . .

Yea, he who acts liberally through his liberality becomes lord;
So, my sons, act liberally and you will be lords over the tribes.
At a call for aid[18] rise as a body, all!
At the shock of battle clash with the foe *en masse*.[19]

The actual date of composition of these folk-verses in *ḥumaynī*[20] seems impossible to determine, but they may be very old, and are certainly in an ancient tradition which has survived up to the present day.

Verse played, as it still does, an important part in war and politics, the prime example in the literature being the large body of poetry quoted by al-Hamdānī in his *Iklīl*, and the verse of his own composition. Al-Ḥasan b. Aḥmad b. Yaᶜqūb al-Hamdānī (280–334/894–945) was known as Ibn al-Ḥāʾik, "Son of the Weaver", because, it is thought, his father "wove" verses, and not that he was of humble non-tribal birth – al-Hamdānī calls himself "Tongue of the Yemen" (*Lisān al-Yaman*). Al-Hamdānī was not only a voluminous writer of wide interests, antiquarian, literary and scientific, as indicated by the published titles listed in the bibliography to this chapter, but a poet so prolific that the ninth/fifteenth-century polymath al-Suyūṭī declared that his poems, if collected together, would fill six volumes. He was the protagonist of Qaḥṭān, the southern Arabs, and extolled his own tribe of Hamdān, but his pride lay also in the glories of the

[16] See *CHALUP*, 117. [17] *Amānah* – perhaps in the sense of safe-conduct, etc?
[18] *Ghārah*; for this sense of the word, see Serjeant and Lewcock, *Ṣanᶜāʾ*, 578a.
[19] Griffini, "Il poemetto", 346. [20] See pp. 452, 465.

Yemen of ancient times, the evidence of which lay everywhere around. The famous route-poem by Aḥmad b. ʿĪsā al-Radāʿī (d. *c.* 230/845), which Hamdānī quotes in his *Ṣifat Jazīrat al-ʿArab* ("Description of the Arabian Peninsula"),[21] boasts, in the same vein, of:

Ṣanʿāʾ of the mansions and towers tall,
High in antiquity, from time afore,
Proud in resisting covetous assault,
Founded through Noah's son Shem's prescience,
Prescience of a lord, a king most wise –
For Shem 'twas who with sureness sought it out,
Sought it more than two thousand years ago,
Set 'tween the hills of Nuqum al-Naqqām
And lofty ʿAybān where [men] dig for springs.
In bygone former days he founded it.

A land wherein are found Ghumdān and al-Qalīs.
The man of valour built them, the Chief, *al-Raʾīs*,
Tubbaʿ who held sway there; where also built Bilqīs.[22]

Al-Hamdānī's strongly partisan sentiment comes out in his famous *qaṣīdah* of over 600 verses, *al-Dāmighah* ("The Mortal Wound Cleaving the Brain"), which was, it is said, a riposte to an attack assailing the honour of Hamdān tribesmen (Qaḥṭānīs) by a group of ʿAdnānī (northern Arab) poets in Ṣaʿdāh. In the quarrels that ensued, al-Hamdānī departed Ṣaʿdāh for Ṣanʿāʾ, where the Yuʿfirid amir of the city imprisoned and subsequently banished him (this amir he satirized in his poem *Qaṣīdat al-Jār*).[23] His *Dāmighah* is one of a series of *dawāmigh* in verse of identical rhyme and metre, one of the first known examples of the genre being Abū ʾl-Dhulfāʾ's riposte to the pro-Hāshimī poet al-Kumayt's *Qaṣīdah Mudhahhabah* ("Golden Ode") at which Diʿbil al-Khuzāʿī also aimed a "*dāmighah*" blow.[24] While the protagonists in this battle of the poets were partisans of ʿAdnān or Qaḥṭān respectively, this antagonism also included the rivalry of the Hāshimīs, the House of the Prophet, and their opponents. Al-Hamdānī flaunts the honour of Qaḥṭān:[25]

The earliest pre-eminent in glory were we not?
In it the foremost were we, the ancients,
By race, in speech the pure Arabs are we. To this feign not blindness,
You part-Arabs, later insinuated among us![26]

[21] Ṣifah, ed. Müller, 235–79/ed. Akwaʿ, 401–58. The numerous faults in this and other of Akwaʿ's writings on Hamdānī are censured in Shāmī's *Jarīmat al-Akwaʿ ʿalā dhakhāʾir al-Hamdānī* ("Al-Akwaʿ's Crimes against the Treasures of al-Hamdānī") (Beirut, 1400/1980).

[22] Trans. Serjeant and Lewcock, *Ṣanʿāʾ*, 6; Ghumdān: fortress of Ṣanʿāʾ; al-Qalīs: ancient castle/church of Ṣanʿāʾ, see ibid.; and Hamdānī, *Iklīl*, VIII, 3–10, trans. (sometimes not very satisfactorily) Faris, *Antiquities*, 8–20. Tubbaʿ: title of the ancient kings of Ḥimyar; Bilqīs: the "queen of Sheba".

[23] In *Iklīl* (Cairo, 1963), I, introd., 49–56.

[24] Cf. p. 191.; Kumayt uses the *wāfir* metre, but later poets sometimes employ *basīṭ*. For a discussion of the genre, see Shāmī, *Dāmighat al-dawāmigh*.

[25] Ibid., 47ff.

[26] Pure and part-Arabs, *ʿāribūn* and *mustaʿribūn*, defined respectively as "those who spoke the language

You have learned to speak our tongue, you are become,
Through the grace of our tribesfolk, adept at it.
When you were yet unborn, of mankind we were the kings.
We it was whose sway dominated all.

Throughout all ages you have remained our followers,[27]
Be you ruled or rulers.

Allāh, when He willed upon you to confer benevolence,
To you sent the son of Āminah, the Trustworthy (*Amīn*),
That he might instruct you in a Book
Which until then [you had not], to recite;
Of al-Raḥmān, the Merciful, to bring you tidings,
Of whom, from ignorance, you were uncomprehending.[28]

The poet then goes on to blame Quraysh for the fate of ʿAlī b. Abī Ṭālib. The contentious nature of al-Hamdānī's poem brought down upon him a number of *naqāʾiḍ* (flytings),[29] in contradiction, but if al-Hamdānī is deeply animated by his bias in favour of Qaḥṭān, the first two volumes of his *Iklīl* were themselves to suffer from the editing of the sixth/twelfth-century scholar and writer Muḥammad b. Nashwān al-Ḥimyarī,[30] who, for political and ethnic reasons, cut out what he disliked and added what he favoured. In the century following al-Hamdānī's death, the traditions he had exemplified were continued by Muḥammad b. Ḥusayn al-Kalaʿī (d. 404/1014), who composed several works on the glories (*mafākhir*) of Qaḥṭān as well as a *dāmighah*.

Yemeni poets continued to follow the pre-Islamic tradition of poetry both in its themes and language; their verse was characterized by a certain fieriness of spirit; it vaunts lineage and heroic deeds, describes strife and tragedy, exults in victory. The tribal *zāmil* (pl. *zawāmil*), basically two rhymed half-verses in *rajaz* metre declaimed by tribesmen moving in a body, is remarked upon by al-Hamdānī: "I have heard men of Banū Nahd reciting in their verses and chanting *zāmil*s (*tuzawmil*) in their wars ... 'Sons we are of the shaykh pure of race, fair of face, Quḍāʿah b. Mālik b. Ḥimyar'."[31] It is, then, apparent that the *zāmil* has a respectable antiquity, alongside the more formal *qaṣīdah*.

Celebrated poets of heroic verse are Muḥammad b. Abān (d. 175/791)[32]

of Yaʿrub b. Qaḥṭān, which is the ancient language" (see Nicholson, *Literary History*, 14), and "those who spoke the language of Ismāʿīl the son of Ibrāhīm" (Ishmael), i.e. the dialects of the Hijaz, etc. (see Lane, *Lexicon*); also applied to non-Arabs who adopted Arabic speech and manners, see also pp. 42–3, 46, above.

27 *Tābiʿūn*, here meaning subordinates owing duty to those in authority, see Serjeant, "Interplay", 17, n. 2.

28 Āminah: mother of the Prophet; *al-Amīn*: a title of the Prophet; "a Book": the Qurʾān.

29 See *CHALUP*, 78–9.

30 See p. 466.

31 Shāmī, *Qiṣṣat al-adab*, 204–5. For the *zāmil*, see Landberg, *Glossaire* and *Ḥaḍramoût*, 143; Serjeant, *Prose and Poetry*, pref., 32.

32 For his *Sijill Ḥimyar*, see *CHALUP*, 115.

and his contemporary ᶜAmr b. Zayd al-Ghālibī, who fought the ᶜAbbasid governor Maᶜn b. Zāᵓidah al-Shaybānī. Muḥammad b. Abān swore that no roof would shelter his head nor would he lie with a woman until he had avenged his slain brother; at his death he was succeeded in his capacity as poet and chief by his son-in-law, Aḥmad b. Yazīd al-Qashībī/Qushaybī (d. after 201/816), reckoned an outstanding poet, or "stallion" (*faḥl*), and the finest poet of the Banū ᵓl-Humaysaᶜ. Al-Hamdānī states that he followed the doctrine of al-Kumayt and al-Sayyid al-Ḥimyarī in Shīᶜī partisanship and love for the Prophet's House, yet he nevertheless attacked the ᶜAlid Ibrāhīm b. Mūsā for killing some of his fellow-tribesmen during his abortive Yemeni campaign (referred to at the beginning of this chapter) in plaintive, melancholy verses displaying wounded Shīᶜī sentiment, but also vengeful tribal feeling.[33] Also to be mentioned in this context is Aḥmad b. ᶜĪsā al-Radāᶜī, famous for his route-poem, *Urjūzat al-Ḥajj*, quoted above and described by al-Hamdānī as "quite unrivalled in its technique", the route-poem being a well-established genre of verse;[34] while of the many outstanding poets of the period whose verse is cited in al-Hamdānī's *Iklīl* or his "Description", we may note Bakr b. Mirdās al-Ṣanᶜānī (d. 197/813), a sophisticated love-poem of whose[35] with its pretty conceits was admired by no less a person than Abū Nuwās himself.

The age of the first Zaydī Imām, al-Hādī ilā ᵓl-Ḥaqq, saw poets ranged on his side or against him and his cause, and both al-Hādī and his son al-Murtaḍā Muḥammad also composed poetry.[36] Al-Hādī's poem addressed to one of his sons when the latter was taken prisoner is a panegyric on him, but breathes threats of divine wrath and hell-fire against his enemies.[37] Ibrāhīm b. Abī ᵓl-Balas, a supporter of al-Hādī, praises him as a champion of the faith in somewhat extravagant terms:

> Had your sword been unsheathed on the day he was ordered to prostrate himself before Adam, Iblīs had not [dared] disobey [God].[38]

Ibrāhīm b. al-Jadawiyyah/al-Ḥadūbah, of the *Abnā*ᵓ[39] of Ṣanᶜāᵓ (d. *c.* 320/933), a contemporary of al-Hamdānī, mourns al-Hādī in similar vein:

> Islam's arm has weakened, its withers shrunk, and the misfortunes fallen on it have torn away its sons from among mortals.[40]

33 Shāmī, *Qiṣṣat al-adab*, 265–6, quoting Hamdānī, *Iklīl*, II.
34 For modern examples of the genre, see Serjeant, *Prose and Poetry*, pref., 9ff.
35 Hamdānī, *Ṣifah*, ed. Müller, 56f./ed. Akwaᶜ, 84f. 36 See p. 453.
37 ᶜAlawī, *Sīrat al-Hādī*, 285–6.
38 Hamdānī, *Ṣifah*, ed. Müller, 66/ed. Akwaᶜ, 98. After creating Adam, God commanded the angels to prostrate themselves before him; all obeyed except Iblīs (Satan), Qurᵓān, ii.34.
39 "Sons" (i.e. descendants) of the Persians who settled in the Yemen in the sixth century, see *CHIran*, III, (1), 607; Serjeant and Lewcock, *Ṣanᶜāᵓ*, index, "Al-Abnāᵓ",.
40 Hamdānī, *Ṣifah*, ed. Müller, 58/ed. Akwaᶜ, 87.

A companion of al-Hādī, ᶜAlī b. Aḥmad b. Abī Ḥarīṣah (d. 325/937 or a little later), composed verse after the manner of Abū ᵓl-ᶜAtāhiyah and is believed to have been a Sufi, although Zaydism is generally hostile to Sufism.[41]

The opposition to al-Hādī included two of the most distinguished poets of the age, ᶜAbd al-Khāliq b. Abī Ṭalḥ al-Shihābī and al-Ukaylī. ᶜAbd al-Khāliq was a poet of Ṣanᶜāᵓ and its countryside (*bādiyah*) and fanatically opposed to the ᶜAdnānīs and al-Hādī's allies, the *Abnāᵓ* of Persian descent living in the eastern sector of Ṣanᶜāᵓ, of which the Banū Shihāb controlled the western sector. Of the *Abnāᵓ* he says:

> Of them our hearts so full of hatreds are
> That drunken, you would reckon us, with ire.[42]

Al-Hamdānī describes him as *maṭbūᶜ* (fluent, naturally gifted), and quotes several passages of his verse.[43] He was a panegyrist of the Yuᶜfirids and others, as well as author of a *Mafākhir Qaḥṭān* ("Glories of Qaḥṭān"); he was still living in 275/889. Al-Ukaylī (ᶜAbdullāh b. Muḥammad b. ᶜAbbād al-Khawlānī), whose father was a chief in Ṣaᶜdah but was slain there, went to Baghdad where he sought and obtained aid from the caliph. His son Aḥmad, lord of Khawlān in his turn, also went to appeal to the caliph al-Muᶜtaḍid in 285/898 for support against the Imam al-Hādī against whom he had rebelled. This the caliph promised, but when al-Ukaylī had audience of him a second time, he found the caliph had changed his mind, saying: "The Yemenis attack impetuously, like ravening lions". He composed attractive verses about his journey to Iraq.[44]

Among the poetic output of the time are the notorious verses attributed to a poet of the entourage of ᶜAlī b. al-Faḍl al-Qarmaṭī, one of the two Fāṭimī *dāᶜīs* sent to the Yemen in 268/881, which ᶜAlī b. Faḍl recited in the Jāmiᶜ Mosque of al-Janad, and which begin; "Take up the drum, dance and sing ...", inciting to indiscriminate licence in wine, women and song.[45] Doubt has been cast on their authenticity, but there is substantial evidence of opposition to restrictions imposed by Islam on what was regarded as a part of society's way of life. An attack by al-Hādī's son on the licentious attitude of his father the Imam's foes in the verse which represents them as saying:

> You prevent folk gainst their will
> From enjoying pleasures and desired delights

seems consistent with a Carmathian revolt against this aspect of Islam.[46]

41 See Ḥabshī, *Maṣādir*, 271. 42 Shāmī, *Qiṣṣat al-adab*, 304–5.
43 Hamdānī, *Iklīl* (Cairo, 1963), I, 205, 455, 479, 482–525. 44 Ibid., 333–4, 338, 344ff.
45 De Goeje, *Mémoire*, 226–7 (trans. ibid., 160–1; Kay, *ᶜOmārah*, 198–9); Ibn Samurah, *Ṭabaqāt*, 75–7.
46 Serjeant, "Interplay", 21. On the Carmathians, see pp. 197–8, 444–5, above. For Carmathian numbers in the Yemen at this period, cf. Stern, "Ismāᶜīlīs and Qarmaṭians", 102.

Ḥumaynī verse

At this point it seems appropriate to introduce the question of the first existence of *ḥumaynī* verse. *Ḥumaynī*, a term of unknown origin, today comprises all popular (*shaᶜbī*) verse on a wide range of themes, e.g. love poetry (*ghazal*), Sufi mystical poetry, humorous poetry, and the *zāmil* (see above) sung by individuals or groups on various occasions.[47] *Ḥumaynī* ignores the inflexions of classical Arabic grammar and abbreviates words; it has certain prosodic devices of its own and metres not known to Khalīl b. Aḥmad.[48] Aḥmad b. Fulaytah (d. 762/1361) of the Rasulid period is said to have been its first prominent exponent, but there is evidence of its being much older. Yāqūt (d. 626/1229) quotes the following verses by a local poet of Ṣanᶜāᵓ in *ḥumaynī* (though Yāqūt calls it *malḥūn*):

Alas, O weeping, when the lover be far
From his beloved – to whom makes he his plaint?
To me then will he complain, and to the city,
His tears flowing like [watercourse of] Ghayl al-Barmakī.[49]

Verses of the *bālabāl* type by the poet al-Naqīb al-ᶜAdanī on ᶜAbd al-Raḥmān b. Rāshid, lord of Shiḥr (d. mid-seventh/thirteenth century) are quoted by Abū Makhramah;[50] from earlier periods still, several *ḥumaynī* verses by al-Hamdānī and a verse attributed to the first/seventh-century poet Aᶜshā Hamdān (though rejected by the early philologists) are discussed in al-Shāmī's history of Yemeni literature *Qiṣṣat al-adab fī ᵓl-Yaman*, though in none of these contexts is the term *ḥumaynī* employed.

Historians, traditionists and other ᶜulamāᵓ

The earliest Yemeni historical writers have been discussed in an earlier volume: ᶜAbīd/ᶜUbayd b. Sharyah al-Jurhumī, who lived into the caliph Muᶜāwiyah's time, and Wahb b. Munabbih (d. 114/732), both of whom wrote in a vein more fabulous than historical.[51] A pupil of Wahb's brother

[47] See Shāmī, *Qiṣṣat al-adab*, 213–33.

[48] *CHALUP*, 15–17. At a later period than that discussed here, and in modern times, the distinction is made between *ḥumaynī* and *ḥakamī* verse; the latter must obey the rules of classical grammar and metre; see Serjeant, *Prose and Poetry*, 5–6, and *GAL*, SII, 545, 547.

[49] *Muᶜjam al-buldān*, III, 830; trans. Serjeant and Lewcock, *Ṣanᶜāᵓ*, 22a; for the *ghayl*s (artificial underground water channels) of Ṣanᶜāᵓ, see ibid.

[50] *Tārīkh thaghr ᶜAdan*, II, 65–7; the poem is in uninflected Arabic and in a non-Khalilian metre in which the lines are not divided into hemistichs as in classical prosody.

[51] For editions of their surviving works, see *CHALUP*, 385, 535. *Al-Isrāᵓīliyyāt* and *K. al-Mulūk al-mutawwajah*, dealing respectively with tales of Old Testament times and the pre-Islamic south Arabian kings, and attributed to ᶜAbdullāh b. Wahb in *CHALUP*, 384–5, but to Wahb himself in the Arabic sources, may incorporate material going back to Wahb since ᶜAbdullāh was his *rāwī*.

Hammām (d. ?101/719),[52] Maᶜmar b. Rāshid al-Azdī (d. 154/771), is known for a collection (*jāmiᶜ*) of *sunnah*s used as a source by later compilers.[53] In fact it is claimed that the first to classify (*ṣannaf*) tradition according to subject-matter were ᶜAbd al-Malik b. Jurayj in Mecca, then Maᶜmar in Ṣanᶜāʾ.[54] Another Yemeni traditionist, ᶜAbd al-Razzāq al-Ṣanᶜānī (d. 211/827), was a transmitter of Ibn Jurayj and pupil to Maᶜmar and, like his master, author of a *muṣannaf* and of a Qurʾān commentary (published). An early scholar famed throughout the Yemen for his rhetorical style in which, says al-Hamdānī, he became a model unrivalled before or since, was Bishr b. Abī Kabār al-Balawī (d. *c.* 184/801), but all that has survived of his writings are ten letters,[55] the first addressed to the ᶜAbbasid governor of Ṣanᶜāʾ in 181/799. By the second/eighth century the Yemen had become a fully developed seat of learning with its own group of *ᶜulamāʾ* in the field of tradition, experts in Quranic commentary, *fiqh* and philology (among the scholars of this period may be mentioned Abū Qurrah Mūsā b. Ṭārif, Muṭarrif b. Māzin, *qāḍī* (judge) of Ṣanᶜāʾ, his successor as *qāḍī* Hishām b. Yūsuf, and Bakr b. ᶜAbdullāh . . . Ibn al-Sharūd, a Qurʾān reciter; others are mentioned in the biographical works). In addition the Yemen was visited by celebrated Sunnī traditionists from elsewhere in the Muslim world: al-Shāfiᶜī[56] in 179/795, Aḥmad b. Ḥanbal, who heard tradition from ᶜAbd al-Razzāq, and Yaḥyā b. Maᶜīn al-Murrī (d. 233/847).

The Imam al-Hādī ilā ʾl-Ḥaqq (d. 298/910–11) is the most significant personality of the third/ninth-century Yemen. Acknowledged Imam in 280/894, he was the founder of the Zaydī Imamate at Ṣaᶜdah (though he held Ṣanᶜāʾ briefly). In many fields of learning he was a scholar as well as a writer, orator, and, as we have seen, poet. Zabārah notes the titles of seventy books by him, exluding his poetic *Dīwān*, and Sezgin lists thirty-nine extant titles;[57] his *fiqh* cases, in the recension known as *al-Muntakhab*, have been edited by ᶜA. K. Kāẓī. Al-Hādī's son al-Murtaḍā Muḥammad succeeded him but abdicated in 301/913; seemingly more of a scholar and ascetic than man of action, also an orator and a poet, he resigned in favour of his brother, al-Nāṣir, who battled successfully with the Carmathians. Five of al-Murtaḍā's books and letters are extant, including a Qurʾān commentary in seven parts,[58] and his verse is cited in ᶜAlī al-ᶜAlawī's

[52] Claimed by some to have been the first to make a written record of *ḥadīth*, *CHALUP*, 272.

[53] *CHALUP*, 356; *GAS*, I, 290–1. See Goldziher, *Muslim Studies*, II, 168, n. 6. Ṭabarī quotes from his lost book on the Prophet's *maghāzī* (raids, see *CHALUP*, 344–5).

[54] Goldziher, *Muslim Studies*, II, 196; *CHALUP*, 272.

[55] Text in Hamdānī, *Ṣifah*, ed. Müller, 58–66/ed. Akwaᶜ, 88–96.

[56] See *CHALUP*, 318, and pp. 417–18, above.

[57] Zabārah, *Aʾimmat al-Yaman*, I, 5, 52; *GAS*, I, 563–6; see also n. 10 above.

[58] For his works see *GAS*, I, 567–8; Ḥabshī/Niewöhner–Eberhard, *Muʾallafāt*, 14–19; Madelung, *Streitschrift*.

biography of his father, *Sīrat al-Hādī*. Prominent in al-Nāṣir's day was Abū ᵓl-Ḥusayn Aḥmad b. Mūsā al-Ṭabarī (d. 325/937), a companion of al-Hādī, who entered into disputations with the *ᶜulamāᵓ* of the various schools in the Yemen and through whom the Zaydī school was able to extend its influence. His best-known work is *al-Anwār fī maᶜrifat Allāh wa-rusulih*, a defence of revelation.[59] Other Zaydī *ᶜulamāᵓ* were al-Hādī's brother ᶜAbdullāh (d. after 300/913), known as Ṣāḥib al-Zaᶜfarān, whose *al-Nāsikh wa ᵓl-mansūkh*, on the vexed question of abrogated verses in the Qurᵓān, is extant;[60] al-Hādī's biographer, ᶜAlī b. Muḥammad al-ᶜAlawī (still alive in the reign of the Imam al-Nāṣir); the notable Imam al-Qāsim al-ᶜIyānī (d. 393/1003), author of a large number of works, including *al-Radd ᶜalā ᵓl-Rāfiḍah* (a polemic against extremist Shīᶜīs) and various theological–philosophical writings (the biography of him by al-Ḥasan b. Aḥmad b. Yaᶜqūb is extant);[61] and his son, Imam al-Mahdī al-Ḥusayn al-ᶜIyānī (d. 404/1013), who was a prolific writer in the fields of polemics, politics, philosophy, theology, etc.[62] Also to be mentioned are Muḥammad . . . b. Abī ᶜUmar (d. 320/932), *qāḍī* of Aden, a traditionist from whom Muslim and al-Tirmidhī heard tradition, who compiled a *musnad* (collection of *ḥadīth* arranged according to *isnād* or chain of transmitters),[63] and ᶜUbayd b. Muḥammad al-Kishwarī, who flourished in Ṣanᶜāᵓ in the late third/ninth century; his "History", not now extant, is quoted by al-Hamdānī and the Yemeni historian Aḥmad b. ᶜAbdullāh al-Rāzī (see below), and has information on early Ṣanᶜāᵓ. He was one of the teachers of the well-known traditionist al-Ṭabarānī. Other historians of this period known by citation are Muḥammad b. ᶜAbdullāh al-Yaharī, the teacher of al-Hamdānī, and ᶜAbdullāh b. Muḥammad al-Awsānī, cited by al-Hamdānī in *Iklīl*, II.

THE SULAYHID PERIOD

ᶜAlī b. Muḥammad al-Ṣulayḥī, the son of a chief in the high mountainous Ḥarāz region, was won over to espouse the Fāṭimī *daᶜwah* by the *dāᶜī* Sulaymān b. ᶜĀmir b. ᶜAbdullāh al-Zawāḥī, who declared for it in 439/1047–8. Al-Ṣulayḥī tried to unite and stabilize the Yemen and conquered most of the petty sultanates, but was attacked by surprise and killed in 459/1067 by Saᶜīd al-Aḥwal al-Najāḥī of the Abyssinians (*Aḥbāsh*) of the Tihāmah and his slaves.[64] This refragmented the country and plunged it into civil wars, but the son of al-Ṣulayḥī, al-Mukarram, was able, in the event, to destroy the Najahids. However he handed over control of the affairs of state to his wife, Arwā bint Aḥmad, who moved south to Dhū

[59] See also Madelung, *Der Imam al-Qāsim*, 254; Ḥabshī, *Maṣādir*, 94. [60] *GAS*, I, 42.
[61] Ibid., 568–9; Madelung, *Der Imam al-Qāsim*, 194–6. [62] *GAS*, I, 569–70.
[63] See *CHALUP*, 273–6.
[64] For the Najahids and the Abyssinians of the Tihāmah (the Red Sea coastal plain), see *EI*[1], "Nadjāḥ".

Jiblah where she established her capital. During her reign, a split occurred among Ismāᶜīlīs over the Fatimid succession on the assassination of the tenth Fatimid caliph al-Āmir in 524/1130; many Ismāᶜīlīs eventually recognized his cousin al-Ḥāfiẓ as caliph but others, including the Sulayhids, held the true imam to be al-Āmir's infant son al-Ṭayyib, who had disappeared and was considered to be in concealment (*satr*). Under the protection of Arwā, the Ṭayyibīs of the Yemen founded an independent *daᶜwah* headed by a *dāᶜī muṭlaq* or "absolute *dāᶜī*", who claimed the authority of the concealed imam and headed a hierarchy of lesser *dāᶜīs*. This organization of the Fāṭimī–Ṭayyibī *daᶜwah* survived in the Yemen until the mid-tenth/sixteenth century.[65]

About the beginning of the sixth/twelfth century, the Zurayᶜids independently controlled Aden, and the Ḥātimids, a little earlier, had set up a principality around Ṣanᶜāʾ;[66] then, in 554/1160, Zabīd fell into the hands of ᶜAlī b. Mahdī.[67] Three Zaydī Imams ruled at Ṣaᶜdah during the period but were constantly at war. This phase of Yemeni history terminates with the invasion from Egypt of the Ayyubid Tūrānshāh, whose great armies, in a series of hard-fought campaigns, overran most of the Yemen, destroying the Sulayhid state.

In literary and intellectual development, the Sulayhid era was one of the most fertile ages of Yemeni history. Despite the violent political confusion and destructive sectarian quarrels that marked it, learning, literature and verse flourished, colleges and mosques were built, roads constructed. Most rulers of the time, Imams, sultans or princes, were scholars of distinction, orators, poets and authors in a great variety of fields. As examples, the Zaydī Imam Abū ʾl-Fatḥ al-Daylamī (d. 444/1052) composed books on *fiqh* and its bases – the Qurʾān, *sunnah*, analogical reasoning (*qiyās*) and consensus (*ijmāᶜ*) – as well as a Qurʾān commentary (extant).[68] Imam Aḥmad b. Sulaymān (500–66/1107–71) likewise wrote on *fiqh* but also entered into the scholastic theology (*kalām*) of the period; some of his verse is preserved in Ṣanᶜāʾ Jāmiᶜ Mosque Library.[69] Both Imams wrote polemics against the Muṭarrifiyyah, a Zaydī heresy thought by earlier western scholars, chiefly on the basis of the polemical literature attacking them, to have acquired dualist (*thanawī*) tendencies and traits, reminiscent of the Carmathians (like the latter, the Muṭarrifiyyah were centred on al-Maṣāniᶜ in the mountainous northwest), under the influence of Greek philosophical

[65] Poonawala, *Biobibliography*, 10; Bates, "The chapter on the Fāṭimid *Dāᶜīs*"; Arwā is known variously as al-Ḥurrah al-Malikah and al-Sayyidah al-Ḥurrah; see Hamdānī, "The Dāᶜī Ḥātim"; Serjeant and Lewcock, *Ṣanᶜāʾ*, Index.

[66] For these petty dynastics, see Smith, *The Ayyūbids and Early Rasūlids*, II, 58, 63–7, 68–75.

[67] For the Mahdids (sometimes called "Khārijīs" in the sources, probably as a term of opprobrium), see ibid., 32–3, 56–62.

[68] *GAL*, SI, 698; Ḥabshī/Niewöhner–Eberhard, *Muʾallafāt*, 28–30.

[69] GAL, SI, 699; Ḥabshī/Niewöhner–Eberhard, *Muʾallafāt*, 31–5.

ideas, Magianism, Isma^cilism, etc. More recently, however, evidence appears that they regarded themselves as followers of the first Zaydī Imam, al-Hādī, and that their most conspicuous divergence from later Zaydī Muᶜtazilīs was in their cosmology and natural philosophy; they became heretical only in so far as they continued to follow the Baghdad Muᶜtazilī school at a time when the Yemeni Imams favoured Basran Muᶜtazilī theology.[70] The founder of the Sulayhid dynasty was, the contemporary historian ᶜUmārah al-Ḥakamī remarks, a scholar expert in *fiqh* after the Fāṭimī school, perceptive in "allegorical" interpretation (*taʾwīl*) of the Qurʾān, in which the Fāṭimīs had their own special line.[71] A convert to the Fāṭimī *daᶜwah* and ally of the Sulayhids was the poet and chieftain al-Sulṭān al-Khaṭṭāb b. al-Ḥasan of the Ḥajūr Hamdān tribe. An extremely forceful character, he killed his brother Ḥasan who had murdered his sister on account of a difference over beliefs. This brought al-Khaṭṭāb into conflict with his elder brother, Sulaymān, himself a poet and scholar but a Sunnī. A war between them lasted from 500/1107 to 514/1120, when al-Khaṭṭāb succeeded in assassinating Sulaymān. He took the latter's nephews into his care, but when they grew up they wreaked vengeance for their father upon him (533/1139). Both al-Khaṭṭāb's and Sulaymān's verse have survived[72] and that of the former has been published. Qāḍī ᶜImrān b. al-Faḍl of the Yām tribe, a supporter of the Sulayhid kingdom, was also a poet of some note and a man of learning;[73] his grandson, sultan Ḥātim b. Aḥmad, a shrewd, stubborn, resolute man, became ruler of Ṣanᶜāʾ. The Zaydī Imam Aḥmad b. Sulaymān besieged him there, and, needing paper and soap, despatched a man by an indirect route to purchase them in the city. Sultan Ḥātim interrogated the man but returned him to the Imam with a letter containing the verses:

> For just mere Ṭalḥī paper would you take our land
> Not yet, amid the dust, contended with the spear?
> Would you take Ṣanᶜāʾ, our kingdom's heartland and seat,
> When greedily we guard our country's borders dear?

He was forced none the less to seek quarter of the Imam when besieged in the citadel and obliged to capitulate.[74]

Historians and philologists

Aḥmad b. ᶜAbdullāh al-Rāzī's (d. 460/1068) rambling but nonetheless interesting history of Ṣanᶜāʾ is in fact a collection of legends, *ḥadīth*s and

[70] See Tritton, "Muṭarrifiya". [71] See Poonawala, *Biobibliography*, 19–20; and n. 12, above.
[72] Ibid., 133–7. [73] H. F. Hamdānī, *Ṣulayḥiyyūn*, 95, 137, 152–3.
[74] ᶜUmārah, *Mufīd*, ed. Akwaᶜ, 313, 320.

biographies of some early traditionists interspersed with historical and topographical data. Other biographical collections are those of Muslim b. Muḥammad al-Laḥjī (d. 545/1151) on the Yemeni poets, *al-Utrujjah fī shuʿarāʾ al-Yaman*, and his *Ṭabaqāt mashāhīr al-Yaman* ("Famous Yemenis"),[75] and of ʿUmar b. ʿAlī b. Samurah al-Jaʿdī (Ibn Samurah), who wrote a history of the *fuqahāʾ* (jurisconsults, sing. *faqīh*) of the Yemen; both authors were Sunnīs. Aḥmad b. Muḥammad al-Ashʿarī (d. *c.* 560/1165) compiled *al-Lubāb fī maʿrifat al-ansāb*, on genealogies, a topic of some importance in Yemeni society.[76] ʿUmārah al-Ḥakamī's (d. 569/1174) *al-Mufīd fī akhbār Ṣanʿāʾ wa-Zabīd* is, however, a history in the full sense of the word, composed for the Fatimid chief secretary al-Qāḍī ʾl-Fāḍil (see ch. 22); it commences with the Ziyadids and proceeds dynasty by dynasty up to his own time. Nashwān b. Saʿīd al-Ḥimyarī (d. 573/1178) wrote, in the form of a poem, *al-Qaṣīdah al-Ḥimyariyyah*, a history of the pre-Islamic Tubbaʿ kings (the detailed commentary on it may also be by Nashwān), but he is more famous for his *Shams al-ʿulūm*, a philological encyclopaedia whose great range of narrative, however, makes it much more. The former work has been published several times, but only parts of *Shams al-ʿulūm* have appeared in print. (Other philologists were the Rabʿī brothers, ʿĪsā and Ismāʿīl, in the fifth/eleventh century, Muḥammad b. Yaḥyā of Zabīd, fifth-sixth/eleventh-twelfth century, who wrote on rhetoric and syntax, and ʿAlī b. Sulaymān al-Ḥārithī, sixth/twelfth century, author of *Kashf al-mushkil fī ʾl-naḥw* on problems of grammar.)

The Islamic sciences

In the religious sciences Nashwān b. Saʿīd – who, it should be noted, was a Muʿtazilī – again figures, as author of a Qurʾān commentary, and also of the religious–philosophical *al Ḥūr al-ʿīn*. Meanwhile, scholastic theology/philosophy (*kalām*) had now long become the arena of debate between the schools and sects. The first *dāʿī muṭlaq* of the Fāṭimī–Ṭayyibī *daʿwah* in the Yemen, Dhuʿayb b. Mūsā al-Wādiʿī (d. 546/1151), the leader of the Ismāʿīlī sect there and protagonist of the concealed (*mastūr*) imam al-Ṭayyib b. Āmir during the reign of queen Arwā, was the author of several surviving theological-philosophical treatises.[77] Next in rank to him in the Ismāʿīlī hierarchy with the grade of *maʾdhūn* (licensed, i.e. to preach)[78] was the poet al-Sulṭān al-Khaṭṭāb, whose violent career has been described above, but who was a man of culture as well as a warrior and wrote nine theological-philosophical treatises. His successor in office, Ibrāhīm al-Ḥāmidī (from 536/1141 to 537/1142), in his *Kanz al-walad* (published) makes the earliest

[75] Neither title in *GAL*, SI, 587. [76] Ibid., 558. [77] Poonawala, *Biobibliography*, 137–9.
[78] See ʿA. Hamdānī, "Evolution".

reference in Ṭayyibī literature to the *Rasāʾil* ("Epistles") of the Ikhwān al-Ṣafāʾ.[79] During the Sulayhid regime, a certain Muḥammad b. Mālīk b. Abī ʾl-Faḍāʾil al-Ḥammādī (d. *c.* 473/1081) joined the Fāṭimī *daʿwah* and studied the exoteric and esoteric aspects of the sect until, as he says, "when he ascertained the evil nature of their doctrine, he recanted from it", and turned to account his inside knowledge of the *daʿwah* to attack it in his *Kashf asrār al-Bāṭiniyyah wa-akhbār al-Qarāmiṭah* ("The Exposure of the Secrets of the Esoterics [Ismāʿīlīs] and Histories of the Carmathians", published).

Prominent during this period as a Zaydī shaykh was *qāḍī* Jaʿfar b. Aḥmad b. ʿAbd al-Salām (d. 573/1177), contemporary and supporter of Imam Aḥmad b. Sulaymān (whose attempts to purchase soap while on campaign were described earlier). In addition to treatises on *fiqh*, philosophical and sectarian or doctrinal questions, he wrote a book entitled *Forty ʿAlawī ḥadīths*, and was a distinguished apologist of the Zaydī school.[80] The most eminent authority of the Shāfiʿī school during the ʿAbbasid era was Jaʿfar's opponent Yaḥyā b. Abī ʾl-Khayr al-ʿImrānī, who wrote his anti-Muʿtazilī *al-Intiṣār fī ʾl-radd ʿalā ʾl-Qadariyyah al-ashrār* ("Confutation of the Iniquitous Qadariyyah[= Muʿtazilīs])[81] after being alarmed at hearing that Jaʿfar, on a visit to Ibb, was disseminating such Muʿtazilī doctrines as their tenet that the Qurʾān is created, not coeternal with God. His eleven-volume *Bayān*, completed in 533/1138, is perhaps the Yemen's most celebrated Shāfiʿī treatise. Another Shāfiʿī doctor was Isḥāq b. Yūsuf al-Ṣardafī (d. 500/1107) who lectured at a school established in the Jāmiʿ Mosque of al-Ṣardaf and was an expert on arithmetic (*ḥisāb*) and the law of inheritance, on which subject he compiled *al-Kāfī fī ʾl-farāʾiḍ*.[82] Also in the fields of *fiqh* and *farāʾiḍ* (the fixed shares in the estate of the deceased allotted to his relatives on the basis of Qurʾān, iv.11, 12, 176) may be noted Imam Aḥmad b. Sulaymān's "orator" (*khaṭīb*), Isḥāq b. Aḥmad . . . ʿAbd al-Bāʿith (d. 555/1161), to whom the Zaydī biographer Ibn Abī ʾl-Rijāl (d. 1092/1681) attributes great activity in the systematic compilation of *ḥadīth* according to subject-matter (*taṣnīf*). Sulaymān b. Nāṣir al-Siḥāmī (d. 566/1171) was a pupil of the same Imām Aḥmad and wrote a three-volume legal work, *Shams al-sharīʿah*, while his twin brother ʿAlī, who became an adherent of the deviationist Zaydī Muṭarrifiyyah, subsequently recanted and wrote an exposition of *fiqh*.[83]

Most Sufis of this period were ascetics, whose writings commend austerity and spiritual exaltation. Among them was the poet and *faqīh* Abū ʾl-ʿAbbās Aḥmad b. Khumarṭāsh, author of *al-Maqālāt*, who died some time after 553/1159 while fleeing the harsh rule of sultan ʿAlī b. Mahdī of Zabīd.[84]

[79] For his other works, see Poonawala, *Biobibliography*, 141–3; for the "Sincere Brethren", see ch. 6, n. 14, above. [80] *GAL*, SI, 699–70. [81] Ibn Samurah, *Ṭabaqāt*, 106f.

[82] *GAL*, I, 620; *GAL*, SI, 855. [83] Ḥabshī, *Maṣādir*, 174.

[84] *GAL*, I, 301–2 does not list this title.

(One of Zabīd's most notable Sufis, Aḥmad b. Abī ᵓl-Khayr al-Ṣayyād [d. 579/1184], composed a supplement to this work.) In this context we may note that many of the authors referred to here achieved distinction in several fields. Aḥmad b. Khumarṭāsh was no less typical in this respect than were the Muᶜtazilī historian, philologist and exegete Nashwān b. Saᶜīd al-Ḥimyarī, the Zaydī apologist Jaᶜfar b. . . . ᶜAbd al-Salām, the Ismāᶜīlī historian ᶜUmārah al-Ḥakamī and, earlier, the first Zaydī Imam al-Hādī and his sons. Inevitably, therefore, in the following pages, certain names will recur under different headings.

Poets

Principal sources for this period are ᶜUmārah al-Ḥakamī's *Mufīd*, Nashwān b. Saᶜīd's *al-Ḥūr al-ᶜīn*, Muḥammed b. Ḥātim al-Yāmīᵓs *al-Simṭ al-ghālī*, and Ibn Abī ᵓl-Rijāl's *Maṭlaᶜ al-budūr*. The output of poetry in this period was considerable since most monarchs, Imams and their ministers were active patrons of poetry and of literature in general, some being poets themselves. As examples, at the Sulayhid court the founder of the dynasty ᶜAlī b. Muḥammad, the Fāṭimī *dāᶜī* Sabaᵓ b. Aḥmad and the amir ᶜAbdullāh b. Yaᶜlā al-Ṣulayḥī were all poets of note. Al-Sulṭān al-Khaṭṭāb, who was an ally of the Sulayhids, and his brother Sulaymān b. Ḥasan al-Ḥajūrī, who was not, battled in verse as well as with arms. Ḥātim al-Yāmī, the Hamdānid sultan whose dynasty succeeded that of the Sulayhids and who was also of the Ismāᶜīlī faction, and the Zaydī Imam Aḥmad b. Sulaymān, with whom Ḥātim did battle, were both poets, as were Jayyāsh, the Najahid sultan of Zabīd, who fought the Sulayhids,[85] his minister Khalaf b. Abī ᵓl-Ṭāhir al-Umawī, and ᶜAlī b. Muḥammad, founder of the Mahdid dynasty; some indeed were poets of major rank (*fuḥūl*). ᶜUmārah al-Ḥakamī's *Mufīd* alludes to no less than thirty poets belonging to this period, most of them being reckoned *fuḥūl*; mention may be made here of ᶜAlī b. Abī ᵓl-Ḥasan al-Ḥakamī, a contemporary of ᶜUmārah, and of Abū Bakr al-ᶜAnadī, ᶜUmārah's teacher, many of whose poems ᶜUmārah quotes; of ᶜAmr b. Yaḥyā al-Haythamī, the poet of the Sulayhid monarch, of al-Ḥusayn b. ᶜAlī al-Qummī, panegyrist of the Fāṭimī *dāᶜī* Sabaᵓ b. Aḥmad;[86] and of Ibn al-Hubaynī, the poet of the Mahdid ruler ᶜAlī b. Mahdī.

Yemeni literature, including poetry, its most important branch, came under the influence of new trends and motifs as a result of the close links at this time between Egypt and the Yemen, arising from the Sulayhids'

[85] See Ḥabshī/Niewöhner–Eberhard, *Muᵓallafāt*, 30–1.
[86] For al-Qummī's official correspondence with the Fatimids on behalf of the *dāᶜī*, see H. F. Ḥamdānī, *Ṣulayḥiyyūn*, 308–18.

support for the Fatimid caliphs in Cairo;[87] the cultural and political exchanges which resulted had a perceptible effect on the style of rhetoric and the stamp of poetry in the Yemen. But it is worth noting, in the light of our earlier remarks on the survival of heroic characteristics in the Yemeni poetry, that on the day of the battle of al-Sharazah (552/1158), as reported in Ibn Abī ʾl-Rijāl's *Maṭlaʿ al-budūr*, a prominent Zaydī, the *qāḍī* Muḥammad b. ʿAbdullāh al-Ḥimyarī, congratulated Imam Aḥmad b. Sulaymān on his victory over sultan Ḥātim of Yām in exultant warlike verses in the vein of the Jāhiliyyah poets.

AYYUBIDS AND RASULIDS: THE PERIOD OF FOREIGN INTERVENTION

The period here under review is that of the foreign intervention commencing in 569/1173 with the invasion of the Ayyubid Tūrānshāh from Egypt and concluding in 858/1454 with the fall of the Rasulid dynasty. It is not intended, however, to proceed much beyond the slaying in battle of the Zaydī Imam Aḥmad b. al-Ḥusayn in 656/1258 (the ʿAbbasid caliphate of Baghdad ended in the same year with the Mongol capture of the city).[88] When sultan Tūrānshāh overran the Yemen he subdued it militarily, sweeping away most of the local sultanates and amirates, and turned it into a province subject to the Ayyubid state, the bases of which were in Egypt and Syria. The Yemen became a battlefield for Arabs, the Ayyubids' Ghuzz Turkish mercenaries and Turkomans, Abyssinian slave-soldiers, mamlukes and mercenary horsemen. After the departure of the last Ayyubids, when their successors the Sunnī Rasulids took over (626/1229), controlling most of the Yemen, they continued the fight with the Zaydī Imams and the tribes of the northern Yemen. The Zaydīs had been the sole element the Ayyubids had been unable finally to subdue, and they continued to fight bitterly against the Rasulids until the Imam was killed. The Rasulid al-Muẓaffar became strong enough almost to unite the "Greater Yemen", but when he died in 694/1295 it was once more rent apart.

During this period three Imams rose to power: ʿAbdullāh b. Ḥamzah (d. 614/1218), Yaḥyā b. Muḥassin (d. 636/1239) and Aḥmad b. al-Ḥusayn (d. 656/1258). Sometimes these Imams were opposed by such petty rulers as the amirs of the Ḥamazāt Ashrāf (of al-Jawf); at others they would form a coalition with them against al-Muẓaffar, or the chieftains would ally

[87] See p. 421 for a specimen of correspondence between Fatimids and Sulayhids (*al-Sijillāt al-mustanṣiriyyah*); additional texts are given in H. F. Hamdānī, *Ṣulayḥiyyūn*, 301–7, 319–22. Cf. also ʿUmārah's *al-Nukat al-ʿaṣriyyah*.

[88] For this period of Yemeni history, see Smith, "Transfer", and *Ayyūbids and Early Rasūlids*, II.

themselves with the Rasulids against the Imams. But despite these shifting alliances, literature continued to flourish as before; and it was also an age of building, of colleges, mosques and especially of castles and forts in the high mountains. Kings, amirs, the notables and the wealthy began to vie with one another in ostentation and luxurious display, imitating in their buildings, costume and retinues the monarchs and the wealthy of India, Baghdad and Cairo, as Ibn Baṭṭūṭah later describes in the eighth/fourteenth century. Certain customs were introduced into the towns from abroad; dancing, singing and other amusements, food and drink, jewellery, costume, weaponry and vocabulary were influenced by foreign fashions and tongues (noteworthy were the introduction of the poisoned caltrop and the use of Greek fire – *nafṭ* – on land and sea,[89] the widespread use of slave-concubines and open consumption of wine by some sultans and amirs).

Writings of the Rasulid monarchs

The era of the Rasulid sultans (626–858/1229–1454) who supplanted the Ayyubids is accounted one of the most brilliant of Yemeni civilization. The Rasulid monarchs themselves displayed an interest in a great range of topics, practical and intellectual. The warrior sultan al-Muẓaffar Yūsuf b. ᶜUmar, who reigned nearly half a century from 647–94/1250–94, extended Rasulid power as far as Ḥaḍramawt and Ẓafār, though he was unable to take Ṣanᶜāʾ. Among his writings are a selection of forty *ḥadīth*s, a treatise on the movements of the heavenly bodies (extant), a medical work, a literary *Mufākahāt al-jalīs* on entertainment (both extant, the first published), and, with that practical bent that characterizes the monarchs of this dynasty, a volume of ten chapters on the pen, the manufacture of ink, writing in gold and silver, binders' glues, bindery, soap manufacture, etc.[90] However, the exemplar of Rasulid culture, both in range and depth, is the unique manuscript which was assembled by al-Malik al-Afḍal al-ᶜAbbās b. ᶜAlī (d. 778/1376), a miscellaneous assembly of writings of practical utility, of intellectual interest or of entertainment.[91] There is no very clear arrangement of the contents, which include astronomical and astrological data in profusion, tables, the ascension of the stars, the fixed stars, the astrolabe, Rūmī (Greek) and Arab dates and how to work them out, almanacs, Coptic and Jewish months, the *zīj* (astronomical handbook), sundials, agriculture (in which the Rasulids were much interested), including a summary of al-Malik al-Afḍal's own *Bughyat al-fallāḥīn*,[92]

[89] Cf. Smith, *Ayyūbids and Early Rasūlids*, I, gloss.
[90] Ḥabshī/Niewöhner–Eberhard, *Muʾallafāt*, 54–6.
[91] A facsimile edition by R. B. Serjeant and Daniel Varisco is in preparation.
[92] A work on comparative agriculture; see Serjeant, "The cultivation of cereals".

passages on animals and animal husbandry; genealogies, court etiquette, generalship, warfare, the handling of armies, the mangonel, lexicographical excursus on the names of weapons; fortresses, routes and distances between Yemeni cities and ports and places in India, and other geographical data; much on taxes and tax tables; a treatise on the *ḥajj*; the interpretation of dreams; the distinction between man and other animals; philosophy, Aristotle's *waṣiyyah* (counsel to Alexander);[93] historical material, tables of dates of events, comparative lexical tables of Arabic, Persian, Armenian, Turkish, etc., extracts from various non-Yemeni authors – the list is not exhaustive.

Poets

As in earlier periods, sultans and Imams, leaders and generals were also *ᶜulamāᵓ* and men of letters, often of great merit. Thus Imam ᶜAbdullāh b. Ḥamzah (561–614/1166–1218), scholar, poet, *faqīh* and warrior, one of the most cultured and learned of the Imams, who wrote a thick volume of verse and of versified treatises on many subjects, is credited by Zabārah with over forty books, of which the most famous is the four-volume *al-Shāfī*, concerned with matters of doctrine, while al-Ḥabshī cites eighty-one titles of works attributed to him. The British Library has a copy of his *Dīwān* and of his *rajaz*-poem, with commentary, on the points, care and training of the horse. This Imam engaged in several hard-fought battles with the Hatimid sultans, and crushed the Zaydī Muṭarrifiyyah, destroying their mosque near Ṣanᶜāᵓ – which prompted them to write to the ᶜAbbāsid caliph for aid.[94] A copy of the Imam's replies to questions on the Muṭarrifiyyah is also in the British Library.[95] His son, the amir Muḥammad, known as al-Muḥtasib,[96] wrote a poem in the form of a *mufākharah*, or vaunting war of words, between ᶜAdnān and Qaḥṭān (the Arabs of North and South), entitled *Dhāt al-furūᶜ fī buyūt ᶜAdnān wa-qabāᵓilihā wa-faḍāᵓilihim*, which has twice been printed, besides writing on *kalām* and producing a commentary on his father's *urjūzah* on the horse (also published).[97] His brother Aḥmad was also a poet. Another Imam, al-Ḥasan b. Badr al-Dīn (d. 670/1271), wrote a lengthy *urjūzah* on the imams of the Prophet's family (*ᶜitrah*)[98] and their

[93] See *CHALUP*, 156. [94] See p. 466.

[95] For his writings, see *GAL*, I, 509; *GAL*, SI, 701, Ḥabshī/Niewöhner–Eberhard, *Muᵓallafāt*, 36–48, Tritton, "Muṭarrifiyah", Madelung, *Der Imam al-Qāsim*.

[96] Title given to a substitute or acting Imam, this being his position in the confusion ensuing on his father's death. See Strothmann, *Staatsrecht*, 94f.

[97] See Shāmī, *Dāmighat al-dawāmigh*, introd., 59; *GAL*, SI, 460.

[98] The Prophet's family in direct patrilinear descent from ᶜAlī and Fāṭimah's offspring.

virtues (*manāqib*) up to his own time, which he provided with a bulky commentary entitled *Anwār al-yaqīn* – a favourite genre of composition among the Prophet's descendants.[99]

The House of Ḥātim, like the other ruling families, had its complement of poets, in the persons of three brothers, ᶜAmr, ᶜAlwān and sultan Mudrik b. Bishr b. Ḥātim b. Aḥmad al-Yāmī. ᶜAmr's *qaṣīdah*, in which he appeals to his father sultan Bishr, when he and his brothers were taken prisoner in 585/1189 by the Ghuzz Turks outside Ṣanᶜāᵓ, to ransom them, is quoted in *al-Simṭ al-ghālī*:

> In no way think I fret for what has befallen [us].
> By your troth, truly resolute am I in fortitude,
> Fearing naught save the tattle of meaner men:
> "Has their father fallen short, by neglect to ransom them?"[100]

ᶜAlwān with his cousin held Ṣanᶜāᵓ on behalf of the Rasulid al-Muẓaffar in 619/1223, and engaged in a poetic correspondence with the Zaydī amir-poet Muḥammad b. ᶜAbdullāh b. Ḥamzah,[101] for whose brother Aḥmad he wrote a *qaṣīdah* in praise of al-Muẓaffar, whose generals had treated the Imam's defeated supporters at Ṣaᶜdah with great mercy. It is not at all impossible that he is "the poet of Hamdān" quoted under this name in *al-Simṭ al-ghālī* as author of an outstanding piece of political verse censuring the action of Imam Aḥmad b. al-Ḥusayn for executing several men on mere suspicion when he occupied Ṣanᶜāᵓ following the slaying of the Rasulid sultan Nūr al-Dīn ᶜUmar b. ᶜAlī in 647/1250.[102] The third brother, Mudrik, had shown still greater flexibility, writing a *qaṣīdah* for the two Rasulids, Ḥasan b. ᶜAlī and ᶜUmar b. ᶜAlī, to send to their masters the Ayyubids in Egypt describing their victory over the Zaydīs at Ṣanᶜāᵓ in 619/1223, and composing a poem of consolation on the same event which he sent to the defeated Zaydī amir Muḥammad b. ᶜAbdullāh b. Ḥamzah.[103] Al-Qāsim b. ᶜAlī b. Hutaymil, the greatest poet of the seventh/thirteenth century, was a Zaydī who served both the Imam Aḥmad b. al-Ḥusayn then the Rasulid al-Muẓaffar. According to Ibn Abī ᵓl-Rijāl's *Maṭlaᶜ al-budūr*, he died poor and aged (probably in 696/1297), having outlived the kings and Imams, his patrons, whom he had eulogized. Al-ᶜAqīlī's edition of his *Dīwān* leaves out anything "connected with partisanship, narrow sectarianism, unacceptable hyperbole or uncommendable extremism", and omits the poems on the

[99] *GAL*, SI, 703; Ḥabshī/Niewöhner–Eberhard, *Muᵓallafāt*, 52–3.
[100] Smith, *Ayyūbids and Early Rasūlids*, I, 35.
[101] Khazrajī, *ᶜUqūd*, ed. Asal, III, 4, 36–8/ed. Akwaᶜ, I, 43–5, trans. Redhouse, III, I, 84–6.
[102] Smith, *Ayyūbids and Early Rasūlids*, I, 236–9.
[103] Ibid., 2, 89; I, 187–8 and 186–7; Khazrajī, *ᶜUqūd*, trans. Redhouse, III, I, 86–7.

Zaydī Imams, apparently on this count. Here is Ibn Hutaymil's description of how al-Muẓaffar took prisoner the Imam Ibrāhīm b. Tāj al-Dīn in 674/1275:

Around their lord they rallied, but, become certain
Of death, from him they fled, flying both far and wide,
Raining lashes on their horses, five-year-olds,
In headlong flight from the mares and colts [of the foe][104]
Like falcons, grey plumage white-flecked, by rain wetted,
Swooping swiftly from the skies down on their aeries.
They escaped! But, firm, Ibrāhīm commands himself –
Charge yet again, flee not, fearing very shame,[105]
Till, when white-hot the battle's cauldron grew, so tight –
Pressed, no longer could he the vanguard horse withstand;
His spirit, resolute, bore him, in a castle
To fortify him, not hide skulking in a cave:
Yet none did he encounter turning to his aid,
Nor found he any to fight on behind a wall.[106]

Another panegyrist of the Rasulids was Muḥammad b. Ḥimyar (d. 651/1253), with whom Ibn Hutaymil used to hold poetic dialogue (*muḥāwarah*); his prolific and accomplished verse is quoted occasionally in al-Khazrajī's *al-ᶜUqūd al-luᵓluᵓiyyah*.

Other dynasties also had their representatives. A poet variously called Aḥmad b. Muḥammad al-Ashraqī (in Yāqūt's "Geographical Dictionary") and Aḥmad b. Muḥammad al-Umawī (in *al-Simṭ al-ghālī*) is noteworthy for a *qaṣīdah*, quoted in *al-Simṭ al-ghālī*, which eulogizes the Ayyubid al-Muᶜizz Ismāᶜīl b. Tughtakīn (regn. 577–93/1181–97) and the Umayyad caliphs, from whom al-Muᶜizz, who aspired to autonomy in the Yemen, claimed descent (this poem is in a markedly different vein from al-Hamdānī's *Dāmighah* and other poems of the pro-Qaḥṭānī or pro-ᶜAdnānī class described in this chapter). An Ismāᶜīlī poet whose *Dīwān* is still extant was the fifth Fāṭimī-Ṭayyibī *dāᶜī* ᶜAlī b. Muḥammad al-Anf.[107] Sources for the numerous other poets of this period – as well as for scholars and political leaders – are al-Khazrajī's *al-ᶜUqūd al-luᵓluᵓiyyah*, Muḥammad b. Ḥātim al-Yāmī's *al-Simṭ al-ghālī*, and Abū Makhramah's *Tārīkh thaghr ᶜAdan*.[108] Ismāᶜīlī poets are listed and quoted respectively in two modern sources, Poonawala's *Biobibliography* and H. F. Hamdānī's *al-Ṣulayḥiyyūn*.

The poets of Ḥaḍramawt of this period, the known history of which is still extremely sparse, are recorded in the modern writer ᶜAbdullāh al-Saqqāf's *Tārīkh al-shuᶜarāᵓ al-Ḥaḍramiyyīn*. The best known appears to be

104 *Al-muharāti wa ᵓl-amhārī*, a poetic cliché.
105 *Bi ᵓl-karri wa-lā bi ᵓl-farri, khawfa ᵓl-ᶜārī.*
106 Shāmī, *Qiṣṣat al-adab*, 355.
107 Poonawala, *Biobibliography*, 156–61.
108 Of particular interest is a poem by a shipwrecked merchant quoted in *Tārīkh thaghr ᶜAdan*, II, 32–6; it is in quatrains and remarkable for its complex, non-classical metrical and rhyme-schemes.

Shaykh ʿAlī b. ʿUqbah al-Ziyādī al-Khawlānī of Wādī Dawʿān (d. 695/1295), because he came to the court of the Rasulid al-Muẓaffar in Aden.[109] Al-Saqqāf says that many of these Ḥaḍramī poets wrote "verse of the native (*waṭanī*) type, *al-ḥumaynī*, but I have rarely mentioned it since it is local, restricted". But *ḥumaynī*, *pace* Saqqāf, was far from being confined to Ḥaḍramawt and, as described earlier in this chapter, cannot be said to be restricted. Writing in 1354/1934 and conforming to the literary attitudes of the time, which still persist today, al-Saqqāf takes a conservatively classical line; thus his volume on the thirteenth/nineteenth century ignores the existence of the great *ḥumaynī* poets of the age.

Historians

Biographical literature flourished during this period, notably biographies of individuals. As examples, the historian Nashwān b. Saʿīd's son ʿAlī (d. 614/1218) produced one of the three known biographies of the Imam ʿAbdullāh b. Ḥamzah, the inveterate foe of the Ismāʿīlī Ḥātimid sultans;[110] Yaḥyā b. al-Qāsim b. Yaḥyā b. Ḥamzah, a fine poet and careful critical scholar, wrote a biography of the Imam Aḥmad b. al-Ḥusayn (d. 656/1258); the work is well known and in circulation in the Yemen, and a copy exists in the Egyptian Library.[111] Another such biography was Abū Firās Fāḍil b. ʿAbbās Daghtham's life of the Rasulid al-Manṣūr Nūr al-Dīn ʿUmār, *al-Sīrah al-sharīfah al-Manṣūriyyah*: Abū Firās had been in charge of the drafting of the ruler's official correspondence and documents (he was also a particularly prolific poet).[112]

General histories and group biographies include Yaḥyā b. Sulaymān al-Ḥajūrī's (d. after 636/1239) *Rawḍat al-akhbār* on Islamic history of the first two centuries,[113] while Ḥumayd b. Aḥmad al-Muḥallī (d. 652/1254), *faqīh* and historian, compiled *al-Ḥadāʾiq al-wardiyyah fī manāqib aʾimmat al-Zaydiyyah*, two stout volumes of biographies of the Zaydī Imams and their illustrious deeds from the time of their ancestor ʿAlī b. Abī Ṭālib up to his own day; the British Library has two copies of *al-Ḥadāʾiq* and one of the same author's *Maḥāsin al-azhār fī faḍl al-ʿitrah al-aṭhār* on a similar theme, the virtues of the Prophet's House.[114]

A major source, frequently referred to in the latter part of this chapter, is *al-Simṭ al-ghālī*. It author, Muḥammad b. Ḥātim, belonged to one of the branches of the Hatimid family and became a Rasulid official under al-

[109] Saqqāf, *Tārīkh*, I, 65–71; he also gives biographies of five other poets of this period.
[110] Cf. Ḥabshī/Niewöhner–Eberhard, *Muʾallafāt*, 37. [111] B. 2163; other MSS, *GAL*, I, 388.
[112] Ibn Abī ʾl-Rijāl, *Maṭlaʿ al-budūr*.
[113] Cairo, Dār al-Kutub, History: 5526; other MSS, *GAL*, SI, 587.
[114] Fuʾād Sayyid, *Maṣādir*, 127–8; other MSS, *GAL*, I, 397; *GAL*, SI, 560.

Muẓaffar; *al-Simṭ al-ghālī* covers the complicated political history of the second half of the eighth/thirteenth century and has been edited by G. Rex Smith under the title *The Ayyūbids and Early Rasūlids in the Yemen*.

Philologists and rhetoricians

Muḥammad, son of Nashwān b. Saᶜīd al-Ḥimyarī and brother of the historian ᶜAlī b. Nashwān, abridged, in his *Ḍiyāᵓ al-ḥulūm*, his father's great encyclopaedia *Shams al-ᶜulūm*, and seems to have had a taste for this kind of activity, for he also abridged and altered parts of al-Hamdānī's *Iklīl*.[115] (He was a contemporary of Imam ᶜAbdullāh b. Ḥamzah [d. 614/1218], who appointed him to the post of *qāḍī*, but he came out in opposition against him and indited a treatise attacking the Imams which he entitled *al-Īḍāḥ*, to which ᶜAbdullāh b. Ḥamzah retorted with a refutation, *al-Ifṣāḥ li-ᶜujmat al-Īḍāḥ*.)[116] Other philologists include Muḥammad b. ᶜAlī al-Qalaᶜī, compiler of *al-Lafẓ al-mustaghrab min alfāẓ al-Muhadhdhab* on difficult vocabulary in a famous Shāfiᶜī *fiqh* book, *al-Muhadhdhab* by Ibrāhīm al-Shīrāzī;[117] Ibrāhīm b. ᶜAlī b. ᶜUjayl (d. 646/1249), author of a commentary on the *Niẓām al-gharīb* of ᶜĪsā b. Ibrāhīm al-Rabaᵓī;[118] and the poet Yaḥyā b. Ibrāhīm al-ᶜAmak (d. 681/1282), who made a compendium of prosody.[119] In the field of rhetoric, the Muṭarrifī poet Ḥusayn b. al-Nassākh, a renowned epistolographer, composed the famous letter (referred to on page 461) which was sent to the ᶜAbbāsid caliph in 611/1214 urging him to despatch a military expedition to put down Imam ᶜAbdullāh b. Ḥamzah, warning him against the Imam – whose distinguished qualities both as a scholar and a general he describes – and of the danger he constituted to the ᶜAbbasid caliphate. The letter is couched in verse and prose and is reckoned a masterpiece of the age.

Qurᵓān commentaries and ḥadīth scholars

The following scholars may be held to represent the activity in these fields at this period. ᶜAlī Yaḥyā al-Ṣabāḥī (d. 656/1258), a Zaydī, wrote a four-volume commentary on the Qurᵓān; ᶜAṭiyyah b. Muḥyī ᵓl-Dīn al-Najrānī (603–65/1207), one of the greatest Zaydī scholars, wrote a work on the science of Qurᵓān interpretation.

Muḥammad b. Ismāᶜīl b. Abī ᵓl-Sayf (d. 609/1213), a Shāfiᶜī of Zabīd, was an authority on *ḥadīth* to whom most Yemeni chains of authority (*isnāds*) go

115 See pp. 449, 457.
116 Cf. Ḥabshī/Niewöhner–Eberhard, *Muᵓallafāt*, 43, no. 48.
117 Ḥabshī, *Maṣādir*, 372; cf. *GAL*, I, 485; *GAL*, SI, 669.
118 Ḥabshī, *Maṣādir*, 368; cf. *GAL*, SI, 492.
119 Shāmī, *Qiṣṣat al-adab*, 349.

back. ʿAlī b. Muḥammad b. Jadīd al-Ḥaḍramī (d. 620/1223), of the Ḥaḍramī Bā ʿAlawī Sayyids, taught *ḥadīth* in the Shāfiʿī part of the Yemen. ʿAlī b. Ḥumayd al-Anf (d. *c.* 646/1249), a Zaydī, wrote *Shams al-akhbār* on the sayings of the Prophet (published). Muḥammad b. Ḥamzah b. Abī ʾl-Najm (d. 656/1258), a Zaydī *ḥadīth* expert, collected the *ḥadīth*s cited in Imam al-Hādī's *al-Aḥkām* in his *Durar al-aḥādīth al-nabawiyyah*. Amir Ḥusayn b. Badr al-Dīn (d. 662/1264), another Zaydī, compiled a four-volume work on *ḥadīth*, *Shifāʾ al-uwām*, which is still used as an authority in the Yemen.[120]

Theologians

Here again it is simplest to list the writers on *kalām*, many of whose writings are still little known or completely unknown outside the Yemen.

Zaydīs: al-Ḥasan b. Muḥammad al-Raṣṣāṣ (d. 584/1189) was a pupil of one of the great Zaydī *ʿulamāʾ*, Jaʿfar . . . b. ʿAbd al-Salām,[121] and author of a number of theological or philosophical works. Ḥumaydan b. al-Qāsim (d. 656/1258) wrote, *inter alia*, against Muʿtazilism and Muṭarrifī dialectic.[122] Aḥmad b. Muḥammad al-Muḥallī al-Hamdānī al-Wādiʿī is best known for the three-volume *ʿUmdat al-mustarshidīn fī uṣūl al-dīn*, but he also wrote polemics against the Muṭarrifīs, the Qadariyyah (i.e. the Zaydī Muʿtazilīs), Ashʿarī tenets and the Carmathians, in a treatise with the resounding title of *al-Ḥusām al-battār fī ʾl-radd ʿalā ʾl-Qarāmiṭah al-kuffār* ("The Keen-Edged Sword in Refutation of the Infidel Carmathians"). He was killed fighting for the Imam in 652/1255 by the Rasulids.[123] ʿAbdullāh b. Zayd al-ʿAnsī (d. 667/1269) is chiefly known as a polemicist against the Muṭarrifiyyah, against whom he penned a number of books or treatises, one being on the interesting subject of "The Prohibition of Inter-marriage with the Iniquitous Muṭarrifiyyah Sect"; another demonstrates the distinction between Islam and the Muṭarrifiyyah.[124] The most notable scholar of the Muṭarrifī school itself was Sulaymān b. Muḥammad b. Aḥmad al-Muḥallī (lived probably sixth/twelfth century), author of *al-Burhān al-rāyiq*, which embodies those tenets of the Muṭarrifiyyah which are in conformity with the school of Imam al-Hādī.[125]

Ismāʿīlīs: Muḥammad b. Ṭāhir al-Ḥārithī (d. 584/1188) was a prolific writer, of whom Poonawala remarks that his "*Majmūʿ al-tarbiyah* . . . is a classic chrestomathy of Ismāʿīlī literature, which served as a model for later compilers".[126] The third *dāʿī*, Ḥātim b. Ibrāhīm al-Ḥāmidī (557–96/1162–

[120] Zabārah, *Aʾimmat al-Yaman*, I, 183–4; Ḥabshī, *Maṣādir*, 109.

[121] See p. 458.

[122] *GAL*, SI, 702–3.

[123] Ḥabshī, *Maṣādir*, 107.

[124] Ibid., 110; Madelung, *Der Imam al-Qāsim*, 202, 222.

[125] MS: University of Ṣanʿāʾ Library, Theology: 120.

[126] *Biobibliography*, 143–50.

99) is reckoned one of the greatest Ismāʿīlī scholars; withdrawing from the internecine warfare of the age to al-Ḥaṭīb in the Ḥarāz mountains, he devoted himself to learning and to writing on Ismāʿīlī doctrine, organization, cosmology, etc.[127] The fifth *dāʿī*, ʿAlī b. Muḥammad . . . b. al-Walīd al-Anf al-Qurashī (d. 612/1215),[128] in whose family the office of *dāʿī* was to reside for approximately three centuries, took over the missionary side of the *daʿwah* after the death of ʿAlī b. Ḥātim al-Ḥāmidī; he wrote extensively in the Ismāʿīlī field and engaged in polemics against the Sunnīs, Muʿtazilīs, Zaydīs and others; his *Tāj al-ʿaqāʾid* is available in English translation.[129]

Shāfiʿīs: Ṭāhir (d. 587/1191), son of the famous Yaḥyā b. Abī ʾl-Khayr al-ʿImrānī,[130] became *qāḍī* of Jiblah and wrote a refutation (*radd*) against the notable Zaydī *qāḍī* Jaʿfar . . . b. ʿAbd al-Salām.

Scholars in fiqh and farāʾiḍ; Sufis

One of the most famous Zaydī *faqīh*s of the Yemen was amir ʿAlī b. al-Ḥusayn b. Yaḥyā, a descendant of the first Imam of the Yemen, al-Hādī. His *al-Lumaʿ*, on the *fiqh* of the Prophet's House, is one of the most highly regarded books of the Zaydīs and has been a favourite subject of commentaries. The author was alive in the reign of Imam Aḥmad b. al-Ḥusayn (d. 656/1258).[131] Al-Faḍl b. Abī ʾl-Saʿd al-ʿUṣayfirī (d. 614/1217) composed a gigantic work in ten volumes on *farāʾiḍ*, *al-Fāyiḍ*; he flourished in the time of Imam ʿAbdullāh b. Ḥamzah.[132]

A noted Shāfiʿī *faqīh* was Ismāʿīl b. Muḥammad al-Ḥaḍramī (d. 696/1297), who was made chief *qāḍī* at Zabīd by the Rasulid sultan al-Muẓaffar. He attained more than purely local note, for half a century or so later the Egyptian al-Subkī remarks: "His compilations (*muṣannafāt*) concerning the [Shāfiʿī] school in the Yemen are famous." He is noted for his commentary on al-Shīrāzī's *al-Muhadhdhab*, but also produced a collection of *fatwā*s (legal opinions) and wrote on Sufism.[133]

A source for Sufis of this period is al-Sharjī (d. 893/1488), *Ṭabaqāt al-khawāṣṣ*. The Zaydī rite is in general antipathetic to Sufi practices, but the Shāfiʿīs produced a number of famous mystics, such as Abū ʾl-Ghayth (d. 651/1253), known as the "Sun of Suns" – a converted brigand. His sayings were collected by one of his pupils.[134] Better known to the outside world is the great Sufi saint Shaykh Aḥmad b. ʿAlwān (d. 655/1267), whose shrine is at Yafrus; the ecstatics (*majādhīb*) attached to it once travelled widely. His *Dīwān*, mostly of Sufi verse, is still well known today.[135]

[127] Ibid., 151–5. [128] Ibid., 156–61. [129] In summary in Ivanow, *A Creed*.
[130] See p. 458; for father and son, see Ibn Samurah, *Ṭabaqāt*. [131] Ḥabshī, *Maṣādir*, 178.
[132] Ibid., 260. [133] Ibid., 180. [134] Ibid., 173. [135] Zabārah, *Aʾimmat al-Yaman*, I, 185.

APPENDIX
TABLE OF METRES

The Arabic system of metrics is described in *CHALUP*, 15–17. The following is a simplified table of the principal metres referred to in this volume. The symbol ∪ represents the sequence consonant + short vowel; the symbol – represents the sequence consonant + vowel + consonant; × represents a variable sequence (i.e. either ∪ or – may be used). Feet are separated by a single stroke (/); the end of a hemistich is marked by a double stroke (//). All symbols read from left to right. The symbols are followed by the Arabic mnemonic for each metre, in which rhythmic stress is marked according to the scheme proposed by G. Weil, to whose article "ʿArūḍ" in *EI*[2], the reader is referred.

ṭawīl
∪ – × /∪ – × – /∪ – × /∪ – × – // twice
faʿū́lun mafā́ʿīlun faʿū́lun mafā́ʿīlun

basīṭ
× × ∪ – /× ∪ – /× – ∪ – /$\overline{\cup\cup}$ – // twice
mustafʿilún fāʿilún mustafʿilún fāʿilún

wāfir
∪ – $\overline{\cup\cup}$ – /∪ – $\overline{\cup\cup}$ – /∪ – – // twice
mufā́ʿalatun mufā́ʿalatun faʿū́lun

kāmil
$\overline{\cup\cup}$ – ∪ – /$\overline{\cup\cup}$ – ∪ – /$\overline{\cup\cup}$ – ∪ – // twice
mutafāʿilún mutafāʿilún mutafāʿilún

rajaz
× × ∪ – /× × ∪ – /× × ∪ – // twice
mustafʿilún mustafʿilún mustasfʿilún

ramal
× ∪ – – /× ∪ – – /× ∪ – – // twice
fāʿilā́tun fāʿilā́tun fāʿilā́tun

sarīʿ
× × ∪ – /× × ∪ – /– ∪ – // twice
mustafʿilún mustafʿilún mafʿūlā́tu/fāʿilun

khafīf
× ∪ – – / × – ∪ – / × ∪ – – // twice
fāʿilātun mustáfʿilun fāʿilātun

mutaqārib
∪ – × / ∪ – × / ∪ – × / ∪ – × // twice
faʿūlun faʿūlun faʿūlun faʿūlun

BIBLIOGRAPHY

The bibliography consists of two parts, a general bibliography and chapter bibliographies. The general bibliography lists reference works and editions (other than *dīwāns*) referred to in more than one chapter. The chapter bibliographies are intended only as a listing of sources, and not as a comprehensive guide to further reading. Entries are alphabetical; the definite article and the prefixes *fī*, *Kitāb*, (or *K.*) and *Risālah* (or R.) are disregarded.

GENERAL BIBLIOGRAPHY

Abū ʾl-Faraj al-Iṣfahānī *Kitāb al-Aghānī*, I–XX, Bulaq, 1285 AH; XXI, ed. R. Brünnow, Leiden, 1883.

Abū Nuᶜaym al-Iṣfahānī *Ḥilyat al-awliyāʾ*, Cairo, 1932–8.

Brockelmann, C. *Geschichte der arabischen Litteratur* and suppls. I–III, Leiden, 1943–9.

The Cambridge History of Arabic Literature: Arabic Literature to the End of the Umayyad Period, eds. A. F. L. Beeston, T. M. Johnstone, R. B. Serjeant and G. R. Smith, Cambridge, 1983.

The Cambridge History of Iran, III, ed. E. Yarshater, Cambridge, 1983; IV, ed. R. N. Frye, 1975; V, ed. J. A. Boyle, 1968.

The Cambridge History of Islam, I, eds. P. M. Holt, A. K. S. Lambton and B. Lewis, Cambridge, 1970.

The Encyclopaedia of Islam, Leiden and London, 1913–38.

The Encyclopaedia of Islam, eds. B. Lewis and J. Schacht, Leiden and London, 1960.

Gibb, H. A. R. *Arabic Literature*, Oxford, 1963.

Studies on the Civilization of Islam, eds. Stanford J. Shaw and William R. Polk, London, 1962.

Goldziher, I. *Muslim Studies* (*Muhammedanische Studien*, Halle, 1889–90), ed. S. M. Stern, trans. C. R. Barber and S. M. Stern, London, 1966.

al-Ḥuṣrī *Zahr al-ādāb*, ed. ᶜA. M. al-Bajāwī, Cairo, 1372/1953.

Ibn ᶜAbd Rabbih *al-ᶜIqd al-farīd*, eds. A. Amīn et al., Cairo, 1367–72/1948–53.

Ibn Khallikān *Wafāyāt al-aᶜyān*, ed. I. ᶜAbbās, Beirut, 1968–72; trans. M. de Slane, *Ibn Khallikān's Biographical Dictionary*, London, 1842–71.

Ibn al-Nadīm *al-Fihrist*, ed. R. Tajaddud, Tehran, 1391/1971; trans. B. Dodge, New York, 1970.

Ibn Rashīq *al-ʿUmdah*, ed. M. M. D. ʿAbd al-Ḥamīd, Beirut, 1972.
al-Jāḥiẓ *Kitāb al-Bayān wa ʾl-tabyīn*, ed. ʿA. S. M. Hārūn, Cairo, 1367–9/1948–50.
Kitāb al-Ḥayawān, ed. ʿA. S. M. Hārūn, Cairo, 1938–45.
al-Jurjānī, al-Qāḍī *al-Wasāṭah*, eds. M.ʿA. F. Ibrāhīm and ʿA. M. al-Bajāwī, Cairo, 1951.
Lane, E. W. *An Arabic–English Lexicon*, London, 1863–93.
Nallino, C. A. *La Littérature arabe des origines à l'époque de la dynastie umayyade* (*La letteratura araba*, Rome, 1948), trans. C. Pellat, Paris, 1950.
Nicholson, R. A. *A Literary History of the Arabs*, Cambridge, 1907.
Pellat, C. *Le Milieu basrien et la formation de Ǧāḥiẓ*, Paris, 1953.
Sezgin, F. *Geschichte des arabischen Schrifttums*, Leiden, 1967.
Shorter Encyclopaedia of Islam, eds. H. A. R. Gibb and J. H. Kramers, Leiden and London, 1953.
al-Thaʿālibī *Tatimmat al-Yatīmah*, ed. A. Iqbāl, Tehran, 1353.
Yatīmat al-dahr, ed. M. I. Sāwī, Cairo, 1353/1934.
Yāqūt *Irshād al-arīb*, ed. D. S. Margoliouth, London, 1923–31.

1: *ADAB* AND THE CONCEPT OF *BELLES-LETTRES*

Abū Tammām *al-Ḥamāsah*: see Marzūqī.
al-ʿAskarī *Dīwān al-Maʿānī*, Cairo, 1352/1933–4.
Bashshār b. Burd *Dīwān*, eds. M. b. ʿAshūr et al., Cairo, 1359/1940.
al-Buḥturī *Dīwān*, ed. Ḥ. K. al-Ṣīrafī, 2nd edn, Cairo, 1972–8.
al-Ḥamāsah, ed. L. Cheikho, Beirut, 1387/1967.
al-Bukhārī *al-Ṣaḥīḥ*, Cairo, 1345–7/1927–8.
Ibn al-Qifṭī *Inbāh al-ruwāh ʿalā anbāh al-nuḥāh*, ed. M. A. Ibrāhīm, Cairo, 1369–74/1950–5.
Ibn Qutaybah *Adab al-kātib*, ed. M. Grünert, Leiden, 1900.
Kitāb al-Shiʿr wa ʾl-shuʿarāʾ, ed. M. J. de Goeje, Leiden, 1902.
ʿUyūn al-akhbār, Cairo, 1343–9/1925–30.
Ibn al-Sīd al-Baṭalyawsī *al-Iqtiḍāb fī sharḥ Adab al-kuttāb*, Beirut, 1973.
Keilani, I. *Abū Ḥayyān at-Tawḥīdī*, Beirut, 1950.
Kilito, A. *Les Séances*, Paris, 1983.
Kushājim *Adab al-nadīm*, Cairo, 1298 AH.
al-Marzūqī *Sharḥ Dīwān al-ḥamāsah*, eds. A. Amīn and ʿA. Hārūn, Cairo, 1371–2/1951–2.
Mez, A., ed. *Abulḳâsim, ein bagdâder Sittenbild*, Heidelberg, 1902.
al-Mubarrad *al-Kāmil*, eds. Z. Mubārak and A. M. Shākir, Cairo, 1355–6/1936–7.
Pellat, C. "Variations sur le thème de l'*adab*", *Correspondance d'Orient*, Etudes 5–6, Brussels, 1964.
Rosenthal, F. *Knowledge Triumphant*, Leiden, 1970.
al-Sukkarī *Sharḥ ashʿār al-Hudhaliyyīn*, ed. ʿA. A. Farrāj, Cairo, 1384/1965.
Usāmah b. Munqidh *Lubāb al-ādāb*, ed. A. M. Shakīr, Cairo, 1354/1935.

Wensinck, A. J. et al., eds. *Concordance et indices de la tradition musulmane*, Leiden, 1936–69.

al-Zubaydī *Ṭabaqāt al-naḥwiyyīn wa ʾl-lughawiyyīn*, ed. M. A. Ibrāhīm, Cairo, 1373/1954.

2: *SHUʿŪBIYYAH* IN ARABIC LITERATURE

Dagorn, R. *La Geste d'Ismaël d'après l'onomastique et la tradition arabes*, Geneva and Paris, 1981.

Ibn Qutaybah *Kitāb al-ʿArab*: see Kurd ʿAlī.

Kurd ʿAlī, M., ed. *Rasāʾil al-bulaghāʾ*, Cairo, 1365/1946.

Madelung, W. "The Sufyānī between tradition and history", *Studia Islamica*, LXXIII, 1984.

al-Masʿūdī, *Murūj al-dhahab*, II, ed. C. Pellat, Beirut, 1966.

Monroe, James T. *The Shuʿūbiyya in al-Andalus, the Risāla of Ibn García and Five Refutations*, California, 1970.

Mottahedeh, Roy P. "The Shuʿūbīyah controversy and the social history of early Islamic Iran", *International Journal of Middle East Studies*, VII, 1976.

Vadet, J.-C. "L''Acculturation' des Sud-Arabiques de Fusṭāṭ au lendemain de la conquête arabe", *Bulletin d'Etudes Orientales*, XIII, Damascus, 1969.

3: IBN AL-MUQAFFAʿ AND EARLY ʿABBASID PROSE

ʿAbbās, Iḥsān "Naẓrah jadīdah fī baʿḍī ʾl-kutubi ʾl-mansūbah li-Ibn al-Muqaffaʿ", *Revue de l'Académie Arabe de Damas*, LII, 1977.

Beeston. A. F. L. *Samples of Arabic Prose in its Historical Development*, Oxford, 1977.

Boyce, M., trans. *The Letter of Tansar*, Rome, 1968.

Charles-Dominique, P. "Le Système éthique d'Ibn al-Muqaffaʿ d'après ses deux épîtres dites 'AL-ṢAĠĪR' et 'AL-KABĪR'", *Arabica*, XII, 1965.

Coulson, N. J. *A History of Islamic Law*, Edinburgh, 1964.

Crone, P. *Slaves on Horses*, Cambridge, 1980.

van Ess, J. "Some fragments of the *Muʿāraḍat al-Qurʾān* attributed to Ibn al-Muqaffaʿ", *Studia Arabica et Islamica: Festschrift for Iḥsān ʿAbbās*, ed. W. al-Qāḍī, Beirut, 1981.

Gabrieli, F. "L'opera di Ibn al-Muqaffaʿ", *Rivista degli Studi Orientali*, XIII, 1931–2.

Goitein, S. D. *Studies in Islamic history and Institutions*, Leiden, 1966.

Guidi, M., ed. and trans. *La lotta tra l'Islam e il manicheismo/K. al-radd ʿalā . . . Ibn al-Muqaffaʿ*, Rome, 1927.

Kurd ʿAlī, M., ed. *Rasāʾil al-bulaghāʾ*, Cairo, 1365/1946.

Pellat, C., ed. and trans. *Ibn al-Muqaffaʿ . . . "conseilleur du calife"*, Paris, 1976.

Schacht, J. *An Introduction to Islamic Law*, Oxford, 1964.

The Origins of Muhammadan Jurisprudence, Oxford, 1950.

Shaban, M. *Islamic History: a New Interpretation*, II, Cambridge, 1976.

Sourdel, D. "La Biographie d'Ibn al-Muqaffa^c^ d'après les sources anciennes", *Arabica*, I, 1954.

Wansbrough, J. *Quranic Studies*, Oxford, 1977.

4: AL-JĀḤIẒ

al-Bayhaqī *Kitāb al-Maḥāsin wa ʾl-masāwī*, ed. F. Schwally, Giessen, 1902.

Blau, J. "Notes on syntactic phenomena in classical Arabic as exhibited by Jāḥiẓ's 'K. al-Buxalā'", *Israel Oriental Studies*, V, 1975.

van Ess, J. "Ǧāḥiẓ und die *aṣḥāb al-maʿārif*", *Der Islam*, XLII, 1966.

Das Kitāb al-Nakṯ des Naẓẓām und seine Rezeption im Kitāb al-Futyā des Ǧāḥiẓ, Göttingen, 1972.

Geries, I. Un genre littéraire arabe, al-Maḥāsin wa ʾl-masāwī, Paris, 1977.

"Quelques aspects de la pensée muʿtazilite d'al-Ǧāḥiẓ selon *K. al-Ḥayawān*", *Studia Islamica*, LII, 1980.

Ibn Qutaybah *Taʾwīl mukhtalif al-ḥadīth*, Cairo, 1326/1908; trans. G. Lecomte, *Le traité des divergences du ḥadīṯ d'Ibn Qutayba*, Damascus, 1962.

al-Jāḥiẓ *Collections*:

Al-Ǧāḥiẓ . . . quatre essais, trans. C. Vial, Cairo, 1976–9.

Iḥdā ʿashrata risālah, Cairo, 1906 (*11 Risālah*).

Majmūʿ rasāʾil al-Jāhiẓ, ed. P. Kraus and M. T. al-Ḥājirī, Cairo, 1943, (*Majmūʿ*).

Rasāʾil al-Jāḥiẓ, ed. ʿA. S. M. Hārūn, Cairo, 1964–79 (H).

Rasāʾil al-Jāḥiẓ, ed. Ḥ. al-Sandūbī, Cairo, 1933 (S).

Three Essays of Abū ʿOthmān b. Baḥr al-Jāḥiẓ, ed. J. Finkel, Cairo, 1926.

Tria Opuscula auctore Abu Othman ibn Bahr al-Djahiz Basrensi, ed. G. van Vloten, Leiden, 1903.

Individual works:

K. al-Akhbār wa-kayfa taṣiḥḥ, I, ed. and trans. C. Pellat, *Journal Asiatique*, 1967; II, ed. and trans. J. van Ess, "Ein unbekanntes Fragment des Naẓẓām", *Festschrift für Otto Spies*, Wiesbaden 1967.

K. al-Amṣār wa- ʿajāʾib al-buldān, ed. C. Pellat, *Machriq*, 1966.

K. Aṭʿimat al-ʿArab: see *K. al-Bukhalāʾ*; trans. Pellat, *Arabica*, II, 1955.

K. al-Bayān wa ʾl-tabyīn, ed. ʿA. S. M. Hārūn, Cairo, 1367–9/1948–50.

K. al-Bukhalāʾ, ed. M. T. al-Ḥājirī, Cairo, 1948; trans. C. Pellat, *Le Livre des avares*, Paris, 1951.

K. al-Burṣān, ed. M. Mursī al-Khūlī, Beirut, 1392/1972.

K. al-Futyā: see van Ess, *Das Kitāb al-Nakṯ.*

K. al-Ḥayawān, ed. ʿA. S. M. Hārūn, Cairo, 1938–45.

Hijāʾ Muḥammad b. al-Jahm al-Barmakī, ed. M. T. al-Ḥājirī, *al-Kātib al-miṣrī*, Feb. 1947.

K. al-Masāʾil wa ʾl-jawābāt fī ʾl-maʿrifah, ed. C. Pellat, *Machriq*, 1969.

Fī Mawt Abī Ḥarb al-Ṣaffār, ed. al-Ḥājirī, *al-Kātib al-miṣrī*, June 1946.

R. *fī Nafy al-tashbīh*, ed. Pellat, *Machriq*, 1953.

al-Nubl wa ʾl-tanabbul, ed. and trans. Pellat, *Arabica*, XIV, 1967.

K. al-Qiyān, ed. and trans. A. F. L. Beeston, *The Epistle on Singing-Girls*, Warminster, 1980.
Fī Tafḍīl al-baṭn ᶜalā ʾl-ẓahr, ed. C. Pellat, *Ḥawliyyāt Jāmiᶜat Tūnis*, XIII, 1976.
(attrib.) *K. al-Tāj*, ed. A. Zakī, Cairo, 1322/1914; trans. C. Pellat, *Le Livre de la couronne*, Paris, 1954.
K. al-Tarbīᶜ wa ʾl-tadwīr, ed. C. Pellat, Damascus, 1955; trans. M. Adad, *Arabica* (tirage à part), Leiden, 1968.
K. Taṣwīb ᶜAlī fī taḥkīm al-ḥakamayn, ed. C. Pellat, *Machriq*, 1958.
K. al-ᶜUthmāniyyah, ed. ᶜA. S. M. Hārūn, Cairo, 1374/1955.
Lecomte, G. *Ibn Qutayba*, Damascus, 1965.
Manṣūr, S.Ḥ. *The World-View of al-Jāḥiẓ in Kitāb al-Ḥayawān*, Alexandria, 1977.
Mubārak, M., *Fann al-qaṣaṣ fī Kitāb al-Bukhalāʾ*, Damascus, 1384/1965.
Pellat, C. "Le culte de Muᶜāwiya au IIIe siècle de l'hégire", *Studia Islamica*, VI, 1956.
"Al-Ǧāḥiẓ jugé par la postérité", *Arabica,* XXVII, 1980.
"L'imamat dans la doctrine de Ǧāḥiz", *Studia Islamica*, XV, 1961.
The Life and Works of Jāḥiẓ, trans. D. M. Hawke, London, 1969.
Le Milieu basrien et la formation de Ǧāḥiẓ: see General Bibliography.
"Nouvel essai d'inventaire de l'oeuvre ġāḥiẓienne", *Arabica*, XXI, 1984.
Vajda, G. "La connaissance naturelle de Dieu selon al-Ǧāḥiẓ critiquée par les Muᶜtazilites", *Studia Islamica*, XXIV, 1966.

5: AL-ṢĀḤIB IBN ᶜABBĀD

Abū Shujāᶜ *Dhayl Tajārib al-umam*: see Miskawayh.
Āl Yāsīn, M.Ḥ. *al-Ṣāḥib b. ᶜAbbād ḥayātuh wa-adabuh*, Baghdad, 1376/1957.
al-Amīnī *al-Ghadīr*, IV, Beirut, 1967.
Ibn ᶜAbbād *al-Risālah fī Aḥwāl ᶜAbd al-ᶜAẓīm al-Ḥasanī*, ed. M.Ḥ. Āl Yāsīn, Najaf, 1374/1955.
al-Amthāl al-sāʾirah min shiᶜr al-Mutanabbī (with *al-Rūẓnāmajah*), ed. Āl Yāsīn, Baghdad, 1385/1965.
Dīwān, ed. Āl-Yāsīn, Beirut, 1394/1974.
al-Farq bayna ʾl-ḍād wa ʾl-ẓāʾ, ed. Āl Yāsīn, Baghdad, 1958.
Risālah fī ʾl-Hidāyah, ed. H.ᶜA. Maḥfūẓ, Tehran, 1374/1955.
al-Ibānah ᶜan madhhab ahl al-ᶜadl, ed. Āl Yāsīn, Najaf, 1372/1953.
al-Kashf ᶜan masāwīʾ shiᶜr al-Mutanabbī, ed. Āl Yāsīn, Baghdad, 1385/1965.
al-Muḥīṭ bi ʾl-lughah, I, ed. Āl Yāsīn, Baghdad, 1385/1965.
Nahj al-sabīl fī ʾl-uṣūl: see Amīnī.
(attrib.) *Nuṣrat madhāhib al-Zaydiyyah*, ed. N. Ḥasan, Beirut, 1981.
al-Rasāʾil, ed. ᶜA. W. ᶜAzzām and Shawqī Ḍayf, Cairo, 1366/1947.
al-Rūẓnāmajah: see *al-Amthāl al-sāʾirah*.
al-Tadhkirah fī ʾl-uṣūl al-khamsah, ed. Āl Yāsīn, Najaf, 1373/1954.
ᶜUnwān al-maᶜārif wa-dhikr al-khalāʾif, ed. Āl Yāsīn, Najaf, 1372/1953.
Ibn al-Athīr *al-Kāmil fī ʾl-taʾrīkh*, ed. C. J. Tornberg, Beirut, 1965–7.
Ibn Fāris *al-Ṣāḥibī fī fiqh al-lughah*, ed. M. El-Chouémi, Beirut, 1383/1964.

Kraemer, Joel, L. *Humanism in the Renaissance of Islam*, Leiden, 1986.
Madelung, W. "Imāmism and Muᶜtazilite theology", *Le Shîᶜisme Imâmite, Colloque de Strasbourg . . . 1968*, Paris, 1970.
Miskawayh *Tajārib al-umam*/Abū Shujāᶜ al-Rūdhrāwarī, *Dhayl Tajārib al-umam* (*The Eclipse of the ᶜAbbasid Caliphate*), eds. and trans. H. F. Amedroz and D. S. Margoliouth, Oxford, 1920–1.
Mottahedeh, Roy P. "Administration in Būyid Qazwīn", *Islamic Civilization 950–1150*, ed. D. S. Richards, Oxford, 1973.
al-Tawḥīdī, Abū Hayyān *Akhlāq al-wazīrayn*, ed. M. T. al-Ṭanjī, Damascus, 1965.
al-Imtāᶜ wa ᵓl-muᵓānasah, eds. A. Amīn and A. al-Zayn, Cairo, 1939–44.

6: ABŪ ḤAYYĀN AL-TAWḤĪDĪ

Arkoun, M. "L'humanisme arabe au IVe/Xe siècle, d'après le *Kitâb al-Hawâmil wal-Šawâmil*", *Studia Islamica*, XIV, 1961.
Bergé, M. "Continuité et progression des études tawḥīdiennes modernes, de 1883 à 1965", *Arabica*, XXII, 1975.
Pour un humanisme vécu: Abū Ḥayyān al-Tawḥīdī, Damascus, 1979.
Endress, G., "The limits to reason . . . philosophy in the Būyid period", *Akten des VII Kongresses für Arabistik und Islamwissenschaft*, Göttingen, 1976.
Ibn Ḥajar al-ᶜAsqalānī *Lisān al-Mīzān*, Hyderabad, 1329–31/1911–13.
Jadaane, F. "La philosophie de Sijistânî", *Studia Islamica*, XXXIII, 1971.
Keilani, I. *Abū Ḥayyān at-Tawḥīdī*, Beirut, 1950.
Kraemer, Joel L. *Humanism in the Renaissance of Islam*, Leiden, 1986.
Philosophy in the Renaissance of Islam, Leiden, 1986.
Laoust, H. *Essai sur les doctrines sociales et politiques d'Ibn Taymiyya*, Cairo, 1939.
Les Schismes dans l'Islam, Paris, 1965.
Mahdi, M. "Language and logic in classical Islam", *Logic in Classical Islamic Culture* (First Giorgio Levi della Vida Conference), Wiesbaden, 1970.
Makdisi, G. "The juridical theology of Shâfiᶜî – origins and significance of *Uṣûl al-Fiqh*", *Studia Islamica*, LIX, 1984.
Marquet, Y. *La Philosophie des Ikhwân al-Ṣafâᵓ*, Algiers, 1976.
Miskawayh *al-Hawāmil wa ᵓl-shawāmil*: see Tawḥīdī.
Stern, S. M. "New information about the authors of the 'Epistles of the Sincere Brethern'", *Islamic Studies*, III, 1964.
al-Tawḥīdī, Abū Ḥayyān *Akhlāq al-wazīrayn*, ed. M. b. T. al-Ṭanjī, Damascus, 1965.
al-Baṣāᵓir wa ᵓl-dhakhāᵓir, ed. I. Keilani, Damascus, 1964.
(with Miskawayh) *al-Hawāmil wa ᵓl-shawāmil*, eds. A. Amīn and A. Ṣaqr, Cairo, 1380/1961.
Risālat al-Ḥayāh, trans. C. Audebert, *Bulletin d'Etudes Orientales*, Damascus, XVIII, 1963–4; see also *Thalāth rasāᵓil*.
Risālah fī ᶜIlm al-kitābah, trans. F. Rosenthal, "Abū Ḥaiyān al-Tawḥīdī on penmanship", *Ars Islamica*, XIII–XIV, 1948; see also *Thalāth rasāᵓil*.

al-Imtāʿ wa ʾl-muʾānasah, eds. A. Amīn and A. al-Zayn, Cairo, 1939–44.
al-Muqābasāt, ed. M. T. Ḥusayn, Baghdad, 1970.
al-Ṣadāqah wa ʾl-ṣadīq, ed. I. Keilani, Damascus, 1964.
Thalāth rasāʾil (R. *al-Ḥayāh*, R. *fī ʿIlm al-kitābah*, R. *al-Saqīfah*), ed. I. Keilani, Damascus, 1951.
Risālah fī ʾl-ʿUlūm, ed. and trans. M. Bergé, *Bulletin d'Etudes Orientales*, Damascus, XVIII, 1963–4.

7: AL-HAMADHĀNĪ, AL-ḤARĪRĪ AND THE *MAQĀMĀT* GENRE

Beeston, A. F. L. "The genesis of the *Maqāmāt* genre", *Journal of Arabic Literature*, II, 1971, 1–12.
Samples of Arabic Prose in its Historical Development, Oxford (James Mew Fund), 1977.
Blachère, R. and Masnou, P. *Maqāmāt (Séances) choisies et traduites de l'arabe avec une étude sur le genre*, Paris, 1957.
Bosworth, C. E. *The Medieval Islamic Underworld: the Banū Sāsān in Arabic Society and Literature*, Leiden, 1976.
al-Dīnawārī *Akhbār al-ṭiwāl*, eds. V. Guirgass and I. Kračkovskij, Leiden, 1888–1912.
al-Hamadhānī *Maqāmāt*, ed. M. ʿAbduh, Beirut, 1889; ed. M. M. D. ʿAbd al-Ḥamīd, Cairo, 1304/1923; Istanbul, 1298 AH; trans. W. J. Prendergast, *The Maqámát of Badīʿ al-Zamán al-Hamadhání*, London and Madras, 1915, repr. London and Dublin, 1973.
al-Ḥarīrī *The Assemblies of Ḥarîrî*, ed. F. Steingass, London, 1897.
The Assemblies of al-Ḥarîrî, trans. T. Chenery and F. Steingass. London, 1867–98.
Kilito, A. *Les Séances*, Paris, 1983.
Mattock, J. N. "The early history of the *maqāma*", *Journal of Arabic Literature*, XV, 1984.
Monroe, J. T. *The Art of Badīʿ az-Zamān al-Hamadhānī as Picaresque Narrative*, Beirut, 1983.
al-Muwayliḥī *Ḥadīth ʿĪsā b. Hishām*, Cairo, 1330/1911.
al-Ṭabarī *Taʾrīkh*, Cairo, 1966.
al-Tanūkhī *al-Faraj baʿd al-shiddah*, ed. ʿA. Shāljī, Beirut, 1398/1978.
Nishwār al-muḥāḍarah, ed. ʿA. Shāljī, Beirut, 1391–3/1971–3; trans. D. S. Margoliouth, *The Table-Talk of a Mesopotamian Judge*, London, 1922, Hyderabad, 1933.

8: FABLES AND LEGENDS

Abbott, N. "A ninth-century fragment of the *Thousand Nights*", *Journal of Near Eastern Studies*, VIII, 1949.
Abel, A. *Le Roman d'Alexandre*, Brussels, 1955.

Basset, R. "Les aventures merveilleuses de Temīm el-Dārī", *Giornale della Società Italiana*, v, 1891.

Légendes arabes d'Espagne: la maison fermée de Tolède, Oran, 1898.

Friedländer, I. *Die Chadirlegende und der Alexanderroman*, Leipzig, 1913.

Gerhardt, M. *The Art of Storytelling, a Literary Study of the Thousand and One Nights*, Leiden, 1963.

Gimaret, D., ed. *Kitāb Bilawhar wa-Būḏāsf*, Beirut, 1972; trans., *Le Livre de Bilawhar et Būḏāsf selon la version arabe ismaélienne*, Geneva and Paris, 1971.

Heath, P. "A critical view of modern scholarship on *Sīrat ᶜAntar Ibn Shaddād* and the popular *Sīra*", *Journal of Arabic Literature*, xv, 1984.

Ibn ᶜAbd al-Ḥakam *Futūḥ Miṣr*, ed. H. Massé, Cairo, 1914; trans. A. Gateau, *Conquête de l'Afrique du Nord et de l'Espagne*, Algiers, 1947.

Imruᵓ al-Qays *Dīwān*, Beirut, 1392/1972.

Khoury, R. G. *Les Légendes prophétiques dans l'Islam depuis le Ier jusqu'au IIIe siècle de l'Hégire*, Wiesbaden, 1978.

Mahdi, M., ed. *The Thousand and One Nights (Alf Layla wa-Layla) from the Earliest Known Sources*, I (Ar. text), Leiden, 1984.

Manqūsh, Thurayyā *Sayf b. Dhī Yazan bayna ᵓl-ḥaqīqah wa ᵓl-usṭūrah*, Baghdad, 1980.

Nagel, T. *Alexander der Grosse in der frühislamischen Volksliteratur*, Walldorf–Hessen, 1978.

Die Qiṣaṣ al-anbiyāᵓ, Bonn, 1967.

Schwarzbaum, H. *Biblical and Extra-Biblical Legends in Islamic Folk-Literature*, Walldorf–Hessen, 1982.

Traini, R. "Il poeta ᶜAmr Ibn Maᶜdikarib, *Fāris al-ᶜArab*", *Annali della Facoltà di Scienze Politiche*, Cagliari, IX, 1983.

9: ᶜABBASID POETRY AND ITS ANTECEDENTS

Abū Nuwās: see Monteil.

Abū Tammām *Dīwān*, I, IV, ed. M.ᶜA. ᶜAzzām, Cairo, 1972, 1965.

Badawi, M. M. "The function of rhetoric in medieval Arabic poetry: Abū Tammām's ode on Amorium", *Journal of Arabic Literature*, IX, 1978.

"From Primary to Secondary Qaṣīdas", *Journal of Arabic Literature*, XI, 1980.

Bonebakker, S. A. "Poets and critics in the third century AH", *Logic in Classical Islamic Culture* (First Giorgio Levi della Vida Conference), Wiesbaden, 1970.

al-Buḥturī *Dīwān*, ed. Ḥ. K. al-Ṣīrafī, Cairo, 1972–8.

Ḍayf, Shawqī *al-Taṭawwur wa ᵓl-tajdīd fī ᵓl-shiᶜr al-umawī*, Cairo, 1965.

al-Farazdaq *Dīwān*, ed. ᶜA. al-Sāwī, Cairo, 1936.

Gibb, H. A. R. "Arab poet and Arabic philologist", *Bulletin of the School of Oriental and African Studies*, XII, 1948.

Hamori, A. *On the Art of Medieval Arabic Literature*, Princeton, 1974.

Ibn al-Muᶜtazz *Dīwān*, Beirut, 1961.

Ibn al-Rūmī *Dīwān*, ed. Ḥ. Naṣṣār, Cairo, 1973–8.

Lyall, C. J., ed. and trans. *The Mufaḍḍalīyāt*, Oxford, 1918–21.

al-Maᶜarrī *Shurūḥ Saqṭ al-zand*, III, Cairo, 1945–9.

Monteil, V., trans. and introd. *Abû-Nuwâs, Le Vin, le vent, la vie*, Paris, 1979.
al-Qāḍī, N. ᶜA. M. *Shiᶜr al-futūḥ al-islāmiyyah fī ṣadr al-Islām*, Cairo, 1965.
al-Ṣanawbarī, *Dīwān*, ed. I. ᶜAbbās, Beirut, 1970.
al-Sarī al-Raffāʾ *Dīwān*, Cairo, 1355 AH.
Schoeler, G. *Arabische Naturdichtung*, Beirut, 1974.
Stetkevych, S. P. "The ᶜAbbasid poet interprets history: three qaṣīdahs by Abū Tammām", *Journal of Arabic Literature*, x, 1979.
Zwettler, M. *The Oral Tradition of Classical Arabic Poetry*, Columbia, Ohio, 1978.

10: HUNTING POETRY (*ṬARDIYYĀT*)

Abū Firās *Dīwān*, ed. S. al-Dahhān, Beirut, 1944.
Abū Nuwās *Dīwān*, II, ed. E. Wagner, Wiesbaden, 1972.
Allen, M. J. S. and Smith, G. R. "Some notes on hunting techniques and practices in the Arabian Peninsula", *Arabian Studies*, II, 1975.
al-Bāshā, ᶜA. R. R. *Shiᶜr al-ṭarad*, Beirut, 1974.
Giese, A. *Waṣf bei Kušāǧim*, Berlin, 1981.
Ibn al-Muᶜtazz *Dīwān*, III, IV, ed. B. Lewin, Istanbul, 1945–50.
Kushājim *Kitāb al-Maṣāyid wa ʾl-maṭārid*, ed. A. Ṭalas, Baghdad, 1954.
Möller, D. *Studien zur mittelalterischen arabischen Falknereiliteratur*, Berlin, 1965.
al-Shamardal b. Sharīk *Die Gedichte des Šamardal ibn Šarīk*, ed. and trans. T. Seidensticker, Wiesbaden, 1983.
Smith, G. Rex "The Arabian hound, the *salūqī* – further consideration of the word and other observations on the breed", *Bulletin of the School of Oriental and African Studies*, XLIII, 1980.
al-Tibrīzī *Sharḥ al-qaṣāʾid al-ᶜashr*, ed. C. J. Lyall, Calcutta, 1894.

11: POLITICAL POETRY

ᶜAbbās, I., ed. *Shiᶜr al-Khawārij*, Beirut, n.d.
Barbier de Meynard, C. "Le Séid Himyarite", *Journal Asiatique*, 1874.
"Tableau littéraire du Khorassan et de la Transoxiane au IVe siècle de l'Hégire", *Journal Asiatique*, 1854.
Canard, M. "L'impérialisme des Fatimides et leur propagande", *Annales de l'Institut d'Etudes Orientales*, Algiers, VI, 1942–7.
van Ess, J. "Die Hinrichtung des Ṣāliḥ b. ᶜAbdalquddūs", *Studien . . . Festschrift für B. Spüler*, Leiden, 1981.
Gabrieli, F. "Imâmisme et littérature sous les Bûyides", *Le Shîᶜisme imâmite, Colloque de Strasbourg . . . 1968*, Paris, 1970.
"Note sul divano di Abū Firās", *Rivista dell'Accademia dei Lincei*, Rome, XXXII, 1977.
"La poesia ḫārigita nel secolo degli Omayyadi", *Rivista degli Studi Orientali*, XX, 1942–3.
Gimaret, D., ed. *Kitāb Bilawhar wa-Būḏāsf*, Beirut, 1972; trans., *Le Livre de Bilawhar et Būḏāsf selon la version arabe ismaélienne*, Geneva and Paris, 1971.
de Goeje, M. J. *Mémoire sur les Carmathes du Bahraïn et les Fatimides*, Leiden, 1886.

Goldziher, I. "Salih b. ᶜAbd al-Kuddûs und das Zindîḳthum", *Transactions of the Ninth Congress of Orientalists*, II, London, 1893.

Hawting, G. *The First Dynasty of Islam*, London, 1986.

al-Ḥuṣrī *Dhayl Zahr al-ādāb* (*Jamᶜ al-jawāhir*), ed. ᶜA. M. al-Bajāwī, Cairo, 1372/1953.

Ibn Abī ᵓl-Ḥadīd *Sharḥ Nahj al-balāghah*, VIII, Cairo, 1960.

Ibn Hāniᵓ *Dīwān*, ed. and trans. Z. ᶜAlī, Cairo, 1352/1933–4.

al-Kumayt: see Müller.

Kuthayyir ᶜAzzah *Dīwān*, ed. H. Pérès, Paris and Algiers, 1928.

Massignon, Louis *Opera Minora*, I, Paris, 1969.

al-Masᶜūdī *Murūj al-dhahab*, ed. and trans. C. Barbier de Meynard and Pavet de Courteille, Paris, 1861–9.

Kitāb al-Tanbīh wa ᵓl-ishrāf, ed. M. J. de Goeje, Leiden, 1894.

Moscati, S. "Per una storia dell'antica '*šīᶜa*'", *Rivista degli Studi Orientali*, XXVII, 1955.

Müller, K. *Kritische Untersuchungen zum Diwan des Kumait b. Zaid*, Freiburg, 1979.

Nagel, T. *Untersuchungen zur Entstehung des Abbasidischen Kalifates*, Bonn, 1972.

Pellat, C. "Djāḥiẓ et les Khāridjites", *Folia Orientalia*, XII, 1970.

Rizzitano, U. *Letteratura araba*, Milan, 1969.

Ullmann, M. *Untersuchungen zur Rağazpoesie*, Wiesbaden, 1966.

12: LOVE POETRY (*GHAZAL*)

al-ᶜAbbās b. al-Aḥnaf *Dīwān*, ed. al-Khazrajī, Cairo, 1954.

Abū ᵓl-ᶜAtāhiyah *Abū ᵓl-ᶜAtāhiyah ashᶜāruh wa-akhbāruh*, ed. Shukrī Fayṣal, Damascus, 1965.

Abū Firās *Dīwān*, ed. S. al-Dahhān, Beirut, 1944.

Abū Nuwās *Dīwān*, IV, ed. G. Schoeler, Wiesbaden, 1982.

Abū Tammām *Dīwān*, IV, ed. M.ᶜA. ᶜAzzām, Cairo, 1965.

Alf laylah wa-laylah, Bulaq, 1252/1835.

al-Aᶜmā ᵓl-Tuṭīlī *Dīwān*, ed. I. ᶜAbbās, Beirut, 1963.

al-Bārūdī, ed. *Mukhtārāt*, Cairo, 1329 AH.

Bashshār b. Burd *Dīwān*, eds. M.Ṭ. b. ᶜAshūr et al., Cairo, 1950–66: see also Beeston.

Beeston, A. F. L., ed. and trans. *Selections from the Poetry of Baššār*, Cambridge, 1977.

Bell, J. N. *Love Theory in Later Hanbalite Islam*, Albany, New York, 1979.

al-Buḥturī *Dīwān*, ed. Ḥ. K. al-Ṣīrafī, II, Cairo, 1963.

García Gómez, E. "Convencionalismo e insinceridad en la poesía árabe", *al-Andalus*, V, 1940.

Gibb, H. A. R. *Arabic Literature*, Oxford, 1963.

Giffen, L. A. *Theory of Profane Love Among the Arabs*, New York and London, 1971.

Hell, J. "Al-ᶜAbbās ibn al-Aḥnaf, der Minnesänger am Hofe Hārūn ar-Rašīds", *Islamica*, II, 1926.

Ibn Dāwūd *Kitāb al-Zahrah*, ed. A. R. Nykl, Chicago, 1932.

Ibn Ḥazm *Ṭawq al-ḥamāmah*, ed. al-Ṣīrafī, Cairo, 1959; trans. A. R. Nykl, *The Dove's Neck-Ring*, Paris, 1931.

Ibn al-Mu^{c}tazz *Dīwān*, Beirut, 1961.
Ibn Qayyim al-Jawziyyah *Rawḍat al-muḥibbīn*, ed. A. ^{c}Ubayd, Cairo, 1956.
Ibn Quzmān *Todo Ben Quzman*, ed. E. García Gómez, Madrid, 1972.
Ibn al-Rūmī *Dīwān*, ed. Ḥ. Naṣṣār, Cairo, 1973–8.
Jamīl b. Ma^{c}mar *Dīwān*, ed. Ḥ. Naṣṣār, Cairo, 1967.
Kinany, A. K. *The Development of Gazal in Arabic Literature*, Damascus, 1950.
Kratchkovsky, I. "Die Frühgeschichte der Erzählung von Macnūn und Lailā in der arabischen Literatur", trans. H. Ritter, *Oriens*, VIII, 1955.
Lyall, C. J., ed. and trans. *The Mufaḍḍalīyāt*, Oxford, 1918–21.
Majnūn Laylā *Dīwān*, ed. ^{c}A. A. Farrāj, Cairo, 1963.
Muslim b. al-Walīd *Sharḥ Dīwān Ṣarī^{c} al-Ghawānī*, ed. S. al-Dahhān, Cairo, 1970.
al-Sharīf al-Raḍī *Dīwān*, ed. A. ^{c}Abbās al-Azharī, Beirut, n.d.
al-Ṣūlī *Ash^{c}ār awlād al-khulafā$^{\supset}$*, ed. J. Heyworth Dunne, London, 1936.
^{c}Umar b. Abī Rabī^{c}ah *Dīwān*, ed. M. M. D. ^{c}Abd al-Ḥamīd, Cairo, 1960.
Vadet, J.-C. *L'Esprit courtois en Orient*, Paris, 1968.
Wagner, E. *Grundzüge der klassischen arabischen Dichtung*, Darmstadt, 1987.
al-Washshā$^{\supset}$ *Kitāb al-Muwashshā*, Beirut, 1965.

13: WINE POETRY (*KHAMRIYYĀT*)

Abū Nuwās *Dīwān*, ed. A.^{c}A. M. al-Ghazālī, Cairo, 1953.
al-Akhṭal, *Shi^{c}r al-Akhṭal*, ed. F. D. Qabāwah, Beirut, 1979.
^{c}Alqamah b. ^{c}Abadah *Dīwān*, eds. L. al-Ṣaqqāl and D. al-Khaṭīb, Aleppo, 1969.
al-^{c}Aqqād, ^{c}A. M. *Abū Nuwās*, Beirut, 1968.
Arberry, A. J., trans. *The Seven Odes*, London, 1957.
al-A^{c}shā Maymūn b. Qays *Dīwān*, ed. R. Geyer, London, 1928.
Beeston, A. F. L. "An experiment with Labīd", *Journal of Arabic Literature*, VII, 1976.
Ḍayf, Shawqī *al-^{c}Aṣr al-^{c}abbāsī al-awwal*, Cairo, n.d.
Ḥassān b. Thābit *Dīwān*, ed. W. ^{c}Arafat, London, 1971.
Ḥusayn, Ṭ. *Ḥadīth al-arbi^{c}ā$^{\supset}$*, Cairo, 1937.
Ibn Harmah *Shi^{c}r Ibn Harmah*, eds. M. Nifā^{c} and H. ^{c}Aṭwān, Damascus, n.d.
Ibn al-Mu^{c}tazz *Ṭabaqāt al-shu^{c}arā$^{\supset}$*, ed. ^{c}A. S. Farrāj, Cairo, 1968.
Ibn Sa^{c}īd *al-Mughrib fī ḥulā $^{\supset}$l-Maghrib*, I, eds. Shawqī Ḍayf et al., Cairo, 1953.
Massignon, L., and Kraus, P. *Akhbār al-Ḥallāj*, Paris, 1957.
Muslim b. al-Walīd *Dīwān*, ed. M. J. de Goeje, Leiden, 1875.
Sharḥ Dīwān Ṣarī^{c} al-Ghawānī, ed. S. al-Dahhān, Cairo, 1970.
Naṣr ^{c}A. J. *al-Ramz al-shi^{c}rī ^{c}inda $^{\supset}$l-ṣūfiyyah*, Beirut, 1978.
al-Nawājī *Ḥalbat al-kumayt*, Bulaq, 1276 AH.
Nicholson, R. A. *Studies in Islamic Mysticism*, Cambridge, 1921.
al-Rāghib al-Iṣfahānī *Muḥāḍarāt al-udabā$^{\supset}$*, Beirut, n.d.
al-Raqīq al-Nadīm *Quṭb al-surūr*, ed. A. al-Jundī, Damascus, n.d.
Ritter, H. "Die Trinkschale von Abū Nuwās", *Orientalia*, I, Istanbul, 1933.
al-Walīd b. Yazīd *Dīwān*, ed. F. Gabrieli, Damascus, 1937.

14: MYSTICAL POETRY

Badawī, ᶜA. R. *Shahīdat al-ᶜishq al-ilāhī*, Cairo, 1962.

al-Ghazālī: see Pedersen.

al-Ḥallāj *Le Dîwân d'al-Ḥallâj*, ed. and trans. L. Massignon, Paris, 1955.

al-Ḥurayfīsh al-Makkī *al-Rawḍ al-fāʾiq*, Bulaq, 1280/1863.

Ibn ᶜAjībah: see Michon.

Ibn ᶜAlīwah, Aḥmad b. Muṣṭafā al-ᶜAlawī al-Mustaghānimī *al-Minaḥ al-quddūsiyyah*, ed. ᶜA.Ṣ. al-Ustādh, trans. ᶜA. K. al-Munawwarah, Norwich, 1981; see also Lings.

Ibn (al-) ᶜArabī *The Tarjumán al-Ashwáq*, ed. and trans. R. A. Nicholson, London, 1911.

Ibn al-Fāriḍ *Dīwān*, ed. M. Tawfīq, Cairo, n.d.

The Mystical Poems of Ibn al-Fāriḍ, ed. A. J. Arberry, London, 1952; trans. A. J. Arberry, Dublin, 1956.

The Poem of the Way, trans. A. J. Arberry, London, 1952.

Ibn al-Zayyāt *al-Tashawwuf ilā rijāl al-taṣawwuf*, ed. A. Faure, Rabat, 1958.

al-Jīlānī *al-Fuyūḍāt al-rabbāniyyah*, ed. I. b. M. b. S. al-Qādirī al-Jīlānī, Delhi, 1330/1912.

Jurjī, E. J., trans. *Illumination in Islamic Mysticism*, Princeton, 1938.

al-Kalābādhī *al-Taᶜarruf li-madhhab ahl al-taṣawwuf*, eds. ᶜA.Ḥ. Mahmud and T.ᶜA. B. Surūr, Cairo, 1960; trans. A. J. Arberry, *The Doctrine of the Ṣūfīs*, Cambridge, 1935; trans. R. Deladrière, *Traité de soufisme*, Paris, 1981.

The Korân trans. George Sale, London, 1734.

Lings, Martin *A Sufi Saint of the Twentieth Century, Shaikh Ahmad al-ᶜAlawi*, London, 1971.

al-Makkī *Qūt al-qulūb*, Cairo, 1310/1893.

Massignon, Louis *Essai sur les origines du lexique technique de la mystique musulmane*, Paris, 1922.

"Investigaciones sobre Šuštarī, poeta andaloz", *al-Andalus*, XIV, 1949.

Recueil de textes inédits concernant l'histoire de la mystique en pays d'Islam, Paris, 1929.

Michon, J.-L., ed. and trans. *Le Soufi marocain Aḥmad ibn ᶜAjîba . . . et son Miᶜrâj*, Paris, 1973.

al-Nābulusī *al-Kawkab al-mutalaʾliʾ*: see Pedersen.

Nadeem, S. H. *A Critical Appreciation of Arabic Mystical Poetry*, Lahore, 1979.

Nicholson, R. A. *Studies in Islamic Mysticism*, Cambridge, 1921.

al-Nīsābūrī *ᶜUqalāʾ al-majānīn*, ed. W. F. al-Kīlānī, Cairo, 1924.

Pedersen, J. "Ein Gedicht al-Ġazālī's", *Le Monde Oriental*, XXV, 1931.

al-Sarrāj *The Kitāb al-Lumaᶜ fī ʾl-taṣawwuf*, ed. R. A. Nicholson, Leiden and London, 1914.

al-Shādhilī *Qawānīn ḥikam al-ishrāq*: see Jurjī.

al-Shaᶜrānī *al-Ṭabaqāt al-kubrā*, Cairo, 1299/1881.

al-Shiblī *Dīwān*, ed. K. M. al-Shaybī, Baghdad, 1386/1967.

al-Shushtarī *Dīwān*, ed. ᶜA. S. al-Nashshār, Alexandria, 1960.

Smith, Margaret *Al-Ghazālī the Mystic*, London, 1944.
Rābiʿa the Mystic and Her Fellow-Saints in Islam, Cambridge, 1928.
al-Sulamī *Ṭabaqāt al-ṣufiyyah*, ed. Shuraybah, Cairo, 1953; ed. J. Pedersen, Leiden, 1960.

15: ASCETIC POETRY (*ZUHDIYYĀT*)

ʿAbbās, I., ed. *Shiʿr al-Khawārij*, Beirut, n.d.
Abū ʾl-ʿAtāhiyah *Abū ʾl-ʿAtāhiyah ashʿāruh wa-akhbāruh*, ed. Shukrī Fayṣal, Damascus, 1965.
Abū Nuwās *Dīwān*, ed. A.ʿA. M. al-Ghazālī, Cairo, 1953; eds. E. Wagner and G. Schoeler, I, Cairo, 1958, II, IV, Wiesbaden, 1972–82; see also Monteil.
ʿAdī b. Zayd *Dīwān*, ed. M. J. al-Muʿaybid, Baghdad, 1965.
Arberry, A. J. *Sufism*, London, 1950.
Becker, C. H. "Ubi sunt qui ante nos in mundo fuere", *Aufsätze zur Kultur- und Sprachgeschichte (Ernst Kuhn Festschrift)*, Breslau, 1916.
Goldziher, I. *Introduction to Islamic Theology and Law* (*Vorlesungen über den Islam*, Heidelberg, 1910), trans. R. and A. Hamori, Princeton, 1981.
Ibn al-Muʿtazz *Dīwān*, Beirut, 1961.
Ibn Qutaybah *ʿUyūn al-akhbār*, Cairo, 1343–9/1925–30.
Ibn al-Rūmī *Dīwān*, ed. Ḥ. Naṣṣār, Cairo, 1973–8.
el-Kafrawy, M. A. A., and Latham, J. D. "Perspective of Abū ʾl-ʿAtahiyah", *Islamic Quarterly*, XVII, 1973.
Kannūn, ʿA. A. *Sābiq al-Barbarī*, Damascus, 1969.
al-Khaṭīb, ʿA. A. *Ṣāliḥ b. ʿAbd al-Quddūs al-Baṣrī*, Basra, 1968.
al-Maʿarrī *Luzūm mā lā yalzam*, ed. I. al-Aʿrābī, Beirut, n.d.
Maḥmūd al-Warrāq *Dīwān*, ed. ʿA. R. al-ʿUbaydī, Baghdad, 1969.
Vajda, G. "Les zindiqs en pays d'Islam au début de la période abbaside", *Rivista degli Studi Orientali*, XVII, 1937.

16: BASHSHĀR B. BURD, ABŪ ʾL-ʿATĀHIYAH AND ABŪ NUWĀS

Abū ʾl-ʿAtāhiyah *Abū ʾl-ʿAtāhiyah ashʿāruh wa-akhbāruh*, ed. Shukrī Fayṣal, Damascus, 1965.
Die Zuhdijjāt, trans. O. Rescher, Stuttgart, 1928.
Abū Nuwās *Dīwān*, ed. A.ʿA. M. al-Ghazālī, Cairo, 1953; eds. E. Wagner and G. Schoeler, I, Cairo, 1958, II, IV, Wiesbaden, 1972–82; see also Ibn Jinnī, Monteil.
Bashshār b. Burd *Dīwān*, eds. M.Ṭ. b. ʿAshūr et al., Cairo, 1950–66.
Beeston, A. F. L., ed. and trans. *Selections from the Poetry of Baššār*, Cambridge, 1977.
Blachère, R. *Analecta*, ed. E. Paret, Damascus, 1975.
Hamori, A. *On the Art of Medieval Arabic Literature*, Princeton, New Jersey, 1974.
Heinrichs, W. "Istiʿārah and badīʿ", *Zeitschrift für Geschichte der arabisch–islamischen Wissenschaften*, I, 1984.

Ibn Jinnī *Tafsīr urjūzat Abī Nuwās fī taqrīẓ al-Faḍl b. Rabī*ᶜ, ed. M. B. al-Atharī, Damascus, 1386/1966.

Jacobi, R. "Die Anfänge der arabischen Ġazalpoesie: Abū D̲u'aib al-Hud̲alī", *Der Islam*, LXI, 1984.

"The camel-section of the panegyrical ode", *Journal of Arabic Literature*, XIV, 1983.

Martin, J. D. "The religious beliefs of Abū ᵓl-ᶜAtāhiya according to the Zuhdīyāt", *Glasgow Oriental Society Transactions*, XXIII, 1969–70.

Meisami, J. S. "The uses of the *qaṣīda*: thematic and structural patterns in a poem of Bashshār", *Journal of Arabic Literature*, XVI, 1985.

Monteil, V., trans. and introd. *Abû-Nuwâs. Le Vin, le vent, la vie*, Paris, 1979.

Roman, A., ed. and trans. *Baššār et son expérience courtoise. Les vers à ᶜAbda*, Beirut, 1972.

"Les thèmes de l'oeuvre de Baššār inspirée par ᶜAbda", *Bulletin d'Etudes Orientales*, XXIV, Damascus 1971.

Schoeler, G. *Arabische Naturdichtung*, Beirut, 1974.

"Die Hispano–arabische Strophendichtung. Entstehung und Beziehung zur Troubadour-Lyrik", *La Signification du bas moyen-âge dans l'histoire et la culture du monde musulman*, Actes du 8ème congrès de l'Union Européenne des Arabisants et Islamisants, Aix-en-Provence, 1976.

"Ein Wendepunkt in der Geschichte der arabischen Literatur", *Saeculum*, XXXV, 1984.

Vadet, J.-C. *L'Esprit courtois en Orient*, Paris, 1968.

Wagner, E. *Abū Nuwās*, Wiesbaden, 1964.

17: AL-MUTANABBĪ

Arberry, A. J. *Arabic Poetry: A Primer for Students*, Cambridge, 1965.

Poems of al-Mutanabbī, Cambridge, 1967.

ᶜAwwād, G. and M., eds. *Rāᵓid al-dirāsah ᶜan al-Mutanabbī*, Baghdad, 1979.

al-Badīᶜī *al-Ṣubḥ al-munbiᵓ ᶜan ḥaythiyyat al-Mutanabbī*, eds. M. al-Saqqā et al., Cairo, 1963.

Blachère, R. *Un Poète arabe du IVe siècle de l'Hégire . . . Abou t-Tayyib al-Motanabbi*, Paris, 1935.

Boustani, Fouad, E., ed. "Ar-Risālat al-Ḥātimiyyat (parallèle d'Aristote et d'al-Motanabbi) de Abī ᶜAlī Moḥammad . . . al-Ḥātimī", *al-Mashriq*, Beirut, 1931.

Gabrieli, F. *Studi su al-Mutanabbi*, Rome, 1972.

Hamori, A. "Reading al-Mutanabbī's ode on the siege of al-Ḥadat̲", *Studia Arabica et Islamica: Festschrift for Iḥsān ᶜAbbās*, ed. W. al-Qāḍī, Beirut, 1981.

al-Ḥātimī: see Boustani.

Ḥusayn, Ṭ. *Maᶜa ᵓl-Mutanabbī*, Cairo, 1936.

Latham, J. D. "Toward a better understanding of al-Mutanabbī's poem on the battle of al-Ḥadath", *Journal of Arabic Literature*, X, 1979.

Massignon, Louis "Mutanabbī devant le siècle ismaélien de l'Islam", *Mutanabbi:*

recueil publié à l'occasion de son millénaire, Mémoires de l'Institut français de Damas, Beirut, 1936.
al-Mutanabbī *Dīwān* with commentary of al-Wāḥidī, ed. Dieterici, Berlin, 1861.
Dīwān with commentary of al-Yāzijī, Beirut, 1964.
Scheindlin, R. *Form and Structure in the Poetry of al-Muᶜtamid Ibn ᶜAbbād*, Leiden, 1974.

18: ABŪ FIRĀS AL-ḤAMDĀNĪ

Abū Firās *Dīwān*, ed. S. al-Dahhān, Beirut, 1944.
Freytag, G. W., ed. *Selecta ex historia Halabi*, Paris, 1819.
Gabrieli, F. *Abu Firas, poeta ed eroe arabo del X secolo*, Rome, 1977.
al-Mutanabbī *Dīwān* with commentary of al-Yāzijī, Beirut, 1964.
Dīwān with commentary of al-Barqūqī, Cairo, 1938.
Stetkevych, S. P. "The ᶜAbbasid poet interprets history: three qaṣīdahs by Abū Tammām", *Journal of Arabic Literature*, x, 1979.

19: ABŪ ᵓL-ᶜALĀᵓ AL-MAᶜARRĪ

ᶜAbd al-Raḥmān, ᶜĀᵓishah ("Bint al-Shāṭiᵓ") *Madkhal ilā Risālat al-Ṣāhil wa ᵓl-shāḥij*, Cairo, 1974.
Qirāᵓah jadīdah li-Risālat al-Ghufrān, Cairo, 1970.
Asín Palacios, M. *La Escatologia musulmana en la Divina Comedia*, Madrid, 1919; trans. H. Sutherland, *Islam and the Divine Comedy*, London, 1926.
Badawi, M. M. "Medieval Arabic drama: Ibn Dāniyāl", *Journal of Arabic Literature*, XIII, 1982.
Cachia, P. J. "The dramatic monologues of al-Maᶜarrī", *Journal of Arabic Literature*, I, 1970.
Ghali, E. S. "Le végétalisme et le doute chez Abū ᵓl-ᶜAlāᵓ al-Maᶜarri", *Bulletin des Etudes Orientales*, XXXII–III, 1980–1.
Ḥusayn, Ṭ *Dhikrā Abī ᵓl-ᶜAlāᵓ*, Cairo, 1915.
al-Jundī, M. S. *al-Jāmiᶜ fī akhbār Abī ᵓl-ᶜAlāᵓ al-Maᶜarrī wa-āthārih*, Damascus, 1382–4/1962–4.
al-Maᶜarrī *ᶜAbath al-Walīd*, ed. M. ᶜA. A. al-Madanī, Cairo, 1970.
"Abū ᵓl-ᶜAlāᵓ al-Maᶜarrī's correspondence on vegetarianism", ed. and trans. D. S. Margoliouth, *Journal of the Royal Asiatic Society*, 1902.
Ḍawᵓ al-saqṭ, Beirut, 1884.
al-Fuṣūl wa ᵓl-ghāyāt, I, ed. M. Ḥ. Zanātī, Cairo, 1356/1938.
The Letters of Abū ᵓl-ᶜAlāᵓ of Maᶜarrat al-Nuᶜmān, ed. and trans. D. S. Margoliouth, Oxford, 1898.
Luzūm mā lā yalzam/al-Luzūmiyyāt, ed. ᶜA. Zand, Cairo, 1891–5.
Mulqā ᵓl-sabīl, see Ibn Taymiyyah, *Fatwā fī ᵓl-qiyām*, ed. S. D. al-Munajjid, Beirut, 1963.
"The *Risâlat ul Ghufrân*", ed. and trans. R. A. Nicholson, *Journal of the Royal*

Asiatic Society, 1900–2; trans. V.-M. Monteil, *L'Epître du pardon*, Paris, 1984.
Rasāʾil: see *Letters*.
Risālat al-Malāʾikah, ed. al-Jundī, Damascus, 1944.
Risālat al-Ṣāhil wa ʾl-shāḥij, ed. ʿA. ʿAbd al-Raḥmān, Cairo, 1975.
Saqṭ al-zand: see *Shurūḥ Saqṭ al-zand*.
Shurūḥ Saqṭ al-zand, bk. 2, Cairo, 1945–9.
Nicholson, R. A. *Studies in Islamic Poetry*, Cambridge, 1921.
Smoor, P. "Enigmatic allusion and double meaning in Maʿarrī's newly discovered *Letter of a Horse and a Mule*", I, II, *Journal of Arabic Literature*, XII, 1981, XIII, 1982.
Kings and Bedouins in the Palace of Aleppo as Reflected in Maʿarrī's Works, Manchester, 1985.
Verity, A. C. F. "Two Poems of Abū ʾl-ʿAlāʾ al-Maʿarrī", *Journal of Arabic Literature*, II, 1971.

20: LITERARY CRITICISM

ʿAbbās, I. *Tārīkh al-naqd al-adabī ʿinda ʾl-ʿArab*, Beirut, 1971.
ʿAbd al-Jabbār *al-Mughnī*, ed. A. al-Khūlī, Cairo, 1960.
Abu Deeb, K. "Al-Jurjānī's classification of *istiʿāra*", *Journal of Arabic Literature*, II, 1971.
Al-Jurjānī's Theory of Poetic Imagery, Warminster, 1979.
"Studies in Arabic literary criticism: the concept of organic unity", *Edebiyât*, III, 1977.
Abū Ḥātim al-Rāzī *Kitāb al-Zīnah*, ed. Ḥ. b. F. al-Hamadānī, Cairo, 1956.
Abū ʿUbaydah *Majāz al-Qurʾān*, ed. F. Sezgin, Cairo, 1954.
Adūnīs (ʿAlī Aḥmad Saʿīd) *al-Thābit wa ʾl-mutaḥawwil*, Beirut, 1977.
al-Āmidī *al-Muwāzanah*, ed. A. Ṣaqr, Cairo, 1972.
al-ʿAskarī *Kitāb al-Ṣināʿatayn*, eds. ʿA. M. al-Bajāwī and M. A. F. Ibrāhīm, Cairo, 1952.
al-Bāqillānī *Iʿjāz al-Qurʾān*, ed. A. Ṣaqr, Cairo, 1954: see also von Grunebaum.
al-Fārābī, ed. and trans. A. J. Arberry "Fārābī's canons of poetry", *Rivista degli Studi Orientali*, XVII, 1938.
van Gelder, G. J. H. *Beyond the Line. Classical Arabic Literary Critics on the Coherence and Unity of the Poem*, Leiden, 1982.
"Critic and craftsman: al-Qarṭājannī and the structure of the poem", *Journal of Arabic Literature*, x, 1979.
von Grunebaum, G. E. *A Tenth-Century Document of Arabic Literary Theory and Criticism*, Chicago, 1950.
Ḥāzim al-Qarṭājannī *Minhāj al-bulaghāʾ*, ed. M.Ḥ. Belkhodja, Tunis, 1966.
Ibn Abī ʿAwn *Kitāb al-Tashbīhāt*, ed. M. A. M. Khān, Cambridge, 1950.
Ibn al-Jarrāḥ *Kitāb al-Waraqah*, eds. ʿA. W. ʿAzzām and ʿA. Farrāj, Cairo, n.d.
Ibn al-Muʿtazz *Kitāb al-Badīʿ*, ed. I. Kratchkovsky, London, 1935.
Ṭabaqāt al-shuʿarāʾ, ed. ʿA. S. Farrāj, Cairo, 1968.

Ibn Qutaybah *Introduction au Livre de la poésie et des poètes*, ed. and trans. M. Gaudefroy-Desmombynes, Paris, 1947.
Kitāb al-Shiʿr wa ʾl-shuʿarāʾ, ed. M. J. de Goeje, Leiden, 1902.
Taʾwīl mushkil al-Qurʾān, ed. A. Ṣaqr, Cairo, 1954.
Ibn Sallām al-Jumaḥī *Ṭabaqāt fuḥūl al-shuʿarāʾ*, ed. M. M. Shākir, Cairo, 1974.
Ibn Sinān al-Khafājī *Sirr al-faṣāḥah*, ed. ʿA. M. al-Saʿīdī, Cairo, 1969.
Ibn Ṭabāṭabā *ʿIyār al-shiʿr*, eds. Ṭ. al-Ḥājirī and M. Z. Sallām, Cairo, 1956.
Ibn Wahb *al-Burhān fī wujūh al-bayān*, eds. K. Ḥadīthī and A. Maṭlūb, Baghdad, 1967.
al-Jurjānī, ʿAbd al-Qāhir *Asrār al-balāghah*, ed. H. Ritter, Istanbul, 1954; trans. H. Ritter, *Die Geheimnisse der Wortkunst*, Wiesbaden, 1959.
Dalāʾil al-iʿjāz, ed. R. Riḍā, Cairo, 1366/1946.
al-Risālah al-Shāfiyah: see *Thalāth rasāʾil*.
al-Khaṭṭābī *Bayān iʿjāz al-Qurʾān*: see *Thalāth rasāʾil*.
Qudāmah b. Jaʿfar *Naqd al-shiʿr*, ed. S. A. Bonebakker, Leiden, 1956.
al-Rummānī *al-Nukat fī iʿjāz al-Qurʾān*: see *Thalāth rasāʾil*.
al-Sharīf al-Raḍī *al-Majāzāt al-nabawiyyah*, Baghdad, 1328/1910.
Talkhīṣ al-bayān fī majāzāt al-Qurʾān, ed. M. A. G. Ḥasan, Cairo, 1955.
al-Sijilmāsī *al-Manziʿ*, ed. ʿA. al-Ghāzī, Rabat, 1980.
Stetkevych, S. P. "Toward a redefinition of *Badīʿ* poetry", *Journal of Arabic Literature*, XII, 1981.
Thaʿlab *Qawāʿid al-shiʿr*, ed. R. ʿAbd al-Tawwāb, Cairo, 1966.
Thalāth rasāʾil fī iʿjāz al-Qurʾān, eds. M. K. Aḥmad and M. Z. Sallām, Cairo, n.d.
ʿUṣfūr, J. *al-Ṣūrah al-fanniyyah fī ʾl-turāth al-naqdī wa ʾl-balāghī*, Cairo, 1977.

21: IBN AL-MUʿTAZZ AND *KITĀB AL-BADĪʿ*

al-Āmidī *al-Muwāzanah*, I, ed. A. Ṣaqr, Cairo, 1972.
al-ʿAskarī *Kitāb al-Ṣināʿatayn*, eds. ʿA. M. al-Bajāwī and M. A. Ibrāhīm, Cairo, 1371/1952.
al-Bāqillānī *Iʿjāz al-Qurʾān*, ed. A. Ṣaqr, Cairo, 1374/1954.
Bonebakker, S. A. "Ibn Abī ʾl-Iṣbaʿʾs text of the *Kitāb al-Badīʿ* of Ibn al-Muʿtazz", *Israel Oriental Studies*, II, 1972.
"Materials for the history of Arabic rhetoric from the *Ḥilyat al-Muḥāḍara* of Ḥātimī", *Annali*, Istituto Orientale, Naples, XXXV, iii (suppl. 4), 1975.
Notes on the Kitāb Naḍrat al-Ighrīḍ of al-Muẓaffar al-Ḥusaynī, Istanbul, 1968.
"Poets and critics in the third century AH", *Logic in Classical Islamic Culture*, ed. G. E. von Grunebaum, Wiesbaden, 1970.
"Reflections on the 'Kitāb al-Badīʿ' of Ibn al-Muʿtazz", *Atti del III Congresso di Studi Arabi e Islamici*, Naples, 1967.
Bürgel, J. C. "Remarques sur une relation entre la logique aristotélienne et la poésie arabo–persane", *Actes du Ve Congrès International d'Arabisants et d'Islamisants*, Brussels, 1971.
Freytag, G. W. *Darstellung der arabischen Verskunst*, Bonn, 1830.

al-Ḥātimī *Ḥilyat al-muḥāḍarah*, ed. H. Nājī, Beirut, 1978.
Heinrichs, W. *Arabische Dichtung und griechische Poetik*, Beirut, 1969.
The Hand of the Northwind: Opinions on Metaphor and the Early Meaning of Istiʿāra in Arabic Poetics, Wiesbaden, 1977.
"Literary theory: the problem of its efficiency", *Arabic Poetry: Theory and Development*, ed. G. E. von Grunebaum, Wiesbaden, 1973.
Ibn Abī ʾl-Iṣbaʿ *Taḥrīr al-taḥbīr*, ed. Ḥ. M. Sharaf, Cairo, 1383/1963.
Ibn al-Muʿtazz *Kitāb al-Badīʿ*, ed. I. Kratchkovsky, London, 1935.
Rasāʾil Ibn al-Muʿtazz, ed. M.ʿA. Khafājī, Cairo, 1375/1946.
Ṭabaqāt al-shuʿarāʾ, ed. ʿA. A. Farrāj, Cairo, 1968.
Ibn Qutaybah, *Kitāb al-Shiʿr wa ʾl-shuʿarāʾ*, ed. M. J. de Goeje, Leiden, 1902.
Kratchkovsky, I. "Deux chapitres inédits de l'oeuvre de Kratchkovsky sur Ibn al-Muʿtazz", trans. M. Canard, *Annales de l'Institut des Etudes Orientales*, xx, Algiers, 1962.
Mandūr, M. *al-Naqd al-manhajī ʿinda ʾl-ʿArab*, Cairo, n.d.
al-Marzubānī *al-Muwashshaḥ*, Cairo, 1343/1924–5.
Mehren, A. F. *Die Rhetorik der Araber*, Copenhagen, 1853.
al-Mihzamī *Akhbār Abī Nuwās*, ed. ʿA. A. Farrāj, Cairo, 1373/1953.
Qudāmah b. Jaʿfar *Naqd al-shiʿr*, ed. S. A. Bonebakker, Leiden, 1956.
Stetkevych, S. P. "Toward a redefinition of *Badīʿ* poetry", *Journal of Arabic Literature*, xii, 1981.
al-Ṣūlī *Akhbār Abī Tammām*, eds. Kh. M. ʿAsākir et al., Cairo, 1356/1937.
Thaʿlab *Qawāʿid al-shiʿr*, ed. R. ʿAbd al-Tawwāb, Cairo, 1966.
Wagner, E. *Abū Nuwās*, Wiesbaden, 1965.

22: REGIONAL LITERATURE: EGYPT

ʿAbd al-Rāziq, M. *Al-Bahāʾ Zuhayr*, Cairo, 1930.
Abū Tammām *Dīwān*, iv, ed. M.ʿA ʿAzzām, Cairo, 1965.
al-Ahwānī, ʿA.ʿA. *Ibn Sanāʾ al-Mulk wa-mushkilat al-ʿuqm wa ʾl-ibtikār fī ʾl-shiʿr*, Cairo, 1962.
al-Bahāʾ Zuhayr/Bahāʾ al-Dīn Zuhayr *Dīwān*, Cairo, 1977; ed. and trans. E. H. Palmer, *Behà-Ed-Dìn Zoheir of Egypt, The Poetical Works*, Cambridge, 1876–7.
al-Balawī *Sīrat Aḥmad b. Ṭūlūn*, ed. M. Kurd ʿAlī, Damascus, 1358 AH.
Becker, C. *Beiträge zur Geschichte Aegyptens*, Strasburg, 1902–3.
Fuʾād Sayyid, A. "Lumières nouvelles sur quelques sources de l'histoire fatimide en Egypte", *Annales Islamologiques*, xiii, 1977.
"Nuṣūṣ ḍāʾiʿah min Akhbār Miṣr li ʾl-Musabbiḥī", *Annales Islamologiques*, xvii, 1981.
Hamdānī, H. F. "The letters of al-Mustanṣir biʾillāh", *Bulletin of the School of Oriental and African Studies*, vii, 1933–5.
Ḥāzim al-Qarṭājannī *Minhāj al-bulaghāʾ*, ed. M. H. Belkhodja, Tunis, 1966.
Ḥusayn, M. K. *Fī adab Miṣr al-fāṭimiyyah*, Cairo, 1950.

Adabunā al-ʿarabī fī ʿaṣr al-wulāh, Cairo, 1950.

Dirāsāt fī ʾl-shiʿr fī ʿaṣr al-Ayyūbiyyīn, Cairo, 1967.

Ibn ʿAbd al-Ḥakam *Futūḥ Miṣr*, ed. H. Massé, Cairo, 1914.

Ibn al-Dāyah *al-Mukāfaʾah*, eds. A. Amīn and ʿA. al-Jārim, Cairo, 1941; trans. F. Gabrieli, "Il *Kitāb al-Mukāfaʾa* di Ibn al-Dāya", *Rivista degli Studi Orientali*, LII, 1978.

Ibn Hishām *al-Sīrah al-nabawiyyah*, Cairo, 1955.

Ibn al-Kīzānī *Ibn al-Kīzānī . . . ḥayātuh wa-dīwānuh*, ed. ʿA.Ṣ. Ḥusayn, Cairo [1967].

Ibn al-Muqaffaʿ, Sāwīris *Alexandrinische Patriarchengeschichte . . . 61–767*, ed. C. F. Seybold, Hamburg, 1912.

History of the Patriarchs of the Egyptian Church . . . (AD 849–880), eds. and trans. Y. ʿAbd al-Masīḥ and O. H. E. Burmester, Cairo, 1943.

Historia Patriarcharum Alexandrinorum, I, pt. I, ed. C. F. Seybold, Beirut, Paris and Leipzig, 1904.

Ibn Saʿīd *al-Mughrib fī ḥulā ʾl-Maghrib*, Egyptian section, pt. 1., eds. Z. M. Ḥasan, Shawqī Ḍayf and Sayyidah Kāshif, Cairo, 1953.

al-Nujūm al-ẓāhirah/Mughrib, Egyptian section, pt. 2., ed. Ḥ. Naṣṣār, Cairo, 1970.

Ibn Sanāʾ al-Mulk *Dīwān*, eds. M. I. Naṣr and Ḥ. Naṣṣār, Cairo, 1969.

Ibn al-Ṣayrafī *Qānūn dīwān al-rasāʾil*, ed. ʿA. Bahjat, Cairo, 1905; trans. H. Massé, "Code de la chancellerie", *Bulletin de l'Institut Français d'Archéologie Orientale*, XI, 1914.

Ibn Zūlāq *Akhbār Sībawayh al-miṣrī*, eds. M. I. Saʿd and Ḥ. al-Dīb, Cairo, 1933.

ʿImād al-Dīn al-Iṣfahānī *Kharīdat al-qaṣr*, Egyptian sections, eds. A. Amīn, Shawqī Ḍayf and I. ʿAbbās, Cairo, 1951.

ʿInān, M. *Muʾarrikhū Miṣr al-islāmiyyah wa-maṣādir al-tārīkh al-miṣrī*, Cairo, 1969.

al-Jawdharī *Sīrat al-Ustādh Jawdhar*, eds. M. K. Ḥusayn and M.ʿA. H. Shaʿīrah, Cairo, 1954; trans. M. Canard, *Vie de l'Ustadh Jaudhar*, Algiers, 1958.

al-Kindī *The Governors and Judges of Egypt* (*K. al-Wulāh* and *K. al-Quḍāh*), ed. R. Guest, Leiden and London, 1912.

al-Maqrīzī *al-Mawāʿiẓ wa ʾl-iʿtibār*, Bulaq, 1270 AH.

Muʾnis, Ḥ. "Tārīkh Miṣr min al-fatḥ al-ʿarabī", *Tārīkh al-ḥaḍārah al-miṣriyyah*, I, Cairo, 1963.

al-Musabbiḥī *Tome quarantième de la Chronique d'Egypte*, eds. Ayman Fuʾād Sayyid and T. Bianqui, Cairo, 1978–84; see also Becker; Sayyid.

al-Mutanabbī *Dīwān* with commentary of al-Yāzijī, Beirut, 1384/1964.

Palmer, E. H.: see al-Bahāʾ Zuhayr.

al-Qāḍī ʾl-Fāḍil *Dīwān*, ed. A. A. Badawī, Cairo, 1962.

Rasāʾil, ed. M. Naghsh, Cairo, 1398/1978.

al-Qalqashandī *Ṣubḥ al-aʿshā*, Cairo, 1910–20.

al-Sharīf al-ʿAqīlī *Dīwān*, ed. Z. al-Maḥāsinī, Cairo, n.d.

al-Sijillāt al-mustanṣiriyyah, ed. ʿA. M. Mājid, Cairo, 1954.

Stern, S. M. *Fāṭimid Decrees*, London, 1964.

Tamīm b. al-Muʿizz *Dīwān*, Cairo, 1957; ed. M.Ḥ. al-Aʿẓamī, Beirut, 1970.

al-Wahrānī *Manāmāt*, eds. I. Shaʿbān and M. Naghsh, Cairo, 1968.
Ẓāfir al-Ḥaddād *Dīwān*, ed. Ḥ. Naṣṣār, Cairo, 1969.

23: REGIONAL LITERATURE: THE YEMEN

Abū/Bā Makhramah: see Löfgren.

Aḥmad al-Nāṣir, Imām: see Madelung, *Streitschrift*.

al-ʿAlawī, ʿAlī b. Muḥammad al-ʿAbbāsī *Sīrat Yaḥyā b. al-Ḥusayn al-Hādī ilā ʾl-Ḥaqq*, ed. S. Zakkār, Beirut, 1392/1972.

ʿAlī b. Muḥammad b. . . . al-Walīd al-Anf al-Qurashī *Risālat al-Īḍāḥ waʾl-tabyīn*, ed. R. Strothmann, *Gnosistexte der Ismailiten*, Göttingen, 1943.

al-ʿAmrī, Ḥ. b. ʿA. *The Yemeni Manuscripts in the British Library/Maṣādir al-turāth al-yamanī fīʾl-Mathaf al-Brīṭānī*, Damascus, 1400/1980.

van Arendonk, C., trans. J. Ryckmans, *Les Débuts de l'imāmat zaidite au Yemen*, Leiden, 1970.

Bates, Michael L. "The chapter on the Fāṭimid *Dāʿīs* in Yemen in the Tārīkh of ʿUmāra al-Ḥakamī (d. 569/1174): an interpolation", *Sources for the History of Arabia*, II, Riyadh, 1979.

Cahen, C. and Serjeant, R. B. "A fiscal survey of the mediaeval Yemen", *Arabica*, IV, 1957.

Derenbourg, H. *ʿOumara du Yemen, sa vie et son oeuvre*, Paris, 1897–1902.

Fihrist kutub al-Khazīnah al-Mutawakkiliyyah al-ʿĀmirah bi ʾl-Jāmiʿ al-muqaddas bi-Ṣanʿāʾ, Ṣanʿāʾ, n.d.

Fuʾād Sayyid, A. *Sources de l'histoire du Yemen à l'époque musulmane/Maṣādir tārīkh al-Yaman fīʾl-ʿaṣr al-islāmī*, Cairo, 1974.

Geddes, Charles L. "The aspostacy of ʿAlī b. al-Faḍl", *Arabian and Islamic Studies . . . presented to R. B. Serjeant*, ed. R. L. Bidwell and G. R. Smith, London, 1983.

Gochenour, D. T. "A revised bibliography of medieval Yemeni history in light of recent publications and discoveries", *Der Islam*, LXIII, 1986.

de Goeje, M. J. *Mémoire sur les Carmathes du Bahraïn et les Fatimides*, Leiden, 1886.

Griffini, E. "Il poemetto di Qudam Ben Qādim", *Rivista degli Studi Orientali*, VII, 1916–18.

al-Ḥabshī/Ḥibshī, ʿA. b. M. *Maṣādir al-fikr al-ʿarabī al-islāmī fīʾl-Yaman*, Ṣanʿāʾ, n.d.

al-Ḥabshī/Ḥibshī, ʿA. b. M. and Niewöhner-Eberhard, E., eds. *The Works of the Rulers of Yemen/Muʾallafāt ḥukkām al-Yaman*, Wiesbaden, 1979.

al-Hādī ilā ʾl-Ḥaqq "Kitāb al-Muntakhab fī ʾl-fiqh of Muḥammad b. Sulaymān al-Kūfī", ed. ʿAbd al-Khāliq Kāẓī, unpublished Ph. D. thesis, University of London, SOAS 45.

Hamdānī, ʿAbbās "the Dāʿī Ḥātim ibn Ibrāhīm al-Ḥāmidī (d. 596 H/1199 AD) and his book *Tuḥfat al-qulūb*", *Oriens*, XXIII–IV, 1970–1.

"Evolution of the organisational structure of the Fāṭimī Daʿwah: the Yemeni and Persian contribution", *Arabian Studies*, III, 1976.

al-Hamdānī, al-Ḥasan b. Aḥmad *al-Dāmighah*: see Shāmī, *Dāmighat al-dawāmigh*.

al-Iklīl, I, ed. M. al-Akwaᶜ, Cairo, 1963; ed. O. Löfgren, *al-Iklīl in der Rezension von Muḥammad bin Naśwān bin Saᶜīd al-Ḥimyarī*, Uppsala, 1954; I, II, ed. al-Akwaᶜ, Cairo, 1386/1966; ed. Löfgren, Uppsala, 1965; VIII, ed. A.-M. al-Kirmilī, Baghdad, 1350/1931; trans. N. A. Faris, *The Antiquities of South Arabia*, Princeton, 1938; x, ed. M. D. al-Khaṭīb, Cairo, 1368/1948.

Kitāb al-Jawharatayn (Die beiden Edelmetalle Gold und Silber), ed. and trans. C. Toll, Uppsala, 1968.

al-Maqālat al-ᶜāshirah min asrār al-ḥikmah fī ᶜilm al-nujūm, ed. M. al-Akwaᶜ, Cairo?, 1978.

Ṣifat Jazīrat al-ᶜArab, ed. D. H. Müller, Leiden, 1884–91; ed. M. al-Akwaᶜ, Riyadh, 1394/1974; trans. L. Forrer, *Südarbien nach al-Hamdānī's Beschriebung der arabischen Ḥalbinsel*, Leipzig, 1942.

Südarabishes Muśtabih, ed. O. Löfgren, Uppsala, 1953; see also Yūsuf Muḥammad.

Hamdānī, H. F. *al-Ṣulayḥiyyūn wa ʾl-ḥarakah al-fāṭimiyyah fī ʾl-Yaman*, Cairo, 1955.

al-Ḥāmidī, Ibrāhīm b. al-Ḥusayn *Kanz al-walad*, ed. M. Ghālib, Wiesbaden, 1971.

al-Ḥammādī, Muḥammad b. Mālik b. Abī ʾl-Faḍāʾil *Kashf asrār al-Bāṭiniyyah*, ed. ᶜI. al-ᶜAṭṭār, Cairo, 1357/1938.

Ibn Hutaymil, al-Qāsim b. ᶜAlī *Dīwān*, ed. M. al-ᶜAqīlī, Cairo, 1381/1961.

Ibn Samurah, *Ṭabaqāt fuqahāʾ al-Yaman*, ed. A. Fuʾād Sayyid, Cairo, 1957.

Ivanow, W. *A Creed of the Fatimids*, Bombay, 1936.

Kay, H. Cassels *Yaman: Its Early Medieval History by ᶜOmārah al-Ḥakamī, Ibn Khaldūn and al-Janadī*, London, 1892.

al-Khazrajī *al-Khazrajī's History of the Resúlí Dynasty of Yemen* (*al-ᶜUqūd al-luʾluʾiyyah*), ed. Sir J. Redhouse and M. Asal, London and Leiden, 1906–18; *al-ᶜUqūd al-luʾluʾiyyah*, ed. M. al-Akwaᶜ, Beirut, 1403/1983.

King, David A. *Mathematical Astronomy in Medieval Yemen: a Bibliographical Survey*, Malibu, 1983.

Landberg, Comte de *Etudes sur les dialectes de l'Arabie méridionale, I, Ḥaḍramoût*, Leiden, 1901.

Glossaire datînois, Leiden, 1920–42.

Löfgren, O. *Arabische Texte zur Kenntnis der Stadt Aden im Mittelalter* (Abū Makhramah, *Tārīkh thaghr ᶜAdan*), Uppsala, 1936–50.

Löfgren, O. and Traini, R. *Catalogue of the Arabic Manuscripts in the Biblioteca Ambrosiana*, Vicenza, 1975–81.

Madelung, W. *Arabic Texts Concerning the History of the Zaydī Imāms of Ṭabaristān, Daylamān and Gīlān*, Beirut, 1987.

Der Imam al-Qāsim ibn Ibrāhīm und die Glaubenslehre der Zaiditen, Berlin, 1965.

Streitschrift des Zaiditen-imams Aḥmad an-Nāṣir: wider die ibaditische Prädestinationslehre, Wiesbaden, 1985.

"*The Sīrat al-amīrayn . . . al-Qāsim wa-Muḥammad ibnay Jaᶜfar b. al-Imām al-Qāsim ibn ᶜAlī al-ᶜIyānī* as a historical source", *Sources for the History of Arabia*, II, Riyadh, 1979.

"The sources of Ismāʿīlī law", *Journal of Near Eastern Studies*, XXXV, 1976.
Madi, M. *Jaḥjā b. al-Ḥusain . . . "Anbāʾ az-zamān fī aḫbār al-Jaman"*, Berlin, 1936.
Manṣūr al-Yaman (Ibn Ḥawshab) *Faṣl min K. al-Rushd wa ʾl-hidāyah*, ed. M. K. Ḥusayn, *Collectanea*, I, Leiden, 1948.
Muḥammad, A. and al-Malīḥ, M. S., eds. *Fihrist makhṭūṭāt al-Maktabah al-gharbiyyah bi ʾl-Jāmiʿ al-kabīr bi-Ṣanʿāʾ*, Alexandria, 1978.
Muḥammad b. Ḥātim al-Yāmī *al-Simṭ al-ghālī*: see Smith.
Nashwān b. Saʿīd al-Ḥimyarī *al-Ḥūr al-ʿīn*, ed. K. Muṣṭafā, Cairo, 1948.
al-Qaṣīdah al-Ḥimyariyyah, ed. and trans. A. von Kremer, Leipzig, 1865; eds. ʿA. al-Muʾayyad and I. al-Jarāfī as *Mulūk Ḥimyar wa-aqyāl al-Yaman*, Cairo, 1378/1958.
Shams al-ʿulūm (letters *alif* to *shīn*), ed. ʿA. A. b. ʿA. K. al-Jarāfī, Beirut, 1982; *Die auf Südarabien bezuglichen Angaben Našwān's im Šams al-ʿulūm* (extracts from letters *alif* to *yāʾ*), ed. A. ʿAẓīmuddīn, Leiden and London, 1916.
Poonawala, Ismail K. *Biobibliography of Ismāʿīlī Literature*, Malibu, 1977.
al-Sulṭān al-Khaṭṭāb, ḥayātuh wa-shiʿruh, Cairo, 1967.
al-Rāzī, Aḥmad b. ʿAbdullah *Tārīkh madīnat Ṣanʿāʾ*, eds. H. A. al-ʿAmrī and ʿAbd al-Jabbār Zakkār, Damascus, 1394/1974.
al-Ruqayḥī, A. ʿA. R., al-Ḥabshī, ʿA. M. and al-Anisī, ʿA. W. eds. *Fihrist makhṭūṭāt al-Jāmiʿ al-Kabīr*, Damascus and Ṣanʿāʾ, 1984.
Ṣanʿāʾ: see *Fihrist*; Muḥammad, ed. *Fihrist*; al-Ruqayḥī, ed., *Fihrist*.
al-Saqqāf, ʿA. *Tārīkh al-shuʿarāʾ al-ḥaḍramiyyīn*, I, Cairo, 1353 AH.
Serjeant, R. B. "The cultivation of cereals in mediaeval Yemen. A translation of the *Bughyat al-fallāḥīn* of the Rasūlid Sultan, al-Malik al-Afḍal . . . composed circa 1370 AD", *Arabian Studies*, I, 1974.
"The interplay between tribal and religious (Zaydī) authority in the Yemen", *al-Abḥāth*, XXX, 1982.
Prose and Poetry from Ḥaḍramawt, London, 1951.
"The Zaydīs", A. J. Arberry and C. F. Beckingham eds., *Religion in the Middle East*, II, *Islam*, Cambridge, 1969.
Serjeant, R. B. and Lewcock, R. *Ṣanʿāʾ: an Arabian Islamic City*, London, 1983.
al-Shāmī, A. b. M., ed. *Dāmighat al-dawāmigh*, Hertford and London, 1966.
Qiṣṣat al-adab fī ʾl-Yaman, Beirut, 1385/1965.
Tārīkh al-Yaman al-fikrī fī ʾl-ʿaṣr al-ʿabbāsī, Beirut, 1407/1987.
al-Sharjī, Aḥmad b. Aḥmad *Ṭabaqāt al-khawāṣṣ*, Cairo, 1903.
Smith, G. Rex *The Ayyūbids and Early Rasūlids in the Yemen* (I = Muḥammad b. Ḥātim al-Yāmī, *al-Simṭ al-ghālī*).
"The Ayyūbids and Rasūlids – the transfer of power in 7th/13th century Yemen", *Islamic Culture*, XLIII, 1969.
Stern, S. M. "Ismāʿīlīs and Qarmaṭians", *L'Élaboration de l'Islam, Colloque de Strasbourg, 1959*, Paris, 1961.
Strothmann, R. *Das Staatsrecht der Zaiditen*, Strasburg, 1912.
al-Sulṭān al-Khaṭṭāb: see Poonawala.
Tritton, A. S. "The Muṭarrifiya", *Le Muséon*, LXIII, 1950.

The Rise of the Imams of Sanaa, Oxford and Madras, 1925.

ʿUmārah b. ʿAlī al-Ḥakamī *Dīwān*, (selections), *al-Nukat al-ʿaṣriyyah* and *Rasāʾil* (selections): see Derenbourg.

al-Mufīd fī akhbār Ṣanʿāʾ wa-Zabīd, ed. M. al-Akwaʿ, Cairo, 1976; see also Kay.

al-Wādiʿī, ʿAlī b. Ḥanẓalah *al-Qaṣīdah . . . Simṭ al-ḥaqāʾiq*, ed. ʿA. al-ʿAzāwī, Damascus, 1953.

Wiedemann, E. *Naturschilderungen bei Hamdânī*, Halle, 1909.

Yaḥyā b. al-Ḥusayn *Anbāʾ al-zamān*: see Madi.

Ghāyat al-amānī, ed. S.ʿA. F. ʿAshūr, Cairo, 1968.

Yajima, Hikoichi *A Chronicle of the Rasūlid Dynasty of the Yemen*, Tokyo, 1974.

Yāqūt *Muʿjam al-buldān*, ed. F. Wüstenfeld, Leipzig, 1866–73.

Yūsuf Muḥammad, ʿA., ed. *Al-Hamdānī: . . . Studies on the Occasion of his Millenial Anniversary*, Ṣanʿāʾ, 1407/1986.

Zabārah, M. b. M. *Aʾimmat al-Yaman*, I, Taʿizz, 1375 AH.

INDEX

al-Ṣulayḥī, ᶜAlī b. Muḥammad, 421, 444, 454, 459
al-Ṣulayḥi, al-Mukarram b. ᶜAlī b. Muḥammad, 454
Sulayhids (Yemeni dynasty), 14, 443, 444, 459–60; *see also* Arwā bint Aḥmad
Sulaymān b. ᶜAbd al-Malik (caliph), 152
Sulaymān b. ᶜAlī b. ᶜAbdullāh b. al-ᶜAbbās, 49, 50
Sulaymān b. ᶜĀmir b.ᶜAbdullāh al-Zawāhī, 454
Sulaymān b. Ḥasan al-Ḥajūrī, 456, 459
Sulaymān b. Nāṣir al-Siḥāmī, 458
al-Ṣūlī, Abū Bakr Muḥammad b. Yaḥyā, 80n, 290, 401, 406, 407, 415
al-Ṣūlī, Ibrāhīm b. al-ᶜAbbās, 80
al-Sulṭān al-Khaṭṭāb b. al-Ḥasan, 456, 457, 459
Sumnūn b. Ḥamzah al-Baṣrī, 243–4
sundials, 461
sunnah, pre-Islamic concept of, 24–5
sunnah (sayings and practice of Prophet), 117, 416; caliphal authority to interpret, 2; Muᶜtazilism and, 5; *see also* Sunnism
Sunnism: ᶜAbbasids and, 2, 10, 191, 195; Baghdad as centre, 5–6; Buyid period, 201; in Fatimid Egypt, 13–14; and Muᶜtazilism, 5, 94; and Qurʾān, 5; Saljuqs, 13, 15; Shīᶜīs and, 9, 116; al-Tawḥīdī, 112, 113, 123; Yemen, 443, 445, 460
Suwayd b. Abī Kāhil, 148
al-Suyūṭī, 447
synechdoche, 387
Syria: Arabicization, 413; bedouins, 15; Carmarthian rebellion, 8; independence under Aḥmad b. Ṭūlūn, 12; Fatimids and, 13, 199; Hamdanids, 7–8, 10, 315–18, 326 al-Manṣūr's reign, 64–5, 69; al-Mutanabbī's attempted revolt, 300, 303, 305; Saljuqs, 15; wine poetry, 232
Syriac, 267

ṭabaqāt (biographical literature), 92, 425, (classification of poets), 341–6
al-Ṭabarānī, 454
al-Ṭabarī, Abū ʾl-Ḥusayn Aḥmad b. Mūsā, 454
al-Ṭabarī, Abū Jaᶜfar Muḥammad b. Jarīr, 4, 126, 142, 424, 453n
Ṭabaristān, 99, 103
taḍmīn (construction of poetry around quotations), 232
tafsīr (Quranic exegesis), 138, 445; mystical, 241; *see also* Qurʾān
Taghlib (tribe), 318, 325
Ṭāhir b. al-Ḥusayn, 4, 5
Taᶜizz, 443, 445
tajnīs (paronomasia), 254, 285, 403, 406; Ibn al-Fāriḍ, 254; Ibn al-Muᶜtazz and, 346, 347, 393; al-Qāḍī, 'l-Jurjānī on, 378; Qudāmah on, 371, 372; *see also* puns
takhalluṣ, *see* transition
takrār (anaphora), 288–9, 325
Ṭālaqān, 97
Ṭalāʾiᶜ b. Ruzzīk (Egyptian ruler), 434
talmīḥ, *see under* allusion
Tamīm (tribe), 227
Tamīm al-Dārī, legend of, 139–41
Tamīm b. al-Muᶜizz, 431
tanāsukh (metempsychosis), 189, 190
Tangier, 280
al-Tanūkhī, Abū ᶜAlī al-Muḥassin, 126, 127, 129, 426
Tanūkh (tribe), 303–4, 328
taqiyyah (tactical dissimulation of beliefs), 191
taqsīm (distributio), 298, 378
Ṭarafah b. al-ᶜAbd, 219–20, 220, 221
ṭardiyyāt, *see* hunting poetry
Ṭāriq the Berber (Ṭāriq b. Ziyād), 141
Tatar invasions, 441
tawakkul (trust in God), 270, 271
al-Tawḥīdī, Abū Ḥayyān ᶜAlī b. Muḥammad b. al-ᶜAbbās, 112–24; *Akhlāq al-waẓīrayn*, 101–2, 109, 114, 115, 118, 120, 121; as copyist 101, 118, 120; *al-Imtāᶜ wa ʾl-muʾānasah*, 101, 114, 116–23; *al-Ishārāt al-ilāhiyyah*, 29, 114, 115, 122; and al-Jāḥiẓ, 94, 114, 118; preserves fragments from early critics, 342 and al-Ṣāḥib Ibn ᶜAbbād, 97, 98, 100–1, 106, 109, 114, 118, 120–1
taʾwīl (esoterical interpretation of Qurʾān), 420, 446, 456
taxation, 2, 3, 4, 9, 106, 107, 152, 462; Ibn al-Muqaffaᶜ on, 66, 67, 70
tax-collectors, 48, 70, 107
al-Ṭayyib b. Āmir (concealed Fāṭimī imam), 455, 457
al-Thaᶜālibī, Abū Manṣūr ᶜAbd al-Malik b. Muḥammad: on Abū Firās, 318, 327; on Hamdanids, 315; and Ibn al-Fāriḍ, 255; medicine, 107; on al-Mutanabbī, 301, 302, 307, 318; and al-Ṣāḥib Ibn ᶜAbbād, 106, 107, 109; *Yatīmah*, 107n, 208, 212, 213, 214, 301, 302, 307, 318, 428
Thābit Quṭnah, 192
Thaᶜlab, Abū ʾl-ᶜAbbās Aḥmad b. Yaḥyā, 106, 356, 390, 403–4, 405, 407
Thamūd, 75
thanawiyyah, *see* dualism
theology (*kalām*), 347, 349, 383; Ibāḍiyyah, 188; al-Jāḥiẓ, 81, 82, 83–6; al-Naẓẓām, 81, 85; polemic, 467–8; al-Ṣāḥib Ibn ᶜAbbād, 97, 102–3, 103–4; al-Tawḥīdī on, 113; and wine poetry, 227; Yemen, 445, 457–8, 467–8; *see also* Ashᶜarism; Muᶜtazilīs
Thousand and One Nights, 4, 137, 143, 210, 218, 299
Thumāmah b. Ashras, 41, 80
ṭibāq, *see* antithesis
al-Tibrīzī, al-Khaṭīb, 29, 146
tiercel goshawk, 170, 171, 177, 181–2
al-Tilimsānī, Abū Madyan (Shuᶜayb b. al-Ḥasan al-Andalusī), *see* Abū Madyan al-Tilimsānī